ORDNANCE SURVEY

STREET ATLAS
West Essex

Contents

IV *Key to maps*

VI *Administrative boundaries*

1 *Street maps*

196 *Index explanation and abbreviations*

197 *Index of towns, villages and rural localities*

198 *Index of street names*

PHILIP'S

First published 1990
Second edition published 1994 by

Ordnance Survey	and	Philip's
Romsey Road		an imprint of Reed Consumer Books Limited
Maybush		Michelin House, 81 Fulham Road, London, SW3 6RB
Southampton SO9 4DH		and Auckland, Melbourne, Singapore and Toronto

ISBN 0-540-05849-1 (Philip's, hardback)
ISBN 0-540-05867-X (Philip's, softback)
ISBN 0-319-00403-1 (Ordnance Survey, hardback)
ISBN 0-319-00404-X (Ordnance Survey, softback)

Printed and bound in Great Britain by
Butler & Tanner Ltd, Frome and London

Key to map symbols

	British Rail station
	London transport station
	Private railway station
	Bus or coach station
	Heliport
	Police station (may not be open 24 hours)
	Hospital with casualty facilities (may not be open 24 hours)
	Post office
+	**Place of worship**
	Important building
P	**Parking**
120	**Adjoining page indicator**
	Motorway or dual carriageway
A27(T)	**Main or through road** (with Department of Transport number)
	Gate or obstruction to traffic (restrictions may not apply at all times or to all vehicles)
	Footpath
	Bridleway
	Path
	Track

The representation in this atlas of a road, track or path is no evidence of the existence of a right of way

Amb Sta	**Ambulance station**	LC	**Level crossing**
Coll	**College**	Liby	**Library**
FB	**Footbridge**	Mus	**Museum**
F Sta	**Fire station**	Sch	**School**
Hospl	**Hospital**	TH	**Town hall**

0 | ¼ | ½ | ¾ | 1 mile

0 | 250m | 500m | 250m | 1 Kilometre

The scale of the maps is 3½ inches to 1 mile (1:18103)

Key to map pages

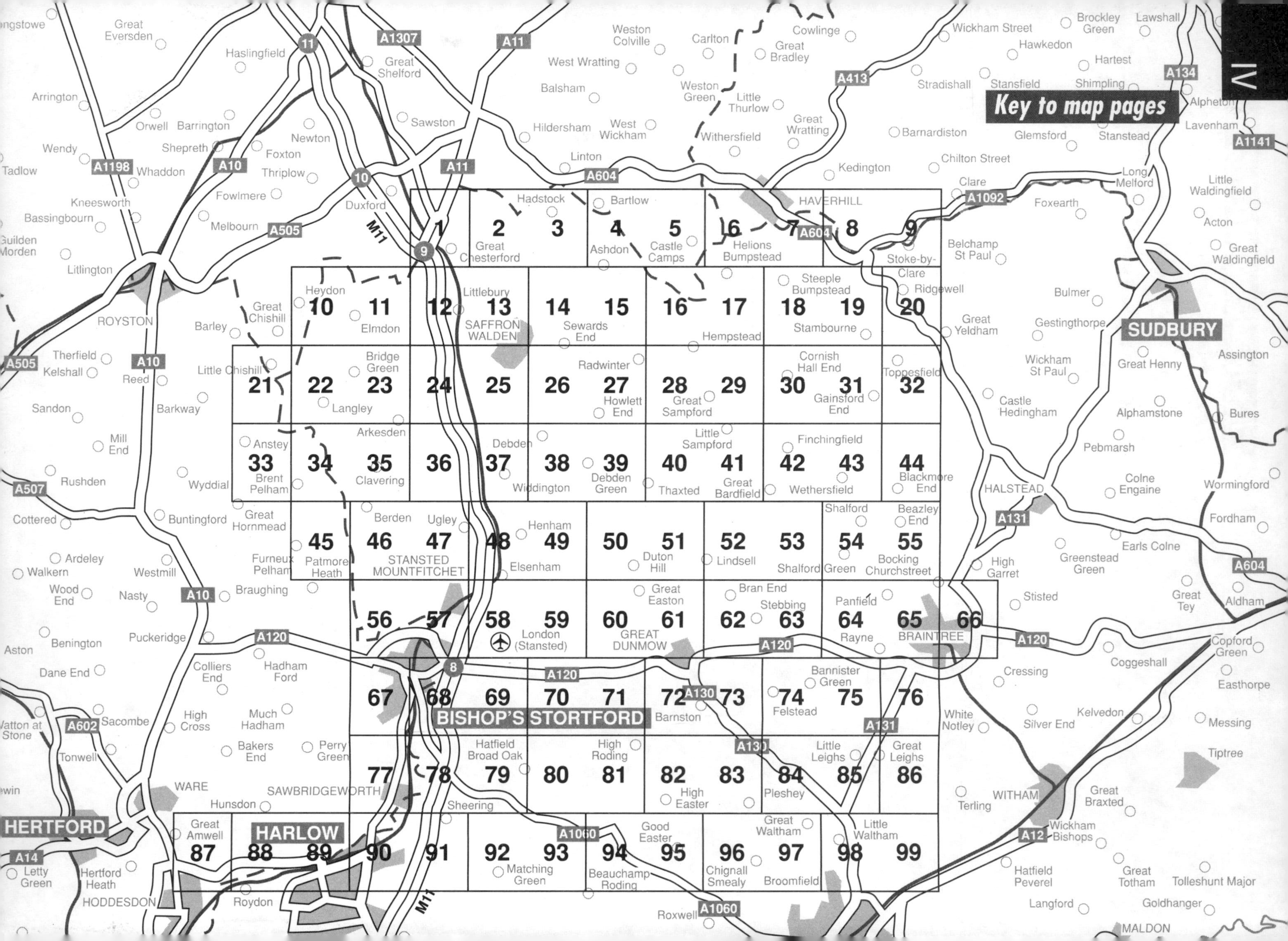

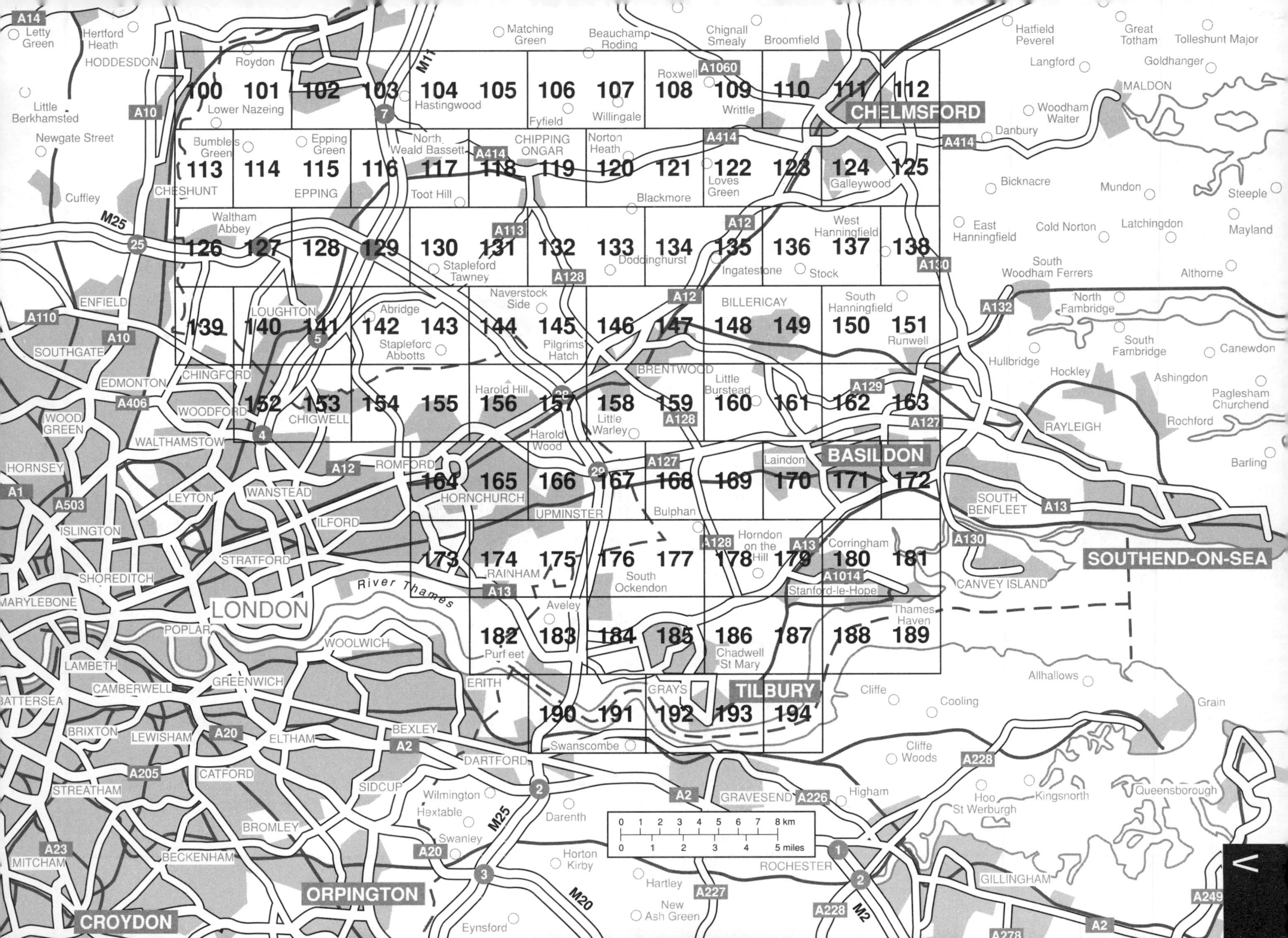

V
100 101 102 103 104 105 106 107 108 109 110 111 112
113 114 115 116 117 118 119 120 121 122 123 124 125
126 127 128 129 130 131 132 133 134 135 136 137 138
139 140 141 142 143 144 145 146 147 148 149 150 151
152 153 154 155 156 157 158 159 160 161 162 163
164 165 166 167 168 169 170 171 172
173 174 175 176 177 178 179 180 181
182 183 184 185 186 187 188 189
190 191 192 193 194
CHELMSFORD
BASILDON
SOUTHEND-ON-SEA
TILBURY
LONDON
ORPINGTON
CROYDON
Letty Green
Hertford Heath
HODDESDON
Little Berkhamsted
Newgate Street
Cuffley
Roydon
Lower Nazeing
Hastingwood
Matching Green
Beauchamp Roding
Fyfield
Willingale
Chignall Smealy
Roxwell
Writtle
Broomfield
Hatfield Peverel
Great Totham
Tolleshunt Major
Langford
Goldhanger
MALDON
Woodham Walter
Danbury
Bumbles Green
CHESHUNT
Epping Green
EPPING
North Weald Bassett
Toot Hill
CHIPPING ONGAR
Norton Heath
Blackmore
Loves Green
Galleywood
Bicknacre
Mundon
Steeple
Mayland
Waltham Abbey
Stapleford Tawney
Doddinghurst
Ingatestone
Stock
West Hanningfield
East Hanningfield
Cold Norton
Latchingdon
South Woodham Ferrers
Althorne
ENFIELD
SOUTHGATE
LOUGHTON
Abridge
Stapleford Abbotts
Naverstock Side
Pilgrims Hatch
BILLERICAY
South Hanningfield
Runwell
North Fambridge
South Fambridge
Canewdon
Hullbridge
Hockley
Ashingdon
Paglesham Churchend
EDMONTON
CHINGFORD
WOODFORD
CHIGWELL
Harold Hill
BRENTWOOD
Little Warley
Little Burstead
RAYLEIGH
Rochford
WOOD GREEN
WALTHAMSTOW
Harold Wood
Laindon
HORNSEY
ROMFORD
Barling
LEYTON
WANSTEAD
HORNCHURCH
UPMINSTER
Bulphan
SOUTH BENFLEET
ISLINGTON
ILFORD
STRATFORD
RAINHAM
South Ockendon
Horndon on the Hill
Corringham
Stanford-le-Hope
CANVEY ISLAND
SHOREDITCH
MARYLEBONE
River Thames
Aveley
Thames Haven
POPLAR
WOOLWICH
Purfleet
Chadwell St Mary
LAMBETH
GREENWICH
CAMBERWELL
ERITH
GRAYS
Allhallows
BATTERSEA
Cliffe
Cooling
Grain
BRIXTON
LEWISHAM
ELTHAM
BEXLEY
Swanscombe
Cliffe Woods
DARTFORD
STREATHAM
CATFORD
SIDCUP
Wilmington
Hextable
GRAVESEND
Higham
Hoo St Werburgh
Kingsnorth
Queensborough
BROMLEY
Darenth
Swanley
MITCHAM
BECKENHAM
Horton Kirby
ROCHESTER
GILLINGHAM
Hartley
New Ash Green
Eynsford
0 1 2 3 4 5 6 7 8 km
0 1 2 3 4 5 miles
M11 M25 M20 M2
A14 A10 A110 A406 A1 A503 A12 A1060 A414 A113 A128 A130 A132 A129 A127 A13 A1014 A23 A205 A20 A2 A226 A228 A227 A249 A278

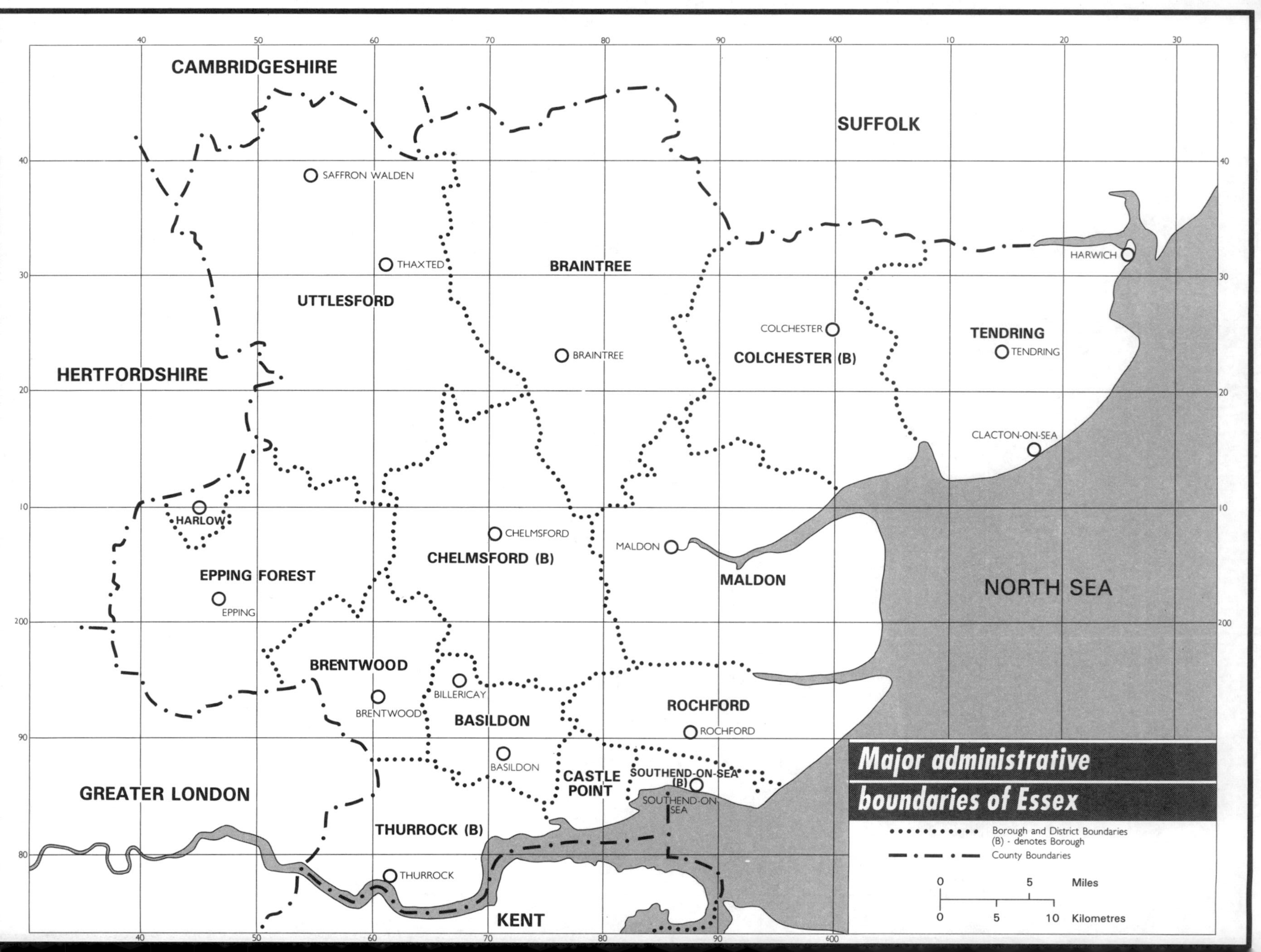
Major administrative boundaries of Essex
Borough and District Boundaries
(B) - denotes Borough
County Boundaries
Miles
Kilometres
CAMBRIDGESHIRE
SUFFOLK
HERTFORDSHIRE
GREATER LONDON
KENT
NORTH SEA
UTTLESFORD
BRAINTREE
COLCHESTER (B)
TENDRING
EPPING FOREST
CHELMSFORD (B)
MALDON
BRENTWOOD
BASILDON
ROCHFORD
CASTLE POINT
SOUTHEND-ON-SEA (B)
THURROCK (B)
SAFFRON WALDEN
THAXTED
BRAINTREE
COLCHESTER
TENDRING
HARWICH
CLACTON-ON-SEA
HARLOW
EPPING
CHELMSFORD
MALDON
BILLERICAY
BRENTWOOD
BASILDON
ROCHFORD
SOUTHEND-ON-SEA
THURROCK

not continued, see key diagram

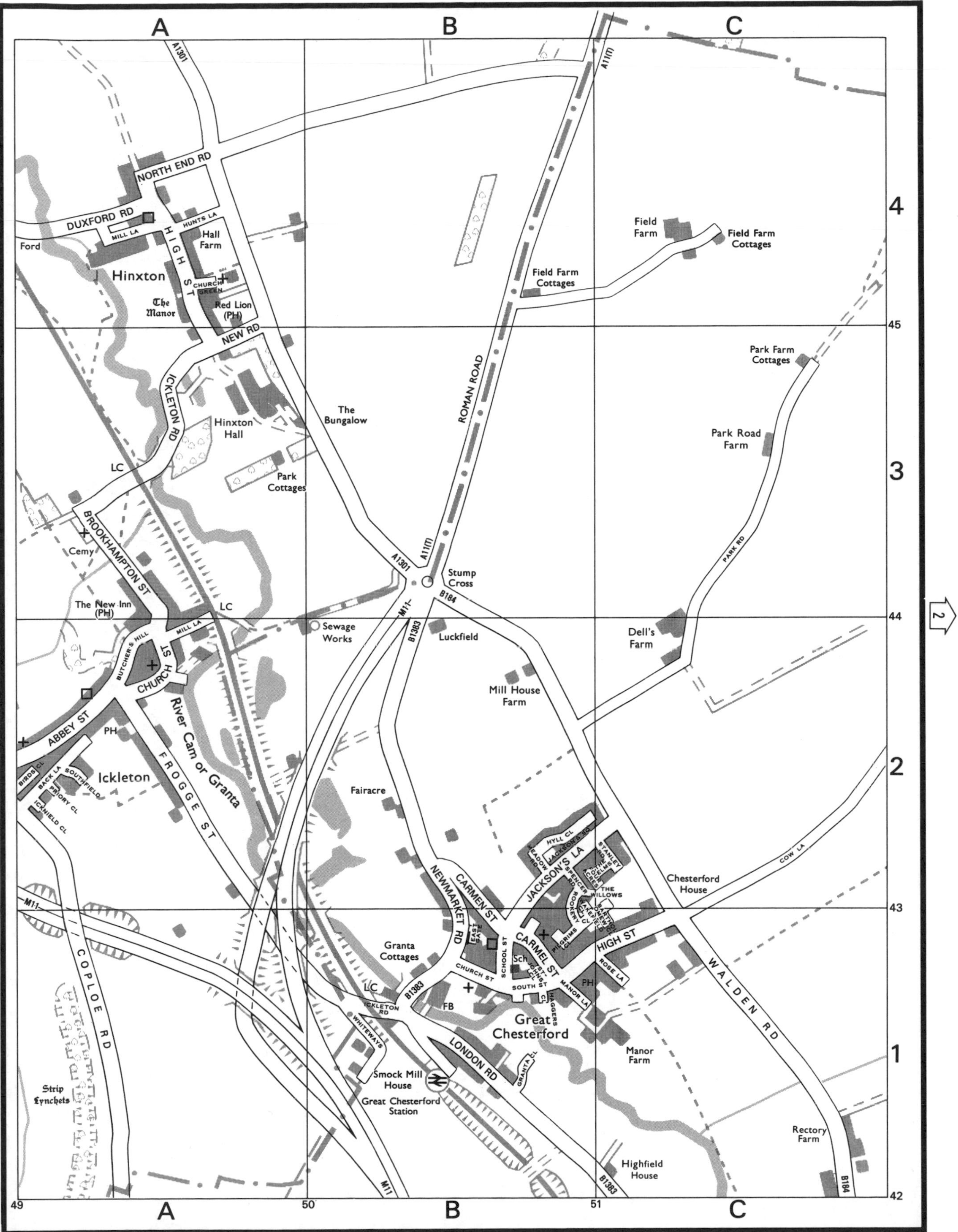

12

not continued, see key diagram

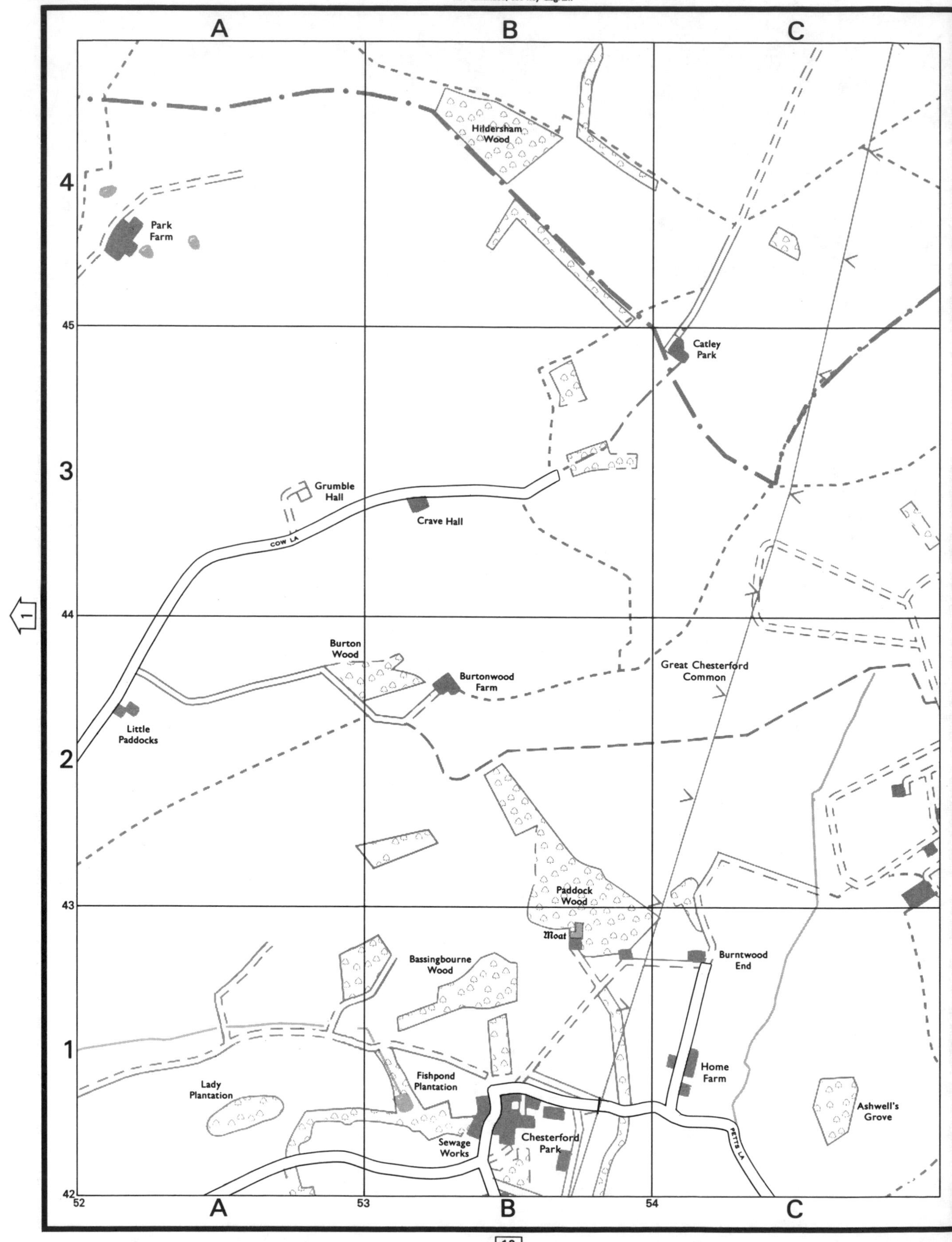

1

13

not continued, see key diagram

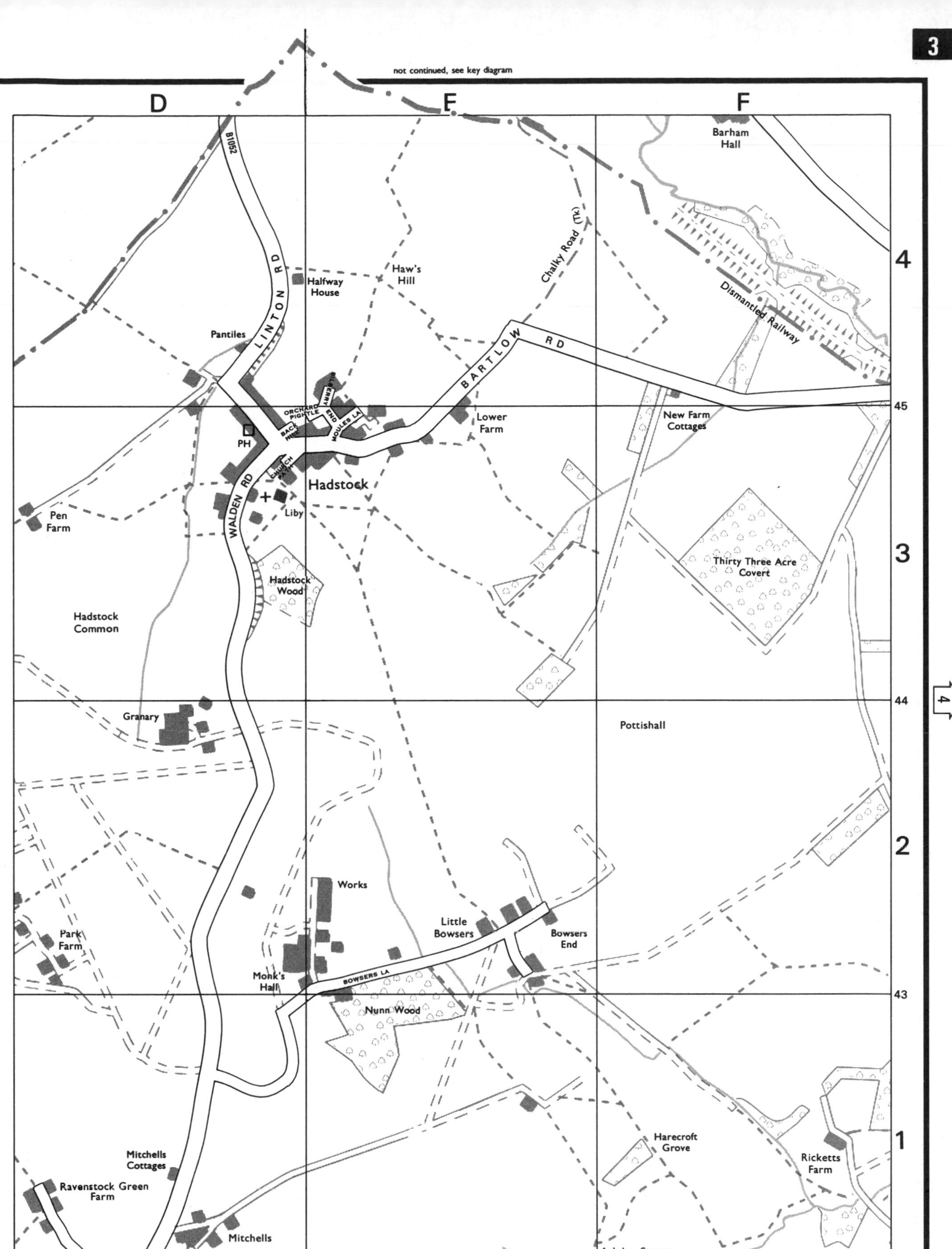

4

14

not continued, see key diagram

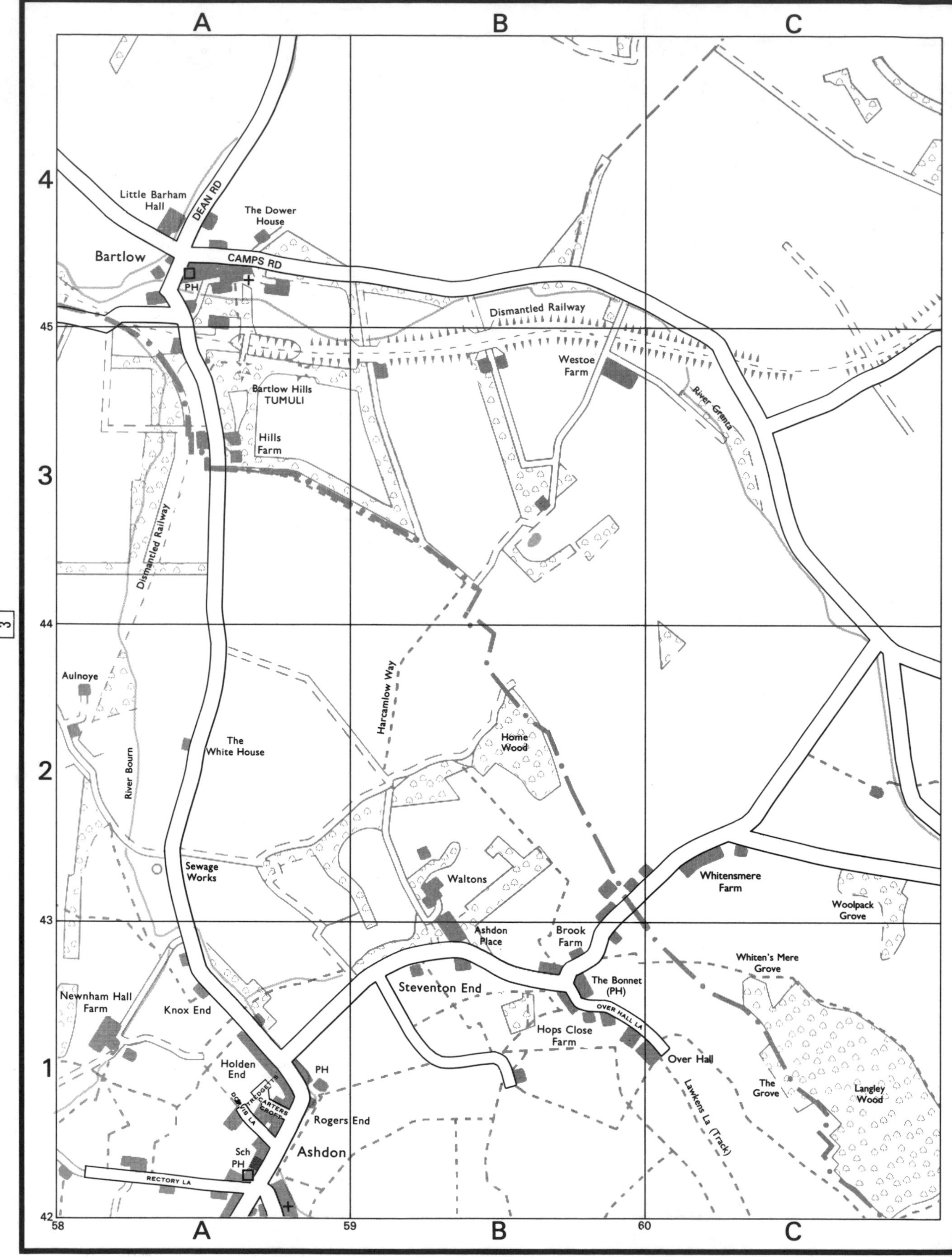

not continued, see key diagram

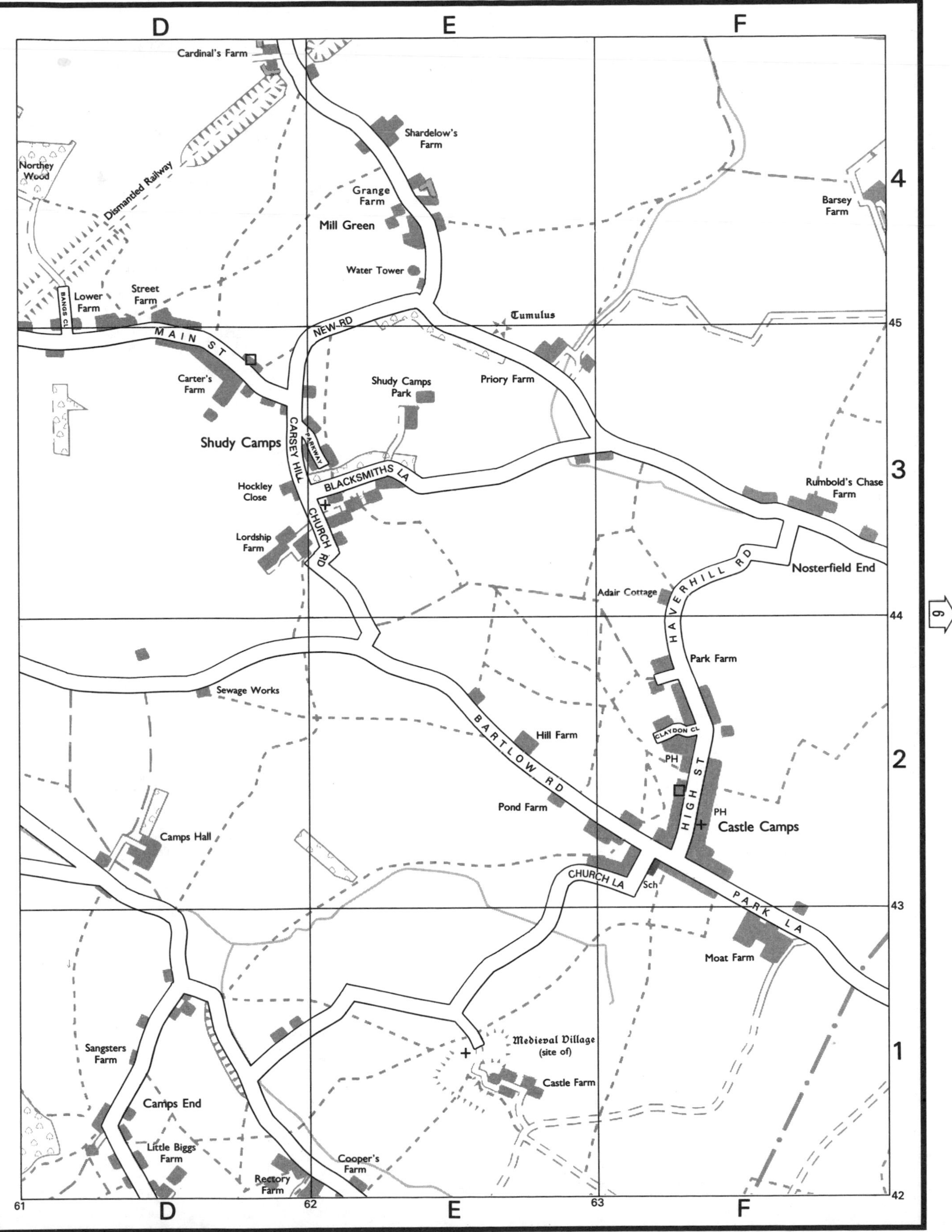

9

16

not continued, see key diagram

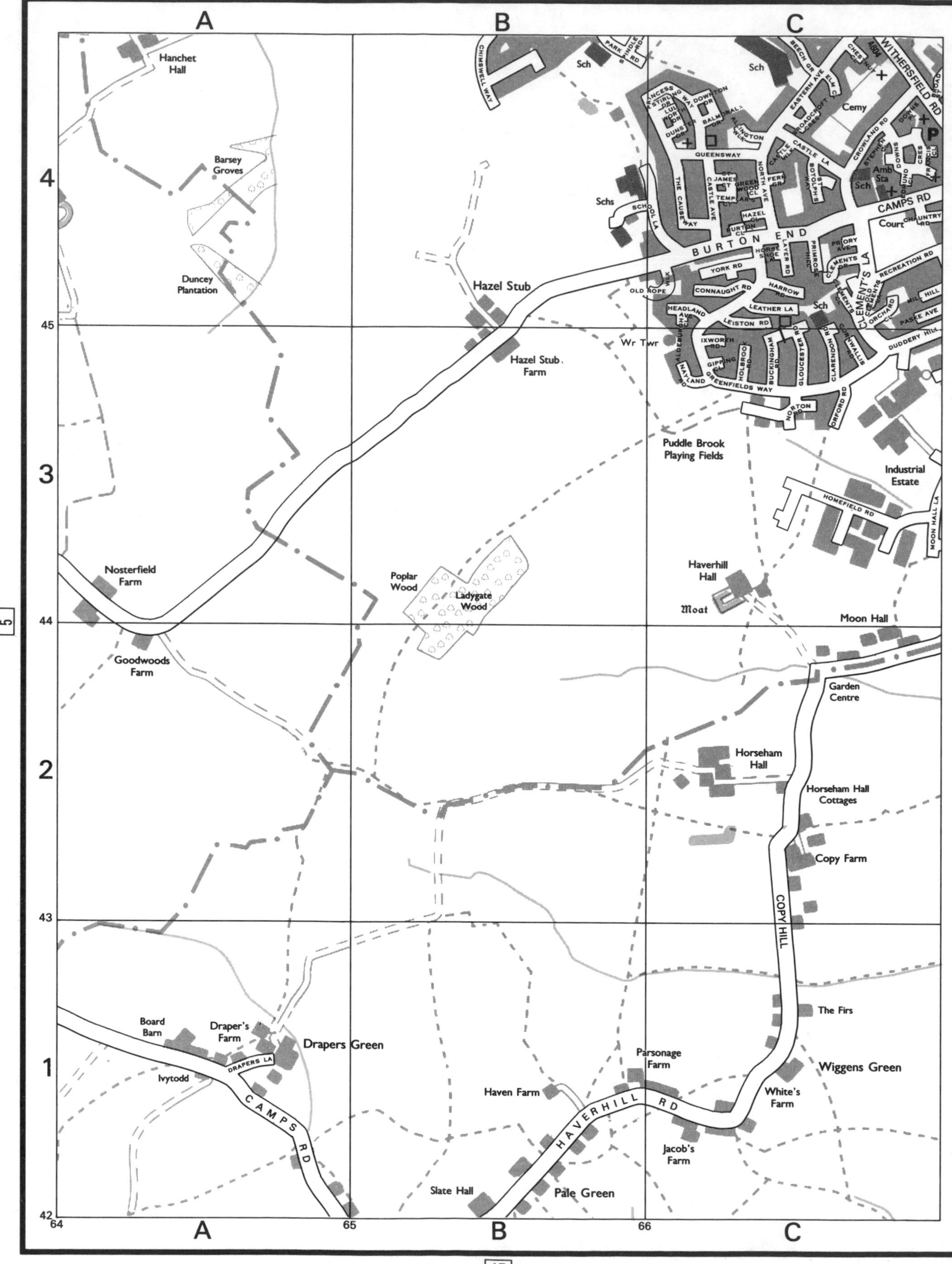

5

17

not continued, see key diagram

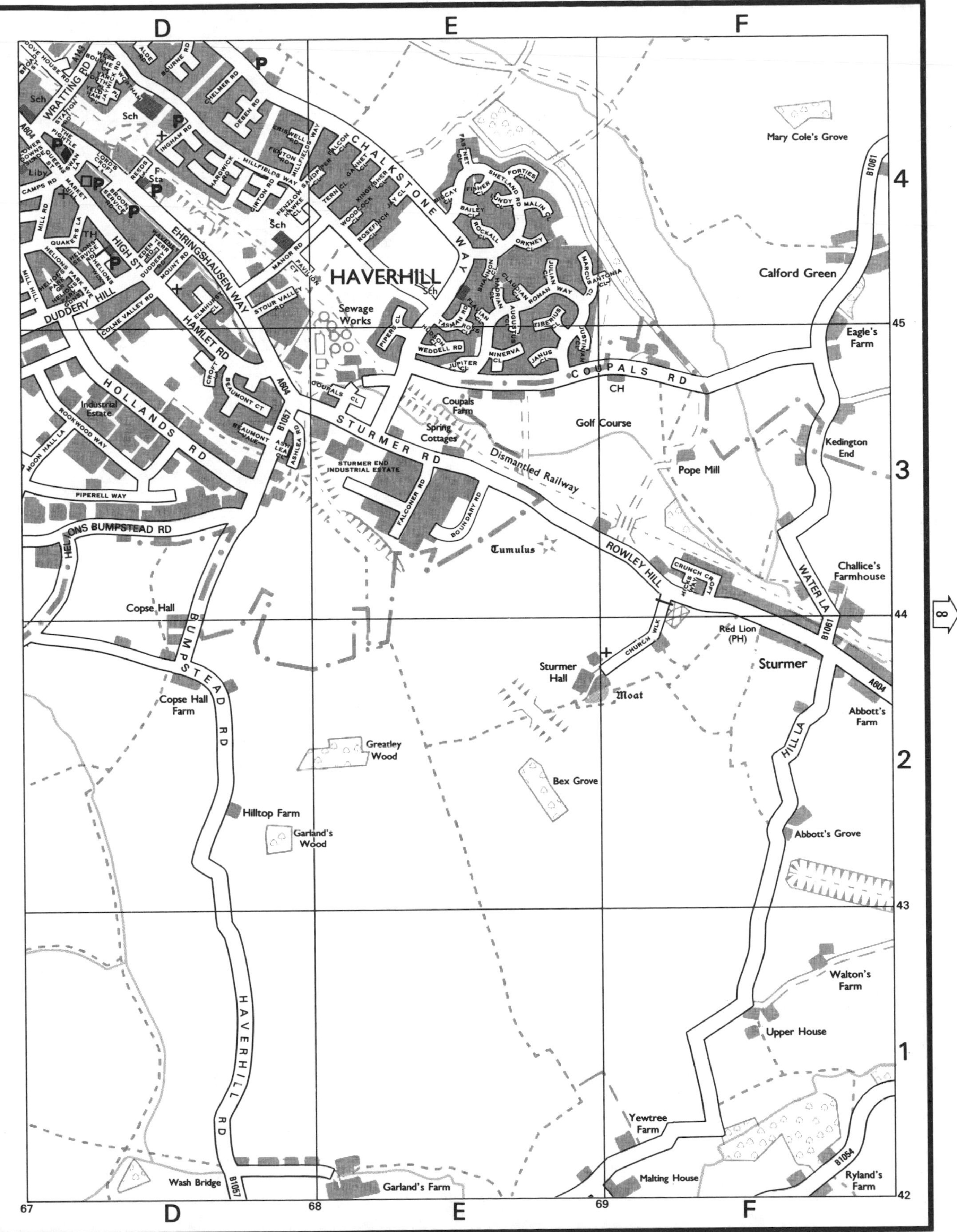

8

not continued, see key diagram

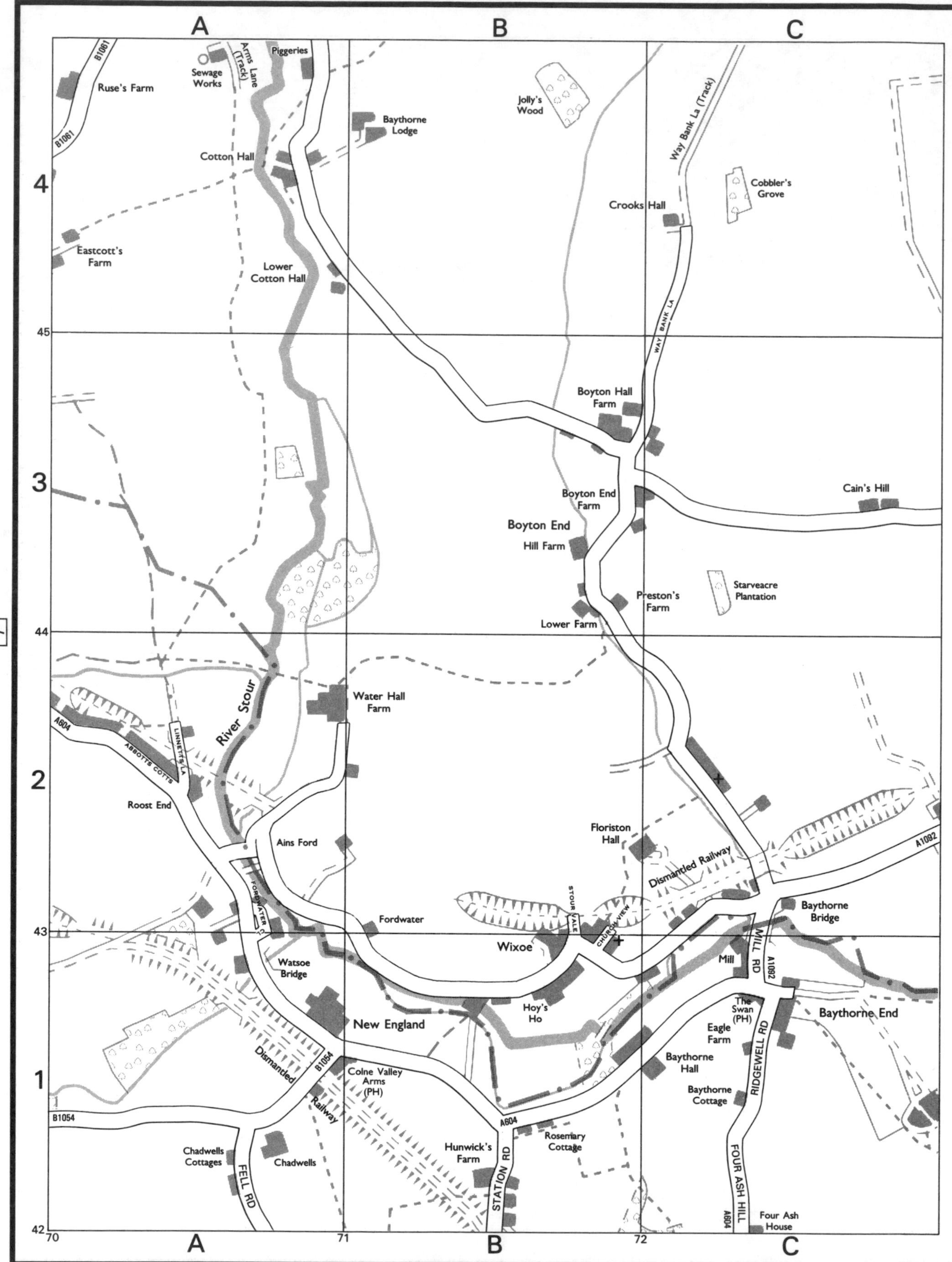

7

19

not continued, see key diagram

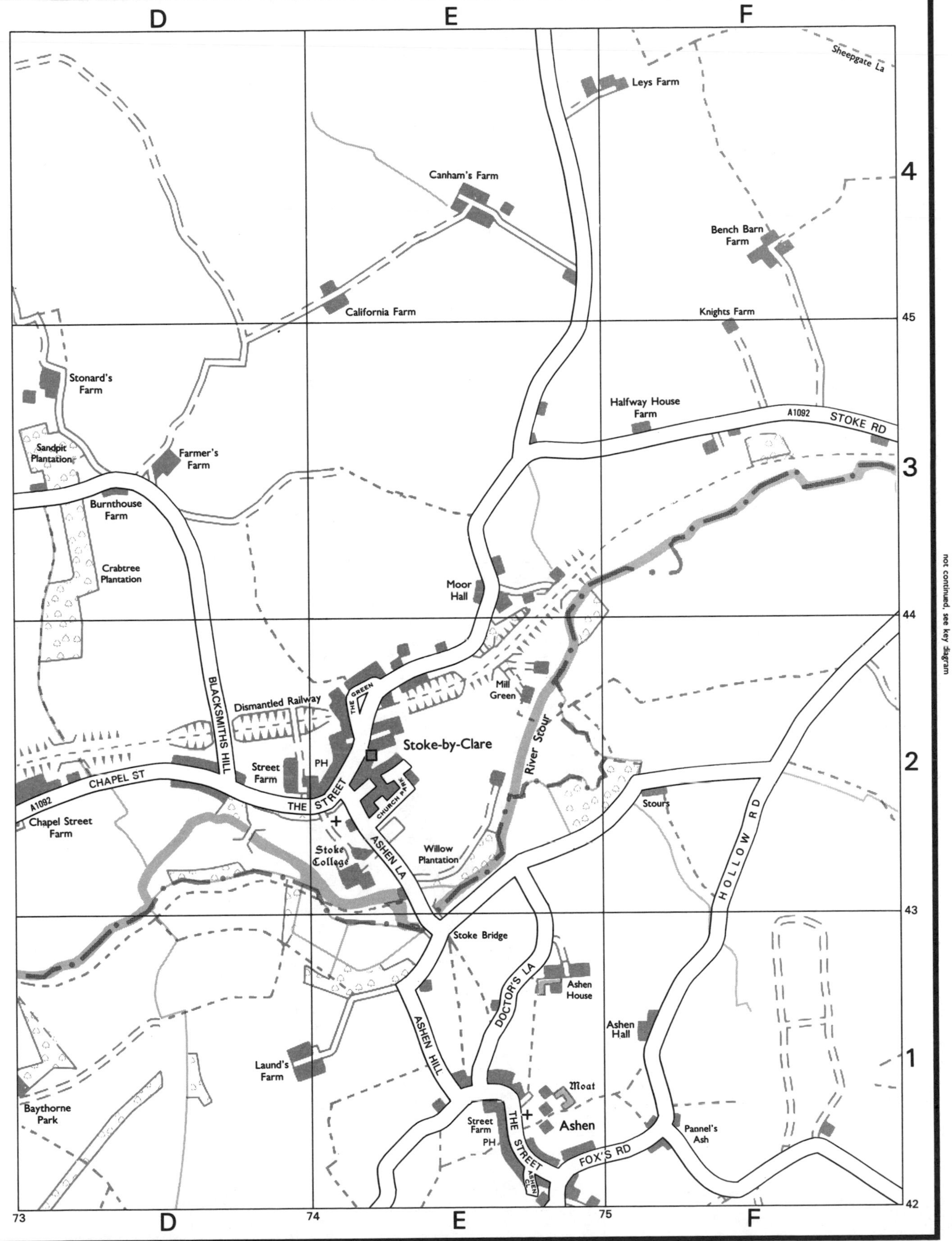

not continued, see key diagram

20

not continued, see key diagram

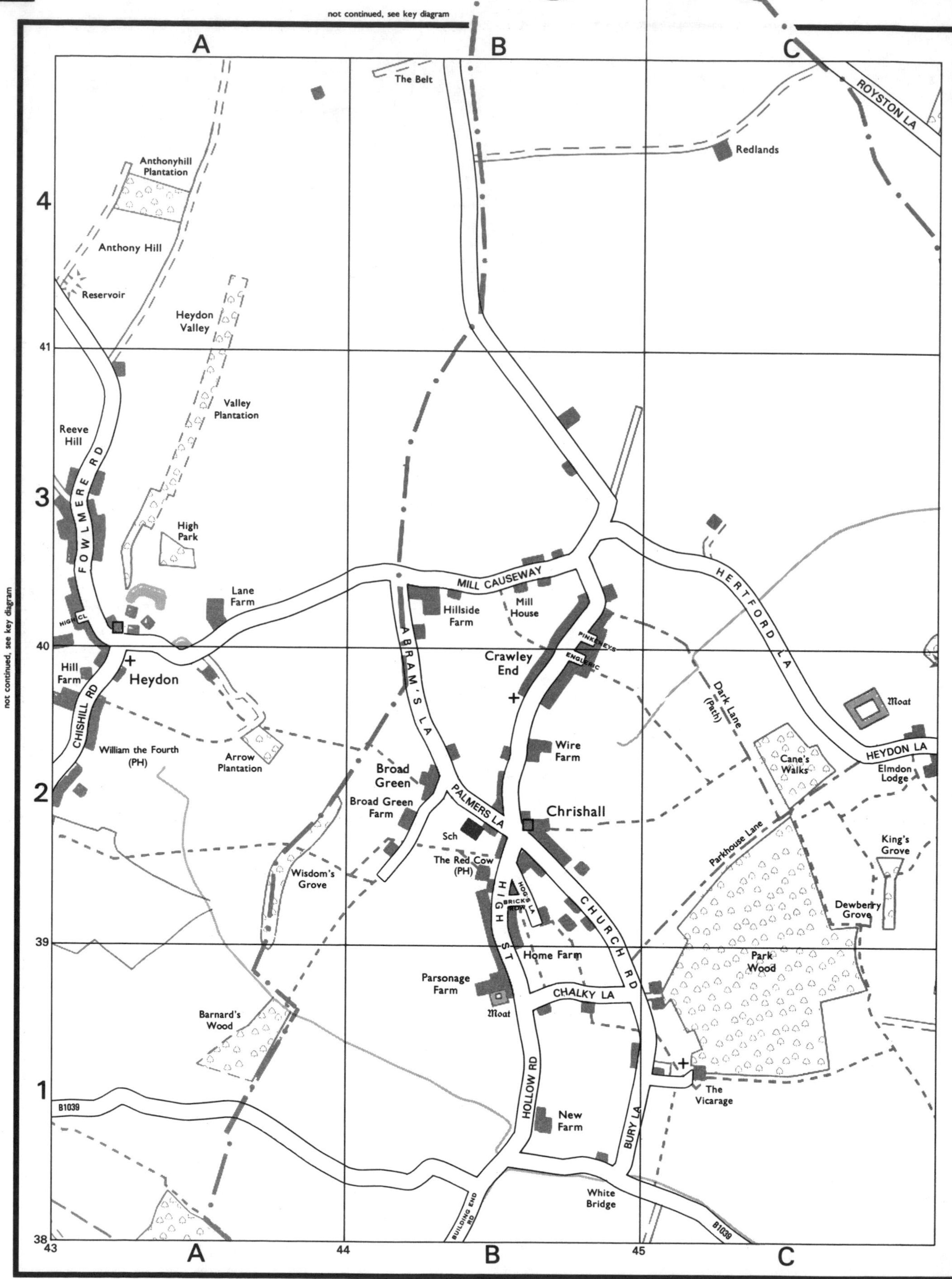

not continued, see key diagram

22

not continued, see key diagram

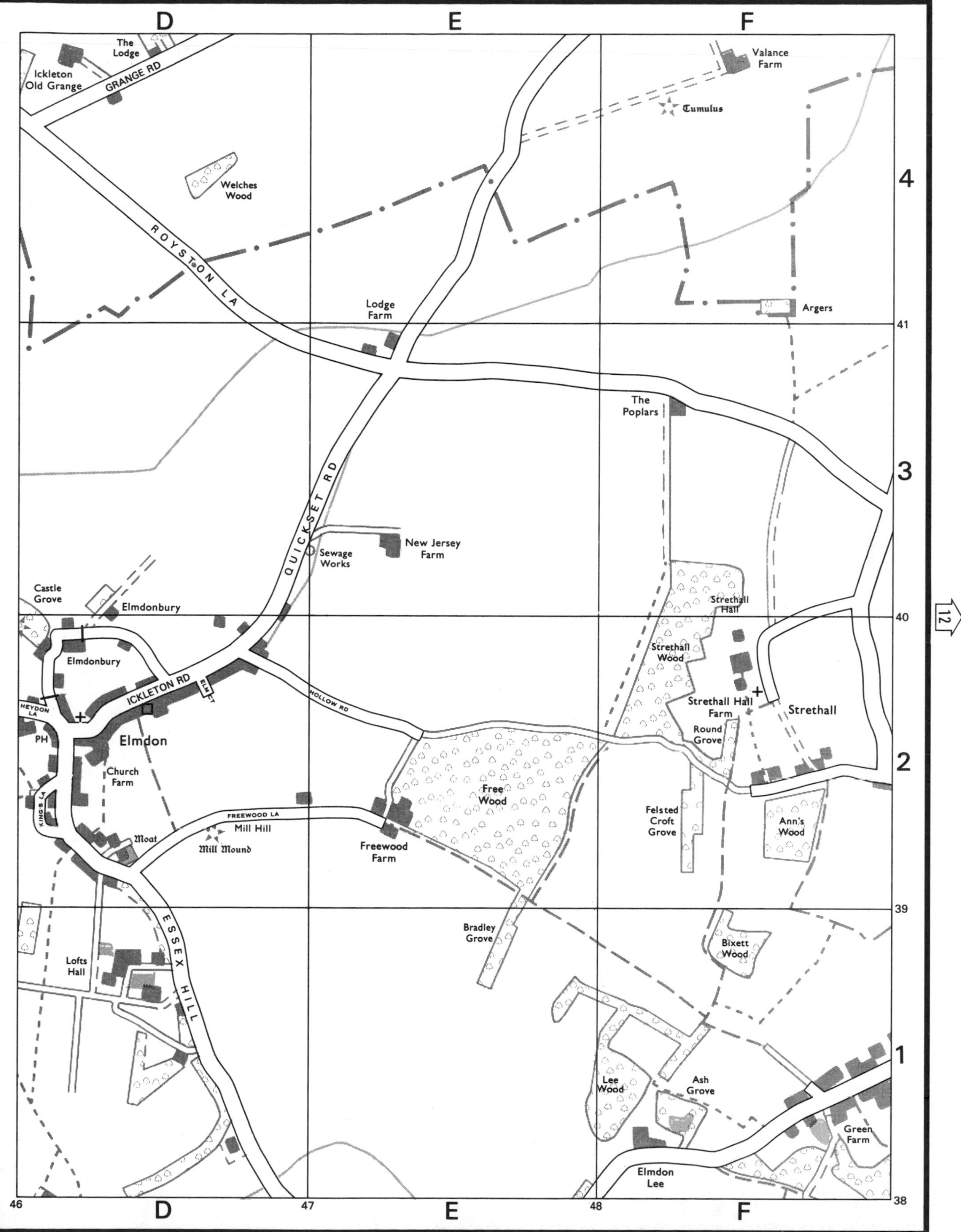

12

23

1

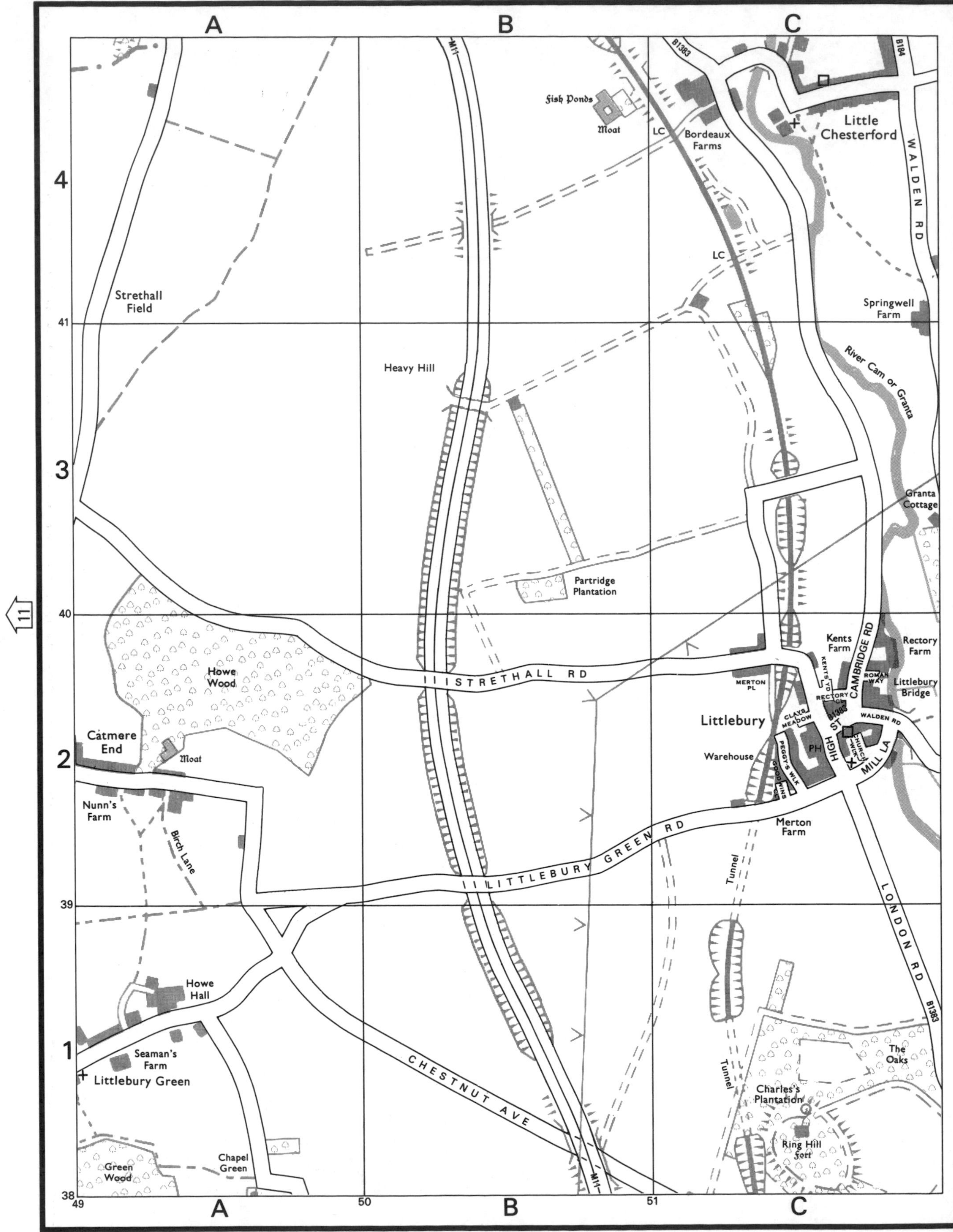
A
B
C
4
3
2
1
41
40
39
38
49
50
51
M11
B1383
B184
Fish Ponds
Moat
LC
Bordeaux Farms
Little Chesterford
WALDEN RD
Strethall Field
Springwell Farm
Heavy Hill
River Cam or Granta
Granta Cottage
Partridge Plantation
Kents Farm
Rectory Farm
CAMBRIDGE RD
KENTS YD
ROMAN WAY
Littlebury Bridge
Howe Wood
STRETHALL RD
MERTON PL
RECTORY CL
Littlebury
CLAYS MEADOW
WALDEN RD
Catmere End
Moat
HIGH ST
PH
CHURCH WLK
MILL LA
Warehouse
PEGGY'S WLK
GOODWINS
Nunn's Farm
Birch Lane
Merton Farm
LITTLEBURY GREEN RD
Tunnel
LONDON RD
Howe Hall
The Oaks
Seaman's Farm
Littlebury Green
CHESTNUT AVE
Charles's Plantation
Ring Hill Fort
Chapel Green
Green Wood

11

24

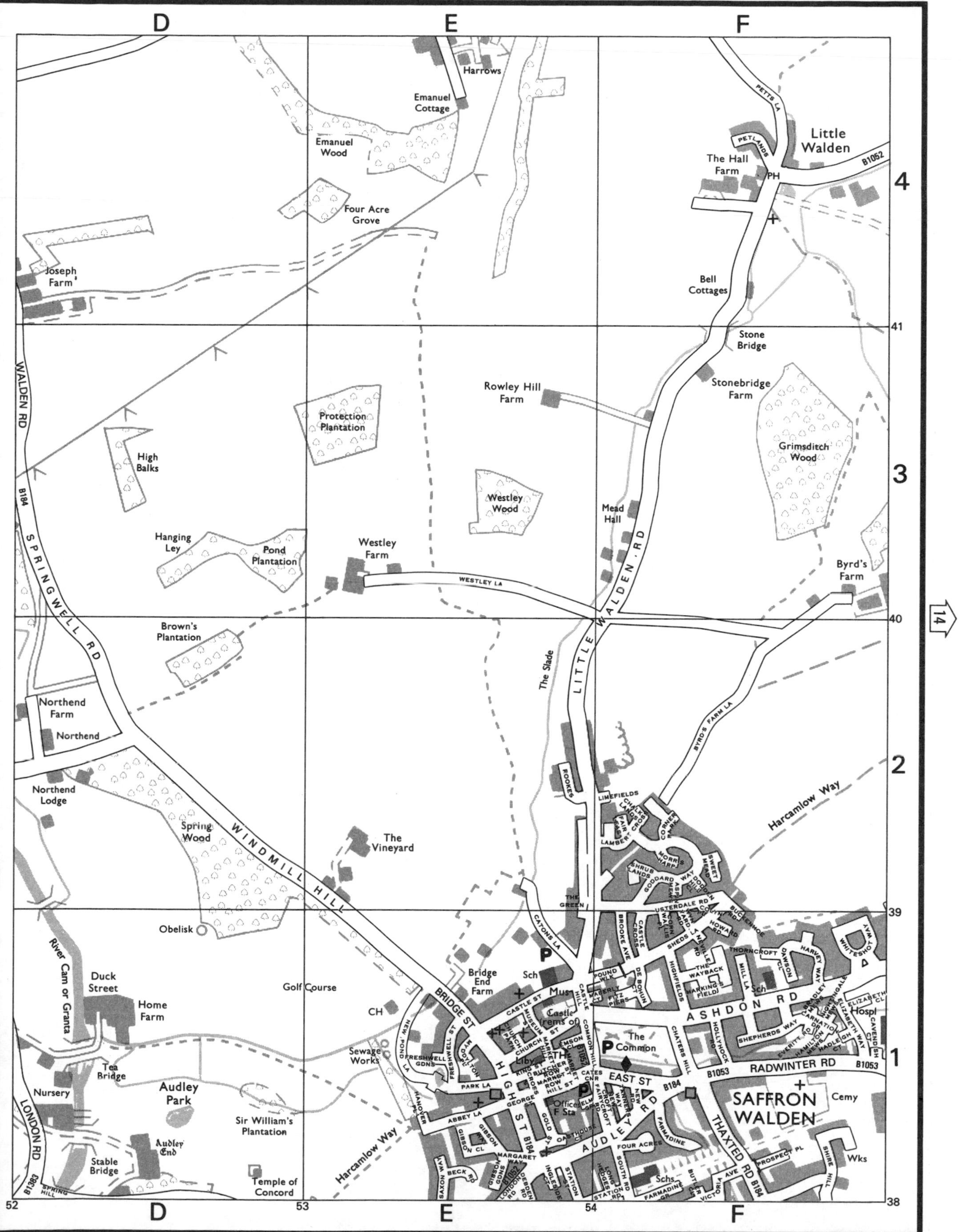
2
D
E
F
Harrows
Emanuel Cottage
Emanuel Wood
Four Acre Grove
Joseph Farm
Little Walden
The Hall Farm
PH
B1052
Bell Cottages
Stone Bridge
Stonebridge Farm
Rowley Hill Farm
Protection Plantation
High Balks
Grimsditch Wood
Westley Wood
Mead Hall
Hanging Ley
Pond Plantation
Westley Farm
WESTLEY LA
Byrd's Farm
WALDEN RD
B184
SPRINGWELL RD
LITTLE WALDEN RD
Brown's Plantation
The Slade
BYRD'S FARM LA
Northend Farm
Northend
Northend Lodge
Harcamlow Way
Spring Wood
WINDMILL HILL
The Vineyard
Obelisk
River Cam or Granta
Duck Street
Home Farm
Golf Course
Bridge End Farm
CH
Sch
Mus
Castle (rems of)
The Common
ASHDON RD
RADWINTER RD
B1053
EAST ST
Sewage Works
Tea Bridge
Nursery
Audley Park
Sir William's Plantation
Audley End
LONDON RD
Stable Bridge
Temple of Concord
Harcamlow Way
SAFFRON WALDEN
Cemy
Hospl
Wks
THAXTED RD
AUDLEY RD
HIGH ST
BRIDGE ST
B1383
4
3
2
1
41
40
39
38
52
53
54
14
25

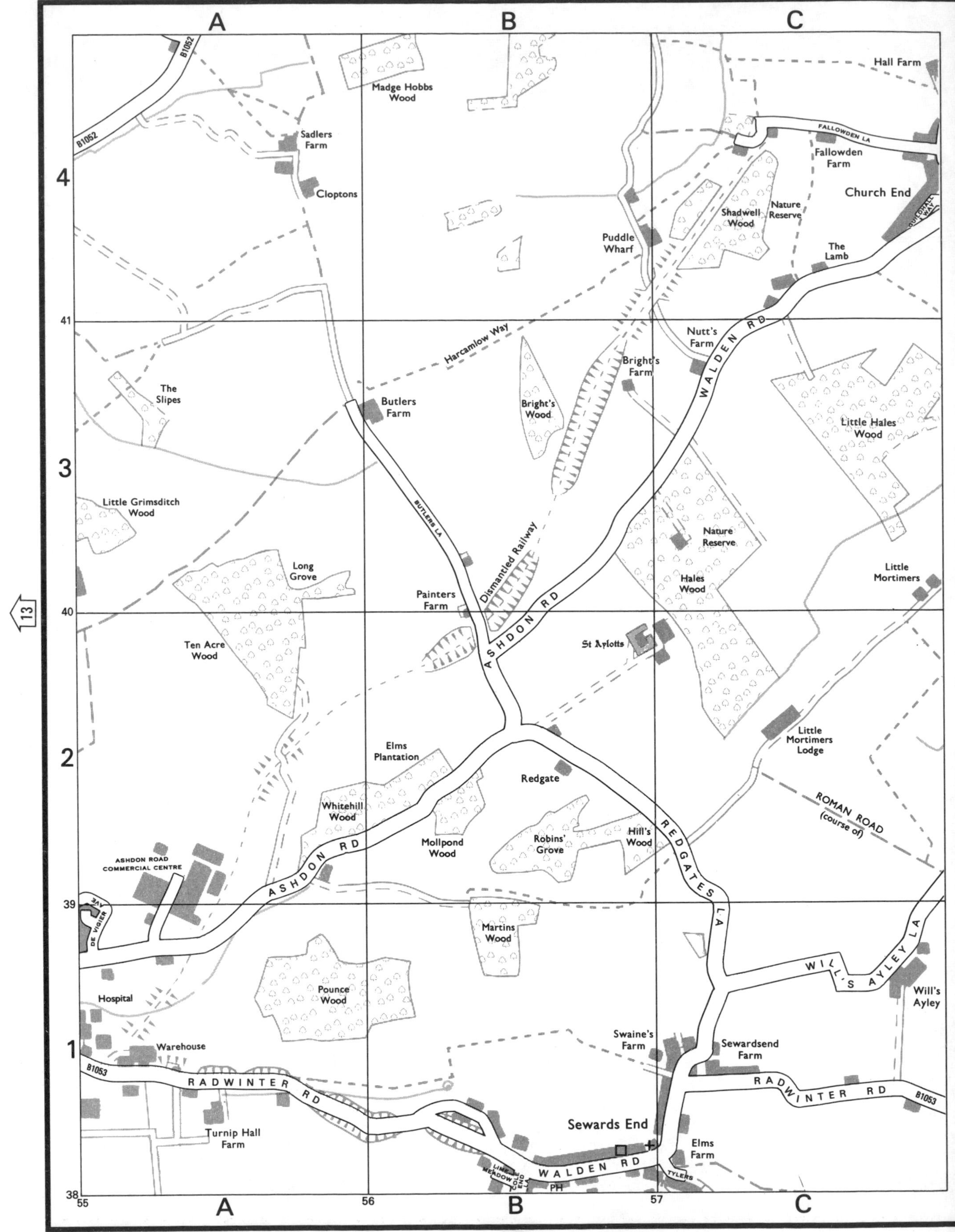
3
A
B
C
Hall Farm
B1052
Madge Hobbs Wood
Sadlers Farm
B1052
FALLOWDEN LA
Fallowden Farm
4
Cloptons
Church End
Shadwell Wood
Nature Reserve
GUILDHALL WAY
Puddle Wharf
The Lamb
41
Nutt's Farm
WALDEN RD
Harcamlow Way
Bright's Farm
The Slipes
Butlers Farm
Bright's Wood
Little Hales Wood
3
Little Grimsditch Wood
BUTLERS LA
Dismantled Railway
Nature Reserve
Long Grove
Little Mortimers
Hales Wood
Painters Farm
13
40
ASHDON RD
St Aylotts
Ten Acre Wood
Little Mortimers Lodge
2
Elms Plantation
Redgate
ROMAN ROAD (course of)
Whitehill Wood
Robins' Grove
Hill's Wood
Mollpond Wood
ASHDON RD
REDGATES LA
ASHDON ROAD COMMERCIAL CENTRE
39
DE VIGIER AVE
Martins Wood
WILL'S AYLEY LA
Hospital
Pounce Wood
Will's Ayley
Swaine's Farm
Sewardsend Farm
1
Warehouse
B1053
RADWINTER RD
RADWINTER RD
B1053
Sewards End
Turnip Hall Farm
Elms Farm
LIME MEADOW
COLE END LA
WALDEN RD
TYLERS
PH
38
55
56
57
A
B
C
26

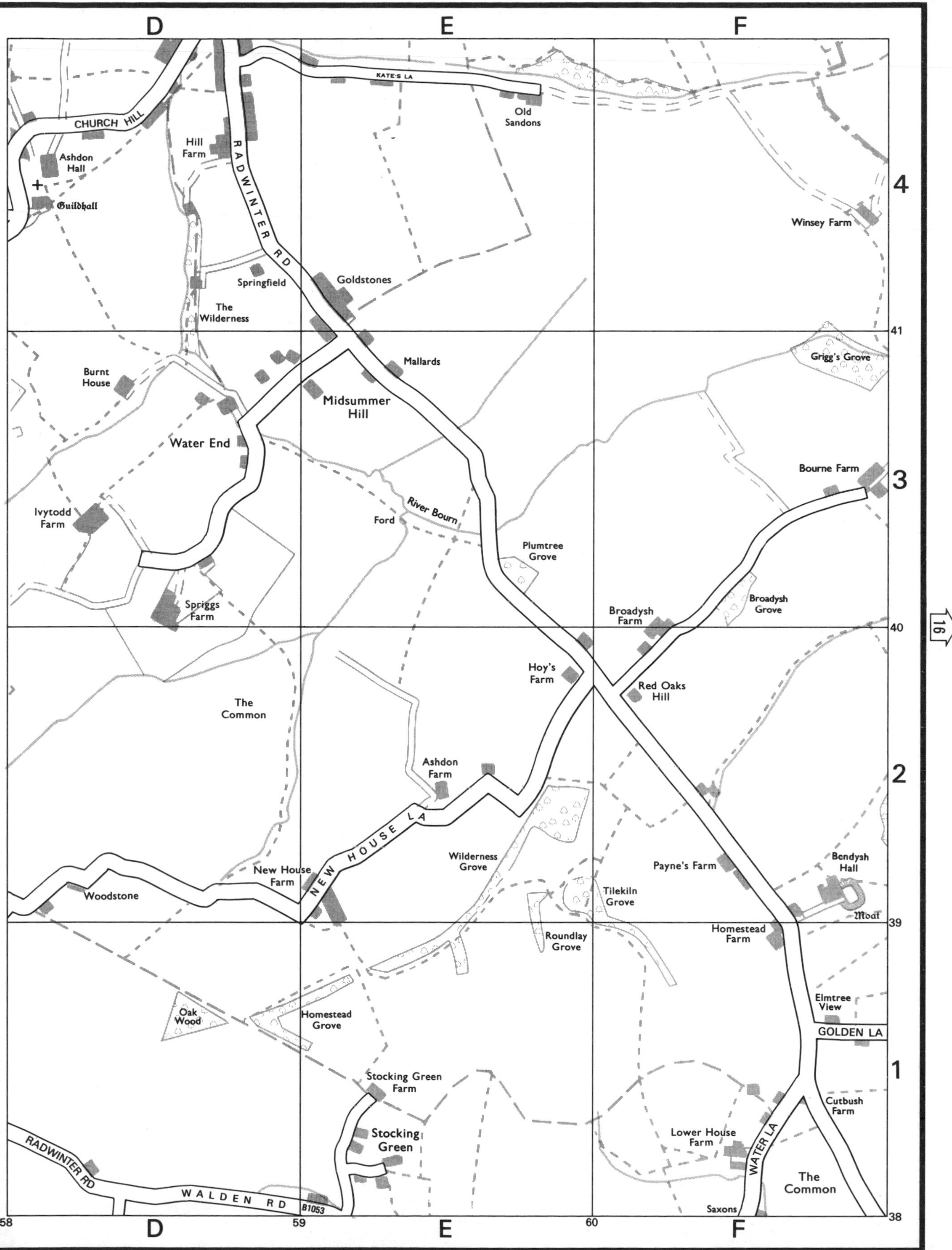
4
D
E
F
CHURCH HILL
RADWINTER RD
KATE'S LA
Old Sandons
Hill Farm
Ashdon Hall
Guildhall
Winsey Farm
Springfield
Goldstones
The Wilderness
Mallards
Grigg's Grove
Burnt House
Midsummer Hill
Water End
Bourne Farm
Ivytodd Farm
River Bourn
Ford
Plumtree Grove
Spriggs Farm
Broadysh Grove
Broadysh Farm
Hoy's Farm
Red Oaks Hill
The Common
Ashdon Farm
NEW HOUSE LA
Wilderness Grove
New House Farm
Payne's Farm
Bendysh Hall
Woodstone
Tilekiln Grove
Moat
Homestead Farm
Roundlay Grove
Elmtree View
Oak Wood
Homestead Grove
GOLDEN LA
Stocking Green Farm
Cutbush Farm
Stocking Green
Lower House Farm
WATER LA
RADWINTER RD
WALDEN RD
B1053
The Common
Saxons
4
41
3
40
16
2
39
1
38
58
59
60
27

5

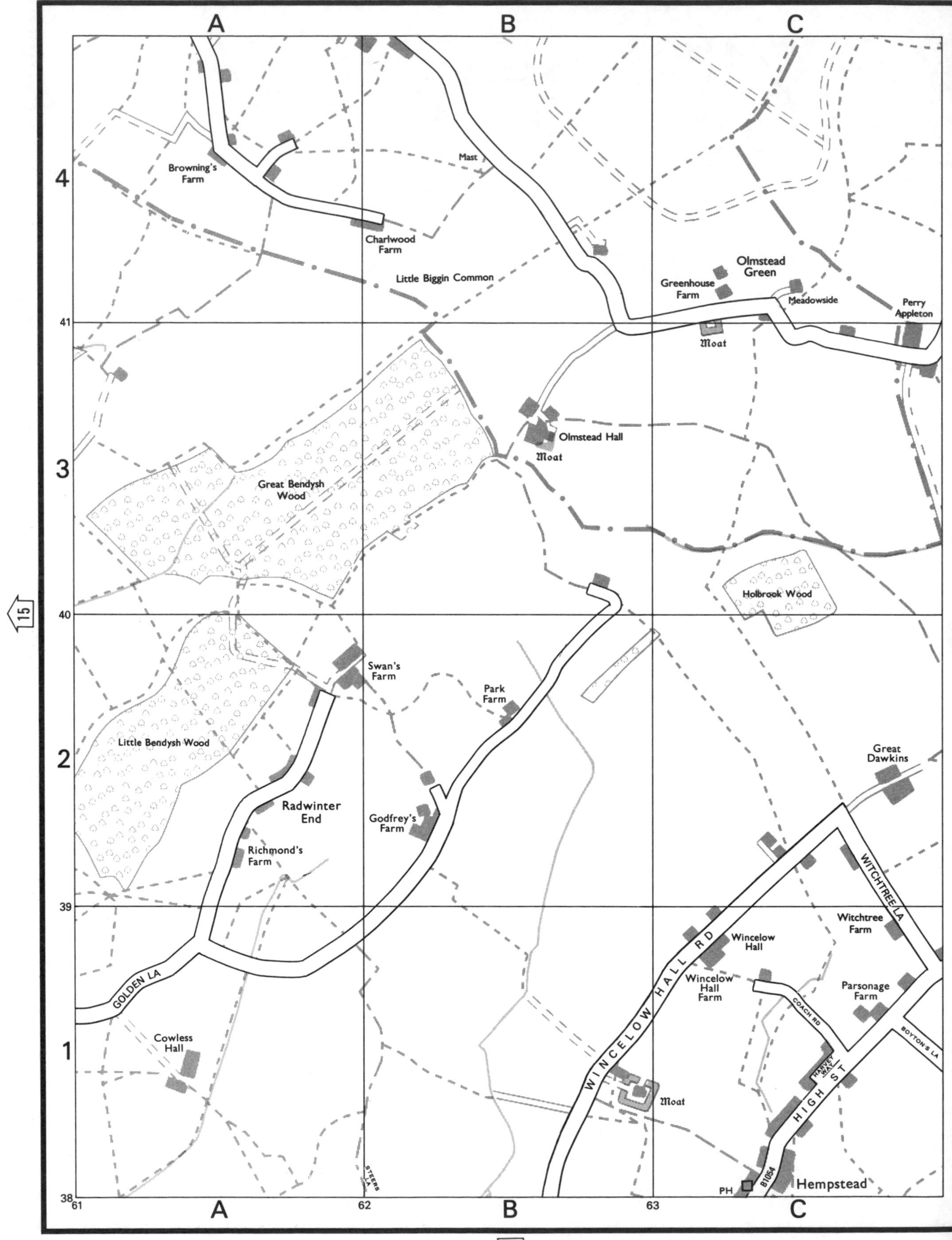

A
B
C
4
3
2
1
41
40
39
38
61
62
63
Browning's Farm
Mast
Charlwood Farm
Little Biggin Common
Olmstead Green
Greenhouse Farm
Meadowside
Perry Appleton
Moat
Olmstead Hall
Moat
Great Bendysh Wood
Holbrook Wood
Swan's Farm
Park Farm
Little Bendysh Wood
Great Dawkins
Radwinter End
Godfrey's Farm
Richmond's Farm
WITCHTREE LA
Witchtree Farm
Wincelow Hall
WINCELOW HALL RD
Wincelow Hall Farm
Parsonage Farm
GOLDEN LA
COACH RD
BOYTON'S LA
Cowless Hall
HARVEY WAY
HIGH ST
Moat
STEERS LA
PH
B1054
Hempstead

15

28

6

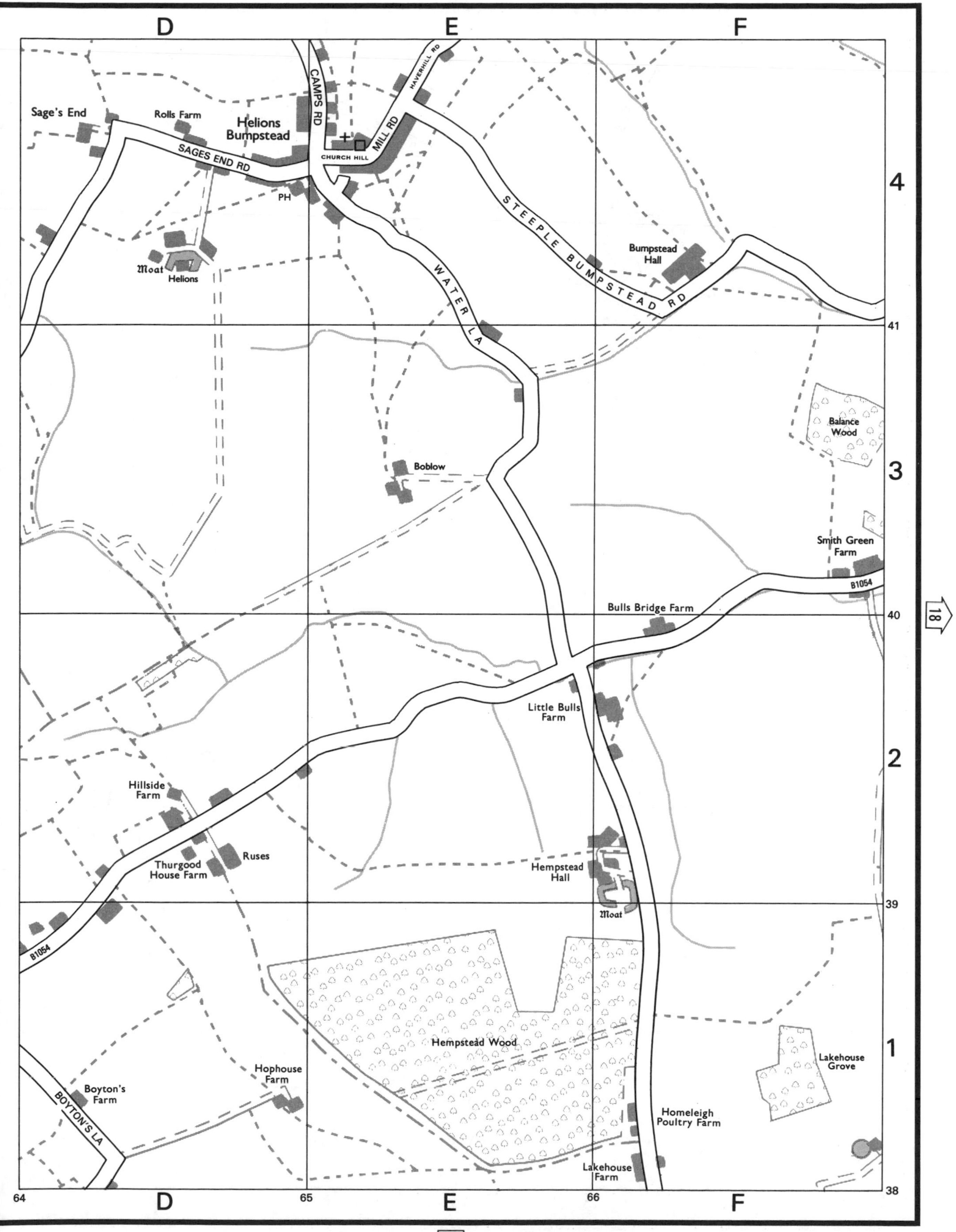
D
E
F
Sage's End
Rolls Farm
Helions Bumpstead
CAMPS RD
HAVERHILL RD
MILL RD
CHURCH HILL
SAGES END RD
PH
Moat
Helions
WATER LA
STEEPLE BUMPSTEAD RD
Bumpstead Hall
4
41
Balance Wood
Boblow
3
Smith Green Farm
B1054
Bulls Bridge Farm
40
Little Bulls Farm
2
Hillside Farm
Ruses
Thurgood House Farm
Hempstead Hall
Moat
39
B1054
Hempstead Wood
1
Lakehouse Grove
Hophouse Farm
Boyton's Farm
BOYTON'S LA
Homeleigh Poultry Farm
Lakehouse Farm
64
65
66
38
D
E
F

18

29

7

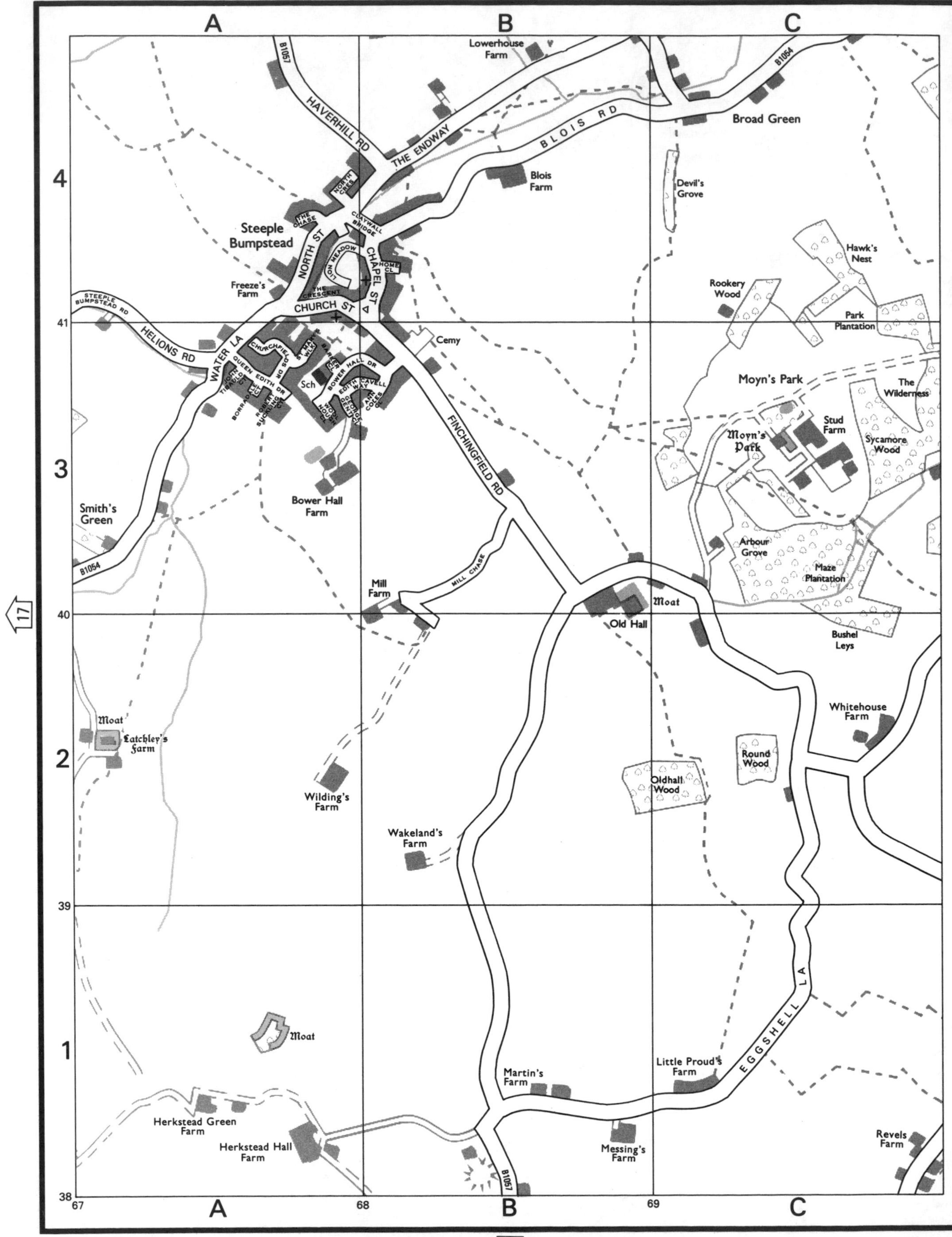
A
B
C
Lowerhouse Farm
B1057
B1054
HAVERHILL RD
THE ENDWAY
BLOIS RD
Broad Green
Blois Farm
Devil's Grove
Steeple Bumpstead
NORTH ST
CHAPEL ST
CHURCH ST
LION MEADOW
THE CRESCENT
HOME CL
Freeze's Farm
STEEPLE BUMPSTEAD RD
HELIONS RD
WATER LA
QUEEN EDITH DR
BOWER HALL DR
Sch
Cemy
FINCHINGFIELD RD
Hawk's Nest
Rookery Wood
Park Plantation
Moyn's Park
The Wilderness
Stud Farm
Moyn's Park
Sycamore Wood
Smith's Green
Bower Hall Farm
Arbour Grove
Maze Plantation
Mill Farm
MILL CHASE
Moat
Old Hall
Bushel Leys
Moat
Latchley's Farm
Whitehouse Farm
Round Wood
Oldhall Wood
Wilding's Farm
Wakeland's Farm
EGGSHELL LA
Moat
Martin's Farm
Little Proud's Farm
Herkstead Green Farm
Herkstead Hall Farm
Messing's Farm
Revels Farm
4
3
2
1
41
40
39
38
67
68
69

17

30

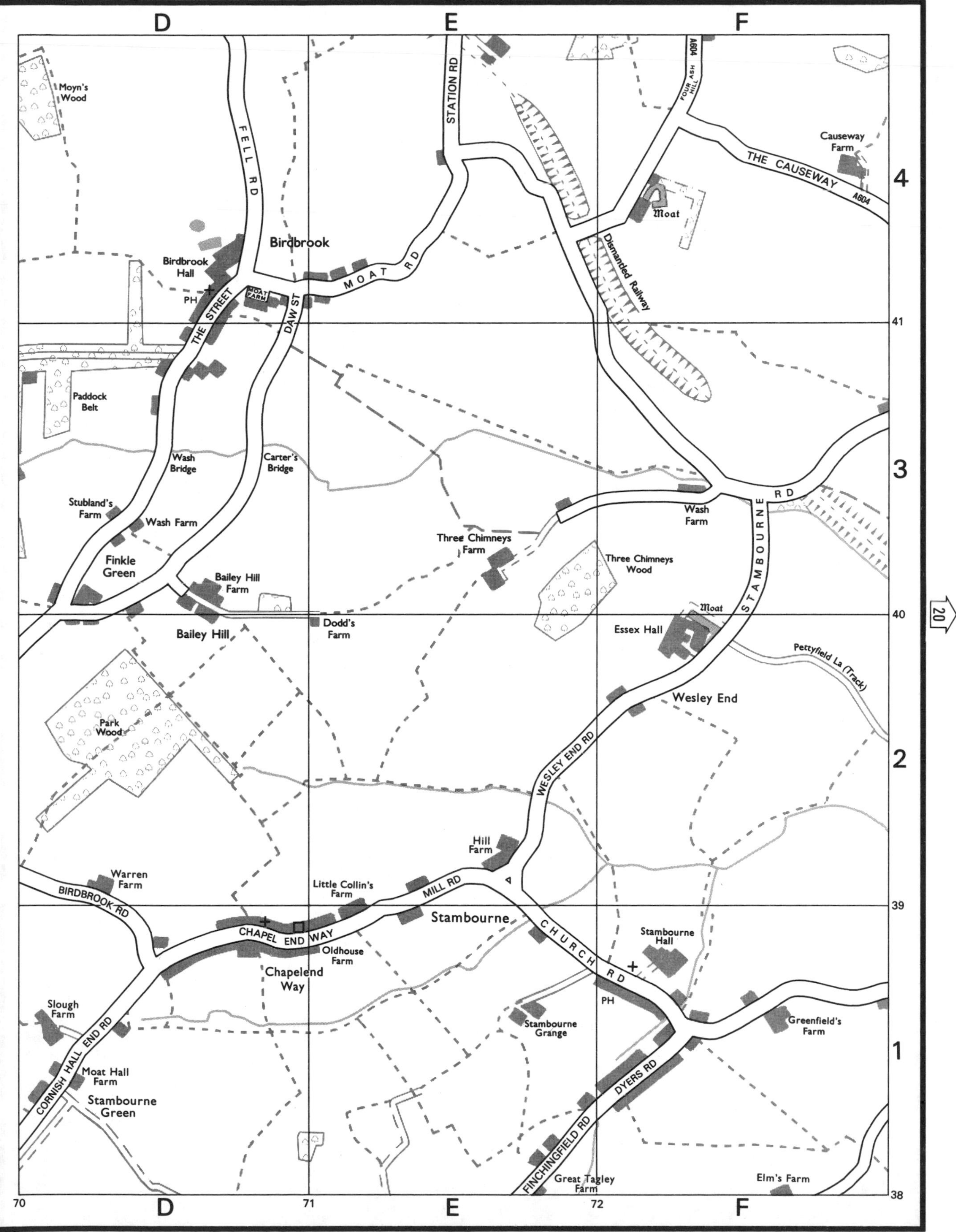
8
D
E
F
Moyn's Wood
FELL RD
STATION RD
A604
FOUR ASH HILL
Causeway Farm
THE CAUSEWAY
A604
4
Moat
Birdbrook
Birdbrook Hall
MOAT RD
Dismantled Railway
PH
THE STREET
MOAT FARM
DAW ST
41
Paddock Belt
Wash Bridge
Carter's Bridge
3
Stubland's Farm
Wash Farm
Wash Farm
RD
Three Chimneys Farm
Three Chimneys Wood
STAMBOURNE
Finkle Green
Bailey Hill Farm
Moat
20
Dodd's Farm
40
Bailey Hill
Essex Hall
Pettyfield La (Track)
Wesley End
Park Wood
WESLEY END RD
2
Hill Farm
Warren Farm
Little Collin's Farm
MILL RD
BIRDBROOK RD
39
CHAPEL END WAY
Stambourne
CHURCH RD
Stambourne Hall
Oldhouse Farm
Chapelend Way
PH
Slough Farm
Stambourne Grange
Greenfield's Farm
CORNISH HALL END RD
1
Moat Hall Farm
DYERS RD
Stambourne Green
FINCHINGFIELD RD
Great Tagley Farm
Elm's Farm
70
71
72
38
D
E
F
31

9

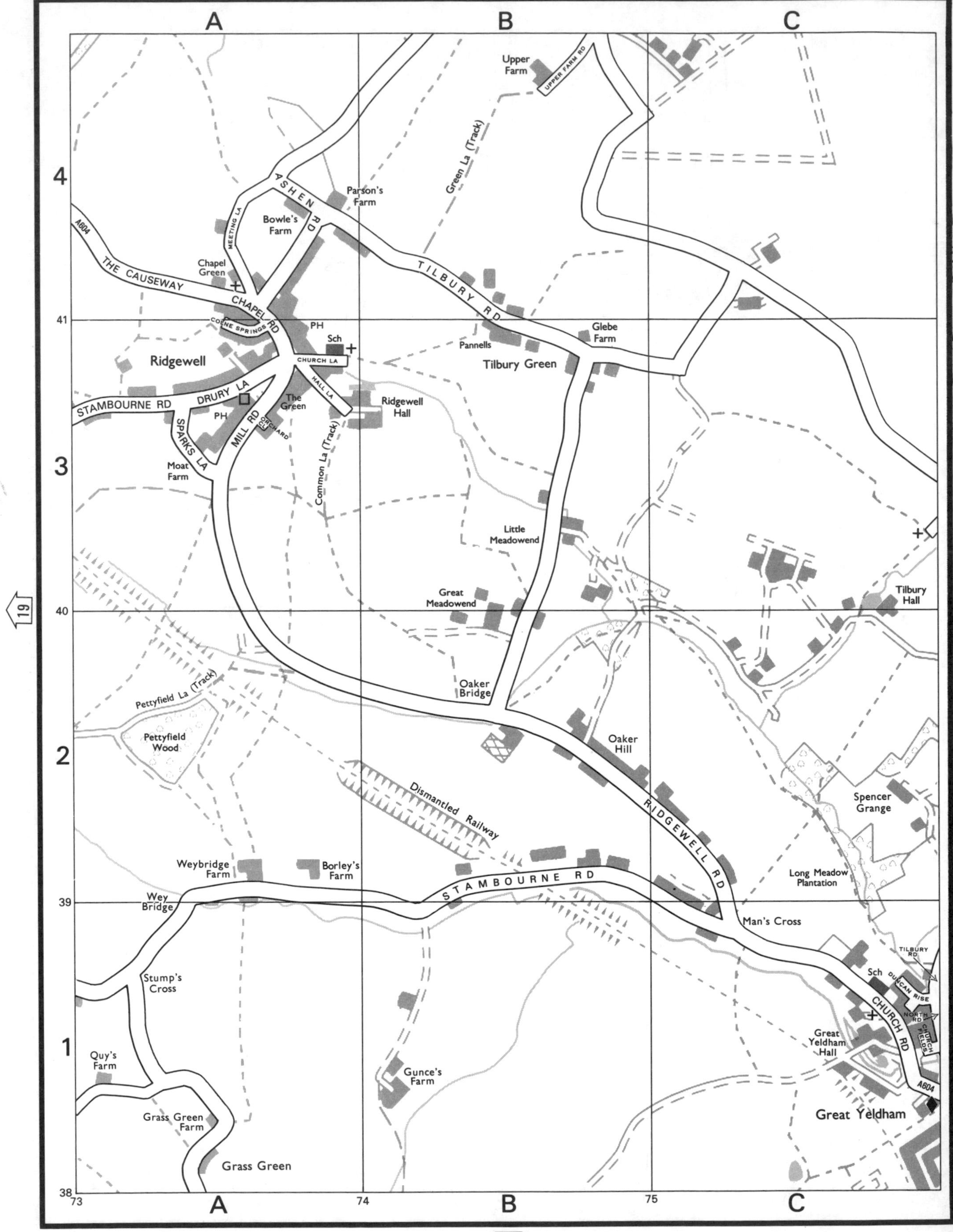

A
B
C
4
3
2
1
41
40
39
38
73
74
75
Upper Farm
UPPER FARM RD
Green La (Track)
ASHEN RD
Parson's Farm
Bowle's Farm
MEETING LA
A604
THE CAUSEWAY
Chapel Green
CHAPEL RD
TILBURY RD
COLNE SPRINGS
PH
Sch
Glebe Farm
Pannells
Ridgewell
CHURCH LA
Tilbury Green
STAMBOURNE RD
DRURY LA
HALL LA
The Green
Ridgewell Hall
PH
MILL RD
ORCHARD
SPARKS LA
Moat Farm
Common La (Track)
Little Meadowend
Tilbury Hall
Great Meadowend
Oaker Bridge
Pettyfield La (Track)
Pettyfield Wood
Oaker Hill
Dismantled Railway
RIDGEWELL RD
Spencer Grange
Weybridge Farm
Borley's Farm
Long Meadow Plantation
STAMBOURNE RD
Wey Bridge
Man's Cross
TILBURY RD
Sch
DUNCAN RISE
Stump's Cross
NORTH RD
CHURCH RD
CHURCH FIELDS
Great Yeldham Hall
Quy's Farm
Gunce's Farm
A604
Great Yeldham
Grass Green Farm
Grass Green

19

32

not continued, see key diagram

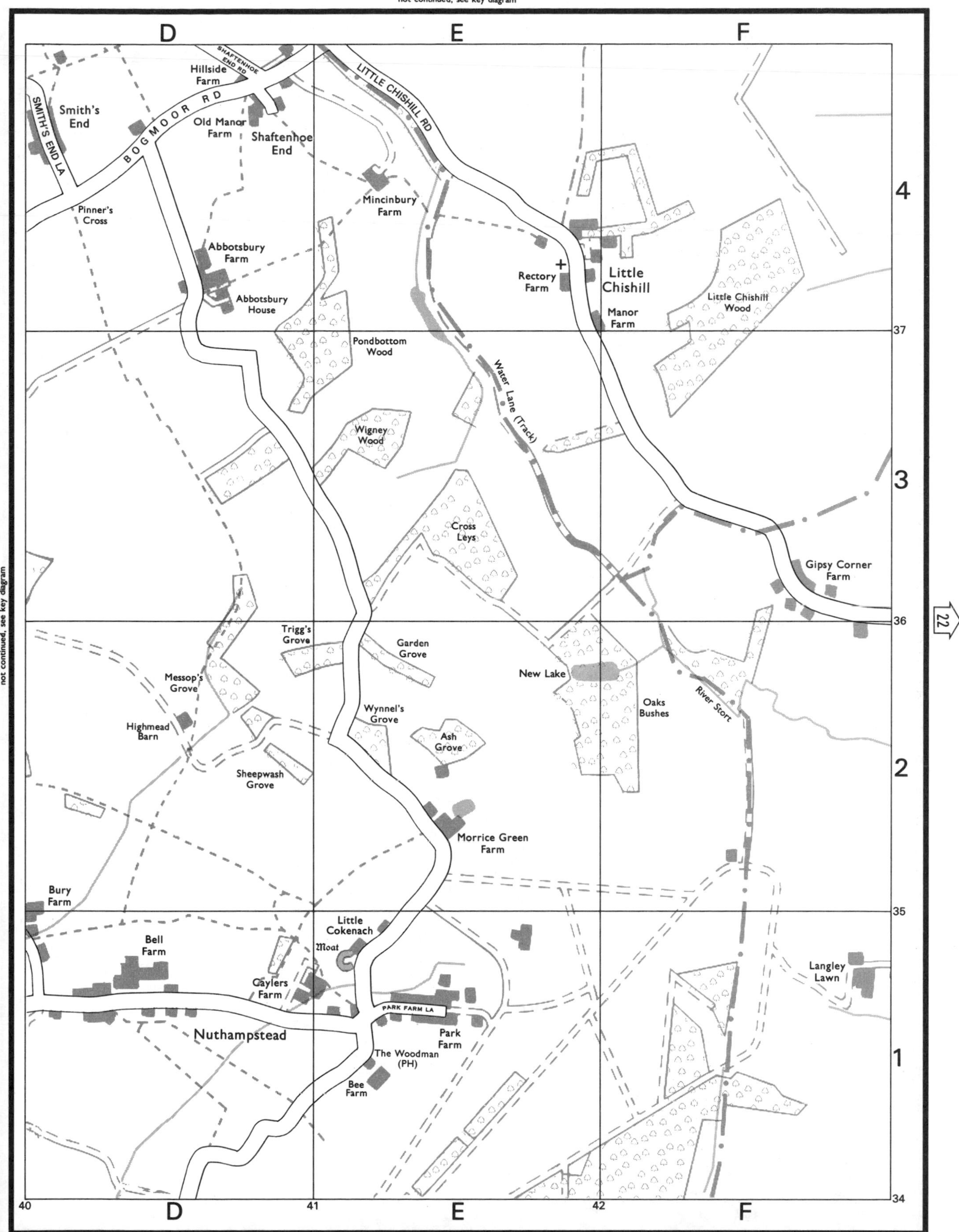

not continued, see key diagram

22

33

10

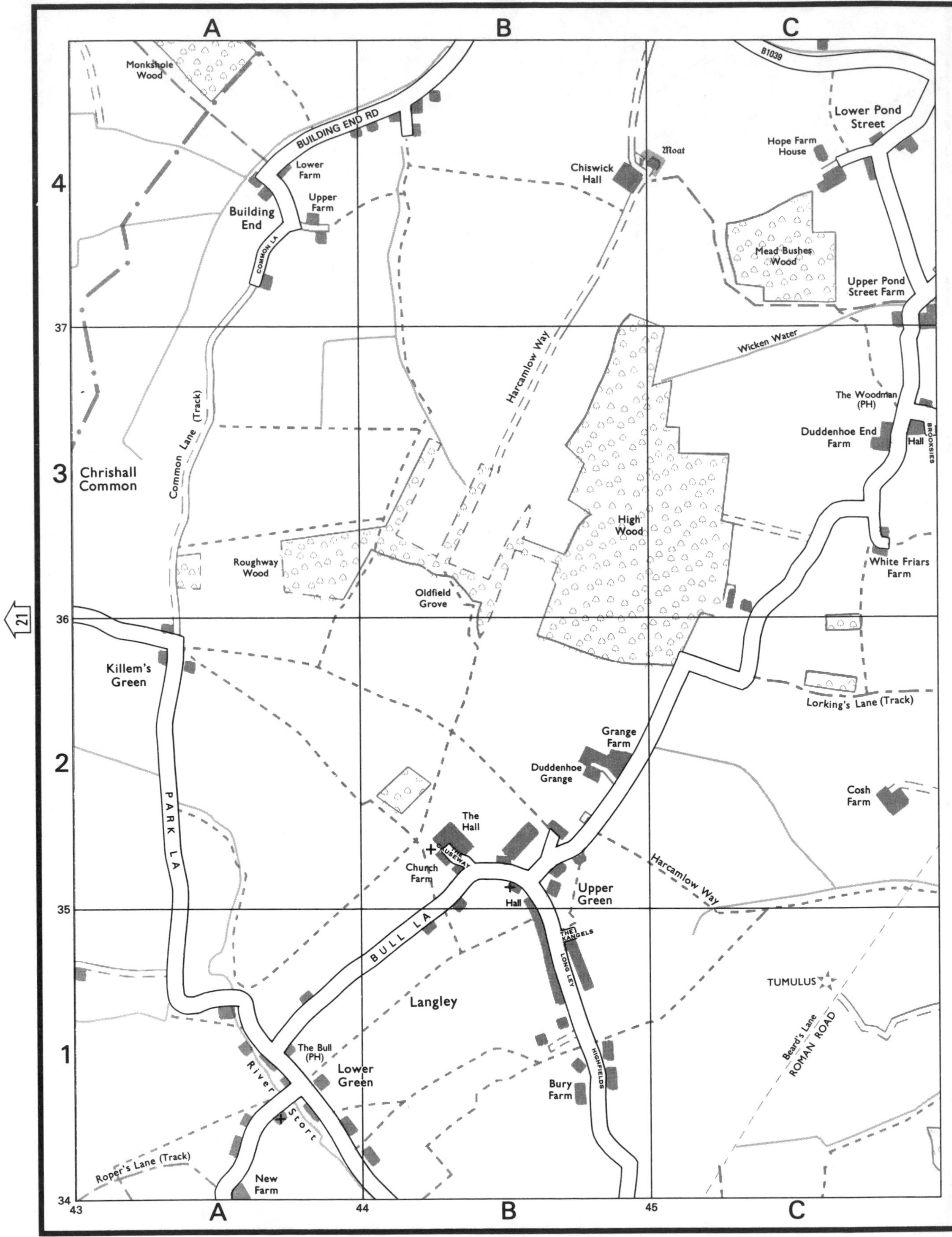
A
B
C
Monkshole Wood
BUILDING END RD
Lower Farm
Upper Farm
Building End
COMMON LA
B1039
Lower Pond Street
Hope Farm House
Moat
Chiswick Hall
Mead Bushes Wood
Upper Pond Street Farm
Wicken Water
Harcamlow Way
The Woodman (PH)
Duddenhoe End Farm
Hall
BROOKSIES
Common Lane (Track)
Chrishall Common
High Wood
Roughway Wood
Oldfield Grove
White Friars Farm
Killem's Green
Lorking's Lane (Track)
Grange Farm
Duddenhoe Grange
Cosh Farm
PARK LA
The Hall
THE CAUSEWAY
Church Farm
Hall
Upper Green
Harcamlow Way
THE TANGELS
LONG LEY
BULL LA
TUMULUS
Langley
Beard's Lane
ROMAN ROAD
The Bull (PH)
Lower Green
River Stort
HIGHFIELDS
Bury Farm
Roper's Lane (Track)
New Farm
4
37
3
36
2
35
1
34
43
44
45
A
B
C

21

34

11

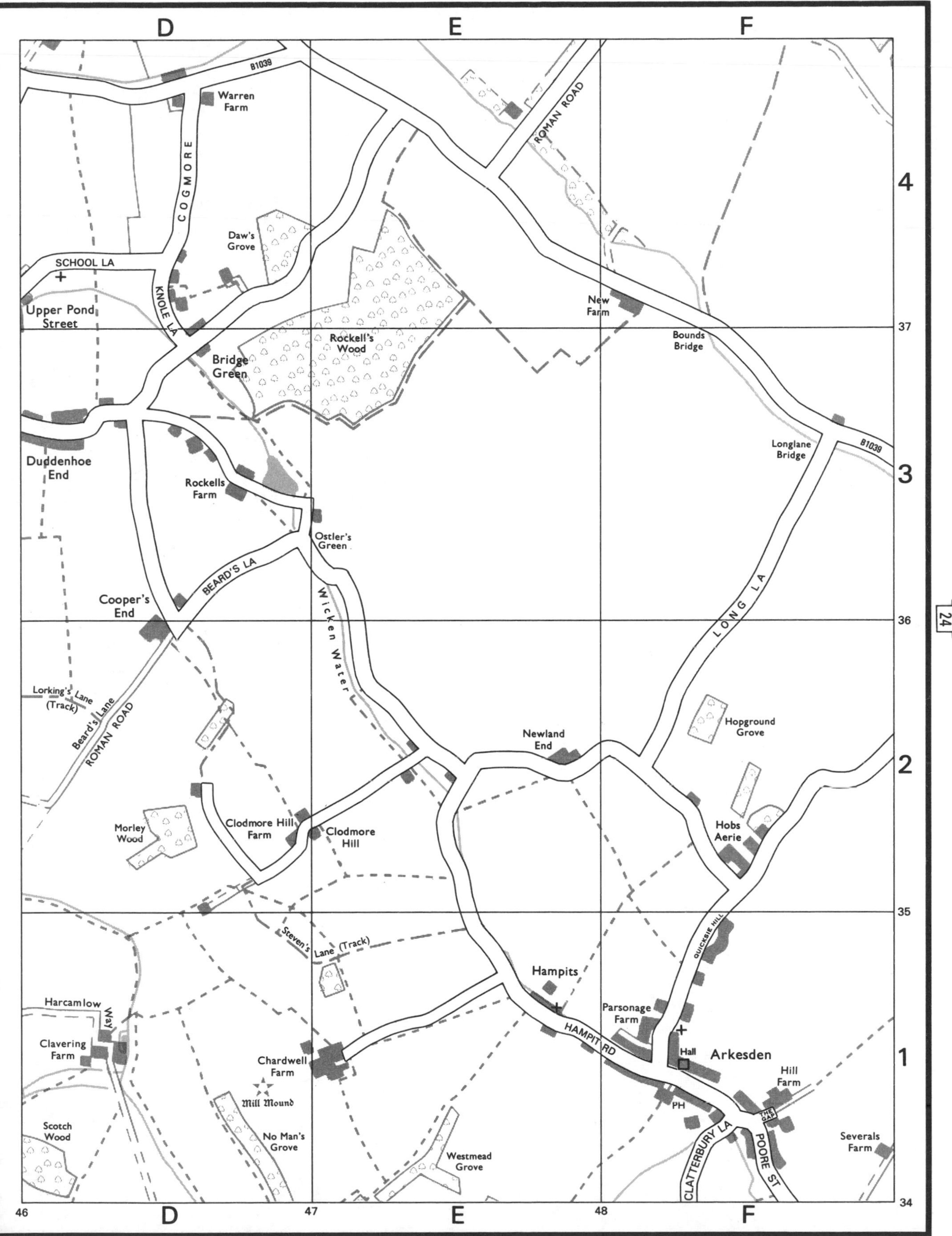

D
E
F
B1039
Warren Farm
COGMORE
ROMAN ROAD
4
Daw's Grove
SCHOOL LA
KNOLE LA
Upper Pond Street
New Farm
37
Bounds Bridge
Rockell's Wood
Bridge Green
Longlane Bridge
B1039
Duddenhoe End
3
Rockells Farm
Ostler's Green
LONG LA
BEARD'S LA
Cooper's End
Wicken Water
36
Lorking's Lane (Track)
Beard's Lane
ROMAN ROAD
Hopground Grove
Newland End
2
Morley Wood
Clodmore Hill Farm
Clodmore Hill
Hobs Aerie
35
Steven's Lane (Track)
QUICKSIE HILL
Hampits
Harcamlow Way
Parsonage Farm
HAMPIT RD
Clavering Farm
Hall
Arkesden
1
Chardwell Farm
Mill Mound
Hill Farm
PH
THE GAP
Scotch Wood
No Man's Grove
CLATTERBURY LA
POORE ST
Severals Farm
Westmead Grove
34
46
D
47
E
48
F

24

35

12

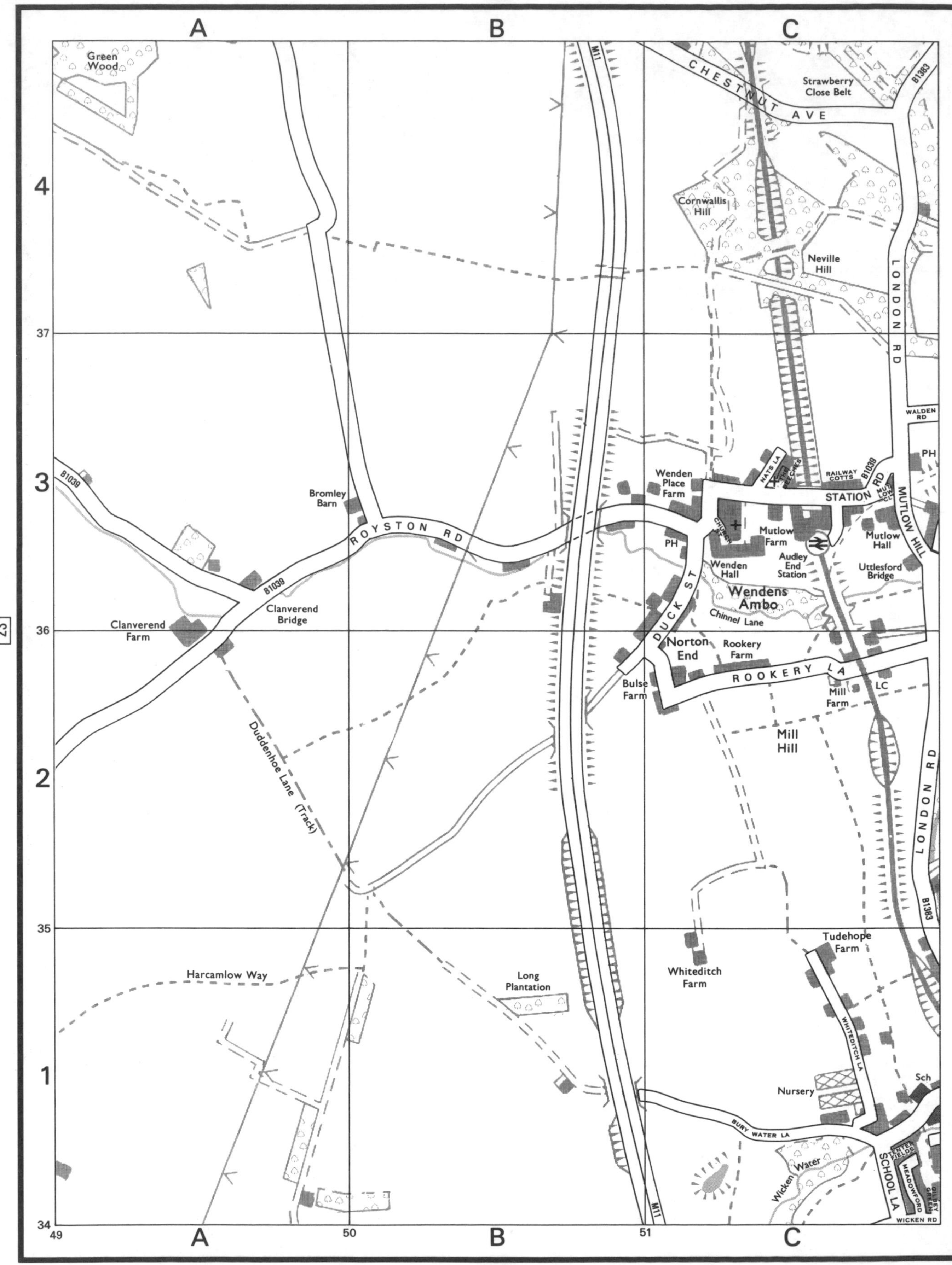

A
B
C
4
37
3
36
2
35
1
34
49
50
51
Green Wood
M11
CHESTNUT AVE
Strawberry Close Belt
B1383
Cornwallis Hill
Neville Hill
LONDON RD
WALDEN RD
PH
NATS LA
THE BEECHES
RAILWAY COTTS
B1039
STATION RD
MUTLOW HILL
Wenden Place Farm
Bromley Barn
ROYSTON RD
B1039
CHURCH ST
Mutlow Farm
Mutlow Hall
PH
Audley End Station
Wenden Hall
Uttlesford Bridge
Wendens Ambo
Chinnel Lane
DUCK ST
Clanverend Bridge
Clanverend Farm
Norton End
Rookery Farm
ROOKERY LA
Bulse Farm
Mill Farm
LC
Mill Hill
Duddenhoe Lane (Track)
LONDON RD
B1383
Tudehope Farm
Harcamlow Way
Long Plantation
Whiteditch Farm
WHITEDITCH LA
Nursery
Sch
BURY WATER LA
Wicken Water
SCHOOL LA
MEADOWFORD
WICKEN RD

23

36

13

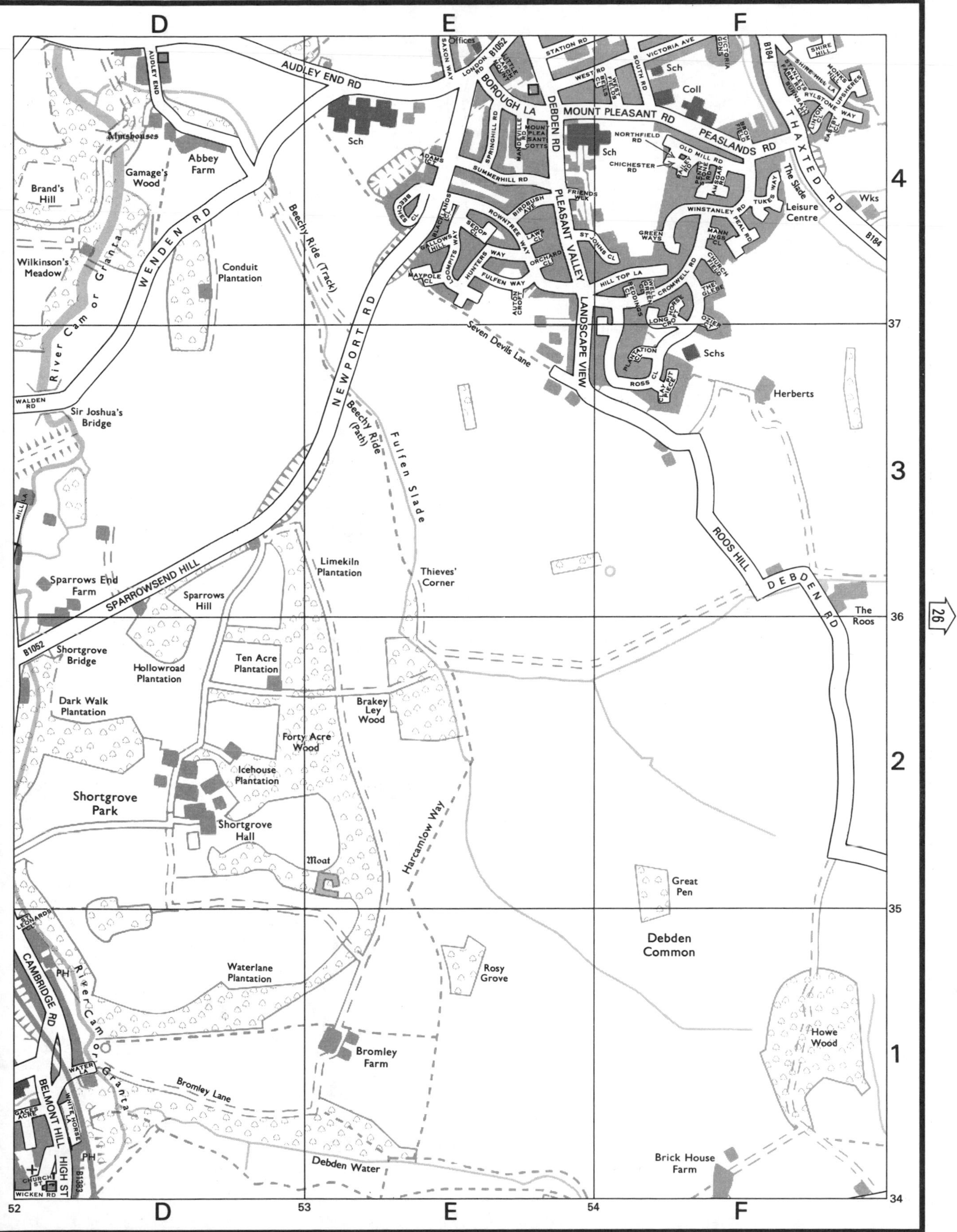
D
E
F
AUDLEY END RD
AUDLEY END
Almshouses
Abbey Farm
Gamage's Wood
Brand's Hill
WENDEN RD
Wilkinson's Meadow
River Cam or Granta
Conduit Plantation
Beechy Ride (Track)
NEWPORT RD
Sch
Offices
SAXON WAY
LONDON RD
B1052
BOROUGH LA
DEBDEN RD
MOUNT PLEASANT RD
STATION RD
WEST RD
SOUTH RD
VICTORIA AVE
Coll
PEASLANDS RD
THAXTED RD
B184
SHIRE HILL
The Slade
Leisure Centre
Wks
SUMMERHILL RD
PLEASANT VALLEY
WINSTANLEY RD
HILL TOP LA
CROMWELL RD
Seven Devils Lane
LANDSCAPE VIEW
Schs
Herberts
ROSS CL
WALDEN RD
Sir Joshua's Bridge
Beechy Ride (Path)
Fulfen Slade
MILL LA
ROOS HILL
DEBDEN RD
The Roos
Sparrows End Farm
SPARROWSEND HILL
Sparrows Hill
Limekiln Plantation
Thieves' Corner
B1052
Shortgrove Bridge
Hollowroad Plantation
Ten Acre Plantation
Dark Walk Plantation
Brakey Ley Wood
Forty Acre Wood
Icehouse Plantation
Shortgrove Park
Shortgrove Hall
Moat
Harcamlow Way
Great Pen
Debden Common
ST LEONARDS
CAMBRIDGE RD
PH
Waterlane Plantation
Rosy Grove
Howe Wood
Bromley Farm
WATER LA
BELMONT HILL
Bromley Lane
WHITE HORSE
HIGH ST
B1383
CHURCH ST
WICKEN RD
Debden Water
Brick House Farm
4
3
2
1
37
36
35
34
52
53
54

26

37

14

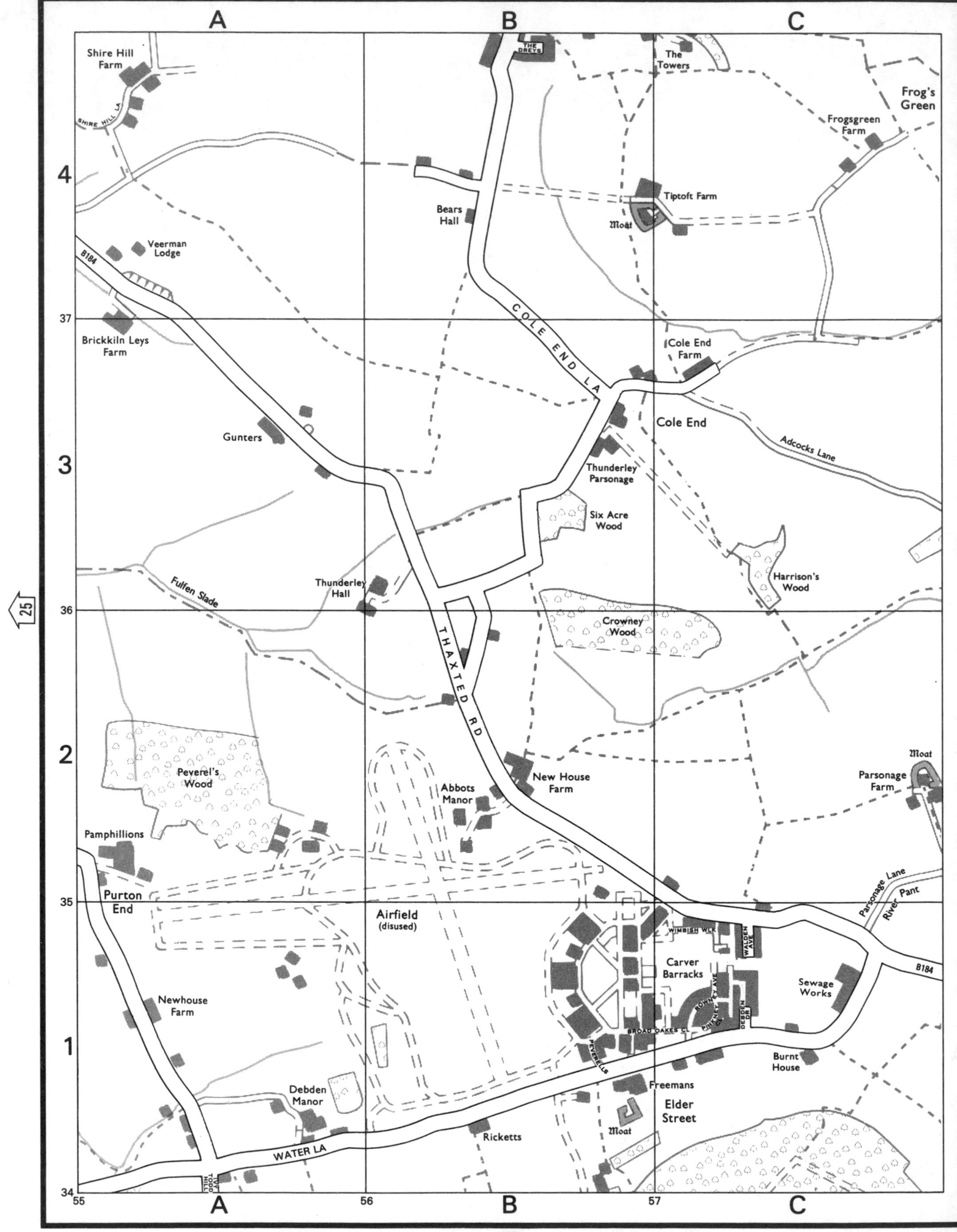
A
B
C
4
3
2
1
37
36
35
34
55
56
57
Shire Hill Farm
SHIRE HILL LA
THE DREYS
The Towers
Frog's Green
Frogsgreen Farm
Bears Hall
Tiptoft Farm
Moat
Veerman Lodge
B184
COLE END LA
Brickkiln Leys Farm
Cole End Farm
Cole End
Gunters
Adcocks Lane
Thunderley Parsonage
Six Acre Wood
Harrison's Wood
Thunderley Hall
Fulfen Slade
THAXTED RD
Crowney Wood
Peverel's Wood
Abbots Manor
New House Farm
Moat
Parsonage Farm
Pamphillions
Purton End
Airfield
(disused)
Parsonage Lane
River Pant
WIMBISH WLK
WALDEN AVE
Carver Barracks
Sewage Works
B184
ROWNEY AVE
DEBDEN DR
PINKNEY CL
BROAD OAKES CL
PEVERELLS
Newhouse Farm
Burnt House
Freemans
Debden Manor
Elder Street
Ricketts
Moat
WATER LA
IVY TODD HILL

25

15

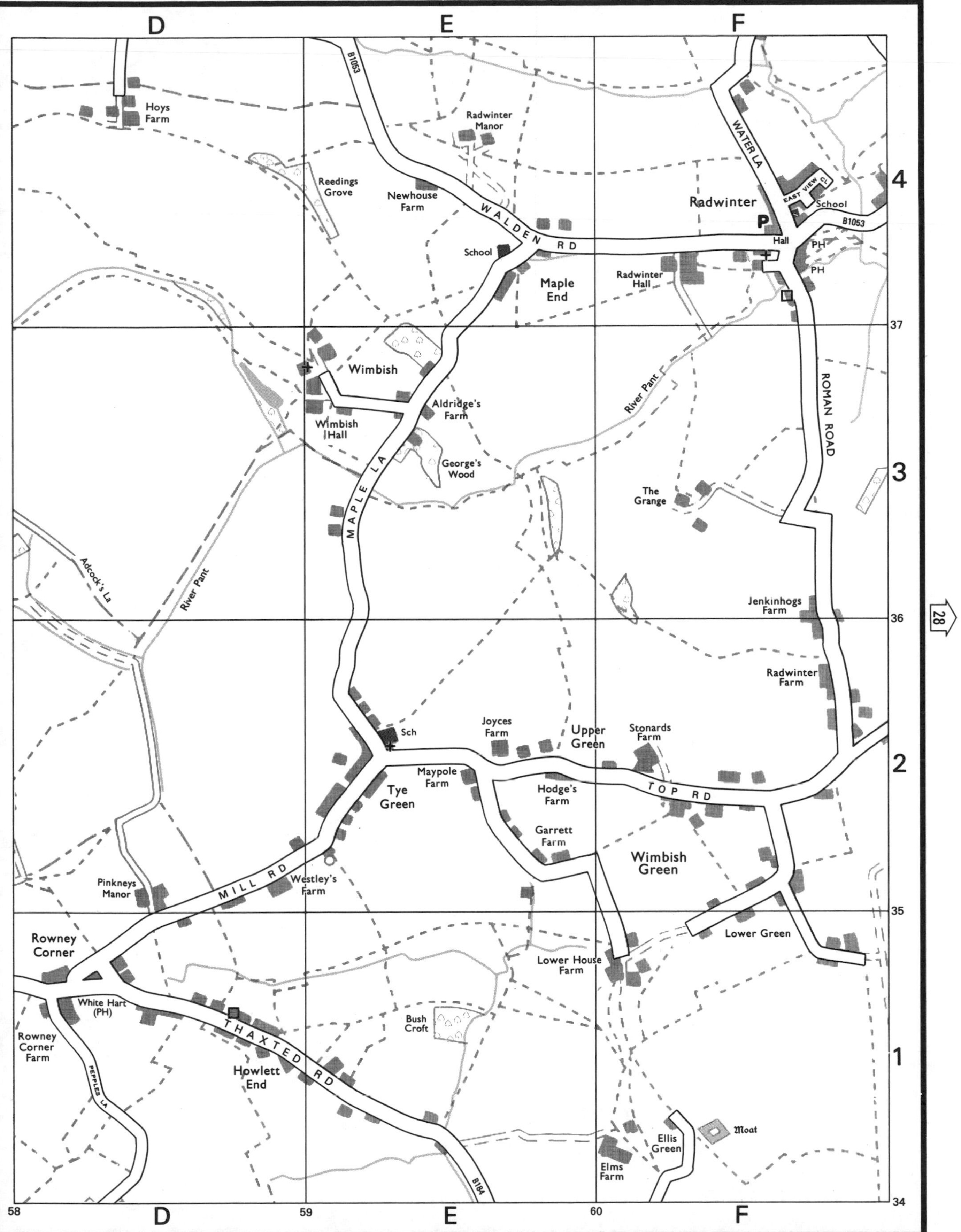
D
E
F
Hoys Farm
Radwinter Manor
Reedings Grove
Newhouse Farm
WALDEN RD
B1053
WATER LA
EAST VIEW CL
School
Radwinter
Hall
PH
PH
School
Maple End
Radwinter Hall
Wimbish
Aldridge's Farm
Wimbish Hall
George's Wood
River Pant
MAPLE LA
ROMAN ROAD
The Grange
Adcock's La
Jenkinhogs Farm
Radwinter Farm
Sch
Joyces Farm
Upper Green
Stonards Farm
Maypole Farm
Tye Green
Hodge's Farm
TOP RD
Garrett Farm
Wimbish Green
Pinkneys Manor
MILL RD
Westley's Farm
Rowney Corner
Lower Green
Lower House Farm
White Hart (PH)
Rowney Corner Farm
THAXTED RD
Bush Croft
Howlett End
PEPPLES LA
Moat
Ellis Green
Elms Farm
B184
4
3
2
1
37
36
35
34
58
59
60

28

39

16

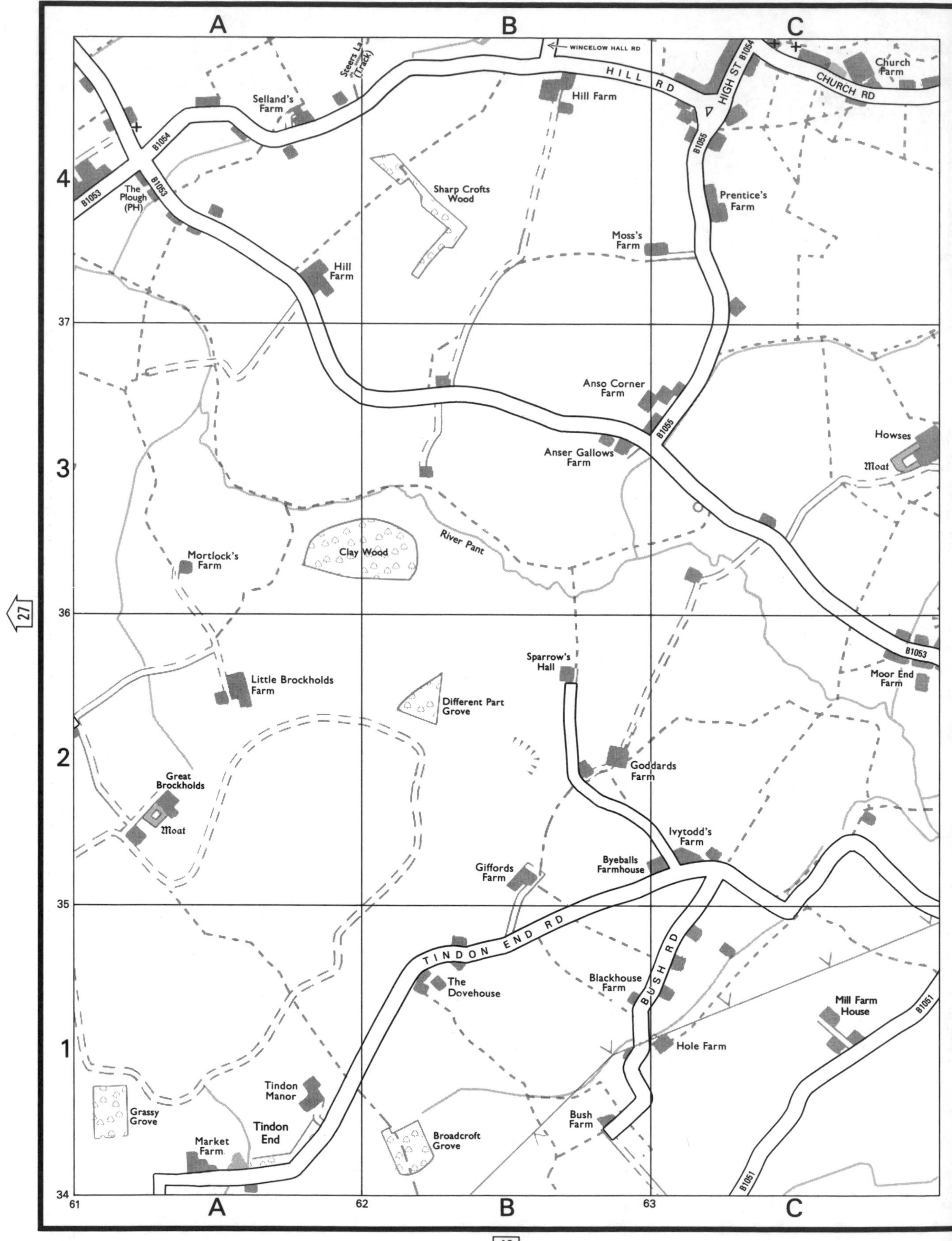

A
B
C
WINCELOW HALL RD
Steers La (Track)
HILL RD
HIGH ST B1054
CHURCH RD
Church Farm
Selland's Farm
Hill Farm
B1054
B1053
The Plough (PH)
B1065
Sharp Crofts Wood
Prentice's Farm
Moss's Farm
Hill Farm
Anso Corner Farm
Anser Gallows Farm
B1065
Howses
Moat
Clay Wood
River Pant
Mortlock's Farm
Sparrow's Hall
Little Brockholds Farm
Different Part Grove
B1053
Moor End Farm
Goddards Farm
Great Brockholds
Moat
Ivytodd's Farm
Byeballs Farmhouse
Giffords Farm
TINDON END RD
BUSH RD
The Dovehouse
Blackhouse Farm
Mill Farm House
B1051
Hole Farm
Tindon Manor
Grassy Grove
Tindon End
Bush Farm
Market Farm
Broadcroft Grove
B1051
4
37
3
36
2
35
1
34
61
62
63

27

40

17

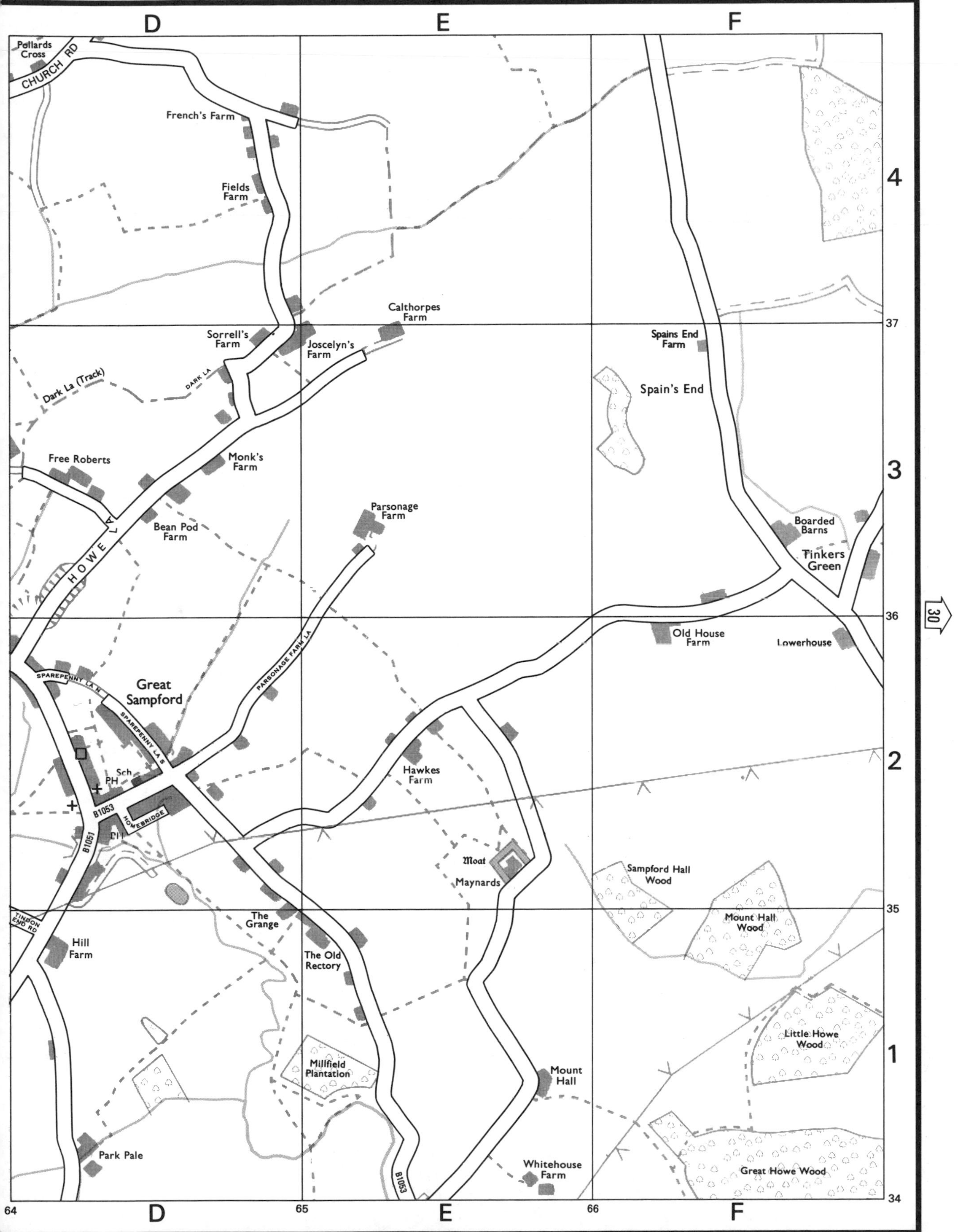
D
E
F
Pollards Cross
CHURCH RD
French's Farm
Fields Farm
4
Calthorpes Farm
37
Sorrell's Farm
Joscelyn's Farm
Spains End Farm
Dark La (Track)
DARK LA
Spain's End
Free Roberts
Monk's Farm
3
Parsonage Farm
Bean Pod Farm
Boarded Barns
Tinkers Green
HOWE LA
36
Old House Farm
Lowerhouse
SPAREPENNY LA N
Great Sampford
PARSONAGE FARM LA
SPAREPENNY LA S
2
Sch
PH
Hawkes Farm
B1053
HOMEBRIDGE
PH
B1051
Moat
Maynards
Sampford Hall Wood
35
TINDON END RD
The Grange
Mount Hall Wood
Hill Farm
The Old Rectory
Little Howe Wood
1
Millfield Plantation
Mount Hall
Park Pale
Whitehouse Farm
Great Howe Wood
B1053
34
64
D
65
E
66
F

30

41

18
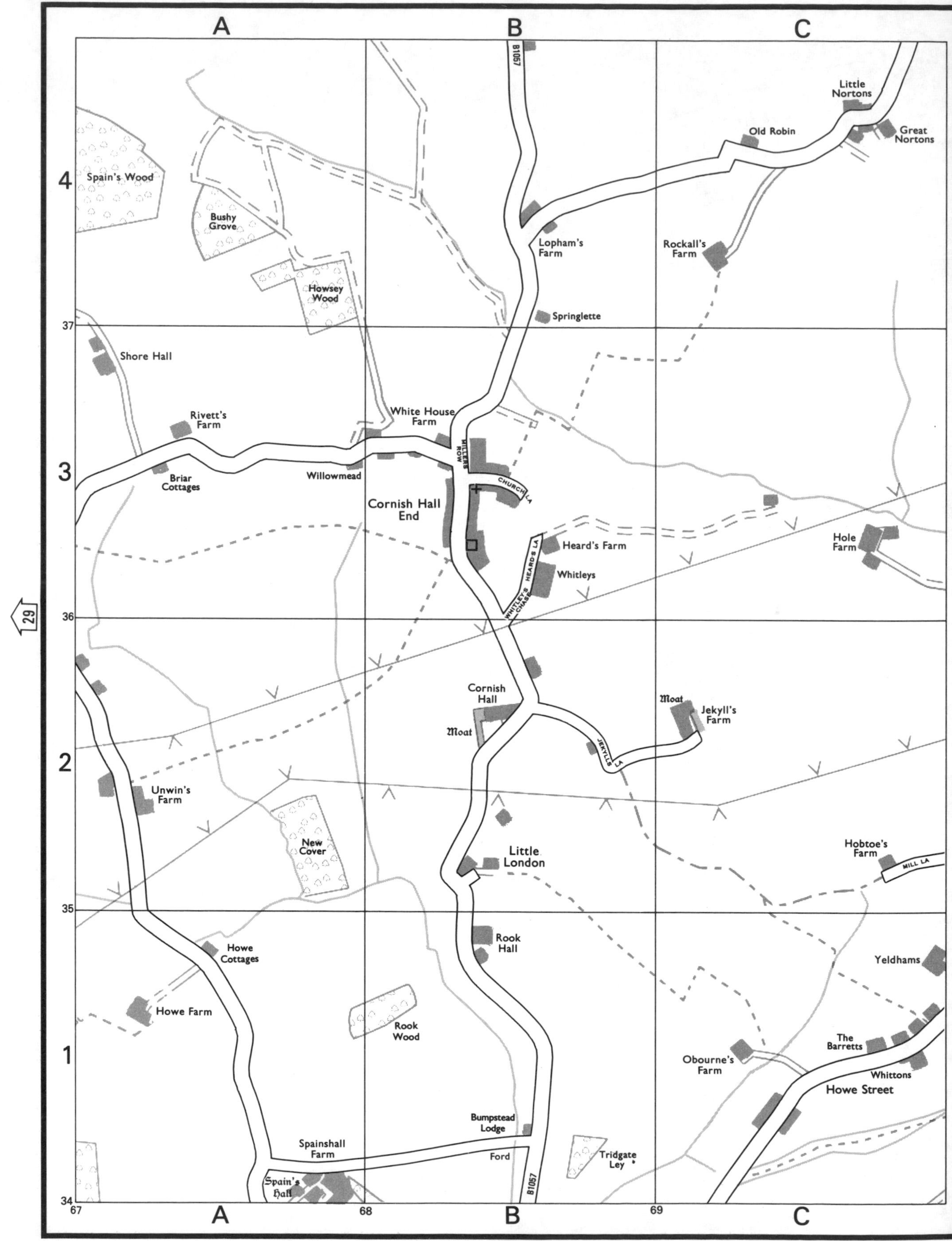

A
B
C
B1057
Little Nortons
Old Robin
Great Nortons
Spain's Wood
4
Bushy Grove
Lopham's Farm
Rockall's Farm
Howsey Wood
Springlette
37
Shore Hall
Rivett's Farm
White House Farm
MILLERS ROW
3
Briar Cottages
Willowmead
CHURCH LA
Cornish Hall End
HEARD'S LA
Heard's Farm
Hole Farm
Whitleys
WHITLEY'S CHASE
36
Cornish Hall
Moat
Jekyll's Farm
Moat
JEKYLLS LA
2
Unwin's Farm
New Cover
Little London
Hobtoe's Farm
MILL LA
35
Rook Hall
Howe Cottages
Yeldhams
Howe Farm
Rook Wood
1
The Barretts
Obourne's Farm
Whittons
Howe Street
Bumpstead Lodge
Spainshall Farm
Ford
Tridgate Ley
Spain's Hall
B1057
34
67
68
69
A
B
C

29
42

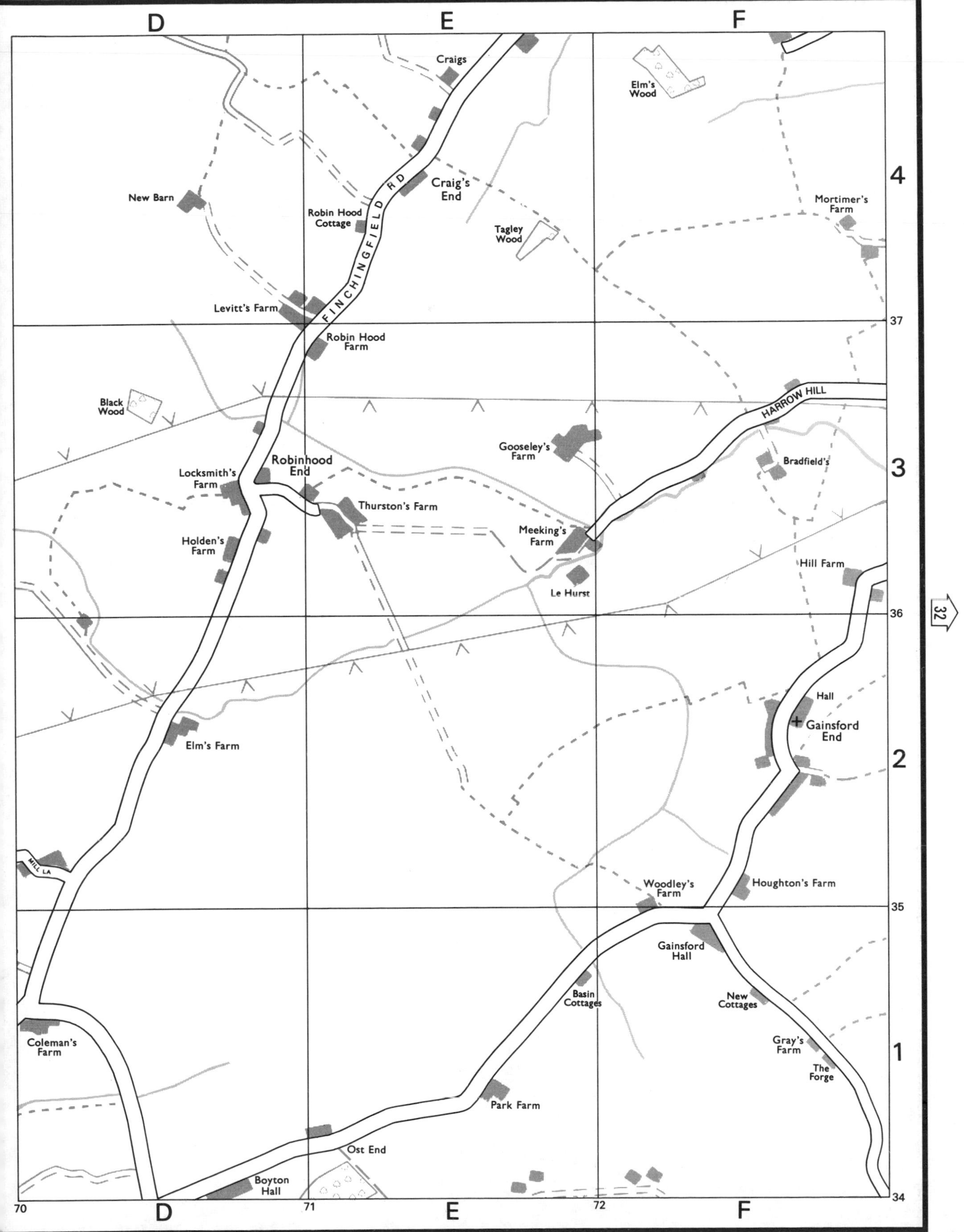
19
D
E
F
Craigs
Elm's Wood
4
New Barn
Robin Hood Cottage
Craig's End
Mortimer's Farm
Tagley Wood
FINCHINGFIELD RD
Levitt's Farm
37
Robin Hood Farm
Black Wood
HARROW HILL
Gooseley's Farm
Robinhood End
Locksmith's Farm
Bradfield's
3
Thurston's Farm
Meeking's Farm
Holden's Farm
Hill Farm
Le Hurst
36
32
Hall
Gainsford End
Elm's Farm
2
MILL LA
Woodley's Farm
Houghton's Farm
35
Gainsford Hall
Basin Cottages
New Cottages
Coleman's Farm
Gray's Farm
1
The Forge
Park Farm
Ost End
Boyton Hall
34
70
D
71
E
72
F
43

20

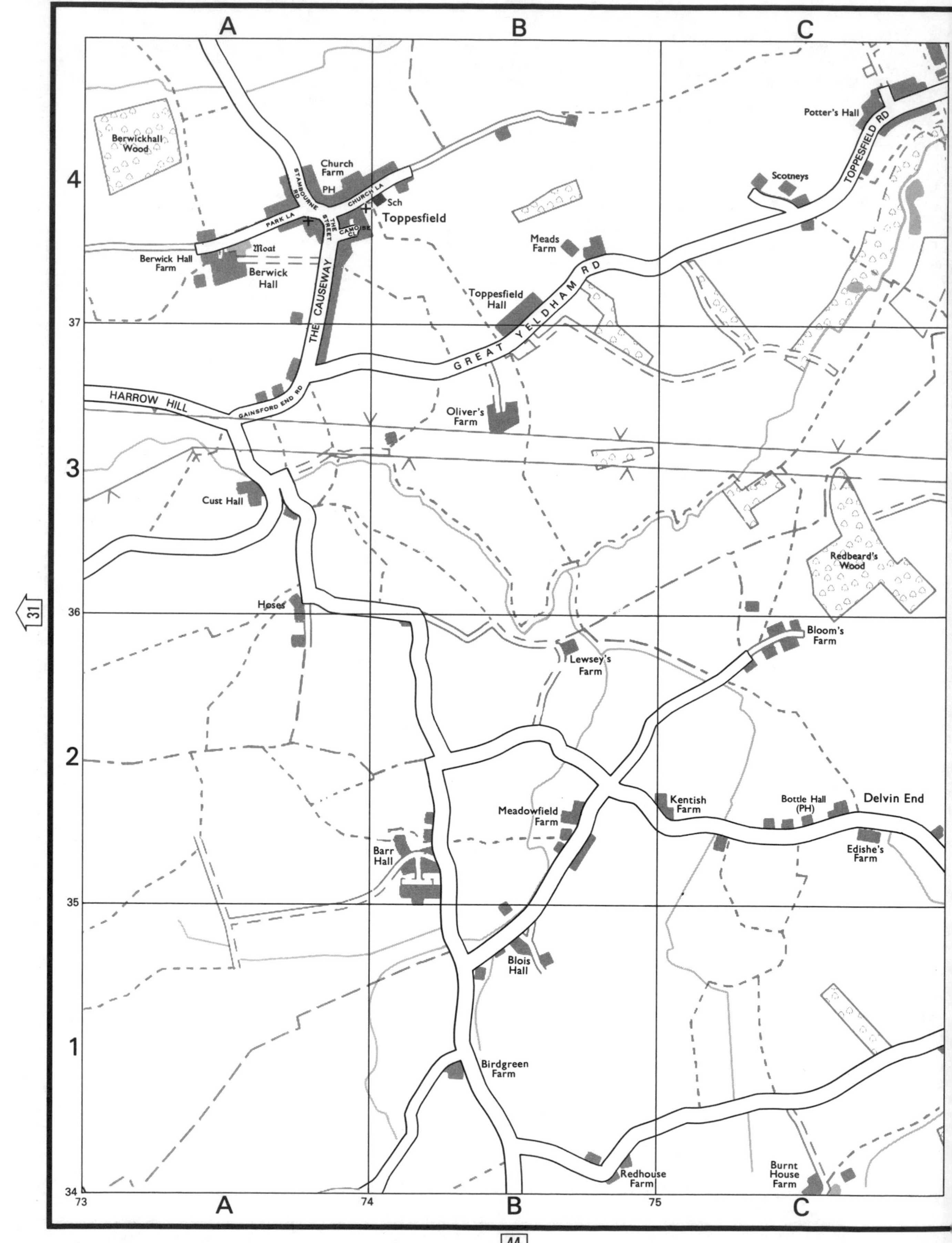
A
B
C
4
3
2
1
37
36
35
34
73
74
75
Berwickhall Wood
Church Farm
PH
Sch
Toppesfield
STAMBOURNE RD
CHURCH LA
PARK LA
THE STREET
CAMOISE CL
Moat
Berwick Hall Farm
Berwick Hall
THE CAUSEWAY
Meads Farm
Toppesfield Hall
GREAT YELDHAM RD
Potter's Hall
TOPPESFIELD RD
Scotneys
HARROW HILL
GAINSFORD END RD
Oliver's Farm
Cust Hall
Redbeard's Wood
Hoses
Bloom's Farm
Lewsey's Farm
Kentish Farm
Bottle Hall (PH)
Delvin End
Meadowfield Farm
Edishe's Farm
Barr Hall
Blois Hall
Birdgreen Farm
Redhouse Farm
Burnt House Farm

31

44

21

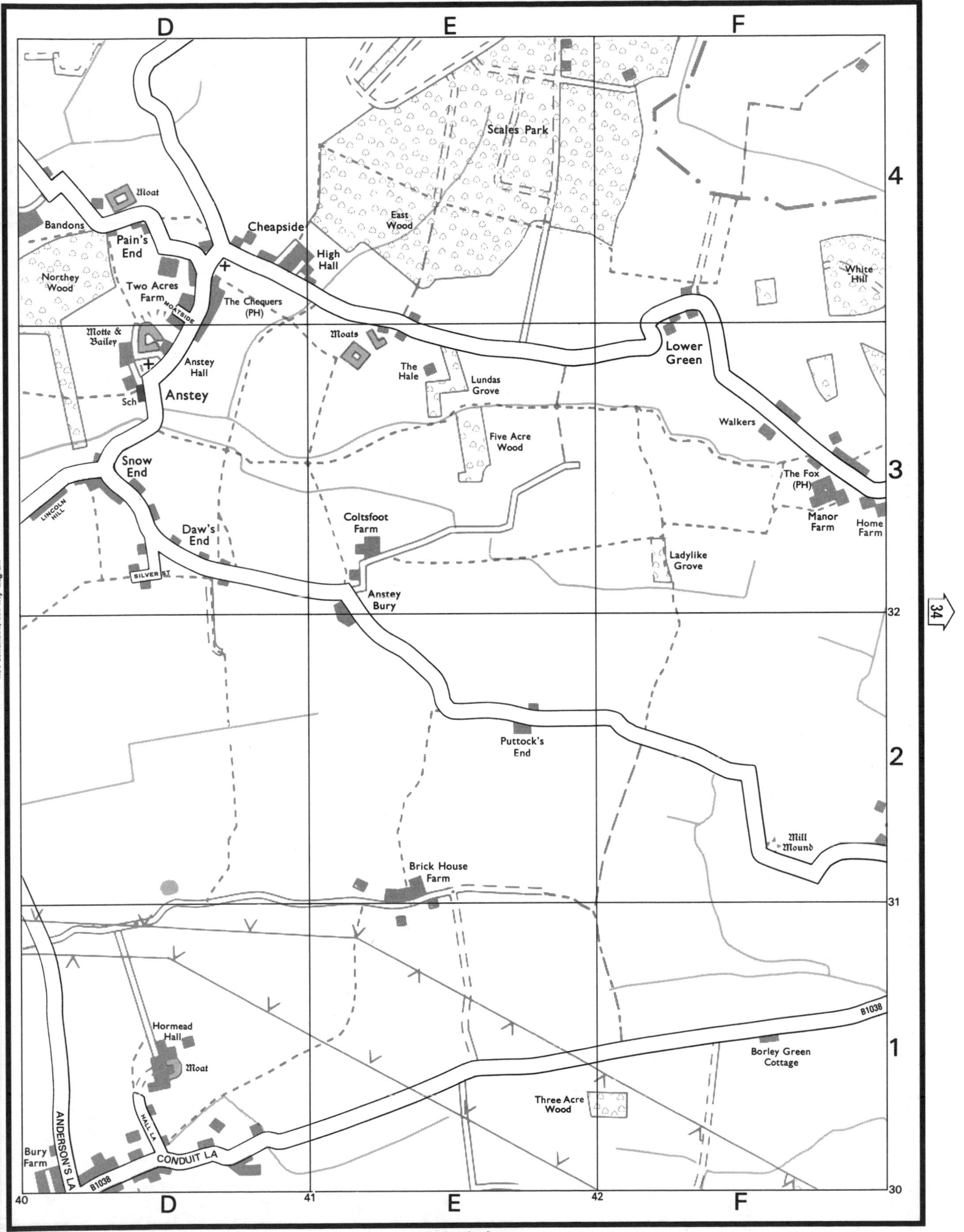

34

not continued, see key diagram

22

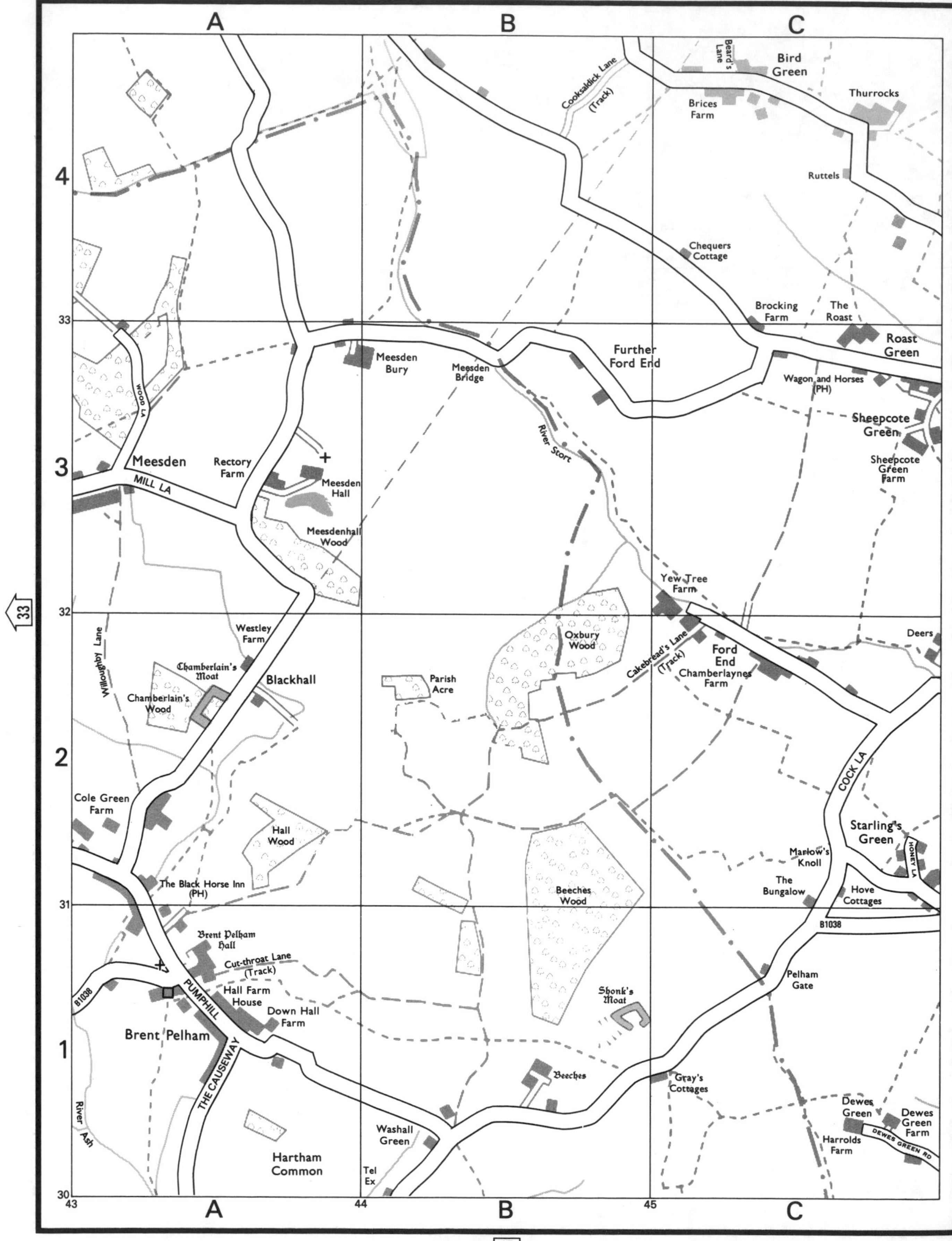

A
B
C
4
3
2
1
33
32
31
30
43
44
45
Bird Green
Beard's Lane
Cooksaldick Lane (Track)
Brices Farm
Thurrocks
Ruttels
Chequers Cottage
Brocking Farm
The Roast
Roast Green
Further Ford End
Meesden Bury
Meesden Bridge
Wagon and Horses (PH)
Sheepcote Green
Sheepcote Green Farm
WOOD LA
River Stort
Meesden
Rectory Farm
Meesden Hall
MILL LA
Meesdenhall Wood
Yew Tree Farm
Ford End
Chamberlaynes Farm
Cakebread's Lane (Track)
Deers
Oxbury Wood
Westley Farm
Willoughby Lane
Chamberlain's Moat
Chamberlain's Wood
Blackhall
Parish Acre
COCK LA
Cole Green Farm
Hall Wood
Starling's Green
HONEY LA
Marlow's Knoll
The Bungalow
Hove Cottages
The Black Horse Inn (PH)
Beeches Wood
B1038
Brent Pelham Hall
Cut-throat Lane (Track)
Pelham Gate
B1038
PUMPHILL
Hall Farm House
Down Hall Farm
Shonk's Moat
Brent Pelham
THE CAUSEWAY
Beeches
Gray's Cottages
Dewes Green
Dewes Green Farm
Harrolds Farm
DEWES GREEN RD
River Ash
Washall Green
Hartham Common
Tel Ex

33

45

23

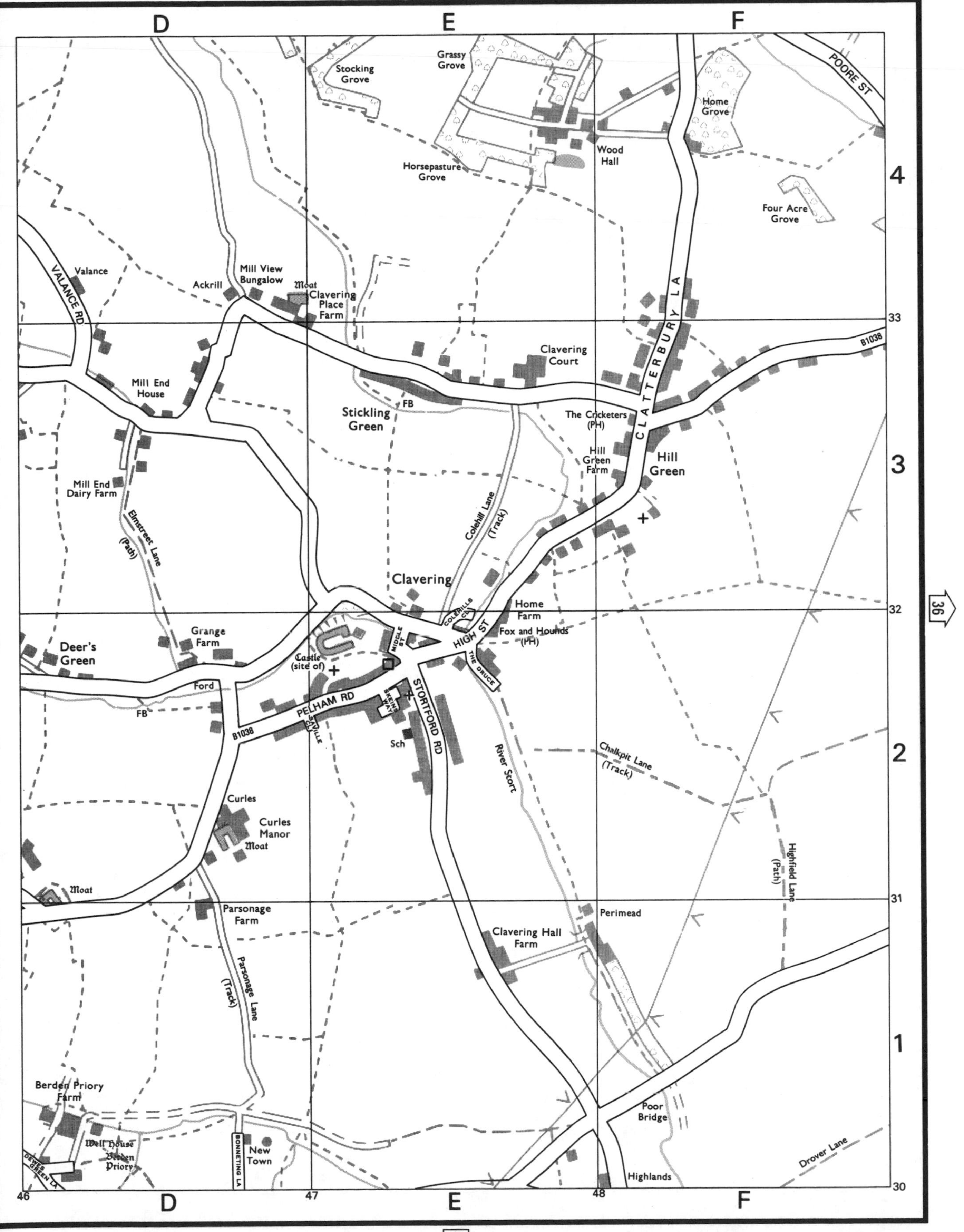
D
E
F
Stocking Grove
Grassy Grove
POORE ST
Home Grove
Wood Hall
Horsepasture Grove
4
Four Acre Grove
VALANCE RD
Valance
Ackrill
Mill View Bungalow
Moat
Clavering Place Farm
CLATTERBURY LA
33
B1038
Clavering Court
Mill End House
Stickling Green
FB
The Cricketers (PH)
Hill Green Farm
Hill Green
3
Mill End Dairy Farm
Elmstreet Lane (Path)
Colehill Lane (Track)
Clavering
Home Farm
COLEHILLS CL
32
Deer's Green
Grange Farm
MIDDLE ST
HIGH ST
Fox and Hounds (PH)
Castle (site of)
THE DRUCE
STORTFORD RD
SKEINS WAY
PELHAM RD
Ford
FB
B1038
SAVILLE
Sch
River Stort
Chalkpit Lane (Track)
2
Curles
Curles Manor
Moat
Highfield Lane (Path)
Moat
31
Parsonage Farm
Perimead
Clavering Hall Farm
Parsonage Lane (Track)
1
Berden Priory Farm
Poor Bridge
Well House
Berden Priory
DEWES GREEN LA
BONNETING LA
New Town
Highlands
Drover Lane
30
46
47
48
D
E
F

36

46

24

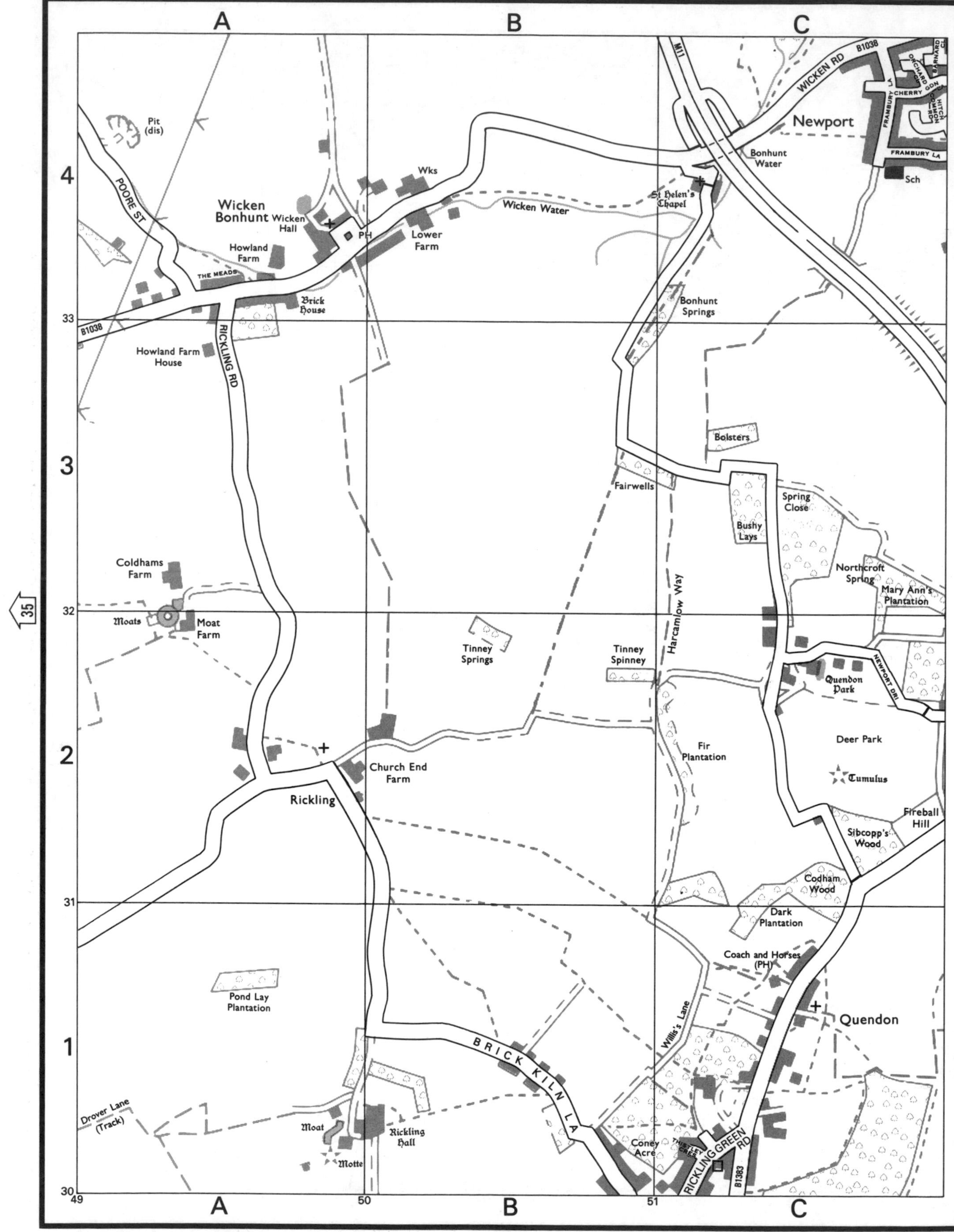
A
B
C
4
3
2
1
33
32
31
30
49
50
51
Pit (dis)
POORE ST
Wicken Bonhunt
Wicken Hall
Wks
PH
Lower Farm
Howland Farm
THE MEADS
Brick House
B1038
Howland Farm House
RICKLING RD
Wicken Water
St Helen's Chapel
Bonhunt Water
M11
WICKEN RD
Newport
FRAMBURY LA
Sch
ORCHARD
CHERRY GDN
COMMON RD
HITCH
BARNARD
Bonhunt Springs
Bolsters
Fairwells
Bushy Lays
Spring Close
Northcroft Spring
Mary Ann's Plantation
Coldhams Farm
Moats
Moat Farm
Tinney Springs
Tinney Spinney
Harcamlow Way
Quendon Park
NEWPORT DRI
Deer Park
Cumulus
Fir Plantation
Church End Farm
Rickling
Fireball Hill
Sibcopp's Wood
Codham Wood
Dark Plantation
Coach and Horses (PH)
Quendon
Willis's Lane
Pond Lay Plantation
BRICK KILN LA
Drover Lane (Track)
Moat
Motte
Rickling Hall
Coney Acre
THISTLEY CRES
RICKLING GREEN RD
B1383

35

47

25

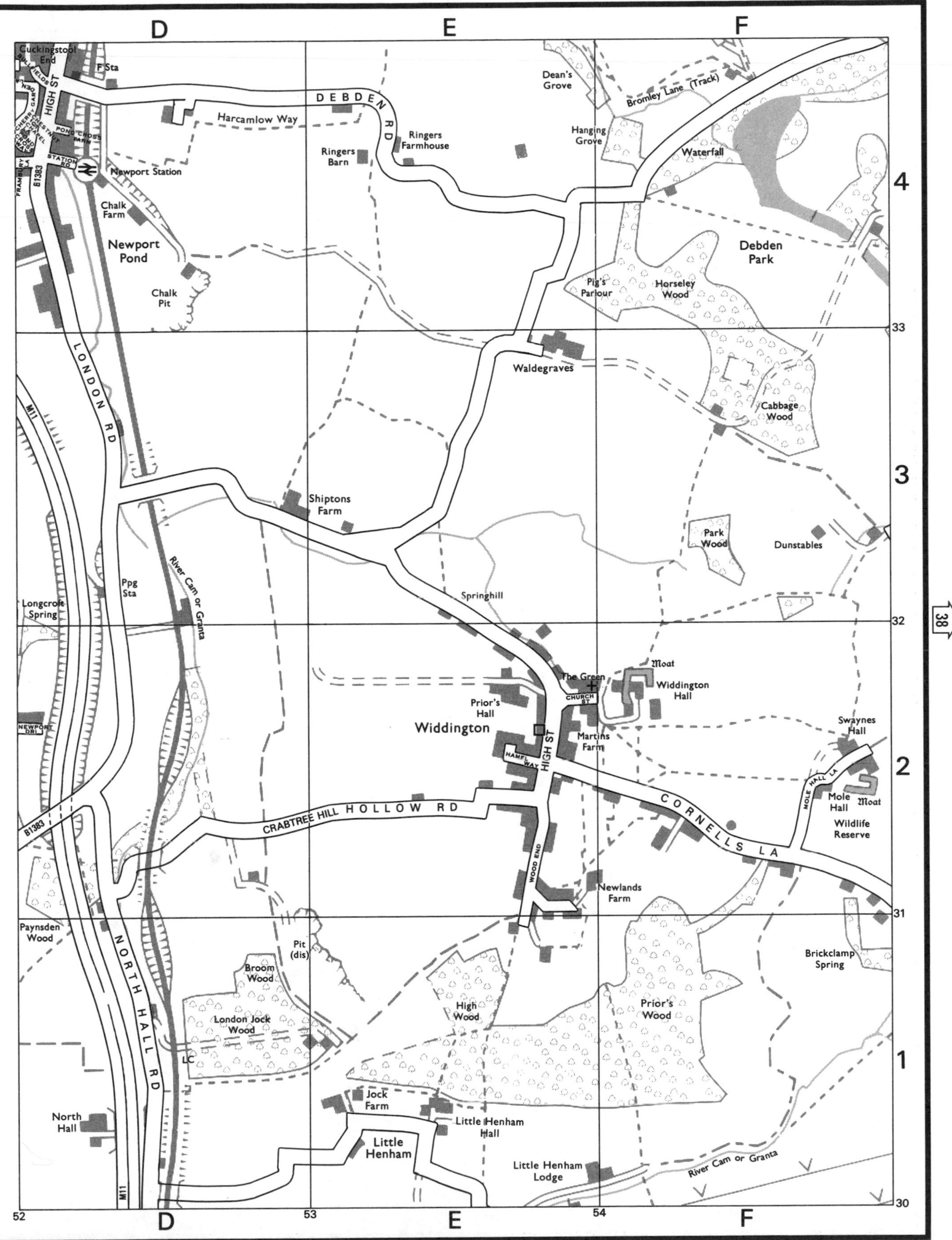

D
E
F
Cuckingstool End
F Sta
HIGH ST
DEBDEN RD
Harcamlow Way
Ringers Farmhouse
Ringers Barn
Dean's Grove
Bromley Lane (Track)
Hanging Grove
Waterfall
Newport Station
STATION RD
B1383
Chalk Farm
Newport Pond
Chalk Pit
Debden Park
Pig's Parlour
Horseley Wood
Waldegraves
Cabbage Wood
LONDON RD
M11
Shiptons Farm
Park Wood
Dunstables
Ppg Sta
River Cam or Granta
Longcroft Spring
Springhill
The Green
CHURCH ST
Moat
Widdington Hall
Prior's Hall
Widdington
Martins Farm
Swaynes Hall
HAMFL WAY
HIGH ST
CRABTREE HILL HOLLOW RD
CORNELLS LA
MOLE HALL LA
Mole Hall
Moat
Wildlife Reserve
WOOD END
Newlands Farm
NEWPORT DRI
Paynsden Wood
NORTH HALL RD
Pit (dis)
Broom Wood
London Jock Wood
LC
High Wood
Prior's Wood
Brickclamp Spring
Jock Farm
Little Henham Hall
North Hall
Little Henham
Little Henham Lodge
River Cam or Granta
4
3
2
1
33
32
31
30
52
53
54

38

48

26

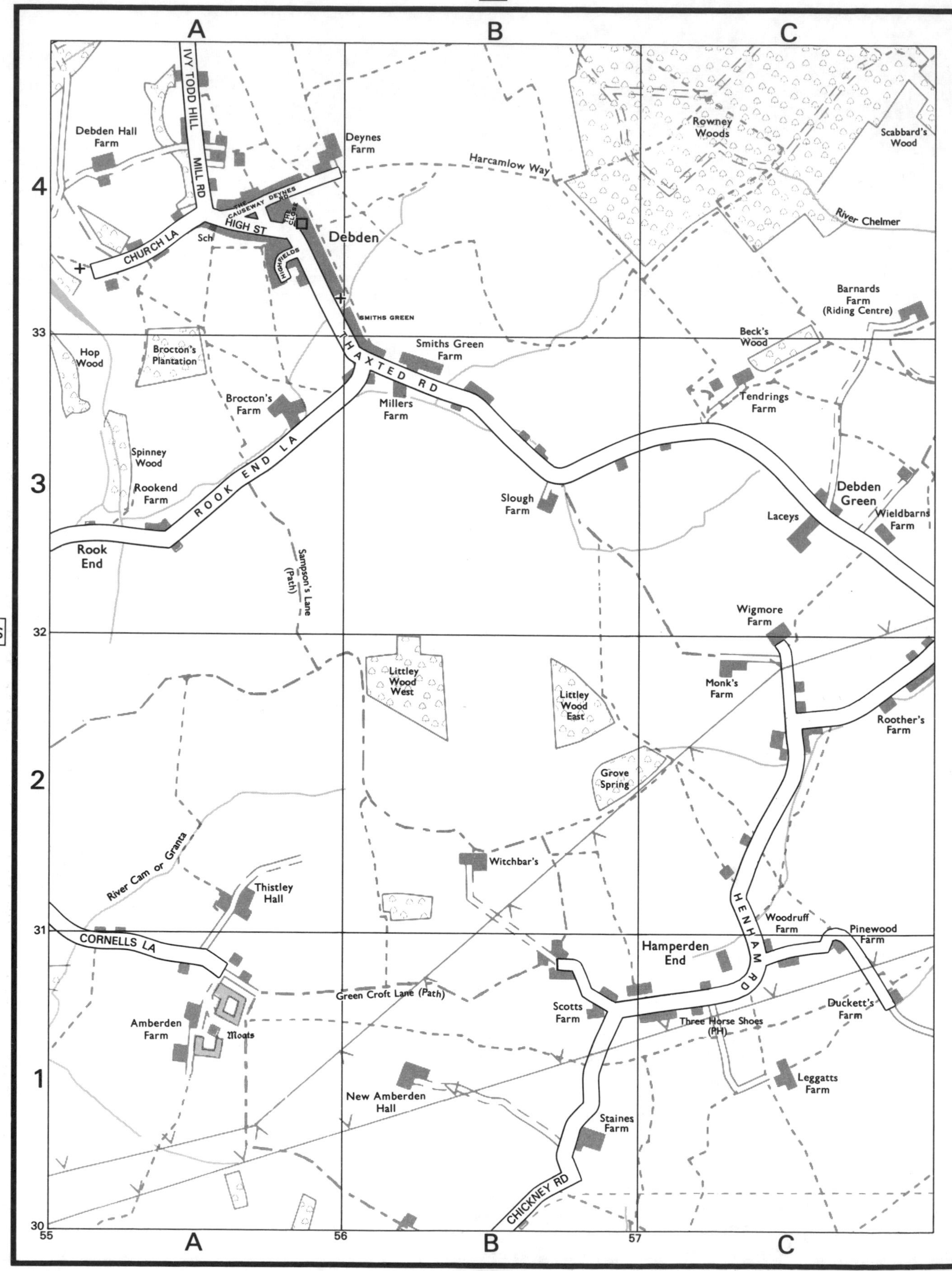

A
B
C
IVY TODD HILL
MILL RD
Debden Hall Farm
Deynes Farm
Harcamlow Way
Rowney Woods
Scabbard's Wood
River Chelmer
THE CAUSEWAY
DEYNES RD
THE CLOSE
HIGH ST
CHURCH LA
Sch
HIGHFIELDS
Debden
SMITHS GREEN
Barnards Farm (Riding Centre)
Beck's Wood
Hop Wood
Brocton's Plantation
Smiths Green Farm
THAXTED RD
Brocton's Farm
Millers Farm
Tendrings Farm
Spinney Wood
Rookend Farm
ROOK END LA
Slough Farm
Debden Green
Laceys
Wieldbarns Farm
Rook End
Sampson's Lane (Path)
Wigmore Farm
Littley Wood West
Littley Wood East
Monk's Farm
Roother's Farm
Grove Spring
Witchbar's
River Cam or Granta
Thistley Hall
HENHAM RD
Woodruff Farm
Pinewood Farm
CORNELLS LA
Hamperden End
Green Croft Lane (Path)
Scotts Farm
Three Horse Shoes (PH)
Duckett's Farm
Amberden Farm
Moats
Leggatts Farm
New Amberden Hall
Staines Farm
CHICKNEY RD
4
3
2
1
33
32
31
30
55
56
57

37

49

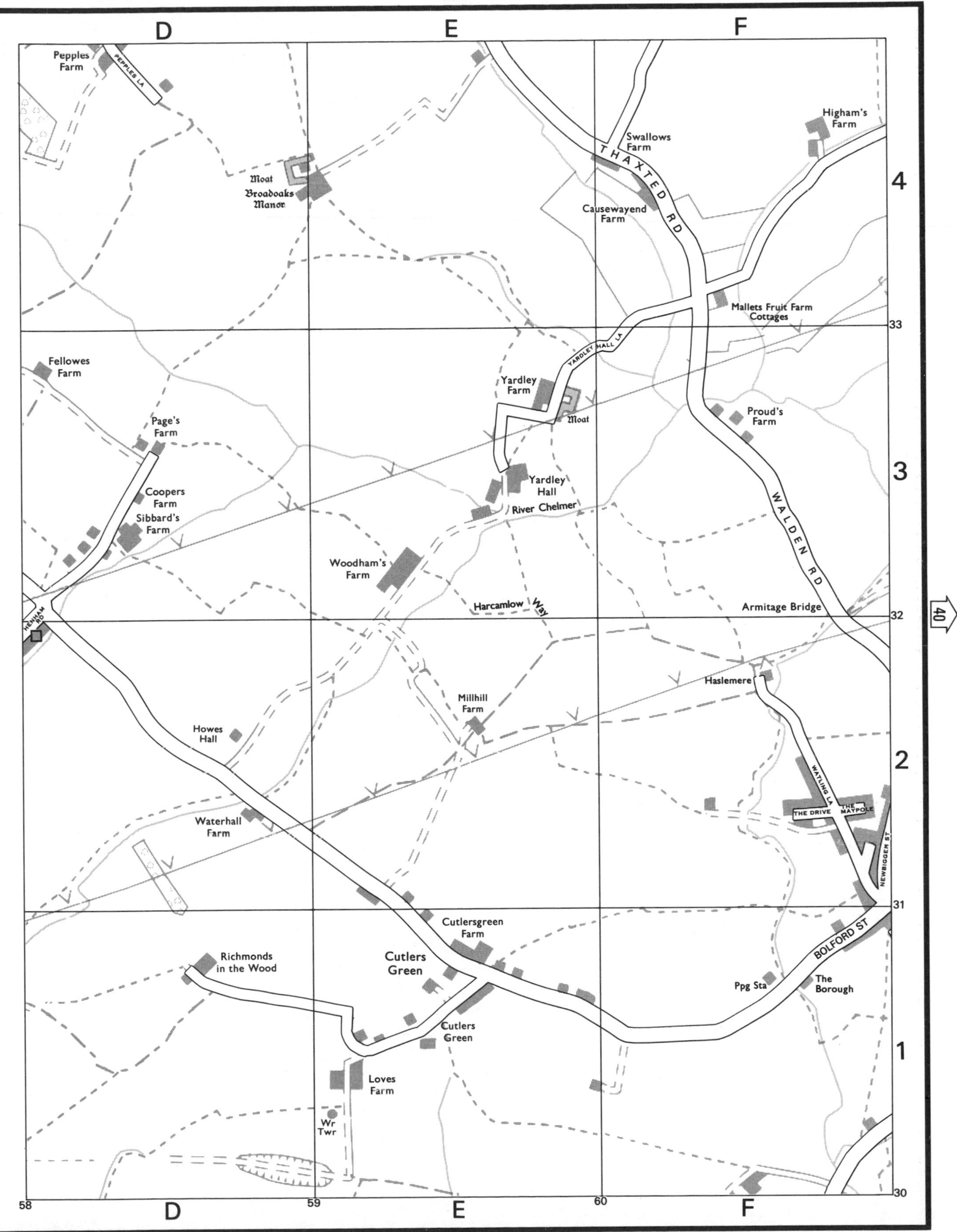

27
D
E
F
Pepples Farm
PEPPLES LA
Moat
Broadoaks Manor
Swallows Farm
THAXTED RD
Higham's Farm
Causewayend Farm
Mallets Fruit Farm Cottages
YARDLEY HALL LA
Fellowes Farm
Yardley Farm
Moat
Proud's Farm
Page's Farm
Yardley Hall
River Chelmer
Coopers Farm
Sibbard's Farm
WALDEN RD
Woodham's Farm
Harcamlow Way
Armitage Bridge
HENHAM RD
Haslemere
Millhill Farm
Howes Hall
WATLING LA
THE DRIVE
THE MAYPOLE
Waterhall Farm
NEWBIGGEN ST
Cutlersgreen Farm
Cutlers Green
BOLFORD ST
Richmonds in the Wood
Ppg Sta
The Borough
Cutlers Green
Loves Farm
Wr Twr
4
3
2
1
33
32
31
30
58
59
60
D
E
F
40
50

28

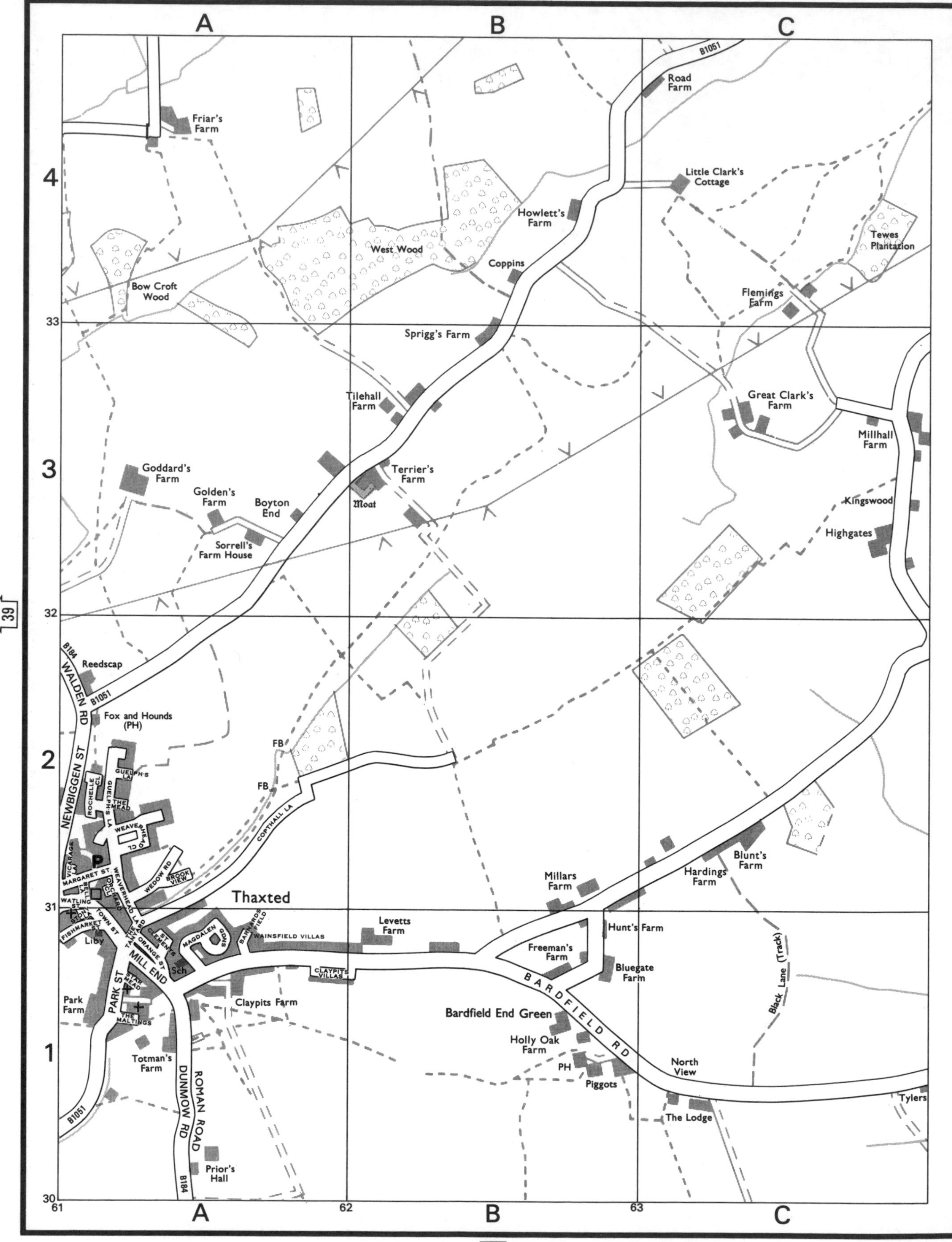

A
B
C
4
3
2
1
33
32
31
30
61
62
63
B1051
Road Farm
Friar's Farm
Little Clark's Cottage
Howlett's Farm
West Wood
Tewes Plantation
Coppins
Bow Croft Wood
Flemings Farm
Sprigg's Farm
Great Clark's Farm
Tilehall Farm
Millhall Farm
Goddard's Farm
Terrier's Farm
Golden's Farm
Boyton End
Moat
Kingswood
Highgates
Sorrell's Farm House
B184
Reedscap
WALDEN RD
Fox and Hounds (PH)
NEWBIGGEN ST
FB
GUELPH'S LA
ROCHELLE CL
THE MEAD
WEAVERHEAD CL
WEDOW RD
BROOK VIEW
COPTHALL LA
VICARAGE
MARGARET ST
WEAVERHEAD LA
WATLING ST
TOWN ST
FISHMARKET ST
Thaxted
Levetts Farm
Millars Farm
Hardings Farm
Blunt's Farm
Hunt's Farm
Freeman's Farm
MAGDALEN GDNS
BARNARDS FIELD
WAINSFIELD VILLAS
ST CLEMENTS
ORANGE ST
MILL END
Sch
Liby
CLAYPITS VILLAS
Bluegate Farm
BARDFIELD RD
Black Lane (Track)
Claypits Farm
Park Farm
PARK ST
STAR MEAD
THE MALTINGS
Bardfield End Green
Holly Oak Farm
North View
Totman's Farm
PH
Piggots
Tylers
The Lodge
ROMAN ROAD
DUNMOW RD
Prior's Hall

39

51

29

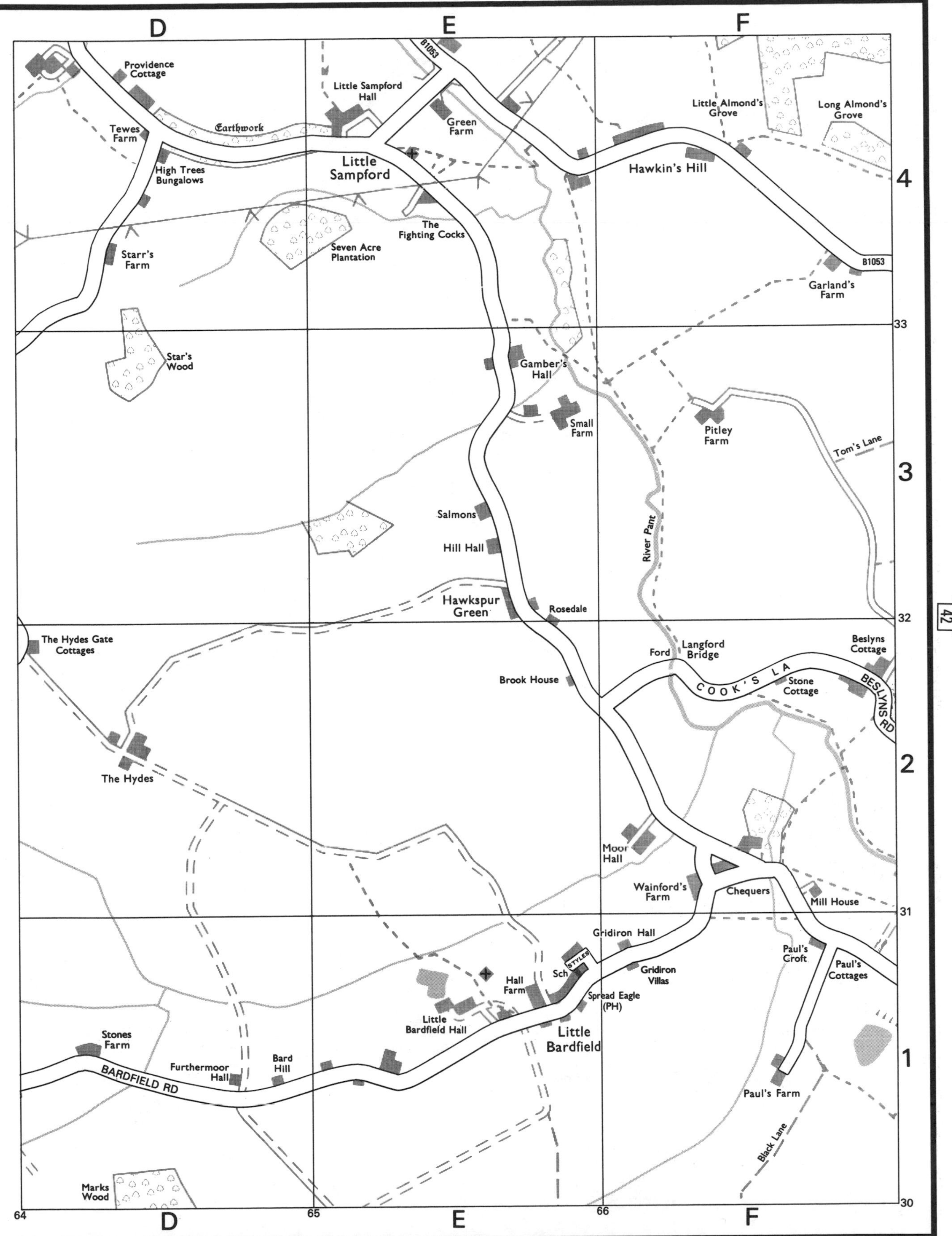
D
E
F
Providence Cottage
Little Sampford Hall
B1053
Green Farm
Little Almond's Grove
Long Almond's Grove
Tewes Farm
Earthwork
Little Sampford
Hawkin's Hill
High Trees Bungalows
The Fighting Cocks
Seven Acre Plantation
Starr's Farm
Garland's Farm
Star's Wood
Gamber's Hall
Small Farm
Pitley Farm
Tom's Lane
Salmons
Hill Hall
River Pant
Hawkspur Green
Rosedale
The Hydes Gate Cottages
Ford
Langford Bridge
Beslyns Cottage
Brook House
COOK'S LA
Stone Cottage
BESLYNS RD
The Hydes
Moor Hall
Wainford's Farm
Chequers
Mill House
Gridiron Hall
Paul's Croft
Paul's Cottages
STYLES
Sch
Gridiron Villas
Hall Farm
Spread Eagle (PH)
Little Bardfield Hall
Little Bardfield
Stones Farm
Furthermoor Hall
Bard Hill
BARDFIELD RD
Paul's Farm
Black Lane
Marks Wood
4
3
2
1
33
32
31
30
64
65
66

42

52

30

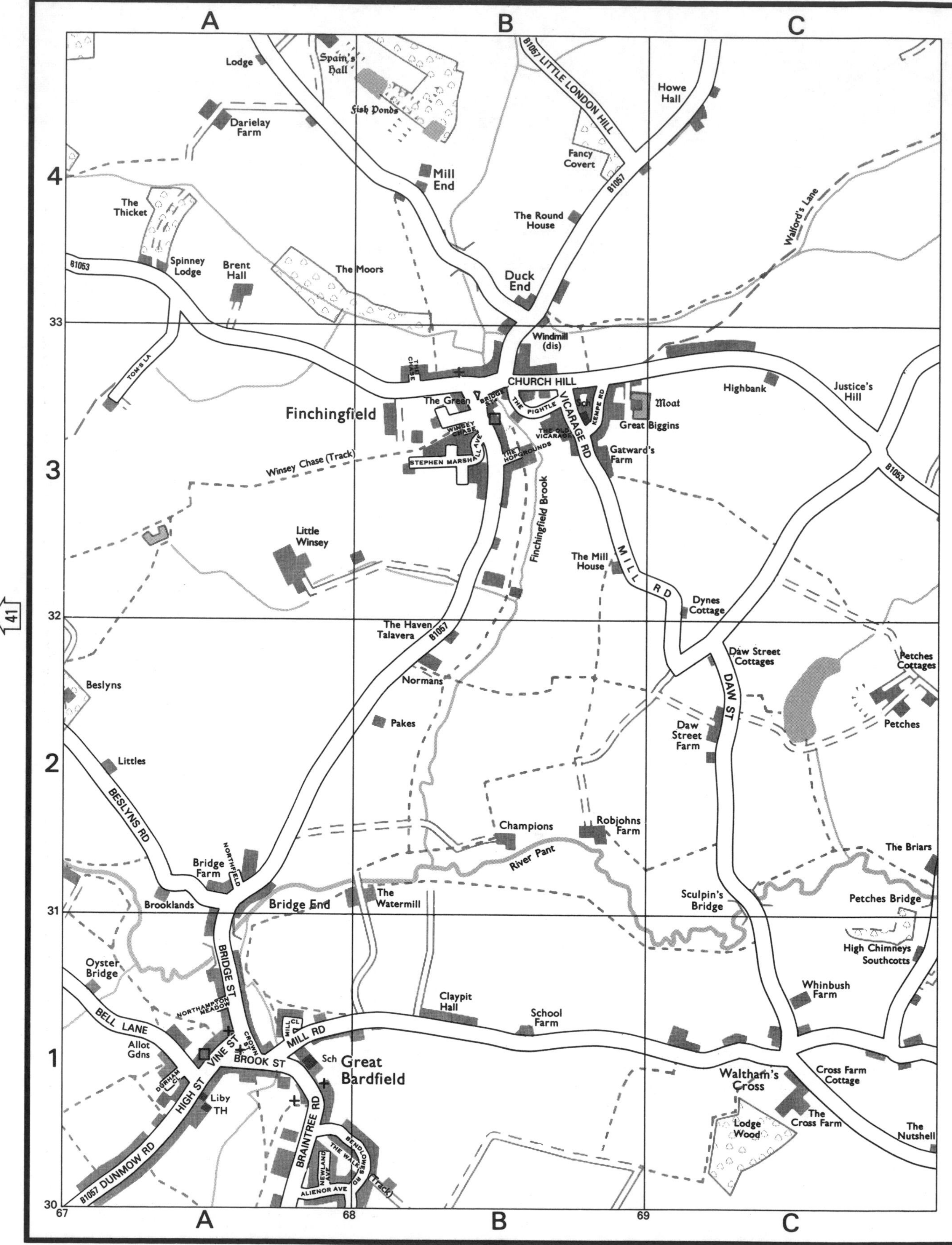

A
B
C
4
3
2
1
33
32
31
30
67
68
69
Lodge
Spain's Hall
Fish Ponds
LITTLE LONDON HILL
B1057
Howe Hall
Darielay Farm
Fancy Covert
Mill End
The Thicket
The Round House
Walford's Lane
B1053
Spinney Lodge
Brent Hall
The Moors
Duck End
TOM'S LA
Windmill (dis)
CHURCH HILL
Justice's Hill
Highbank
The Green
Finchingfield
THE PIGHTLE
Sch
KEMPE RD
Moat
Great Biggins
VICARAGE RD
WINSEY CHASE
THE OLD VICARAGE
THE HOPGROUNDS
Gatward's Farm
Winsey Chase (Track)
STEPHEN MARSHALL AVE
Finchingfield Brook
Little Winsey
The Mill House
MILL RD
Dynes Cottage
The Haven
Talavera
Normans
Daw Street Cottages
DAW ST
Petches Cottages
Beslyns
Pakes
Daw Street Farm
Petches
Littles
BESLYNS RD
Champions
Robjohns Farm
The Briars
River Pant
Bridge Farm
NORTHFIELD
Brooklands
Bridge End
The Watermill
Sculpin's Bridge
Petches Bridge
High Chimneys
Southcotts
Oyster Bridge
BRIDGE ST
Claypit Hall
School Farm
Whinbush Farm
BELL LANE
NORTHAMPTON MEADOW
MILL CL
MILL RD
Allot Gdns
VINE ST
CROWN ST
BROOK ST
Sch
Great Bardfield
Waltham's Cross
Cross Farm Cottage
HIGH ST
DURHAM CL
Liby
TH
The Cross Farm
Lodge Wood
The Nutshell
BRAINTREE RD
BENDLOWES RD
THE WALK
NEWLAND AVE
ALIENOR AVE
(Track)
B1057 DUNMOW RD

41

53

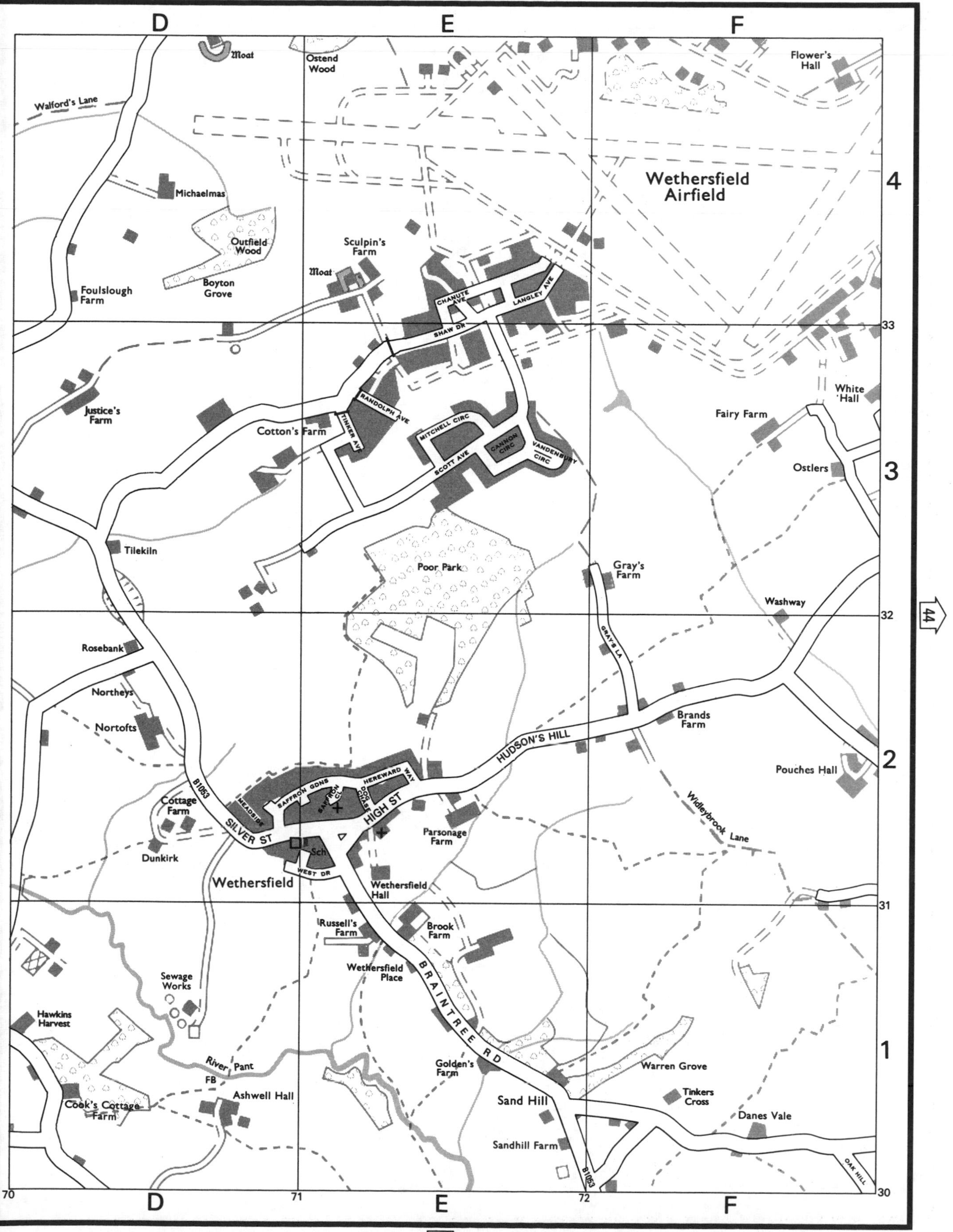
31
D
E
F
Moat
Ostend Wood
Flower's Hall
Walford's Lane
Wethersfield Airfield
4
Michaelmas
Outfield Wood
Sculpin's Farm
Moat
Boyton Grove
Foulslough Farm
CHANUTE AVE
LANGLEY AVE
SHAW DR
33
White Hall
Justice's Farm
RANDOLPH AVE
TINKER AVE
MITCHELL CIRC
Cotton's Farm
CANNON CIRC
VANDENBURY CIRC
SCOTT AVE
Fairy Farm
Ostlers
3
Tilekiln
Poor Park
Gray's Farm
Washway
32
44
Rosebank
GRAY'S LA
Northeys
Nortofts
Brands Farm
HUDSON'S HILL
2
Pouches Hall
B1053
SAFFRON GDNS
SAFFRON CL
HEREWARD WAY
DOCK CHASE
MEADSIDE
HIGH ST
Widleybrook Lane
Cottage Farm
SILVER ST
Parsonage Farm
Dunkirk
Sch
WEST DR
Wethersfield
Wethersfield Hall
31
Russell's Farm
Brook Farm
Wethersfield Place
BRAINTREE RD
Sewage Works
Hawkins Harvest
1
River Pant
Golden's Farm
Warren Grove
FB
Ashwell Hall
Sand Hill
Tinkers Cross
Cook's Cottage Farm
Danes Vale
Sandhill Farm
OAK HILL
B1053
70
71
72
30
D
E
F
54

32

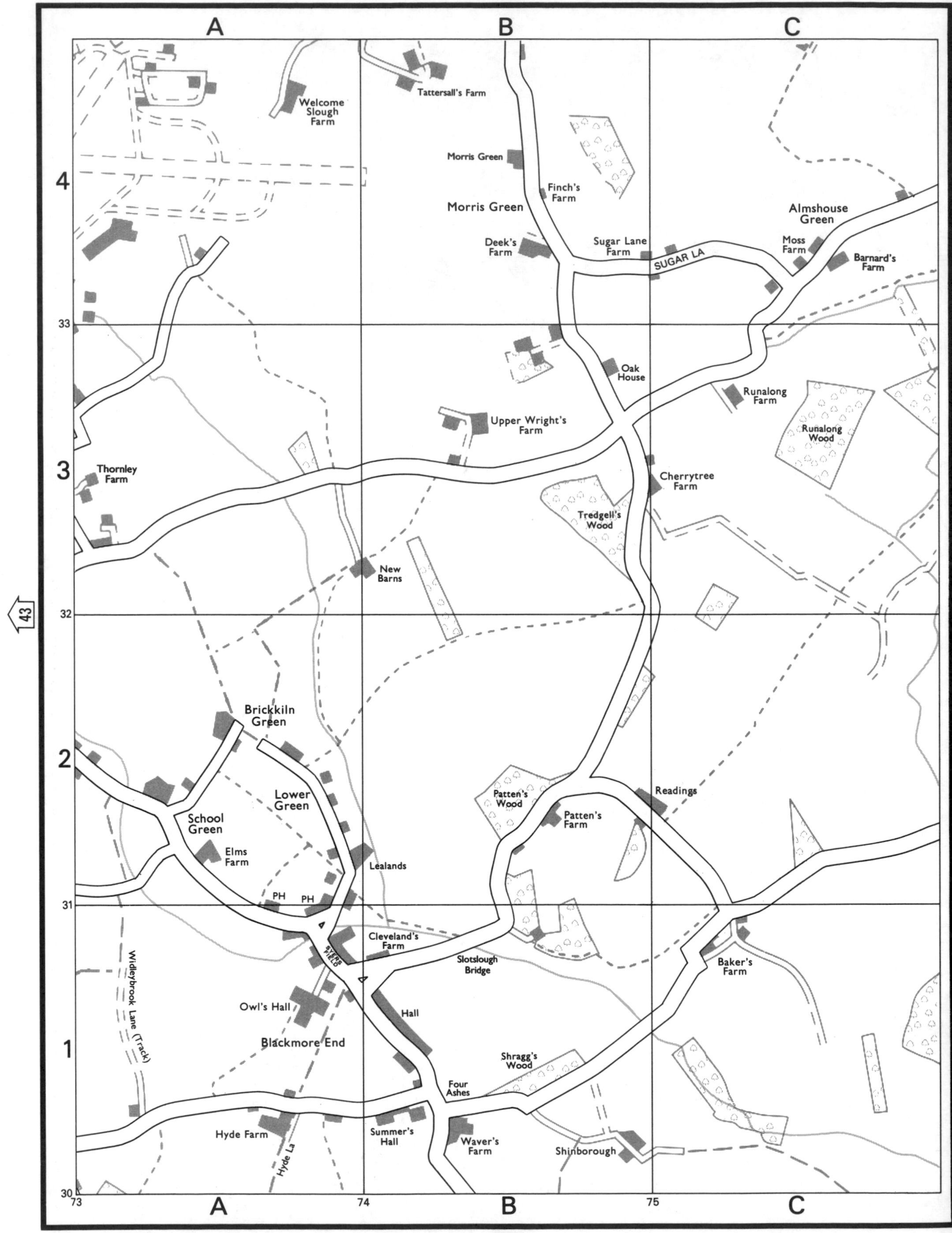
A
B
C
Welcome Slough Farm
Tattersall's Farm
Morris Green
Finch's Farm
Morris Green
Almshouse Green
Deek's Farm
Sugar Lane Farm
SUGAR LA
Moss Farm
Barnard's Farm
Oak House
Runalong Farm
Runalong Wood
Upper Wright's Farm
Thornley Farm
Cherrytree Farm
Tredgell's Wood
New Barns
Brickkiln Green
Lower Green
School Green
Elms Farm
Lealands
Patten's Wood
Patten's Farm
Readings
PH
PH
Cleveland's Farm
Slotslough Bridge
Baker's Farm
Widleybrook Lane (Track)
Owl's Hall
Hall
Blackmore End
Shragg's Wood
Four Ashes
Hyde Farm
Summer's Hall
Waver's Farm
Shinborough
Hyde La
4
3
2
1
33
32
31
30
73
74
75

43

55

34

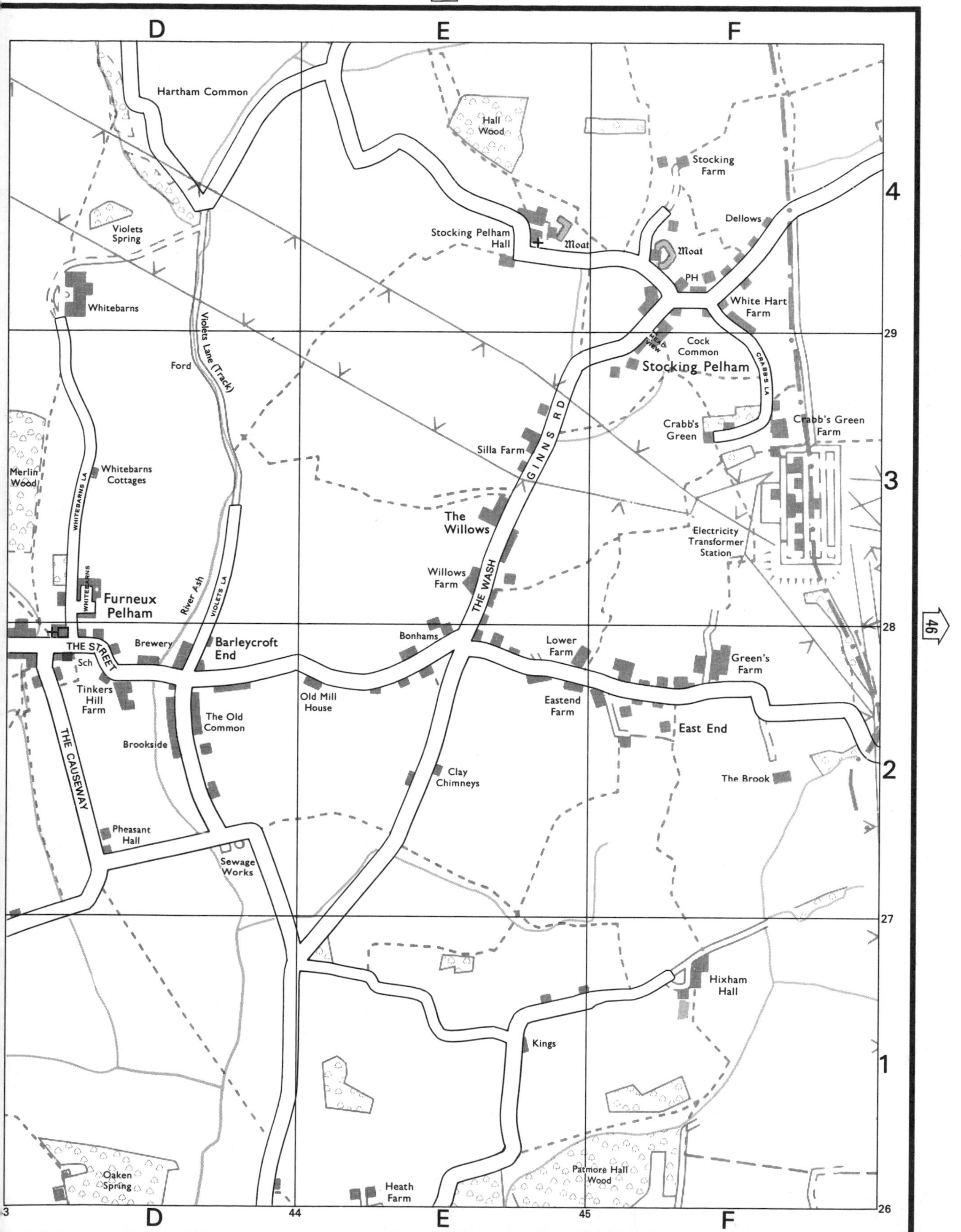

46

not continued, see key diagram

35

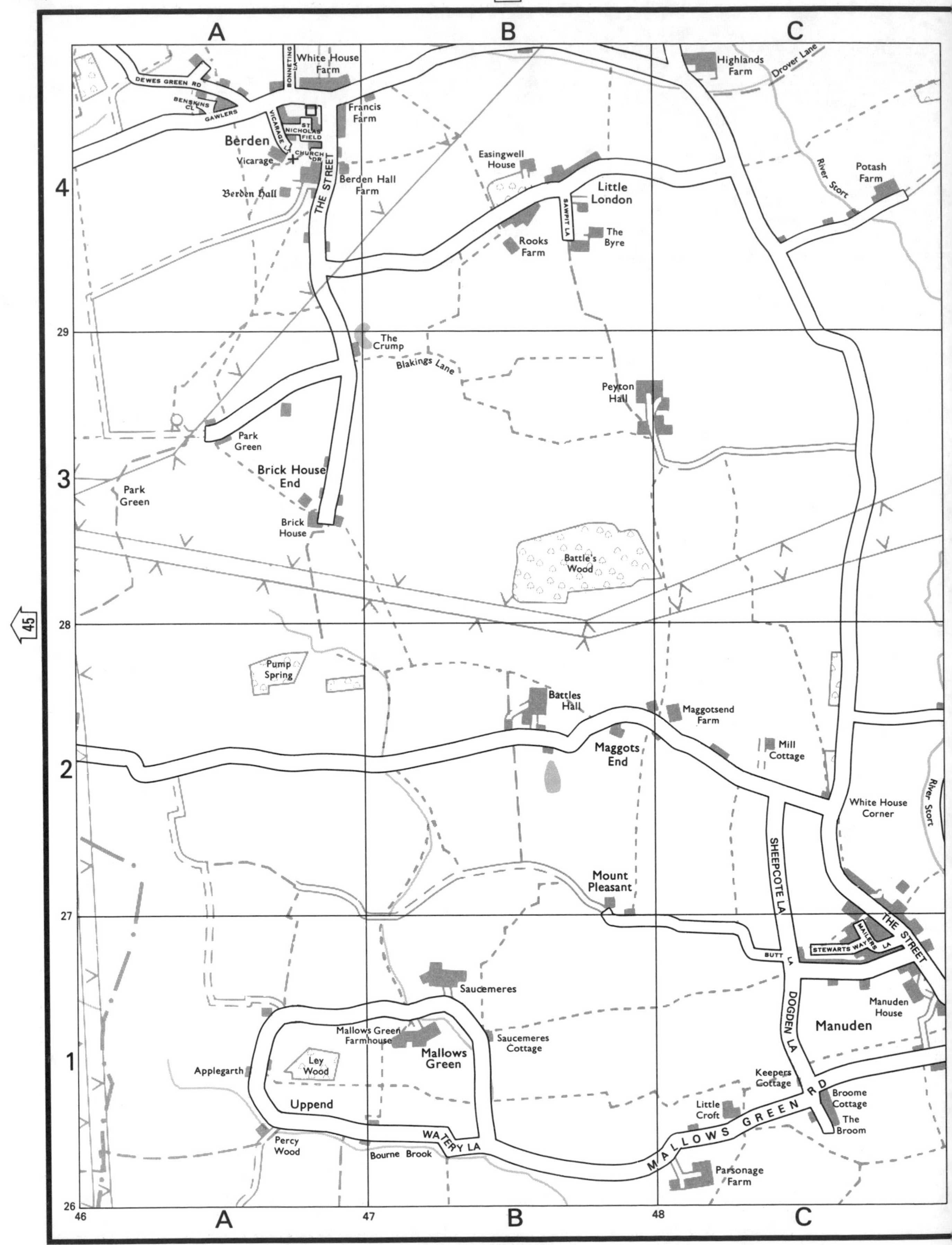

A
B
C
White House Farm
Highlands Farm
Drover Lane
DEWES GREEN RD
BONNETING LA
BENSKINS CL
GAWLERS
VICARAGE LA
ST NICHOLAS FIELD
CHURCH DR
Francis Farm
Berden
Vicarage
Easingwell House
Potash Farm
River Stort
Berden Hall
THE STREET
Berden Hall Farm
Little London
SAWPIT LA
The Byre
Rooks Farm
The Crump
Blakings Lane
Peyton Hall
Park Green
Brick House End
Park Green
Brick House
Battle's Wood
Pump Spring
Battles Hall
Maggotsend Farm
Mill Cottage
Maggots End
White House Corner
River Stort
SHEEPCOTE LA
Mount Pleasant
THE STREET
MAILERS LA
STEWARTS WAY
BUTT LA
Saucemeres
DOGDEN LA
Manuden House
Manuden
Mallows Green Farmhouse
Saucemeres Cottage
Mallows Green
Ley Wood
Applegarth
Keepers Cottage
Broome Cottage
The Broom
Little Croft
Uppend
MALLOWS GREEN RD
WATERY LA
Percy Wood
Bourne Brook
Parsonage Farm
1
2
3
4
26
27
28
29
46
47
48

45

56

36

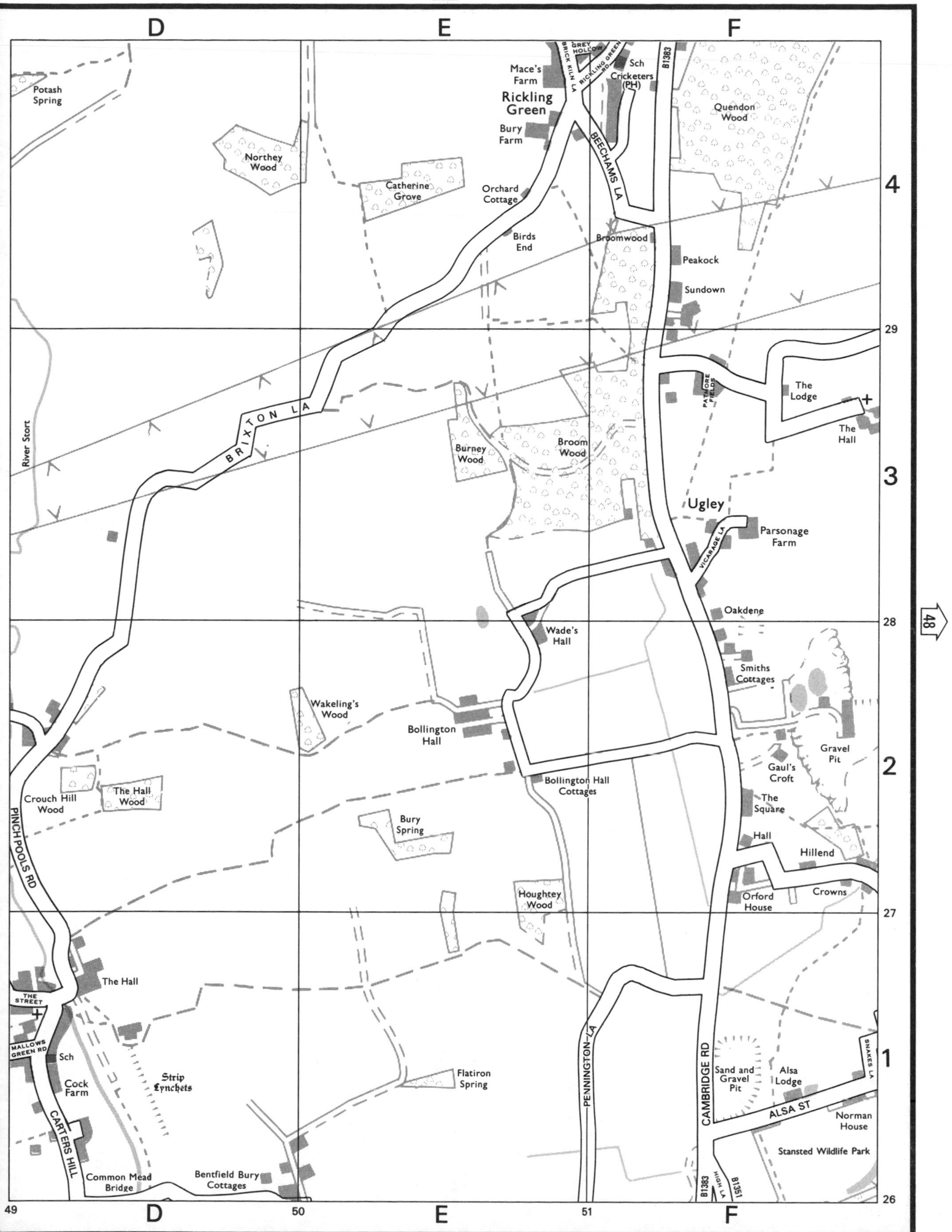
D
E
F
Potash Spring
Northey Wood
Catherine Grove
Mace's Farm
Rickling Green
Bury Farm
Grey Hollow
Brick Kiln La
Rickling Green Rd
Sch
Cricketers (PH)
B1383
Quendon Wood
Beechams La
Orchard Cottage
Birds End
Broomwood
Peakock
Sundown
The Lodge
The Hall
Brixton La
River Stort
Burney Wood
Broom Wood
Ugley
Parsonage Farm
Vicarage La
Oakdene
Wade's Hall
Smiths Cottages
Wakeling's Wood
Bollington Hall
Gravel Pit
Gaul's Croft
Bollington Hall Cottages
Crouch Hill Wood
The Hall Wood
Pinchpools Rd
Bury Spring
The Square
Hall
Hillend
Houghtey Wood
Orford House
Crowns
The Hall
The Street
Mallows Green Rd
Sch
Cock Farm
Strip Lynchets
Flatiron Spring
Pennington La
Cambridge Rd
Sand and Gravel Pit
Alsa Lodge
Snakes La
Alsa St
Norman House
Stansted Wildlife Park
Carters Hill
Common Mead Bridge
Bentfield Bury Cottages
High La
B1351
4
3
2
1
29
28
27
26
49
50
51

48

57

37

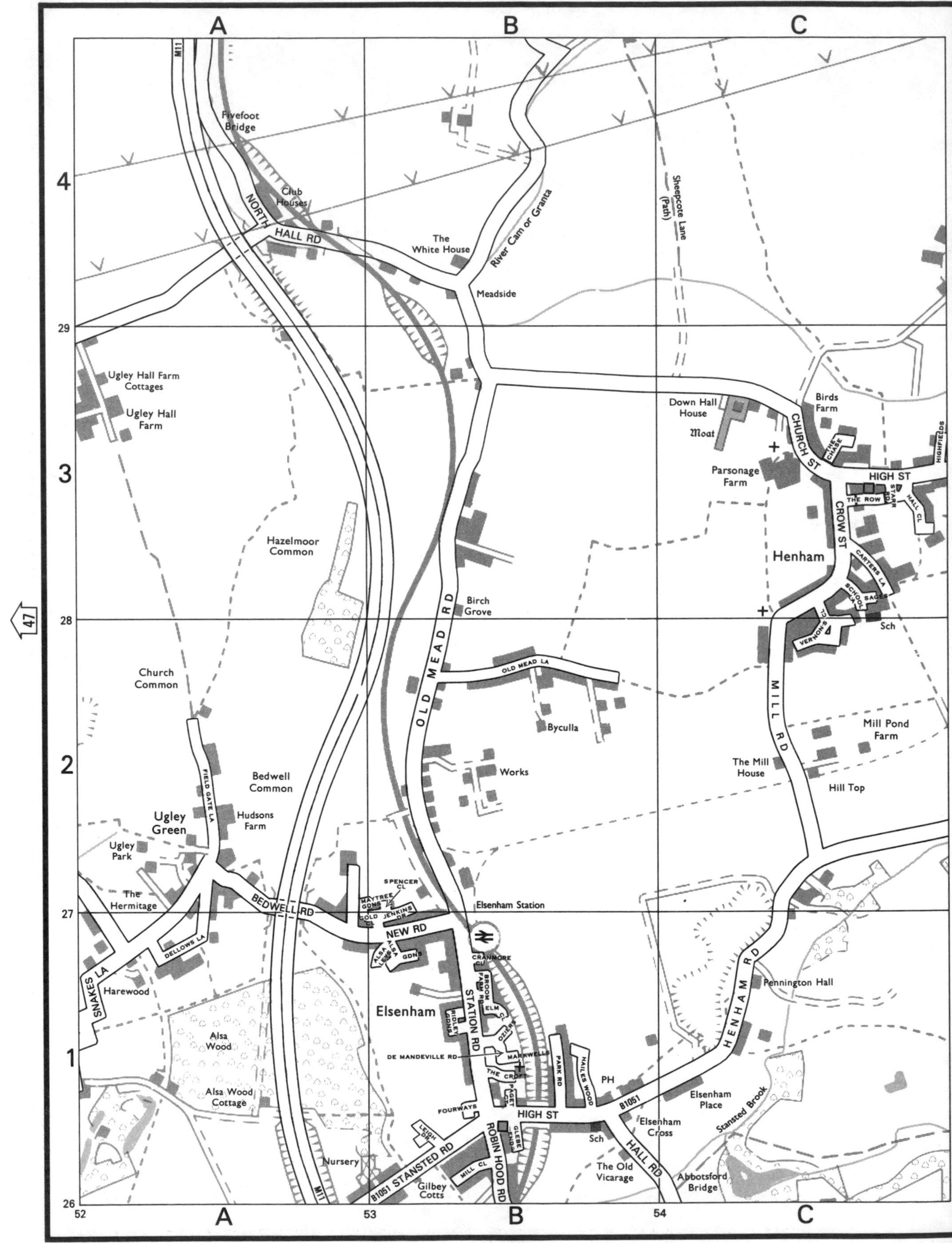
A
B
C
Fivefoot Bridge
Club Houses
NORTH HALL RD
The White House
River Cam or Granta
Sheepcote Lane (Path)
Meadside
Ugley Hall Farm Cottages
Ugley Hall Farm
Down Hall House
Moat
Birds Farm
CHURCH ST
Parsonage Farm
HIGH ST
THE ROW
CROW ST
Henham
CARTERS LA
SCHOOL LA
SAGES
Sch
VERNON'S CL
Hazelmoor Common
Birch Grove
OLD MEAD RD
OLD MEAD LA
Church Common
Byculla
MILL RD
Mill Pond Farm
The Mill House
Hill Top
Bedwell Common
Works
FIELD GATE LA
Ugley Green
Hudsons Farm
Ugley Park
The Hermitage
BEDWELL RD
SPENCER CL
JENKINS DR
Elsenham Station
NEW RD
DELLOWS LA
CRANMORE CL
SNAKES LA
Harewood
Pennington Hall
HENHAM RD
Elsenham
STATION RD
ELM CL
RIDLEY GDNS
Alsa Wood
DE MANDEVILLE RD
MARKWELLS
THE CROFT
PARK RD
HAILES WOOD
PH
Alsa Wood Cottage
FOURWAYS
HIGH ST
B1051
Elsenham Place
Elsenham Cross
Stansted Brook
Sch
HALL RD
ROBIN HOOD RD
STANSTED RD
MILL CL
Nursery
The Old Vicarage
Abbotsford Bridge
Gilbey Cotts
M11
52
53
54
26
27
28
29
1
2
3
4

47

58

38

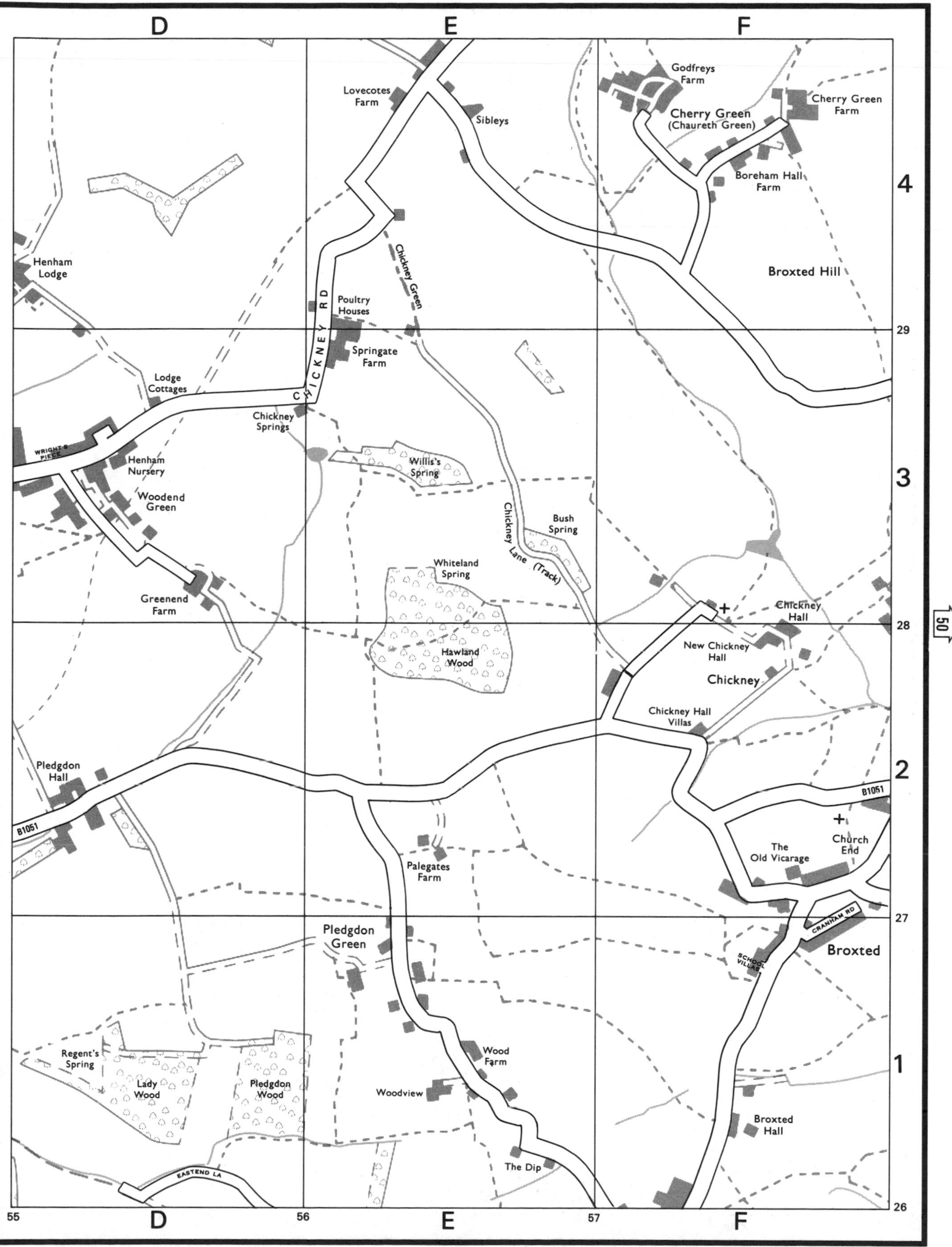
D
E
F
Godfreys Farm
Lovecotes Farm
Sibleys
Cherry Green
(Chaureth Green)
Cherry Green Farm
Boreham Hall Farm
4
Henham Lodge
Broxted Hill
Chickney Green
CHICKNEY RD
Poultry Houses
Springate Farm
29
Lodge Cottages
Chickney Springs
WRIGHT'S PIECE
Henham Nursery
Willis's Spring
3
Woodend Green
Bush Spring
Chickney Lane (Track)
Whiteland Spring
Greenend Farm
Chickney Hall
28
Hawland Wood
New Chickney Hall
Chickney
Chickney Hall Villas
Pledgdon Hall
2
B1051
B1051
Church End
The Old Vicarage
Palegates Farm
27
Pledgdon Green
CRANHAM RD
Broxted
SCHOOL VILLAS
Regent's Spring
Wood Farm
1
Lady Wood
Pledgdon Wood
Woodview
Broxted Hall
The Dip
EASTEND LA
26
55
56
57
D
E
F

50

59

39

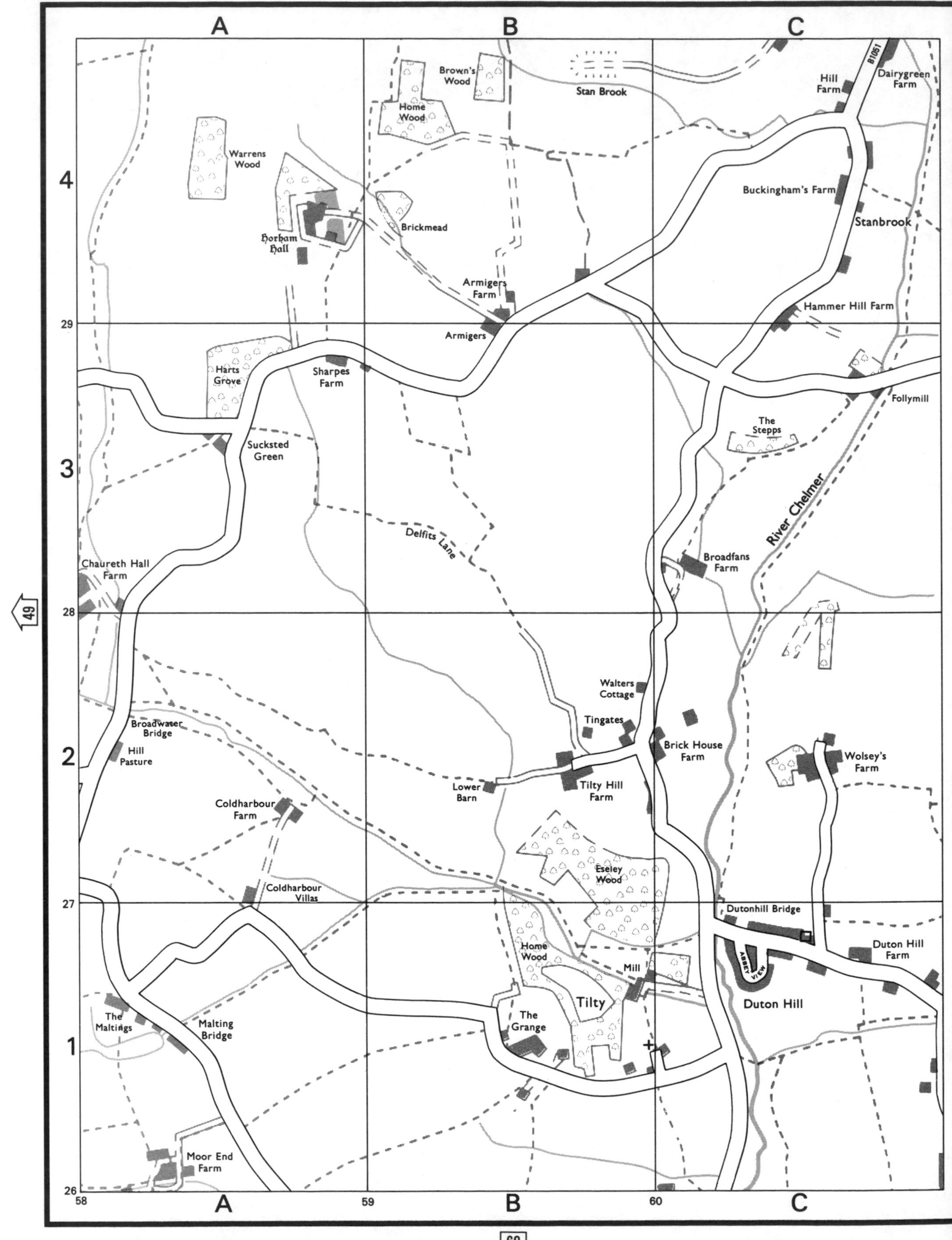
A
B
C
4
3
2
1
29
28
27
26
58
59
60
Brown's Wood
Home Wood
Stan Brook
Hill Farm
Dairygreen Farm
B1051
Warrens Wood
Horham Hall
Brickmead
Buckingham's Farm
Stanbrook
Armigers Farm
Armigers
Hammer Hill Farm
Harts Grove
Sharpes Farm
Follymill
The Stepps
Sucksted Green
River Chelmer
Delfits Lane
Chaureth Hall Farm
Broadfans Farm
Walters Cottage
Tingates
Broadwater Bridge
Hill Pasture
Brick House Farm
Wolsey's Farm
Lower Barn
Tilty Hill Farm
Coldharbour Farm
Eseley Wood
Coldharbour Villas
Dutonhill Bridge
Home Wood
Duton Hill Farm
Mill
Abbey View
The Maltings
Malting Bridge
Tilty
Duton Hill
The Grange
Moor End Farm

49

60

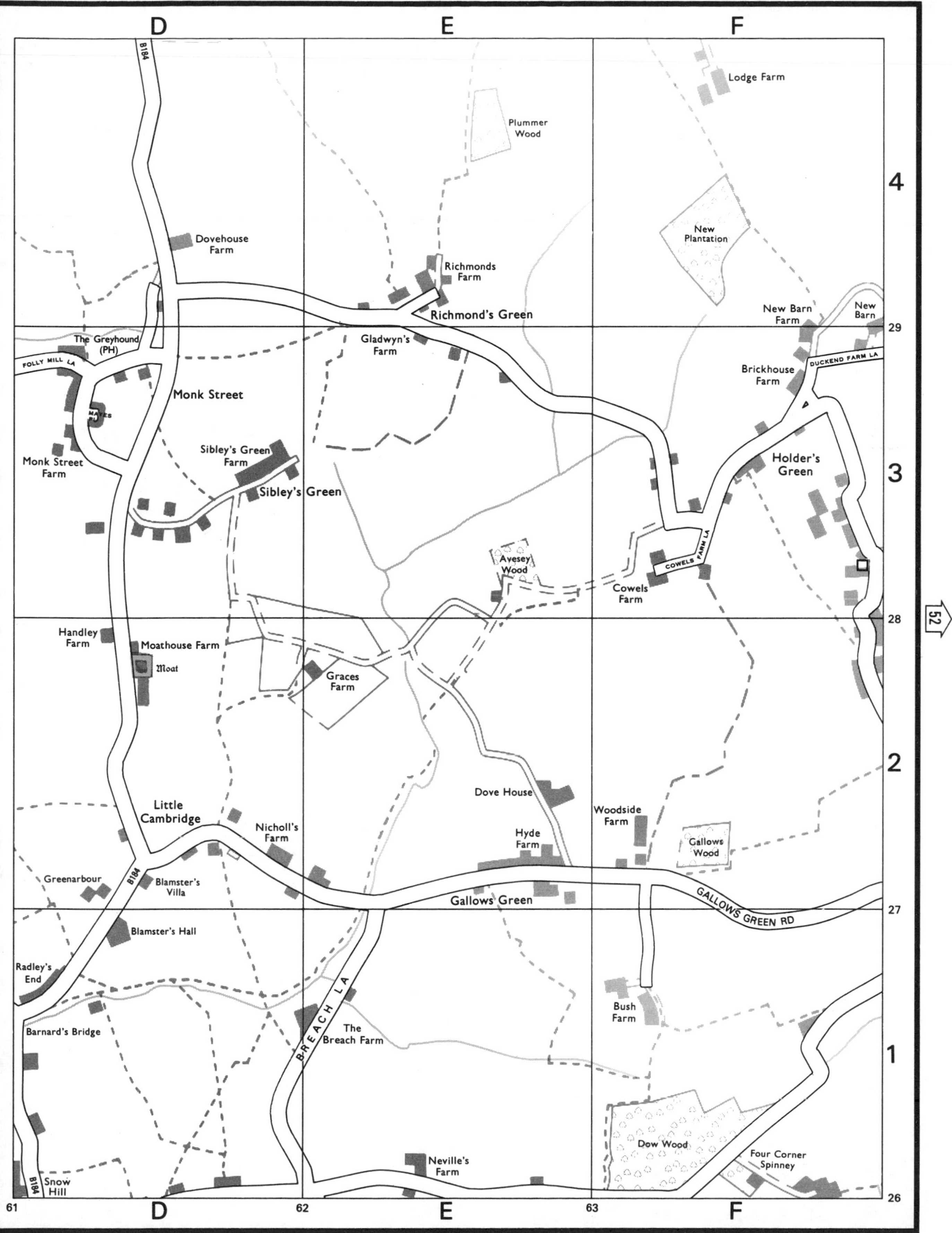
40
D
E
F
B184
Lodge Farm
Plummer Wood
4
New Plantation
Dovehouse Farm
Richmonds Farm
Richmond's Green
New Barn Farm
New Barn
29
The Greyhound (PH)
FOLLY MILL LA
Gladwyn's Farm
DUCKEND FARM LA
Brickhouse Farm
Monk Street
MAYES PL
Monk Street Farm
Sibley's Green Farm
Sibley's Green
Holder's Green
3
COWELS FARM LA
Avesey Wood
Cowels Farm
28
52
Handley Farm
Moathouse Farm
Moat
Graces Farm
2
Dove House
Little Cambridge
Woodside Farm
Nicholl's Farm
Hyde Farm
Gallows Wood
Greenarbour
B184
Blamster's Villa
Gallows Green
GALLOWS GREEN RD
27
Blamster's Hall
Radley's End
BREACH LA
Bush Farm
Barnard's Bridge
The Breach Farm
1
Dow Wood
Four Corner Spinney
Neville's Farm
B184
Snow Hill
26
61
62
63
D
E
F
61

41

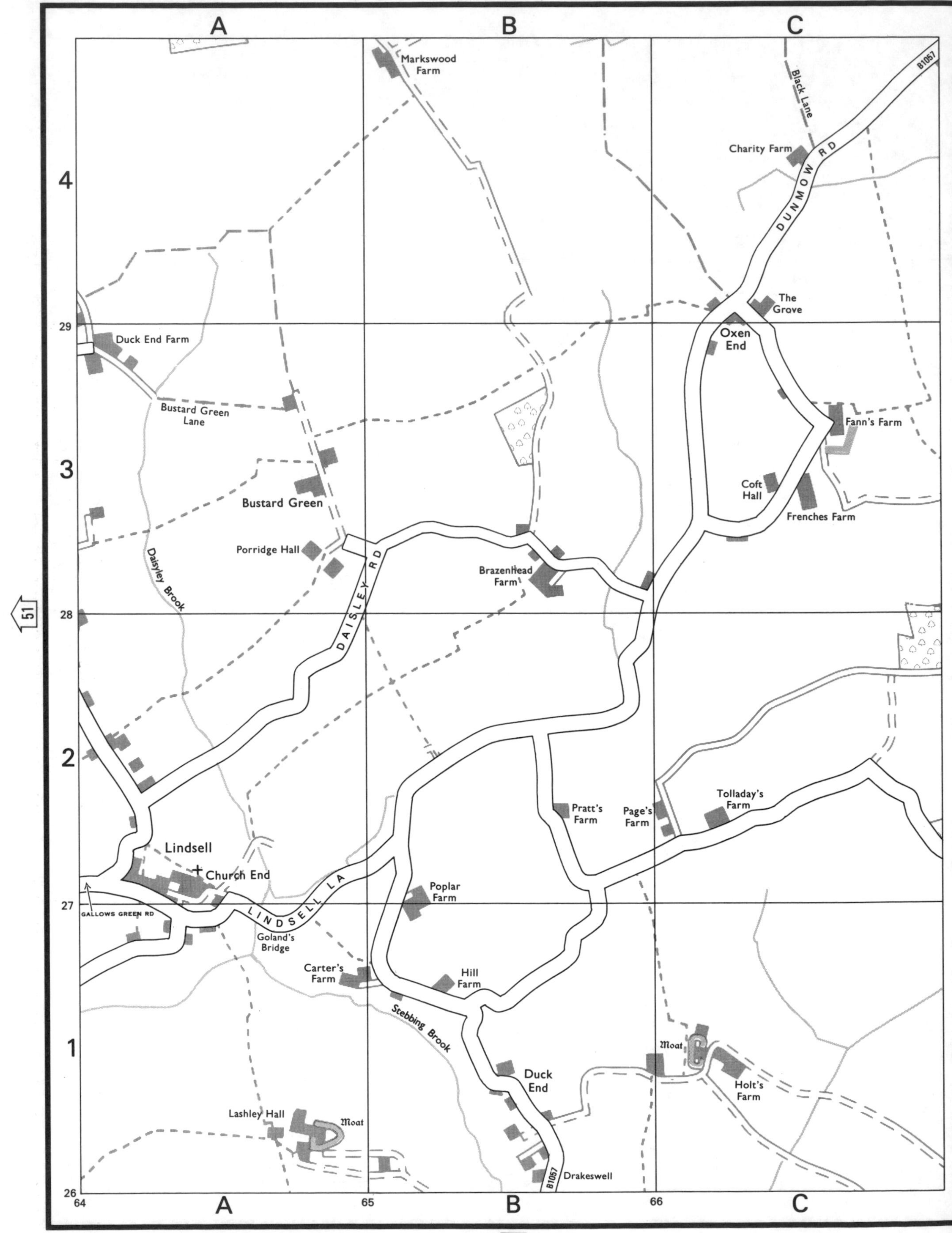

A
B
C
Markswood Farm
B1057
Black Lane
Charity Farm
DUNMOW RD
4
The Grove
29
Duck End Farm
Oxen End
Bustard Green Lane
Fann's Farm
3
Bustard Green
Coft Hall
Frenches Farm
Porridge Hall
Daisyley Brook
DAISLEY RD
Brazenhead Farm
51
28
2
Pratt's Farm
Page's Farm
Tolladay's Farm
Lindsell
Church End
Poplar Farm
GALLOWS GREEN RD
27
LINDSELL LA
Goland's Bridge
Carter's Farm
Hill Farm
Stebbing Brook
1
Moat
Duck End
Holt's Farm
Lashley Hall
Moat
B1057
Drakeswell
26
64
65
66
A
B
C

62

42

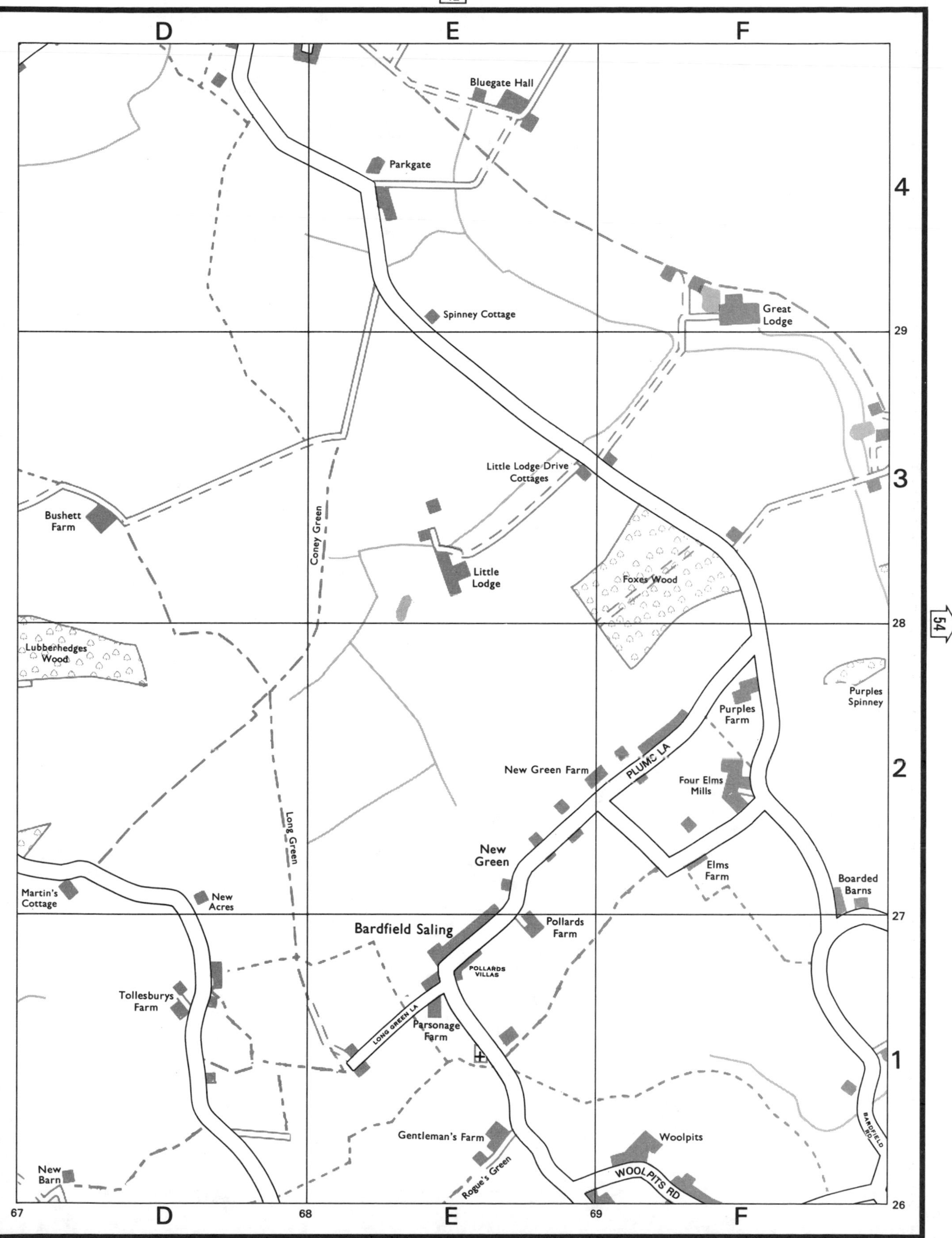
D
E
F
Bluegate Hall
Parkgate
4
Spinney Cottage
Great
Lodge
29
Little Lodge Drive
Cottages
3
Bushett
Farm
Coney Green
Little
Lodge
Foxes Wood
28
Lubberhedges
Wood
Purples
Spinney
Purples
Farm
New Green Farm
PLUMC LA
2
Four Elms
Mills
Long Green
New
Green
Elms
Farm
Boarded
Barns
Martin's
Cottage
New
Acres
27
Bardfield Saling
Pollards
Farm
POLLARDS
VILLAS
Tollesburys
Farm
LONG GREEN LA
Parsonage
Farm
1
BARDFIELD
RD
Gentleman's Farm
Woolpits
WOOLPITS RD
Rogue's Green
New
Barn
26
67
68
69
D
E
F

54

63

43

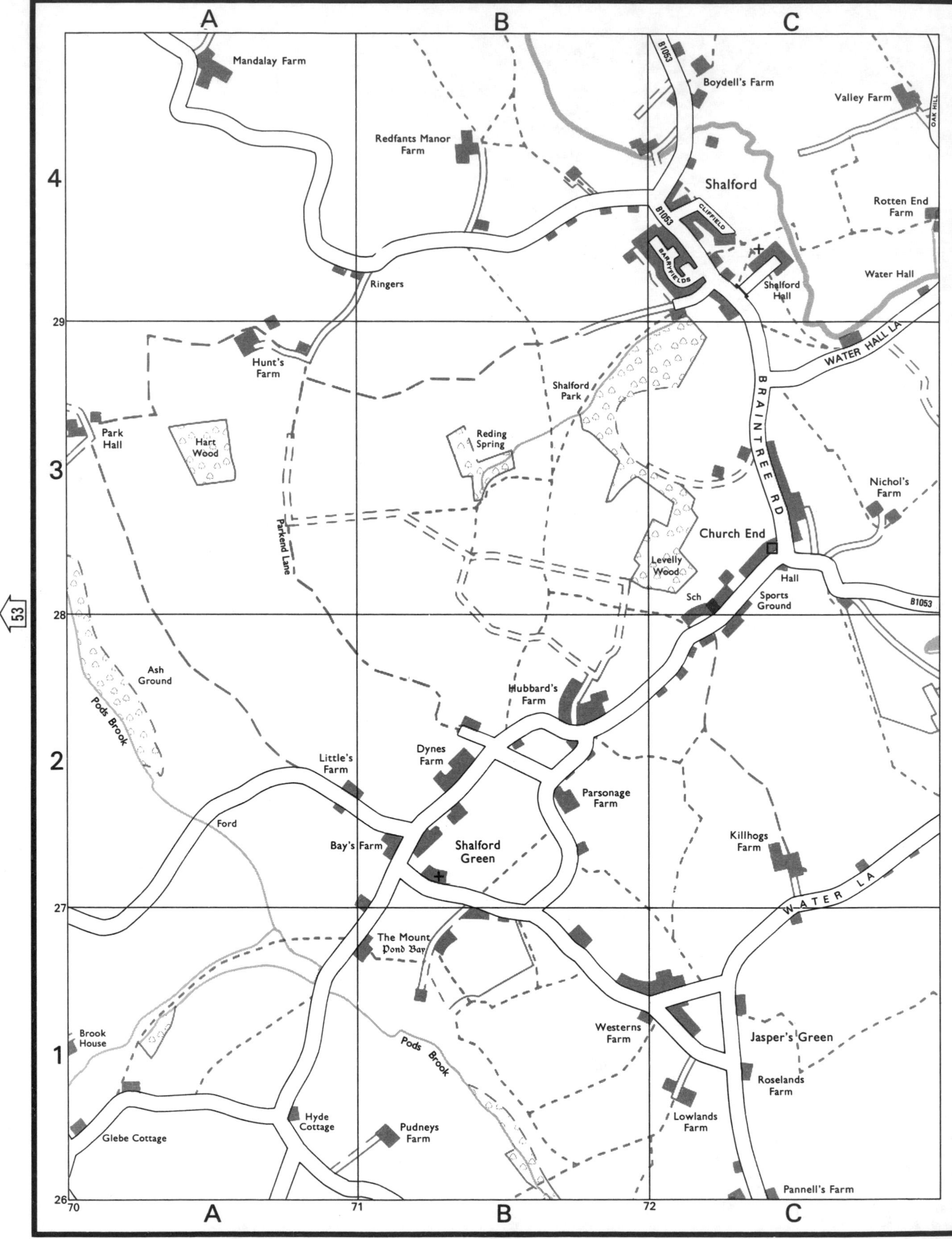
A
B
C
4
3
2
1
29
28
27
26
70
71
72
Mandalay Farm
Redfants Manor Farm
B1053
Boydell's Farm
Valley Farm
OAK HILL
Shalford
Rotten End Farm
CLIFFIELD
BARRYFIELDS
Water Hall
Shelford Hall
Ringers
Hunt's Farm
WATER HALL LA
Shalford Park
BRAINTREE RD
Park Hall
Hart Wood
Reding Spring
Nichol's Farm
Church End
Parkend Lane
Levelly Wood
Hall
Sch
Sports Ground
B1053
Ash Ground
Pods Brook
Hubbard's Farm
Dynes Farm
Little's Farm
Parsonage Farm
Ford
Killhogs Farm
Bay's Farm
Shalford Green
WATER LA
The Mount
Pond Bay
Westerns Farm
Brook House
Pods Brook
Jasper's Green
Roselands Farm
Lowlands Farm
Hyde Cottage
Glebe Cottage
Pudneys Farm
Pannell's Farm

53

64

44

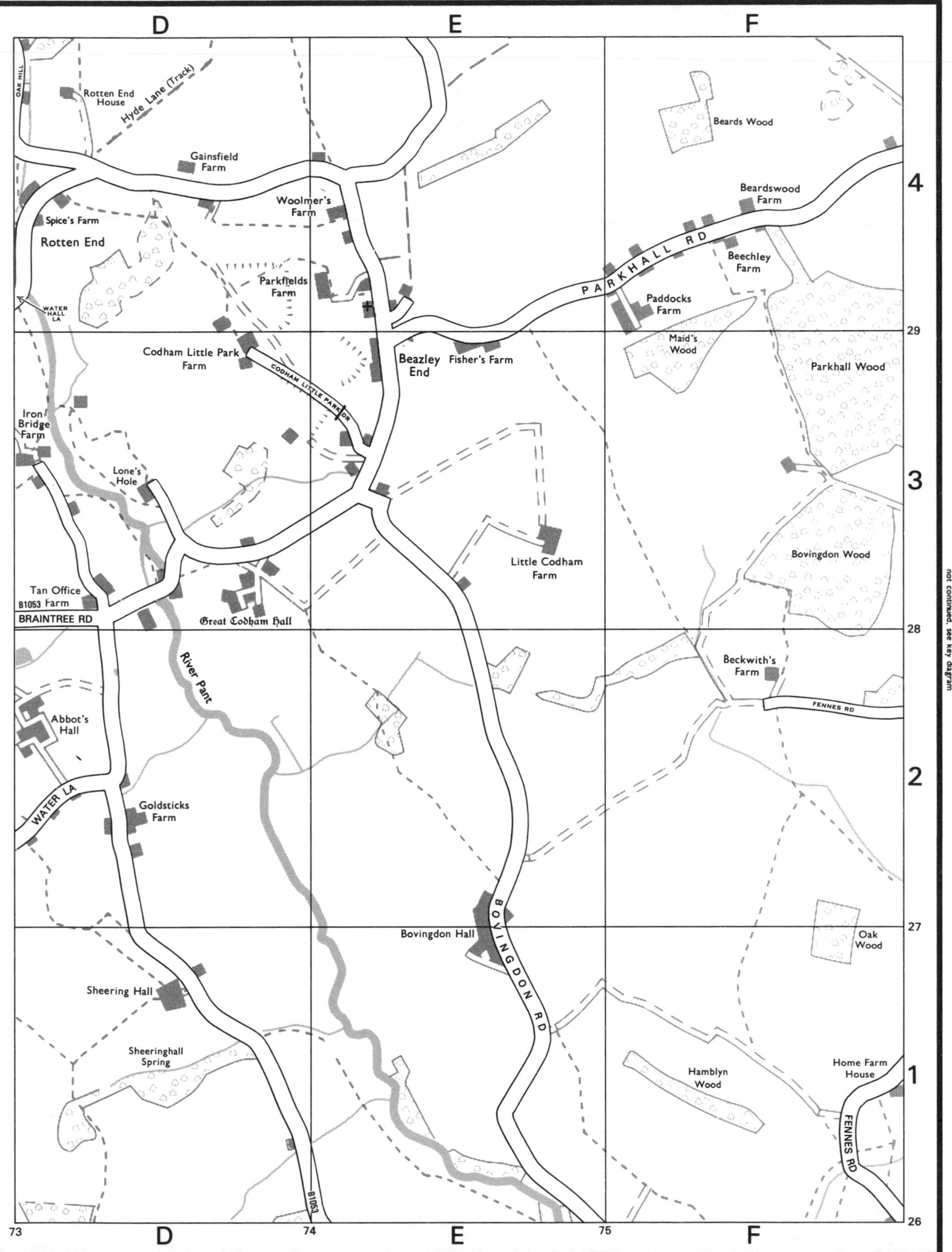
D
E
F
Rotten End House
Hyde Lane (Track)
Gainsfield Farm
Woolmer's Farm
Spice's Farm
Rotten End
Parkfields Farm
WATER HALL LA
Beards Wood
Beardswood Farm
PARKHALL RD
Beechley Farm
Paddocks Farm
Maid's Wood
Parkhall Wood
Codham Little Park Farm
CODHAM LITTLE PARK DR
Beazley End
Fisher's Farm
Iron Bridge Farm
Lone's Hole
Little Codham Farm
Bovingdon Wood
Tan Office Farm
B1053
BRAINTREE RD
Great Codham Hall
River Pant
Beckwith's Farm
FENNES RD
Abbot's Hall
WATER LA
Goldsticks Farm
Bovingdon Hall
BOVINGDON RD
Oak Wood
Sheering Hall
Sheeringhall Spring
Hamblyn Wood
Home Farm House
B1053
73
74
75
26
27
28
29
1
2
3
4
not continued, see key diagram

65

46

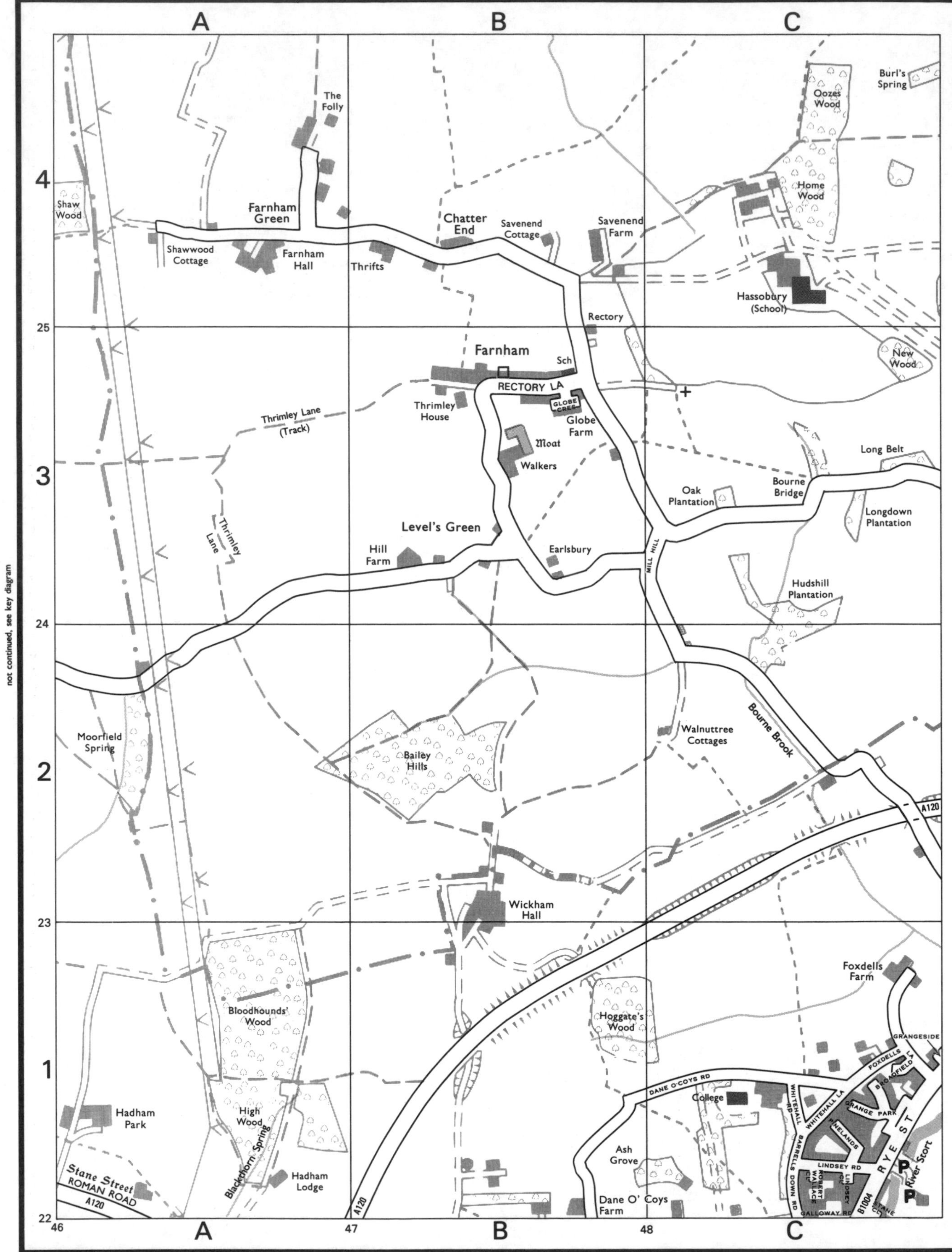
A
B
C
The Folly
Burl's Spring
Oozes Wood
Shaw Wood
Farnham Green
Chatter End
Savenend Cottage
Savenend Farm
Home Wood
Shawwood Cottage
Farnham Hall
Thrifts
Hassobury (School)
Rectory
Farnham
Sch
New Wood
RECTORY LA
GLOBE CRES
Thrimley House
Globe Farm
Thrimley Lane (Track)
Moat
Walkers
Long Belt
Oak Plantation
Bourne Bridge
Longdown Plantation
Thrimley Lane
Level's Green
Hill Farm
Earlsbury
MILL HILL
Hudshill Plantation
Moorfield Spring
Walnuttree Cottages
Bourne Brook
Bailey Hills
A120
Wickham Hall
Foxdells Farm
Bloodhounds' Wood
Hoggate's Wood
GRANGESIDE
FOXDELLS LA
BROADFIELD
DANE O'COYS RD
College
WHITEHALL RD
WHITEHALL LA
GRANGE PARK
PINELANDS
Hadham Park
High Wood
Ash Grove
RYE ST
River Stort
LINDSEY RD
BARRELLS DOWN RD
ROBERT WALLACE CL
LINDSEY CL
B1004
Stane Street ROMAN ROAD
Blackthorn Spring
Hadham Lodge
Dane O' Coys Farm
GALLOWAY RD
STANE CL
A120
A120
4
3
2
1
25
24
23
22
46
47
48
not continued, see key diagram

67

47

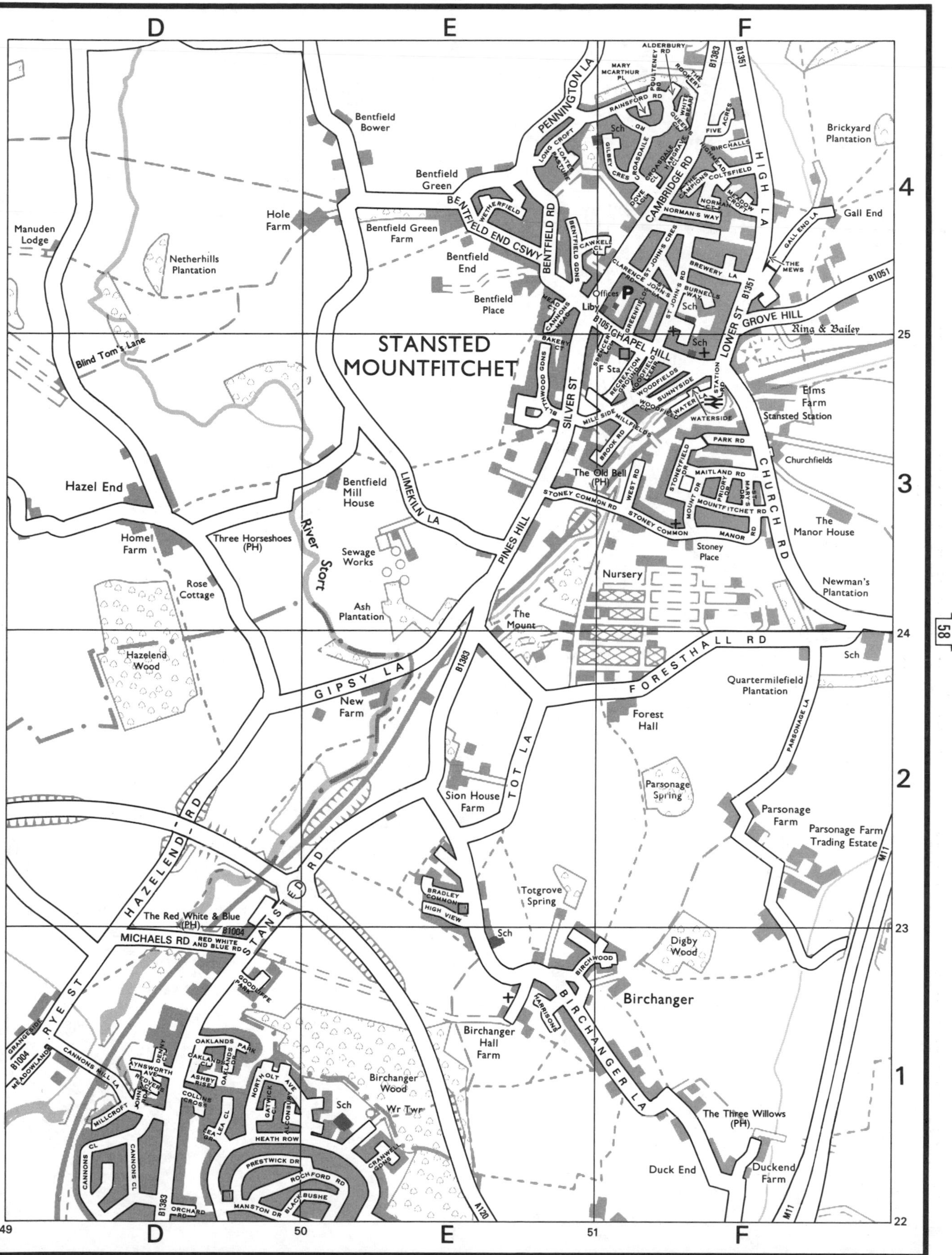

STANSTED MOUNTFITCHET
Bentfield Bower
Bentfield Green
Bentfield Green Farm
Bentfield End
Bentfield Place
Hole Farm
Manuden Lodge
Netherhills Plantation
Blind Tom's Lane
Hazel End
Home Farm
Three Horseshoes (PH)
Rose Cottage
Hazelend Wood
Bentfield Mill House
Sewage Works
Ash Plantation
River Stort
LIMEKILN LA
PINES HILL
GIPSY LA
New Farm
The Mount
Nursery
Stoney Place
The Old Bell (PH)
Brickyard Plantation
Gall End
Ring & Bailey
Elms Farm
Stansted Station
Churchfields
The Manor House
Newman's Plantation
Sch
Quartermilefield Plantation
FORESTHALL RD
Forest Hall
Parsonage Spring
Parsonage Farm
Parsonage Farm Trading Estate
PARSONAGE LA
Sion House Farm
TOT LA
Totgrove Spring
Digby Wood
Birchanger
Birchanger Hall Farm
Birchanger Wood
Wr Twr
The Three Willows (PH)
Duck End
Duckend Farm
The Red White & Blue (PH)
HAZELEND RD
STANSTED RD
MICHAELS RD
RYE ST
CANNONS MILL LA
BIRCHANGER LA
PENNINGTON LA
BENTFIELD END CSWY
BENTFIELD RD
CAMBRIDGE RD
HIGH LA
GROVE HILL
LOWER ST
CHAPEL HILL
SILVER ST
CHURCH RD
STONEY COMMON RD
STONEY COMMON
Offices
Liby
F Sta
M11
A120
B1383
B1351
B1051
B1004

58

68

48

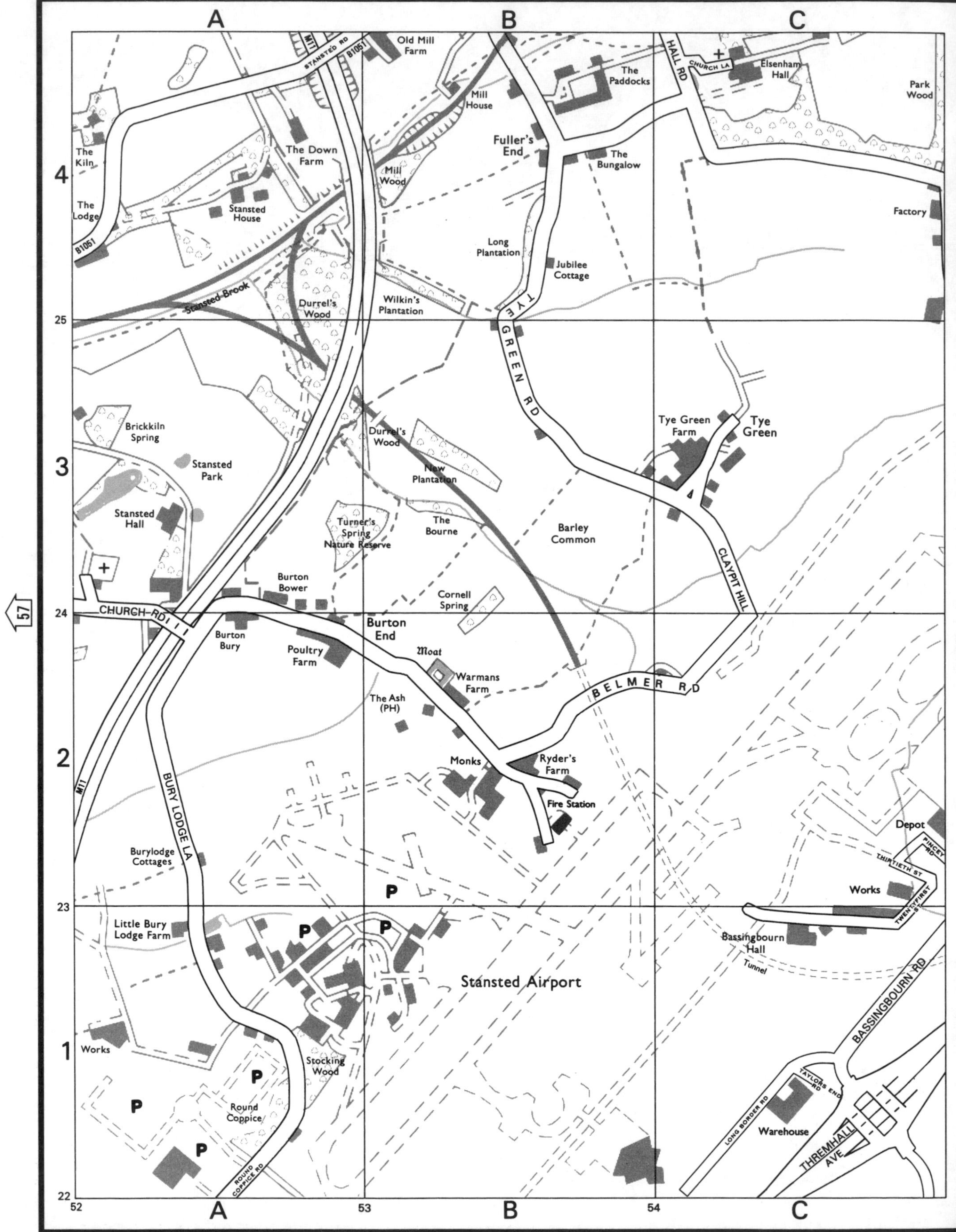

A
B
C
Old Mill Farm
Elsenham Hall
The Paddocks
Park Wood
Mill House
The Kiln
The Down Farm
Fuller's End
The Bungalow
Mill Wood
The Lodge
Stansted House
Factory
Long Plantation
Jubilee Cottage
Stansted Brook
Durrel's Wood
Wilkin's Plantation
TYE GREEN RD
HALL RD
CHURCH LA
STANSTED RD
B1051
M11
Brickkiln Spring
Tye Green Farm
Tye Green
Stansted Park
Durrel's Wood
New Plantation
Stansted Hall
Turner's Spring Nature Reserve
The Bourne
Barley Common
CLAYPIT HILL
Burton Bower
Cornell Spring
CHURCH RD
Burton End
Burton Bury
Poultry Farm
Moat
Warmans Farm
BELMER RD
The Ash (PH)
Monks
Ryder's Farm
Fire Station
BURY LODGE LA
Depot
PINCEY RD
THIRTIETH ST
Burylodge Cottages
Works
TWENTYFIRST ST
Little Bury Lodge Farm
Bassingbourn Hall
Tunnel
Stansted Airport
BASSINGBOURN RD
Works
Stocking Wood
TAYLORS END RD
Round Coppice
LONG BORDER RD
Warehouse
THREMHALL AVE
ROUND COPPICE RD
P
4
3
2
1
25
24
23
22
52
53
54

57

69

49

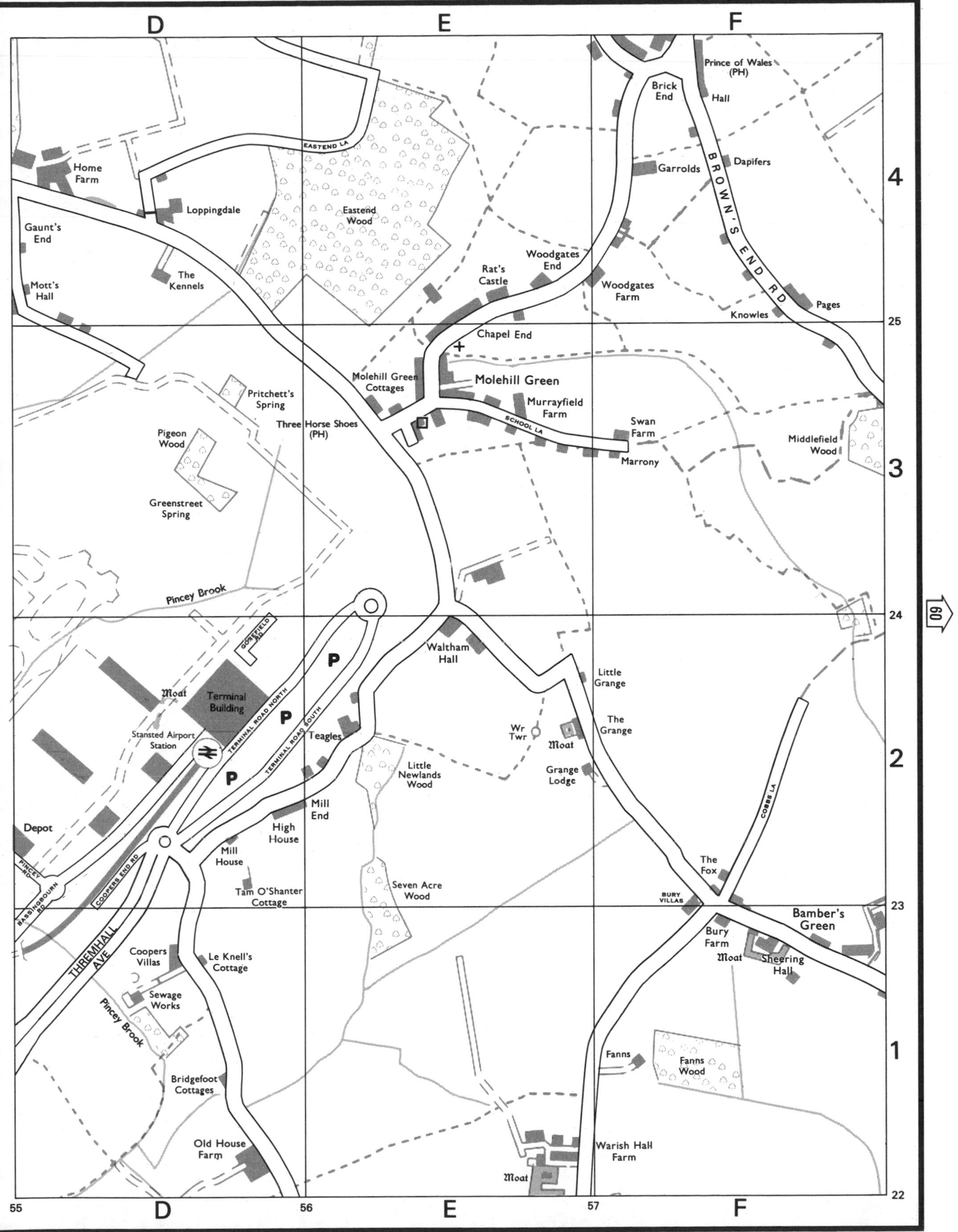

D
E
F
4
3
2
1
25
24
23
22
55
56
57
Prince of Wales (PH)
Hall
Brick End
EASTEND LA
Home Farm
Loppingdale
Gaunt's End
Eastend Wood
Garrolds
BROWN'S END RD
Dapifers
Mott's Hall
The Kennels
Woodgates End
Rat's Castle
Woodgates Farm
Knowles
Pages
Chapel End
Molehill Green Cottages
Molehill Green
Murrayfield Farm
Pritchett's Spring
Three Horse Shoes (PH)
SCHOOL LA
Swan Farm
Marrony
Middlefield Wood
Pigeon Wood
Greenstreet Spring
Pincey Brook
GOREFIELD RD
Waltham Hall
Little Grange
Moat
Terminal Building
TERMINAL ROAD NORTH
TERMINAL ROAD SOUTH
P
Teagles
Wr Twr
The Grange
Stansted Airport Station
Grange Lodge
Little Newlands Wood
Mill End
High House
COBBS LA
Depot
Mill House
PINCEY RD
BASSINGBOURN RD
COOPERS END RD
Tam O'Shanter Cottage
Seven Acre Wood
The Fox
BURY VILLAS
Bamber's Green
THREMHALL AVE
Coopers Villas
Le Knell's Cottage
Bury Farm
Sheering Hall
Sewage Works
Pincey Brook
Fanns
Fanns Wood
Bridgefoot Cottages
Old House Farm
Warish Hall Farm

60

70

50

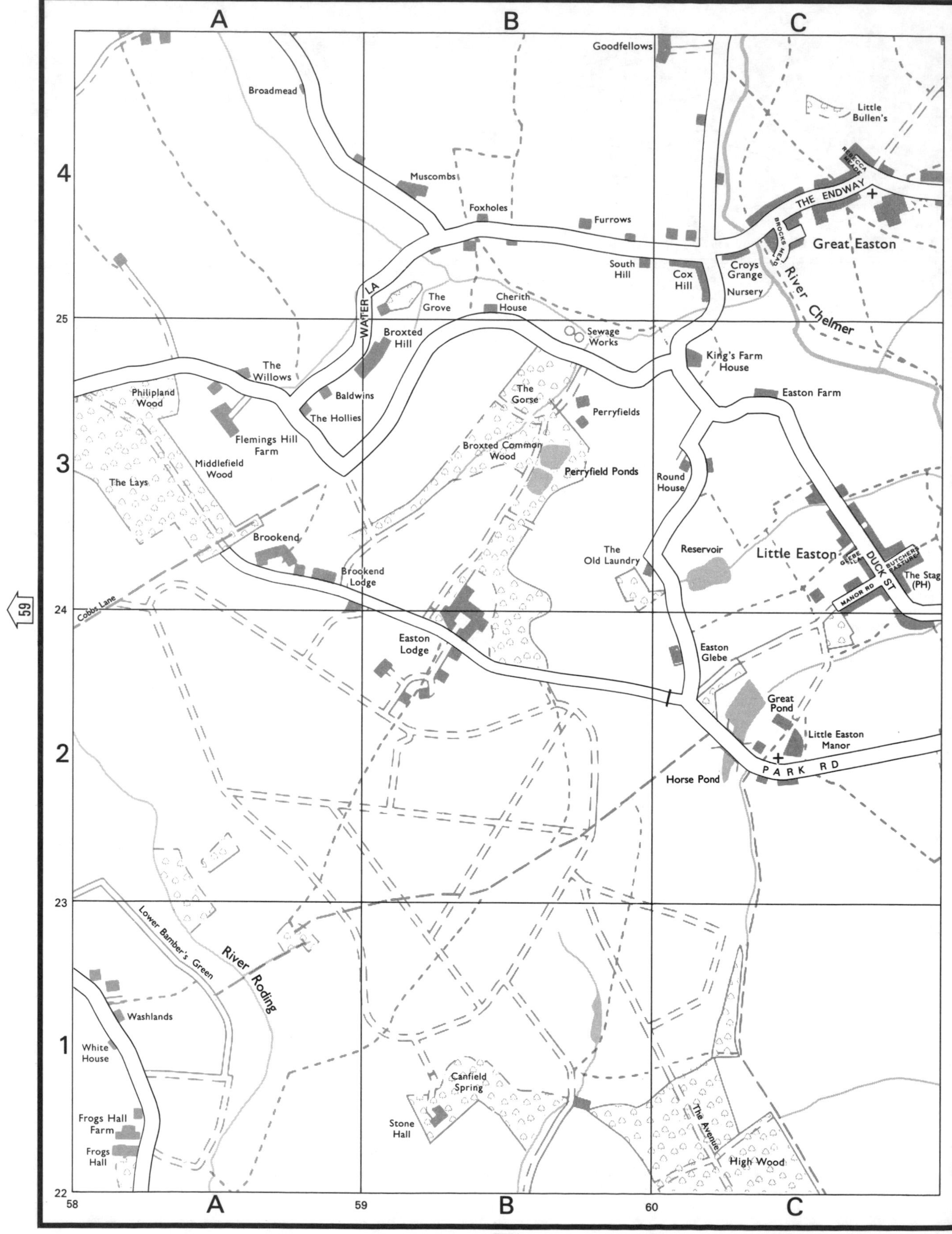

A
B
C
4
3
2
1
25
24
23
22
58
59
60
Goodfellows
Broadmead
Little Bullen's
REBECCA MEADE
THE ENDWAY
Muscombs
Foxholes
Furrows
BROCKS MEAD
Great Easton
South Hill
Cox Hill
Croys Grange
Nursery
River Chelmer
WATER LA
The Grove
Cherith House
Broxted Hill
Sewage Works
The Willows
King's Farm House
Philipland Wood
Baldwins
The Gorse
Easton Farm
The Hollies
Perryfields
Flemings Hill Farm
Broxted Common Wood
Middlefield Wood
Perryfield Ponds
Round House
The Lays
Brookend
The Old Laundry
Reservoir
Little Easton
GLEBE LA
DUCK ST
BUTCHERS PASTURE
The Stag (PH)
Brookend Lodge
MANOR RD
Cobbs Lane
Easton Lodge
Easton Glebe
Great Pond
Little Easton Manor
PARK RD
Horse Pond
Lower Bamber's Green
River Roding
Washlands
White House
Canfield Spring
Stone Hall
Frogs Hall Farm
Frogs Hall
The Avenue
High Wood

59

71

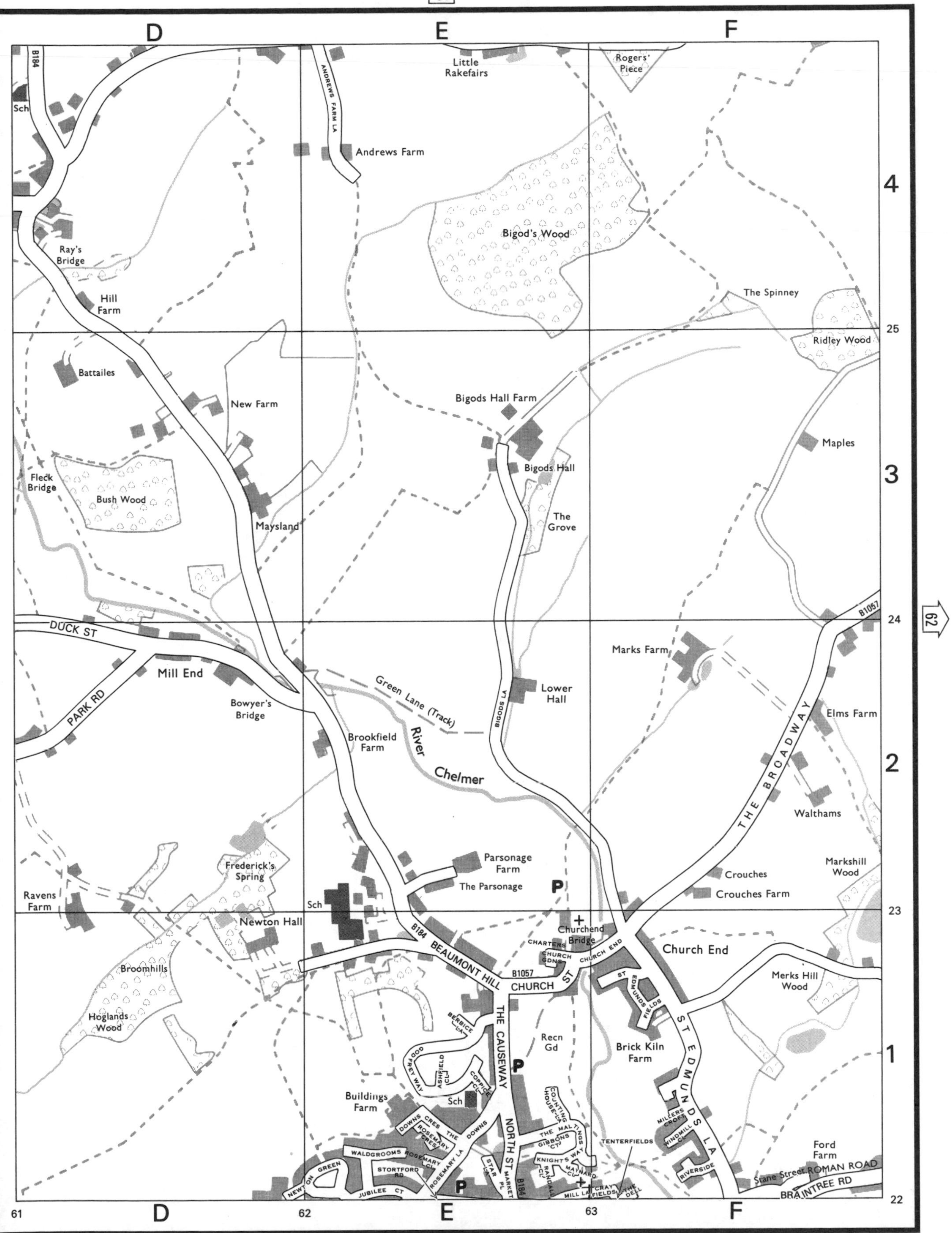

51
D
E
F
Little Rakefairs
Rogers' Piece
ANDREWS FARM LA
Andrews Farm
Sch
B184
Ray's Bridge
Bigod's Wood
Hill Farm
The Spinney
Ridley Wood
Battailes
New Farm
Bigods Hall Farm
Maples
Fleck Bridge
Bush Wood
Bigods Hall
The Grove
Maysland
DUCK ST
Mill End
PARK RD
Bowyer's Bridge
Green Lane (Track)
Marks Farm
BIGODS LA
Lower Hall
Elms Farm
B1057
Brookfield Farm
River Chelmer
THE BROADWAY
Walthams
Frederick's Spring
Parsonage Farm
The Parsonage
Markshill Wood
Crouches
Crouches Farm
Ravens Farm
Newton Hall
Churchend Bridge
Church End
CHARTERS
CHURCH GDNS
CHURCH END
BEAUMONT HILL
CHURCH ST
Broomhills
ST EDMUNDS FIELDS
Merks Hill Wood
Hoglands Wood
BERBICE LA
THE CAUSEWAY
Recn Gd
Brick Kiln Farm
ST EDMUNDS LA
GODFREY WAY
ASHFIELD CL
COPPICE CL
COUNTING HOUSE LA
Buildings Farm
Sch
DOWNS CRES
ROSEMARY CRES
THE DOWNS
NORTH ST
THE MALTINGS
GIBBONS CT
MILLERS CROFT
WINDMILL CL
TENTERFIELDS
WALDGROOMS
ROSEMARY CL
KNIGHT'S WAY
RANDALL CL
MAYNARD CL
Ford Farm
STORTFORD RD
ROSEMARY LA
STAR LA
MARKET PL
NEWTON GREEN
JUBILEE CT
MILL LA
CRAY FIELDS
THE DELL
RIVERSIDE
Stane Street
ROMAN ROAD
BRAINTREE RD
P
4
3
2
1
25
24
23
22
61
62
63
62
72

52

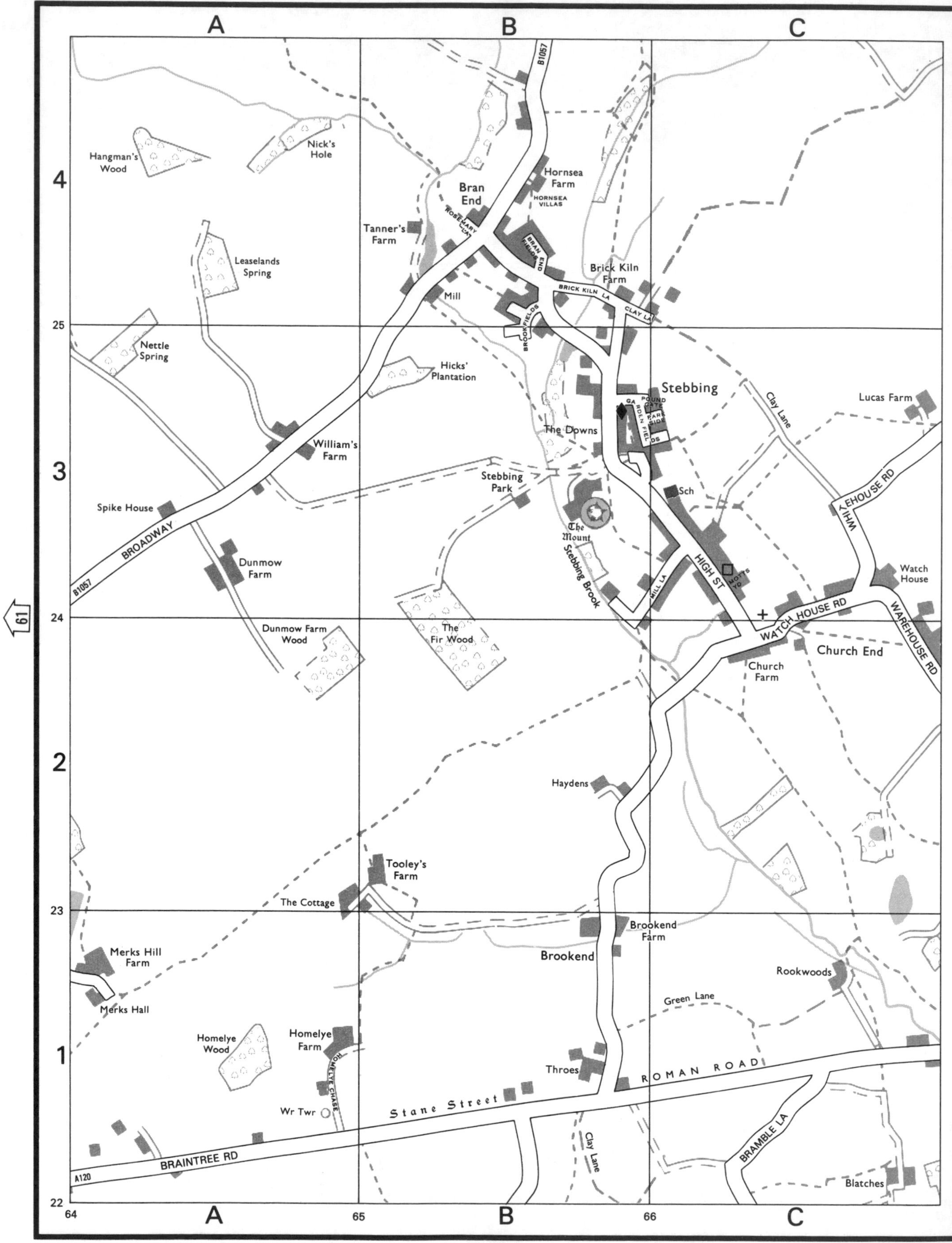
A
B
C
4
3
2
1
25
24
23
22
64
65
66
Hangman's Wood
Nick's Hole
Bran End
Hornsea Farm
HORNSEA VILLAS
Tanner's Farm
ROSEMARY LA
BRAN END FIELDS
Leaselands Spring
Brick Kiln Farm
BRICK KILN LA
CLAY LA
Mill
BROOKFIELDS
B1057
Nettle Spring
Hicks' Plantation
Stebbing
POUND GATE
PARK SIDE
GARDEN FIELDS
Lucas Farm
Clay Lane
The Downs
William's Farm
Stebbing Park
Sch
WHITEHOUSE RD
Spike House
BROADWAY
The Mount
Stebbing Brook
Dunmow Farm
MILL LA
HIGH ST
MOTTS YD
Watch House
WATCH HOUSE RD
WAREHOUSE RD
Dunmow Farm Wood
The Fir Wood
Church End
Church Farm
Haydens
Tooley's Farm
The Cottage
Brookend Farm
Brookend
Merks Hill Farm
Merks Hall
Rookwoods
Green Lane
Homelye Wood
Homelye Farm
HOMELYE CHASE
Throes
ROMAN ROAD
Stane Street
Wr Twr
BRAINTREE RD
A120
Clay Lane
BRAMBLE LA
Blatches

61

73

53

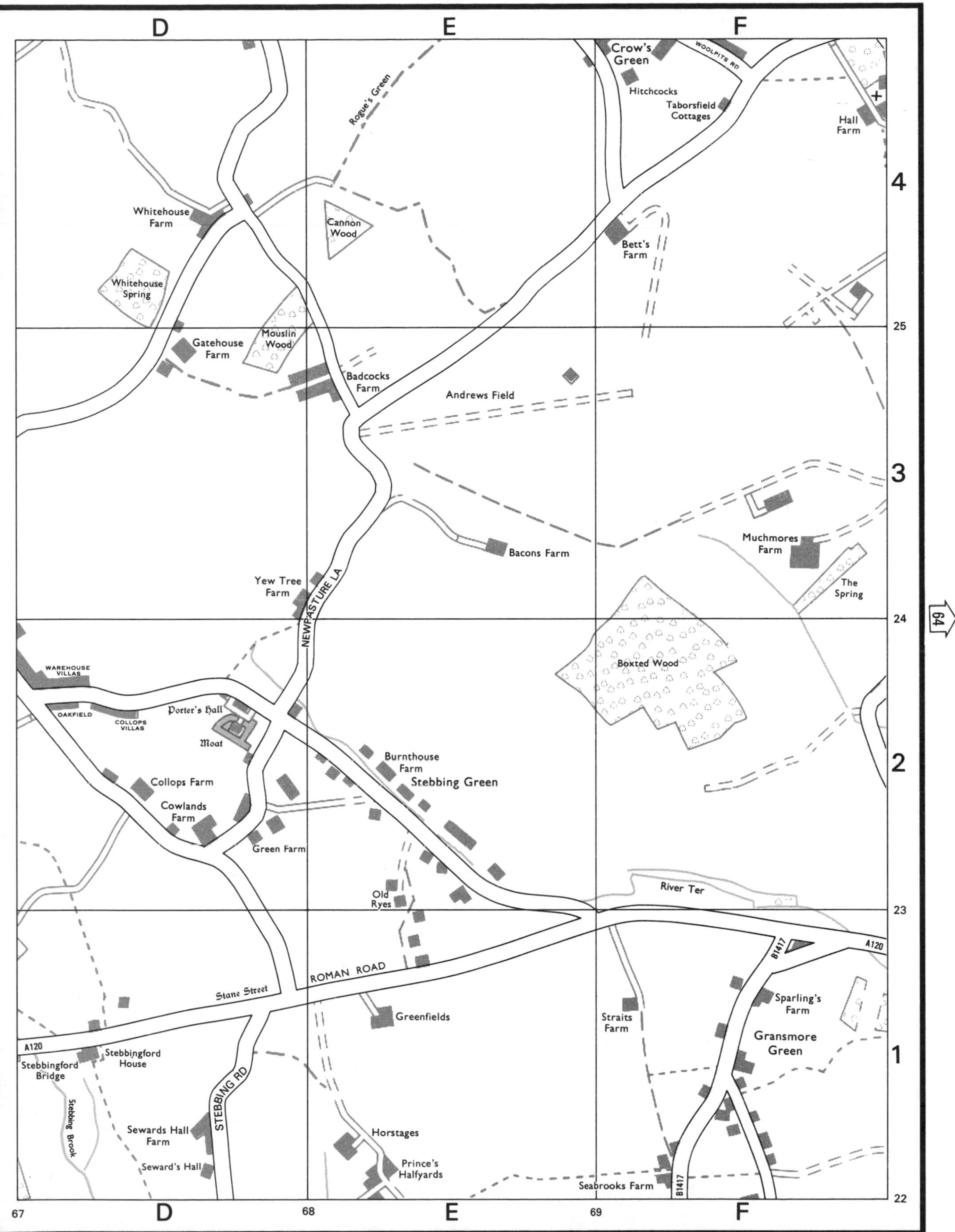
D
E
F
Crow's Green
WOOLPITS RD
Hitchcocks
Taborsfield Cottages
Hall Farm
Rogue's Green
4
Whitehouse Farm
Cannon Wood
Bett's Farm
Whitehouse Spring
Mouslin Wood
25
Gatehouse Farm
Badcocks Farm
Andrews Field
3
Bacons Farm
Muchmores Farm
Yew Tree Farm
The Spring
NEWPASTURE LA
24
WAREHOUSE VILLAS
Boxted Wood
OAKFIELD
COLLOPS VILLAS
Porter's Hall
Moat
Burnthouse Farm
2
Collops Farm
Stebbing Green
Cowlands Farm
Green Farm
River Ter
Old Ryes
23
ROMAN ROAD
B1417
A120
Stane Street
Greenfields
Sparling's Farm
Straits Farm
A120
Stebbingford Bridge
Stebbingford House
Gransmore Green
1
Stebbing Brook
STEBBING RD
Sewards Hall Farm
Horstages
Seward's Hall
Prince's Halfyards
Seabrooks Farm
B1417
22
67
D
68
E
69
F

64

74

54

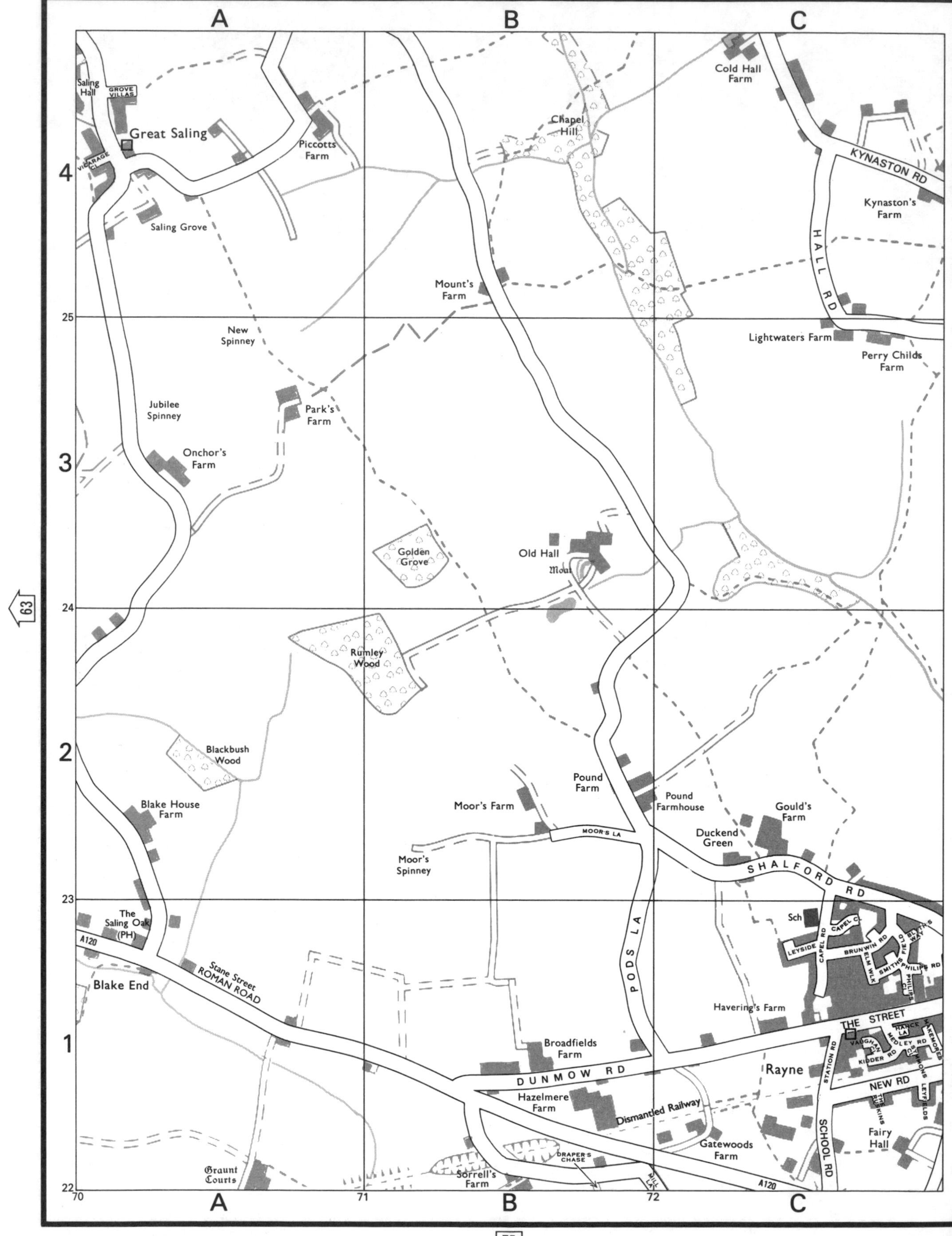
A
B
C
1
2
3
4
22
23
24
25
70
71
72
Saling Hall
GROVE VILLAS
Great Saling
VICARAGE CL
Piccotts Farm
Saling Grove
Cold Hall Farm
Chapel Hill
KYNASTON RD
Kynaston's Farm
HALL RD
Mount's Farm
New Spinney
Lightwaters Farm
Perry Childs Farm
Jubilee Spinney
Park's Farm
Onchor's Farm
Golden Grove
Old Hall
Moat
Rumley Wood
Blackbush Wood
Pound Farm
Pound Farmhouse
Gould's Farm
Blake House Farm
Moor's Farm
MOOR'S LA
Moor's Spinney
Duckend Green
SHALFORD RD
The Saling Oak (PH)
Sch
LEYSIDE
CAPEL RD
CAPEL CL
BRUNWIN RD
ELM WLK
SMITHS FIELD
BLYTH'S WAY
PHILIPS RD
A120
Stane Street
ROMAN ROAD
Blake End
PODS LA
Havering's Farm
THE STREET
HANCE LA
Broadfields Farm
DUNMOW RD
Rayne
STATION RD
VAUGHAN
MEDLEY RD
KIDDER RD
NEW RD
LEYFIELDS
Hazelmere Farm
Dismantled Railway
SCHOOL RD
Fairy Hall
Gatewoods Farm
DRAPER'S CHASE
Graunt Courts
Sorrell's Farm
MILL LA

63

75

55

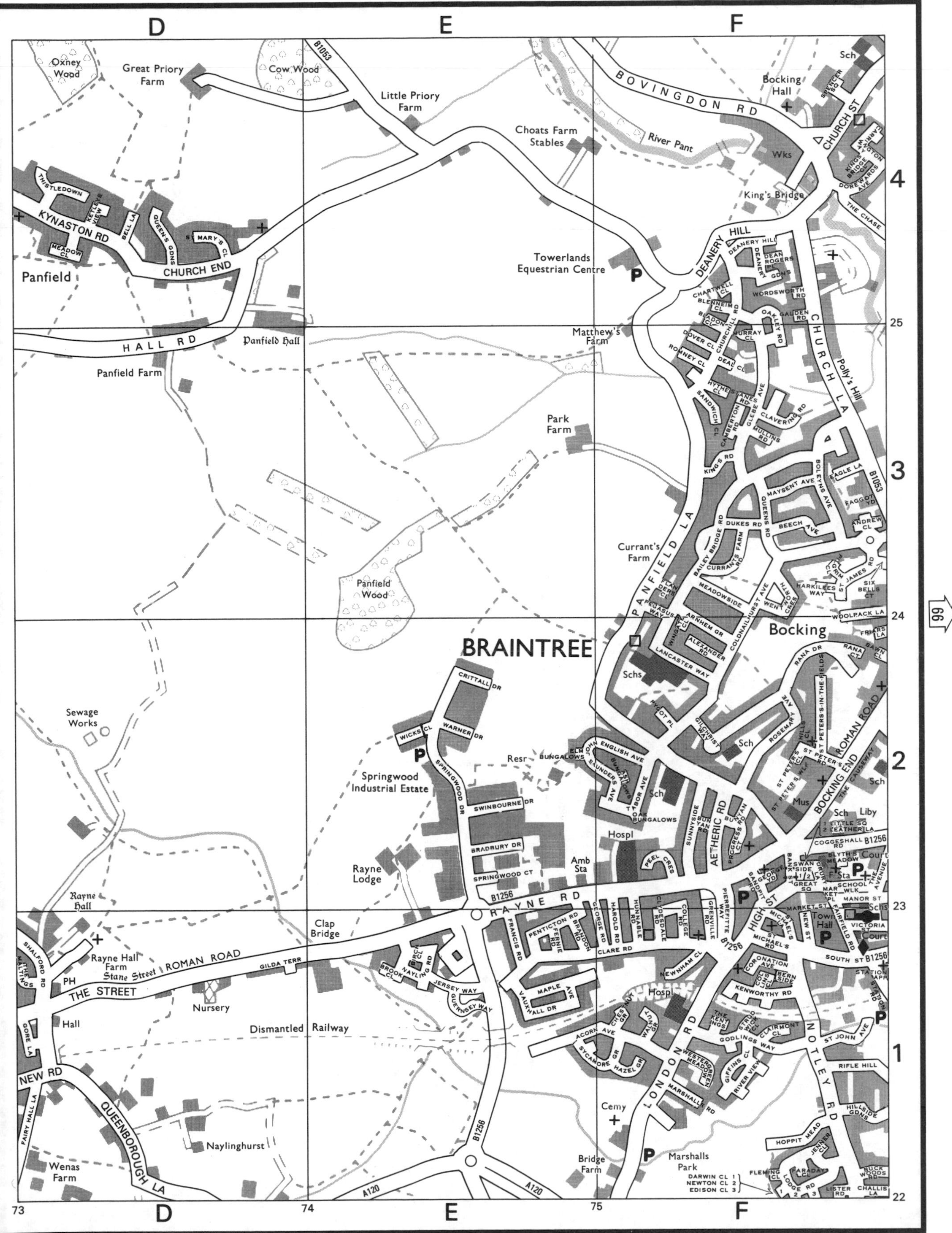
D
E
F
Oxney Wood
Great Priory Farm
Cow Wood
B1053
Little Priory Farm
BOVINGDON RD
Bocking Hall
Sch
River Pant
Choats Farm Stables
Wks
CHURCH ST
King's Bridge
THE CHASE
4
THISTLEDOWN
KYNASTON RD
BELL LA
QUEEN'S GDNS
ST MARY'S CL
MEADOW CL
CHURCH END
Panfield
Towerlands Equestrian Centre
DEANERY HILL
WORDSWORTH RD
CHURCH LA
25
HALL RD
Panfield Hall
Panfield Farm
Matthew's Farm
Polly's Hill
Park Farm
3
Panfield Wood
Currant's Farm
PANFIELD LA
BRAINTREE
Bocking
24
Sewage Works
Springwood Industrial Estate
Schs
Sch
ROMAN ROAD
BOCKING END
2
Resr
Hospl
Amb Sta
Rayne Lodge
Rayne Hall
RAYNE RD
B1256
Clap Bridge
Rayne Hall Farm
Stane Street ROMAN ROAD
THE STREET
PH
Nursery
HIGH ST
Town Hall
23
Hall
Dismantled Railway
LONDON RD
NOTLEY RD
1
NEW RD
QUEENBOROUGH LA
Naylinghurst
Wenas Farm
Cemy
Bridge Farm
Marshalls Park
DARWIN CL 1
NEWTON CL 2
EDISON CL 3
A120
22
73
74
75
99

76

not continued, see key diagram

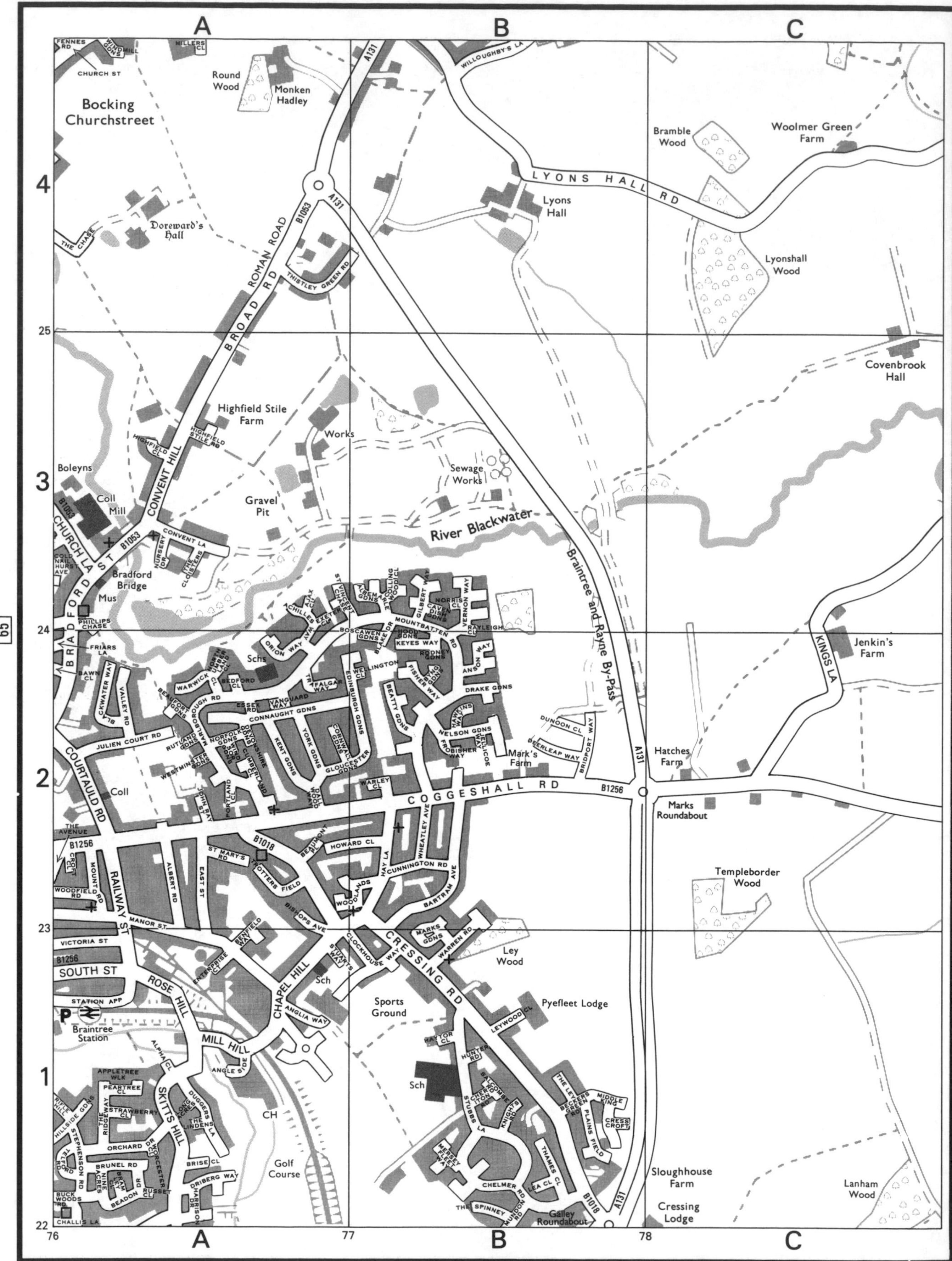

65

not continued, see key diagram

56

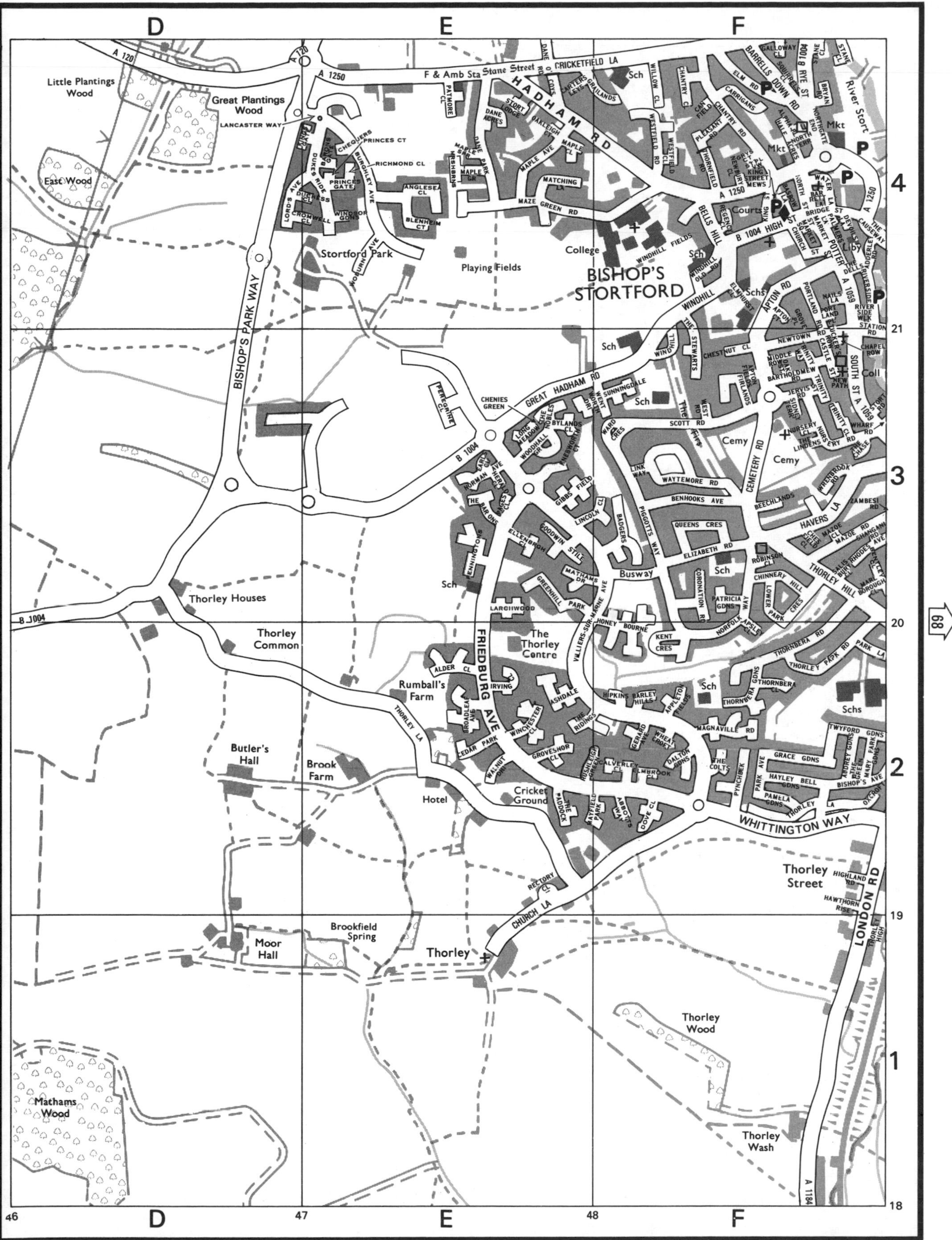
D
E
F
Little Plantings Wood
Great Plantings Wood
East Wood
Stortford Park
Playing Fields
College
BISHOP'S STORTFORD
BISHOP'S PARK WAY
HADHAM RD
GREAT HADHAM RD
WINDHILL
MAZE GREEN RD
Thorley Houses
Thorley Common
The Thorley Centre
FRIEDBURG AVE
Rumball's Farm
Butler's Hall
Brook Farm
Hotel
Cricket Ground
WHITTINGTON WAY
Thorley Street
LONDON RD
CHURCH LA
THORLEY LA
Moor Hall
Brookfield Spring
Thorley
Thorley Wood
Thorley Wash
Mathams Wood
Cemy
Busway
Schs
THORLEY HILL
River Stort
46
47
48
18
19
20
21
1
2
3
4

68

77

57

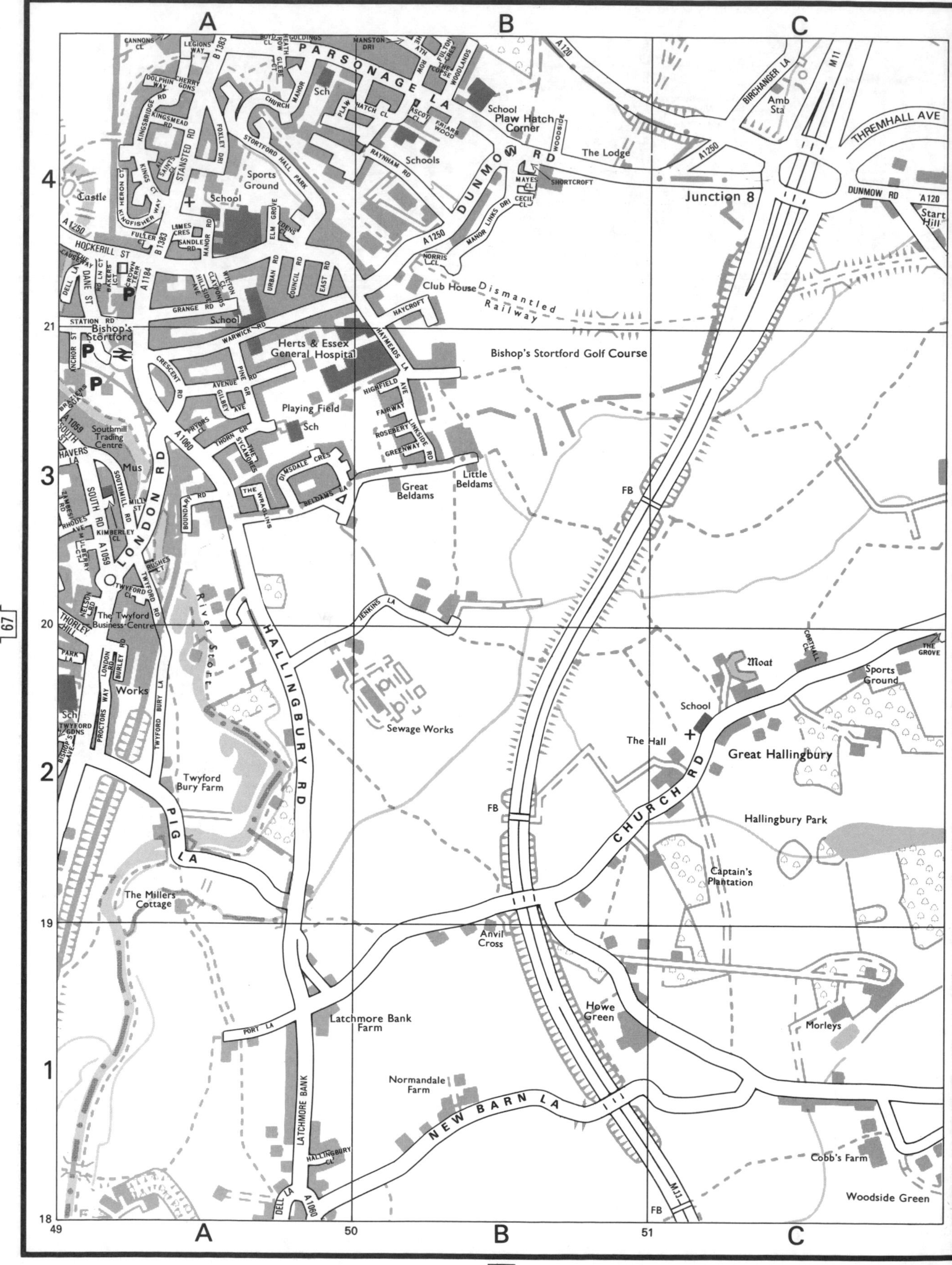
A
B
C
4
3
2
1
21
20
19
18
49
50
51
PARSONAGE LA
School
Plaw Hatch Corner
DUNMOW RD
The Lodge
Junction 8
THREMHALL AVE
DUNMOW RD
A120
Start Hill
Amb Sta
BIRCHANGER LA
M11
A1250
Castle
Sports Ground
School
Schools
STANSTED RD
HOCKERILL ST
Club House
Dismantled Railway
Bishop's Stortford Golf Course
Bishop's Stortford
Herts & Essex General Hospital
Playing Field
Sch
School
Southmill Trading Centre
Mus
LONDON RD
Great Beldams
Little Beldams
FB
The Twyford Business Centre
River Stort
HALLINGBURY RD
JENKINS LA
Sewage Works
Works
Moat
Sports Ground
School
The Hall
Great Hallingbury
CHURCH RD
Hallingbury Park
Twyford Bury Farm
PIG LA
The Millers Cottage
Captain's Plantation
Anvil Cross
PORT LA
Latchmore Bank Farm
Howe Green
Morleys
Normandale Farm
NEW BARN LA
LATCHMORE BANK
HALLINGBURY CL
DELL LA
A1060
Cobb's Farm
Woodside Green

67

78

58

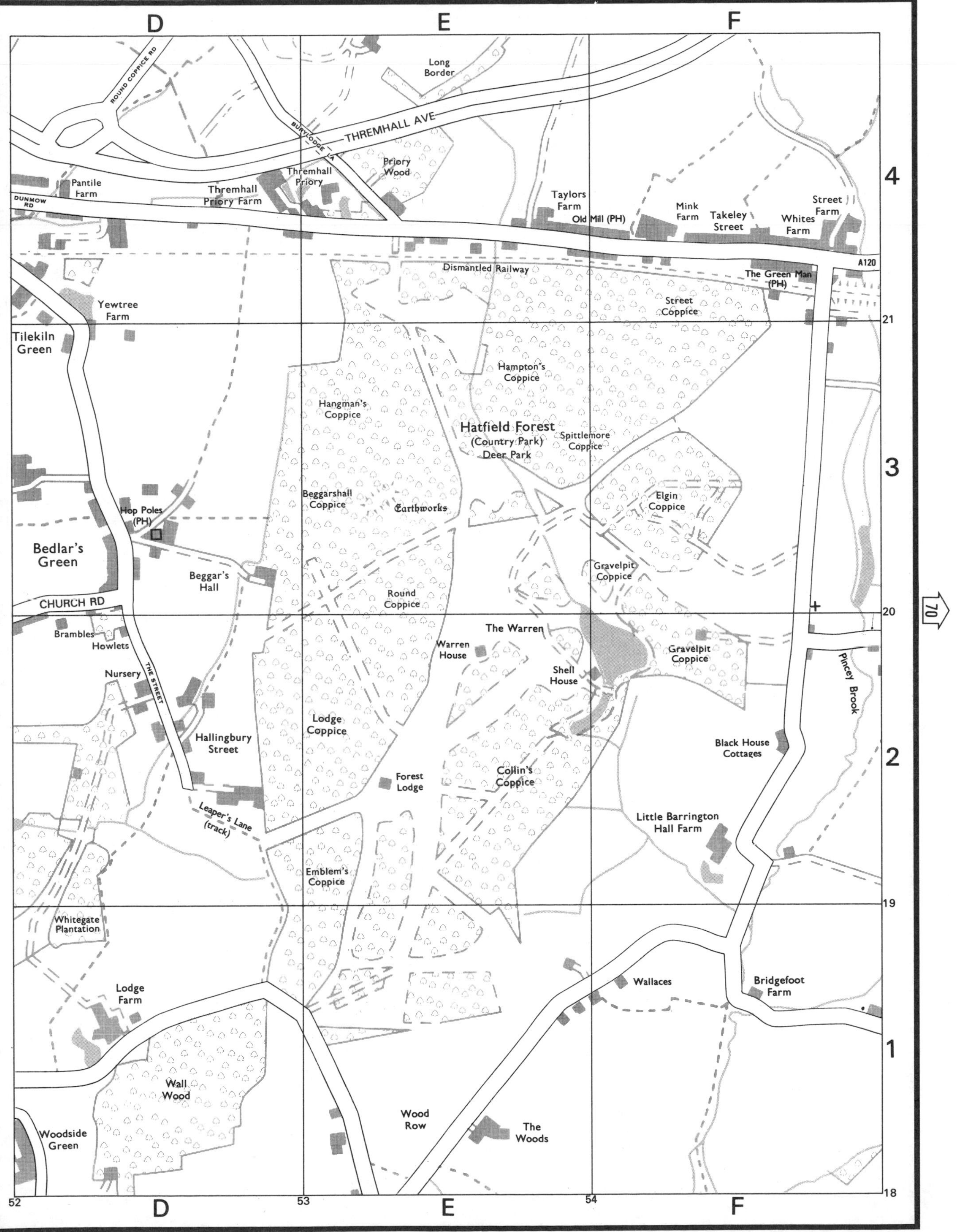

D
E
F
Long Border
ROUND COPPICE RD
BURY LODGE LA
THREMHALL AVE
Priory Wood
Thremhall Priory
Pantile Farm
Thremhall Priory Farm
DUNMOW RD
Taylors Farm
Old Mill (PH)
Mink Farm
Takeley Street
Street Farm
Whites Farm
A120
Dismantled Railway
The Green Man (PH)
Street Coppice
Yewtree Farm
Tilekiln Green
Hampton's Coppice
Hangman's Coppice
Hatfield Forest
(Country Park)
Deer Park
Spittlemore Coppice
Elgin Coppice
Beggarshall Coppice
Earthworks
Hop Poles (PH)
Bedlar's Green
Gravelpit Coppice
Beggar's Hall
Round Coppice
CHURCH RD
The Warren
Brambles
Howlets
Warren House
Gravelpit Coppice
Shell House
Pincey Brook
Nursery
THE STREET
Hallingbury Street
Lodge Coppice
Black House Cottages
Forest Lodge
Collin's Coppice
Leaper's Lane (track)
Little Barrington Hall Farm
Emblem's Coppice
Whitegate Plantation
Wallaces
Bridgefoot Farm
Lodge Farm
Wall Wood
Wood Row
The Woods
Woodside Green
52
53
54
18
19
20
21
1
2
3
4
D
E
F

70

79

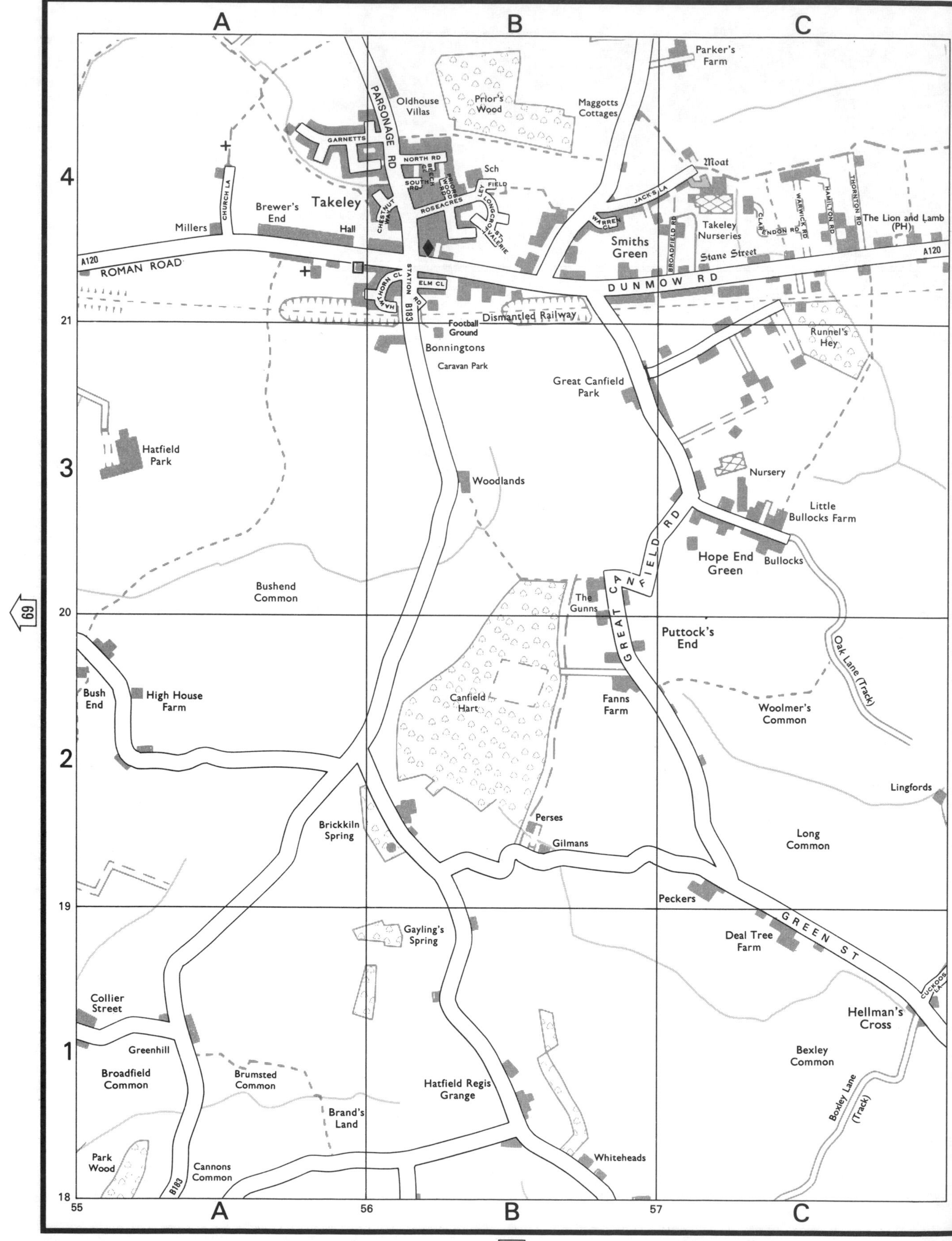
59
A
B
C
Parker's Farm
Oldhouse Villas
Prior's Wood
Maggotts Cottages
PARSONAGE RD
GARNETTS
NORTH RD
SOUTH RD
Sch
Moat
JACK'S LA
Takeley
Brewer's End
Millers
CHURCH LA
Hall
ROSEACRES
Smiths Green
Takeley Nurseries
The Lion and Lamb (PH)
A120
ROMAN ROAD
Stane Street
DUNMOW RD
STATION RD
B183
ELM CL
Dismantled Railway
Football Ground
Bonningtons
Caravan Park
Runnel's Hey
Great Canfield Park
Hatfield Park
Woodlands
Nursery
Little Bullocks Farm
GREAT CANFIELD RD
Hope End Green
Bullocks
Bushend Common
The Gunns
Puttock's End
Oak Lane (Track)
Bush End
High House Farm
Canfield Hart
Fanns Farm
Woolmer's Common
Lingfords
Perses
Gilmans
Brickkiln Spring
Long Common
Peckers
GREEN ST
Gayling's Spring
Deal Tree Farm
Collier Street
Hellman's Cross
Greenhill
Bexley Common
Broadfield Common
Brumsted Common
Hatfield Regis Grange
Brand's Land
Boxley Lane (Track)
Park Wood
Cannons Common
Whiteheads
4
3
2
1
21
20
19
18
55
56
57
69
80

60

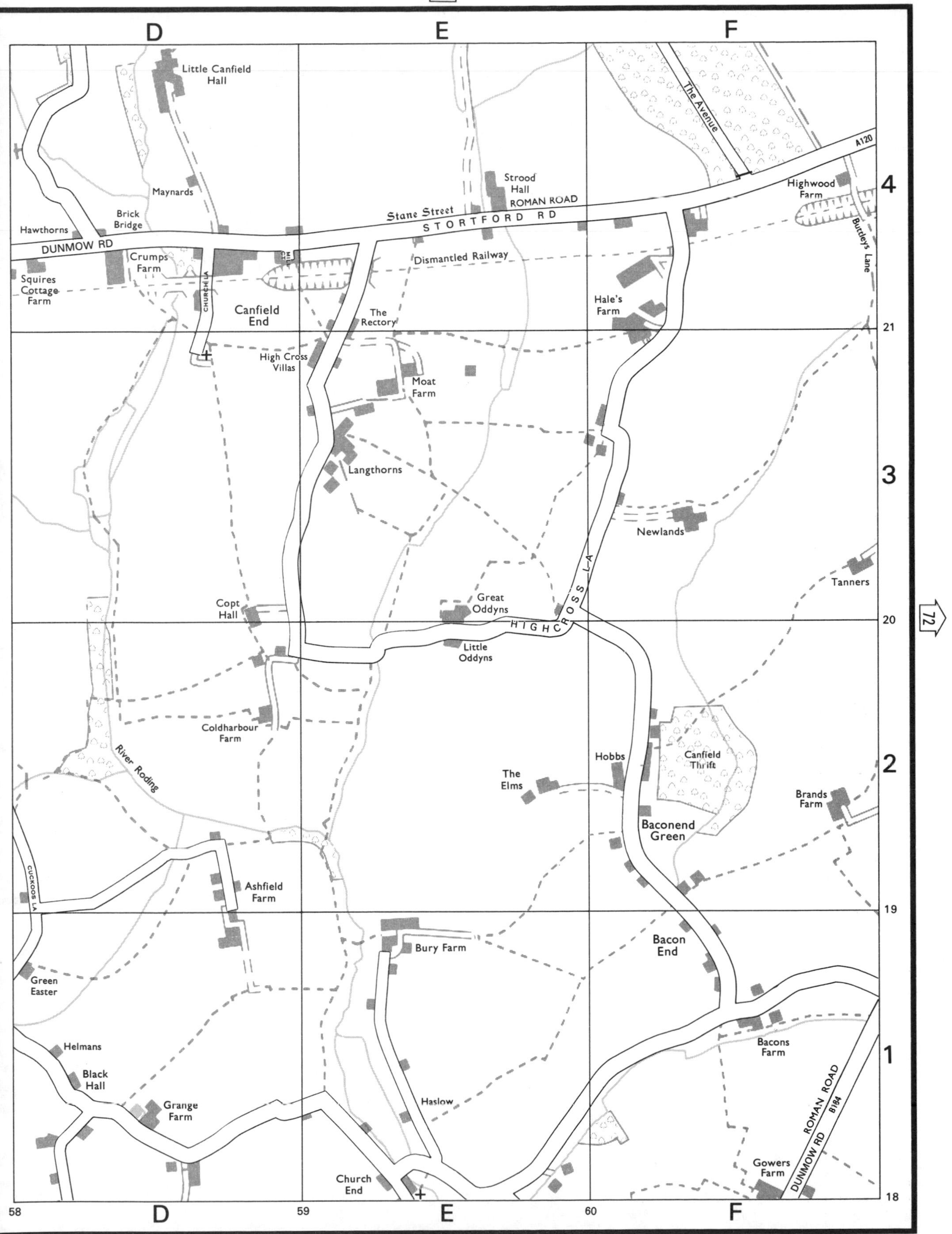
D
E
F
Little Canfield Hall
Maynards
Brick Bridge
Hawthorns
DUNMOW RD
Crumps Farm
Squires Cottage Farm
CHURCH LA
MILL
Canfield End
Stane Street
STORTFORD RD
Strood Hall
ROMAN ROAD
Dismantled Railway
The Rectory
High Cross Villas
Moat Farm
The Avenue
A120
Highwood Farm
Buttleys Lane
Hale's Farm
Langthorns
Newlands
Tanners
Copt Hall
Great Oddyns
HIGH CROSS LA
Little Oddyns
Coldharbour Farm
River Roding
Hobbs
Canfield Thrift
The Elms
Brands Farm
Baconend Green
Ashfield Farm
CUCKOOS LA
Bury Farm
Bacon End
Green Easter
Helmans
Black Hall
Grange Farm
Haslow
Bacons Farm
ROMAN ROAD
DUNMOW RD
B184
Gowers Farm
Church End
4
3
2
1
21
20
19
18
58
59
60

72

81

61

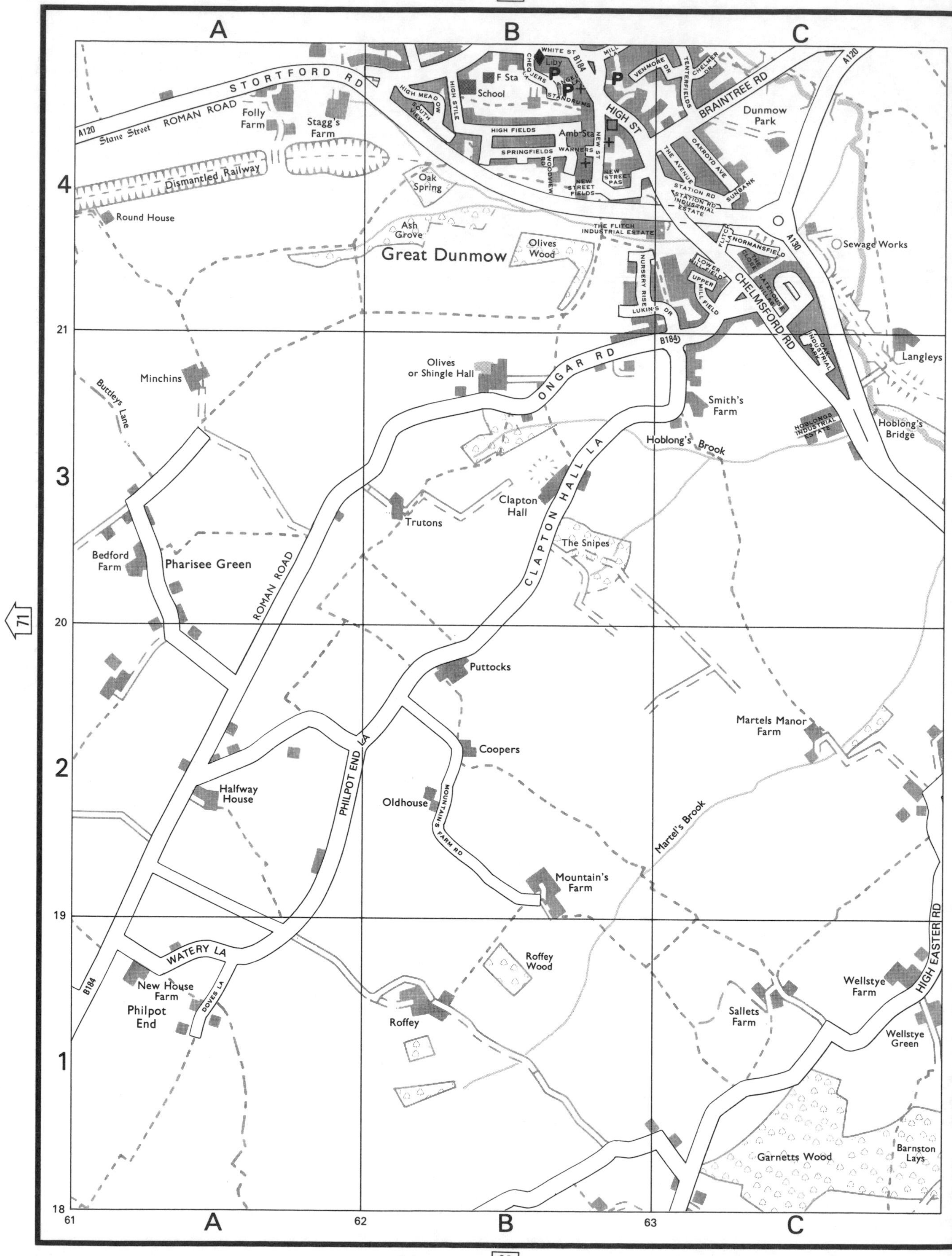

A
B
C
4
3
2
1
21
20
19
18
61
62
63
STORTFORD RD
ROMAN ROAD
Stane Street
A120
Folly Farm
Stagg's Farm
Dismantled Railway
Round House
Oak Spring
Ash Grove
Great Dunmow
Olives Wood
F Sta
School
Liby
WHITE ST
HIGH MEADOW
SOUTH VIEW
HIGH STILE
HIGH FIELDS
SPRINGFIELDS
Amb Sta
WARNERS
NEW ST
NEW STREET FIELDS
NEW STREET PAS
HIGH ST
B184
VENMORE DR
TENTERFIELDS
CHELMER DR
BRAINTREE RD
Dunmow Park
OAKROYD AVE
THE AVENUE
STATION RD
STATION RD INDUSTRIAL ESTATE
SUNBANK
THE FLITCH INDUSTRIAL ESTATE
NORMANSFIELD
THE CLOSE
A130
Sewage Works
A120
LOWER MILL FIELD
UPPER MILL FIELD
NURSERY RISE
LUKIN'S DR
CHELMSFORD RD
OAK INDUSTRIAL PARK
Langleys
ONGAR RD
Olives or Shingle Hall
Minchins
Buttleys Lane
Smith's Farm
Hoblong's Brook
HOBLONGS INDUSTRIAL ESTATE
Hoblong's Bridge
CLAPTON HALL LA
Clapton Hall
Trutons
The Snipes
Bedford Farm
Pharisee Green
ROMAN ROAD
Puttocks
Coopers
Martels Manor Farm
Halfway House
PHILPOT END LA
Oldhouse
MOUNTAIN'S FARM RD
Martel's Brook
Mountain's Farm
WATERY LA
B184
New House Farm
Philpot End
DOVES LA
Roffey Wood
Roffey
Sallets Farm
Wellstye Farm
HIGH EASTER RD
Wellstye Green
Garnetts Wood
Barnston Lays

71

82

62

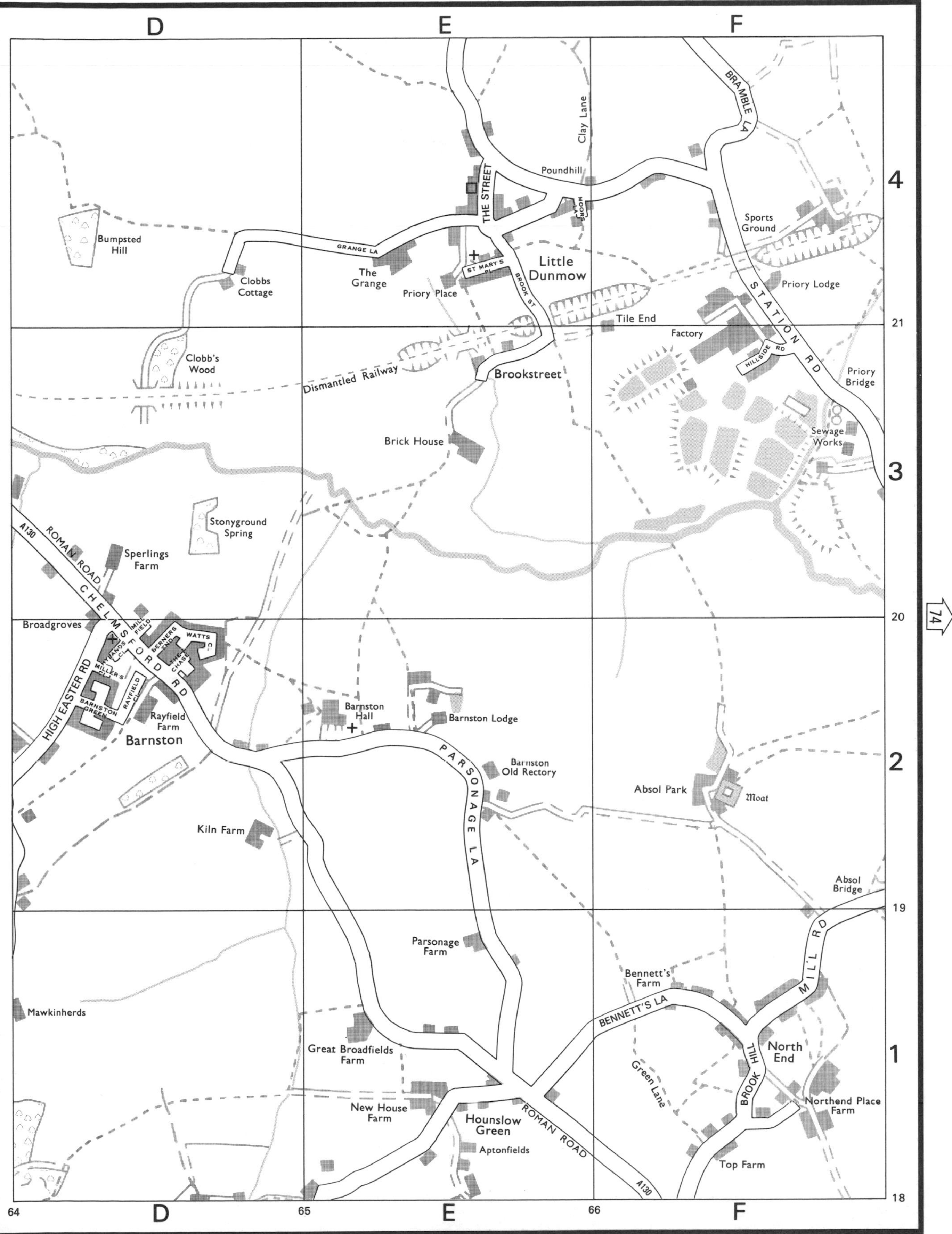

D
E
F
4
3
2
1
21
20
19
18
64
65
66
Bumpsted Hill
Clobbs Cottage
Clobb's Wood
GRANGE LA
The Grange
THE STREET
Priory Place
ST MARY'S PL
BROOK ST
Little Dunmow
Poundhill
Clay Lane
MOORS LA
BRAMBLE LA
Sports Ground
Priory Lodge
STATION RD
Tile End
Factory
HILLSIDE RD
Priory Bridge
Dismantled Railway
Brookstreet
Brick House
Sewage Works
Stonyground Spring
A130
ROMAN ROAD
Sperlings Farm
CHELMSFORD RD
Broadgroves
MILL FIELD
BERNERS END
WATTS CL
THE CHASE
HYLANDS CL
MILLER'S CL
HIGH EASTER RD
RAYFIELD CL
BARNSTON GREEN
Rayfield Farm
Barnston
Barnston Hall
Barnston Lodge
PARSONAGE LA
Barnston Old Rectory
Absol Park
Moat
Kiln Farm
Absol Bridge
MILL RD
Parsonage Farm
Bennett's Farm
BENNETT'S LA
Mawkinherds
Great Broadfields Farm
BROOK HILL
North End
Green Lane
Northend Place Farm
New House Farm
Hounslow Green
ROMAN ROAD
Aptonfields
Top Farm
A130
D
E
F

74

83

63

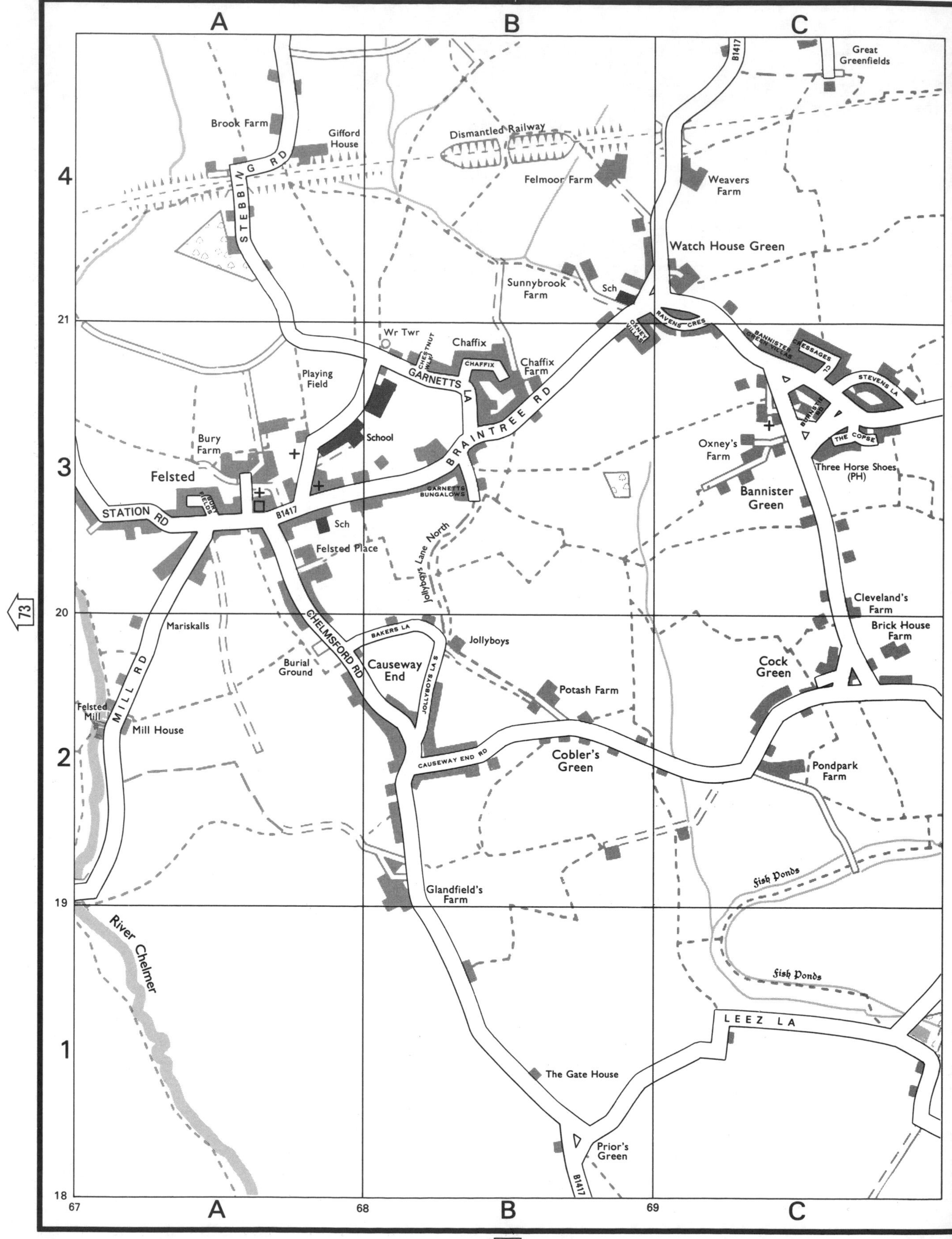

A
B
C
Great Greenfields
Brook Farm
Gifford House
Dismantled Railway
Felmoor Farm
Weavers Farm
STEBBING RD
B1417
Watch House Green
Sunnybrook Farm
Sch
Wr Twr
Chaffix
CHESTNUT WALK
CHAFFIX
Chaffix Farm
OXNEY VILLAS
RAVENS CRES
BANNISTER GREEN VILLAS
CRESSAGES CL
STEVENS LA
BURNSIDE RD
THE COPSE
Playing Field
GARNETTS LA
School
BRAINTREE RD
Bury Farm
Oxney's Farm
Three Horse Shoes (PH)
Felsted
BURY FIELDS
STATION RD
B1417
GARNETTS BUNGALOWS
Bannister Green
Sch
Felsted Place
Jollyboys Lane North
Cleveland's Farm
Mariskalls
CHELMSFORD RD
BAKERS LA
Jollyboys
Brick House Farm
Burial Ground
Causeway End
JOLLYBOYS LA S
Cock Green
Felsted Mill
MILL RD
Mill House
Potash Farm
CAUSEWAY END RD
Cobler's Green
Pondpark Farm
Glandfield's Farm
Fish Ponds
River Chelmer
Fish Ponds
LEEZ LA
The Gate House
Prior's Green
B1417
4
21
3
20
2
19
1
18
67
68
69

73

84

64

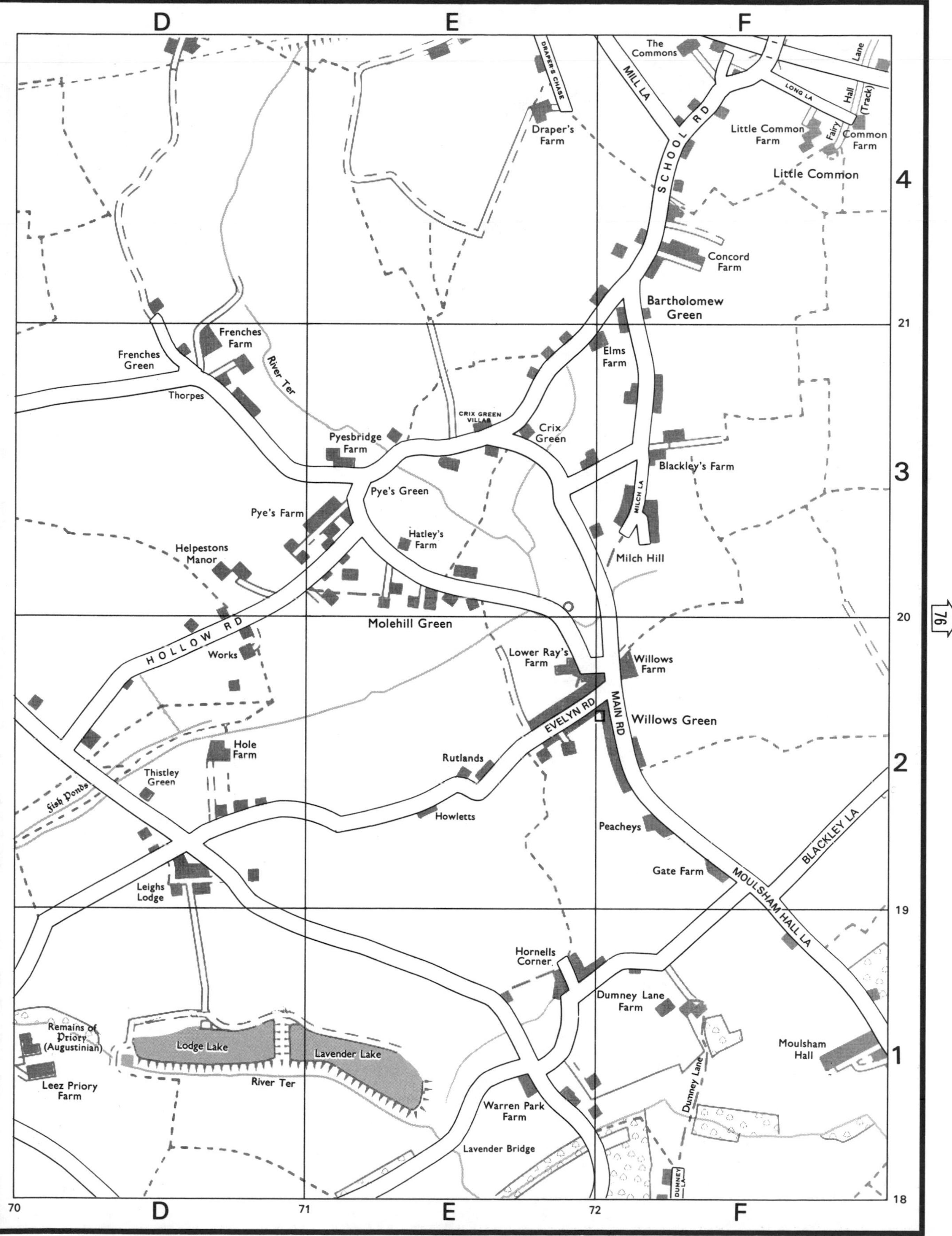
D
E
F
The Commons
DRAPER'S CHASE
MILL LA
SCHOOL RD
Lane
LONG LA
Hall
(Track)
Fairy
Little Common Farm
Common Farm
Draper's Farm
Little Common
4
Concord Farm
Bartholomew Green
21
Frenches Farm
Frenches Green
River Ter
Thorpes
Elms Farm
CRIX GREEN VILLAS
Crix Green
Pyesbridge Farm
Blackley's Farm
3
Pye's Green
Pye's Farm
MILCH LA
Hatley's Farm
Helpestons Manor
Milch Hill
HOLLOW RD
Molehill Green
20
Works
Lower Ray's Farm
Willows Farm
EVELYN RD
MAIN RD
Willows Green
Hole Farm
Rutlands
2
Thistley Green
Fish Ponds
Howletts
Peacheys
BLACKLEY LA
Gate Farm
MOULSHAM HALL LA
Leighs Lodge
19
Hornells Corner
Dumney Lane Farm
Remains of Priory (Augustinian)
Lodge Lake
Lavender Lake
Moulsham Hall
1
Leez Priory Farm
River Ter
Dumney Lane
Warren Park Farm
Lavender Bridge
DUMNEY LA
18
70
71
72

76

85

65

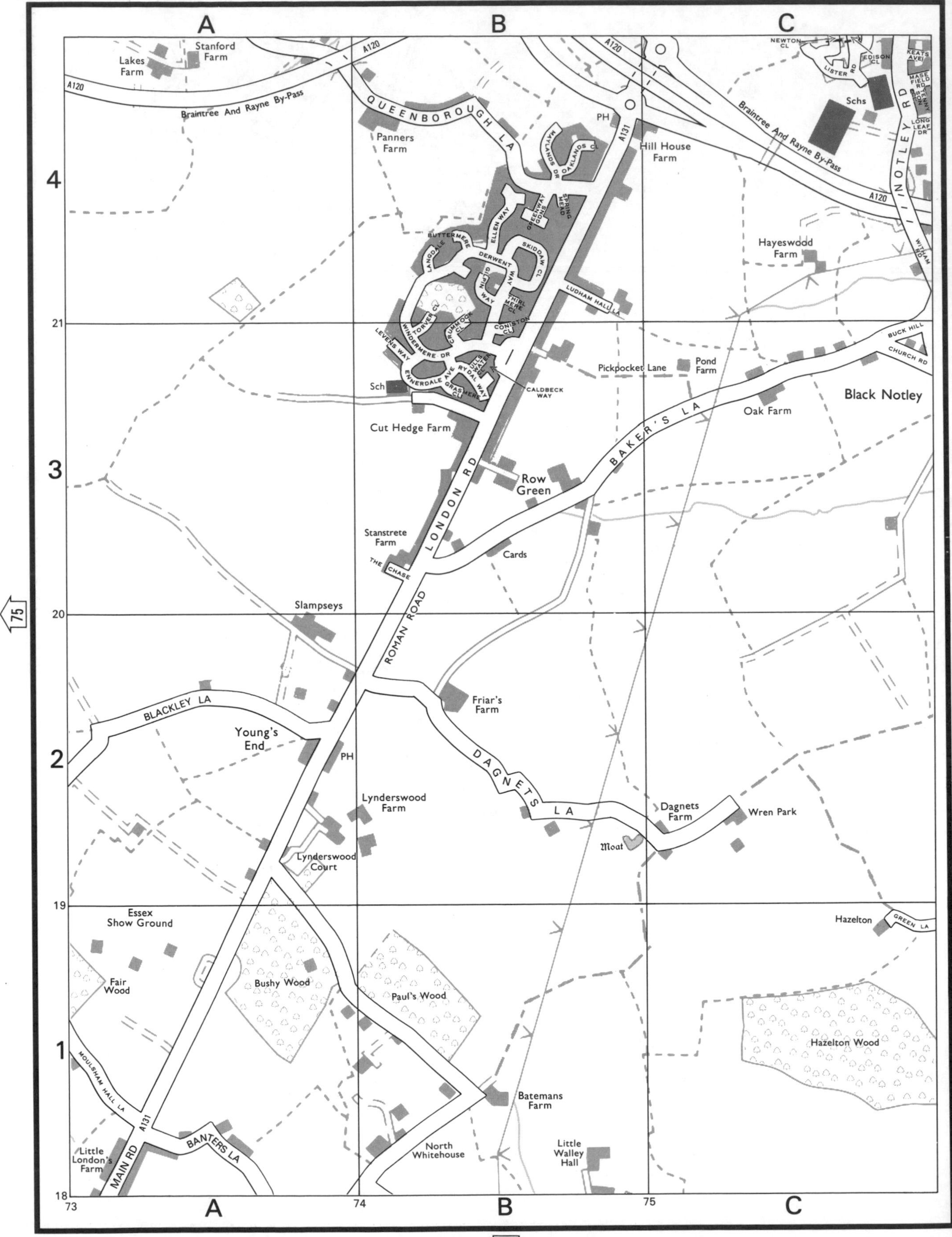
A
B
C
Lakes Farm
Stanford Farm
A120
Braintree And Rayne By-Pass
QUEENBOROUGH LA
Panners Farm
PH
A131
Hill House Farm
Schs
Braintree And Rayne By-Pass
NOTLEY RD
Hayeswood Farm
LUDHAM HALL LA
BUCK HILL
CHURCH RD
Pickpocket Lane
Pond Farm
Black Notley
Oak Farm
BAKER'S LA
Sch
CALDBECK WAY
Cut Hedge Farm
Row Green
LONDON RD
Stanstrete Farm
THE CHASE
Cards
Slampseys
ROMAN ROAD
Friar's Farm
BLACKLEY LA
Young's End
PH
DAGNETS LA
Lynderswood Farm
Dagnets Farm
Wren Park
Moat
Lynderswood Court
Essex Show Ground
Hazelton
GREEN LA
Fair Wood
Bushy Wood
Paul's Wood
Hazelton Wood
MOULSHAM HALL LA
A131
Batemans Farm
Little London's Farm
MAIN RD
BANTERS LA
North Whitehouse
Little Walley Hall
4
3
2
1
21
20
19
18
73
74
75

75

86

67

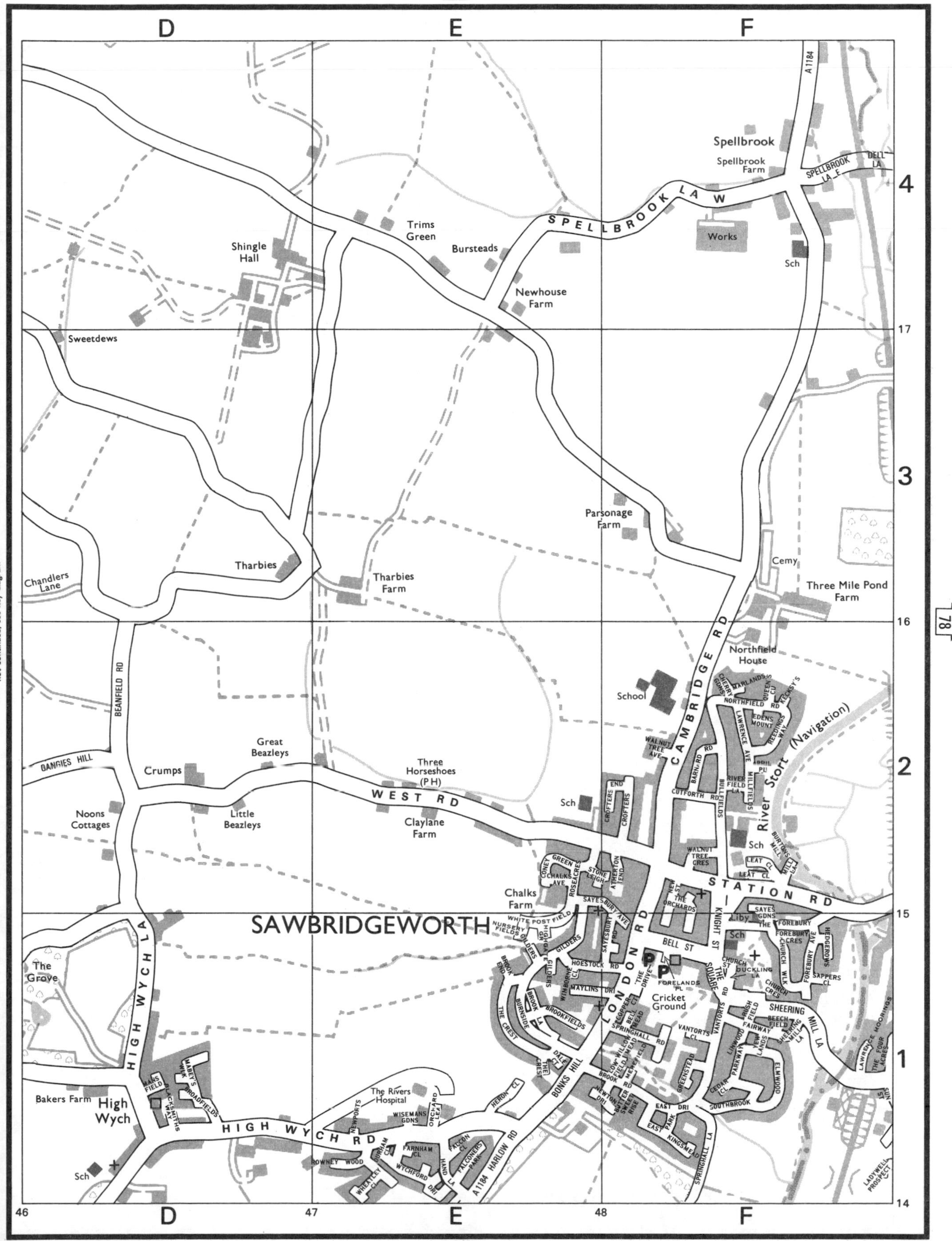

D
E
F
4
3
2
1
17
16
15
14
46
47
48
Spellbrook
Spellbrook Farm
SPELLBROOK LA W
SPELLBROOK LA E
DELL LA
A1184
Works
Sch
Trims Green
Bursteads
Shingle Hall
Newhouse Farm
Sweetdews
Parsonage Farm
Cemy
Three Mile Pond Farm
Chandlers Lane
Tharbies
Tharbies Farm
Northfield House
School
CAMBRIDGE RD
BEANFIELD RD
GANGIES HILL
Great Beazleys
Crumps
Three Horseshoes (P H)
WEST RD
Noons Cottages
Little Beazleys
Claylane Farm
River Stort (Navigation)
STATION RD
Chalks Farm
SAWBRIDGEWORTH
LONDON RD
BELL ST
KNIGHT ST
THE SQUARE
Cricket Ground
SHEERING MILL LA
The Grove
HIGH WYCH LA
Bakers Farm
High Wych
HIGH WYCH RD
The Rivers Hospital
A1184 HARLOW RD
BONKS HILL
EAST DRI
SPRINGHALL LA
KINGSMEAD
SOUTHBROOK
LADYWELL PROSPECT
THE FOUR ACRES
LAWRENCE MOORINGS

78

90

68

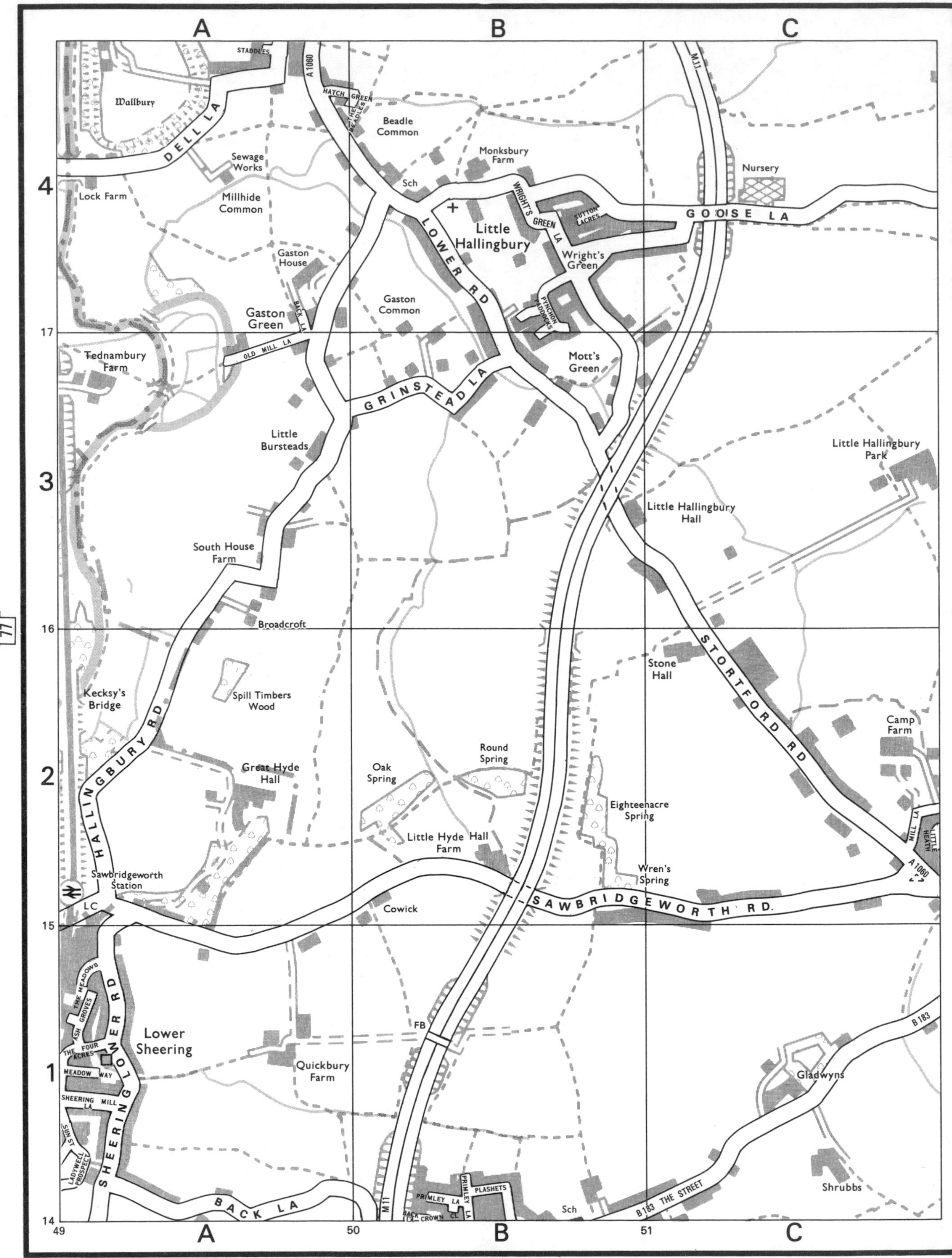
A
B
C
4
3
2
1
17
16
15
14
49
50
51
Wallbury
DELL LA
STADDLES
A 1060
HATCH GREEN
THE BEADLES
Beadle Common
Sewage Works
Monksbury Farm
M11
Nursery
Lock Farm
Millhide Common
Sch
WRIGHT'S GREEN LA
SUTTON ACRES
GOOSE LA
Little Hallingbury
LOWER RD
Wright's Green
Gaston House
Gaston Common
PINCHON PADDOCKS
BACK LA
Gaston Green
OLD MILL LA
Tednambury Farm
Mott's Green
GRINSTEAD LA
Little Bursteads
Little Hallingbury Park
Little Hallingbury Hall
South House Farm
Broadcroft
STORTFORD RD
Stone Hall
Spill Timbers Wood
Kecksy's Bridge
HALLINGBURY RD
Camp Farm
Round Spring
Great Hyde Hall
Oak Spring
Eighteenacre Spring
MILL LA
LITTLE HEATH
Little Hyde Hall Farm
Wren's Spring
A 1060
Sawbridgeworth Station
LC
SAWBRIDGEWORTH RD.
Cowick
THE MEADOWS
ASH GROVES
LOWER RD
Lower Sheering
FB
B 183
THE FOUR ACRES
MEADOW WAY
Quickbury Farm
Gladwyns
SHEERING MILL LA
SHEERING
SUN ST
LADYWELL PROSPECT
BACK LA
M11
PRIMLEY LA
PLASHETS
BACK LA
CROWN CL
Sch
B183 THE STREET
Shrubbs

77

91

69

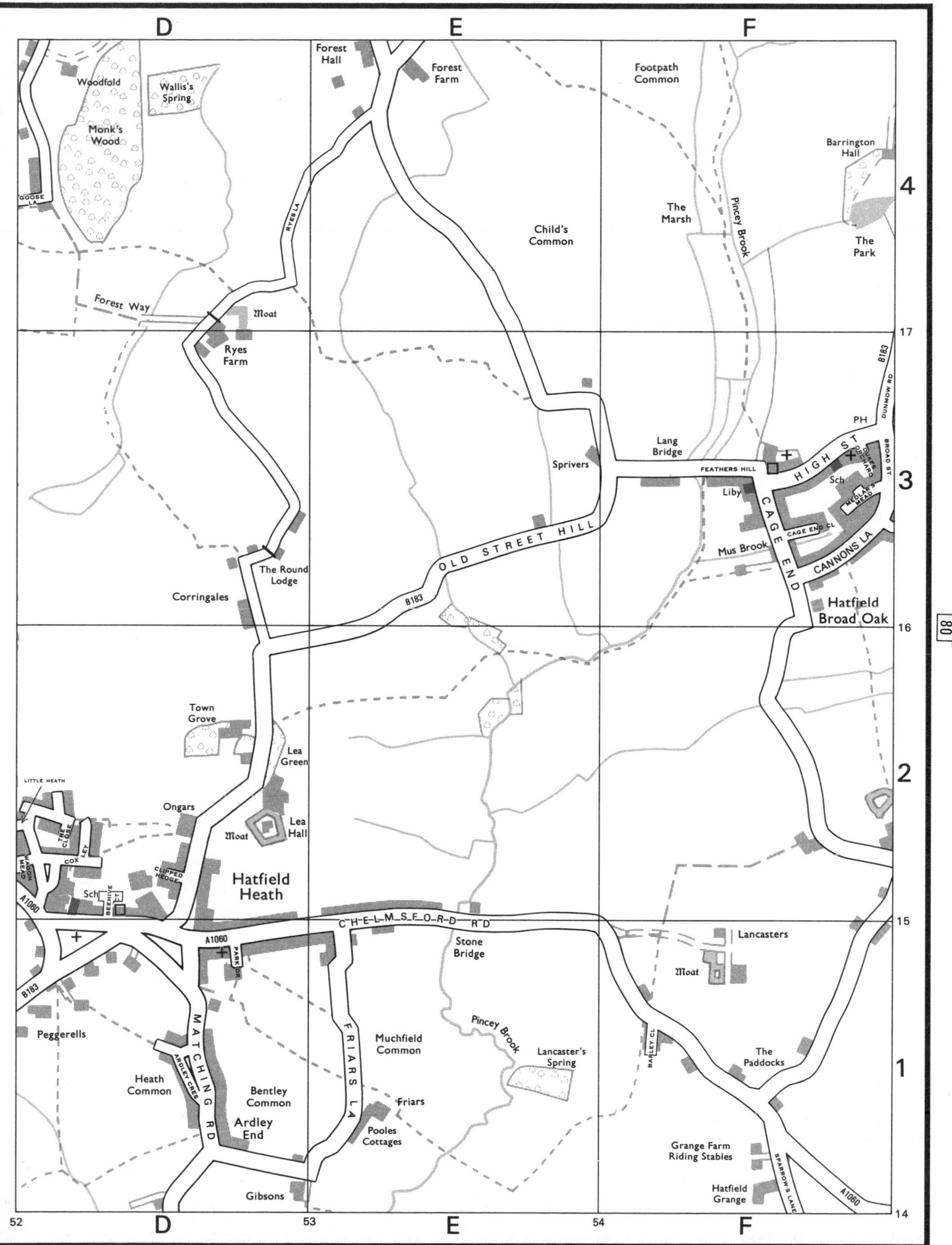
D
E
F
Forest Hall
Forest Farm
Footpath Common
Woodfold
Wallis's Spring
Monk's Wood
Barrington Hall
GOOSE LA
RYES LA
The Marsh
Pincey Brook
Child's Common
The Park
4
Forest Way
Moat
17
Ryes Farm
B183
DUNMOW RD
PH
Lang Bridge
Sprivers
FEATHERS HILL
HIGH ST
BROAD ST
Sch
Liby
CAGE END
MEDLAR'S MEAD
3
OLD STREET HILL
CAGE END CL
Mus Brook
CANNONS LA
The Round Lodge
Corringales
B183
Hatfield Broad Oak
16
Town Grove
Lea Green
LITTLE HEATH
2
Ongars
THE CLOSE
Lea Hall
Moat
COX LEY
CLIPPED HEDGE
Hatfield Heath
A1060
Sch
BEEHIVE CT
15
CHELMSFORD RD
A1060
Lancasters
Stone Bridge
PARK DR
Moat
B183
MATCHING RD
Peggerells
FRIARS LA
Muchfield Common
Pincey Brook
Lancaster's Spring
BARLEY CL
The Paddocks
1
Heath Common
ARDLEY CRES
Bentley Common
Friars
Ardley End
Pooles Cottages
Grange Farm Riding Stables
SPARROW'S LANE
A1060
Hatfield Grange
Gibsons
14
52
53
54
D
E
F

80

92

70

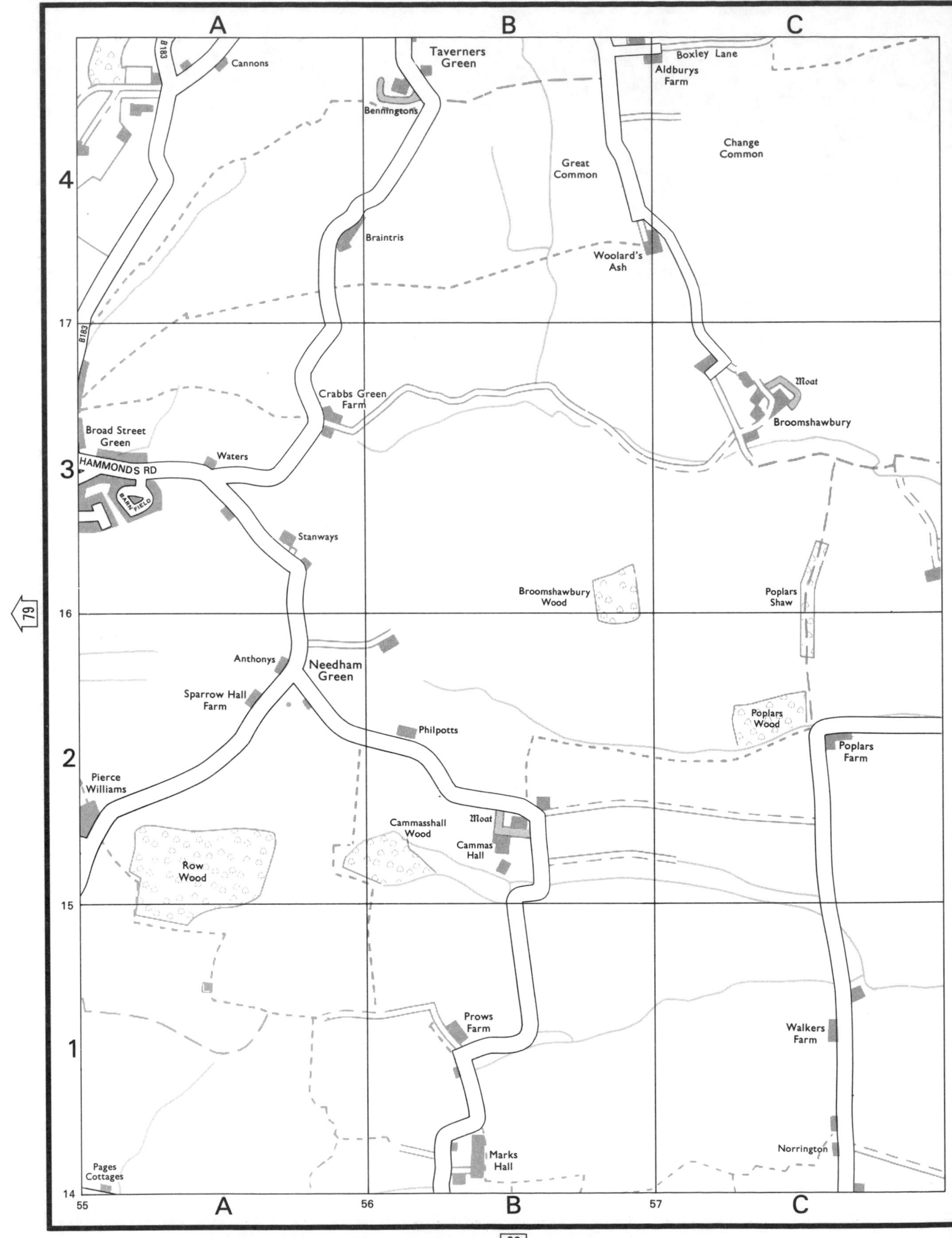
A
B
C
Cannons
Taverners Green
Benningtons
Boxley Lane
Aldburys Farm
Change Common
Great Common
Braintris
Woolard's Ash
Moat
Broomshawbury
Crabbs Green Farm
Broad Street Green
Waters
HAMMONDS RD
BARN FIELD
Stanways
Broomshawbury Wood
Poplars Shaw
Anthonys
Needham Green
Sparrow Hall Farm
Poplars Wood
Philpotts
Poplars Farm
Pierce Williams
Cammasshall Wood
Moat
Cammas Hall
Row Wood
Prows Farm
Walkers Farm
Marks Hall
Norrington
Pages Cottages
B183
4
3
2
1
17
16
15
14
55
56
57

79

93

71

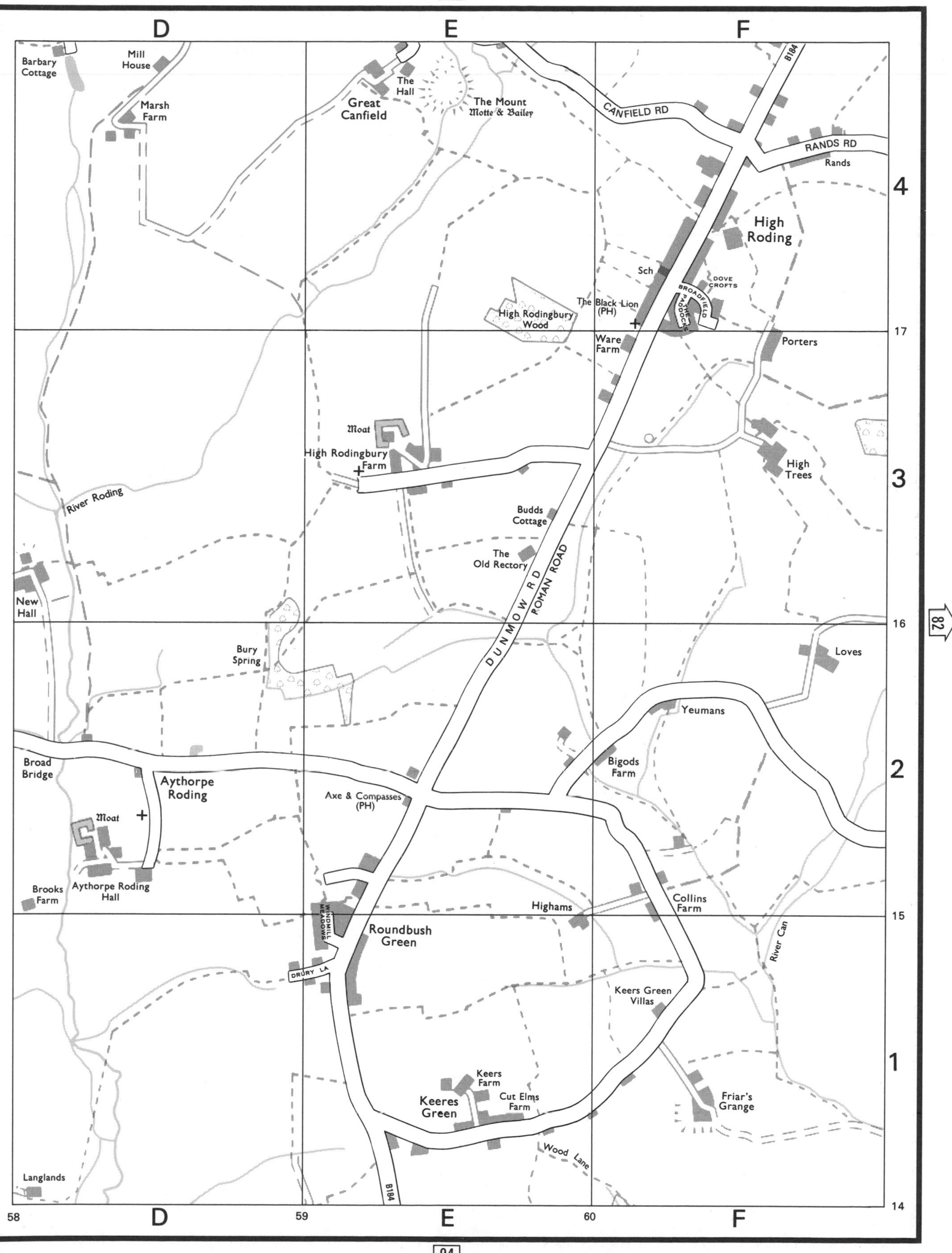
D
E
F
Barbary Cottage
Mill House
Marsh Farm
The Hall
Great Canfield
The Mount
Motte & Bailey
CANFIELD RD
B184
RANDS RD
Rands
High Roding
Sch
DOVE CROFTS
BROADFIELD
THE PADDOCKS
The Black Lion (PH)
High Rodingbury Wood
Ware Farm
Porters
Moat
High Rodingbury Farm
High Trees
River Roding
Budds Cottage
The Old Rectory
DUNMOW RD
ROMAN ROAD
New Hall
Bury Spring
Loves
Yeumans
Broad Bridge
Aythorpe Roding
Bigods Farm
Axe & Compasses (PH)
Moat
Brooks Farm
Aythorpe Roding Hall
Highams
Collins Farm
WINDMILL MEADOWS
Roundbush Green
DRURY LA
River Can
Keers Green Villas
Keers Farm
Cut Elms Farm
Keeres Green
Friar's Grange
Wood Lane
Langlands
B184
4
3
2
1
17
16
15
14
58
59
60
D
E
F

82

94

72

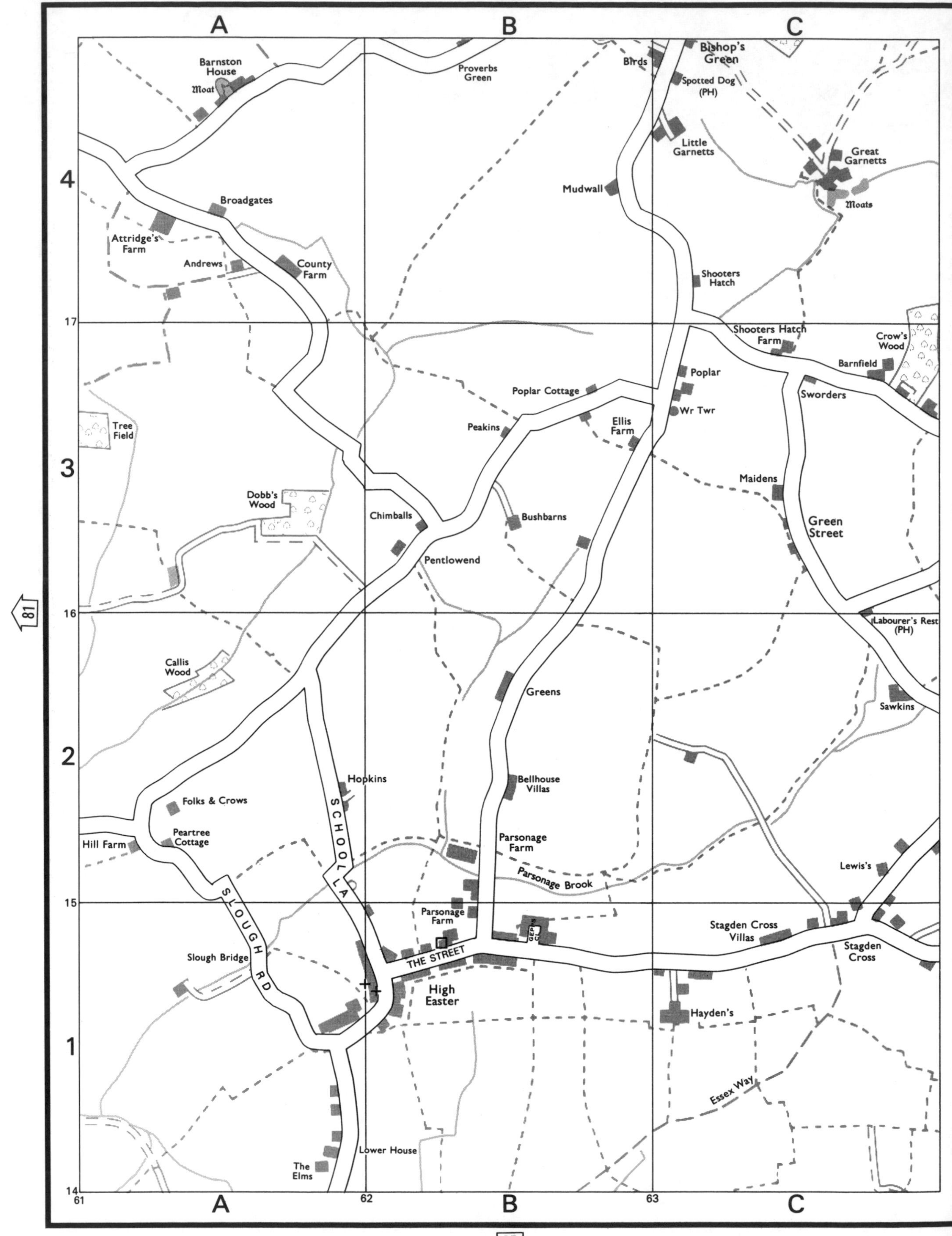
A
B
C
4
3
2
1
17
16
15
14
61
62
63
Barnston House
Moat
Proverbs Green
Birds
Bishop's Green
Spotted Dog (PH)
Little Garnetts
Great Garnetts
Moats
Mudwall
Broadgates
Attridge's Farm
Andrews
County Farm
Shooters Hatch
Shooters Hatch Farm
Crow's Wood
Barnfield
Poplar
Sworders
Poplar Cottage
Wr Twr
Ellis Farm
Peakins
Tree Field
Maidens
Green Street
Dobb's Wood
Chimballs
Bushbarns
Pentlowend
Labourer's Rest (PH)
Callis Wood
Greens
Sawkins
Hopkins
Bellhouse Villas
Folks & Crows
Peartree Cottage
Hill Farm
SCHOOL LA
Parsonage Farm
Parsonage Brook
Lewis's
SLOUGH RD
Parsonage Farm
GEPPS CL
Stagden Cross Villas
Stagden Cross
Slough Bridge
THE STREET
High Easter
Hayden's
Essex Way
Lower House
The Elms

81

95

73

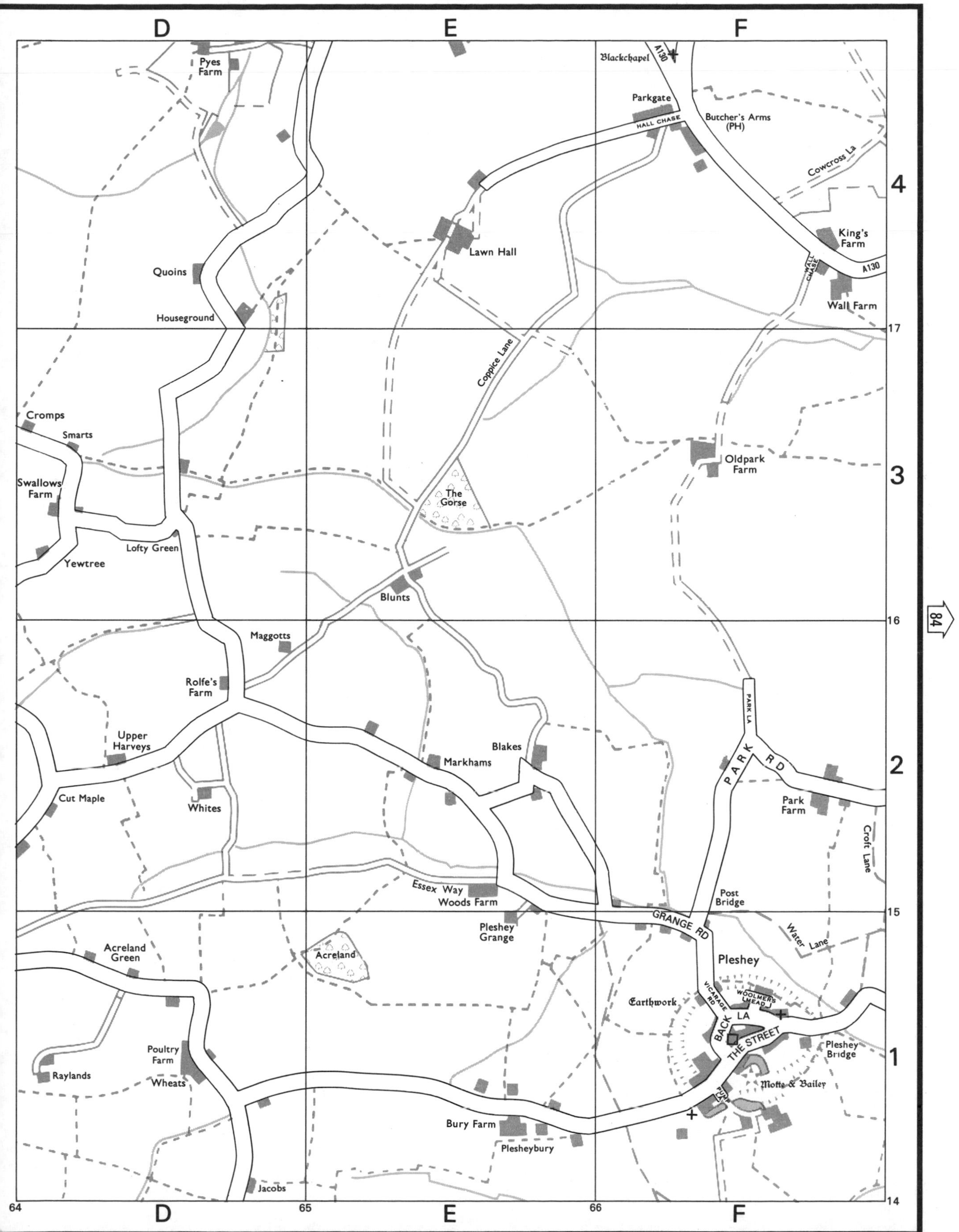
D
E
F
Pyes Farm
Blackchapel
A130
Parkgate
Hall Chase
Butcher's Arms (PH)
Cowcross La
4
King's Farm
Lawn Hall
Quoins
Wall Chase
A130
Wall Farm
Houseground
17
Coppice Lane
Cromps
Smarts
Oldpark Farm
3
Swallows Farm
The Gorse
Lofty Green
Yewtree
Blunts
16
Maggotts
Rolfe's Farm
Park La
Upper Harveys
Blakes
Park Rd
2
Markhams
Cut Maple
Whites
Park Farm
Croft Lane
Essex Way
Woods Farm
Post Bridge
15
Grange Rd
Pleshey Grange
Water Lane
Acreland Green
Acreland
Pleshey
Vicarage Rd
Woolmers Mead
Earthwork
Back La
The Street
Pleshey Bridge
1
Poultry Farm
Raylands
Wheats
Pump La
Motte & Bailey
Bury Farm
Plesheybury
Jacobs
64
65
66
14
D
E
F

84

96

74

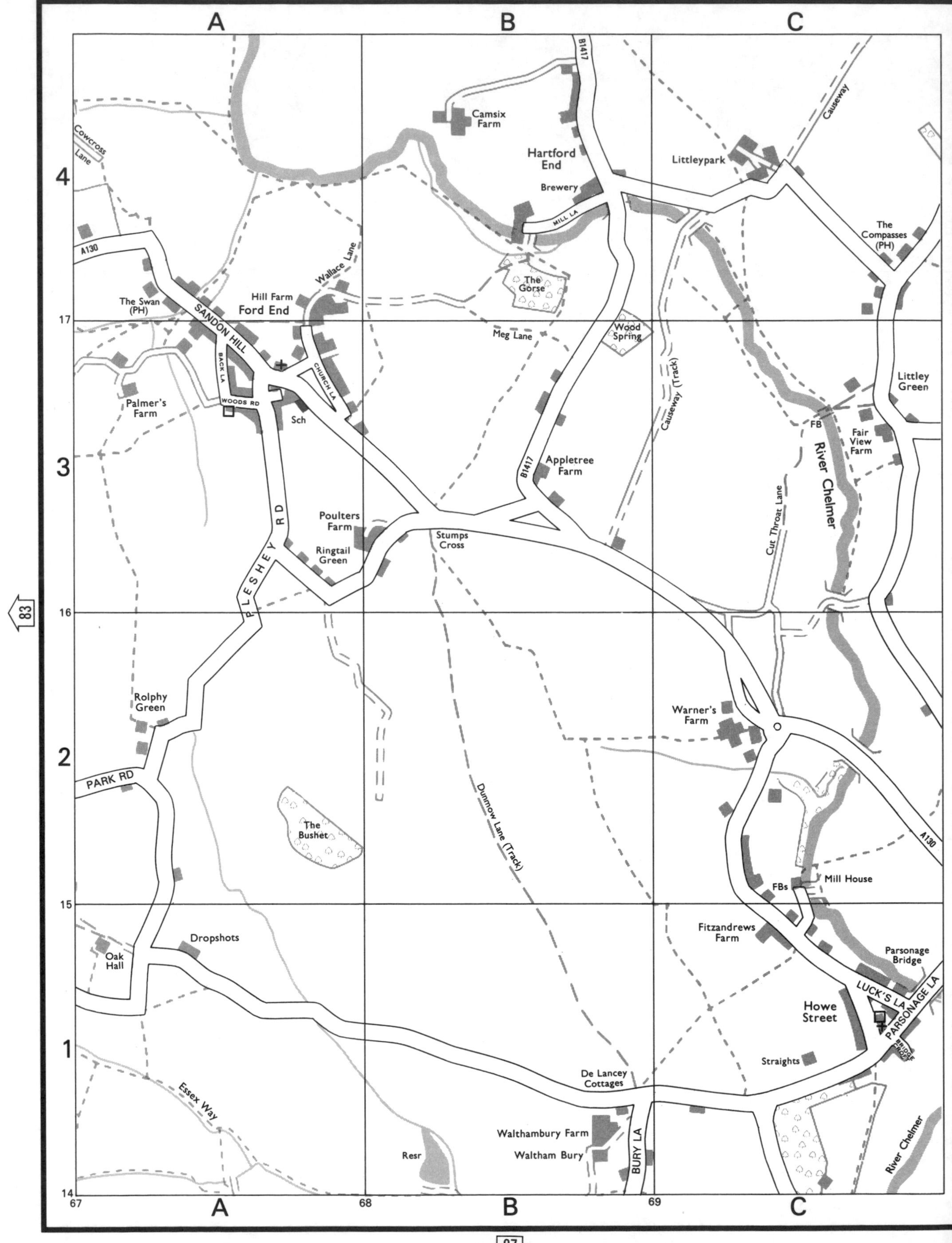
A
B
C
4
3
2
1
17
16
15
14
67
68
69
Cowcross Lane
Camsix Farm
Hartford End
Brewery
MILL LA
B1417
Littleypark
Causeway
The Compasses (PH)
A130
The Swan (PH)
SANDON HILL
Hill Farm
Ford End
Wallace Lane
The Gorse
Meg Lane
Wood Spring
BACK LA
CHURCH LA
WOODS RD
Sch
Palmer's Farm
Littley Green
Causeway (Track)
FB
Fair View Farm
River Chelmer
Appletree Farm
Cut Throat Lane
Poulters Farm
Ringtail Green
Stumps Cross
PLESHEY RD
Rolphy Green
Warner's Farm
PARK RD
The Bushet
Dunmow Lane (Track)
Mill House
FBs
Dropshots
Oak Hall
Fitzandrews Farm
Parsonage Bridge
LUCK'S LA
PARSONAGE LA
Howe Street
BRIDGE CROFT
Straights
Essex Way
De Lancey Cottages
Walthambury Farm
Waltham Bury
Resr
BURY LA
River Chelmer

83

97

75

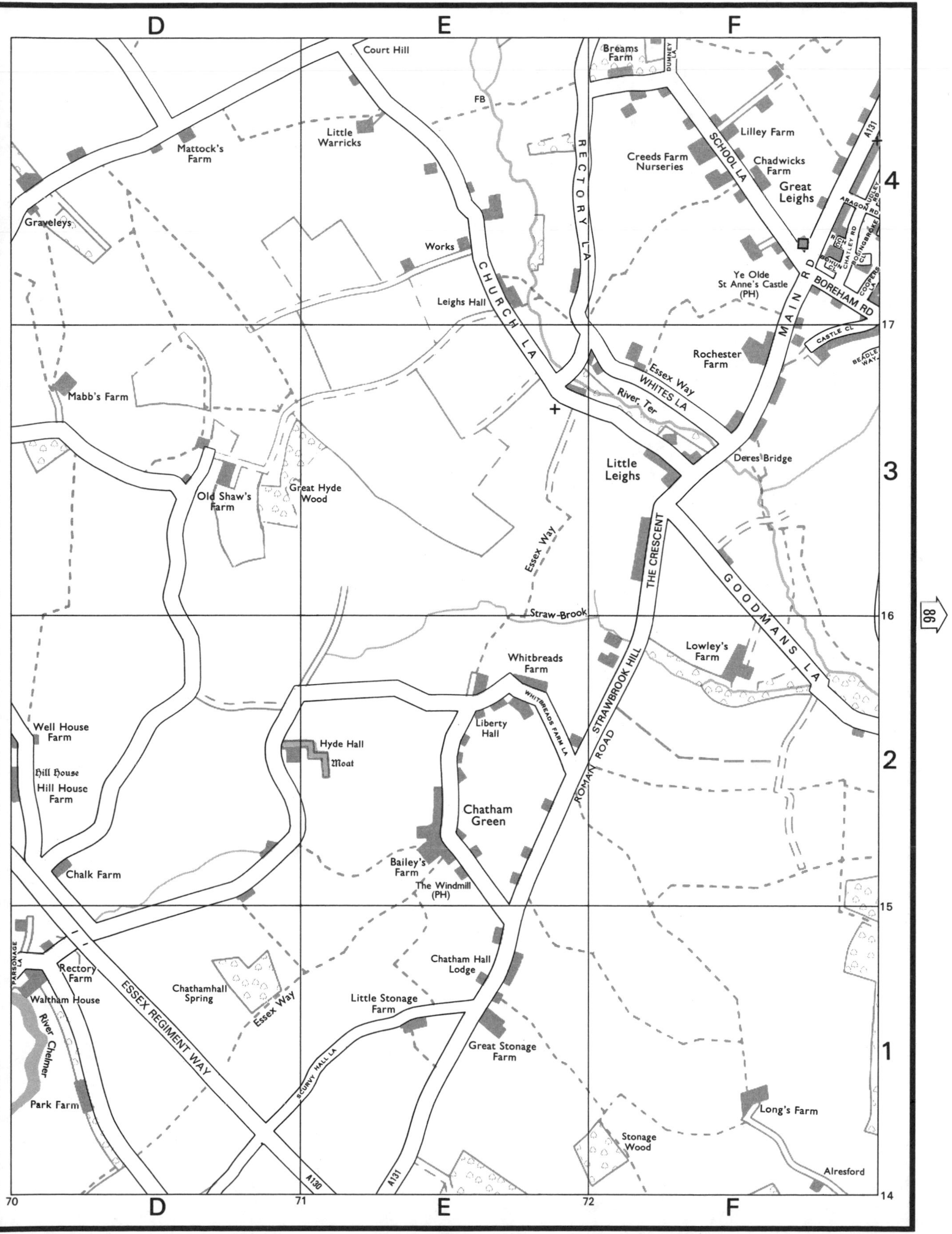

D
E
F
Court Hill
Breams Farm
DUMNEY LA
FB
Mattock's Farm
Little Warricks
RECTORY LA
Creeds Farm Nurseries
SCHOOL LA
Lilley Farm
Chadwicks Farm
Great Leighs
A131
Graveleys
Works
CHURCH LA
Leighs Hall
Ye Olde St Anne's Castle (PH)
MAIN RD
BOREHAM RD
CASTLE CL
Rochester Farm
Essex Way
WHITES LA
River Ter
Mabb's Farm
Deres Bridge
Little Leighs
Old Shaw's Farm
Great Hyde Wood
THE CRESCENT
Essex Way
GOODMANS LA
Straw Brook
Lowley's Farm
Whitbreads Farm
STRAWBROOK HILL
WHITBREADS FARM LA
Liberty Hall
Well House Farm
Hyde Hall
Moat
ROMAN ROAD
Hill House
Hill House Farm
Chatham Green
Chalk Farm
Bailey's Farm
The Windmill (PH)
PARSONAGE LA
Rectory Farm
Chatham Hall Lodge
Chathamhall Spring
Essex Way
Little Stonage Farm
Waltham House
ESSEX REGIMENT WAY
Great Stonage Farm
River Chelmer
SCURVY HALL LA
Park Farm
Long's Farm
Stonage Wood
Alresford
A130
A131
70
71
72
17
16
15
14
4
3
2
1

86

98

76

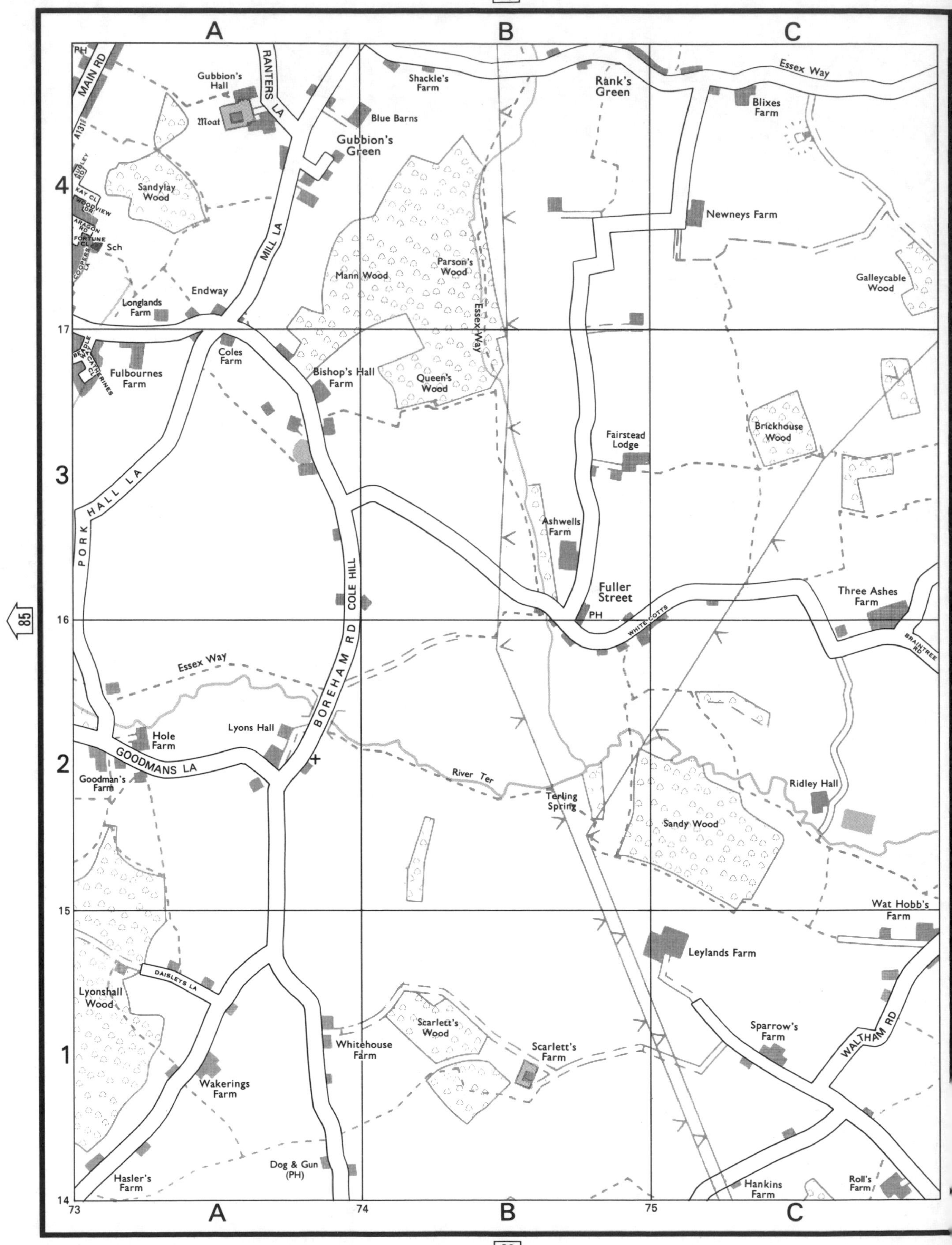

A
B
C
PH
MAIN RD
A131
Gubbion's Hall
Moat
RANTERS LA
Shackle's Farm
Blue Barns
Gubbion's Green
Rank's Green
Essex Way
Blixes Farm
Sandylay Wood
MILL LA
Newneys Farm
Sch
Endway
Longlands Farm
Mann Wood
Parson's Wood
Galleycable Wood
Coles Farm
Fulbournes Farm
Bishop's Hall Farm
Queen's Wood
Brickhouse Wood
Fairstead Lodge
PORK HALL LA
COLE HILL
Ashwells Farm
Fuller Street
PH
WHITE COTTS
Three Ashes Farm
BRAINTREE RD
BOREHAM RD
Hole Farm
Lyons Hall
GOODMANS LA
Goodman's Farm
River Ter
Terling Spring
Sandy Wood
Ridley Hall
Wat Hobb's Farm
Leylands Farm
DAISLEYS LA
Lyonshall Wood
Scarlett's Wood
Whitehouse Farm
Scarlett's Farm
Sparrow's Farm
WALTHAM RD
Wakerings Farm
Hasler's Farm
Dog & Gun (PH)
Hankins Farm
Roll's Farm
4
3
2
1
17
16
15
14
73
74
75

85

99

not continued, see key diagram

100

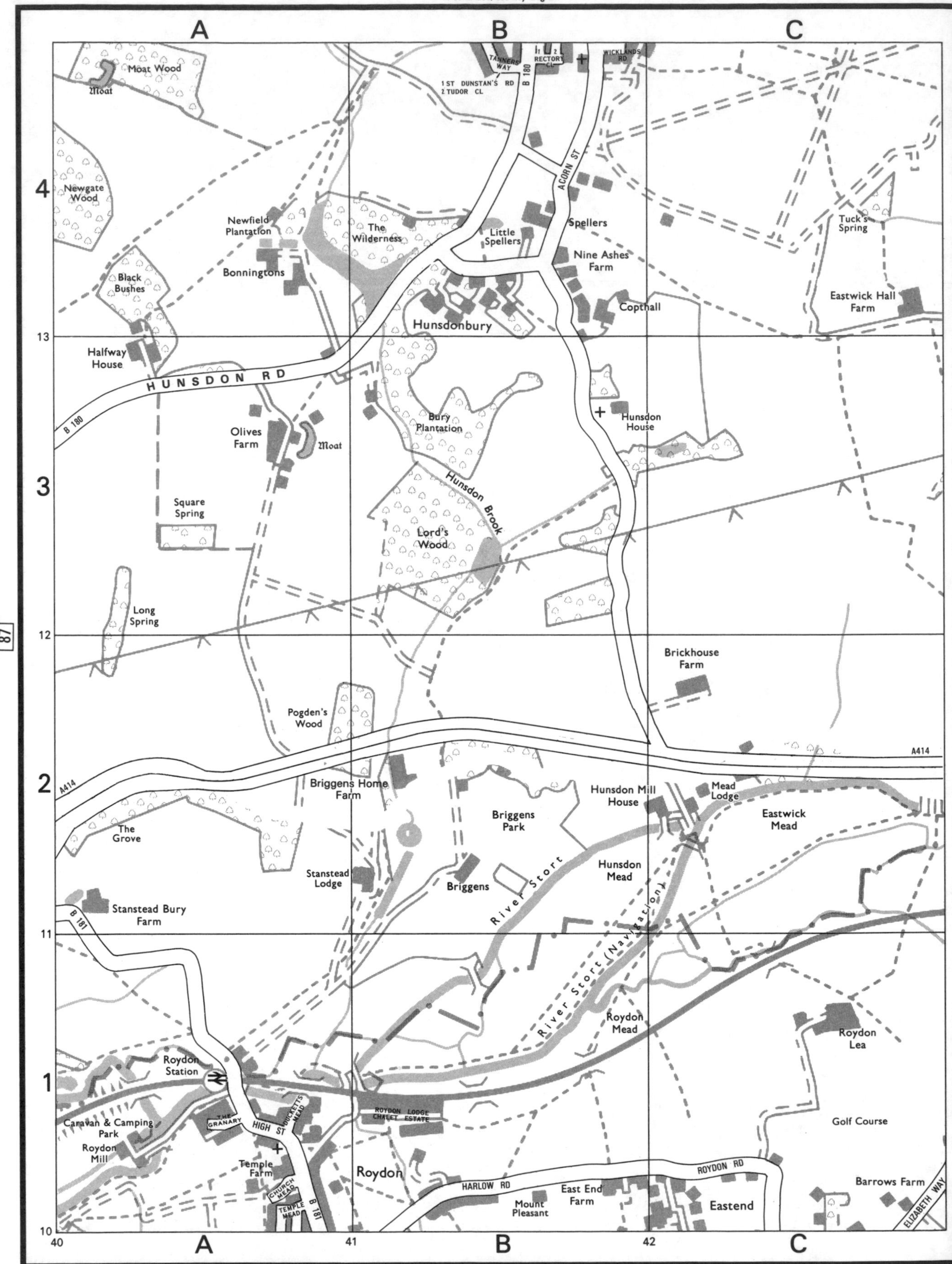

not continued, see key diagram
A
B
C
Moat Wood
Moat
Newgate Wood
Newfield Plantation
The Wilderness
Bonningtons
Black Bushes
Little Spellers
Spellers
Nine Ashes Farm
Copthall
Hunsdonbury
Tuck's Spring
Eastwick Hall Farm
TANNERS WAY
RECTORY CL
WICKLANDS RD
1 ST DUNSTAN'S RD
2 TUDOR CL
B 180
ACORN ST
Halfway House
HUNSDON RD
B 180
Olives Farm
Moat
Bury Plantation
Hunsdon House
Hunsdon Brook
Square Spring
Lord's Wood
Long Spring
Brickhouse Farm
Pogden's Wood
A414
Briggens Home Farm
Hunsdon Mill House
Mead Lodge
Eastwick Mead
The Grove
Briggens Park
Hunsdon Mead
Stanstead Lodge
Briggens
River Stort
Stanstead Bury Farm
B 181
River Stort (Navigation)
Roydon Mead
Roydon Lea
Roydon Station
Caravan & Camping Park
Roydon Mill
THE GRANARY
HIGH ST
DUCKETTS MEAD
ROYDON LODGE CHALET ESTATE
Golf Course
Temple Farm
CHURCH MEAD
TEMPLE MEAD
Roydon
HARLOW RD
ROYDON RD
Mount Pleasant
East End Farm
Eastend
Barrows Farm
ELIZABETH WAY
4
13
3
12
2
11
1
10
40
41
42
87
101

not continued, see key diagram

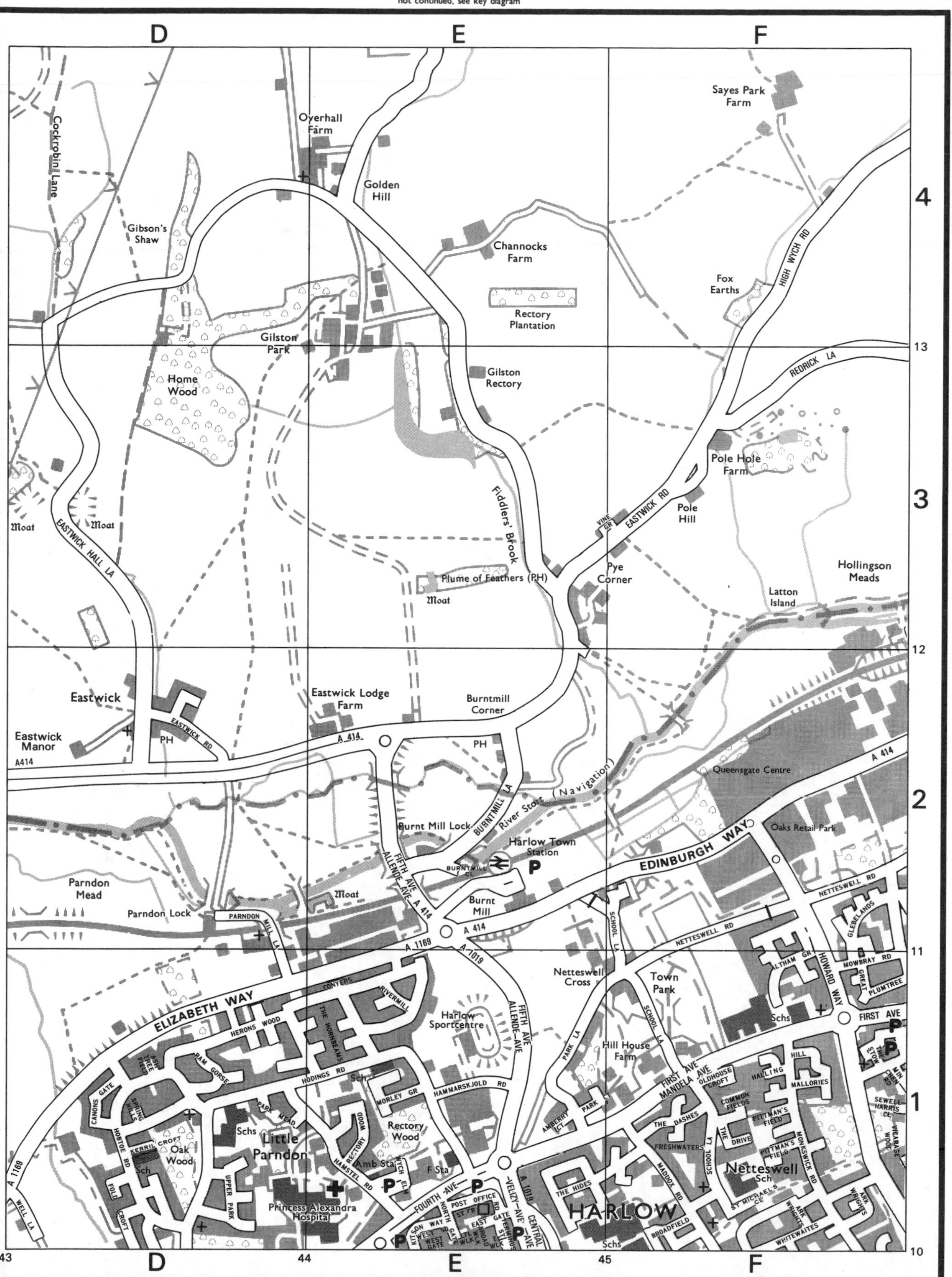

90

102

77

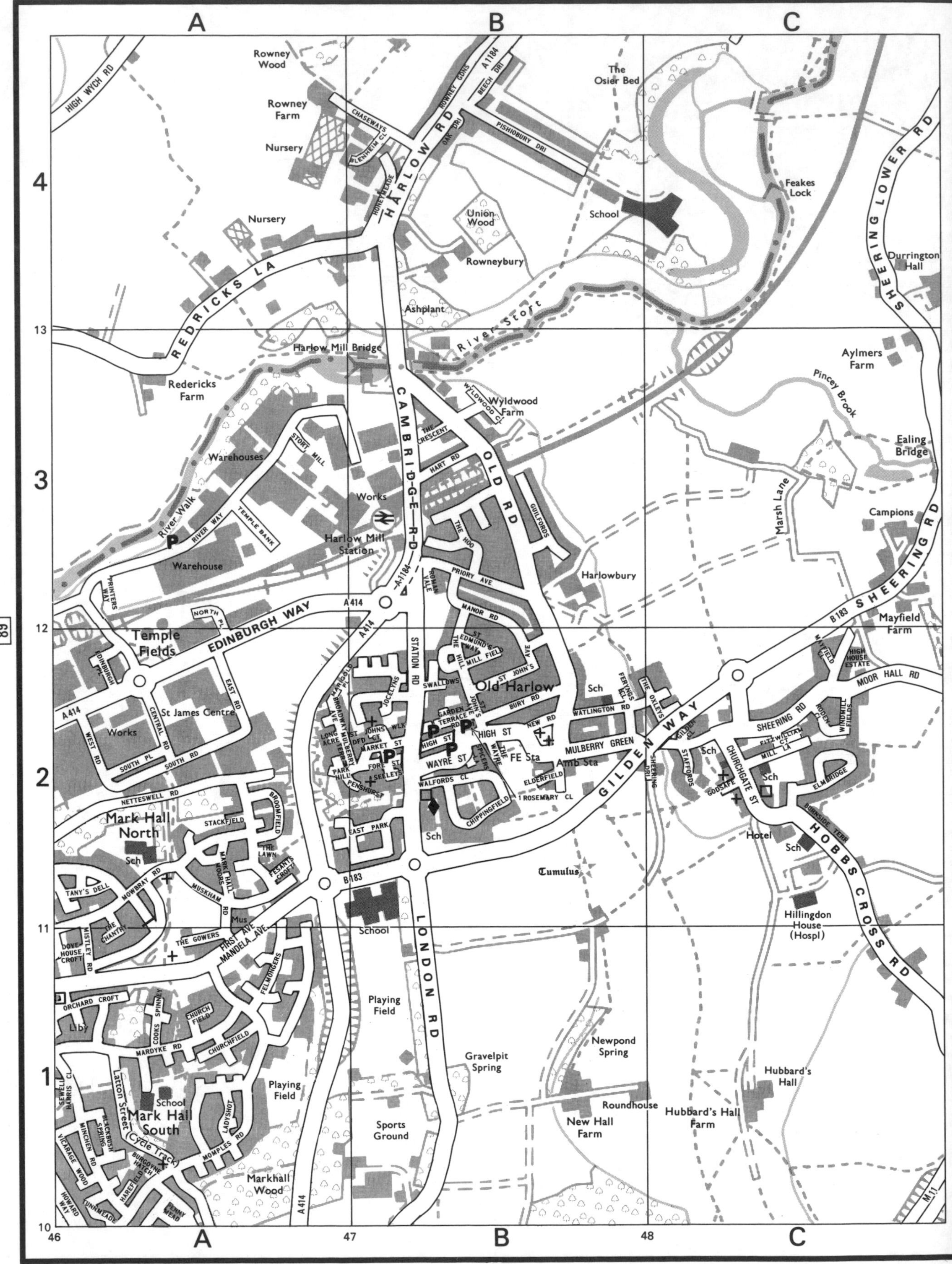

A
B
C
Rowney Wood
Rowney Farm
Nursery
The Osier Bed
School
Feakes Lock
Union Wood
Rowneybury
Durrington Hall
Ashplant
River Stort
Harlow Mill Bridge
Redericks Farm
Aylmers Farm
Pincey Brook
Wyldwood Farm
Warehouses
Works
Harlow Mill Station
Warehouse
Ealing Bridge
Campions
Marsh Lane
Harlowbury
Mayfield Farm
Temple Fields
Old Harlow
St James Centre
Works
FE Sta
Amb Sta
Mark Hall North
Sch
Hotel
Hillingdon House (Hospl)
Cumulus
Mus
School
Playing Field
Liby
Newpond Spring
Gravelpit Spring
Hubbard's Hall
School
Mark Hall South
Playing Field
Sports Ground
Roundhouse
New Hall Farm
Hubbard's Hall Farm
Markhall Wood
Latton Street (Cycle Track)
HIGH WYCH RD
REDERICKS LA
HARLOW RD
CAMBRIDGE RD
OLD RD
EDINBURGH WAY
GILDEN WAY
SHEERING LOWER RD
SHEERING RD
HOBBS CROSS RD
LONDON RD
STATION RD
HIGH ST
MULBERRY GREEN
A414
A1184
B183
M11
4
3
2
1
13
12
11
10
46
47
48

89

103

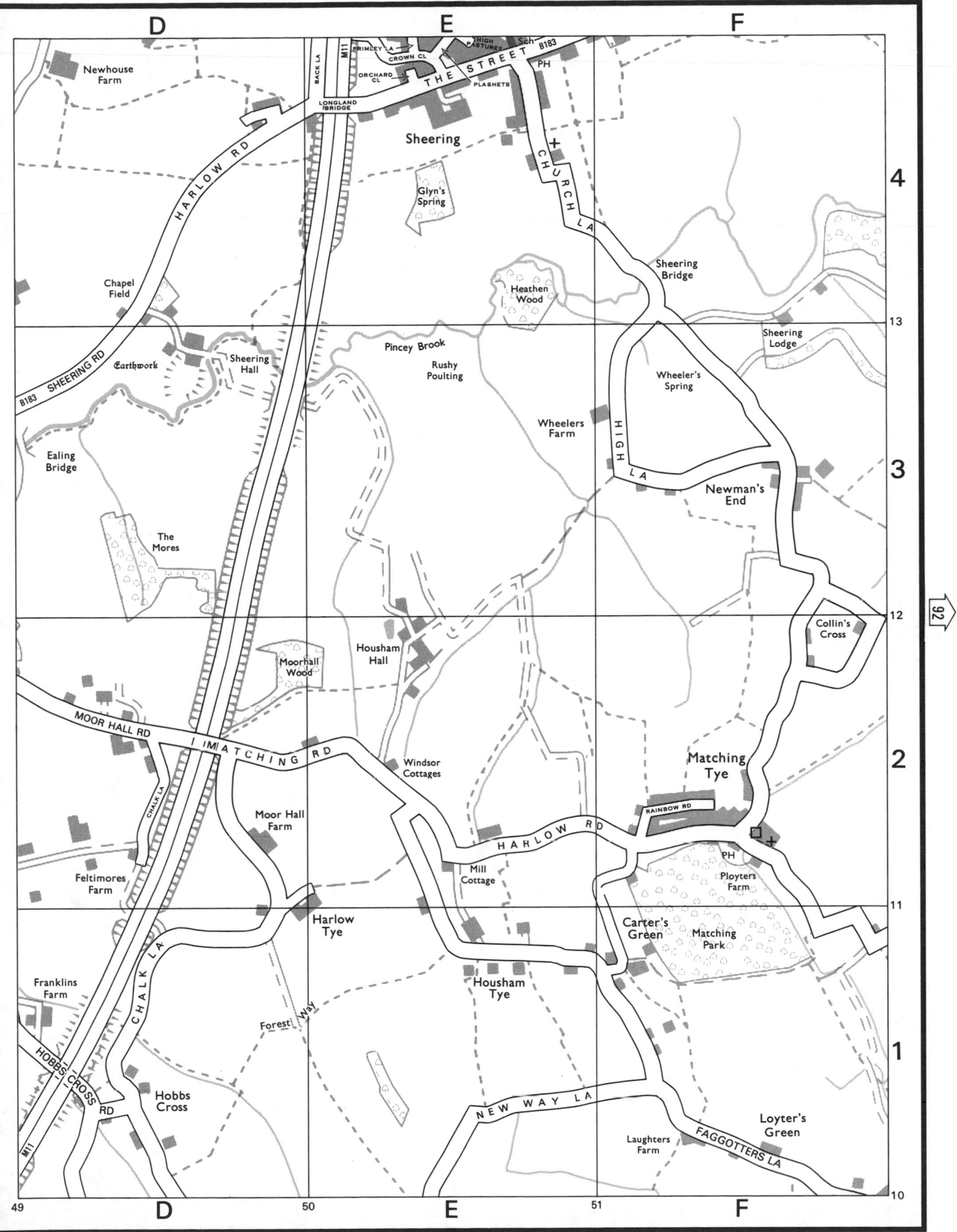
78
D
E
F
Newhouse Farm
PRIMLEY LA
CROWN CL
ORCHARD CL
HIGH PASTURES
Sch
B183
THE STREET
PLASHETS
PH
BACK LA
M11
LONGLAND BRIDGE
Sheering
CHURCH LA
HARLOW RD
Glyn's Spring
Sheering Bridge
Chapel Field
Heathen Wood
Pincey Brook
Rushy Poulting
Sheering Lodge
Sheering Hall
Earthwork
B183 SHEERING RD
Wheeler's Spring
Wheelers Farm
HIGH LA
Ealing Bridge
Newman's End
The Mores
Collin's Cross
92
Housham Hall
Moorhall Wood
MOOR HALL RD
MATCHING RD
Windsor Cottages
Matching Tye
RAINBOW RD
CHALK LA
Moor Hall Farm
HARLOW RD
Mill Cottage
PH
Ployters Farm
Feltimores Farm
Harlow Tye
Carter's Green
Matching Park
Franklins Farm
Housham Tye
Forest Way
HOBBS CROSS RD
Hobbs Cross
NEW WAY LA
Loyter's Green
Laughters Farm
FAGGOTTERS LA
4
3
2
1
13
12
11
10
49
50
51
104

79

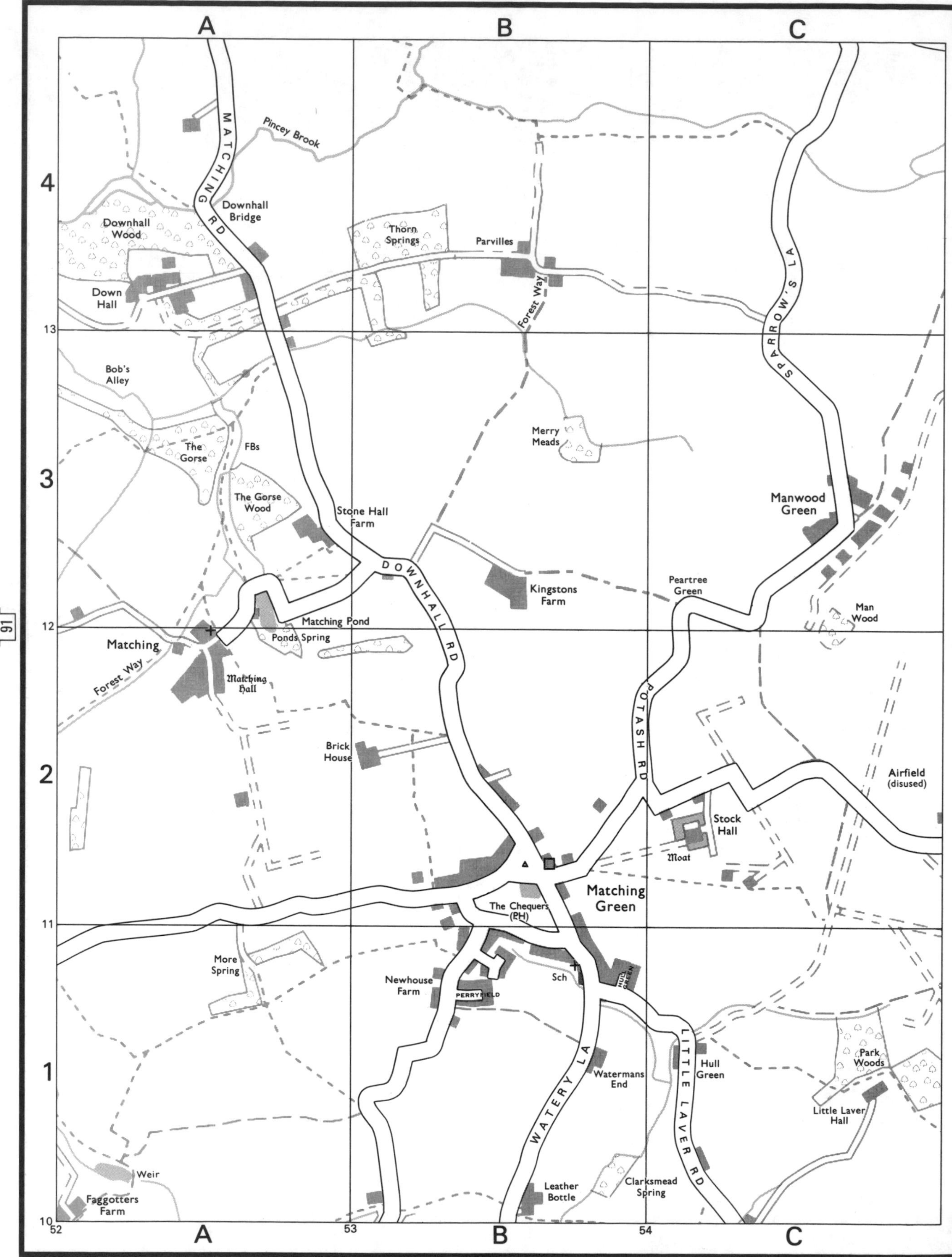
A
B
C
4
3
2
1
13
12
11
10
52
53
54
MATCHING RD
Pincey Brook
Downhall Bridge
Downhall Wood
Down Hall
Thorn Springs
Parvilles
Forest Way
SPARROW'S LA
Bob's Alley
Merry Meads
The Gorse
FBs
The Gorse Wood
Stone Hall Farm
Manwood Green
DOWNHALL RD
Kingstons Farm
Peartree Green
Man Wood
Matching Pond
Matching
Ponds Spring
Forest Way
Matching Hall
POTASH RD
Brick House
Airfield (disused)
Stock Hall
Moat
Matching Green
The Chequers (PH)
More Spring
Newhouse Farm
PERRYFIELD
Sch
HULL GREEN
LITTLE LAVER RD
Hull Green
Park Woods
WATERY LA
Watermans End
Little Laver Hall
Weir
Faggotters Farm
Leather Bottle
Clarksmead Spring

91

105

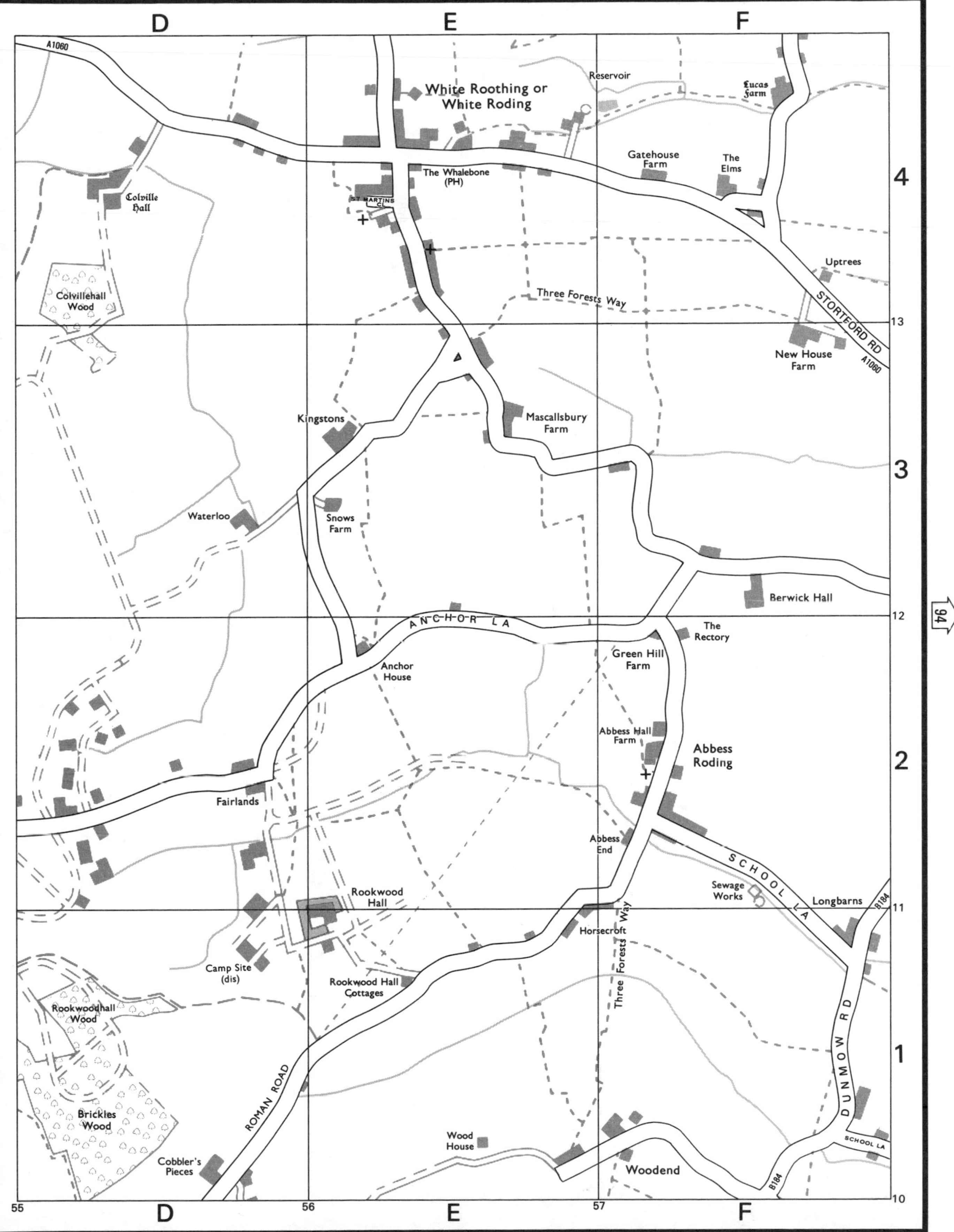
80
D
E
F
A1060
White Roothing or
White Roding
Reservoir
Lucas
Farm
Colville
Hall
The Whalebone
(PH)
ST MARTINS CL
Gatehouse
Farm
The
Elms
4
Uptrees
Colvillehall
Wood
Three Forests Way
STORTFORD RD
13
New House
Farm
A1060
Kingstons
Mascallsbury
Farm
3
Waterloo
Snows
Farm
Berwick Hall
94
12
ANCHOR LA
The
Rectory
Green Hill
Farm
Anchor
House
Abbess Hall
Farm
Abbess
Roding
2
Fairlands
Abbess
End
SCHOOL LA
Sewage
Works
Rookwood
Hall
Longbarns
B184
11
Horsecroft
Camp Site
(dis)
Rookwood Hall
Cottages
Three Forests Way
Rookwoodhall
Wood
DUNMOW RD
1
Brickles
Wood
ROMAN ROAD
Wood
House
SCHOOL LA
Cobbler's
Pieces
Woodend
B184
10
55
56
57
D
E
F
106

81

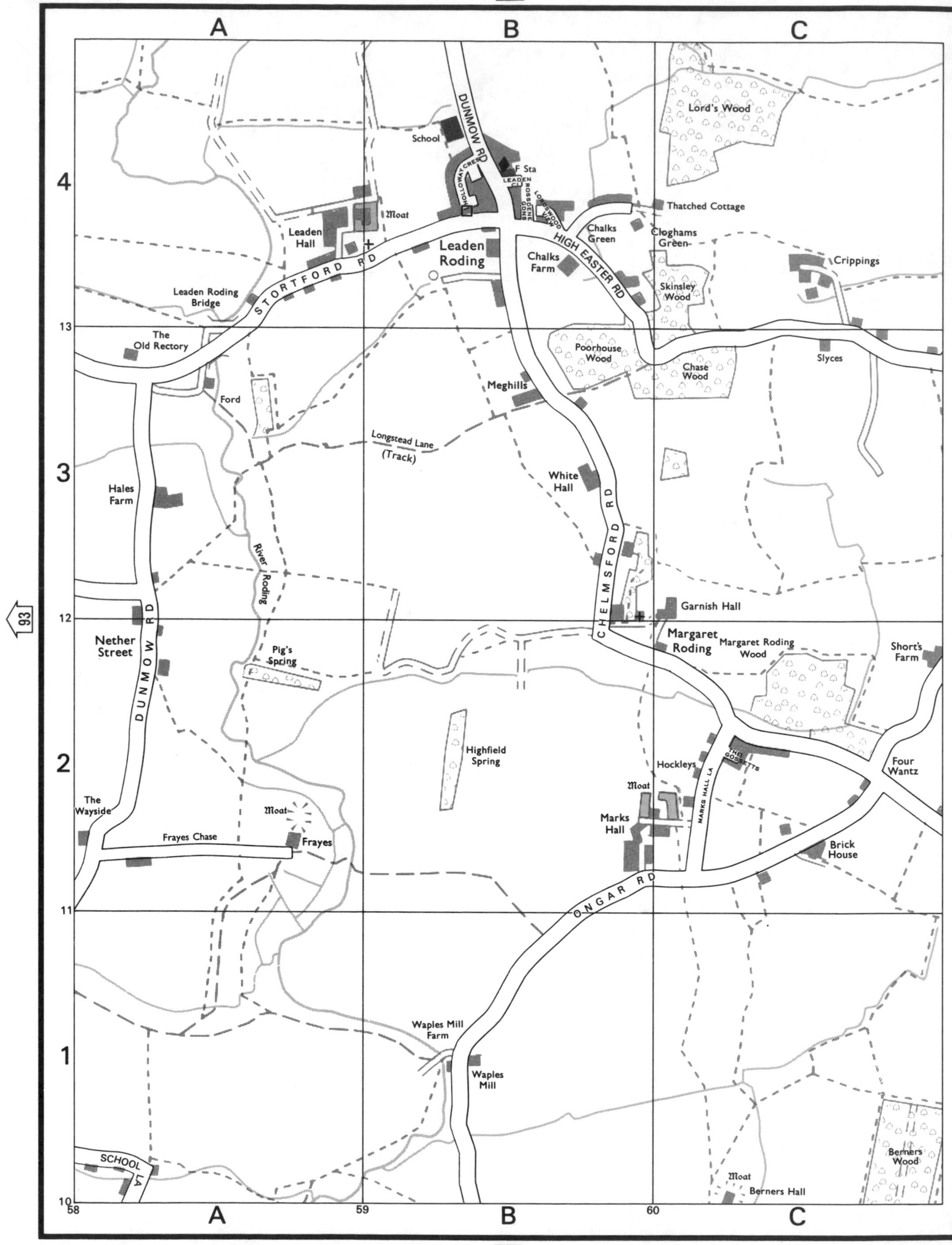
A
B
C
4
3
2
1
13
12
11
10
58
59
60
Lord's Wood
School
DUNMOW RD
F Sta
HOLLOWAY CRES
LEADEN CL
ROSSDENE GDNS
LORDSWOOD VIEW
Moat
Thatched Cottage
Leaden Hall
Leaden Roding
Chalks Green
Cloghams Green
HIGH EASTER RD
Chalks Farm
Crippings
Skinsley Wood
STORTFORD RD
Leaden Roding Bridge
The Old Rectory
Poorhouse Wood
Chase Wood
Slyces
Meghills
Ford
Longstead Lane (Track)
Hales Farm
White Hall
CHELMSFORD RD
River Roding
Garnish Hall
Nether Street
DUNMOW RD
Pig's Spring
Margaret Roding
Margaret Roding Wood
Short's Farm
Highfield Spring
Hockleys
THE GOSSETTS
Four Wantz
MARKS HALL LA
The Wayside
Moat
Marks Hall
Frayes Chase
Frayes
Brick House
ONGAR RD
Waples Mill Farm
Waples Mill
SCHOOL LA
Berners Wood
Berners Hall

93

107

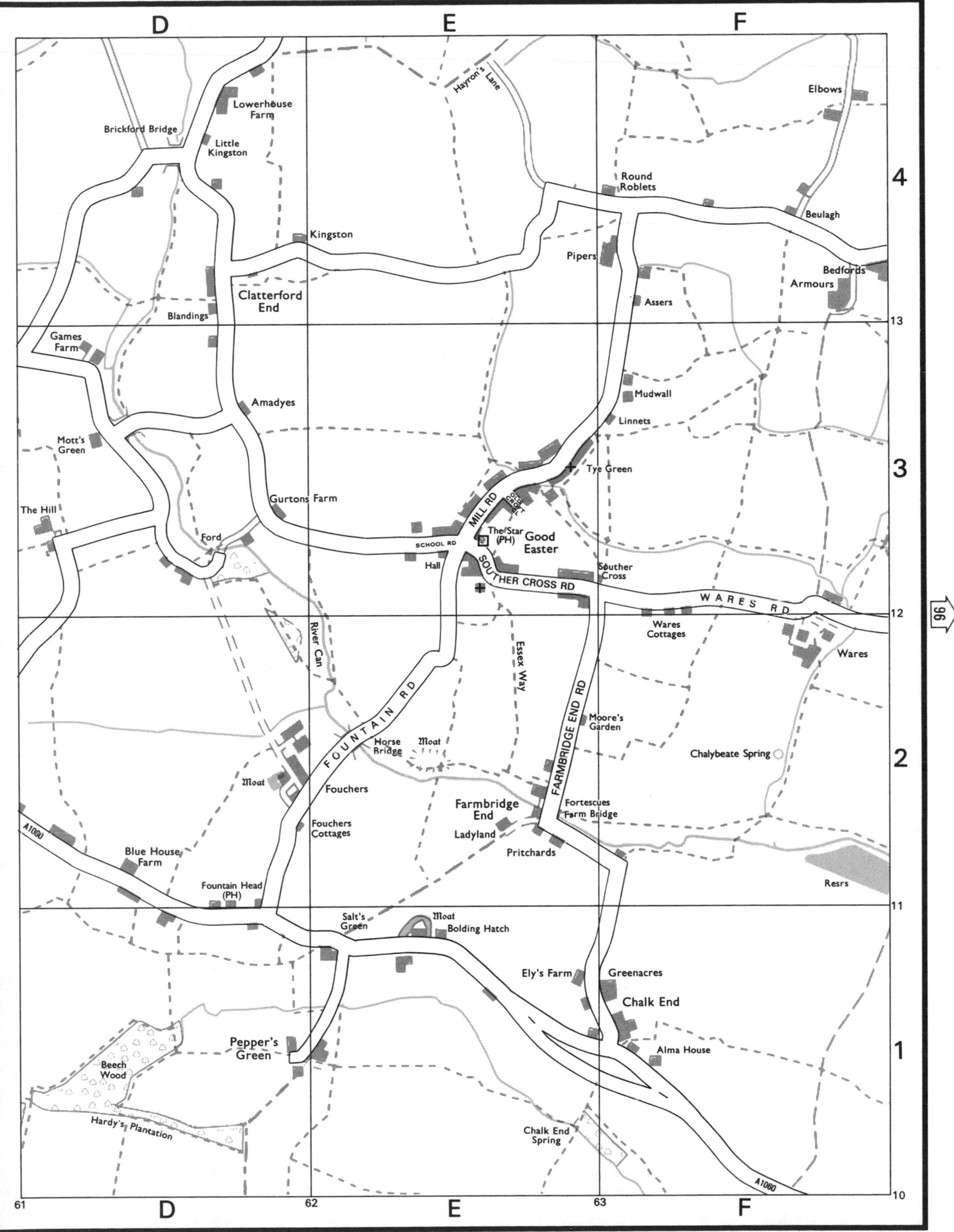
82
D
E
F
Hayron's Lane
Elbows
Lowerhouse Farm
Brickford Bridge
Little Kingston
4
Round Roblets
Beulagh
Kingston
Pipers
Bedfords
Armours
Clatterford End
Assers
Blandings
13
Games Farm
Mudwall
Amadyes
Linnets
Mott's Green
3
Tye Green
Gurtons Farm
MILL RD
OLD CROFT
The Hill
The Star (PH)
Good Easter
Ford
SCHOOL RD
Hall
Souther Cross
SOUTHER CROSS RD
WARES RD
12
96
Wares Cottages
Wares
River Can
Essex Way
FOUNTAIN RD
FARMBRIDGE END RD
Moore's Garden
Horse Bridge
Moat
Chalybeate Spring
2
Moat
Fouchers
Farmbridge End
Fortescues Farm Bridge
A1060
Fouchers Cottages
Ladyland
Pritchards
Blue House Farm
Resrs
Fountain Head (PH)
11
Salt's Green
Moat
Bolding Hatch
Ely's Farm
Greenacres
Chalk End
Pepper's Green
Alma House
1
Beech Wood
Hardy's Plantation
Chalk End Spring
A1060
61
62
63
10
108

83

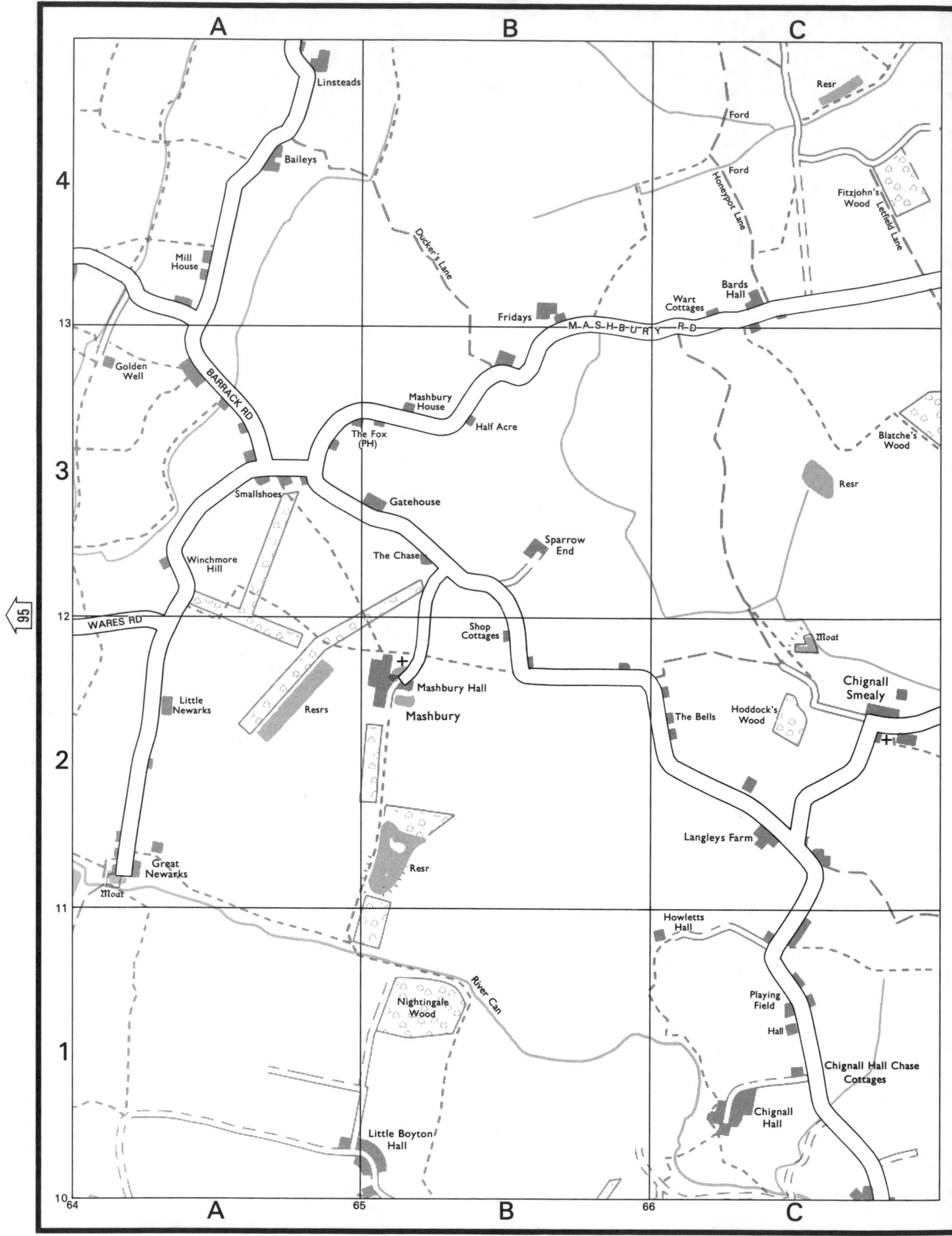

A
B
C
4
3
2
1
13
12
11
10
64
65
66
Linsteads
Baileys
Mill House
Golden Well
BARRACK RD
Ducker's Lane
Fridays
MASHBURY RD
Ford
Ford
Resr
Honeypot Lane
Fitzjohn's Wood
Letfield Lane
Wart Cottages
Bards Hall
Mashbury House
Half Acre
The Fox (PH)
Blatche's Wood
Resr
Smallshoes
Gatehouse
Sparrow End
Winchmore Hill
The Chase
WARES RD
Shop Cottages
Moat
Chignall Smealy
Mashbury Hall
Mashbury
Little Newarks
Resrs
The Bells
Hoddock's Wood
Langleys Farm
Great Newarks
Moat
Resr
Howletts Hall
River Can
Nightingale Wood
Playing Field
Hall
Chignall Hall Chase Cottages
Chignall Hall
Little Boyton Hall

95

109

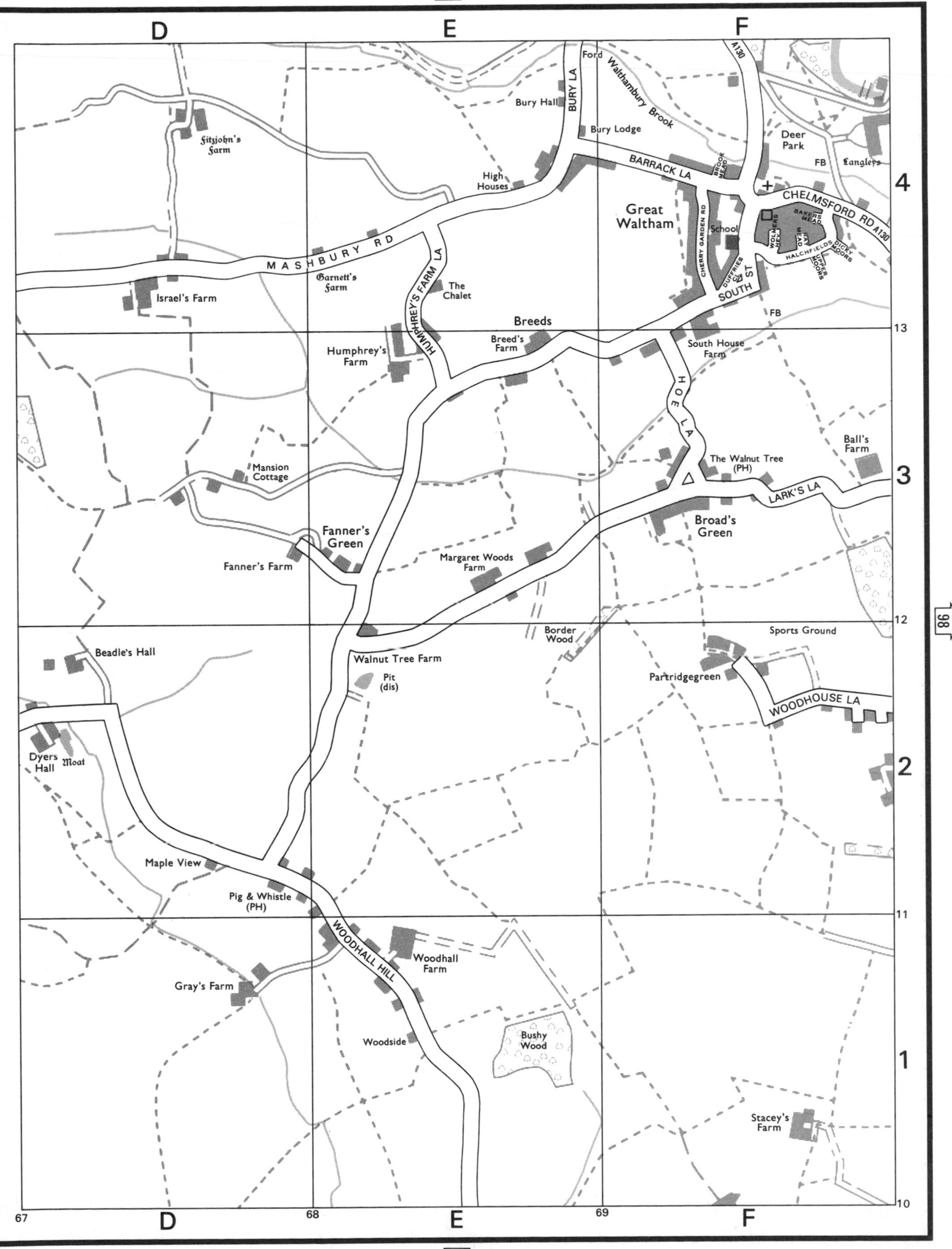
84
D
E
F
Ford
Walthambury Brook
BURY LA
A130
Bury Hall
Bury Lodge
Deer Park
FB
Langleys
Fitzjohn's Farm
BARRACK LA
BROOK MEAD
High Houses
CHELMSFORD RD A130
Great Waltham
CHERRY GARDEN RD
School
BAKERS MEAD
WOLMERS HEY
MAY MEAD
HALCHFIELDS
DICKY MOORS
UPPER MOORS
DUFFRIES CL
SOUTH ST
MASHBURY RD
Garnett's Farm
HUMPHREY'S FARM LA
The Chalet
Israel's Farm
FB
Breeds
Breed's Farm
South House Farm
Humphrey's Farm
HOE LA
Ball's Farm
Mansion Cottage
The Walnut Tree (PH)
LARK'S LA
Broad's Green
Fanner's Green
Fanner's Farm
Margaret Woods Farm
Border Wood
Sports Ground
Beadle's Hall
Walnut Tree Farm
Pit (dis)
Partridgegreen
WOODHOUSE LA
Dyers Hall
Moat
Maple View
Pig & Whistle (PH)
WOODHALL HILL
Woodhall Farm
Gray's Farm
Bushy Wood
Woodside
Stacey's Farm
4
3
2
1
13
12
11
10
67
68
69
98
110

85

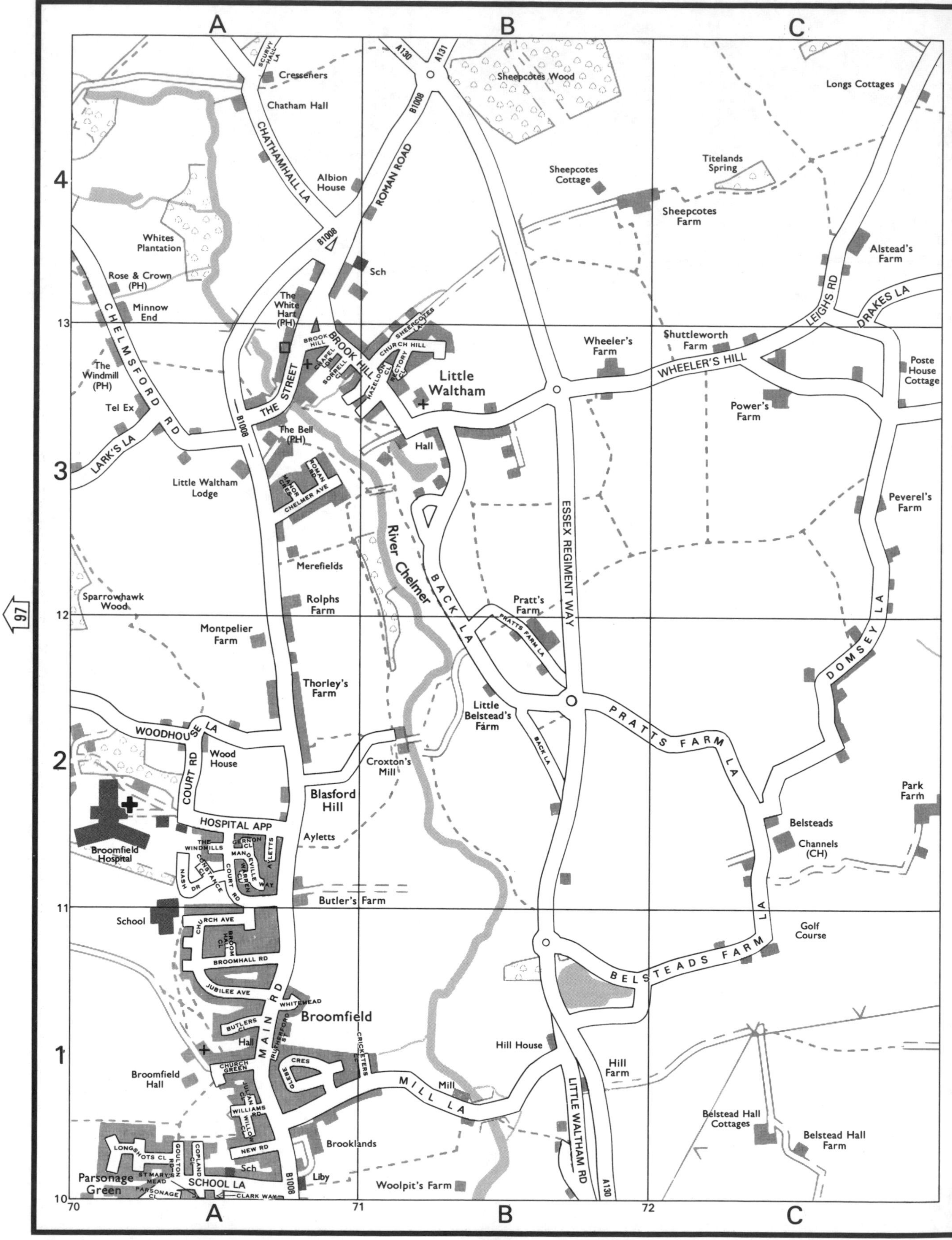
A
B
C
4
13
3
12
2
11
1
10
70
71
72
Cresseners
Chatham Hall
CHATHAMHALL LA
SCURVY HALL LA
A130
A131
B1008
ROMAN ROAD
Sheepcotes Wood
Longs Cottages
Albion House
Titelands Spring
Sheepcotes Cottage
Sheepcotes Farm
Whites Plantation
Sch
Alstead's Farm
Rose & Crown (PH)
Minnow End
The White Hart (PH)
LEIGHS RD
DRAKES LA
CHELMSFORD RD
BROOK HILL
CHURCH HILL
SHEEPCOTES LA
CHAPEL LA
SORRELL
HAZELDON CL
RECTORY CL
Wheeler's Farm
Shuttleworth Farm
WHEELER'S HILL
Poste House Cottage
The Windmill (PH)
THE STREET
Little Waltham
Power's Farm
Tel Ex
LARK'S LA
The Bell (PH)
Hall
ROMAN RD
MANOR CRES
CHELMER AVE
Little Waltham Lodge
Peverel's Farm
ESSEX REGIMENT WAY
River Chelmer
BACK LA
Merefields
Sparrowhawk Wood
Rolphs Farm
Pratt's Farm
PRATTS FARM LA
Montpelier Farm
DOMSEY LA
Thorley's Farm
Little Belstead's Farm
WOODHOUSE LA
COURT RD
Wood House
Croxton's Mill
Blasford Hill
Park Farm
HOSPITAL APP
Ayletts
Belsteads
Channels (CH)
Broomfield Hospital
THE WINDMILLS
GERNON CL
MANDEVILLE WAY
AYLETTS
NASH DR
CONSTANCE CL
WARREN CL
Butler's Farm
School
CHURCH AVE
BROOMHALL CL
BROOMHALL RD
Golf Course
BELSTEADS FARM LA
JUBILEE AVE
WHITEMEAD
MAIN RD
Broomfield
BUTLERS CL
RUTHERFORD ST
CRICKETERS CL
Hall
Hill House
Hill Farm
CRES
GLEBE
CHURCH GREEN
MILL LA
Mill
Broomfield Hall
LITTLE WALTHAM RD
Belstead Hall Cottages
Belstead Hall Farm
WILLIAMS RD
JULIAN CL
WILLOW CL
Brooklands
LONGSHOTS CL
GOULTON RD
COPLAND CL
NEW RD
Sch
Parsonage Green
ST MARY'S MEAD
SCHOOL LA
PARSONAGE CL
CLARK WAY
Liby
Woolpit's Farm

97

111

86

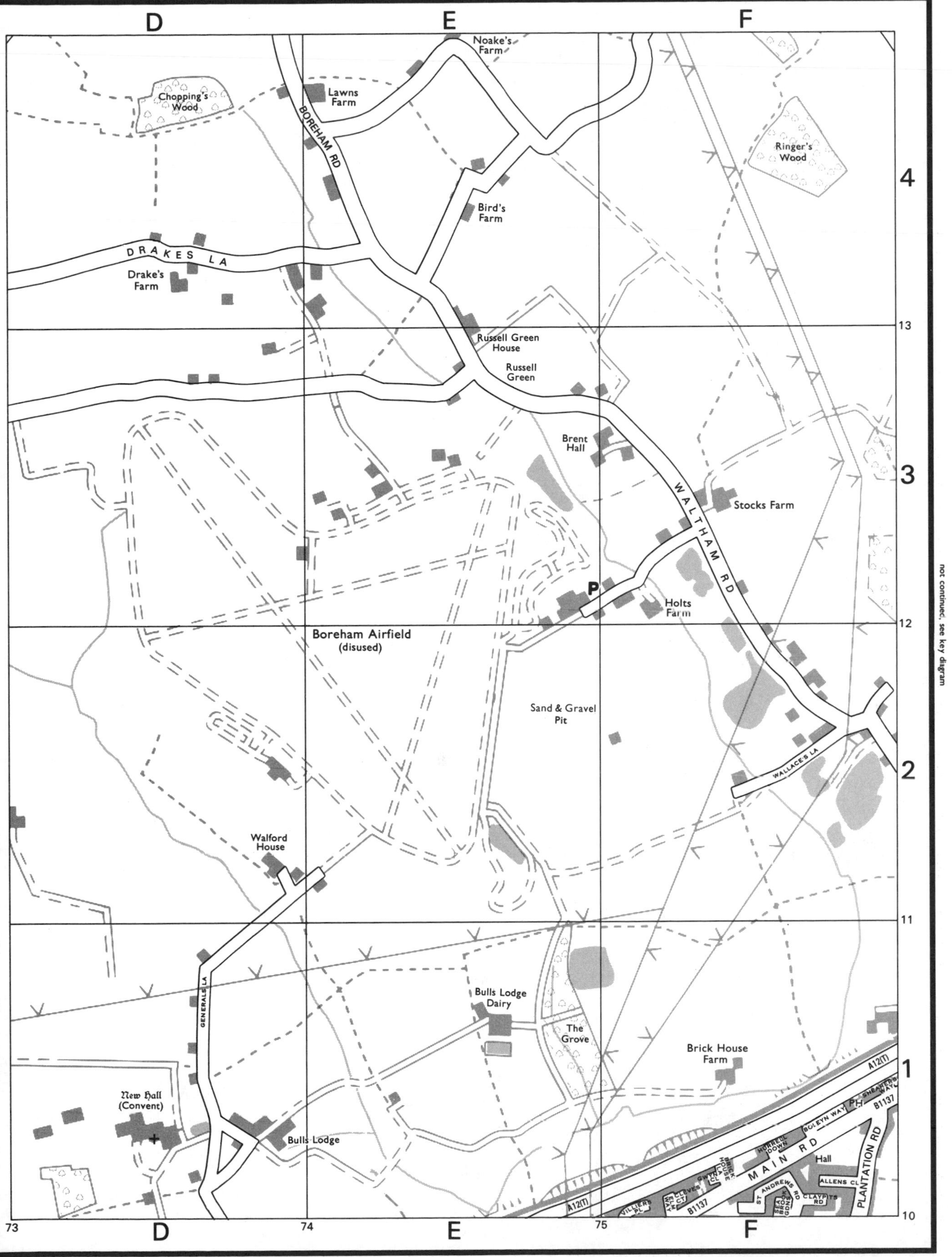

not continued, see key diagram

112

87

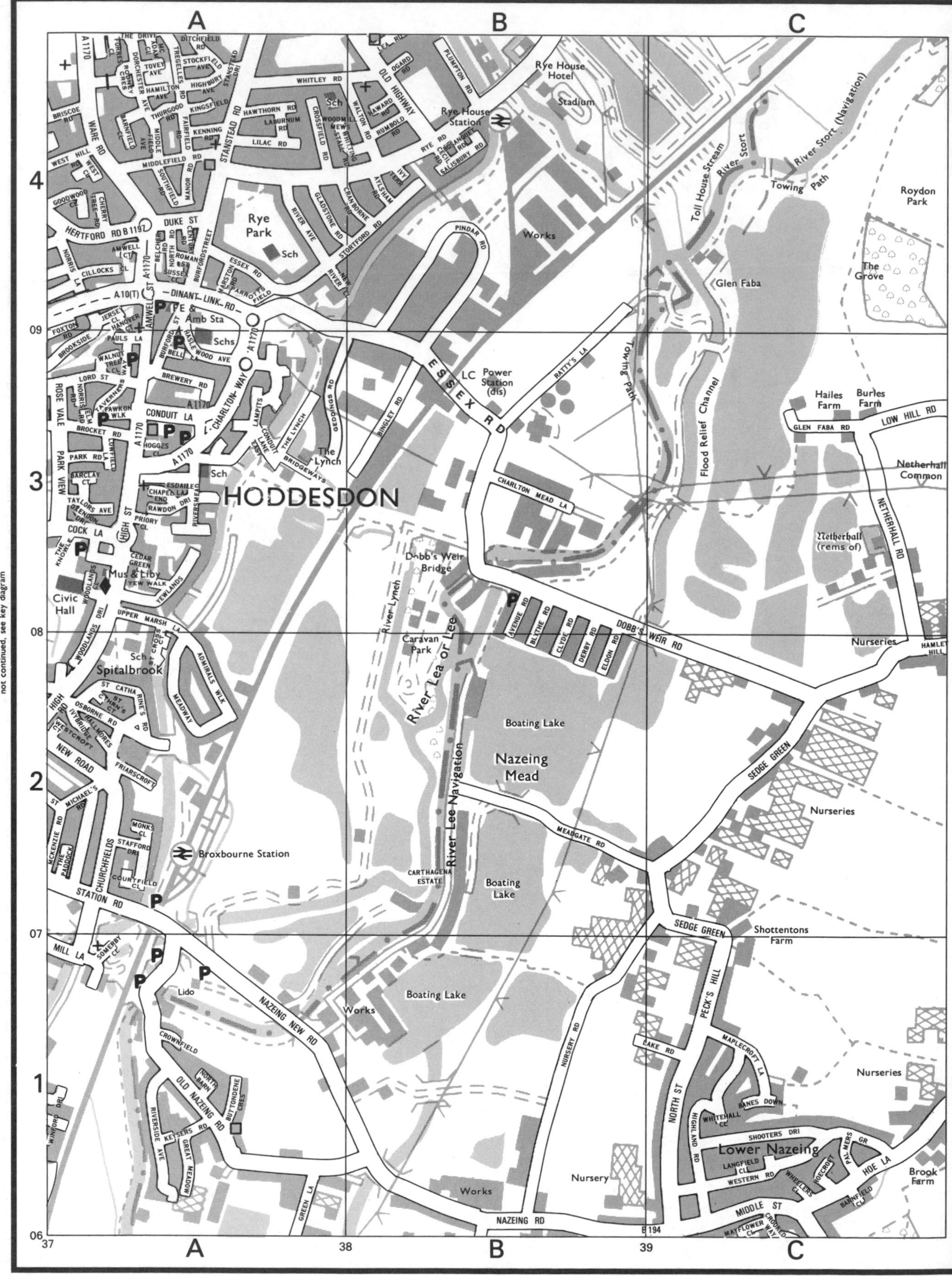

not continued, see key diagram

113

88

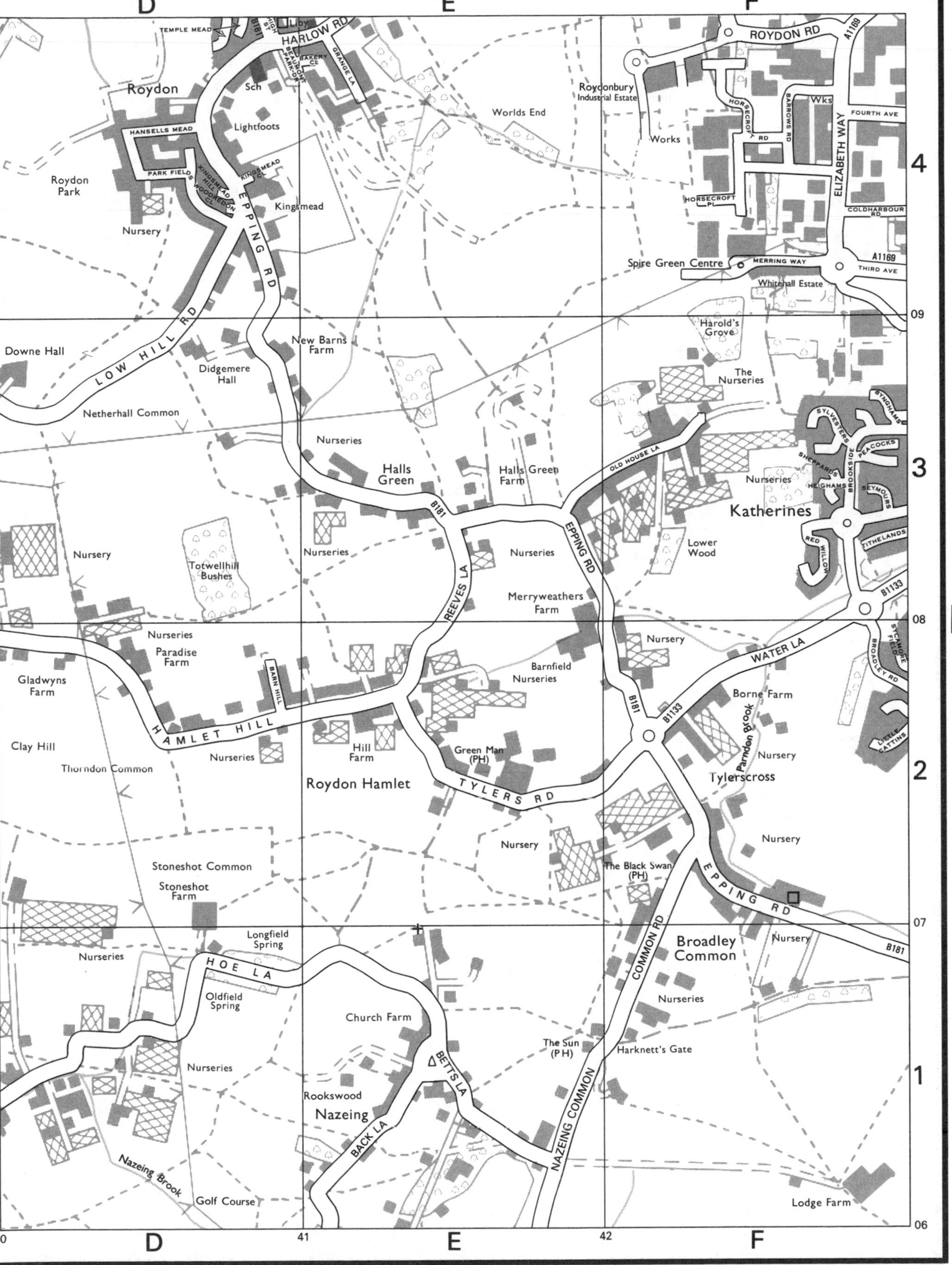

D
E
F
Roydon
Roydon Park
Nursery
Lightfoots
Kingsmead
Sch
HARLOW RD
TEMPLE MEAD
HANSELLS MEAD
PARK FIELDS
EPPING RD
LOW HILL RD
Downe Hall
Didgemere Hall
Netherhall Common
New Barns Farm
Worlds End
Roydonbury Industrial Estate
Works
ROYDON RD
ELIZABETH WAY
FOURTH AVE
COLDHARBOUR RD
HORSECROFT RD
BARROWS RD
Wks
Spire Green Centre
MERRING WAY
A1169
THIRD AVE
Whitehall Estate
Harold's Grove
The Nurseries
Nurseries
Halls Green
Halls Green Farm
OLD HOUSE LA
Katherines
Lower Wood
Nursery
Totwellhill Bushes
REEVES LA
B181
Merryweathers Farm
B1133
Nurseries
Paradise Farm
Gladwyns Farm
Clay Hill
Thorndon Common
HAMLET HILL
BARN HILL
Barnfield Nurseries
WATER LA
Borne Farm
Parndon Brook
Tylerscross
Green Man (PH)
Hill Farm
Roydon Hamlet
TYLERS RD
Stoneshot Common
Stoneshot Farm
The Black Swan (PH)
Broadley Common
COMMON RD
Longfield Spring
HOE LA
Oldfield Spring
Church Farm
The Sun (PH)
Harknett's Gate
BETTS LA
Rookswood
Nazeing
BACK LA
NAZEING COMMON
Nazeing Brook
Golf Course
Lodge Farm
4
3
2
1
09
08
07
06
40
41
42

102

114

89

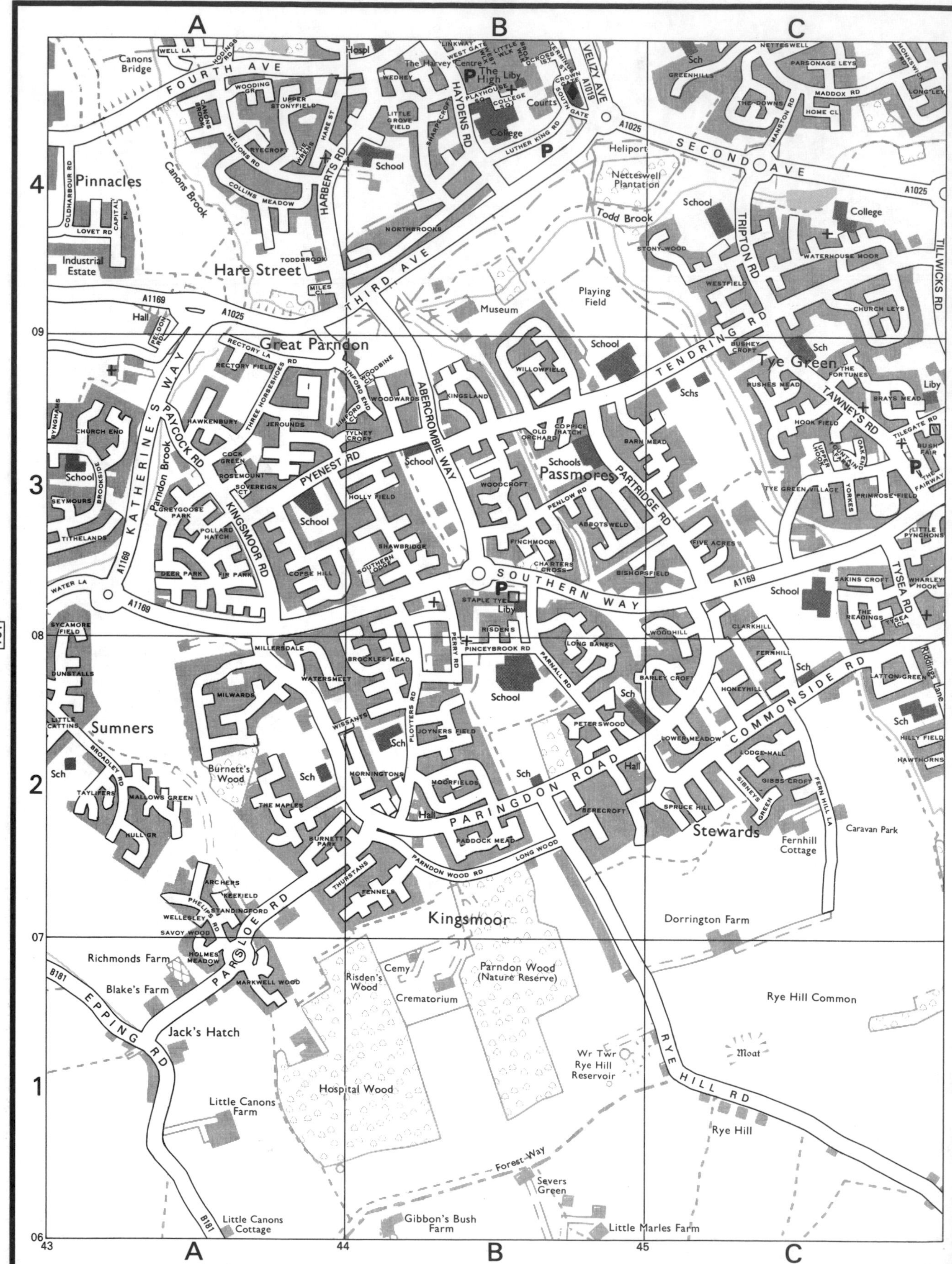

A
B
C
4
3
2
1
09
08
07
06
43
44
45
Canons Bridge
WELL LA
FOURTH AVE
Hospl
The Harvey Centre
The High
Liby
Courts
College
School
HAYDENS RD
VELIZY AVE
A1019
A1025
SECOND AVE
Heliport
Netteswell Plantation
Todd Brook
Pinnacles
Canons Brook
Industrial Estate
Hare Street
HARBERTS RD
COLLINS MEADOW
NORTHBROOKS
THIRD AVE
A1169
Hall
Great Parndon
Museum
Playing Field
TENDRING RD
TRIPTON RD
TILLWICKS RD
Tye Green
TAWNEYS RD
Liby
Schs
Passmores
PARTRIDGE RD
ABERCROMBIE WAY
PYENEST RD
KATHERINE'S WAY
PAYCOCK RD
KINGSMOOR RD
Parndon Brook
SOUTHERN WAY
STAPLE TYE
PERRY RD
PINCEYBROOK RD
School
Sch
COMMONSIDE RD
Riddings Lane
Sumners
Burnett's Wood
PARINGDON ROAD
Stewards
Fernhill Cottage
Caravan Park
PARNDON WOOD RD
LONG WOOD
Kingsmoor
Dorrington Farm
PARSLOE RD
Richmonds Farm
Blake's Farm
B181
EPPING RD
Jack's Hatch
Risden's Wood
Cemy
Crematorium
Parndon Wood (Nature Reserve)
Rye Hill Common
Moat
Wr Twr
Rye Hill Reservoir
RYE HILL RD
Rye Hill
Hospital Wood
Little Canons Farm
Forest Way
Severs Green
Gibbon's Bush Farm
Little Canons Cottage
Little Marles Farm
WATER LA

101

115

90

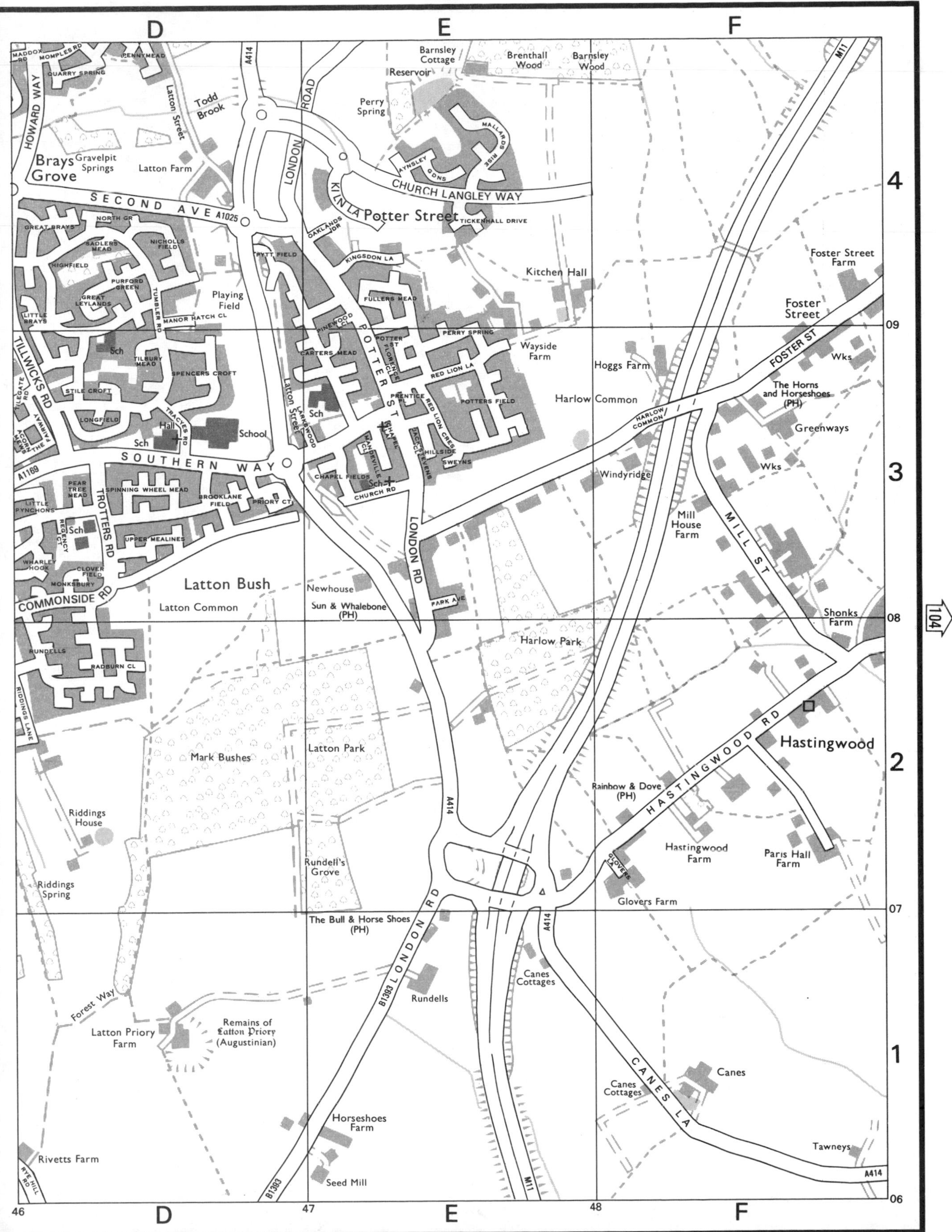

D
E
F
Barnsley Cottage
Brenthall Wood
Barnsley Wood
Reservoir
M11
Todd Brook
Latton Street
Perry Spring
HOWARD WAY
Brays Grove
Gravelpit Springs
Latton Farm
LONDON ROAD
MALLARDS RISE
AYNSLEY GDNS
CHURCH LANGLEY WAY
KILN LA
SECOND AVE A1025
Potter Street
TICKENHALL DRIVE
OAKLANDS DR
KINGSDON LA
Kitchen Hall
Foster Street Farm
Playing Field
FULLERS MEAD
Foster Street
POTTER ST
PERRY SPRING
Wayside Farm
Hoggs Farm
FOSTER ST
Wks
TILLWICKS RD
CARTERS MEAD
RED LION LA
The Horns and Horseshoes (PH)
SPENCERS CROFT
Harlow Common
STILE CROFT
POTTERS FIELD
Sch
LONGFIELD
Hall
School
HARLOW COMMON
Greenways
HILLSIDE
SWEYNS
SOUTHERN WAY
Windyridge
Wks
A1169
SPINNING WHEEL MEAD
CHAPEL FIELDS
CHURCH RD
PRIORY CT
BROOKLANE FIELD
TROTTERS RD
LONDON RD
Mill House Farm
MILL ST
UPPER MEALINES
Latton Bush
Newhouse
COMMONSIDE RD
Latton Common
Sun & Whalebone (PH)
PARK AVE
Shonks Farm
RUNDELLS
RADBURN CL
Harlow Park
RIDDINGS LANE
Mark Bushes
Latton Park
HASTINGWOOD RD
Hastingwood
Riddings House
A414
Rainbow & Dove (PH)
Hastingwood Farm
Paris Hall Farm
Rundell's Grove
GLOVERS LA
Riddings Spring
Glovers Farm
The Bull & Horse Shoes (PH)
LONDON RD
Canes Cottages
Forest Way
Rundells
B1393
Remains of Latton Priory (Augustinian)
Latton Priory Farm
CANES LA
Canes
Canes Cottages
Horseshoes Farm
Tawneys
Rivetts Farm
RYE HILL RD
Seed Mill
A414
46
47
48
4
3
2
1
09
08
07
06
104

116

91

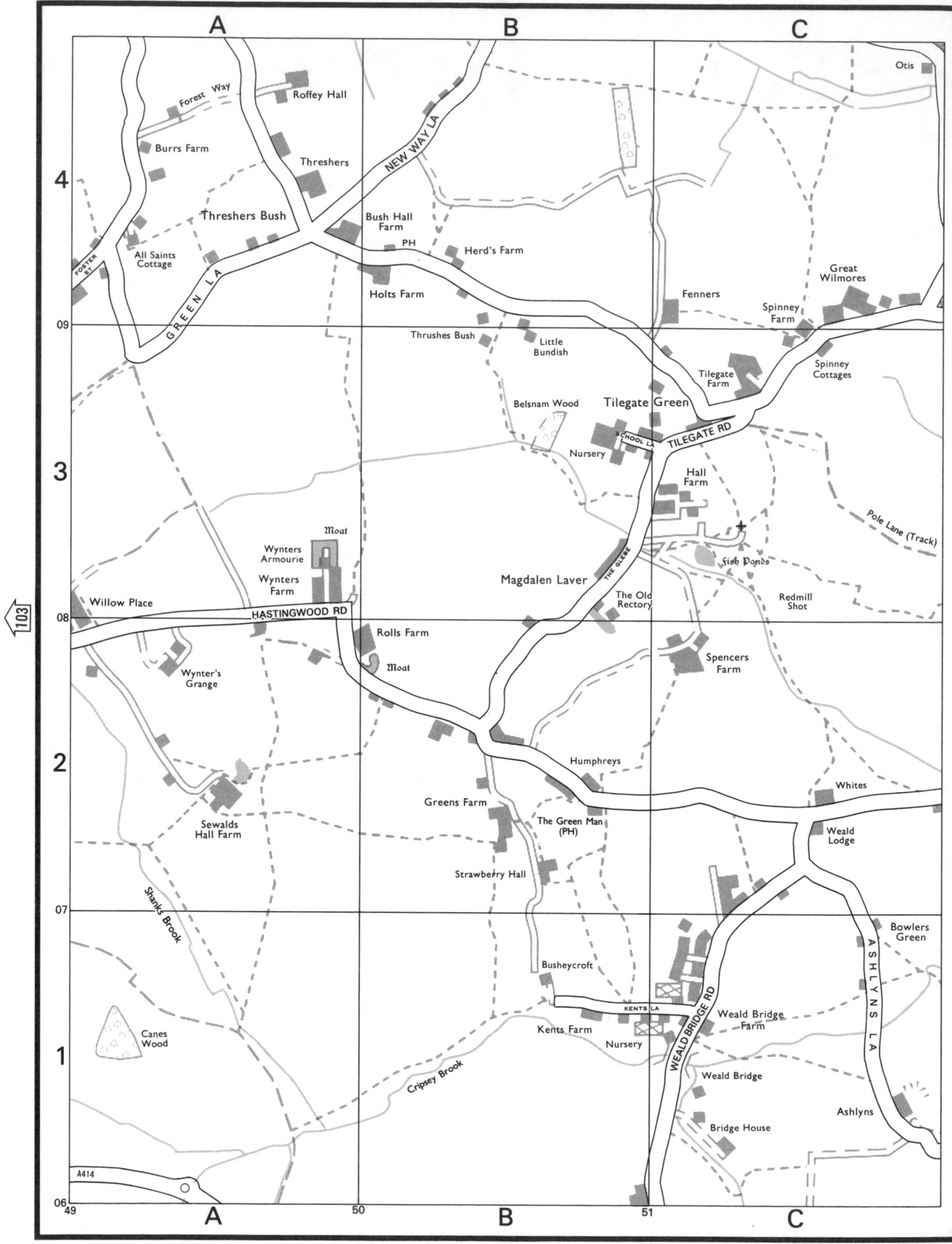
A
B
C
4
3
2
1
09
08
07
06
49
50
51
Otis
Forest Way
Roffey Hall
Burrs Farm
Threshers
NEW WAY LA
Threshers Bush
Bush Hall Farm
PH
Herd's Farm
All Saints Cottage
FOSTER ST
GREEN LA
Holts Farm
Fenners
Great Wilmores
Spinney Farm
Thrushes Bush
Little Bundish
Spinney Cottages
Tilegate Farm
Belsnam Wood
Tilegate Green
SCHOOL LA
TILEGATE RD
Nursery
Hall Farm
Pole Lane (Track)
Moat
Wynters Armourie
Wynters Farm
THE GLEBE
Fish Ponds
Magdalen Laver
The Old Rectory
Redmill Shot
Willow Place
HASTINGWOOD RD
Rolls Farm
Moat
Spencers Farm
Wynter's Grange
Humphreys
Whites
Greens Farm
The Green Man (PH)
Weald Lodge
Sewalds Hall Farm
Strawberry Hall
Shanks Brook
Bowlers Green
ASHLYNS LA
Busheycroft
KENTS LA
WEALD BRIDGE RD
Weald Bridge Farm
Canes Wood
Kents Farm
Nursery
Cripsey Brook
Weald Bridge
Ashlyns
Bridge House
A414

103

117

92

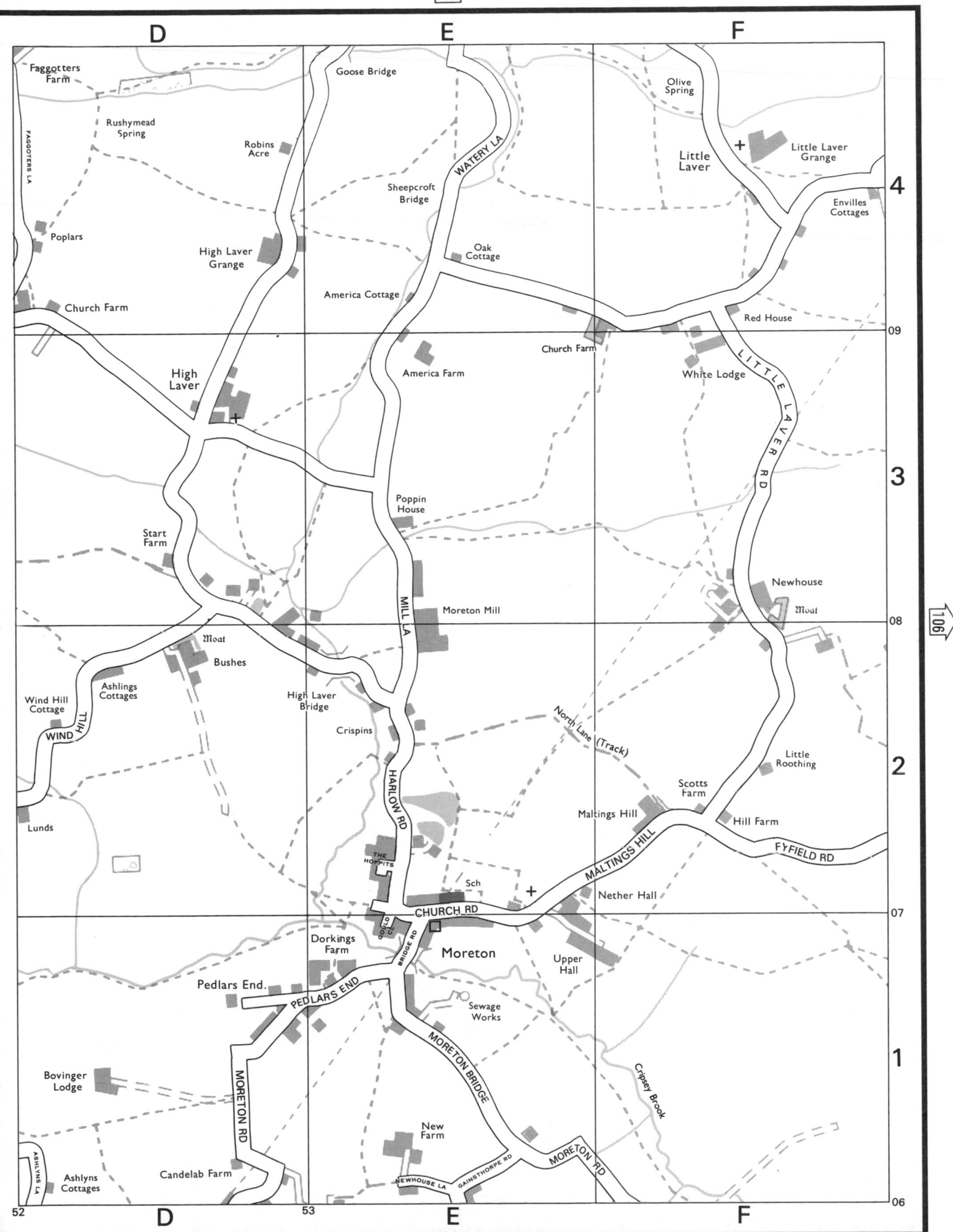

D
E
F
Faggotters Farm
Goose Bridge
Olive Spring
Rushymead Spring
FAGGOTERS LA
Robins Acre
WATERY LA
Little Laver
Little Laver Grange
Sheepcroft Bridge
4
Envilles Cottages
Poplars
High Laver Grange
Oak Cottage
America Cottage
Church Farm
Red House
09
Church Farm
America Farm
White Lodge
High Laver
LITTLE LAVER RD
3
Poppin House
Start Farm
Newhouse
Moat
MILL LA
Moreton Mill
08
Moat
Bushes
Ashlings Cottages
Wind Hill Cottage
High Laver Bridge
WIND HILL
Crispins
North Lane (Track)
Little Roothing
2
HARLOW RD
Scotts Farm
Maltings Hill
Hill Farm
Lunds
FYFIELD RD
THE HOPPITS
MALTINGS HILL
Sch
Nether Hall
CHURCH RD
07
GOULD CL
BRIDGE RD
Dorkings Farm
Moreton
Upper Hall
Pedlars End.
PEDLARS END
Sewage Works
1
MORETON BRIDGE
Bovinger Lodge
Cripsey Brook
MORETON RD
New Farm
ASHLYNS LA
Ashlyns Cottages
Candelab Farm
GAINSTHORPE RD
NEWHOUSE LA
MORETON RD
52
53
06
D
E
F

106

118

93

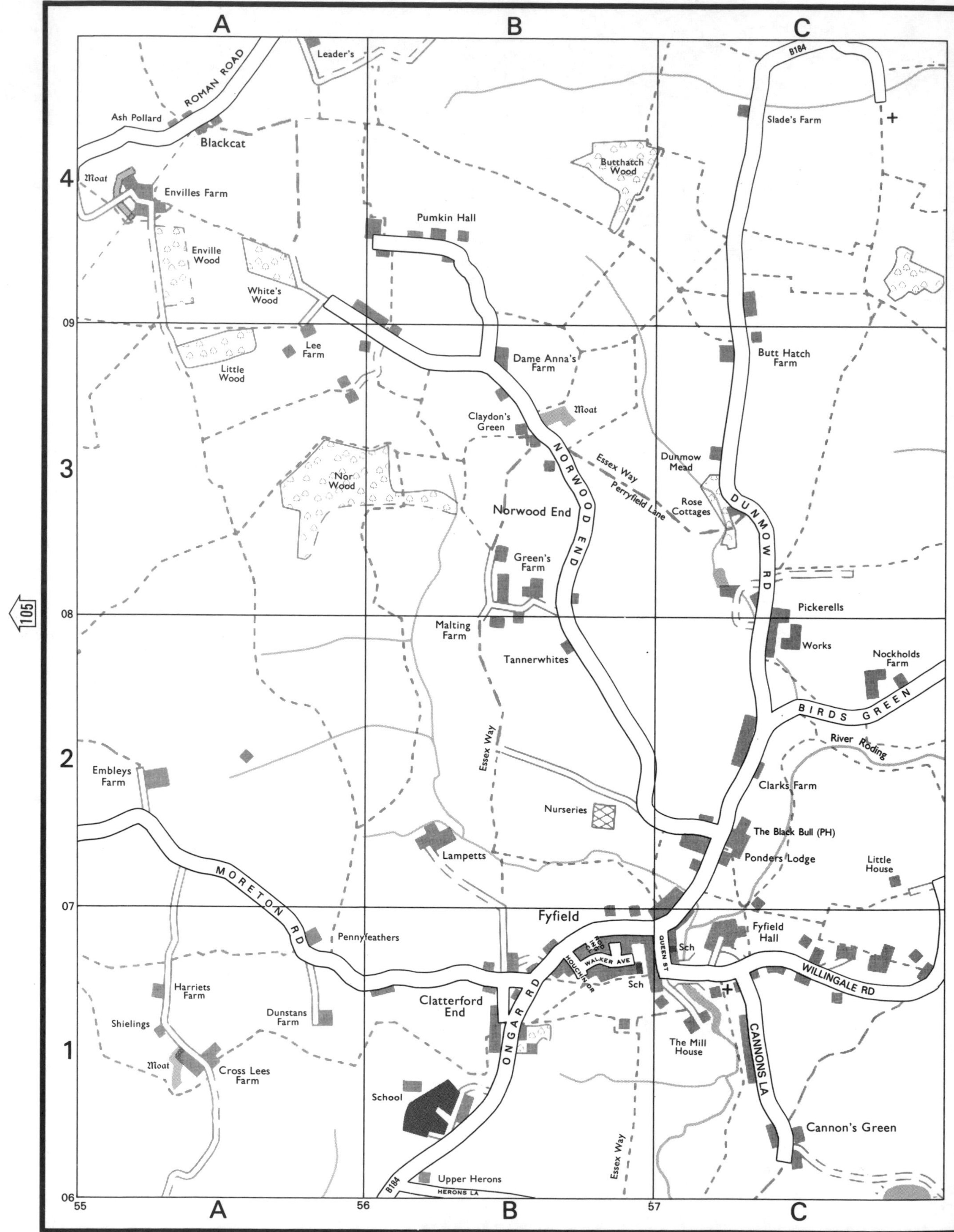

A
B
C
ROMAN ROAD
Leader's
B184
Ash Pollard
Blackcat
Slade's Farm
Butthatch Wood
Moat
Envilles Farm
Pumkin Hall
Enville Wood
White's Wood
Lee Farm
Little Wood
Dame Anna's Farm
Butt Hatch Farm
Moat
Claydon's Green
Dunmow Mead
Essex Way
Perryfield Lane
NORWOOD END
Nor Wood
Norwood End
Rose Cottages
DUNMOW RD
Green's Farm
Pickerells
Malting Farm
Works
Tannerwhites
Nockholds Farm
BIRDS GREEN
River Roding
Essex Way
Embleys Farm
Clarks Farm
Nurseries
The Black Bull (PH)
Lampetts
Ponders Lodge
Little House
MORETON RD
Fyfield
Pennyfeathers
Sch
Fyfield Hall
QUEEN ST
WALKER AVE
HOUCHIN DR
Sch
WILLINGALE RD
Harriets Farm
Clatterford End
Shielings
Dunstans Farm
ONGAR RD
CANNONS LA
The Mill House
Moat
Cross Lees Farm
School
Cannon's Green
Essex Way
Upper Herons
B184
HERONS LA
4
3
2
1
09
08
07
06
55
56
57

105

119

94

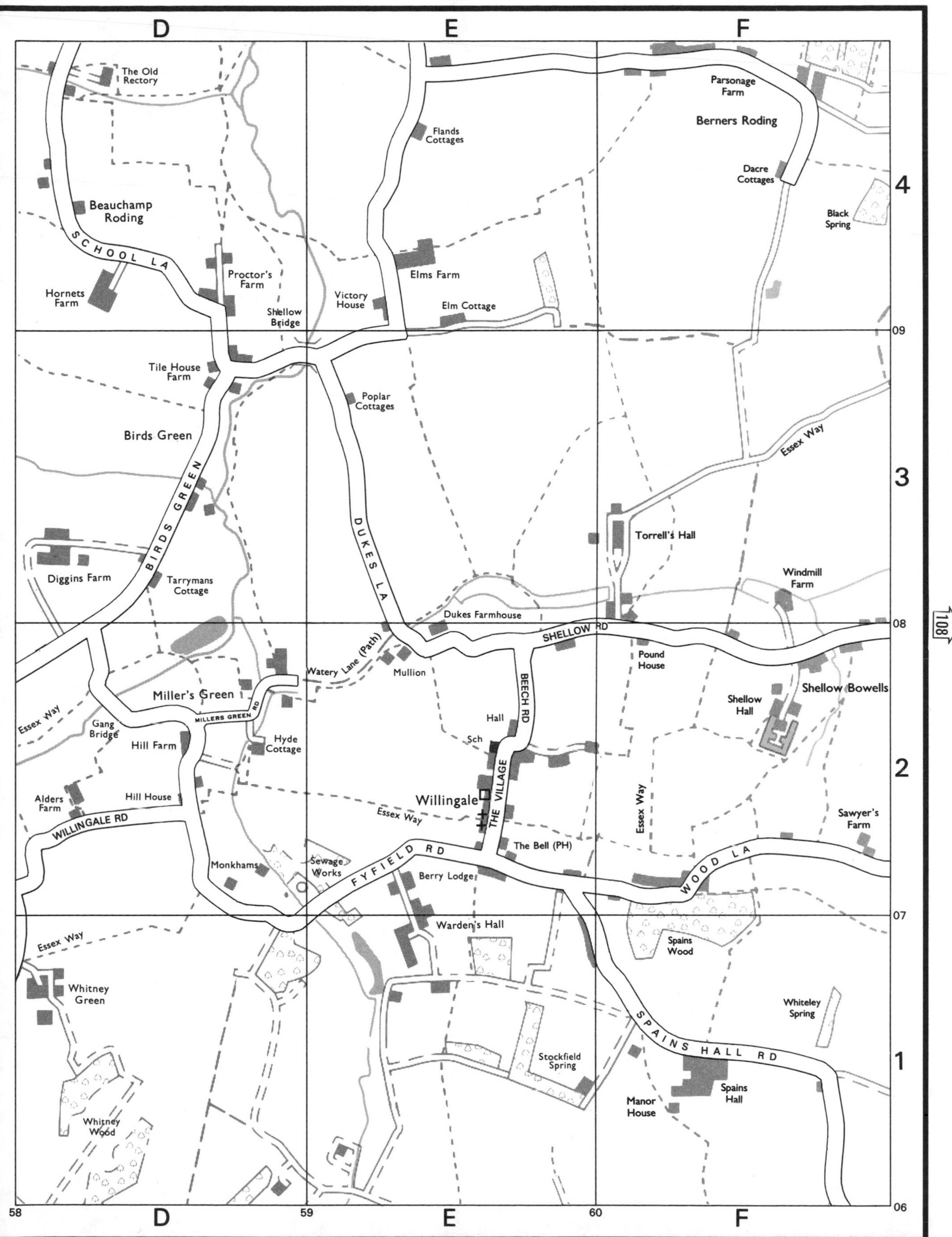
D
E
F
The Old Rectory
Flands Cottages
Parsonage Farm
Berners Roding
Dacre Cottages
Black Spring
Beauchamp Roding
SCHOOL LA
Proctor's Farm
Hornets Farm
Shellow Bridge
Victory House
Elms Farm
Elm Cottage
Tile House Farm
Poplar Cottages
Birds Green
Essex Way
BIRDS GREEN
DUKES LA
Torrell's Hall
Diggins Farm
Tarrymans Cottage
Windmill Farm
Dukes Farmhouse
SHELLOW RD
Pound House
Watery Lane (Path)
Mullion
BEECH RD
Shellow Bowells
Miller's Green
Shellow Hall
MILLERS GREEN RD
Gang Bridge
Hall
Hill Farm
Hyde Cottage
Sch
Alders Farm
Hill House
Willingale
THE VILLAGE
Sawyer's Farm
WILLINGALE RD
The Bell (PH)
Monkhams
Sewage Works
FYFIELD RD
Berry Lodge
WOOD LA
Warden's Hall
Spains Wood
Whitney Green
Whiteley Spring
SPAINS HALL RD
Stockfield Spring
Spains Hall
Manor House
Whitney Wood
4
3
2
1
09
08
07
06
58
59
60

108

120

95

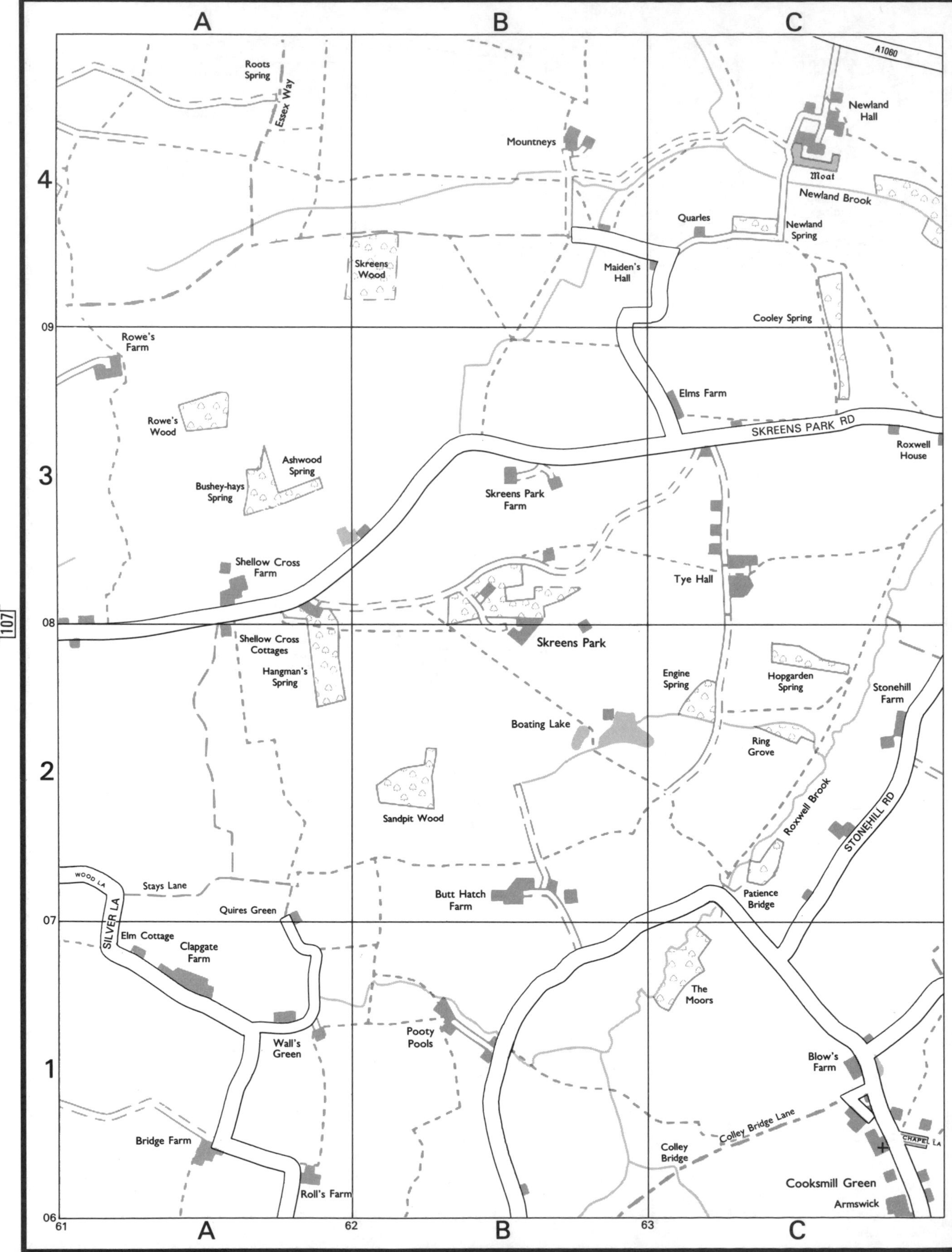
A
B
C
A1060
Roots Spring
Essex Way
Newland Hall
Mountneys
Moat
Newland Brook
Quarles
Newland Spring
Skreens Wood
Maiden's Hall
Cooley Spring
Rowe's Farm
Elms Farm
Rowe's Wood
SKREENS PARK RD
Roxwell House
Ashwood Spring
Bushey-hays Spring
Skreens Park Farm
Shellow Cross Farm
Tye Hall
Skreens Park
Shellow Cross Cottages
Hangman's Spring
Engine Spring
Hopgarden Spring
Stonehill Farm
Boating Lake
Ring Grove
Roxwell Brook
Sandpit Wood
STONEHILL RD
WOOD LA
Stays Lane
Butt Hatch Farm
Patience Bridge
Quires Green
SILVER LA
Elm Cottage
Clapgate Farm
The Moors
Wall's Green
Pooty Pools
Blow's Farm
Colley Bridge Lane
CHAPEL LA
Bridge Farm
Colley Bridge
Cooksmill Green
Roll's Farm
Armswick
4
3
2
1
09
08
07
06
61
62
63

107

121

96

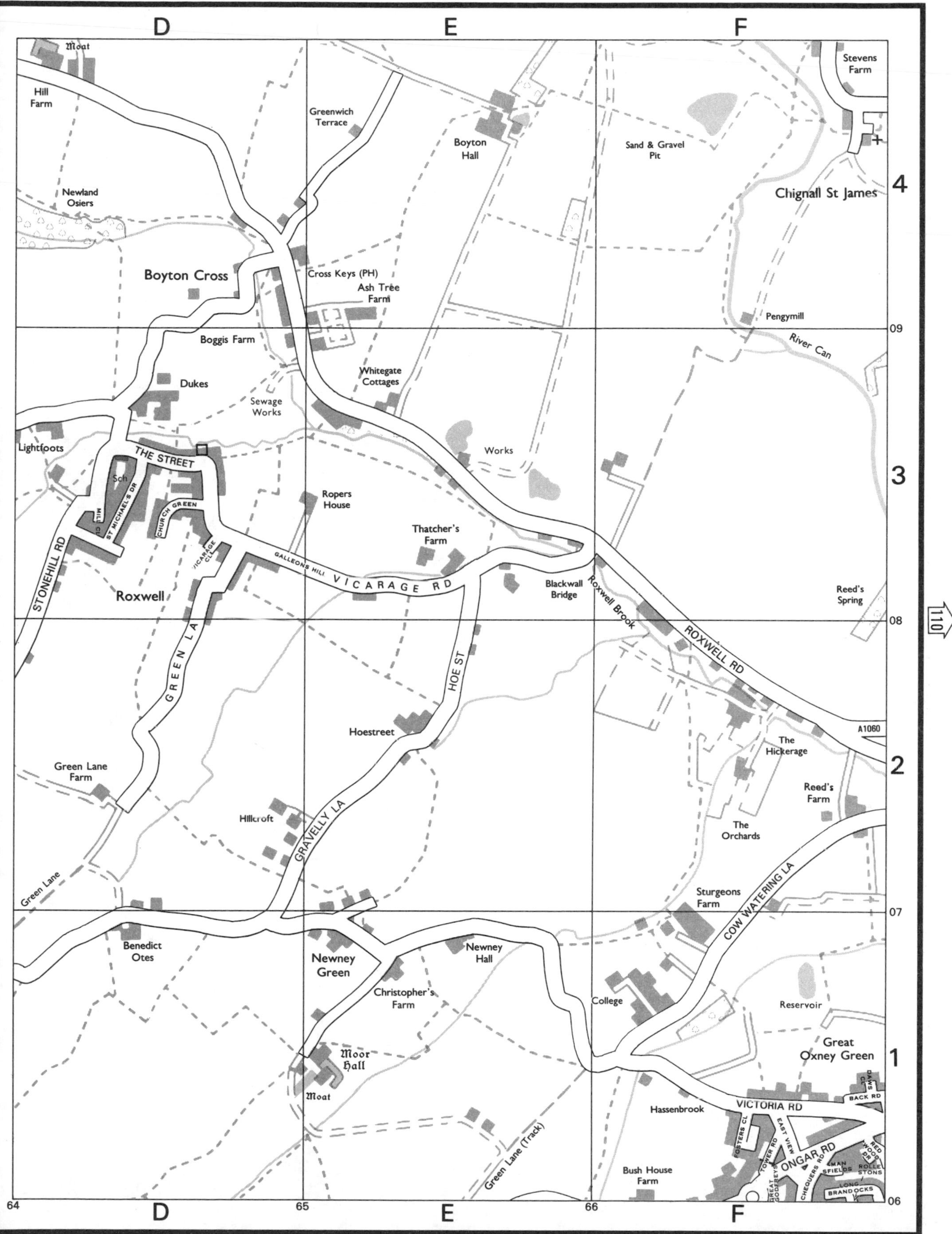

D
E
F
Moat
Hill Farm
Greenwich Terrace
Boyton Hall
Sand & Gravel Pit
Stevens Farm
Chignall St James
Newland Osiers
Boyton Cross
Cross Keys (PH)
Ash Tree Farm
Pengymill
Boggis Farm
River Can
Whitegate Cottages
Dukes
Sewage Works
Works
Lightfoots
THE STREET
Sch
MILL CL
ST MICHAEL'S DR
CHURCH GREEN
Ropers House
Thatcher's Farm
VICARAGE CL
GALLEONS HILL
VICARAGE RD
Blackwall Bridge
Roxwell Brook
STONEHILL RD
Roxwell
Reed's Spring
ROXWELL RD
GREEN LA
HOE ST
Hoestreet
A1060
The Hickerage
Green Lane Farm
Reed's Farm
Hillcroft
GRAVELLY LA
The Orchards
Green Lane
Sturgeons Farm
COW WATERING LA
Benedict Otes
Newney Green
Newney Hall
Christopher's Farm
College
Reservoir
Moor Hall
Moat
Great Oxney Green
DAWS CL
BACK RD
VICTORIA RD
Hassenbrook
Green Lane (Track)
FOSTERS CL
EAST VIEW
TOWER RD
ONGAR RD
CHEQUERS RD
GREAT GODFREYS
Bush House Farm
LONG BRANDOCKS
ROLLESTONS
4
3
2
1
09
08
07
06
64
65
66

110

122

97

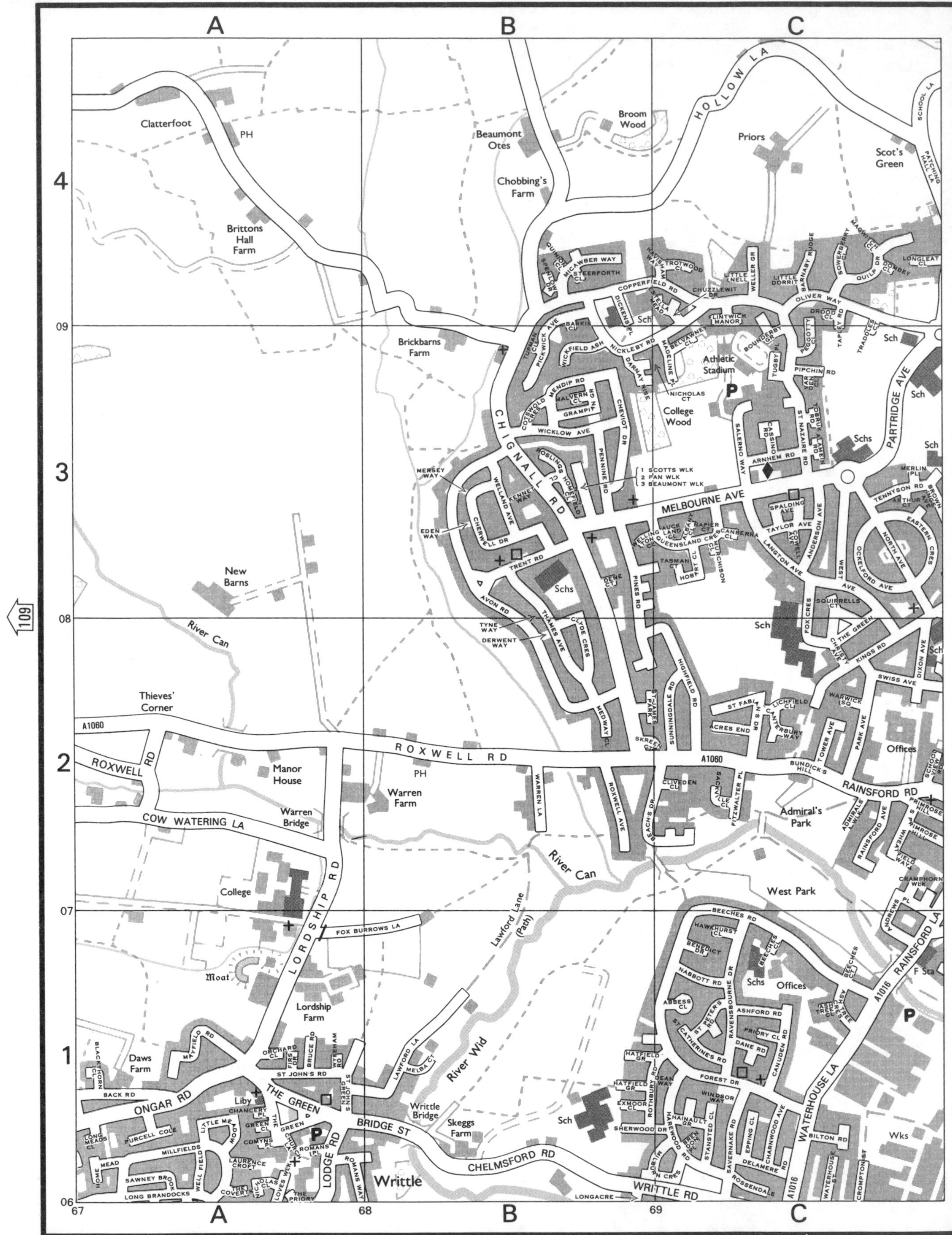

A
B
C
4
3
2
1
09
08
07
06
67
68
69
Clatterfoot
PH
Beaumont Otes
Chobbing's Farm
Broom Wood
HOLLOW LA
Priors
Scot's Green
Brittons Hall Farm
Brickbarns Farm
CHIGNALL RD
Athletic Stadium
College Wood
MELBOURNE AVE
PARTRIDGE AVE
New Barns
River Can
Schs
Sch
Thieves' Corner
A1060
ROXWELL RD
Manor House
Warren Farm
Warren Bridge
COW WATERING LA
RAINSFORD RD
Admiral's Park
West Park
College
LORDSHIP RD
FOX BURROWS LA
Lawford Lane (Path)
Moat
Lordship Farm
River Wid
Daws Farm
ONGAR RD
THE GREEN
BRIDGE ST
Writtle Bridge
Skeggs Farm
CHELMSFORD RD
Writtle
WRITTLE RD
WATERHOUSE LA
RAINSFORD LA
Offices
F Sta
Wks

109

123

98

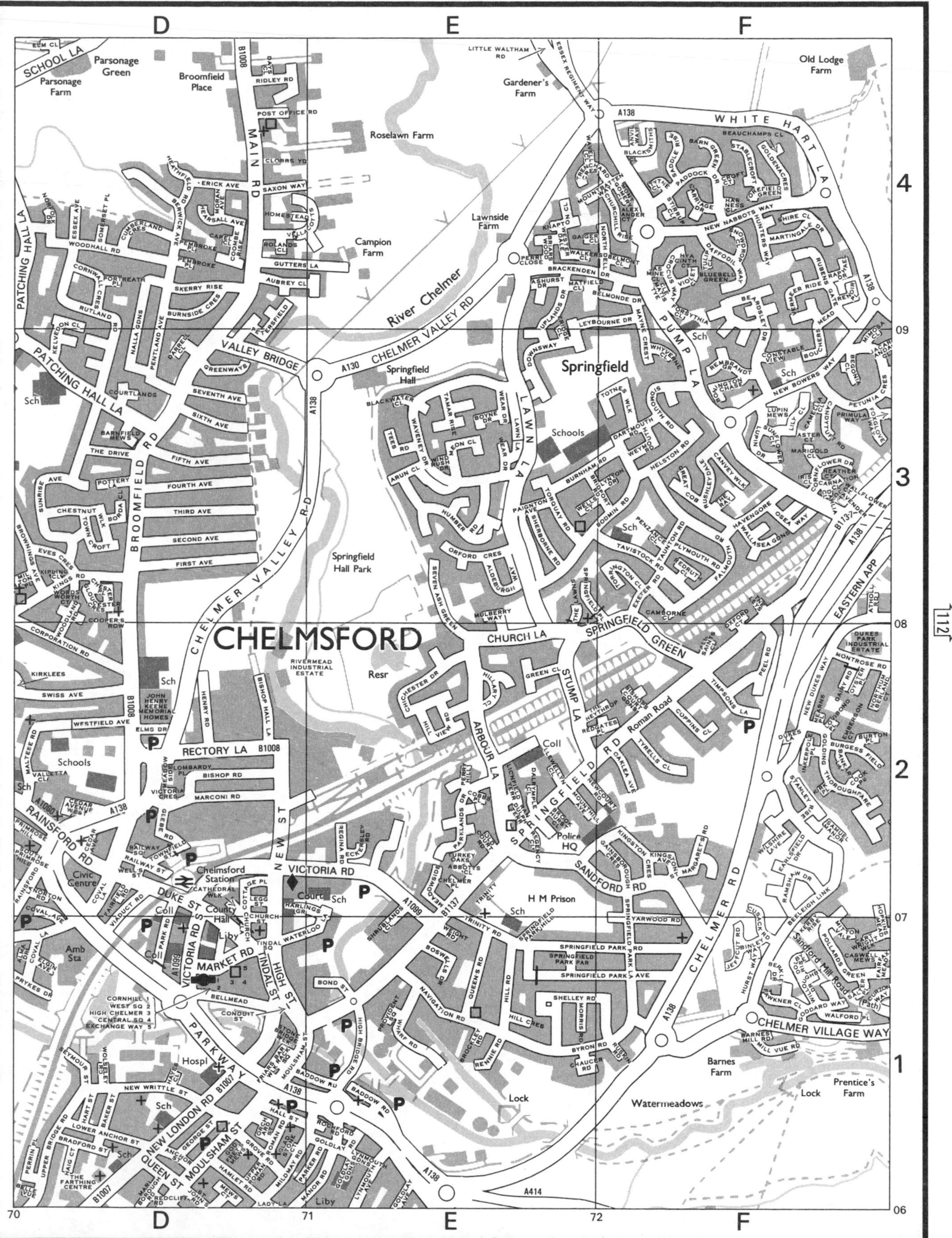
D
E
F
CHELMSFORD
Springfield
River Chelmer
Springfield Hall Park
H M Prison
Chelmsford Station
Broomfield Place
Parsonage Green
Parsonage Farm
Roselawn Farm
Campion Farm
Lawnside Farm
Gardener's Farm
Old Lodge Farm
Barnes Farm
Prentice's Farm
Watermeadows
CHELMER VILLAGE WAY
CHELMER VALLEY RD
WHITE HART LA
PUMP LA
LAWN LA
SPRINGFIELD RD
SPRINGFIELD GREEN
EASTERN APP
PATCHING HALL LA
BROOMFIELD RD
MAIN RD
VALLEY BRIDGE
RIVERMEAD INDUSTRIAL ESTATE
DUKES PARK INDUSTRIAL ESTATE
4
3
2
1
09
08
07
06
70
71
72

112

124

99

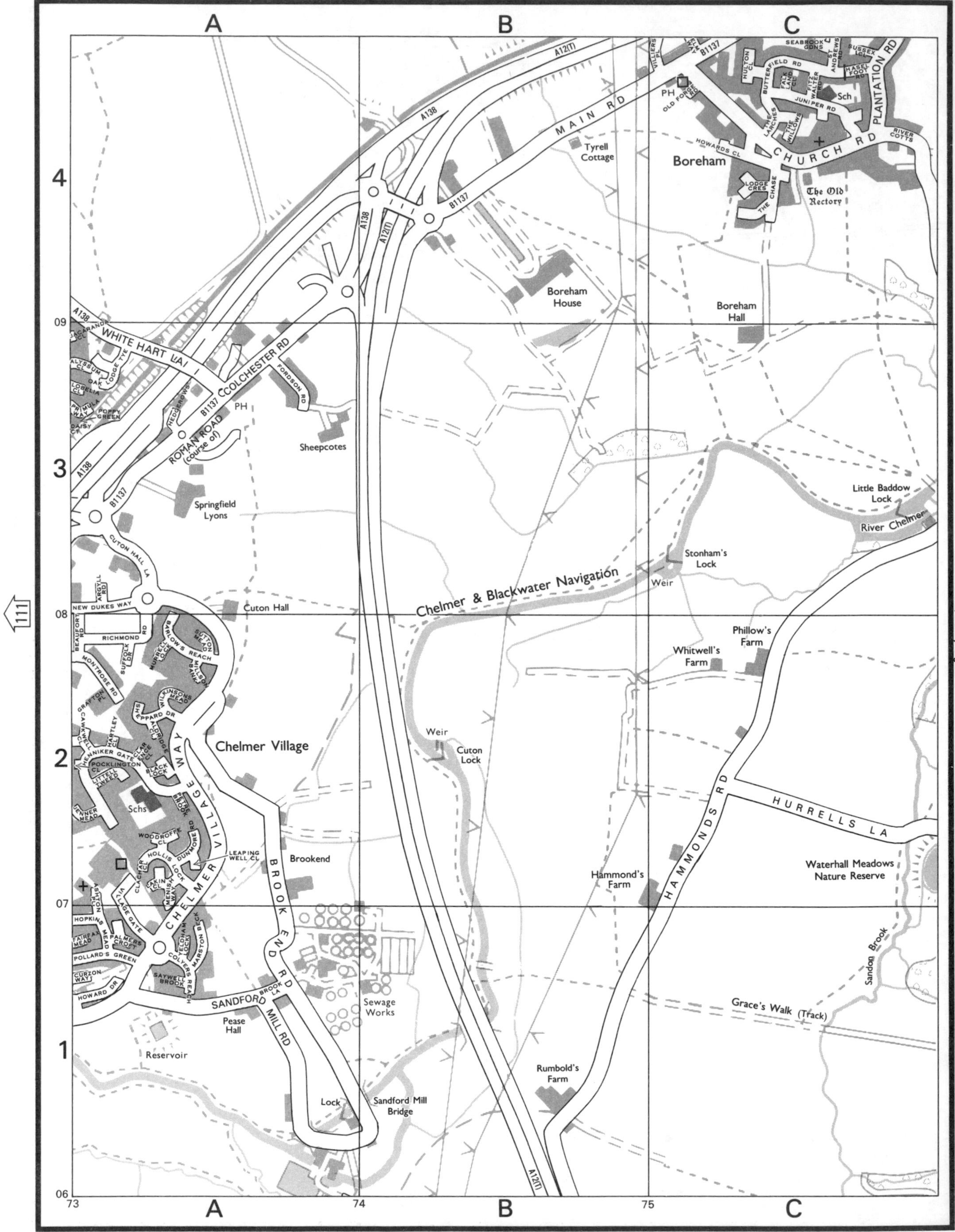

A
B
C
4
3
2
1
09
08
07
06
73
74
75
Boreham
Boreham House
Boreham Hall
Tyrell Cottage
The Old Rectory
MAIN RD
CHURCH RD
PLANTATION RD
B1137
A12(T)
A138
WHITE HART LA
COLCHESTER RD
ROMAN ROAD (course of)
FORDSON RD
Sheepcotes
Springfield Lyons
CUTON HALL LA
Cuton Hall
NEW DUKES WAY
Chelmer & Blackwater Navigation
Weir
Stonham's Lock
Little Baddow Lock
River Chelmer
Phillow's Farm
Whitwell's Farm
Chelmer Village
CHELMER VILLAGE WAY
Schs
Weir
Cuton Lock
HURRELLS LA
HAMMONDS RD
Hammond's Farm
Waterhall Meadows Nature Reserve
Brookend
BROOK END RD
SANDFORD MILL RD
Sewage Works
Pease Hall
Reservoir
Grace's Walk (Track)
Sandon Brook
Rumbold's Farm
Lock
Sandford Mill Bridge
PH
Sch

111

125

100

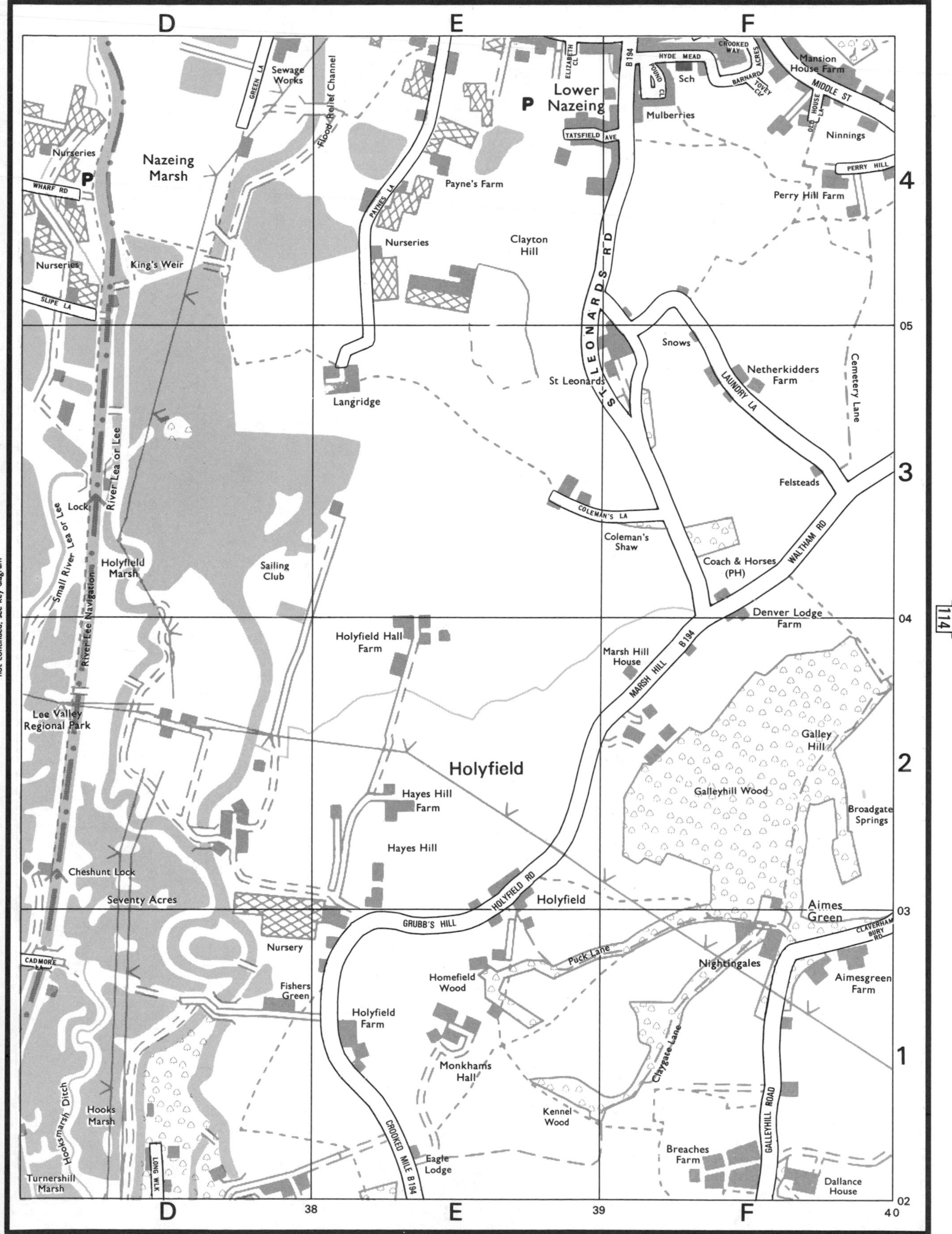

126

not continued, see key diagram

101

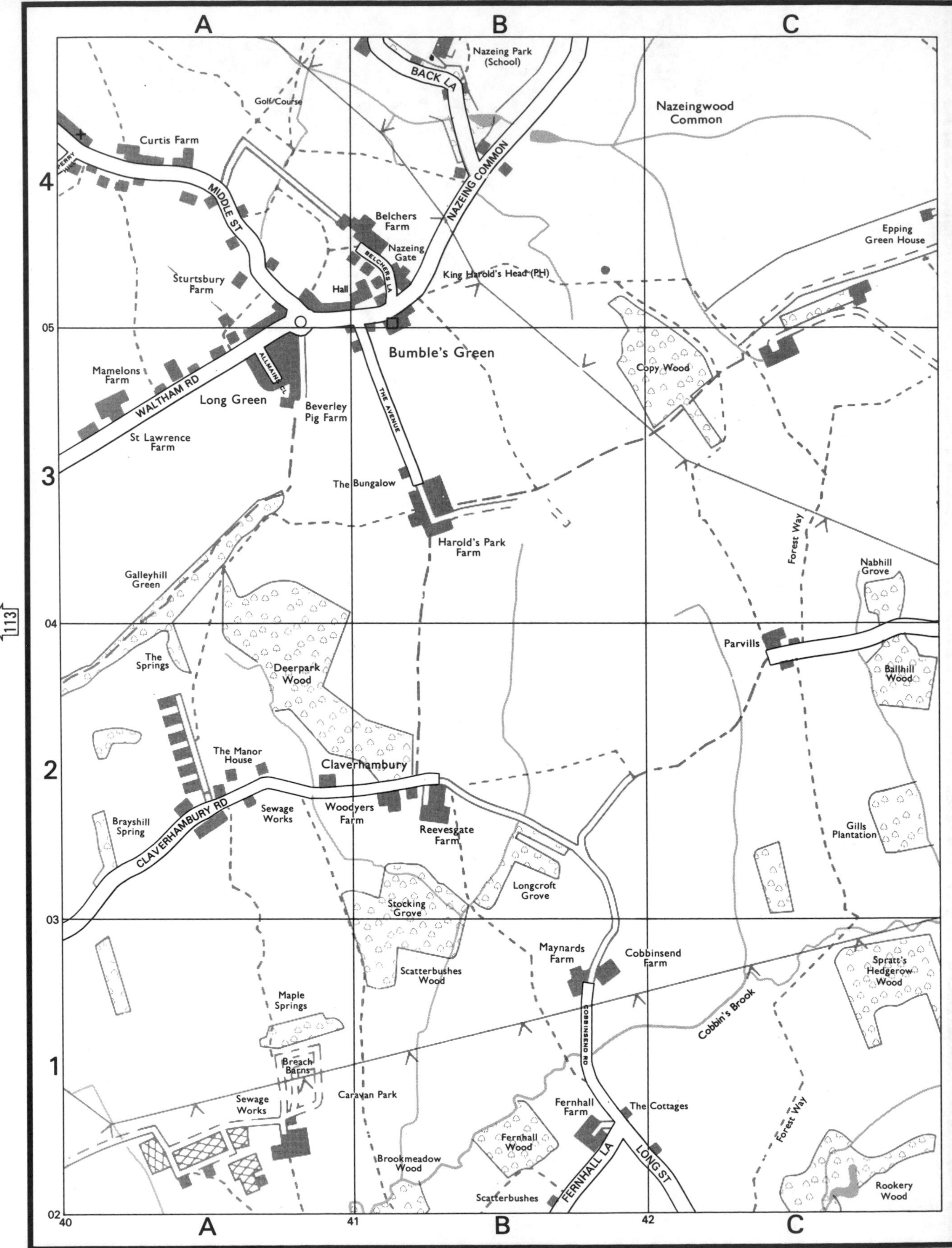

A
B
C
Nazeing Park (School)
BACK LA
Golf Course
Nazeingwood Common
Curtis Farm
PERRY HILL
4
MIDDLE ST
NAZEING COMMON
Belchers Farm
Nazeing Gate
BELCHERS LA
Epping Green House
Sturtsbury Farm
Hall
King Harold's Head (PH)
05
Bumble's Green
Mamelons Farm
ALLMAINS CL
Copy Wood
WALTHAM RD
Long Green
Beverley Pig Farm
THE AVENUE
St Lawrence Farm
3
The Bungalow
Harold's Park Farm
Forest Way
Galleyhill Green
Nabhill Grove
04
Parvills
The Springs
Deerpark Wood
Ballhill Wood
The Manor House
2
Claverhambury
Brayshill Spring
CLAVERHAMBURY RD
Sewage Works
Woodyers Farm
Reevesgate Farm
Gills Plantation
Longcroft Grove
Stocking Grove
03
Maynards Farm
Cobbinsend Farm
Spratt's Hedgerow Wood
Scatterbushes Wood
Maple Springs
COBBINSEND RD
Cobbin's Brook
1
Breach Barns
Sewage Works
Caravan Park
Fernhall Farm
The Cottages
Forest Way
Fernhall Wood
Brookmeadow Wood
FERNHALL LA
LONG ST
Rookery Wood
Scatterbushes
02
40
41
42
A
B
C

113

127

102

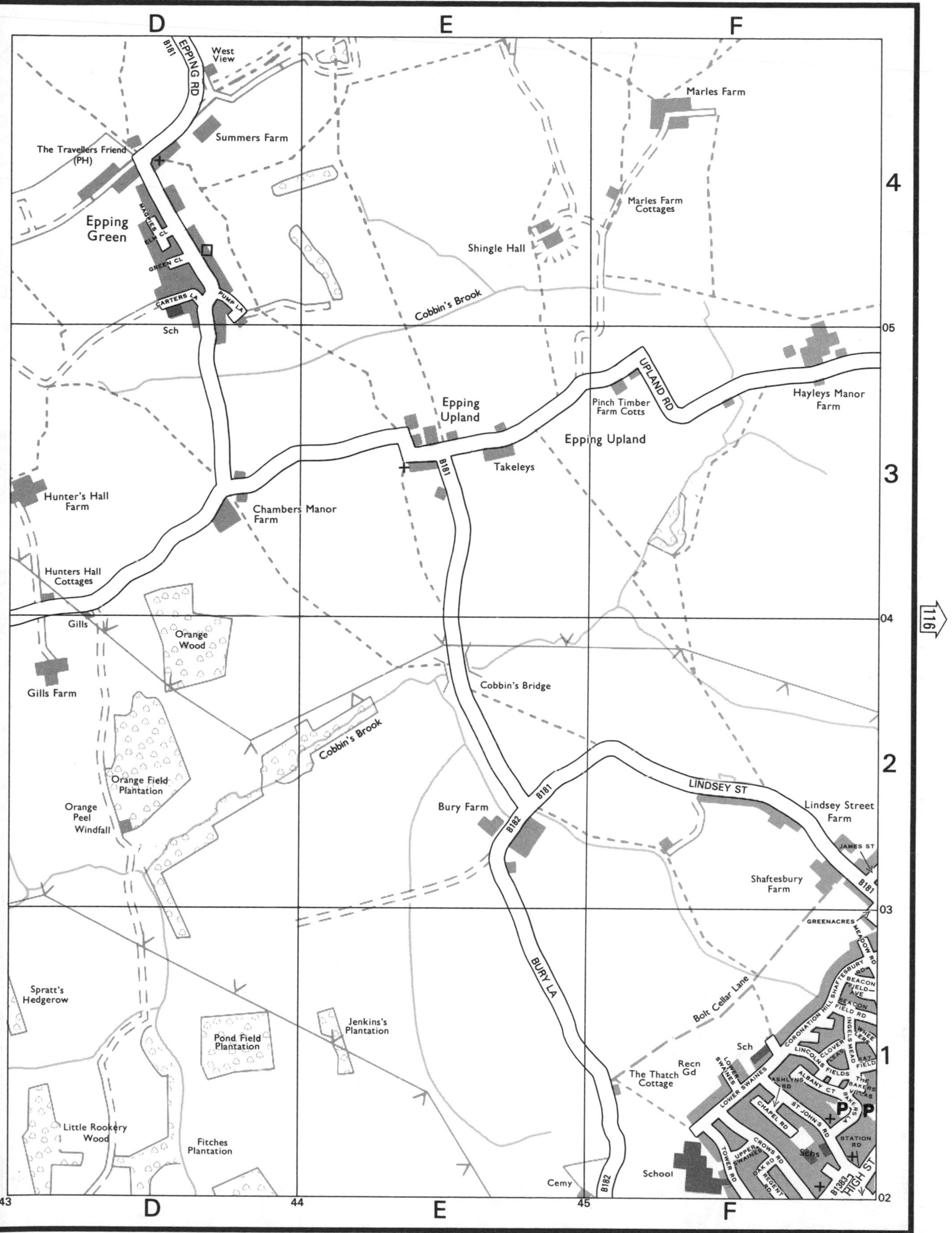
D
E
F
EPPING RD
B181
West View
Marles Farm
Summers Farm
The Travellers Friend (PH)
4
Marles Farm Cottages
Epping Green
MAGPIES CL
ELM CL
GREEN CL
Shingle Hall
CARTERS LA
PUMP LA
Cobbin's Brook
Sch
05
UPLAND RD
Hayleys Manor Farm
Pinch Timber Farm Cotts
Epping Upland
Epping Upland
Takeleys
3
Hunter's Hall Farm
Chambers Manor Farm
Hunters Hall Cottages
04
Gills
Orange Wood
Gills Farm
Cobbin's Bridge
Cobbin's Brook
2
Orange Field Plantation
LINDSEY ST
Lindsey Street Farm
Bury Farm
B182
Orange Peel Windfall
JAMES ST
Shaftesbury Farm
03
GREENACRES
MEADOW RD
BURY LA
SHAFTESBURY RD
BEACON FIELD AVE
BEACON FIELD RD
Spratt's Hedgerow
CORONATION HILL
INGELS MEAD
WHEE LERS
Bolt Cellar Lane
Jenkins's Plantation
Pond Field Plantation
Sch
CLOVER LEAS
RAY FIELD
LINCOLNS FIELDS
1
Recn Gd
LOWER SWAINES
The Thatch Cottage
ASHLYNS RD
ALBANY CT
THE BAKERS VILLAS
LOWER SWAINES
CHAPEL RD
ST JOHN'S RD
P
P
Little Rookery Wood
STATION RD
Fitches Plantation
TOWER RD
UPPER SWAINES
CROWS RD
Schs
OAK RD
REGENT RD
School
Cemy
B182
B1383
HIGH ST
43
44
45
02

116

128

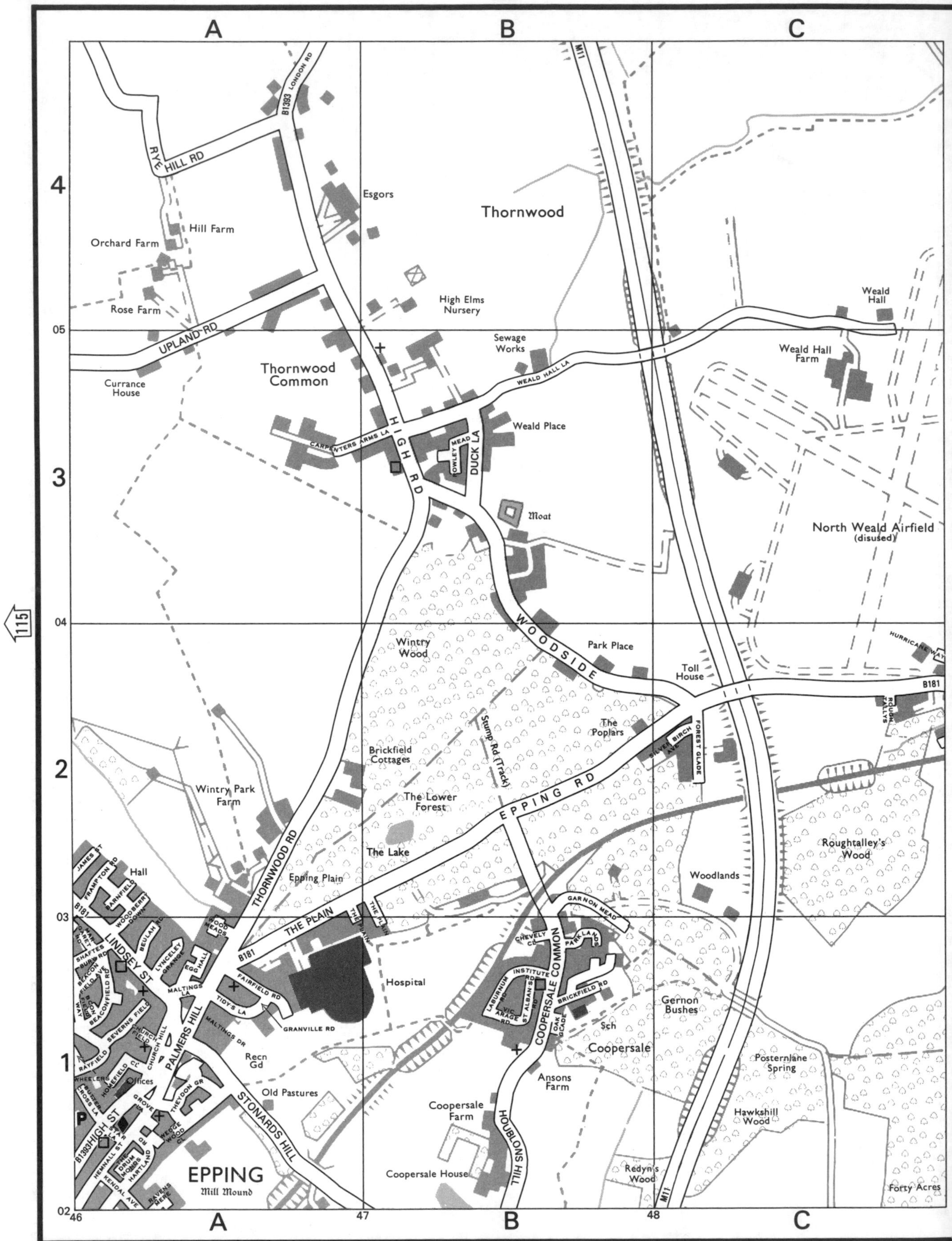
103
A
B
C
4
3
2
1
05
04
03
02
46
47
48
115
129
Thornwood
Thornwood Common
Esgors
Hill Farm
Orchard Farm
Rose Farm
High Elms Nursery
Sewage Works
Weald Hall
Weald Hall Farm
Currance House
Weald Place
Moat
North Weald Airfield
(disused)
Wintry Wood
Park Place
Toll House
The Poplars
Brickfield Cottages
Wintry Park Farm
The Lower Forest
The Lake
Epping Plain
Roughtalley's Wood
Woodlands
Hall
Hospital
Gernon Bushes
Sch
Coopersale
Recn Gd
Offices
Old Pastures
Ansons Farm
Coopersale Farm
Posternlane Spring
Hawkshill Wood
Coopersale House
Redyn's Wood
Forty Acres
EPPING
Mill Mound
RYE HILL RD
UPLAND RD
B1393 LONDON RD
HIGH RD
CARPENTERS ARMS LA
ROWLEY MEAD
DUCK LA
WEALD HALL LA
WOODSIDE
Stump Rd (Track)
EPPING RD
THORNWOOD RD
THE PLAIN
SILVER BIRCH AVE
FOREST GLADE
GARNON MEAD
CHEVELY CL
PARK LANDS
COOPERSALE COMMON
BRICKFIELD RD
INSTITUTE RD
LABURNUM RD
ST ALBAN'S RD
VICARAGE RD
OAK GLADE
HOUBLONS HILL
STONARDS HILL
GRANVILLE RD
FAIRFIELD RD
TIDY'S LA
MALTINGS LA
MALTINGS DR
PALMERS HILL
CHURCH HILL
LINDSEY ST
THEYDON GR
WEDGE WOOD CL
HIGH ST
B1393
B181
HURRICANE WAY
ROUGH TALLYS
M11
JAMES ST
FRAMPTON RD
BARNFIELD
WOODBERRY DOWN
BEULAH RD
LYNCELEY GRANGE
EGG HALL
WOOD MEADS
BEACONFIELD RD
SEVERNS FIELD
RAYFIELD
HOMEFIELD CL
HEMNALL ST
KENDAL AVE
HARTLAND RD
THE DRUM MOBBS
RAVENS MERE
P

104

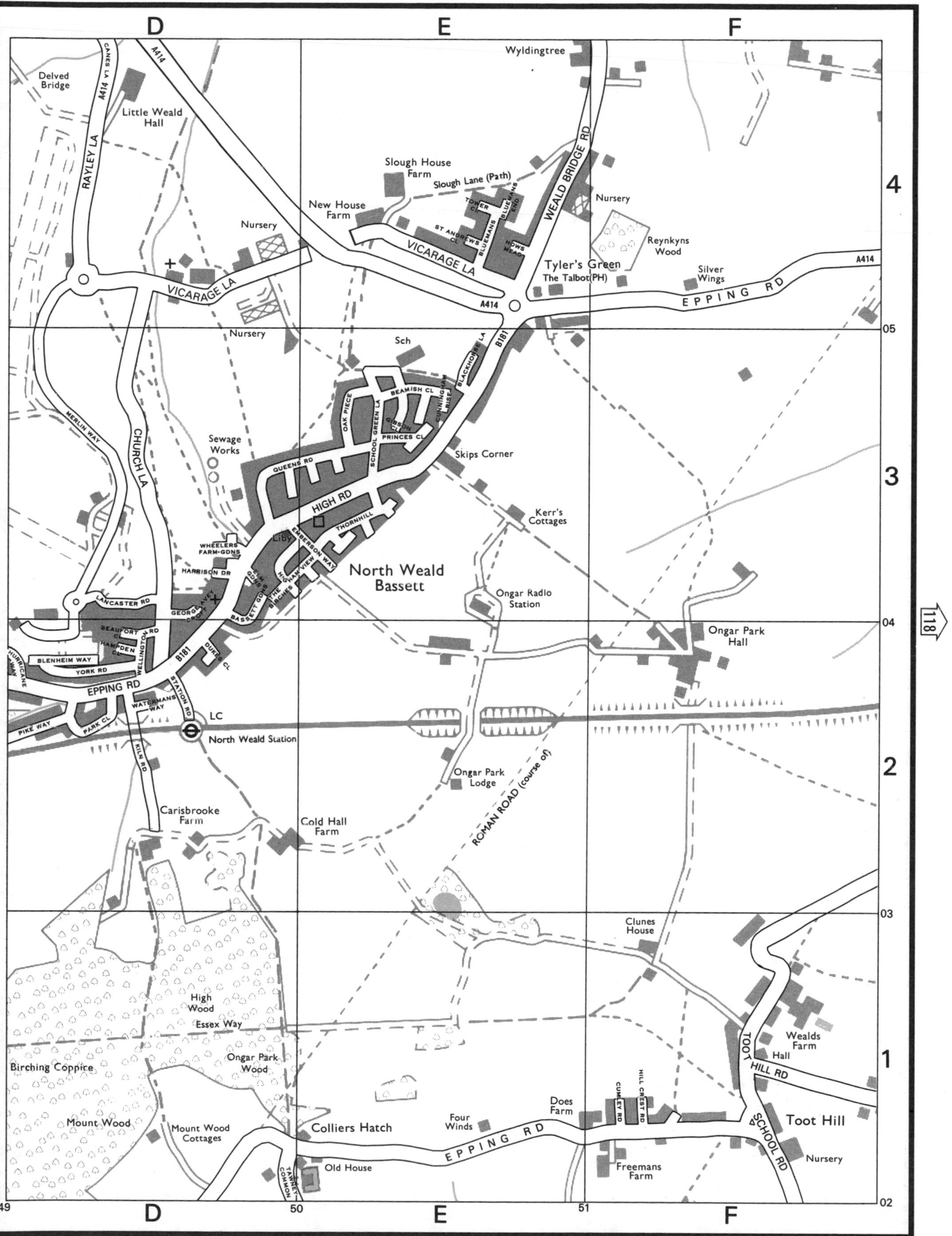

D
E
F
Delved Bridge
Little Weald Hall
RAYLEY LA
CANES LA
A414
Wyldingtree
Slough House Farm
Slough Lane (Path)
New House Farm
Nursery
WEALD BRIDGE RD
Reynkyns Wood
VICARAGE LA
TOWER CL
BLUEMANS END
BLUEMANS
ST ANDREWS CL
HOWS MEAD
Tyler's Green
The Talbot (PH)
Silver Wings
EPPING RD
B181
Sch
Nursery
BLACKHORSE LA
BEAMISH CL
CUNNINGHAM RISE
GIBSON CL
PRINCES CL
OAK PIECE
SCHOOL GREEN LA
QUEENS RD
MERLIN WAY
CHURCH LA
Sewage Works
Skips Corner
HIGH RD
THORNHILL
Kerr's Cottages
WHEELERS FARM GDNS
Liby
EMERSON WAY
North Weald Bassett
HARRISON DR
ELM GDNS
HIGHVIEW
THE BIRCHES
BASSETT GDNS
GEORGE AVEY CROFT
LANCASTER RD
Ongar Radio Station
Ongar Park Hall
BEAUFORT RD
HAMPDEN CL
WELLINGTON RD
BLENHEIM WAY
YORK RD
HURRICANE WAY
DUKES CL
EPPING RD
STATION RD
WATERMANS WAY
PIKE WAY
PARK CL
LC
North Weald Station
KILN RD
Ongar Park Lodge
ROMAN ROAD (course of)
Carisbrooke Farm
Cold Hall Farm
Clunes House
High Wood
Essex Way
Wealds Farm
Hall
TOOT HILL RD
Birching Coppice
Ongar Park Wood
CUMLEY RD
HILL CREST RD
Does Farm
Four Winds
Toot Hill
SCHOOL RD
Mount Wood
Mount Wood Cottages
Colliers Hatch
EPPING RD
TAWNEY COMMON
Old House
Freemans Farm
Nursery
4
3
2
1
05
04
03
02
49
50
51

118

130

105

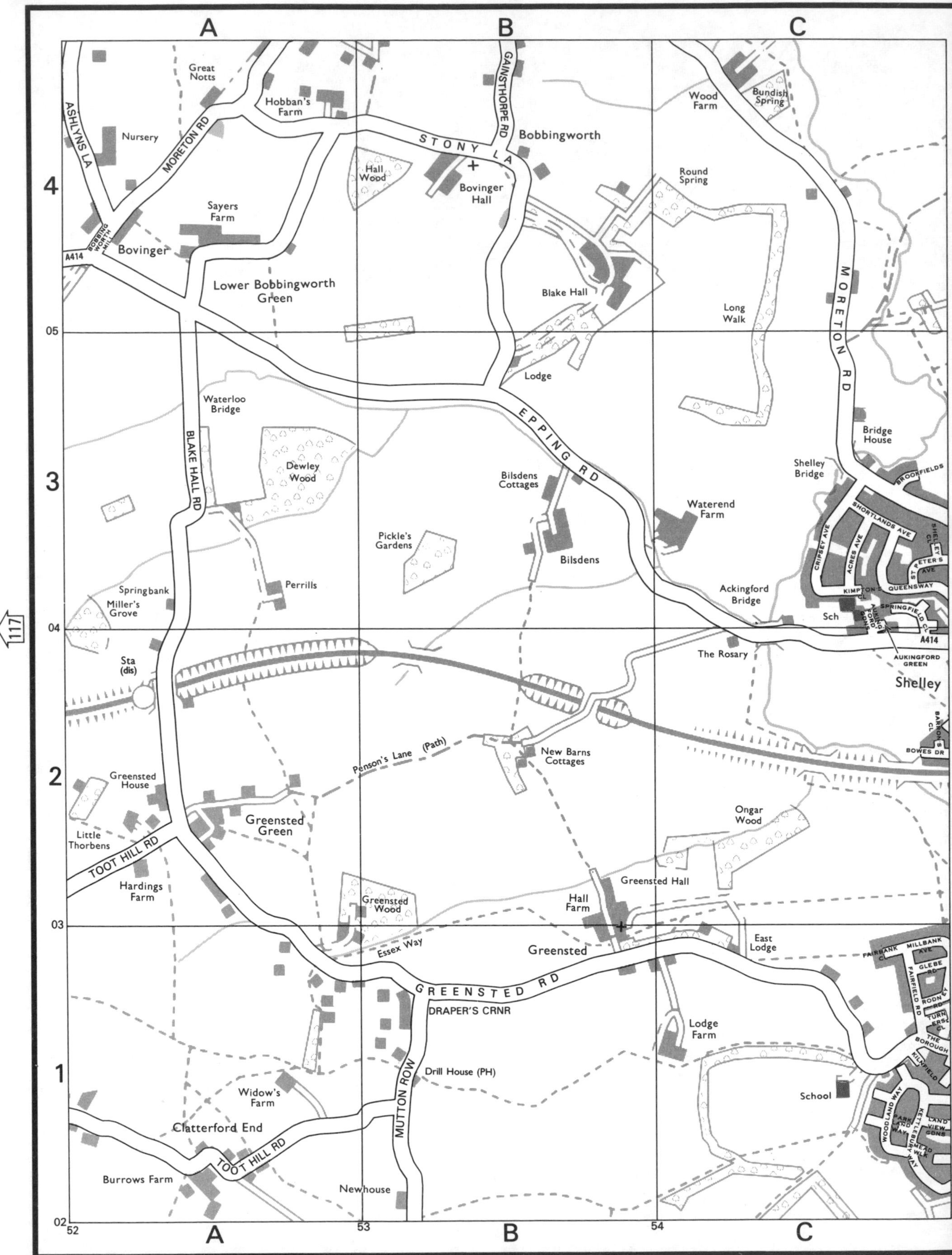
A
B
C
Great Notts
Hobban's Farm
GAINSTHORPE RD
Wood Farm
Bundish Spring
ASHLYNS LA
Nursery
MORETON RD
STONY LA
Bobbingworth
Hall Wood
Bovinger Hall
Round Spring
4
Sayers Farm
A414
BOBBING WORTH MILL
Bovinger
Lower Bobbingworth Green
Blake Hall
Long Walk
MORETON RD
05
Lodge
Waterloo Bridge
EPPING RD
Bridge House
BLAKE HALL RD
Dewley Wood
3
Bilsdens Cottages
Shelley Bridge
BROOKFIELDS
Waterend Farm
SHORTLANDS AVE
Pickle's Gardens
CRIPSEY AVE
ACRES AVE
SHELLEY CL
ST PETER'S AVE
Bilsdens
Perrills
Springbank
Ackingford Bridge
KIMPTONS
QUEENSWAY
Miller's Grove
Sch
SPRINGFIELD CL
A414
04
The Rosary
AUKINGFORD GREEN
Sta (dis)
Shelley
BARRONS CL
BOWES DR
Penson's Lane (Path)
New Barns Cottages
2
Greensted House
Greensted Green
Ongar Wood
Little Thorbens
TOOT HILL RD
Greensted Hall
Hardings Farm
Hall Farm
Greensted Wood
03
Essex Way
Greensted
East Lodge
FAIRBANK CL
MILLBANK AVE
GLEBE RD
GREENSTED RD
FAIRFIELD RD
RODNEY RD
DRAPER'S CRNR
TURNERS CL
Lodge Farm
THE BOROUGH
1
Drill House (PH)
KILNFIELD
MUTTON ROW
School
Widow's Farm
WOODLAND WAY
PARK LAND WAY
KETTLEBURY WAY
LAND VIEW GDNS
Clatterford End
MEAD WLK
TOOT HILL RD
Burrows Farm
Newhouse
02
52
53
54
A
B
C

117

131

106

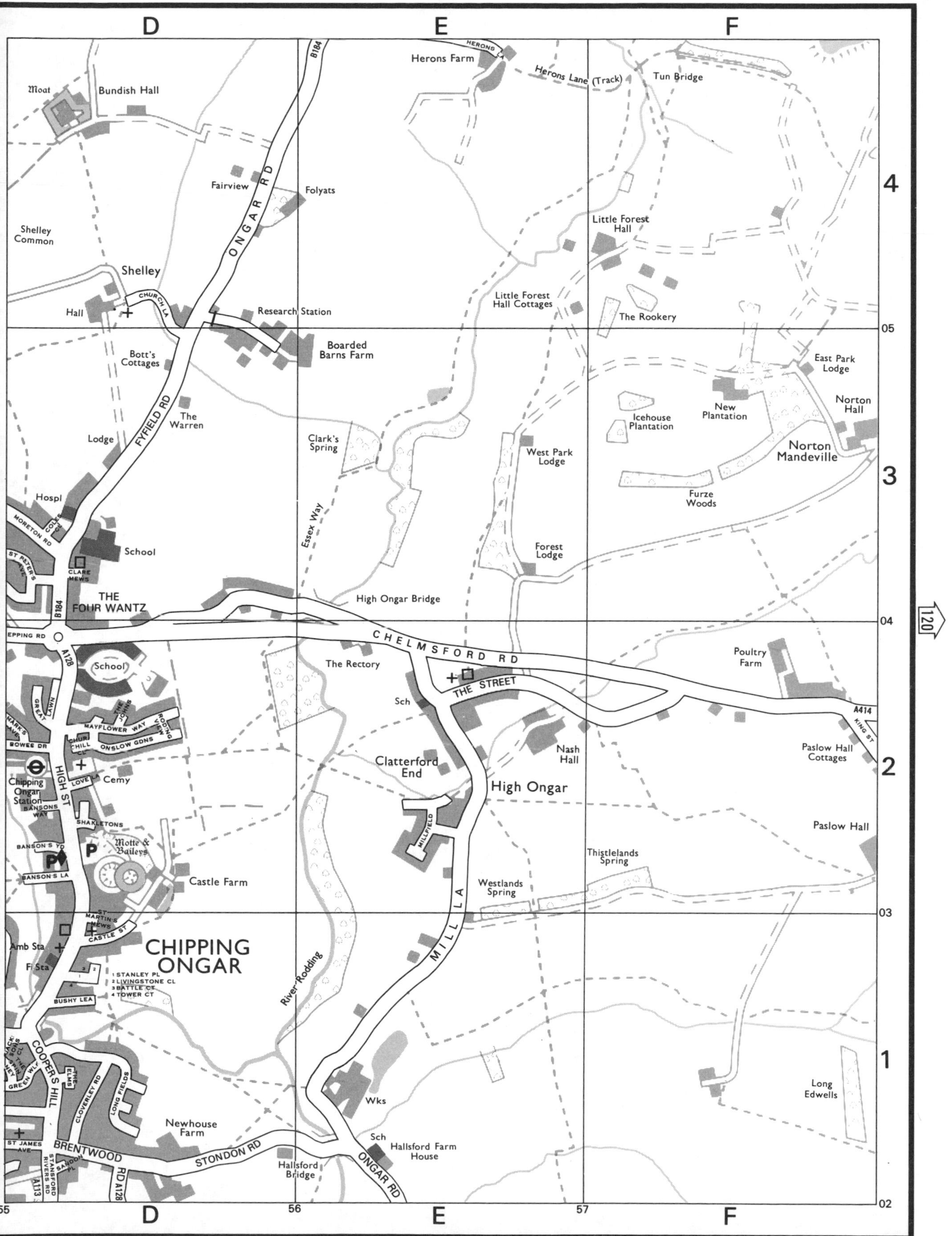
D
E
F
Herons Farm
Herons Lane (Track)
Tun Bridge
Moat
Bundish Hall
Fairview
Folyats
ONGAR RD
Shelley Common
Shelley
Little Forest Hall
Little Forest Hall Cottages
The Rookery
Hall
CHURCH LA
Research Station
Boarded Barns Farm
Bott's Cottages
East Park Lodge
Icehouse Plantation
New Plantation
Norton Hall
FYFIELD RD
The Warren
Lodge
Clark's Spring
West Park Lodge
Norton Mandeville
Hospl
Essex Way
Furze Woods
MORETON RD
School
Forest Lodge
CLARE MEWS
THE FOUR WANTZ
High Ongar Bridge
B184
EPPING RD
A128
CHELMSFORD RD
The Rectory
Poultry Farm
School
THE STREET
Sch
A414
KING ST
MAYFLOWER WAY
ONSLOW GDNS
BOWES DR
Nash Hall
Paslow Hall Cottages
Clatterford End
High Ongar
Chipping Ongar Station
Cemy
HIGH ST
LOVE LA
BANSONS WAY
SHAKLETONS
MILLFIELD
Paslow Hall
Motte & Baileys
BANSON'S LA
Castle Farm
Thistlelands Spring
Westlands Spring
ST MARTIN'S MEWS
CASTLE ST
CHIPPING ONGAR
Amb Sta
Fi Sta
1 STANLEY PL
2 LIVINGSTONE CL
3 BATTLE CT
4 TOWER CT
MILL LA
River Rodding
BUSHY LEA
COOPERS HILL
CLOVERLEY RD
LONG FIELDS
Long Edwells
Wks
Newhouse Farm
BRENTWOOD RD A128
STONDON RD
Sch
Hallsford Farm House
Hallsford Bridge
ONGAR RD
ST JAMES AVE
STANSFORD RIVERS RD
A113
4
05
3
04
2
03
1
02
55
56
57

120

132

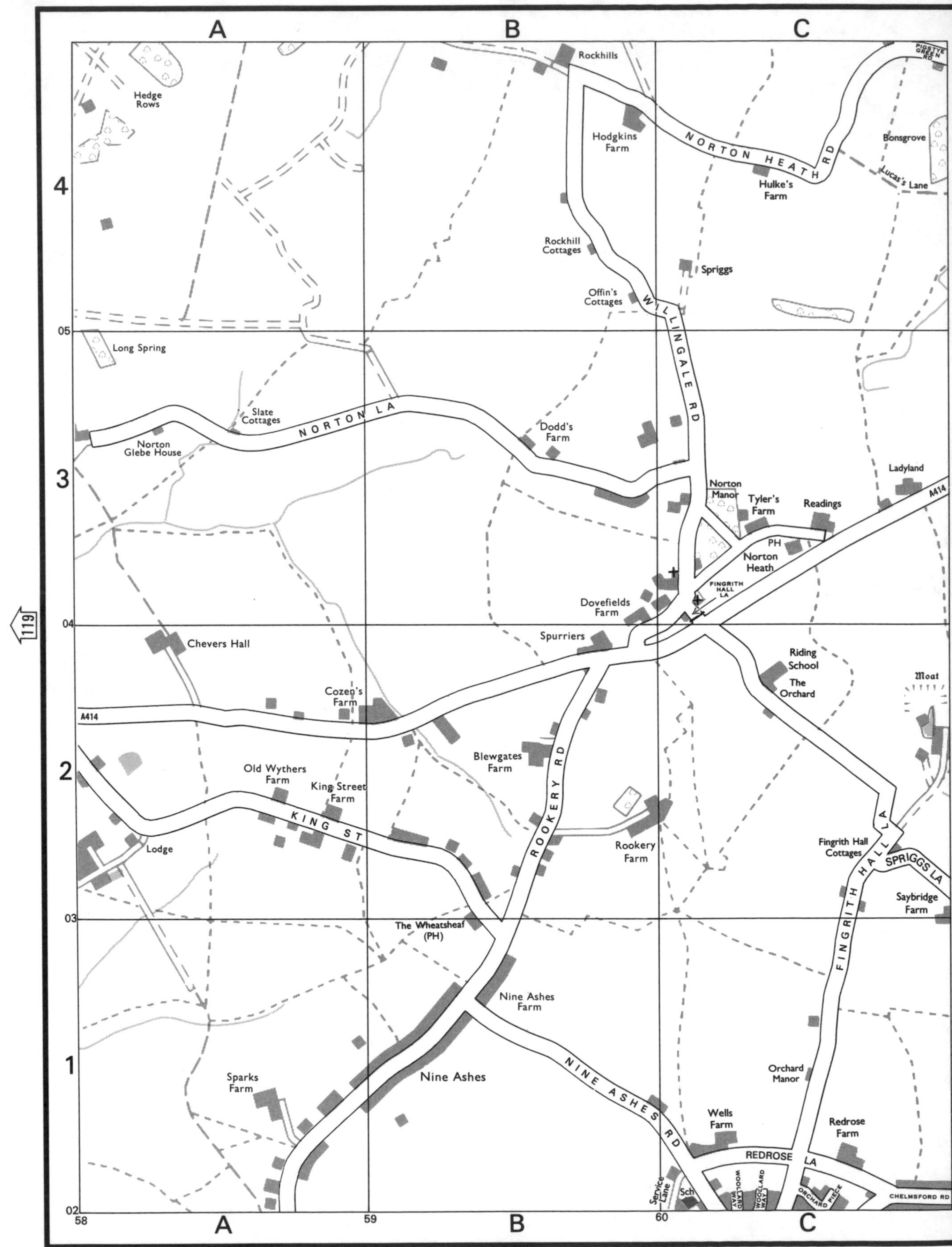
107
A
B
C
Rockhills
PIGSTYE GREEN RD
Hedge Rows
Hodgkins Farm
NORTON HEATH RD
Bonsgrove
Lucas's Lane
Hulke's Farm
4
Rockhill Cottages
Spriggs
Offin's Cottages
WILLINGALE RD
05
Long Spring
Slate Cottages
NORTON LA
Norton Glebe House
Dodd's Farm
3
Norton Manor
Tyler's Farm
Readings
Ladyland
A414
PH
Norton Heath
FINGRITH HALL LA
Dovefields Farm
119
04
Chevers Hall
Spurriers
Riding School
The Orchard
Moat
Cozen's Farm
A414
Blewgates Farm
ROOKERY RD
2
Old Wythers Farm
King Street Farm
KING ST
Lodge
Rookery Farm
Fingrith Hall Cottages
FINGRITH HALL LA
SPRIGGS LA
Saybridge Farm
03
The Wheatsheaf (PH)
Nine Ashes Farm
1
Nine Ashes
NINE ASHES RD
Orchard Manor
Sparks Farm
Wells Farm
Redrose Farm
REDROSE LA
Service Lane
Sch
WOOLLARD WAY
WOOLLARD WAY
ORCHARD PIECE
CHELMSFORD RD
02
58
59
60
A
B
C
133

108

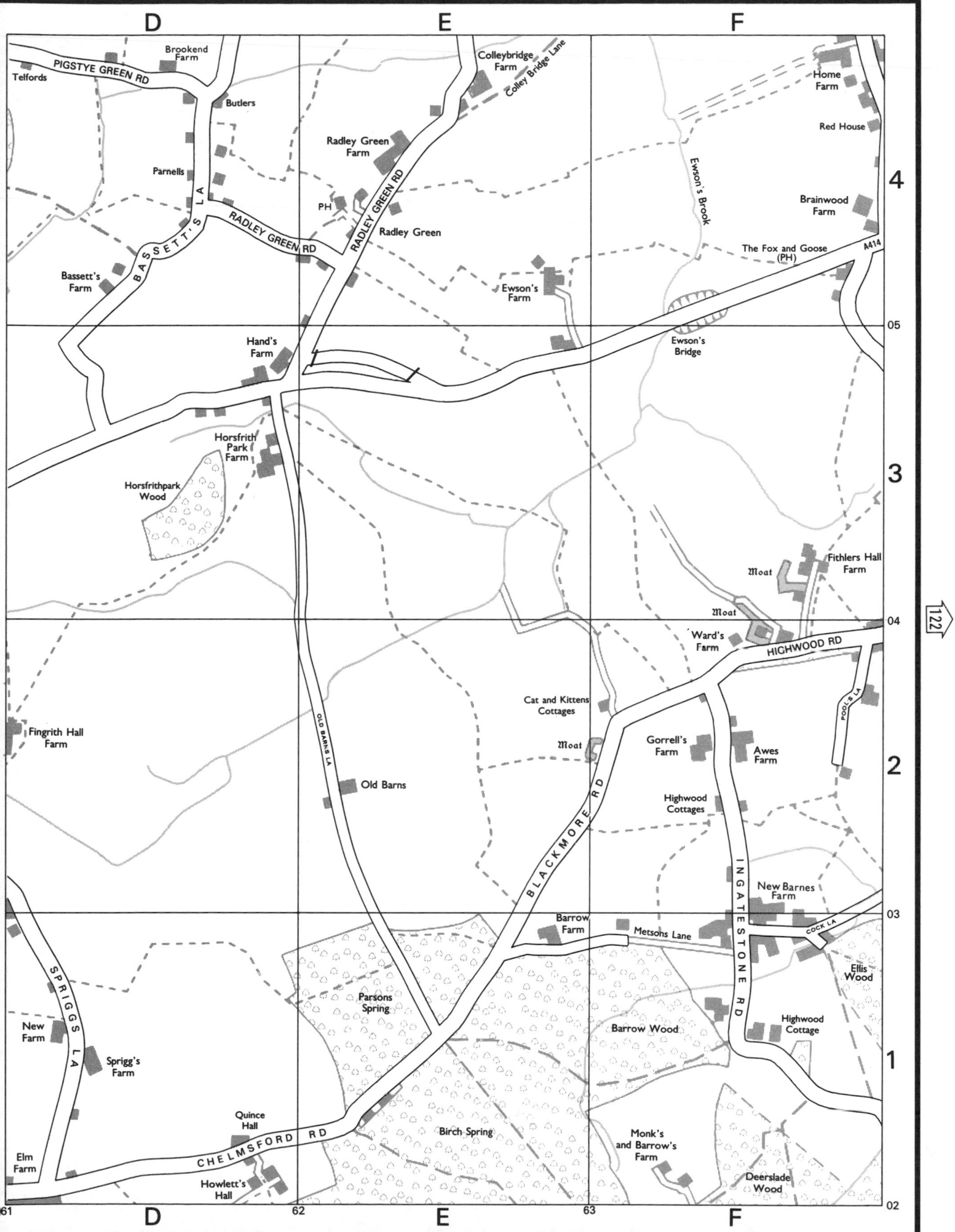
D
E
F
Brookend Farm
Telfords
PIGSTYE GREEN RD
Butlers
Colleybridge Farm
Colley Bridge Lane
Home Farm
Red House
Radley Green Farm
Parnells
PH
RADLEY GREEN RD
Radley Green
Ewson's Brook
Brainwood Farm
The Fox and Goose (PH)
A414
BASSETT'S LA
Bassett's Farm
Ewson's Farm
Hand's Farm
Ewson's Bridge
Horsfrith Park Farm
Horsfrithpark Wood
Moat
Fithlers Hall Farm
Moat
Ward's Farm
HIGHWOOD RD
Cat and Kittens Cottages
POOLS LA
Fingrith Hall Farm
Moat
Gorrell's Farm
Awes Farm
OLD BARNS LA
Old Barns
Highwood Cottages
BLACKMORE RD
INGATESTONE RD
New Barnes Farm
Barrow Farm
Metsons Lane
COCK LA
Ellis Wood
SPRIGGS LA
Parsons Spring
New Farm
Barrow Wood
Highwood Cottage
Sprigg's Farm
Quince Hall
Birch Spring
Elm Farm
CHELMSFORD RD
Monk's and Barrow's Farm
Howlett's Hall
Deerslade Wood
4
05
3
04
2
03
1
02
61
62
63
D
E
F

122

134

109

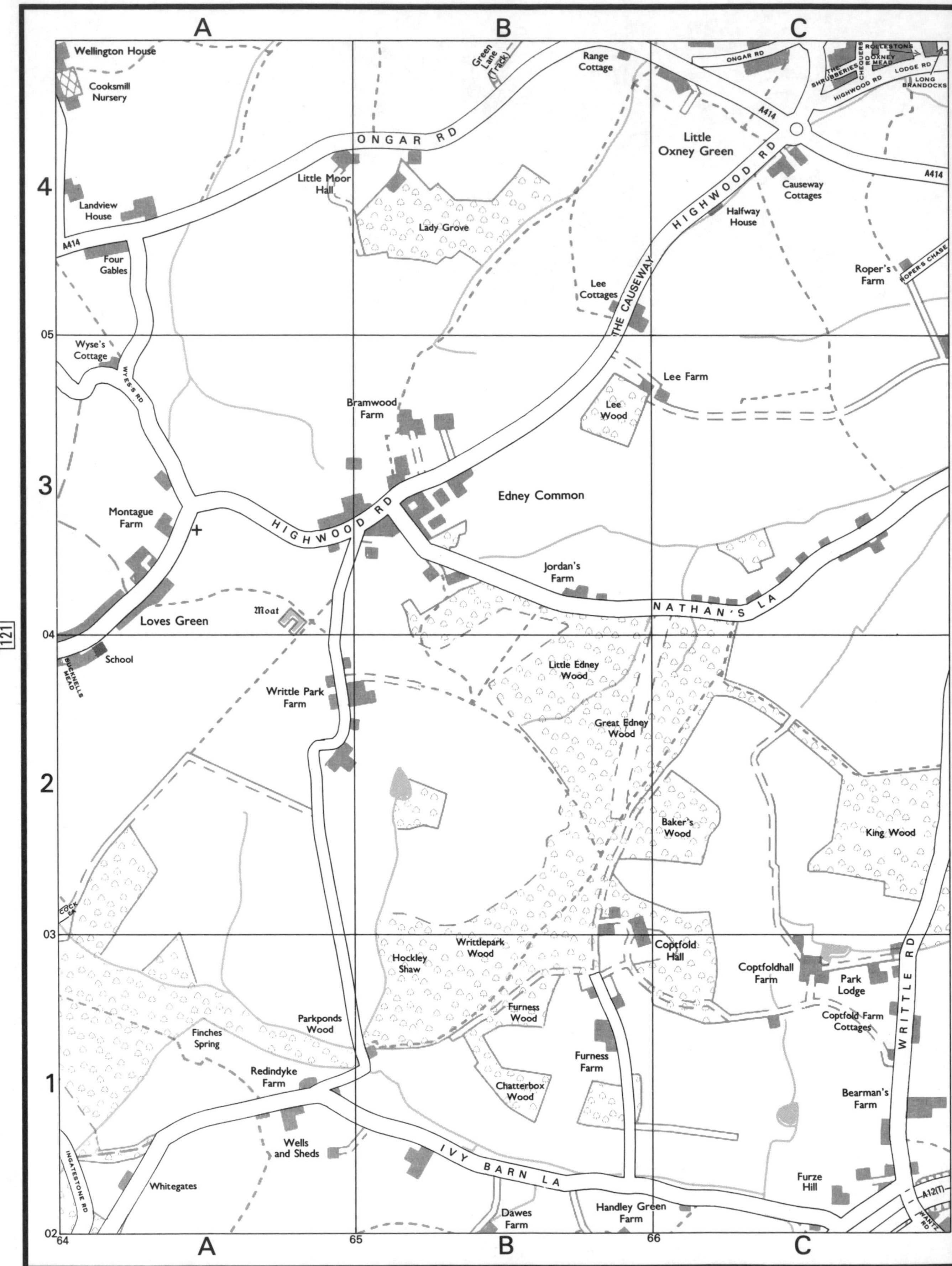

A
B
C
Wellington House
Cooksmill Nursery
Green Lane (Track)
Range Cottage
ONGAR RD
THE SHRUBBERIES
CHEQUERS RD
ROLLESTONS
OXNEY MEAD
LODGE RD
HIGHWOOD RD
LONG BRANDOCKS
A414
Little Oxney Green
ONGAR RD
Little Moor Hall
Landview House
Lady Grove
Causeway Cottages
Halfway House
HIGHWOOD RD
4
A414
Four Gables
Lee Cottages
THE CAUSEWAY
Roper's Farm
ROPER'S CHASE
05
Wyse's Cottage
WYSE'S RD
Lee Farm
Lee Wood
Bramwood Farm
3
Edney Common
Montague Farm
HIGHWOOD RD
Jordan's Farm
Loves Green
Moat
NATHAN'S LA
04
School
BUCKNELLS MEAD
Little Edney Wood
Writtle Park Farm
Great Edney Wood
2
Baker's Wood
King Wood
COCK LA
03
Coptfold Hall
Hockley Shaw
Writtlepark Wood
Coptfoldhall Farm
Park Lodge
Parkponds Wood
Furness Wood
Coptfold Farm Cottages
Finches Spring
WRITTLE RD
Furness Farm
Redindyke Farm
1
Chatterbox Wood
Bearman's Farm
Wells and Sheds
INGATESTONE RD
IVY BARN LA
Whitegates
Furze Hill
A12(T)
Dawes Farm
Handley Green Farm
MANTZ RD
02
64
65
66
A
B
C

121

135

110

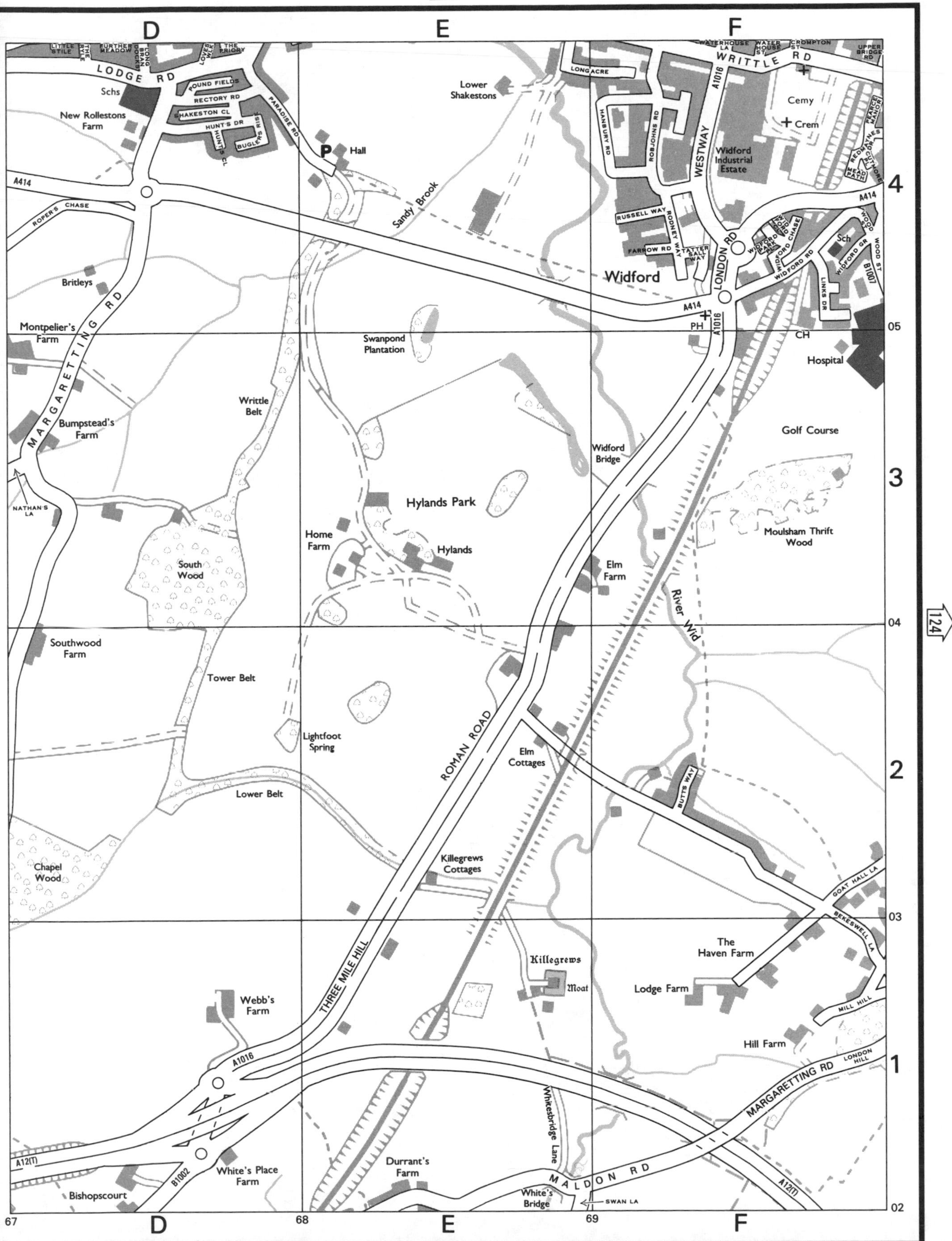
D
E
F
LODGE RD
Schs
New Rollestons Farm
ROUND FIELDS
RECTORY RD
SHAKESTON CL
HUNT'S DR
BUGLERS RISE
PARADISE RD
Hall
Lower Shakestons
LONGACRE
WRITTLE RD
WATERHOUSE LA
CROMPTON ST
UPPER BRIDGE RD
Cemy
Crem
HANBURY RD
ROBJOHNS RD
WESTWAY
Widford Industrial Estate
A414
ROPER'S CHASE
Sandy Brook
RUSSELL WAY
RODNEY WAY
FARROW RD
TATTERSALL WAY
LONDON RD
WIDFORD CHASE
WIDFORD RD
Sch
WIDFORD GR
WOOD ST
B1007
LINKS DR
Widford
Britleys
MARGARETTING RD
Montpelier's Farm
PH
CH
Swanpond Plantation
Hospital
Writtle Belt
Bumpstead's Farm
Golf Course
Widford Bridge
NATHAN'S LA
Hylands Park
Moulsham Thrift Wood
Home Farm
Hylands
South Wood
Elm Farm
River Wid
Southwood Farm
Tower Belt
Lightfoot Spring
ROMAN ROAD
Elm Cottages
BUTTS WAY
Lower Belt
Chapel Wood
Killegrews Cottages
GOAT HALL LA
BEKESWELL LA
The Haven Farm
Killegrews
Moat
Lodge Farm
THREE MILE HILL
Webb's Farm
MILL HILL
Hill Farm
A1016
LONDON HILL
MARGARETTING RD
Whitesbridge Lane
A12(T)
White's Place Farm
B1002
Durrant's Farm
MALDON RD
White's Bridge
SWAN LA
Bishopscourt
4
05
3
04
2
03
1
02
67
68
69

124

136

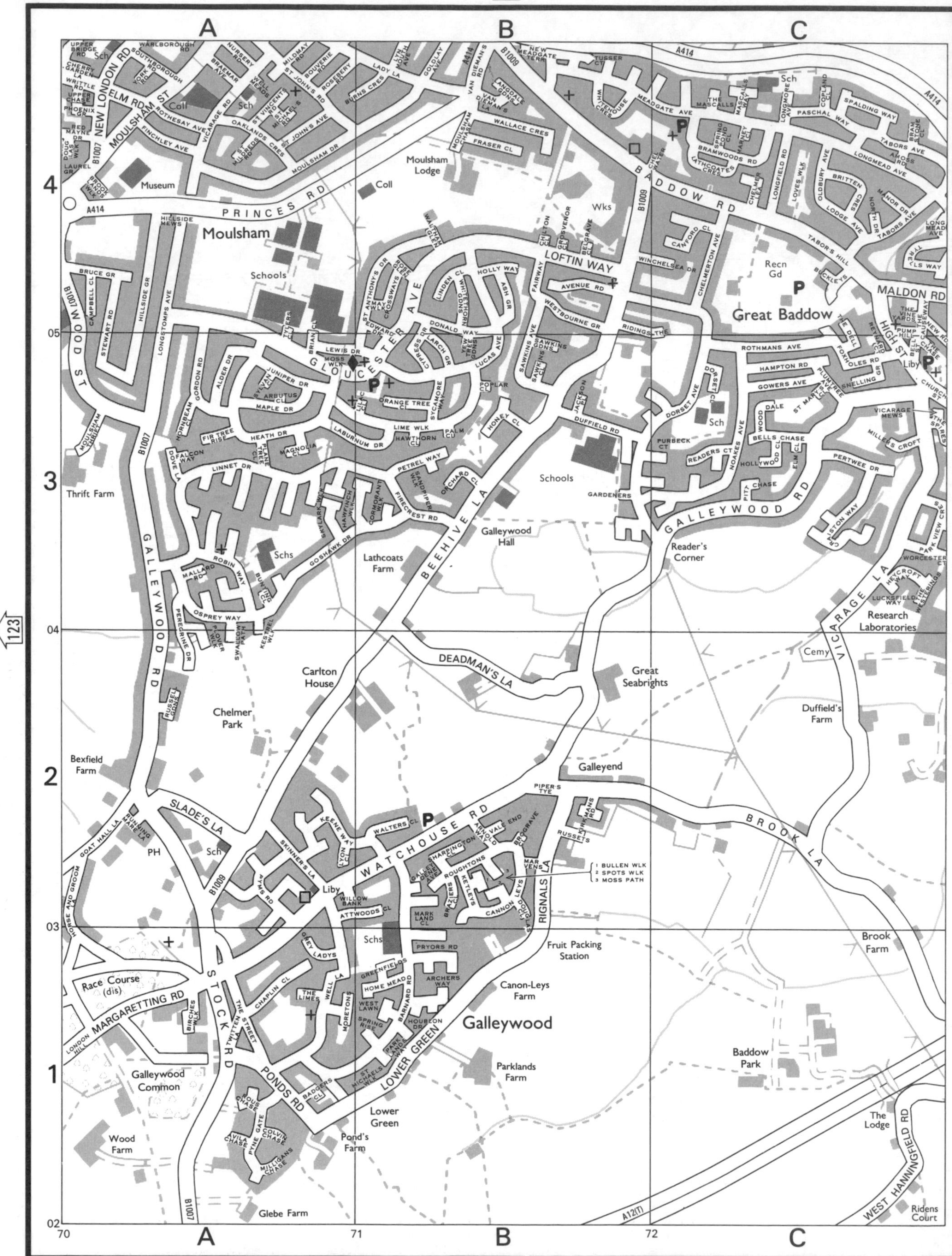
111
A
B
C
Moulsham
Great Baddow
Galleywood
PRINCES RD
BADDOW RD
MALDON RD
LOFTIN WAY
GLOUCESTER AVE
GALLEYWOOD RD
BEEHIVE LA
DEADMAN'S LA
WATCHOUSE RD
BROOK LA
VICARAGE LA
STOCK RD
MARGARETTING RD
SLADE'S LA
WOOD ST
Thrift Farm
Bexfield Farm
Chelmer Park
Carlton House
Lathcoats Farm
Galleywood Hall
Reader's Corner
Great Seabrights
Duffield's Farm
Research Laboratories
Galleyend
Fruit Packing Station
Canon-Leys Farm
Parklands Farm
Lower Green
Pond's Farm
Galleywood Common
Wood Farm
Race Course (dis)
Glebe Farm
Baddow Park
Brook Farm
The Lodge
Ridens Court
WEST HANNINGFIELD RD
A12(T)
1 BULLEN WLK
2 SPOTS WLK
3 MOSS PATH
123
137
70
71
72
02
03
04
05
1
2
3
4

112

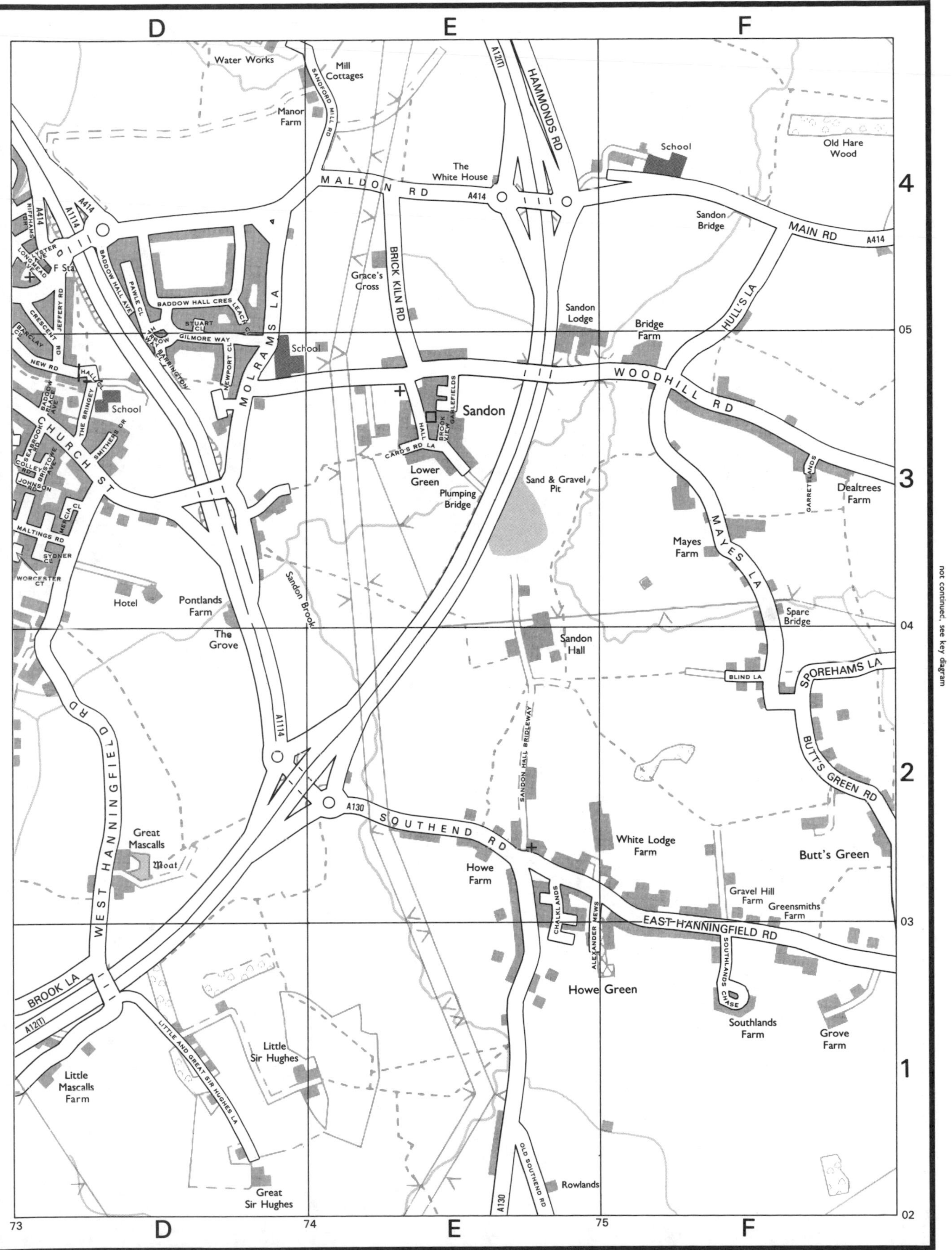
D
E
F
Water Works
Mill Cottages
Manor Farm
SANDFORD MILL RD
A12(T)
HAMMONDS RD
School
Old Hare Wood
The White House
MALDON RD
A414
Sandon Bridge
MAIN RD
A414
4
BRICK KILN RD
Grace's Cross
BADDOW HALL AVE
PAWLE CL
BADDOW HALL CRES
LEACH CL
STUART CL
GILMORE WAY
Sandon Lodge
Bridge Farm
HULL'S LA
05
School
NEWPORT CL
MOLRAMS LA
WOODHILL RD
F Sta
JEFFERY RD
CRESCENT RD
BARCLAY CL
NEW RD
School
CHURCH ST
THE BRINGEY
SMITHERS DR
Sandon
CARD'S RD LA
HALL
BROOK VIEW
GABLEFIELDS
Lower Green
Plumping Bridge
Sand & Gravel Pit
GARRETTLANDS
Dealtrees Farm
3
MAYES LA
Mayes Farm
MERCIA CL
MALTINGS RD
SYDNER CL
WORCESTER CT
Hotel
Pontlands Farm
The Grove
Sandon Brook
Spare Bridge
04
Sandon Hall
BLIND LA
SPOREHAMS LA
A1114
SANDON HALL BRIDLEWAY
BUTT'S GREEN RD
2
WEST HANNINGFIELD RD
Great Mascalls
Moat
A130
SOUTHEND RD
White Lodge Farm
Howe Farm
Butt's Green
Gravel Hill Farm
Greensmiths Farm
CHALKLANDS
ALEXANDER MEWS
EAST HANNINGFIELD RD
03
SOUTHLANDS CHASE
BROOK LA
A12(T)
Howe Green
Southlands Farm
Grove Farm
LITTLE AND GREAT SIR HUGHES LA
Little Sir Hughes
1
Little Mascalls Farm
OLD SOUTHEND RD
A130
Rowlands
Great Sir Hughes
02
73
74
75
D
E
F
not continued, see key diagram

138

113

not continued, see key diagram

139

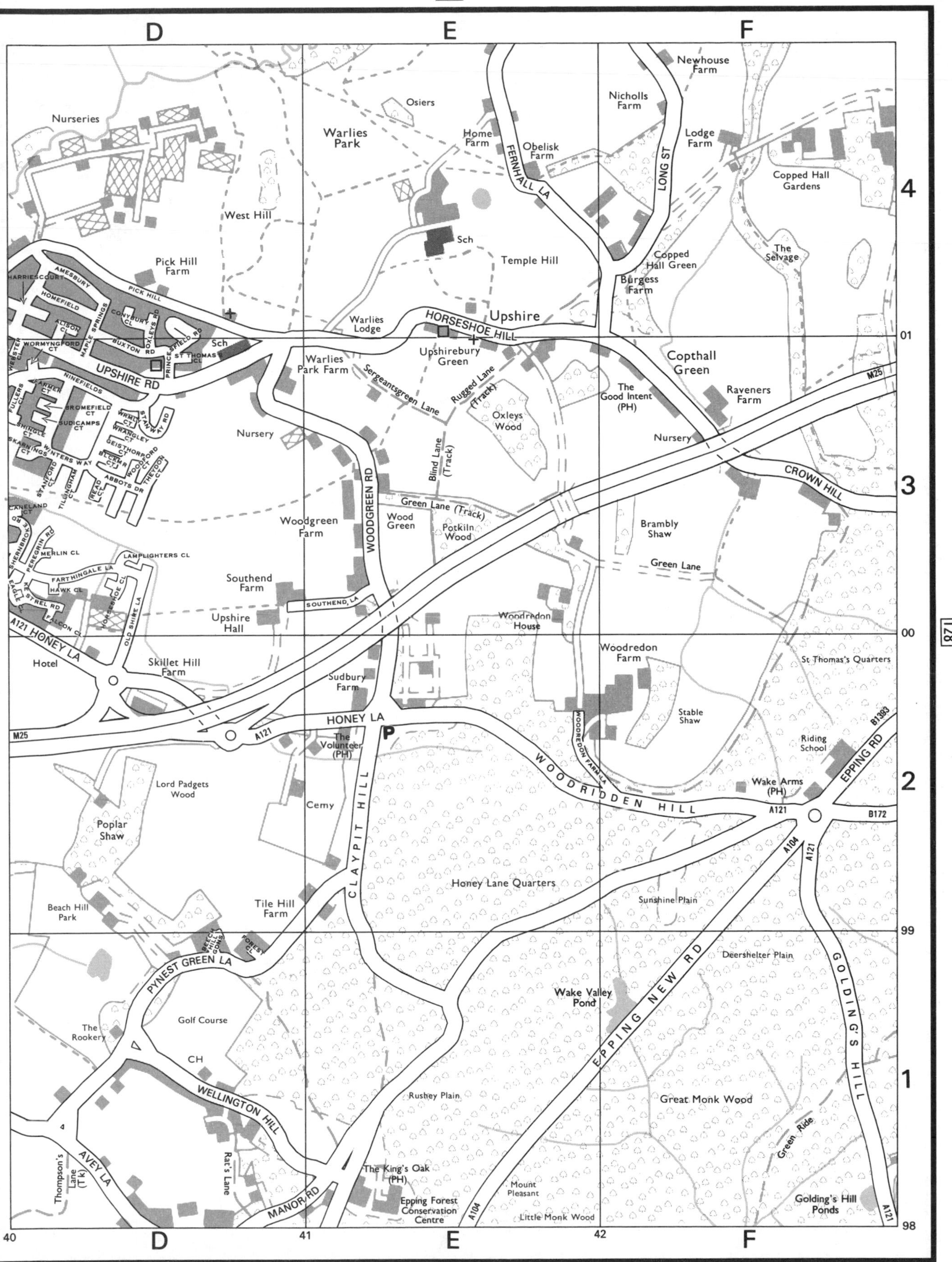

114
D
E
F
Nurseries
Osiers
Warlies Park
Home Farm
Obelisk Farm
Nicholls Farm
Newhouse Farm
Lodge Farm
Copped Hall Gardens
FERNHALL LA
LONG ST
West Hill
Sch
Temple Hill
The Selvage
Copped Hall Green
Burgess Farm
Pick Hill Farm
PICK HILL
AMESBURY
HARRIESCOURT
HOMEFIELD
Warlies Lodge
HORSESHOE HILL
Upshire
Upshirebury Green
Copthall Green
UPSHIRE RD
Sch
Warlies Park Farm
Sergeantsgreen Lane
Rugged Lane (Track)
Oxleys Wood
The Good Intent (PH)
Raveners Farm
M25
Nursery
Nursery
Blind Lane (Track)
CROWN HILL
WOODGREEN RD
Green Lane (Track)
Wood Green
Potkiln Wood
Woodgreen Farm
Brambly Shaw
Green Lane
Southend Farm
SOUTHEND LA
Upshire Hall
Woodredon House
Woodredon Farm
St Thomas's Quarters
A121 HONEY LA
Hotel
Skillet Hill Farm
Sudbury Farm
Stable Shaw
HONEY LA
A121
The Volunteer (PH)
Riding School
EPPING RD
B1393
Lord Padgets Wood
WOODRIDDEN HILL
WOODREDON FARM LA
Wake Arms (PH)
A121
B172
Poplar Shaw
Cemy
CLAYPIT HILL
A104
Honey Lane Quarters
Sunshine Plain
Beach Hill Park
Tile Hill Farm
PYNEST GREEN LA
Deershelter Plain
Golf Course
Wake Valley Pond
EPPING NEW RD
GOLDING'S HILL
The Rookery
CH
WELLINGTON HILL
Rushey Plain
Great Monk Wood
Green Ride
AVEY LA
Thompson's Lane (Tk)
Rat's Lane
MANOR RD
The King's Oak (PH)
Epping Forest Conservation Centre
Mount Pleasant
Little Monk Wood
Golding's Hill Ponds
A104
A121
4
3
2
1
01
00
99
98
40
41
42
128
140

115

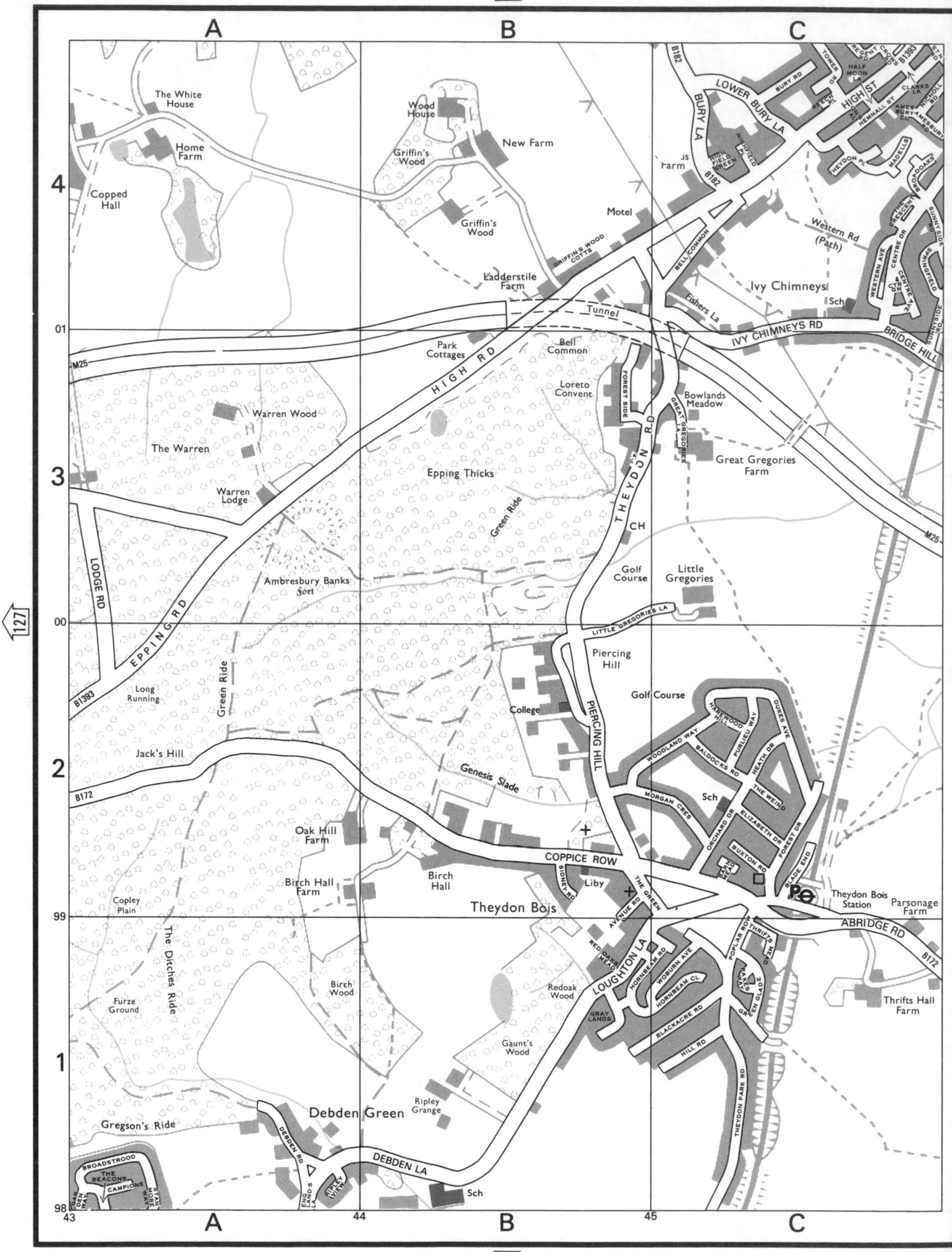

A
B
C
4
3
2
1
01
00
99
98
43
44
45
The White House
Home Farm
Copped Hall
Wood House
Griffin's Wood
New Farm
Griffin's Wood
Motel
Ladderstile Farm
GRIFFIN'S WOOD COTTS
LOWER BURY LA
BURY LA
BURY RD
HIGH ST
B1393
B182
Western Rd (Path)
Ivy Chimneys
Sch
Fishers La
IVY CHIMNEYS RD
BRIDGE HILL
BELL COMMON
Tunnel
M25
Park Cottages
Bell Common
Loreto Convent
FOREST SIDE
Bowlands Meadow
GREAT GREGORIES
Great Gregories Farm
HIGH RD
Warren Wood
The Warren
Epping Thicks
Warren Lodge
THEYDON RD
CH
Green Ride
LODGE RD
Ambresbury Banks Fort
Golf Course
Little Gregories
LITTLE GREGORIES LA
EPPING RD
Piercing Hill
Long Running
B1393
College
PIERCING HILL
Golf Course
Jack's Hill
Green Ride
B172
Genesis Slade
WOODLAND WAY
BALDOCKS RD
HEATH DR
DUKES AVE
MORGAN CRES
Sch
THE WEIND
ORCHARD DR
ELIZABETH DR
FOREST DR
Oak Hill Farm
COPPICE ROW
BUXTON RD
BLADE END
Birch Hall Farm
Birch Hall
Liby
SIDNEY RD
THE GREEN
Theydon Bois Station
Parsonage Farm
Copley Plain
Theydon Bois
AVENUE RD
ABRIDGE RD
B172
The Ditches Ride
LOUGHTON LA
HORNBEAM RD
WOBURN AVE
HORNBEAM CL
POPLAR ROW
THRIFTS MEAD
GREEN GLADE
Birch Wood
Redoak Wood
Furze Ground
GRAY LANDS
BLACKACRE RD
HILL RD
Thrifts Hall Farm
Gaunt's Wood
THEYDON PARK RD
Ripley Grange
Debden Green
Gregson's Ride
DEBDEN RD
DEBDEN LA
Sch
BROADSTROOD
THE BEACONS
CAMPIONS
RIPLEY VIEW

127

141

116

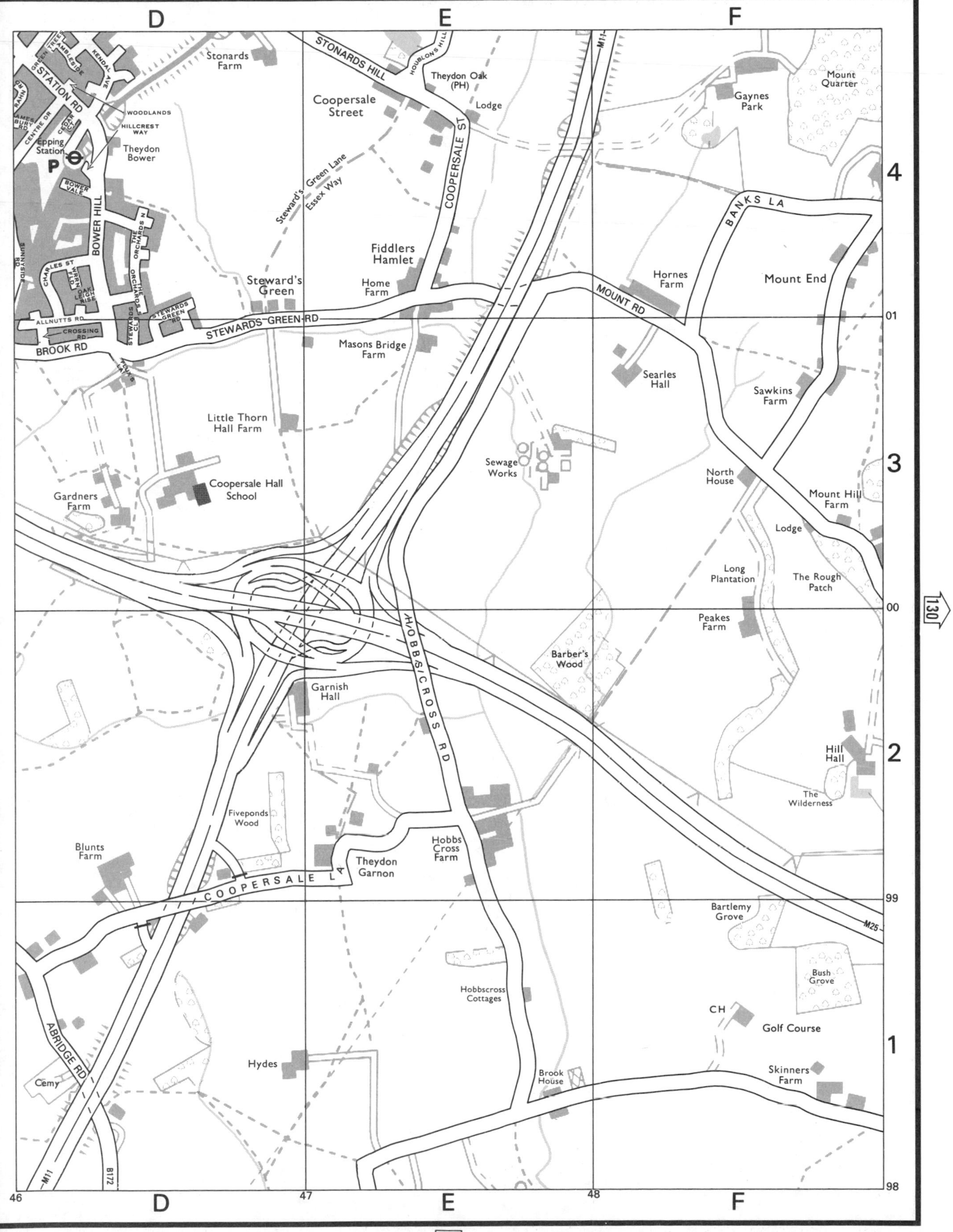

D
E
F
Stonards Farm
STONARDS HILL
HOUBLONS HILL
Theydon Oak (PH)
Lodge
Coopersale Street
Gaynes Park
Mount Quarter
STATION RD
WOODLANDS
HILLCREST WAY
Epping Station
Theydon Bower
BOWER VALE
BOWER HILL
Steward's Green Lane
Essex Way
COOPERSALE ST
BANKS LA
Fiddlers Hamlet
Home Farm
Steward's Green
Hornes Farm
Mount End
MOUNT RD
ALLNUTTS RD
CROSSING RD
STEWARDS GREEN RD
BROOK RD
Masons Bridge Farm
Searles Hall
Sawkins Farm
Little Thorn Hall Farm
Sewage Works
North House
Mount Hill Farm
Gardners Farm
Coopersale Hall School
Lodge
Long Plantation
The Rough Patch
Peakes Farm
Barber's Wood
Garnish Hall
HOBBS CROSS RD
Hill Hall
The Wilderness
Fiveponds Wood
Blunts Farm
COOPERSALE LA
Theydon Garnon
Hobbs Cross Farm
Bartlemy Grove
M25
Bush Grove
Hobbscross Cottages
CH
Golf Course
ABRIDGE RD
Hydes
Cemy
Brook House
Skinners Farm
M11
B172
4
01
3
00
2
99
1
98
46
47
48

130

142

117

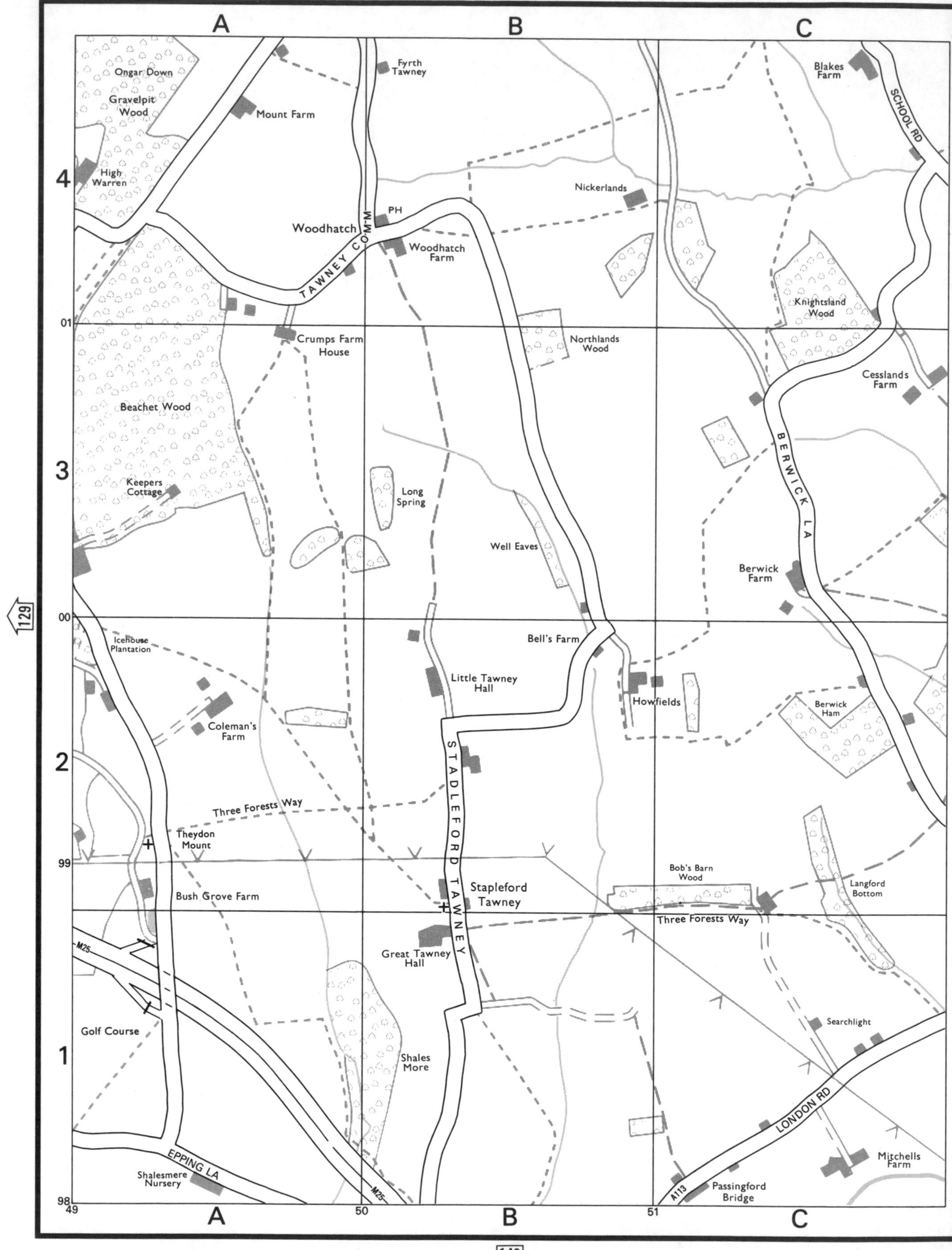
A
B
C
Ongar Down
Gravelpit Wood
Mount Farm
Fyrth Tawney
Blakes Farm
SCHOOL RD
High Warren
4
Nickerlands
PH
Woodhatch
TAWNEY COMM
Woodhatch Farm
Knightsland Wood
01
Crumps Farm House
Northlands Wood
Cesslands Farm
Beachet Wood
BERWICK LA
3
Keepers Cottage
Long Spring
Well Eaves
Berwick Farm
00
Icehouse Plantation
Bell's Farm
Little Tawney Hall
Howfields
Berwick Ham
Coleman's Farm
STADLEFORD TAWNEY
2
Three Forests Way
Theydon Mount
99
Bob's Barn Wood
Langford Bottom
Bush Grove Farm
Stapleford Tawney
Three Forests Way
M25
Great Tawney Hall
Searchlight
Golf Course
1
Shales More
LONDON RD
EPPING LA
Mitchells Farm
Shalesmere Nursery
M25
A113
Passingford Bridge
98
49
50
51
A
B
C

129

143

118

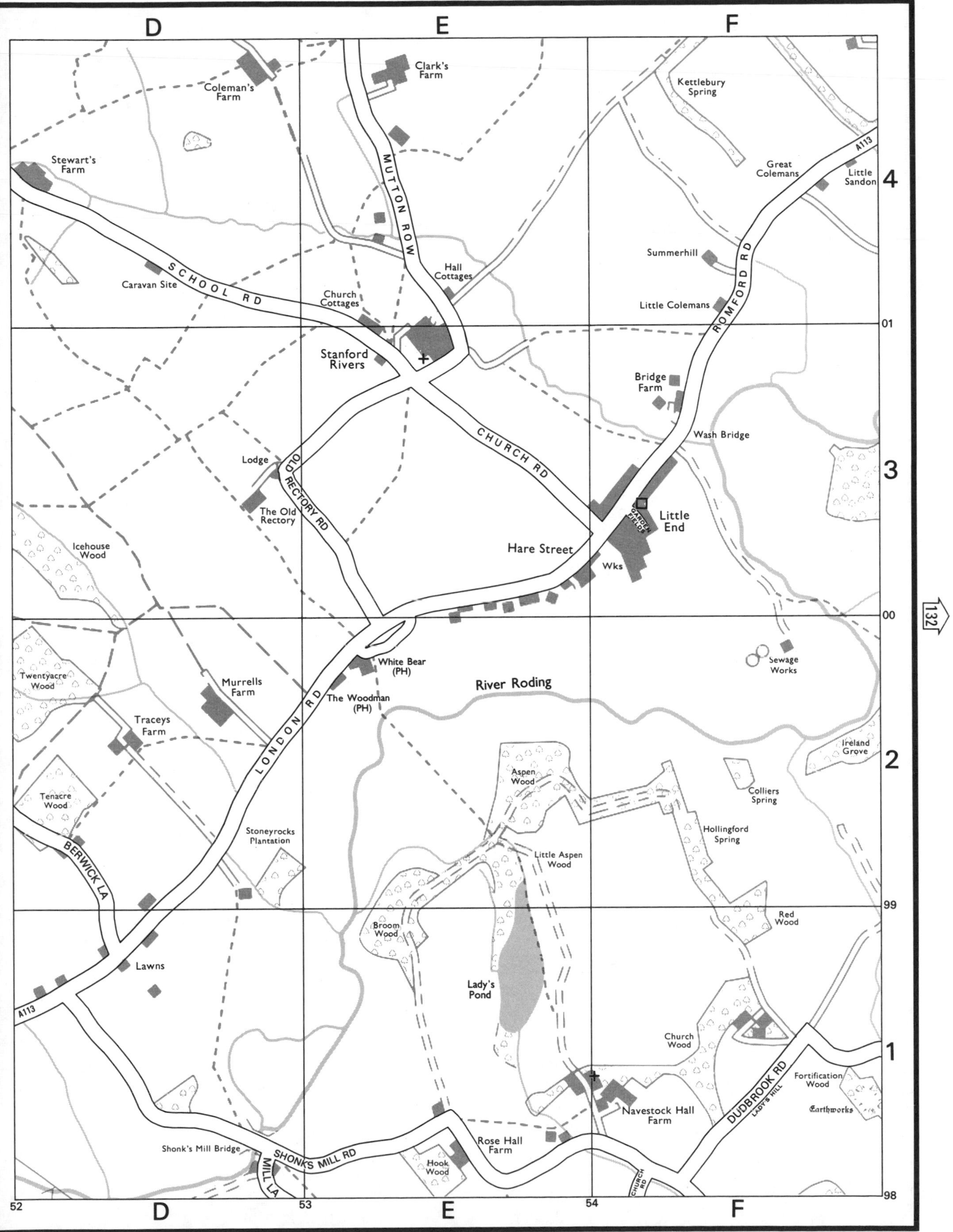
D
E
F
Clark's Farm
Coleman's Farm
Kettlebury Spring
Stewart's Farm
MUTTON ROW
Great Colemans
A113
Little Sandon
4
Summerhill
SCHOOL RD
Caravan Site
Hall Cottages
Church Cottages
Little Colemans
ROMFORD RD
01
Stanford Rivers
Bridge Farm
CHURCH RD
Wash Bridge
Lodge
OLD RECTORY RD
3
The Old Rectory
Little End
GARDEN FIELDS
Icehouse Wood
Hare Street
Wks
00
White Bear (PH)
Sewage Works
River Roding
Twentyacre Wood
Murrells Farm
The Woodman (PH)
Traceys Farm
LONDON RD
Ireland Grove
2
Aspen Wood
Tenacre Wood
Colliers Spring
Hollingford Spring
Stoneyrocks Plantation
BERWICK LA
Little Aspen Wood
99
Red Wood
Broom Wood
Lawns
Lady's Pond
A113
Church Wood
1
Fortification Wood
DUDBROOK RD
LADY'S HILL
Earthworks
Navestock Hall Farm
Rose Hall Farm
Shonk's Mill Bridge
SHONKS MILL RD
MILL LA
Hook Wood
CHURCH RD
52
53
54
98

132

144

119

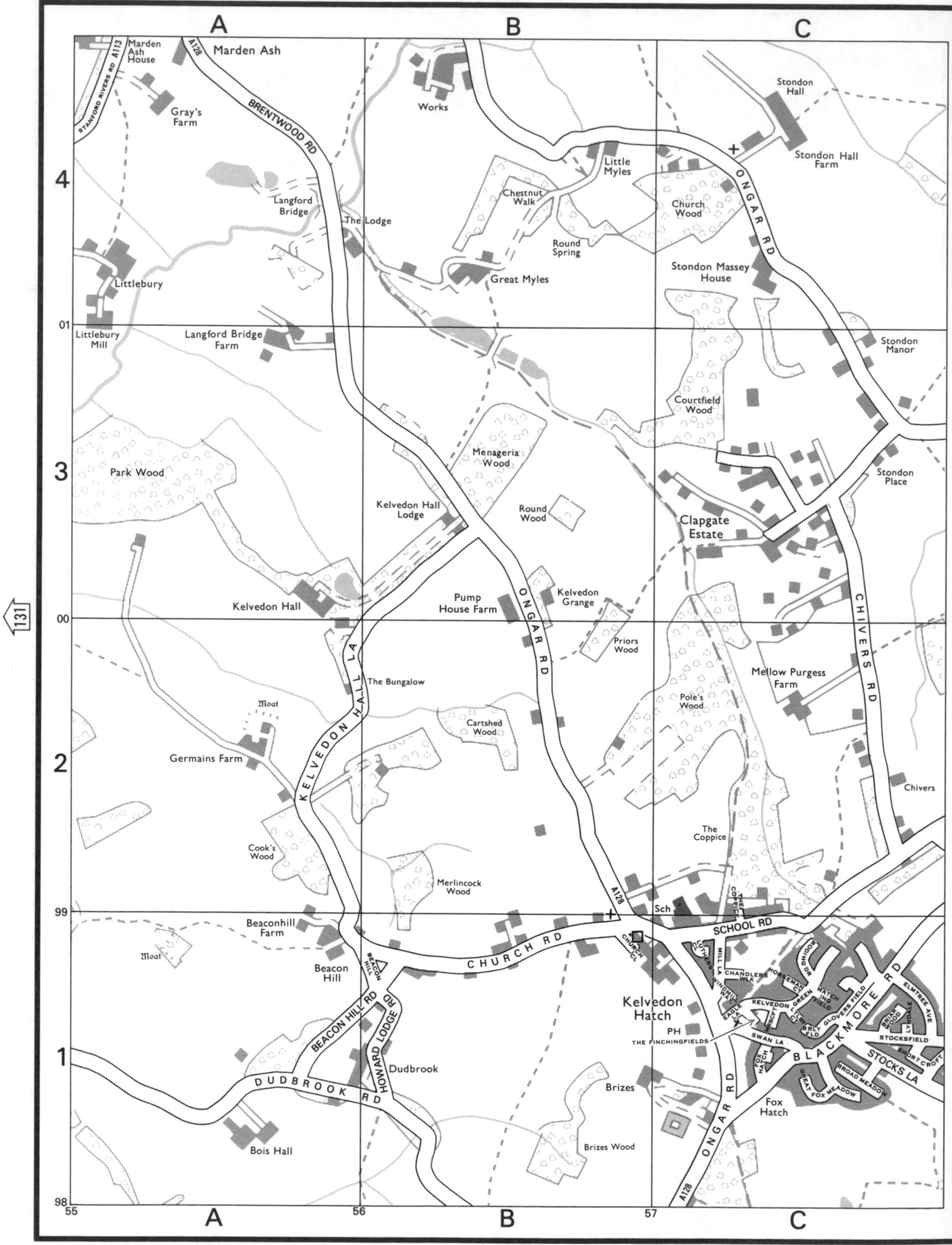

A
B
C
Marden Ash
Marden Ash House
A113
A128
STANFORD RIVERS RD
Gray's Farm
BRENTWOOD RD
Works
Stondon Hall
Stondon Hall Farm
Little Myles
Chestnut Walk
Church Wood
ONGAR RD
Langford Bridge
The Lodge
Round Spring
Littlebury
Great Myles
Stondon Massey House
Littlebury Mill
Langford Bridge Farm
Stondon Manor
Courtfield Wood
Park Wood
Menageria Wood
Stondon Place
Kelvedon Hall Lodge
Round Wood
Clapgate Estate
Kelvedon Hall
Pump House Farm
Kelvedon Grange
ONGAR RD
CHIVERS RD
Priors Wood
The Bungalow
Mellow Purgess Farm
Moat
Pole's Wood
Cartshed Wood
KELVEDON HALL LA
Germains Farm
Chivers
The Coppice
Cook's Wood
Merlincock Wood
Beaconhill Farm
Sch
SCHOOL RD
THE COPPICE
Moat
BEACON HILL
CHURCH RD
CHURCH CL
Beacon Hill
BEACON HILL RD
HOWARD LODGE RD
Kelvedon Hatch
PH
THE FINCHINGFIELDS
BLACKMORE RD
STOCKSFIELD
STOCKS LA
SHORT CROFT
SWAN LA
BROAD MEADOW
GREAT FOX MEADOW
FOX HATCH
MILL LA
CHANDLERS WLK
HORSEMAN CL
OGDEN DR
MATCHING FIELD
GLOVERS FIELD
ELMTREE AVE
LYNDALE
BRIAR WOOD
KELVEDON GREEN
EAGLE
Dudbrook
DUDBROOK RD
Brizes
Fox Hatch
Bois Hall
Brizes Wood
4
3
2
1
01
00
99
98
55
56
57

131

145

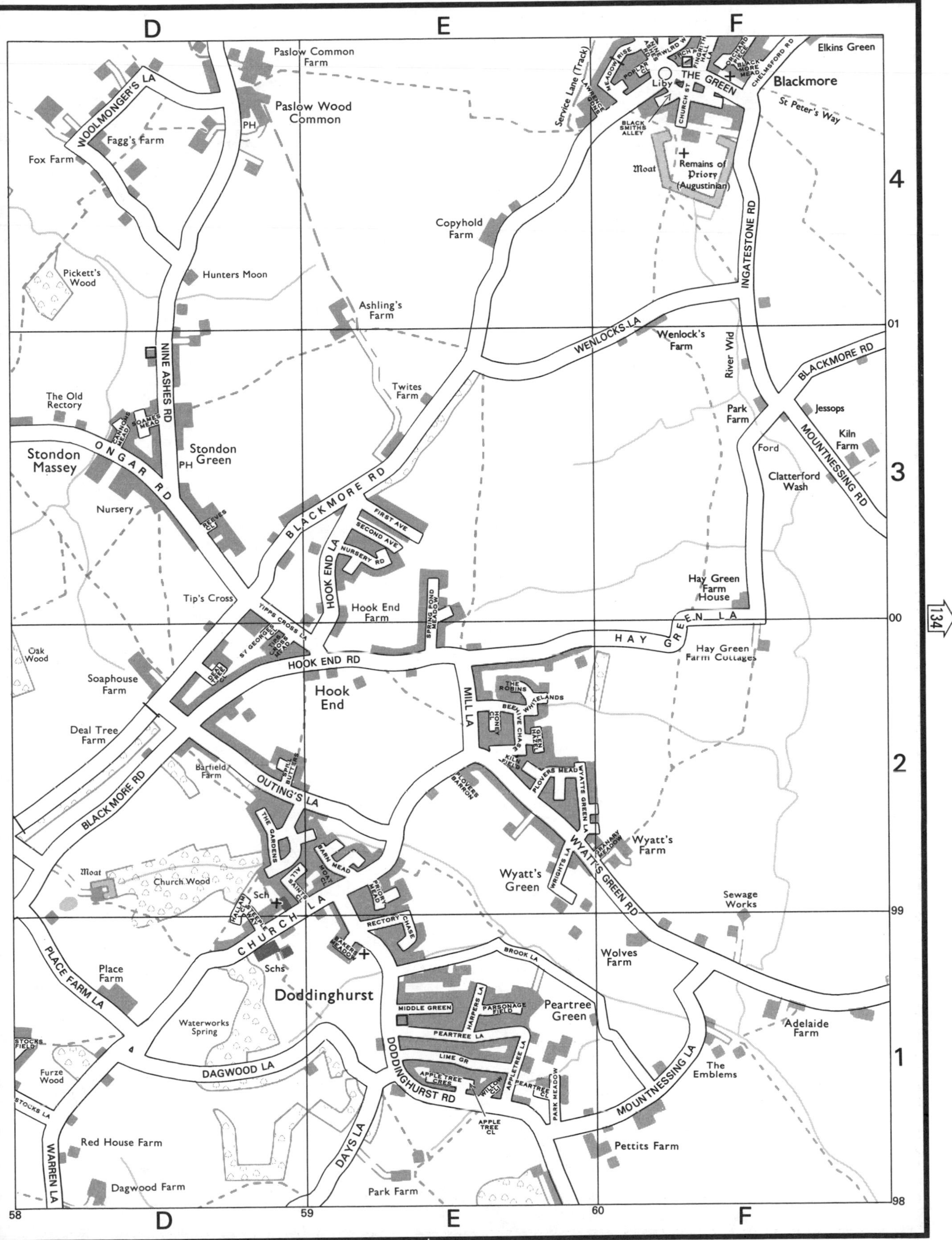

120
D
E
F
Paslow Common Farm
Paslow Wood Common
Woolmonger's La
Fagg's Farm
Fox Farm
PH
Pickett's Wood
Hunters Moon
Nine Ashes Rd
Ashling's Farm
Copyhold Farm
Service Lane (Track)
The Green
Liby
Church St
Black Smiths Alley
Blackmore
Elkins Green
Chelmsford Rd
St Peter's Way
Moat
Remains of Priory (Augustinian)
Ingatestone Rd
Wenlocks La
Wenlock's Farm
River Wid
Blackmore Rd
Jessops
Kiln Farm
Park Farm
Ford
Mountnessing Rd
Clatterford Wash
The Old Rectory
Soames Mead
Cannons Mead
Stondon Massey
Stondon Green
Ongar Rd
Twites Farm
Nursery
Reeves Cl
First Ave
Second Ave
Nursery Rd
Hook End La
Hay Green Farm House
Tip's Cross
Tipps Cross La
Hook End Farm
Spring Pond Meadow
Hay Green La
Hay Green Farm Cottages
Oak Wood
St George's Cl
Hook End Rd
Soaphouse Farm
Deal Tree Cl
Hook End
Mill La
The Robins
Whitelands
Beehive Chase
Honey Cl
Glen Cl
Kiln Field
Plovers Mead
Deal Tree Farm
Barfield Farm
Outing's La
Plovers Barron
Wyatts Green La
Blackmore Rd
The Gardens
Barn Mead
Moat Cl
All Saints Cl
Granary Meadow
Wyatt's Farm
Moat
Church Wood
Sch
Priory Mead
Wyatt's Green
Wrights La
Wyatts Green Rd
Sewage Works
Church La
Rectory Chase
Bakers Meadow
Brook La
Wolves Farm
Place Farm La
Place Farm
Schs
Doddinghurst
Peartree Green
Middle Green
Harpers La
Parsonage Field
Adelaide Farm
Waterworks Spring
Peartree La
Stocks Field
Lime Gr
Appletree La
The Emblems
Furze Wood
Dagwood La
Apple Tree Cres
Willow Cl
Peartree Cl
Park Meadow
Mountnessing La
Stocks La
Doddinghurst Rd
Apple Tree Cl
Red House Farm
Days La
Pettits Farm
Warren La
Dagwood Farm
Park Farm
4
3
2
1
01
00
99
98
58
59
60
134
146

121

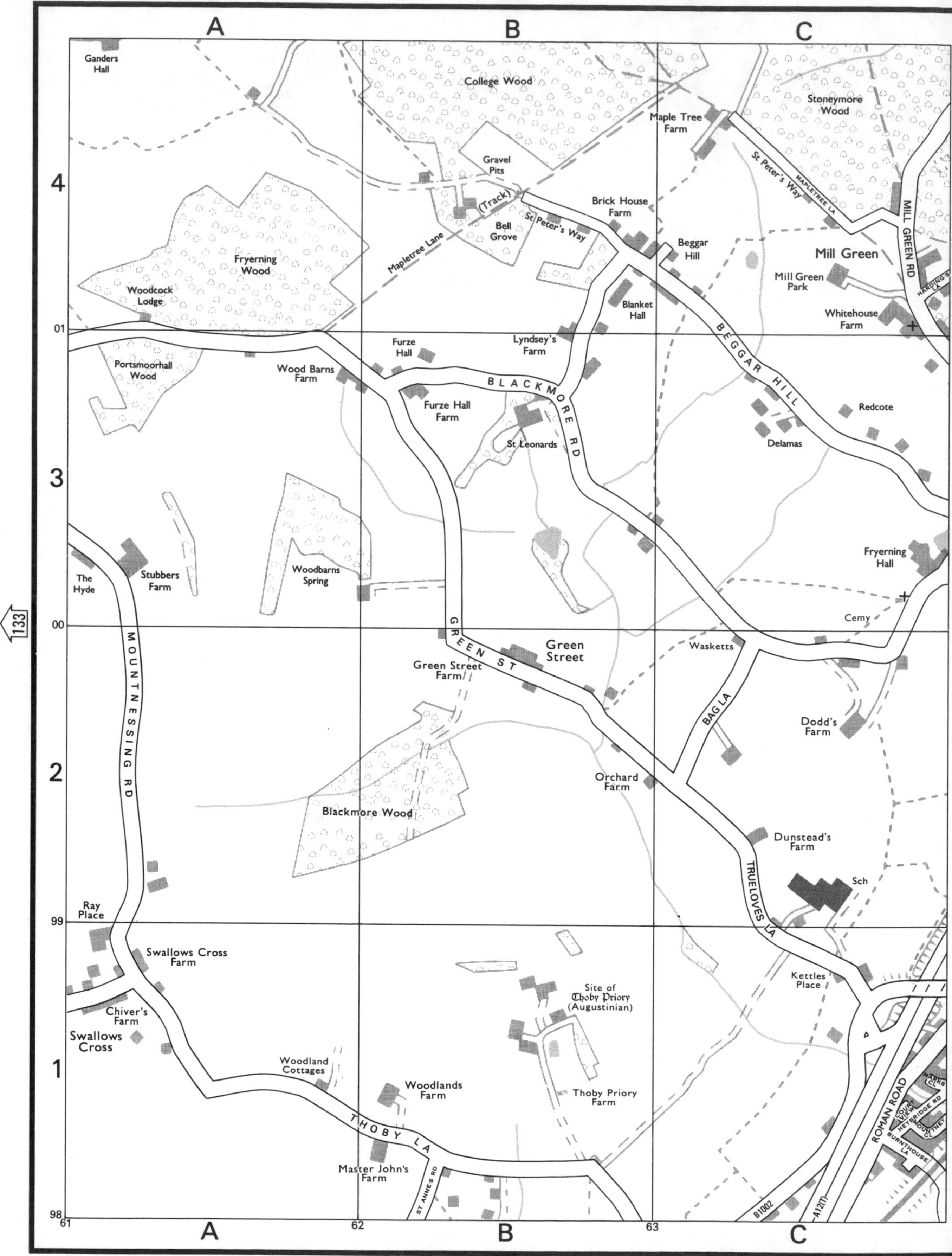

A
B
C
Ganders Hall
College Wood
Stoneymore Wood
Maple Tree Farm
Gravel Pits
(Track)
Bell Grove
St Peter's Way
Mapletree Lane
Brick House Farm
Beggar Hill
MAPLETREE LA
MILL GREEN RD
Mill Green
Mill Green Park
Whitehouse Farm
Fryerning Wood
Woodcock Lodge
Blanket Hall
Lyndsey's Farm
Furze Hall
Wood Barns Farm
Portsmoorhall Wood
BLACKMORE RD
BEGGAR HILL
Furze Hall Farm
St Leonards
Redcote
Delamas
Woodbarns Spring
The Hyde
Stubbers Farm
Fryerning Hall
Cemy
GREEN ST
Green Street
Green Street Farm
Wasketts
MOUNTNESSING RD
BAG LA
Dodd's Farm
Orchard Farm
Blackmore Wood
Dunstead's Farm
TRUELOVES LA
Sch
Ray Place
Swallows Cross Farm
Kettles Place
Site of Thoby Priory (Augustinian)
Chiver's Farm
Swallows Cross
Woodland Cottages
Woodlands Farm
Thoby Priory Farm
ROMAN ROAD
HEYBRIDGE RD
BURNTHOUSE LA
THOBY LA
Master John's Farm
ST ANNE'S RD
B1002
A12(T)
4
3
2
1
01
00
99
98
61
62
63

133

147

122

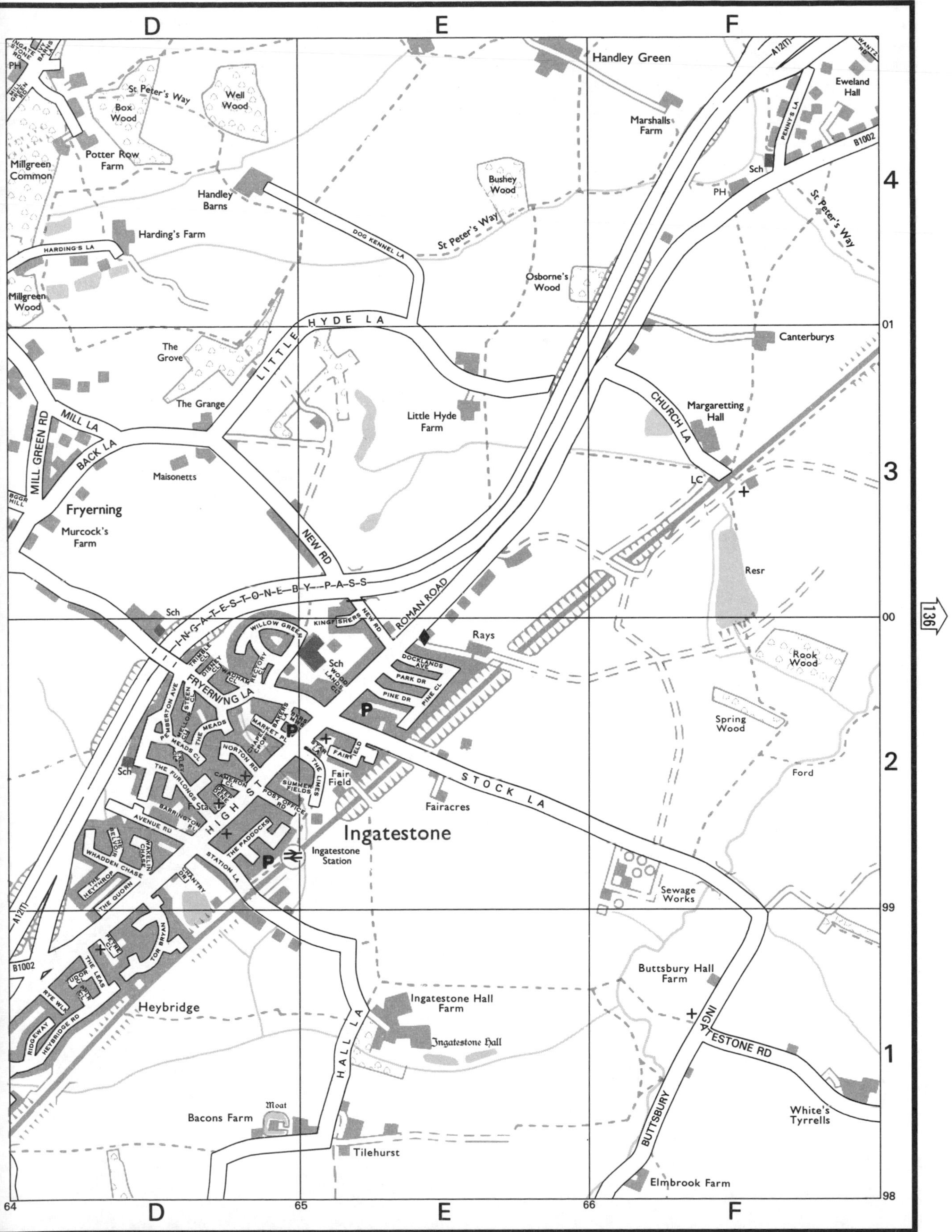
D
E
F
Handley Green
Eweland Hall
Marshalls Farm
St Peter's Way
Box Wood
Well Wood
Potter Row Farm
Millgreen Common
Handley Barns
Bushey Wood
Harding's Farm
HARDING'S LA
DOG KENNEL LA
Osborne's Wood
Millgreen Wood
LITTLE HYDE LA
The Grove
The Grange
Canterburys
Little Hyde Farm
CHURCH LA
Margaretting Hall
MILL LA
MILL GREEN RD
BACK LA
Maisonetts
Fryerning
Murcock's Farm
NEW RD
Resr
INGATESTONE BY-PASS
ROMAN ROAD
Rays
Sch
Rook Wood
Spring Wood
FRYERNING LA
STOCK LA
Ford
Fair Field
Fairacres
HIGH ST
Ingatestone
Ingatestone Station
Sewage Works
STATION LA
B1002
A12(T)
Buttsbury Hall Farm
Heybridge
Ingatestone Hall Farm
Ingatestone Hall
INGATESTONE RD
HALL LA
BUTTSBURY
White's Tyrrells
Moat
Bacons Farm
Tilehurst
Elmbrook Farm
4
3
2
1
01
00
99
98
64
65
66

136

123

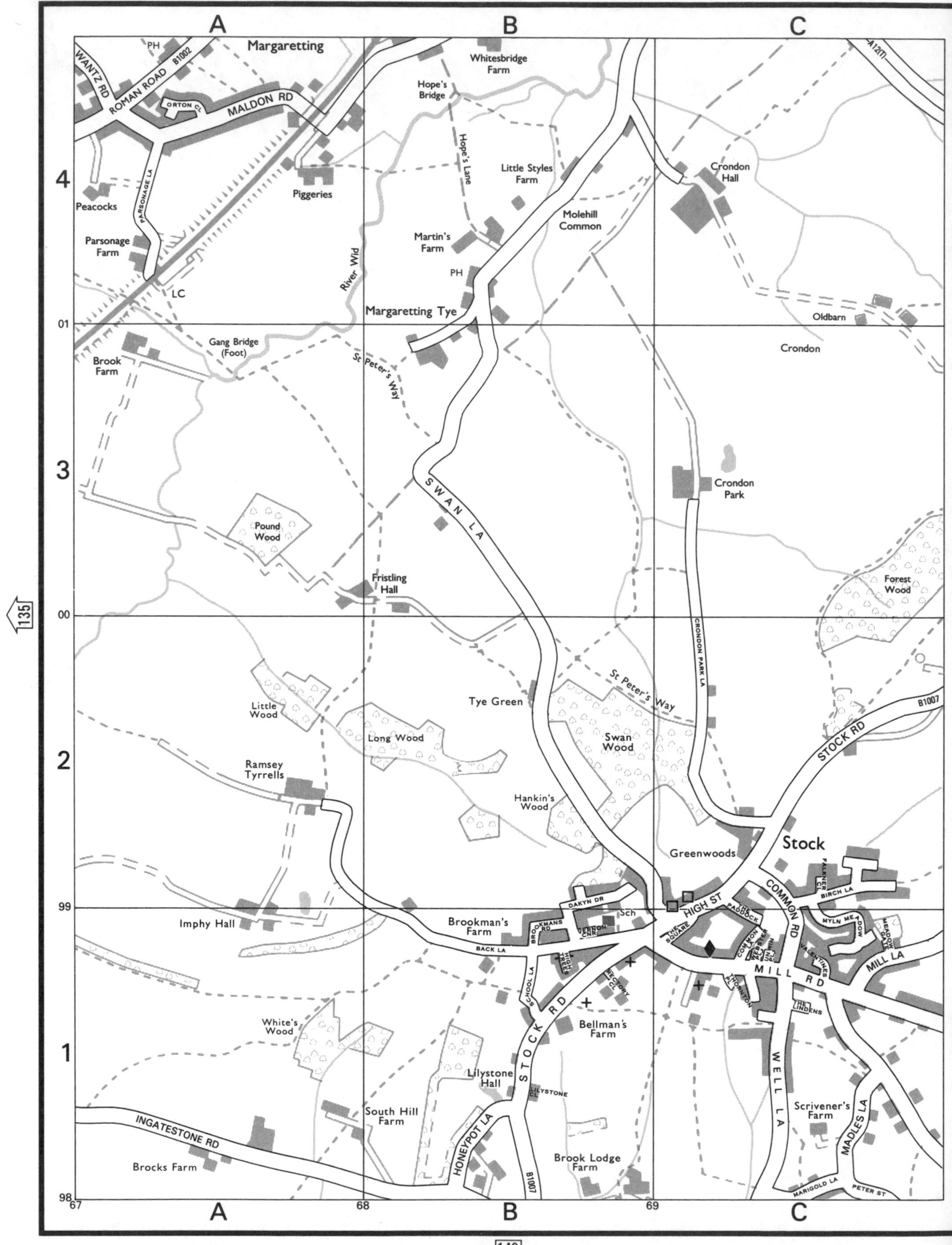

A
B
C
Margaretting
Whitesbridge Farm
Hope's Bridge
Hope's Lane
WANTZ RD
ROMAN ROAD
B1002
ORTON CL
MALDON RD
PH
A12(T)
4
Peacocks
PARSONAGE LA
Parsonage Farm
Piggeries
Little Styles Farm
Crondon Hall
Molehill Common
Martin's Farm
River Wid
LC
Margaretting Tye
01
Oldbarn
Crondon
Gang Bridge (Foot)
Brook Farm
St Peter's Way
3
SWAN LA
Crondon Park
Pound Wood
Fristling Hall
Forest Wood
00
CRONDON PARK LA
St Peter's Way
Tye Green
Little Wood
Long Wood
Swan Wood
STOCK RD
B1007
2
Ramsey Tyrrells
Hankin's Wood
Stock
Greenwoods
COMMON RD
FALKNER CL
BIRCH LA
DAKYN DR
HIGH ST
Sch
99
Imphy Hall
Brookman's Farm
BROOKMANS RD
VERNON CNR
THE SQUARE
THE PADDOCK
COMMON FIELDS
WEBSTER PL
MYLN MEADOW
MEADOW GATE
BACK LA
HIGH TREES
RECTORY CL
VALENTINES
MILL RD
MILL LA
SCHOOL LA
THORNTON PL
THE LINDENS
White's Wood
STOCK RD
Bellman's Farm
1
WELL LA
Lilystone Hall
LILYSTONE CL
Scrivener's Farm
MADLES LA
HONEYPOT LA
South Hill Farm
INGATESTONE RD
Brook Lodge Farm
Brocks Farm
B1007
MARIGOLD LA
PETER ST
98
67
68
69

135

149

124

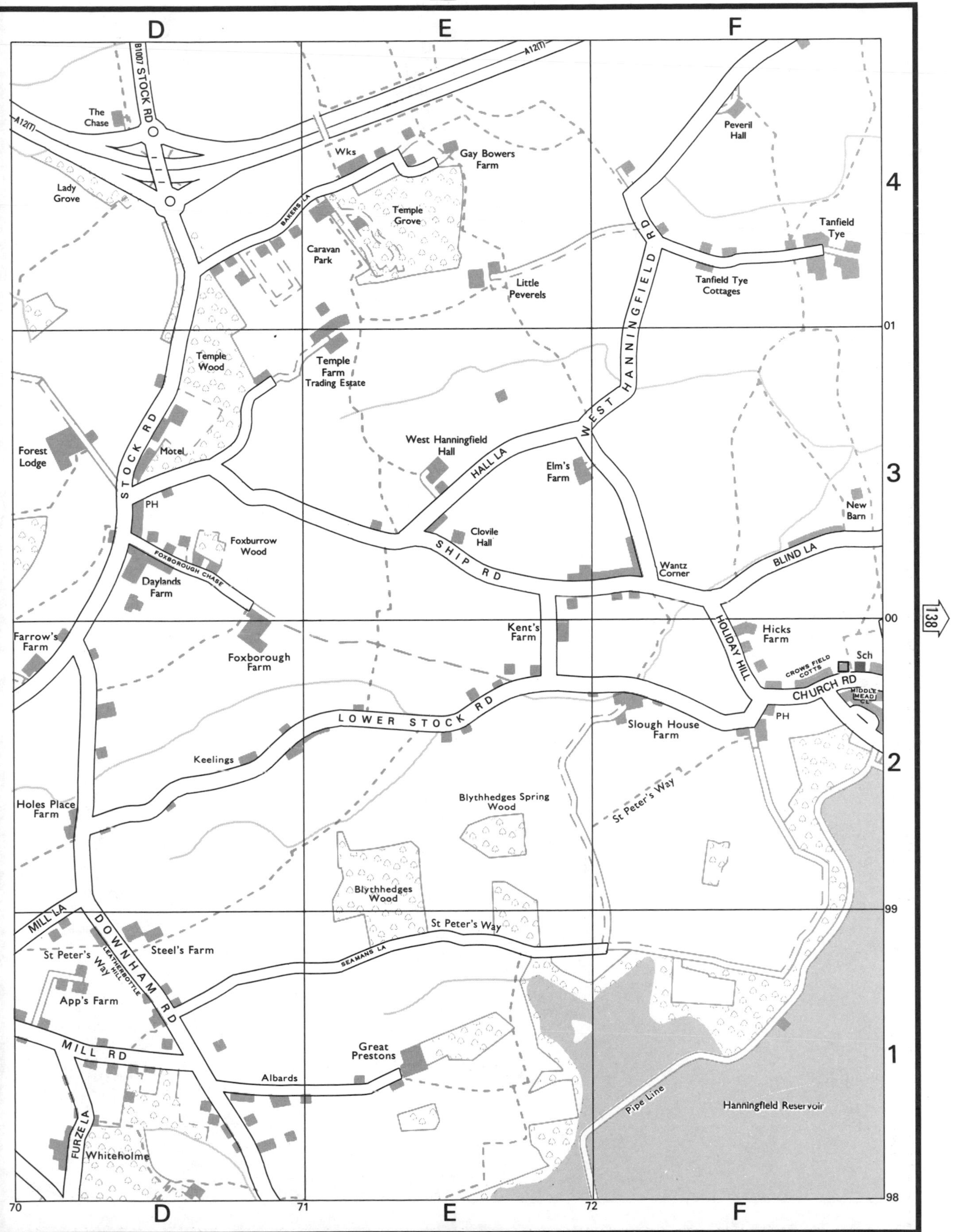
D
E
F
A12(T)
B1007 STOCK RD
The Chase
Lady Grove
Wks
Gay Bowers Farm
Peveril Hall
BAKERS LA
Temple Grove
Caravan Park
Little Peverels
Tanfield Tye
Tanfield Tye Cottages
WEST HANNINGFIELD RD
Temple Wood
Temple Farm Trading Estate
STOCK RD
Forest Lodge
Motel
West Hanningfield Hall
HALL LA
Elm's Farm
PH
Foxburrow Wood
Clovile Hall
New Barn
FOXBOROUGH CHASE
Daylands Farm
SHIP RD
Wantz Corner
BLIND LA
Farrow's Farm
Foxborough Farm
Kent's Farm
HOLIDAY HILL
Hicks Farm
Sch
CROWS FIELD COTTS
CHURCH RD
MIDDLE MEAD CL
LOWER STOCK RD
Slough House Farm
PH
Keelings
Holes Place Farm
Blythhedges Spring Wood
St Peter's Way
Blythhedges Wood
St Peter's Way
MILL LA
DOWNHAM RD
Steel's Farm
St Peter's Way
LEATHERBOTTLE HILL
SEAMANS LA
App's Farm
MILL RD
Great Prestons
Albards
Pipe Line
Hanningfield Reservoir
FURZE LA
Whiteholme
4
3
2
1
01
00
99
98
70
71
72

138

150

125

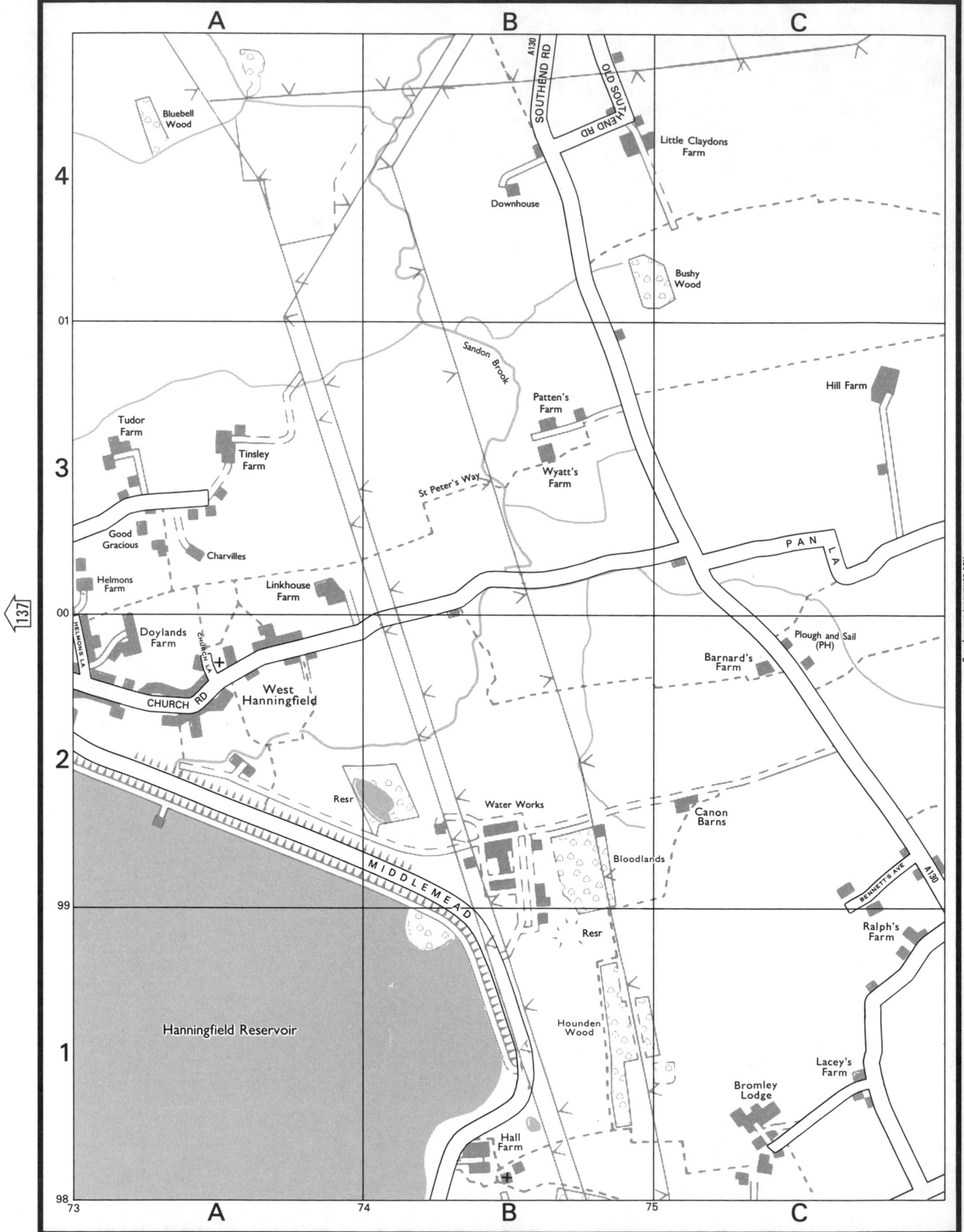
A
B
C
Bluebell Wood
A130
SOUTHEND RD
OLD SOUTHEND RD
Little Claydons Farm
Downhouse
Bushy Wood
Sandon Brook
Hill Farm
Patten's Farm
Tudor Farm
Tinsley Farm
Wyatt's Farm
St Peter's Way
Good Gracious
Charvilles
PAN LA
Helmons Farm
Linkhouse Farm
HELMONS LA
Doylands Farm
CHURCH LA
Plough and Sail (PH)
Barnard's Farm
CHURCH RD
West Hanningfield
Resr
Water Works
Canon Barns
Bloodlands
MIDDLEMEAD
BENNETT'S AVE
A130
Ralph's Farm
Resr
Hounden Wood
Hanningfield Reservoir
Lacey's Farm
Bromley Lodge
Hall Farm
4
3
2
1
01
00
99
98
73
74
75

137

151

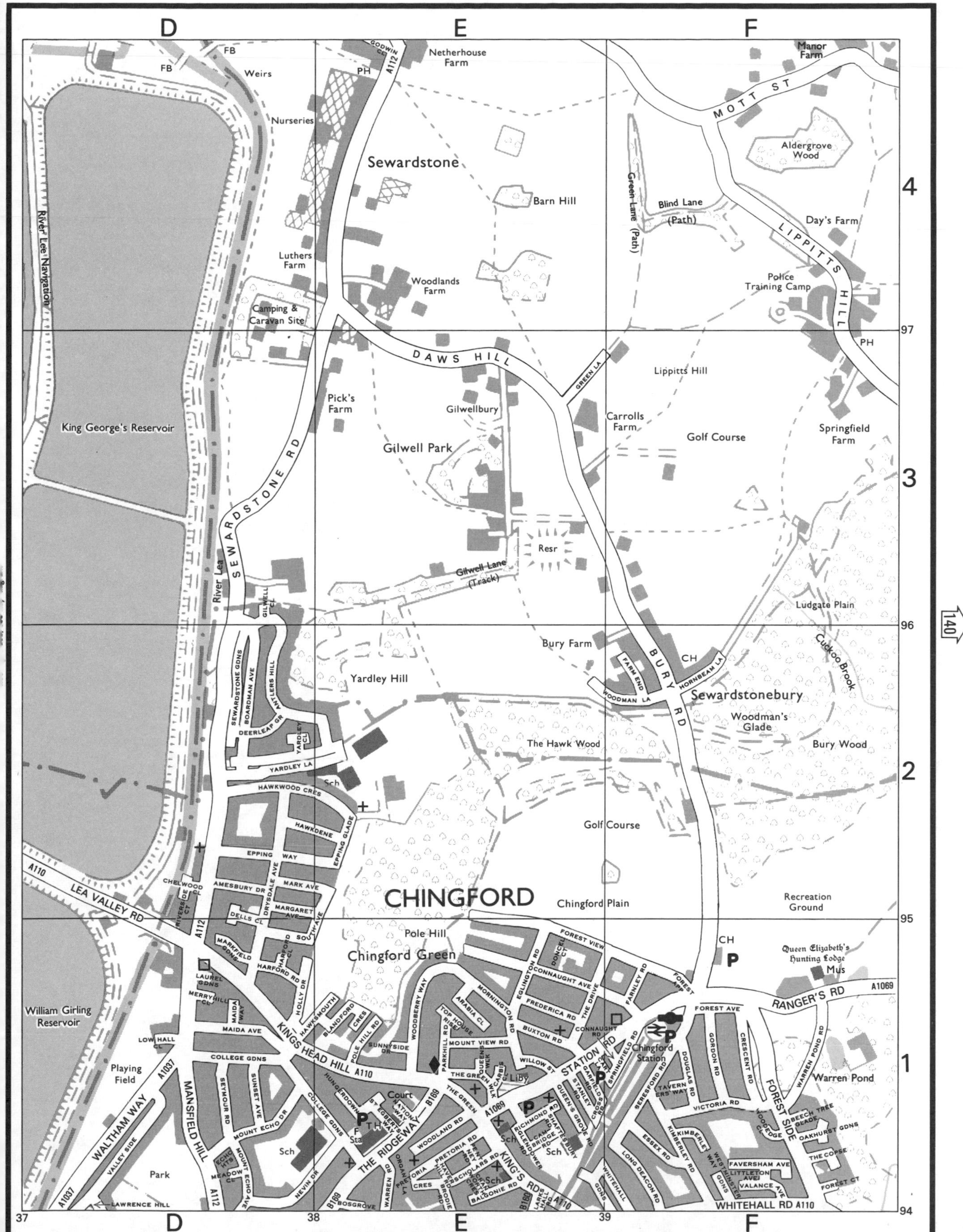

not continued, see key diagram

127

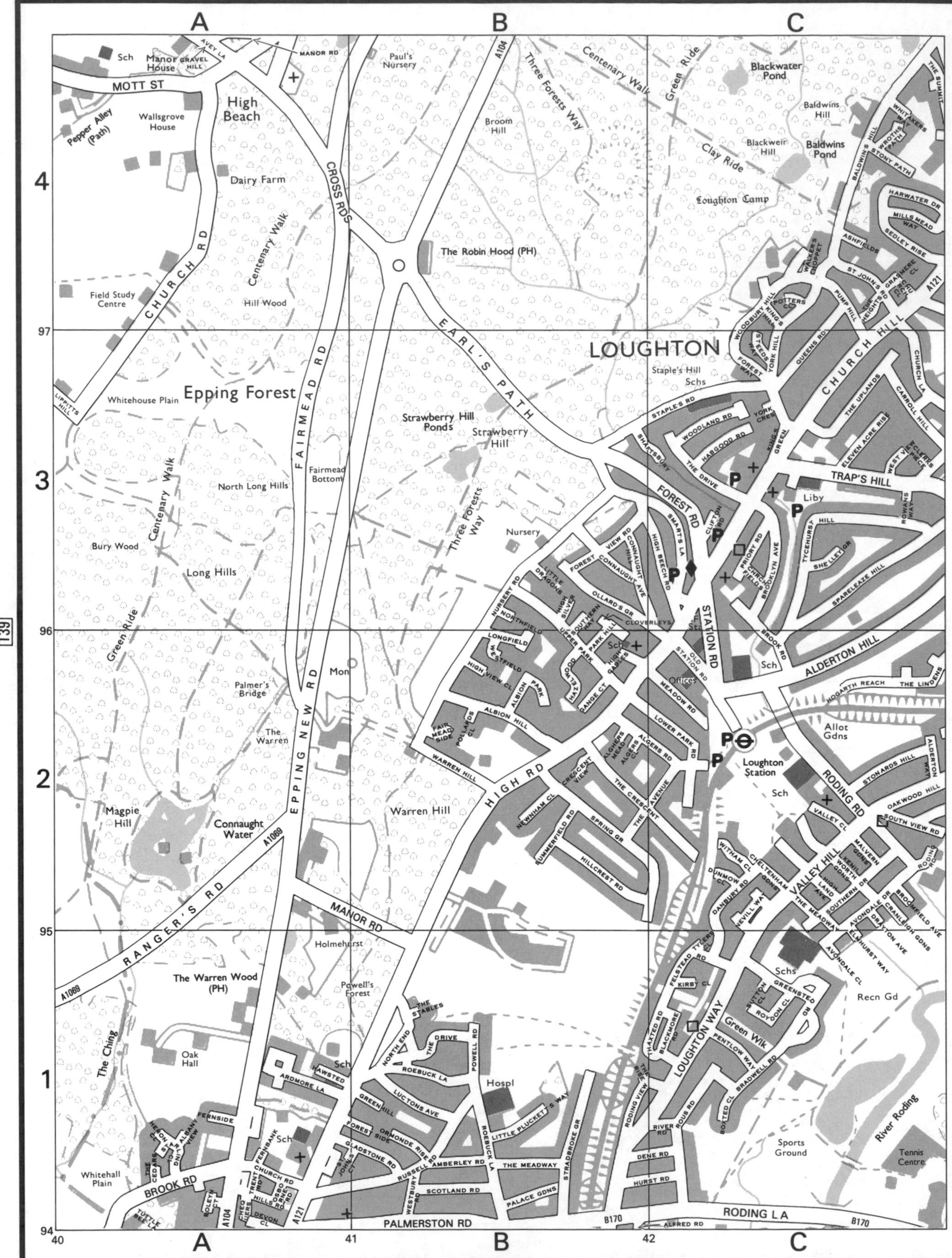

A
B
C
LOUGHTON
Epping Forest
High Beach
MOTT ST
Manor House
GRAVEL HILL
AVEY LA
MANOR RD
Sch
Pepper Alley (Path)
Wallsgrove House
Dairy Farm
CROSS RDS
Paul's Nursery
Broom Hill
Three Forests Way
Centenary Walk
Green Ride
Blackwater Pond
Baldwins Hill
Baldwins Pond
Blackweir Hill
Clay Ride
Loughton Camp
The Robin Hood (PH)
CHURCH RD
Field Study Centre
Hill Wood
EARL'S PATH
FAIRMEAD RD
Whitehouse Plain
LIPPITTS HILL
Staple's Hill
Schs
Strawberry Hill Ponds
Strawberry Hill
Fairmead Bottom
North Long Hills
Bury Wood
Long Hills
Nursery
STAPLE'S RD
WOODLAND RD
HABGOOD RD
THE DRIVE
FOREST RD
SHAFTSBURY
TRAP'S HILL
Liby
CHURCH HILL
QUEENS RD
YORK HILL
STEEDS WAY
FOREST WAY
WOODBURY HILL
POTTERS CL
PUMP HILL
THE HEIGHTS
ST JOHN'S RD
ASHFIELDS
SEDLEY RISE
HARWATER DR
MILLSMEAD WAY
STONY PATH
BALDWINS HILL
WHITAKERS WAY
THE SUMMIT
A121
THE UPLANDS
CARROLL HILL
CHURCH LA
ELEVEN ACRE RISE
WEST VIEW
TYCEHURST HILL
SHELLEY GR
SPARELEAZE HILL
ROWANS WAY
STATION RD
PRIORY RD
BROOKLYN AVE
BROOK RD
ALDERTON HILL
HOGARTH REACH
THE LINDENS
HIGH BEECH RD
SMART'S LA
CONNAUGHT AVE
VIEW RD
FOREST
NURSERY RD
LITTLE DRAGONS
NORTHFIELD
LONGFIELD
WESTFIELD
HIGH VIEW CL
ALBION PARK
ALBION HILL
POLLARDS CL
FAIR MEAD SIDE
WARREN HILL
UPPER PARK
PARK HILL
CLOVERLEYS
OLLARD'S GR
SOUTHERN WAY
HIGH GABLES
OLD STATION RD
Offices
MEADOW RD
LOWER PARK RD
ALGERS RD
ALGERS CL
ALGERS MEAD
CRESCENT VIEW
THE CRESCENT
THE AVENUE
HIGH RD
NEWNHAM CL
SUMMERFIELD RD
SPRING GR
HILLCREST RD
Loughton Station
Allot Gdns
ALDERTON WAY
STONARDS HILL
OAKWOOD HILL
RODING RD
VALLEY CL
SOUTH VIEW RD
VALLEY HILL
MALVERN GDNS
KENILWORTH GDNS
CHELTENHAM GDNS
WITHAM CL
DUNMOW CL
DANBURY RD
REVILL WAY
THE MEADWAY
SOUTHERN DR
AVONDALE DR
BROOMFIELD AVE
CRANLEIGH GDNS
DRAYTON AVE
ELMHURST WAY
AVONDALE CL
Mon
Palmer's Bridge
The Warren
Warren Hill
EPPING NEW RD
Magpie Hill
Connaught Water
A1069
RANGER'S RD
MANOR RD
Holmehurst
Powell's Forest
The Warren Wood (PH)
The Ching
Oak Hall
THE STABLES
NORTH END
THE DRIVE
POWELL RD
ROEBUCK LA
HAWSTED
ARDMORE LA
GREEN HILL
LUCTONS AVE
Hospl
LITTLE PLUCKETT'S WAY
FOREST SIDE
ORMONDE RISE
GLADSTONE RD
RUSSELL RD
AMBERLEY RD
THE MEADWAY
FERNSIDE
FERNBANK
ALBANY VIEW
THE CEDARS
Whitehall Plain
BROOK RD
CHURCH RD
SCOTLAND RD
PALACE GDNS
STRADBROKE GR
WESTBURY RD
PALMERSTON RD
DEVON CL
TUTTLE BEE LA
A104
RODING VIEW
THE RISE
THAXTED RD
BLACKMORE RD
FELSTEAD RD
KIRBY CL
TYLERS CL
LOUGHTON WAY
Green Wlk
PENTLOW WAY
BRADWELL RD
BOXTED CL
GREENSTED RD
ROYDON CL
SUTTON CL
RIVER ROUS RD
DENE RD
HURST RD
ALFRED RD
RODING LA
B170
Recn Gd
Sports Ground
River Roding
Tennis Centre
4
3
2
1
97
96
95
94
40
41
42

139

152

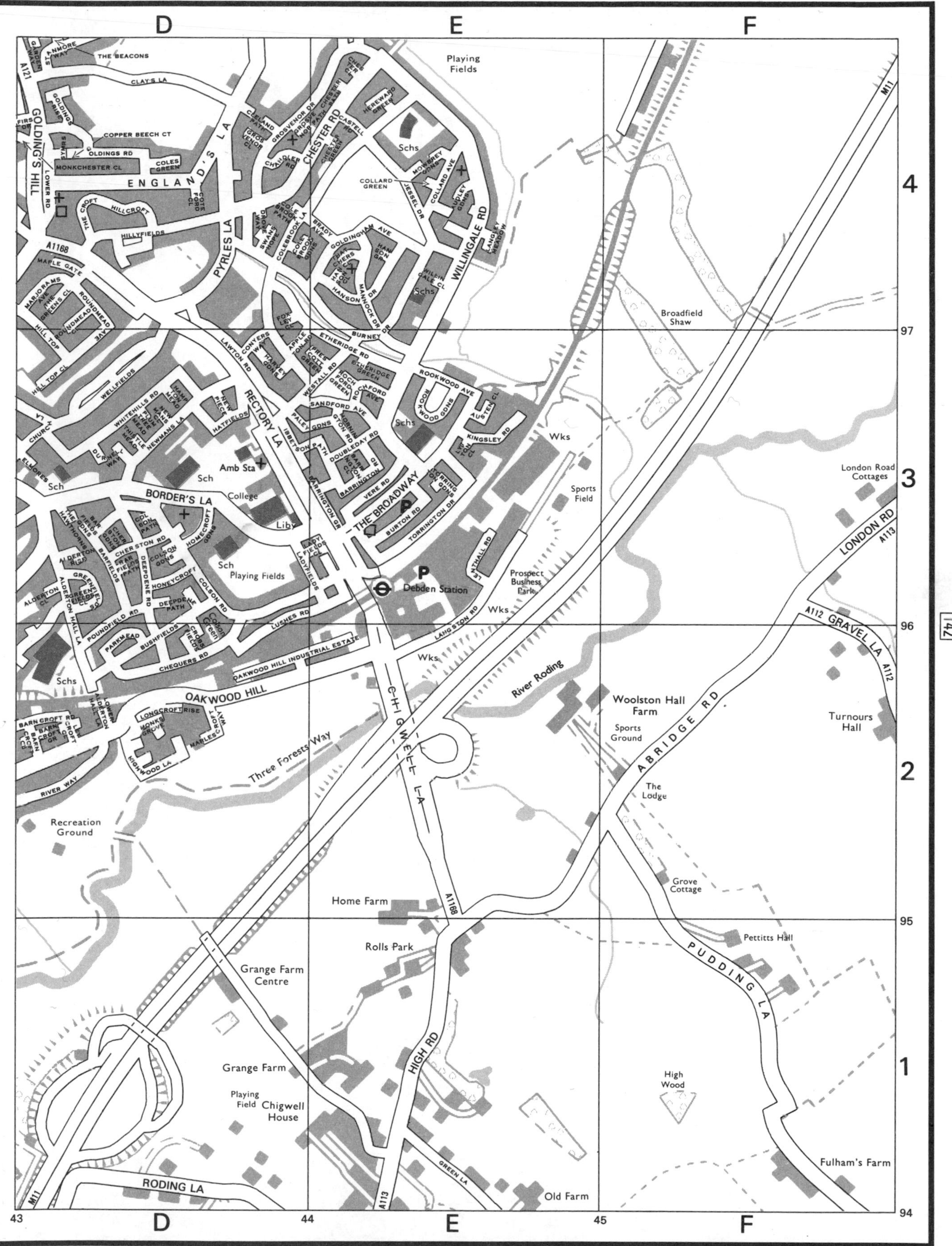
128
153
142
D
E
F
Playing Fields
Schs
Broadfield Shaw
Wks
Sports Field
London Road Cottages
LONDON RD
Prospect Business Park
Debden Station
THE BROADWAY
RECTORY LA
PYRLES LA
CHESTER RD
WILLINGALE RD
ENGLAND'S LA
GOLDING'S HILL
BORDER'S LA
OAKWOOD HILL
OAKWOOD HILL INDUSTRIAL ESTATE
CHIGWELL LA
River Roding
Woolston Hall Farm
Sports Ground
ABRIDGE RD
GRAVEL LA
Turnours Hall
The Lodge
Three Forests Way
Recreation Ground
Grove Cottage
Home Farm
Rolls Park
Pettitts Hall
PUDDING LA
Grange Farm Centre
Grange Farm
Playing Field
Chigwell House
HIGH RD
High Wood
Fulham's Farm
GREEN LA
Old Farm
RODING LA
M11
A113
A1168
A112
43
44
45
94
95
96
97
1
2
3
4

129

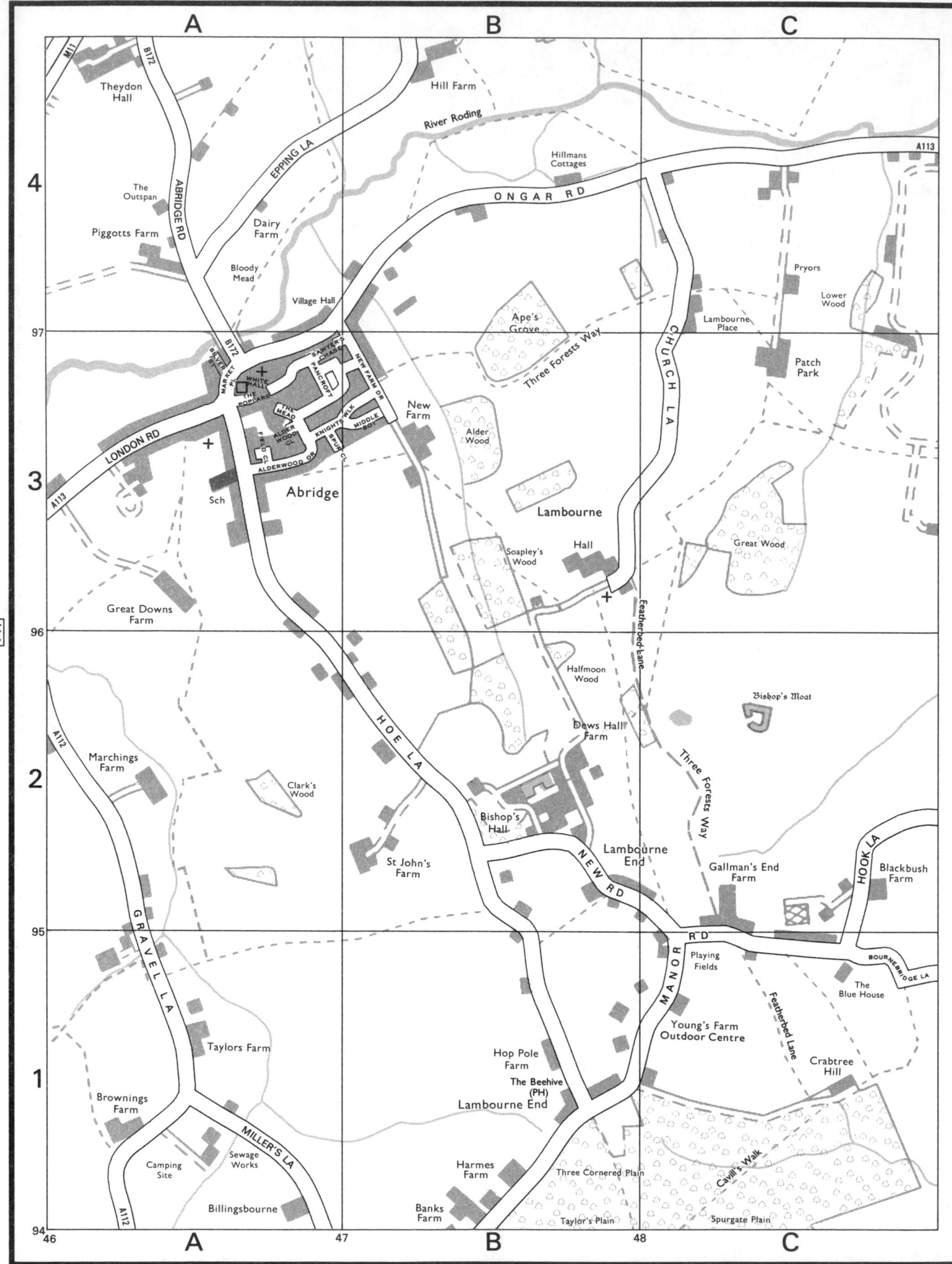

A
B
C
4
3
2
1
97
96
95
94
46
47
48
M11
B172
Theydon Hall
Hill Farm
River Roding
EPPING LA
ABRIDGE RD
Hillmans Cottages
A113
ONGAR RD
The Outspan
Piggotts Farm
Dairy Farm
Bloody Mead
Village Hall
Pryors
Lower Wood
Ape's Grove
Lambourne Place
Three Forests Way
CHURCH LA
Patch Park
SILVER ST
MARKET PL
WHITE HALL
THE POPLARS
SAWYER'S CHASE
PANCROFT
NEW FARM DR
THE MEAD
ALDER WOOD CL
FIELD CL
KNIGHTS WLK
MIDDLE BOY
SPUR CL
ALDERWOOD DR
New Farm
Alder Wood
LONDON RD
Abridge
Sch
Lambourne
Hall
Soapley's Wood
Great Wood
Great Downs Farm
Featherbed Lane
Halfmoon Wood
Bishop's Moat
Dews Hall Farm
HOE LA
A112
Marchings Farm
Clark's Wood
Three Forests Way
Bishop's Hall
St John's Farm
NEW RD
Lambourne End
Gallman's End Farm
HOOK LA
Blackbush Farm
GRAVEL LA
RD
MANOR
Playing Fields
BOURNEBRIDGE LA
The Blue House
Featherbed Lane
Young's Farm Outdoor Centre
Taylors Farm
Hop Pole Farm
Crabtree Hill
The Beehive (PH)
Lambourne End
Brownings Farm
MILLER'S LA
Camping Site
Sewage Works
Harmes Farm
Three Cornered Plain
Cavill's Walk
Billingsbourne
Banks Farm
Taylor's Plain
Spurgate Plain

141

154

130

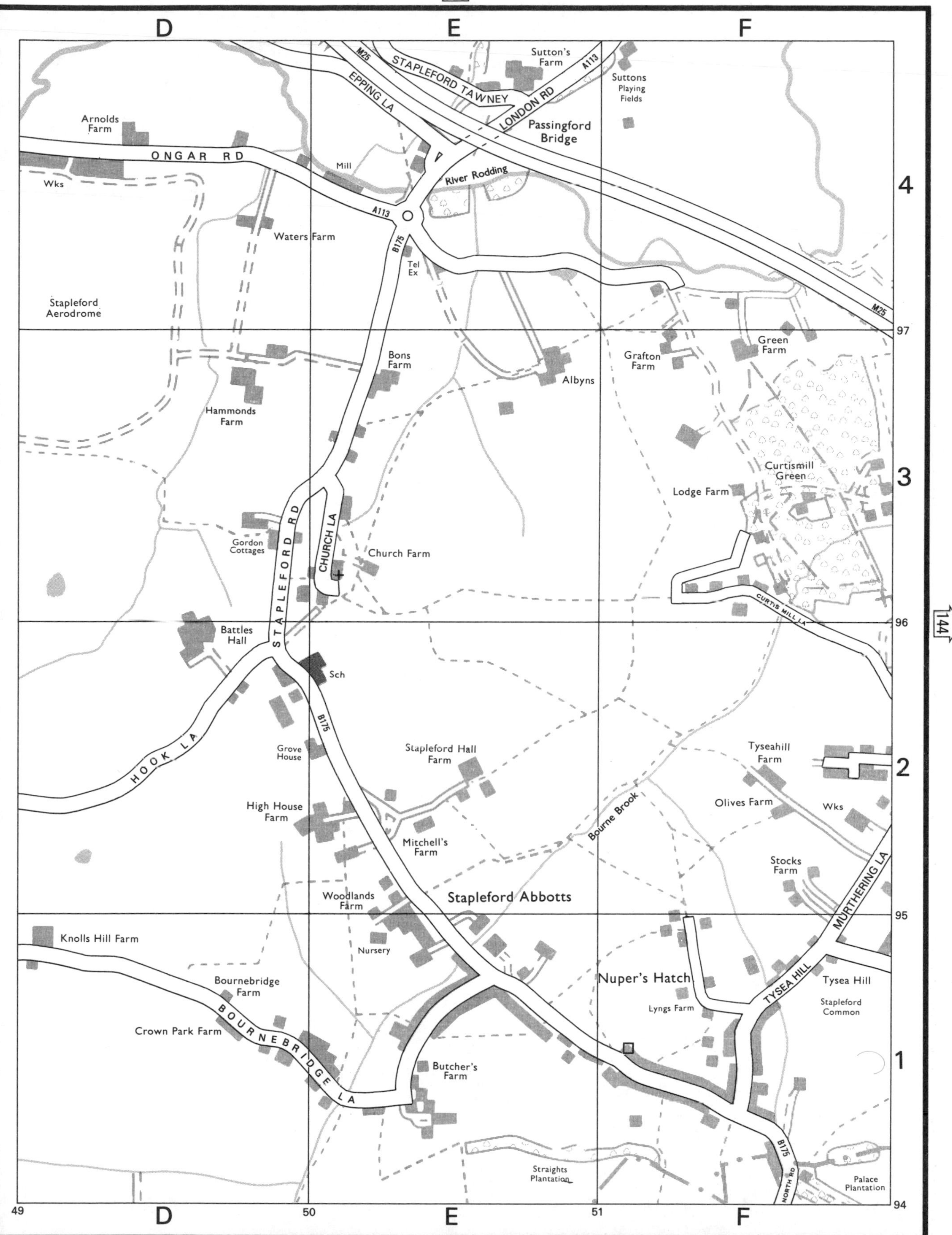
D
E
F
Sutton's Farm
Suttons Playing Fields
STAPLEFORD TAWNEY
EPPING LA
M25
A113
LONDON RD
Passingford Bridge
Arnolds Farm
ONGAR RD
Wks
Mill
River Rodding
A113
B175
Waters Farm
Tel Ex
Stapleford Aerodrome
Bons Farm
Albyns
Grafton Farm
Green Farm
Hammonds Farm
Curtismill Green
Lodge Farm
Gordon Cottages
STAPLEFORD RD
CHURCH LA
Church Farm
CURTIS MILL LA
Battles Hall
Sch
HOOK LA
Grove House
Stapleford Hall Farm
Tyseahill Farm
High House Farm
Olives Farm
Wks
Bourne Brook
Mitchell's Farm
Stocks Farm
MURTHERING LA
Woodlands Farm
Stapleford Abbotts
Knolls Hill Farm
Nursery
Nuper's Hatch
TYSEA HILL
Tysea Hill
Bournebridge Farm
Lyngs Farm
Stapleford Common
Crown Park Farm
BOURNEBRIDGE LA
Butcher's Farm
Straights Plantation
NORTH RD
Palace Plantation
4
3
2
1
97
96
95
94
49
50
51

144

155

131

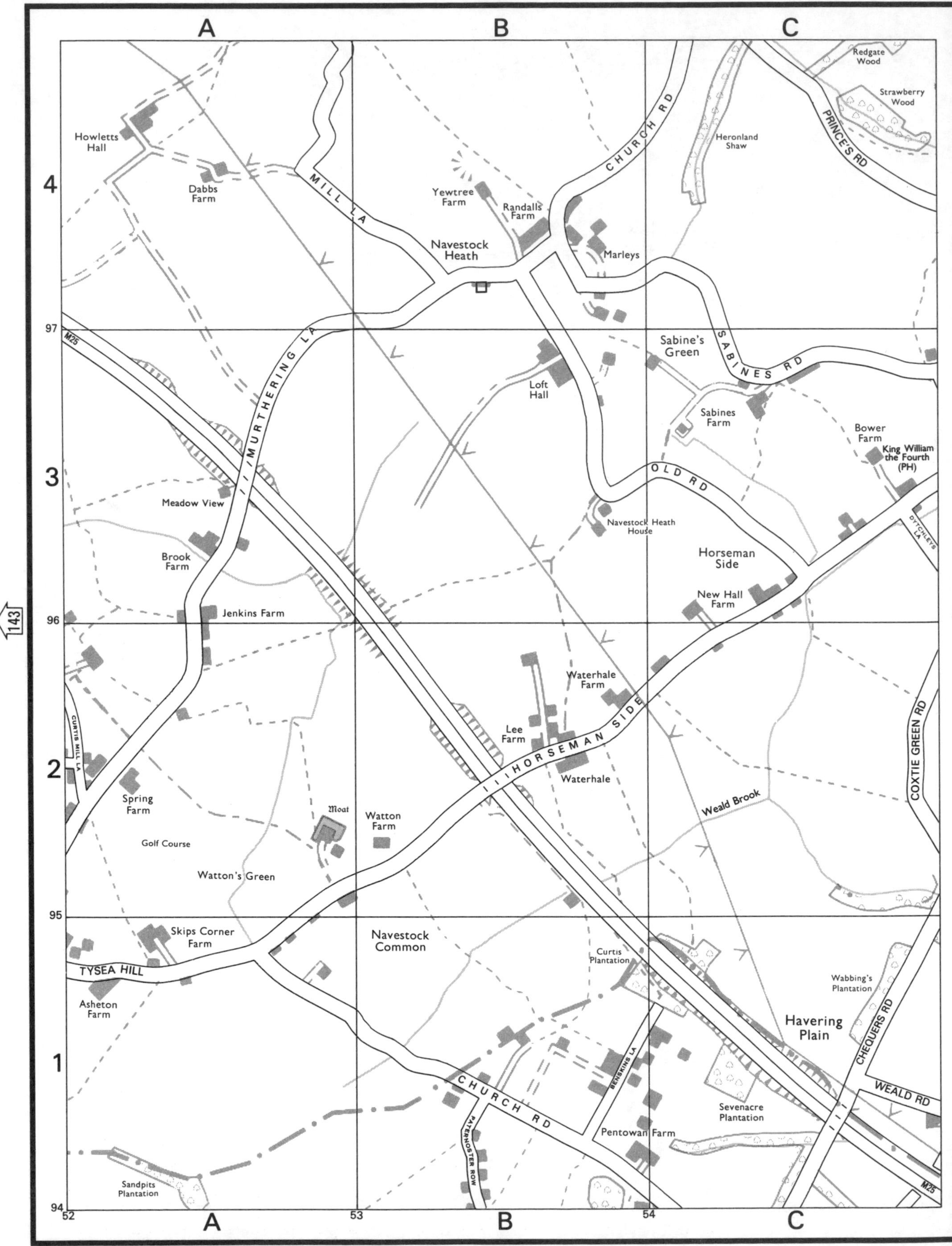
A
B
C
Howletts Hall
Dabbs Farm
MILL LA
Yewtree Farm
Randalls Farm
CHURCH RD
Navestock Heath
Marleys
Heronland Shaw
Redgate Wood
Strawberry Wood
PRINCE'S RD
M25
MURTHERING LA
Sabine's Green
SABINES RD
Loft Hall
Sabines Farm
Bower Farm
King William the Fourth (PH)
OLD RD
Meadow View
Navestock Heath House
Horseman Side
DYTCHLEYS LA
Brook Farm
New Hall Farm
Jenkins Farm
Waterhale Farm
CURTIS MILL LA
Lee Farm
HORSEMAN SIDE
COXTIE GREEN RD
Waterhale
Weald Brook
Spring Farm
Moat
Watton Farm
Golf Course
Watton's Green
Skips Corner Farm
Navestock Common
Curtis Plantation
Wabbing's Plantation
TYSEA HILL
Asheton Farm
Havering Plain
CHEQUERS RD
BENSKINS LA
WEALD RD
CHURCH RD
PATERNOSTER ROW
Sevenacre Plantation
Pentowan Farm
Sandpits Plantation
4
3
2
1
97
96
95
94
52
53
54

143

156

132

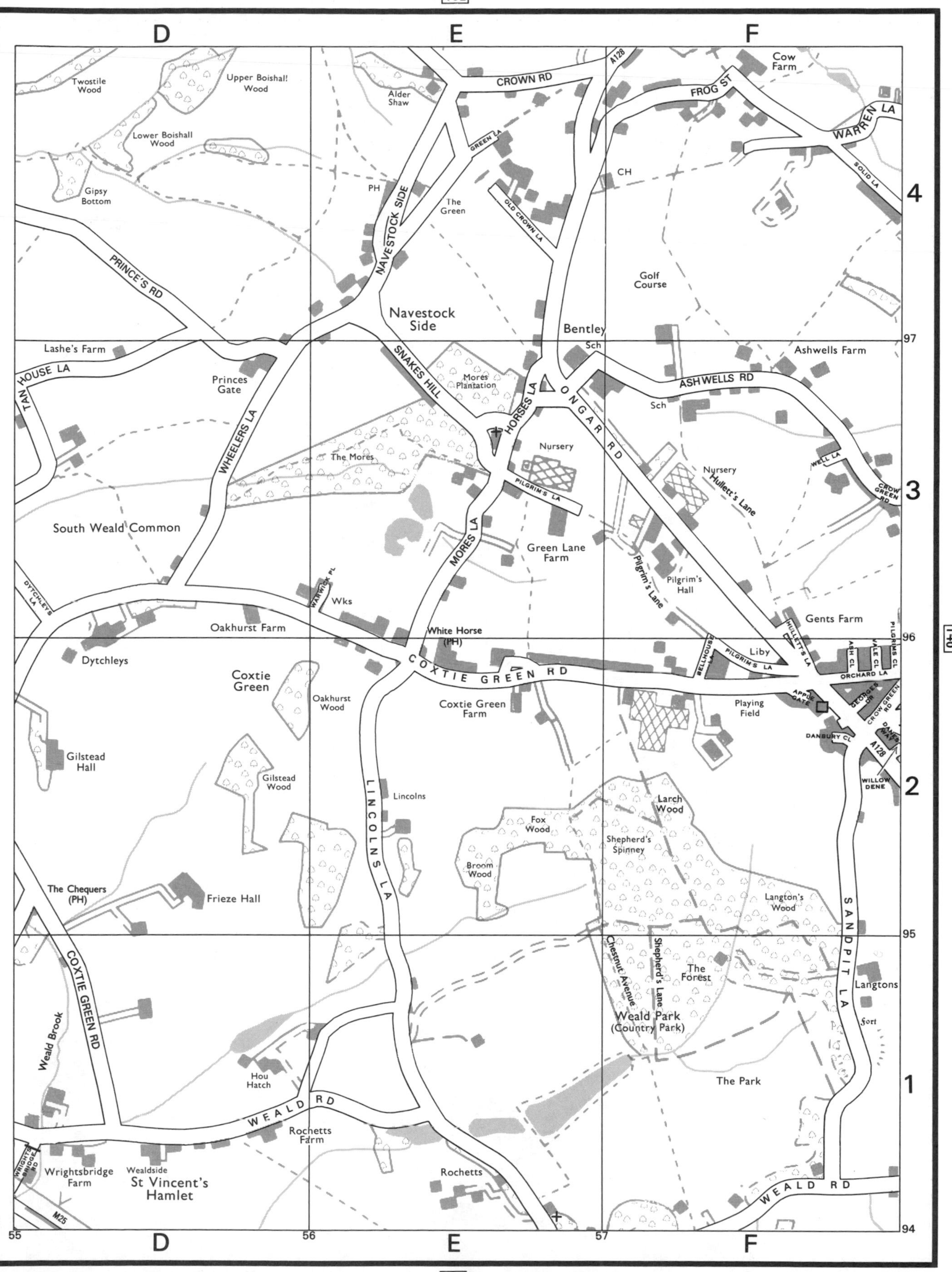

D
E
F
Twostile Wood
Upper Boishall Wood
Lower Boishall Wood
Gipsy Bottom
Alder Shaw
CROWN RD
A128
FROG ST
Cow Farm
WARREN LA
SOLID LA
GREEN LA
PH
The Green
OLD CROWN LA
CH
NAVESTOCK SIDE
PRINCE'S RD
Golf Course
Navestock Side
Bentley
Sch
Lashe's Farm
Ashwells Farm
TAN HOUSE LA
Princes Gate
SNAKES HILL
Mores Plantation
HORSES LA
ONGAR RD
ASHWELLS RD
Sch
WHEELERS LA
The Mores
Nursery
Nursery
Hullett's Lane
WELL LA
CROW GREEN RD
PILGRIM'S LA
South Weald Common
MORES LA
Green Lane Farm
Pilgrim's Lane
Pilgrim's Hall
DYTCHLEYS LA
WARWICK PL
Wks
Oakhurst Farm
White Horse (PH)
Gents Farm
HULLETTS LA
PILGRIMS CL
ASH CL
VALE CL
Dytchleys
COXTIE GREEN RD
BELLHOUSE LA
PILGRIM'S LA
Liby
ORCHARD LA
Coxtie Green
Oakhurst Wood
Coxtie Green Farm
Playing Field
APPLE GATE
GEORGES DR
CROW GREEN RD
DANBURY CL
A128
Gilstead Hall
Gilstead Wood
WILLOW DENE
LINCOLNS LA
Lincolns
Larch Wood
Fox Wood
Shepherd's Spinney
Broom Wood
The Chequers (PH)
Frieze Hall
Langton's Wood
SANDPIT LA
COXTIE GREEN RD
Chestnut Avenue
Shepherd's Lane
The Forest
Langtons
Weald Brook
Weald Park (Country Park)
Fort
Hou Hatch
The Park
WEALD RD
Rochetts Farm
WRIGHTS BRIDGE RD
Wrightsbridge Farm
Wealdside
St Vincent's Hamlet
Rochetts
WEALD RD
M25
55
56
57
94
95
96
97
1
2
3
4

146

157

133

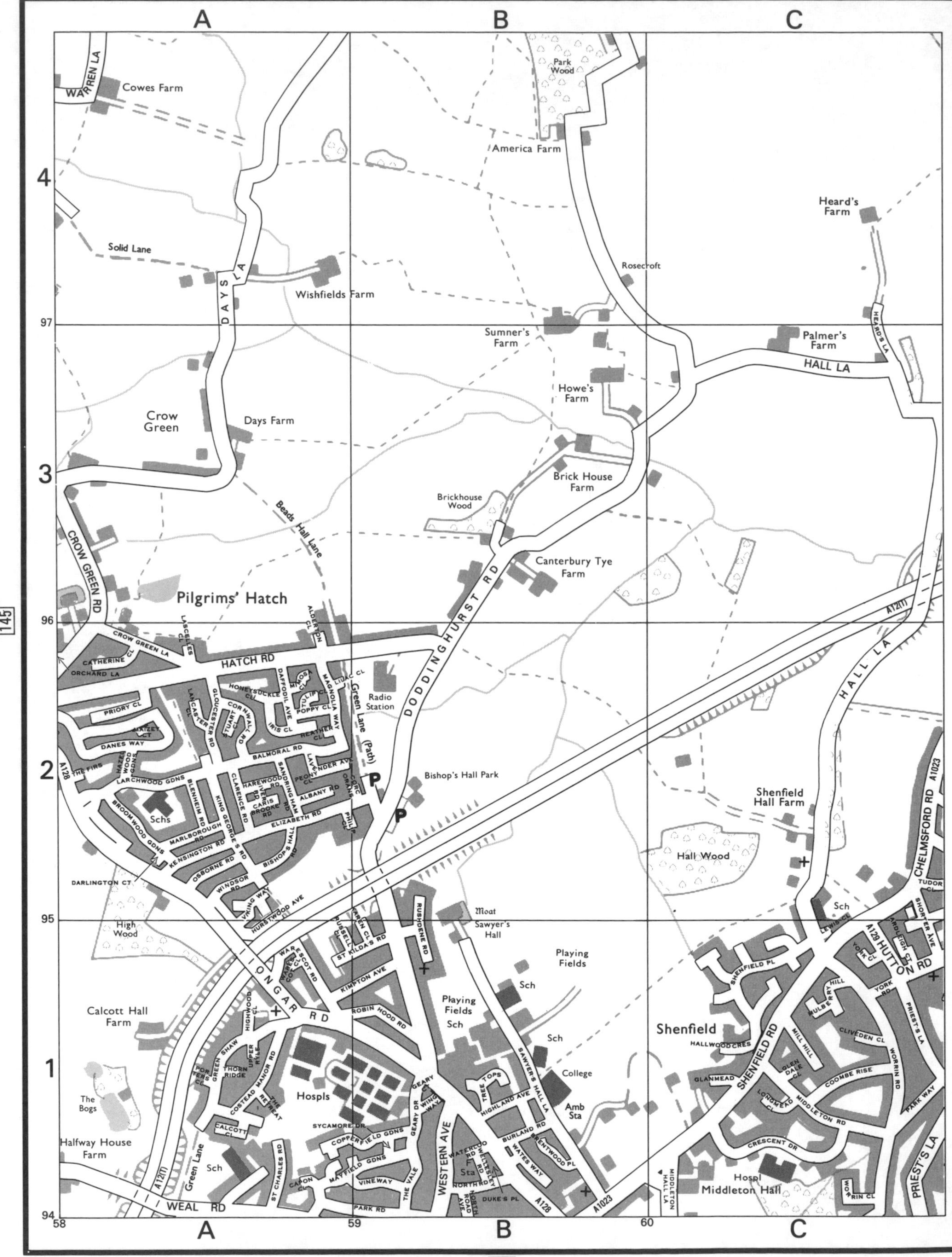
A
B
C
4
3
2
1
97
96
95
94
58
59
60
Cowes Farm
Park Wood
America Farm
Heard's Farm
Solid Lane
Wishfields Farm
Rosecroft
Sumner's Farm
Palmer's Farm
HALL LA
Howe's Farm
Crow Green
Days Farm
Brick House Farm
Brickhouse Wood
Beads Hall Lane
Canterbury Tye Farm
Pilgrims' Hatch
CROW GREEN RD
DAYS LA
DODDINGHURST RD
HATCH RD
CROW GREEN LA
Radio Station
Green Lane (Path)
Bishop's Hall Park
Shenfield Hall Farm
Hall Wood
CHELMSFORD RD
A1023
A12(T)
A128
Schs
BALMORAL RD
DANES WAY
PRIORY CL
LARCHWOOD GDNS
BROOMWOOD GDNS
DARLINGTON CT
High Wood
Moat
Sawyer's Hall
Playing Fields
Sch
HUTTON RD
ONGAR RD
Calcott Hall Farm
Shenfield
SHENFIELD RD
Hospls
College
Amb Sta
The Bogs
Halfway House Farm
WESTERN AVE
Green Lane
WEAL RD
Hospl
Middleton Hall
PRIEST'S LA
CRESCENT DR
MIDDLETON RD
COOMBE RISE

145

158

134

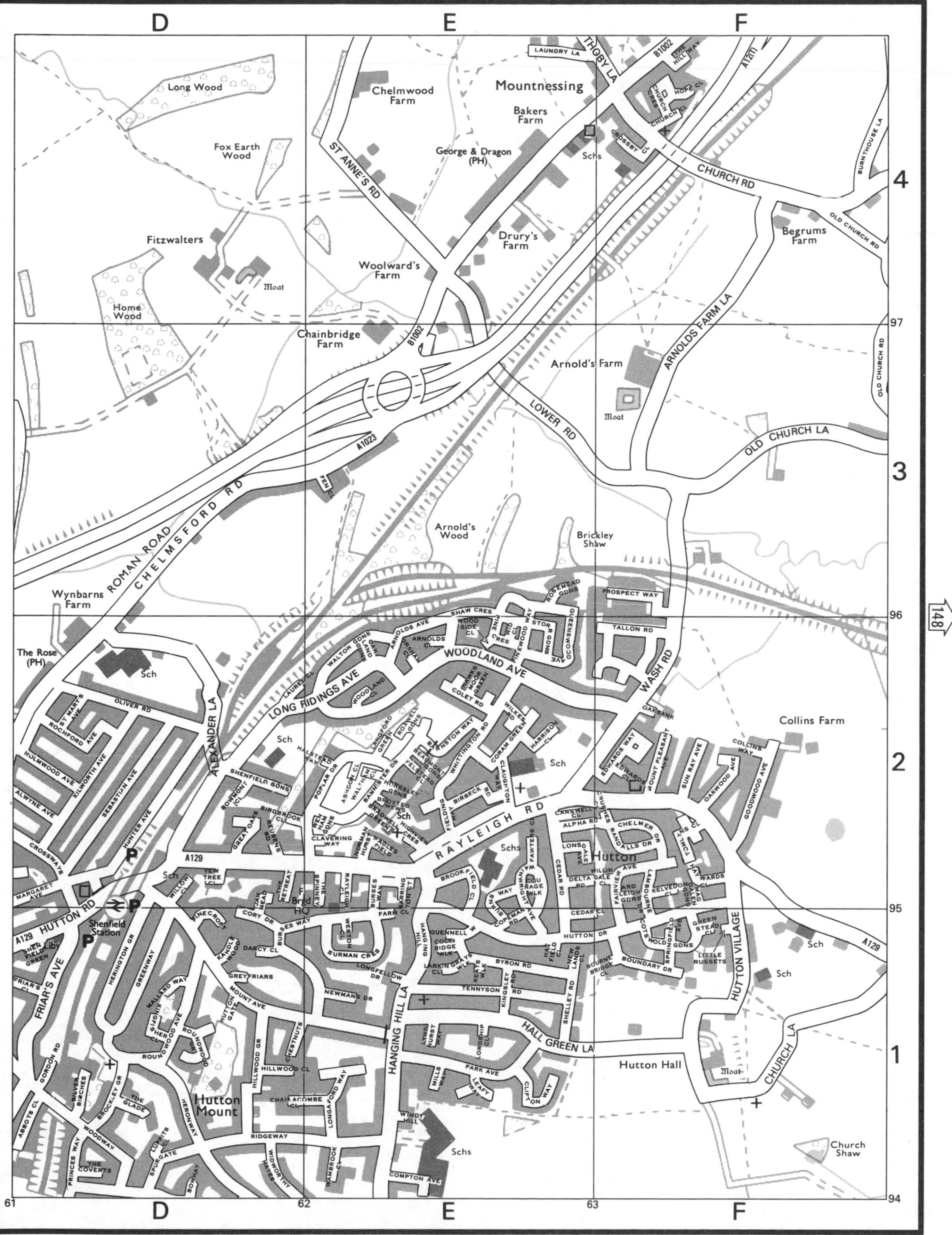
D
E
F
Long Wood
Fox Earth Wood
Fitzwalters
Moat
Home Wood
Chelmwood Farm
Mountnessing
Bakers Farm
George & Dragon (PH)
Schs
Drury's Farm
Woolward's Farm
Chainbridge Farm
Arnold's Farm
Moat
Begrums Farm
LOWER RD
OLD CHURCH LA
ARNOLDS FARM LA
CHURCH RD
OLD CHURCH RD
BURNTHOUSE LA
ST ANNE'S RD
THOBY LA
LAUNDRY LA
B1002
A12(T)
A1023
ROMAN ROAD
CHELMSFORD RD
Arnold's Wood
Brickley Shaw
Wynbarns Farm
The Rose (PH)
Sch
WOODLAND AVE
LONG RIDINGS AVE
WASH RD
PROSPECT WAY
TALLON RD
Collins Farm
ALEXANDER LA
RAYLEIGH RD
Hutton
Schs
A129
HUTTON RD
Shenfield Station
HANGING HILL LA
HALL GREEN LA
Hutton Hall
Moat
CHURCH LA
HUTTON VILLAGE
Hutton Mount
Schs
Church Shaw
4
3
2
1
97
96
95
94
61
62
63

148

159

135

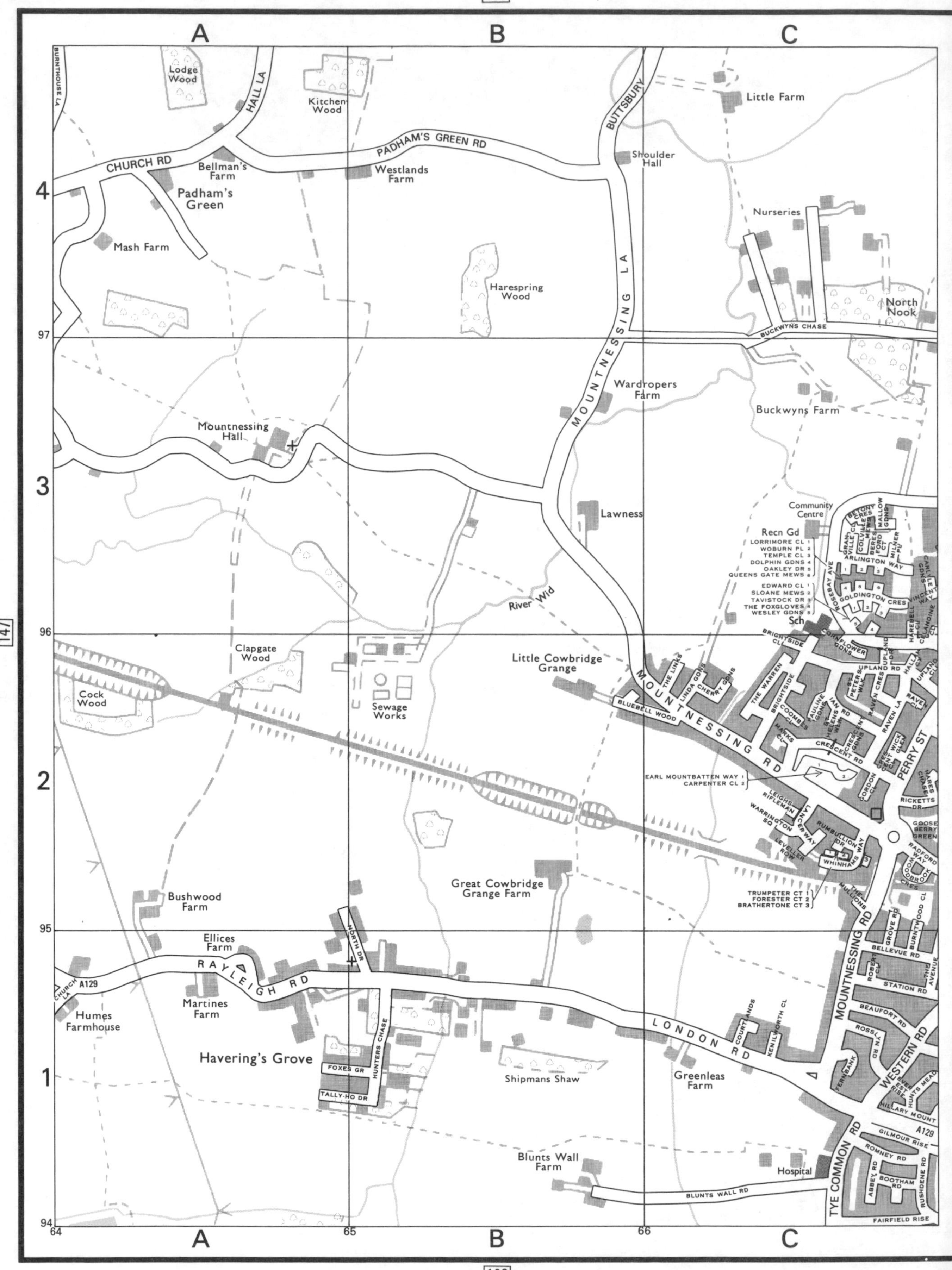
A
B
C
Lodge Wood
Kitchen Wood
HALL LA
BURNTHOUSE LA
BUTTSBURY
Little Farm
CHURCH RD
Bellman's Farm
PADHAM'S GREEN RD
Westlands Farm
Shoulder Hall
Padham's Green
Mash Farm
Nurseries
Harespring Wood
MOUNTNESSING LA
North Nook
BUCKWYNS CHASE
Wardropers Farm
Buckwyns Farm
Mountnessing Hall
Lawness
Community Centre
Recn Gd
LORRIMORE CL 1
WOBURN PL 2
TEMPLE CL 3
DOLPHIN GDNS 4
OAKLEY DR 5
QUEENS GATE MEWS 6
EDWARD CL 1
SLOANE MEWS 2
TAVISTOCK DR 3
THE FOXGLOVES 4
WESLEY GDNS 5
ARLINGTON WAY
GOLDINGTON CRES
ROSEBAY AVE
River Wid
Sch
BRIGHTSIDE CL
CORNFLOWER GDNS
UPLAND RD
Clapgate Wood
Little Cowbridge Grange
Cock Wood
Sewage Works
THE LINKS
LINDA GDNS
CHERRY GDNS
BLUEBELL WOOD
MOUNTNESSING RD
THE WARREN
BRIGHTSIDE
PAULINE GDNS
COOMBES
CRESCENT RD
RAVEN CRES
RAVEN LA
PERRY ST
EARL MOUNTBATTEN WAY 1
CARPENTER CL 2
GORDON CL
RICKETTS DR
LEIGHS RIFLEMAN
WARRINGTON SQ
LANCERS WAY
RUMBULLION DR
LEVELLER ROW
WHINHAMS WAY
GOOSEBERRY GREEN
RADFORD WAY
GOOBROOK
THE MULLIONS
TRUMPETER CT 1
FORESTER CT 2
BRATHERTONE CT 3
Great Cowbridge Grange Farm
Bushwood Farm
Ellices Farm
NORTH DR
RAYLEIGH RD
A129
CHURCH LA
Humes Farmhouse
Martines Farm
Havering's Grove
FOXES GR
HUNTERS CHASE
TALLY-HO DR
Shipmans Shaw
LONDON RD
COURTLANDS
KENILWORTH CL
Greenleas Farm
MOUNTNESSING RD
GROVE RD
BURNTWOOD CL
BELLEVUE RD
ROBERT CL
THE AVENUE
STATION RD
BEAUFORT RD
ROSSLYN RD
WESTERN RD
FERNBANK
HUNTS MEAD
HILLARY MOUNT
GILMOUR RISE
ROMNEY RD
ABBEY RD
BOOTHAM RD
RUSHDENE RD
TYE COMMON RD
Blunts Wall Farm
Hospital
BLUNTS WALL RD
FAIRFIELD RISE
97
96
95
94
64
65
66
4
3
2
1

147

160

136

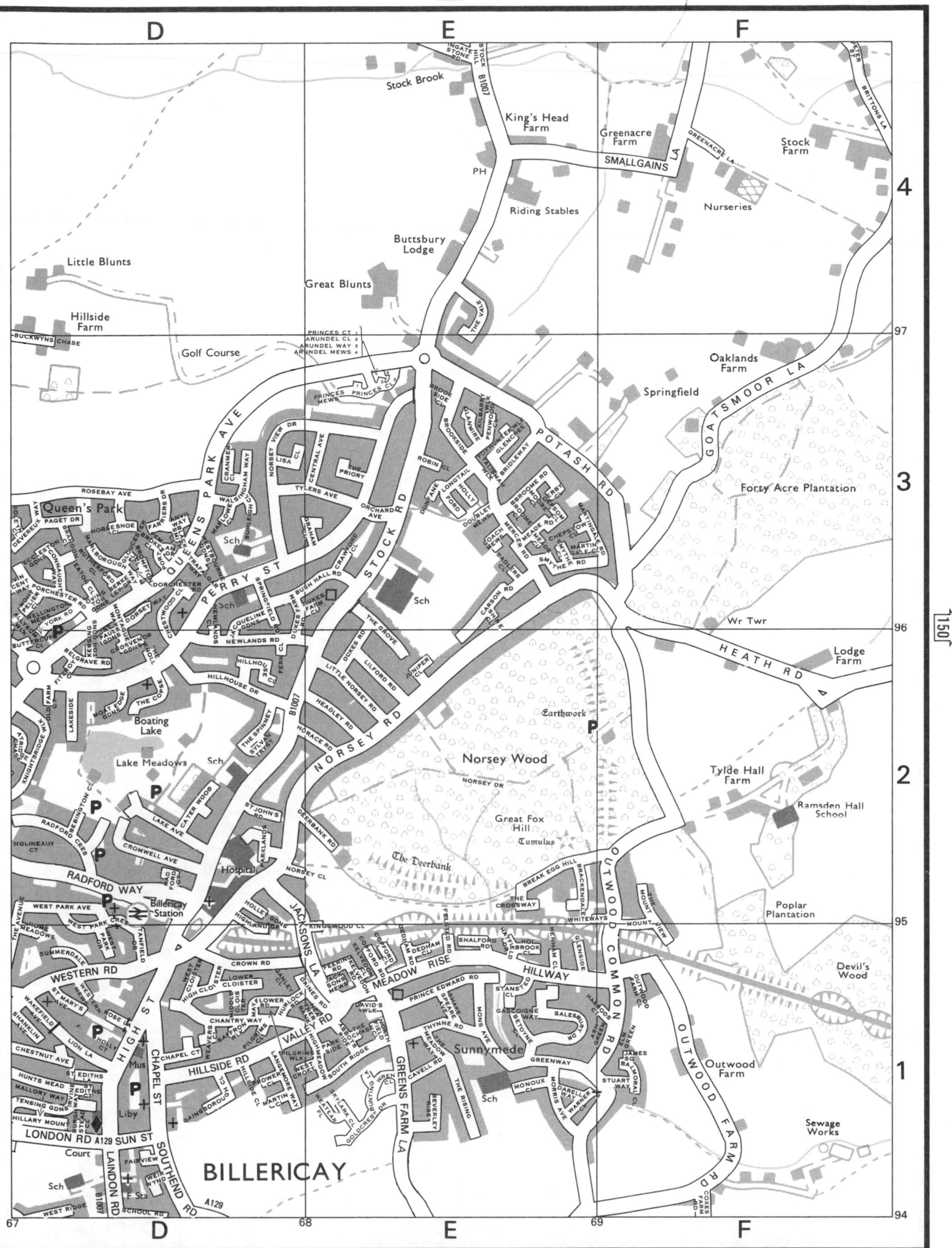

D
E
F
4
3
2
1
97
96
95
94
67
68
69
Stock Brook
King's Head Farm
Greenacre Farm
SMALLGAINS LA
GREENACRE LA
Stock Farm
BRITTONS LA
PH
Riding Stables
Nurseries
Buttsbury Lodge
Little Blunts
Great Blunts
Hillside Farm
BUCKWYNS CHASE
Golf Course
THE VALE
PRINCES CT 1
ARUNDEL CL 2
ARUNDEL WAY 3
ARUNDEL MEWS 4
Oaklands Farm
Springfield
GOATSMOOR LA
POTASH RD
Forty Acre Plantation
Queen's Park
ROSEBAY AVE
QUEENS PARK AVE
PERRY ST
STOCK RD
B1007
Sch
Wr Twr
HEATH RD
Lodge Farm
Earthwork
Norsey Wood
NORSEY DR
NORSEY RD
Great Fox Hill
Tumulus
The Deerbank
Tyldе Hall Farm
Ramsden Hall School
Boating Lake
Lake Meadows
Hospital
RADFORD WAY
Billericay Station
Poplar Plantation
Devil's Wood
OUTWOOD COMMON RD
OUTWOOD FARM RD
Outwood Farm
Sewage Works
JACKSONS LA
MEADOW RISE
HILLWAY
WESTERN RD
CHAPEL ST
HIGH ST
HILLSIDE RD
VALLEY RD
GREENS FARM LA
Sunnymede
Mus
Liby
LONDON RD A129 SUN ST
Court
LAINDON RD
SOUTHEND RD
A129
F Sta
BILLERICAY
WEST RIDGE
SCHOOL RD

150

161

137

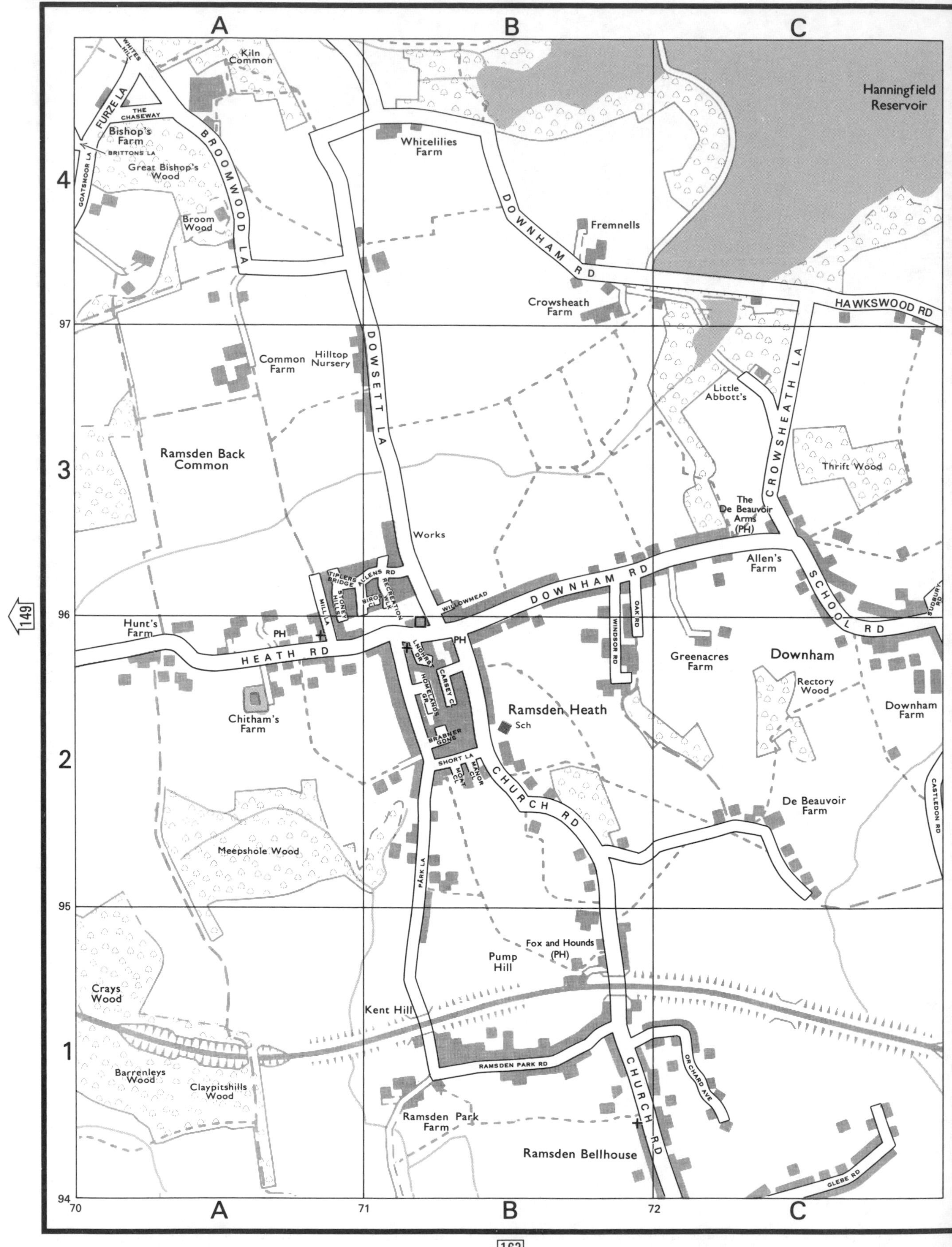

A
B
C
Kiln Common
WHITES HILL
FURZE LA
THE CHASEWAY
Bishop's Farm
BRITTONS LA
GOATSMOOR LA
Great Bishop's Wood
BROOMWOOD LA
Broom Wood
Whitelilies Farm
Hanningfield Reservoir
DOWNHAM RD
Fremnells
Crowsheath Farm
HAWKSWOOD RD
Common Farm
Hilltop Nursery
DOWSETT LA
Little Abbott's
CROWSHEATH LA
Ramsden Back Common
Thrift Wood
The De Beauvoir Arms (PH)
Works
Allen's Farm
TIPLERS BRIDGE
ALLENS RD
RECREATION WLK
STONEY HILLS
MILL LA
BIRD CL
WILLOWMEAD
SCHOOL RD
SUDBURY RD
Hunt's Farm
PH
HEATH RD
LYNDHURST DR
CARSEY CL
HOMELANDS GR
WINDSOR RD
OAK RD
Greenacres Farm
Downham
Rectory Wood
Downham Farm
Chitham's Farm
Ramsden Heath
Sch
BRABNER GDNS
SHORT LA
MOAT CL
MANOR CL
CHURCH RD
De Beauvoir Farm
CASTLEDON RD
Meepshole Wood
PARK LA
Fox and Hounds (PH)
Pump Hill
Crays Wood
Kent Hill
RAMSDEN PARK RD
ORCHARD AVE
Barrenleys Wood
Claypitshills Wood
Ramsden Park Farm
Ramsden Bellhouse
GLEBE RD
4
3
2
1
97
96
95
94
70
71
72

149

162

138

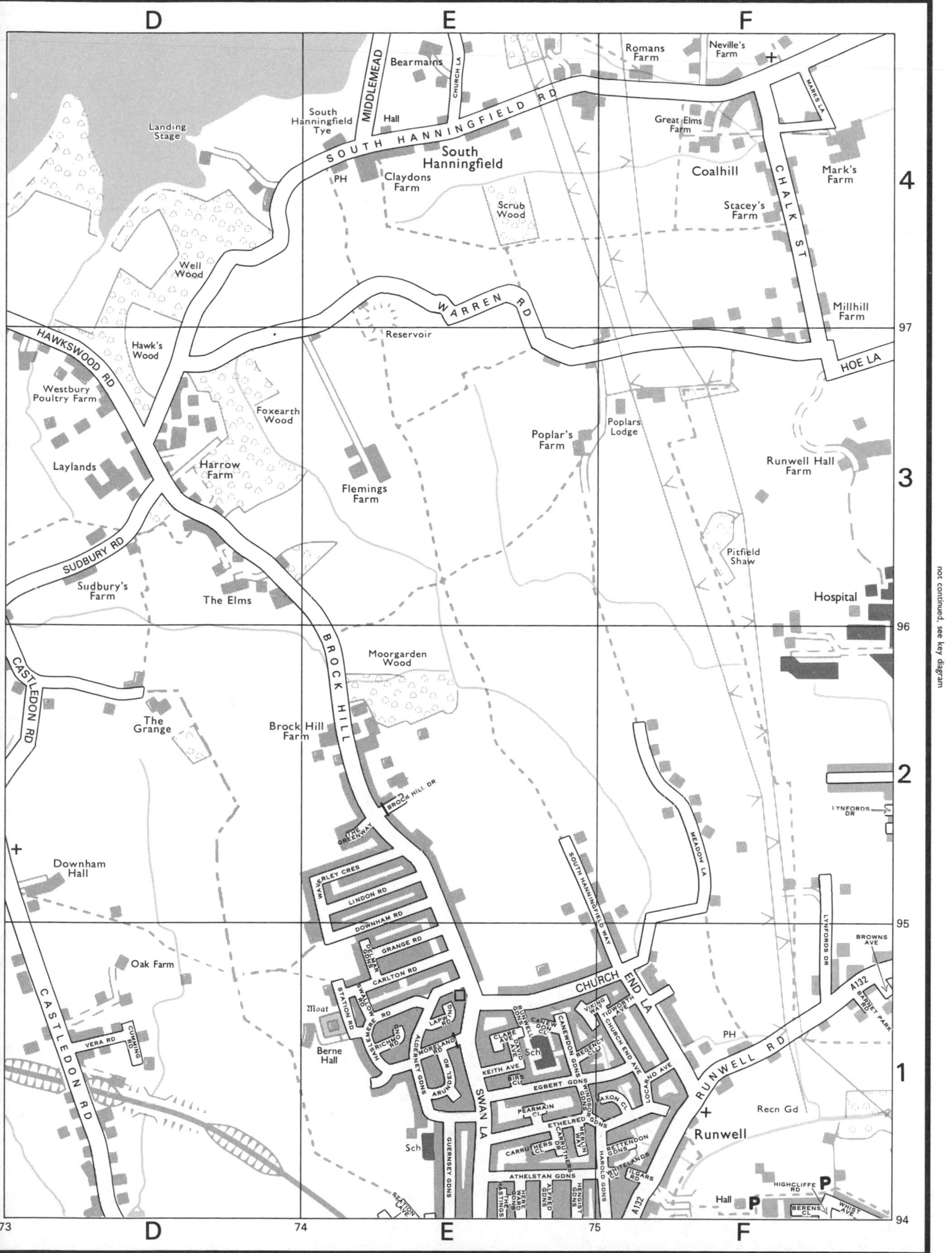

not continued, see key diagram

163

140

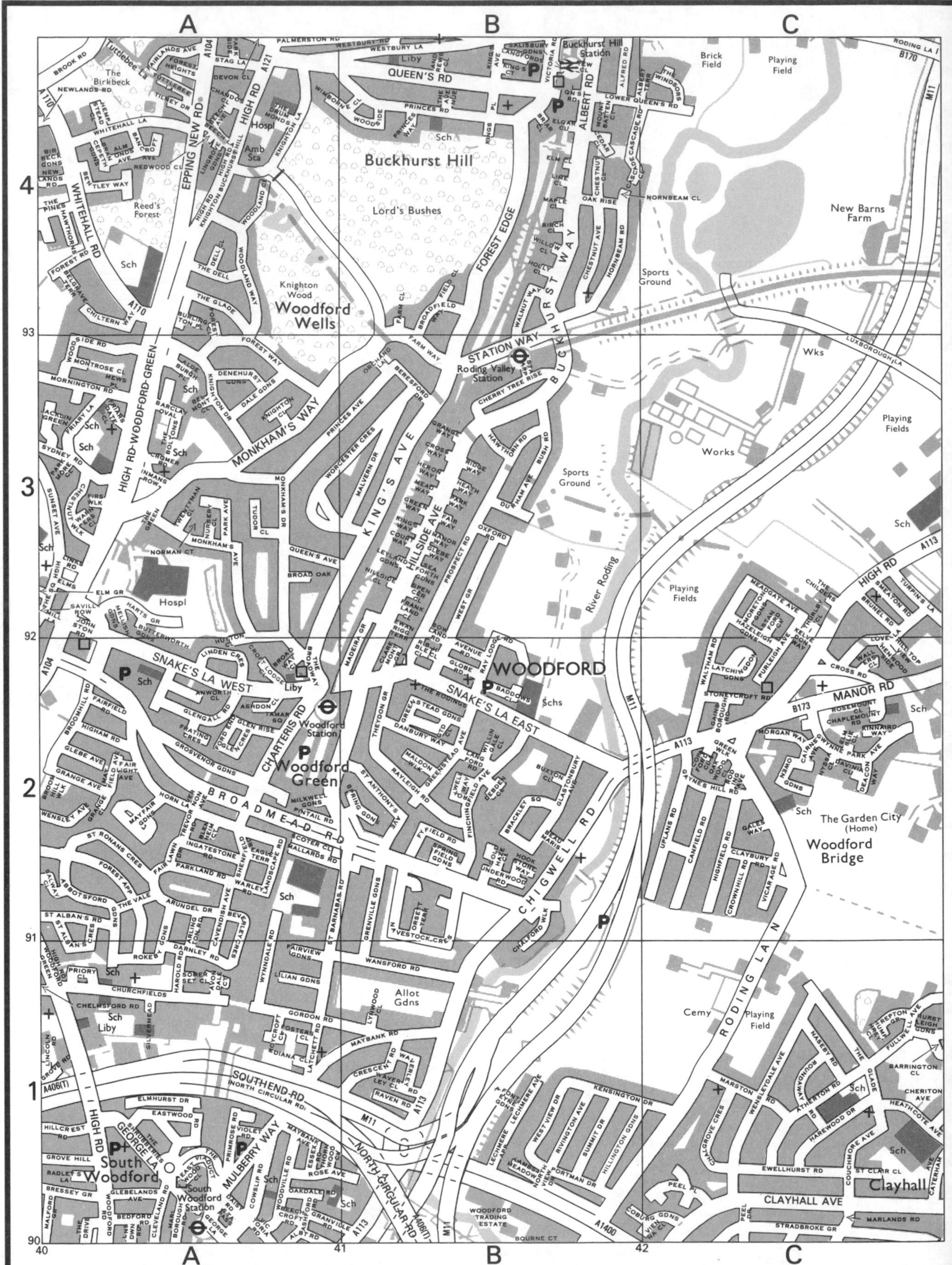

not continued, see key diagram

not continued, see key diagram

141

154

D E F

4 3 2 1

93 92 91 90

43 44 45

CHIGWELL

Chigwell Hall

Chigwell Station

Golf Course

Hospl

Three Forests Way

Oaks Farm

Hillside

Cemy

FOREST HOUSE FIELDS

Grange Hill Station

Grange Hill

Hainault Station

Sports Ground

Hospital Hill Wood

Hospital Hill

Recreation Ground

Playing Field

Wks

FOREST INDUSTRIAL PARK

Fairlop Station

Fullwell Cross

Fairlop

Fairlop Plain Country Park

Allot Gdns

1 HEADINGLEY CL
2 TAUNTON CL

not continued, see key diagram

142

153

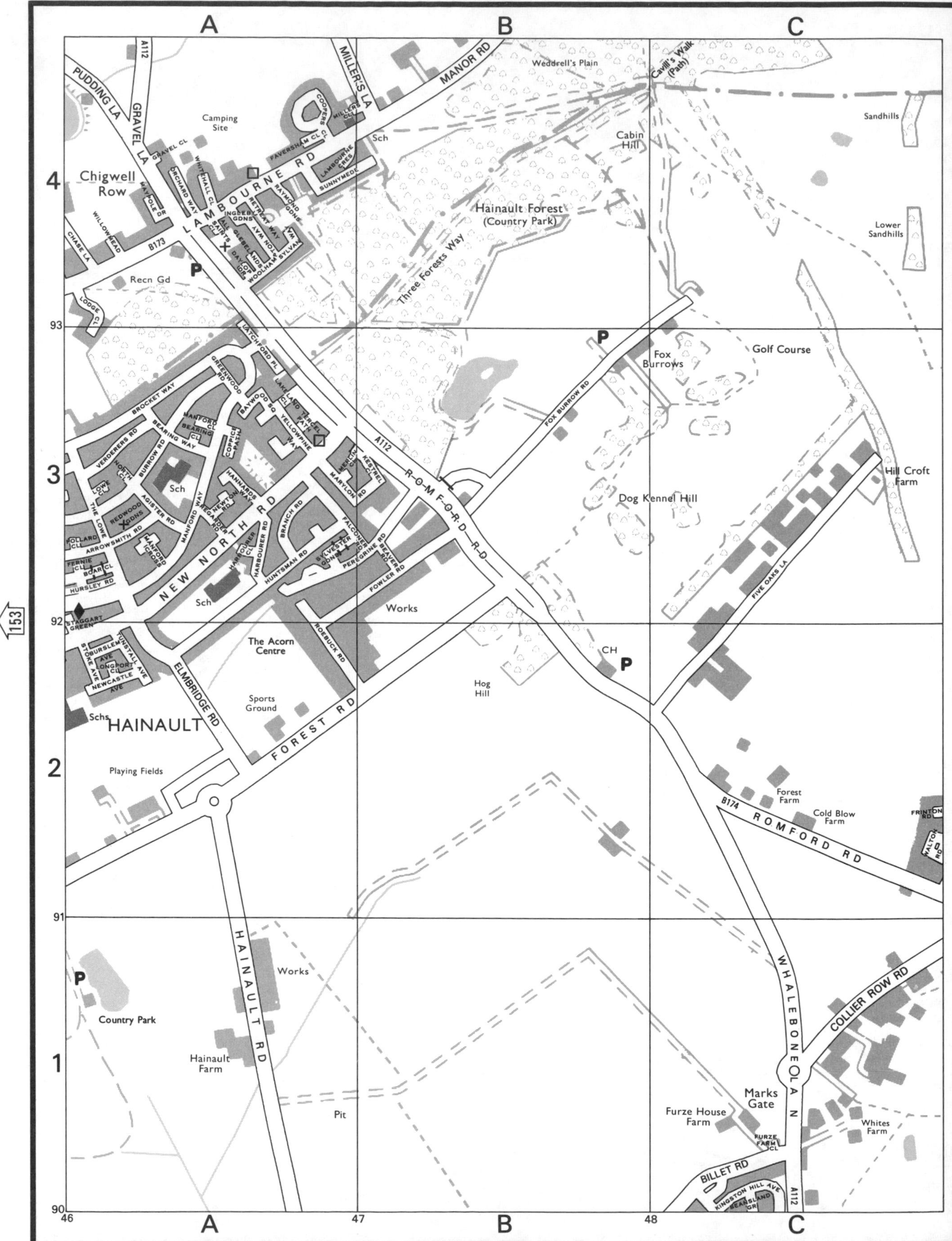

not continued, see key diagram

143

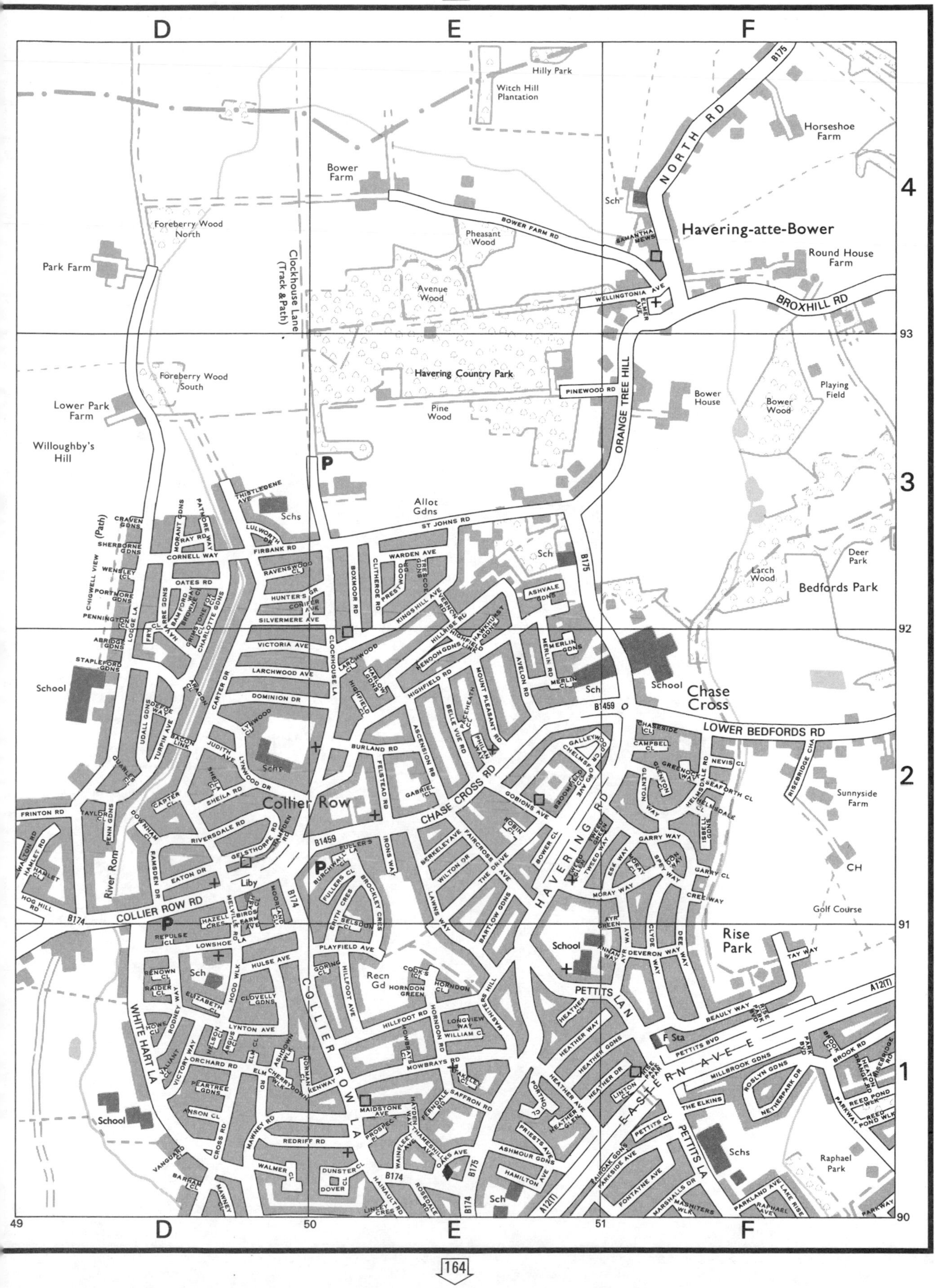

D E F

Hilly Park
Witch Hill Plantation
Horseshoe Farm
NORTH RD
B175
Bower Farm
Sch
Havering-atte-Bower
BOWER FARM RD
SAMANTHA MEWS
Foreberry Wood North
Pheasant Wood
Round House Farm
Park Farm
Clockhouse Lane (Track & Path)
Avenue Wood
WELLINGTONIA AVE
ELMER AVE
BROXHILL RD
Havering Country Park
PINEWOOD RD
ORANGE TREE HILL
Foreberry Wood South
Bower House
Bower Wood
Playing Field
Lower Park Farm
Pine Wood
Willoughby's Hill
P
THISTLEDENE AVE
Allot Gdns
Schs
ST JOHNS RD
(Path)
CRAVEN GDNS
SHERBORNE GDNS
WENSLEY CL
PORTMORE GDNS
PENNINGTON CL
ABRIDGE GDNS
STAPLEFORD GDNS
CHIGWELL VIEW
LODGE LA
PATMORE WAY
MORANT GDNS
RAY RD
CORNELL WAY
OATES RD
LULWORTH DR
FIRBANK RD
RAVENSWOOD CL
HUNTER'S GR
CONIFER AVE
SILVERMERE AVE
VICTORIA AVE
LARCHWOOD AVE
DOMINION DR
BOXMOOR RD
CLITHEROE RD
PRESTWOOD
TRESCOE GDNS
WARDEN AVE
KINGSHILL AVE
ASHVALE GDNS
Sch
B175
Deer Park
Larch Wood
Bedfords Park
MERLIN GDNS
MERLIN RD
MERLIN CL
AVELON RD
MOUNT PLEASANT RD
HIGHFIELD RD
HIGHFIELD LINK
HILLRISE RD
HAWKHURST GDNS
HENDON GDNS
LARCHWOOD
FARLOW GDNS
CLOCKHOUSE LA
School
Chase Cross
B1459
CHASESIDE CL
LOWER BEDFORDS RD
School
FRINTON RD
UDALL GDNS
DEFOE WAY
TURPIN AVE
BACON LINK
JUDITH AVE
LYNWOOD DR
LYNWOOD
CARTER DR
ARAGON
CHARLOTTE GDNS
GRIMSTONE CL
BROWNE CL
BAMFORD WAY
NAVESTOCK CRES
FRIARS CL
BURLAND RD
ASCENSION RD
BELLE VUE RD
PHILAN WAY
CHASE CROSS RD
GALLEYWOOD CR
CHELMSFORD AVE
CAMPBELL CL
NEVIS CL
RISEBRIDGE CHA
GREENOCK WAY
GLENTON WAY
SEAFORTH CL
HELMSDALE
Sunnyside Farm
Schs
SHEILA CL
SHEILA RD
CAPTER CL
Collier Row
FELSTEAD RD
GABRIEL CL
GOBIONS AVE
HAVERING RD
ROBIN CL
QUARLES
TAYLOR
PENN GDNS
DOWNHAM
RIVERSDALE RD
GELSTHORPE RD
HAMPDEN RD
B1459
FULLERS LA
IRONS WAY
BERKELEY AVE
FAIRCROSS AVE
WILTON DR
THE DRIVE
BOWER CL
TWEED WAY
GARRY WAY
ISBELL GDNS
ESK WAY
SPEY WAY
DON WAY
GARRY CL
CH
WALTON RD
HAMLET RD
HAMLET CL
River Rom
FAMSDEN DR
EATON DR
Liby
BURCHWALL CL
FULLERS CL
BROCKLEY CRES
MORAY WAY
CREE WAY
Golf Course
HOG HILL RD
B174
COLLIER ROW RD
MELVILLE RD
BIRDS FARM AVE
B174
MOORLAND CL
ERITH CRES
SELSDON
LAWNS WAY
BARTLOW GDNS
AYR GREEN
CLYDE WAY
DEE WAY
Rise Park
P
HAZEL CRES
REPULSE CL
LOWSHOE LA
PLAYFIELD AVE
School
DEVERON WAY
TAY WAY
RENOWN CL
Sch
HULSE AVE
GORING CL
Recn Gd
COOK'S CL
HORNDON CL
HORNDON GREEN
MASHITERS HILL
PETTITS LA
A12(T)
RAIDER CL
ELIZABETH CL
HOOD WLK
CLOVELLY GDNS
COLLIER ROW LA
HILLFOOT AVE
HILLFOOT RD
HEATHER CL
BEAULY WAY
RISE PARK BVD
WHITE HART LA
RODNEY WAY
HOWE CL
LYNTON AVE
NELSON CL
ARGUS CL
ELM CL
ASHDOWN RD
NORMAN RD
MOWBRAYS CL
HORNDON RD
LONGVIEW WAY
WILLIAM CL
HEATHER WAY
F Sta
PETTITS BVD
PARK BVD
BROOK CL
BROOK RD
VALIANT
VICTORY WAY
ORCHARD RD
ELM RD
CHERRYDOWN WLK
KENWAY
MOWBRAYS RD
OAKLEY CL
HEATHER GDNS
EASTERN AVE
MILLBROOK GDNS
ROSLYN GDNS
NETHERPARK DR
HEATON AVE
GRANGER WAY
WOODBRIDGE
PEARTREE GDNS
MAIDSTONE AVE
SAFFRON RD
FERNDALE RD
PORTNOI CL
HEATHER AVE
HEATHER DR
LINTON CT
THE ELKINS
REED POND WLK
PARKWAY
School
ANSON CL
MAWNEY RD
HAYDEN WAY
PROSPECT PL
HAMESHILL RD
HEATHER GLEN
PRIESTS AVE
PETTITS CL
Schs
Raphael Park
VANGUARD CL
CROSS RD
REDRIFF RD
WAINFLEET AVE
OAKS AVE
ASHMOUR GDNS
BARHAM CL
WALMER CL
DUNSTER CL
DOVER
B174
B175
HAMILTON AVE
TAUROAK GDNS
PARKSIDE AVE
FONTAYNE AVE
MARSHALLS DR
MASHITERS WLK
PARKLAND AVE
LAKE RISE
RAPHAEL AVE
MAWNEY CL
LINLEY CRES
HAINAULT RD
ROSEDALE RD
B174
Sch
A12(T)

4 3 2 1

93 92 91 90

49 50 51

D E F

156

164

144

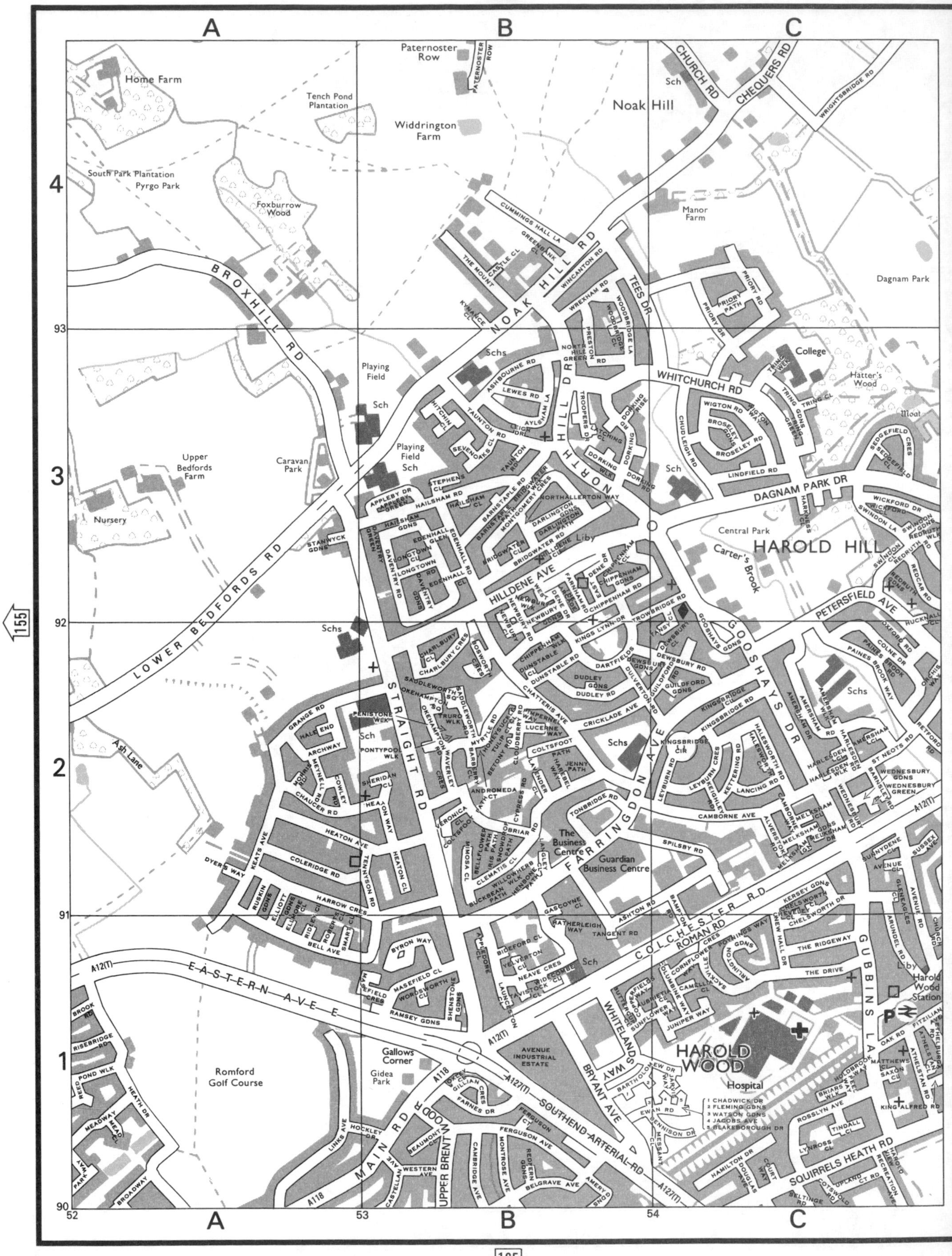
A
B
C
4
3
2
1
93
92
91
90
52
53
54
Home Farm
Paternoster Row
Tench Pond Plantation
Widdrington Farm
Noak Hill
Sch
CHURCH RD
CHEQUERS RD
WRIGHTSBRIDGE RD
South Park Plantation
Pyrgo Park
Foxburrow Wood
Manor Farm
Dagnam Park
BROXHILL RD
CUMMINGS HALL LA
NOAK HILL RD
WINCANTON RD
TEES DR
PRIORY RD
PRIORY PATH
College
Playing Field
Schs
WHITCHURCH RD
Hatter's Wood
Moat
TRING CL
Upper Bedfords Farm
Caravan Park
NORTH HILL DR
DAGNAM PARK DR
SEDGEFIELD CRES
Nursery
LOWER BEDFORDS RD
HAILSHAM RD
NORTHALLERTON WAY
Central Park
HAROLD HILL
Carter's Brook
HILLDENE AVE
Liby
PETERSFIELD AVE
GOOSHAYS DR
STRAIGHT RD
Ash Lane
FARRINGDON AVE
KINGSBRIDGE RD
The Business Centre
Guardian Business Centre
COLCHESTER RD
ROMAN RD
GUBBINS LA
A12(T)
EASTERN AVE E
Harold Wood Station
HAROLD WOOD
Hospital
1 CHADWICK DR
2 FLEMING GDNS
3 WATSON GDNS
4 JACOBS AVE
5 BLAKEBOROUGH DR
Romford Golf Course
Gallows Corner
Gidea Park
AVENUE INDUSTRIAL ESTATE
BRYANT AVE
SOUTHEND ARTERIAL RD
A127(T)
MAIN RD
UPPER BRENTWOOD RD
A118
SQUIRRELS HEATH RD
BROADWAY

155

165

145

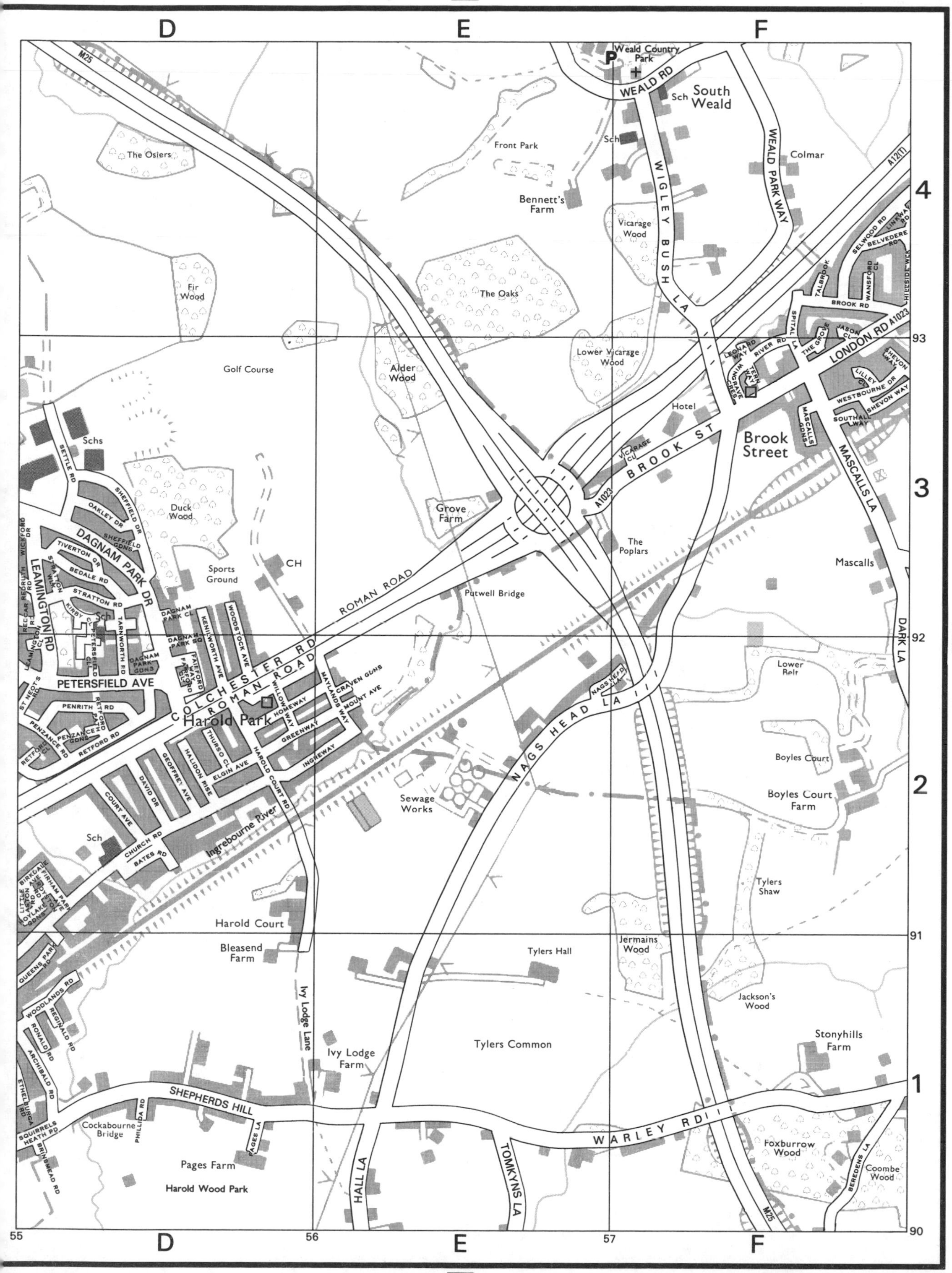

D
E
F
M25
Weald Country Park
WEALD RD
Sch
South Weald
Sch
WIGLEY BUSH LA
WEALD PARK WAY
Colmar
A12(T)
The Osiers
Front Park
Bennett's Farm
Vicarage Wood
4
Fir Wood
The Oaks
Golf Course
Alder Wood
Lower Vicarage Wood
93
Hotel
Brook Street
BROOK ST
VICARAGE CL
A1023
LONDON RD A1023
SPITAL LA
BROOK RD
TALBROOK
SELWOOD RD
BELVEDERE RD
WANSFORD CL
HILLSIDE WALK
LINKWAY
JASON CL
THE GROVE
RIVER RD
LEONARD WAY
FERN WAY
MASCALLS GDNS
MASCALLS LA
LILLEY CL
WESTBOURNE DR
SHEVON WAY
SOUTHALL WAY
Schs
SETTLE RD
SHEFFIELD DR
OAKLEY DR
SHEFFIELD GDNS
Duck Wood
DAGNAM PARK DR
TIVERTON GR
BEDALE RD
STRATTON RD
LEAMINGTON RD
WICKFORD WAY
REDRUTH RD
Grove Farm
3
The Poplars
Mascalls
Sports Ground
CH
ROMAN ROAD
Putwell Bridge
DAGNAM PARK CL
KENILWORTH AVE
WOODSTOCK AVE
DAGNAM PARK SQ
TARNWORTH RD
DAGNAM PARK GDNS
PETERSFIELD CL
PETERSFIELD AVE
COLCHESTER RD
ROMAN ROAD
Harold Park
WILLOWAY WAY
HOMEWAY
NAYLANDS WAY
CRAVEN GDNS
MOUNT AVE
GREENWAY
INGREWAY
92
DARK LA
Lower Belt
NAGS HEAD LA
NAGS HEAD LA
PENRITH RD
PENZANCE GDNS
PENZANCE RD
RETFORD RD
ST NEOTS RD
THURSO CL
HALIDON RISE
GEOFFREY AVE
DAVID DR
ELGIN AVE
HAROLD COURT RD
COURT AVE
Sewage Works
Boyles Court
2
Boyles Court Farm
Sch
CHURCH RD
BATES RD
Ingrebourne River
Tylers Shaw
Harold Court
Bleasend Farm
Tylers Hall
Jermains Wood
91
QUEENS PARK
WOODLANDS RD
REGINALD RD
RONALD RD
ARCHIBALD RD
Ivy Lodge Lane
Jackson's Wood
Ivy Lodge Farm
Tylers Common
Stonyhills Farm
1
SHEPHERDS HILL
WARLEY RD
Cockabourne Bridge
PHILLIDA RD
PAGES LA
SQUIRRELS HEATH RD
BRINSMEAD RD
Foxburrow Wood
Coombe Wood
BEREDENS LA
Pages Farm
Harold Wood Park
HALL LA
TOMKYNS LA
M25
55
56
57
90
D
E
F

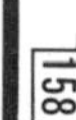

158

166

146

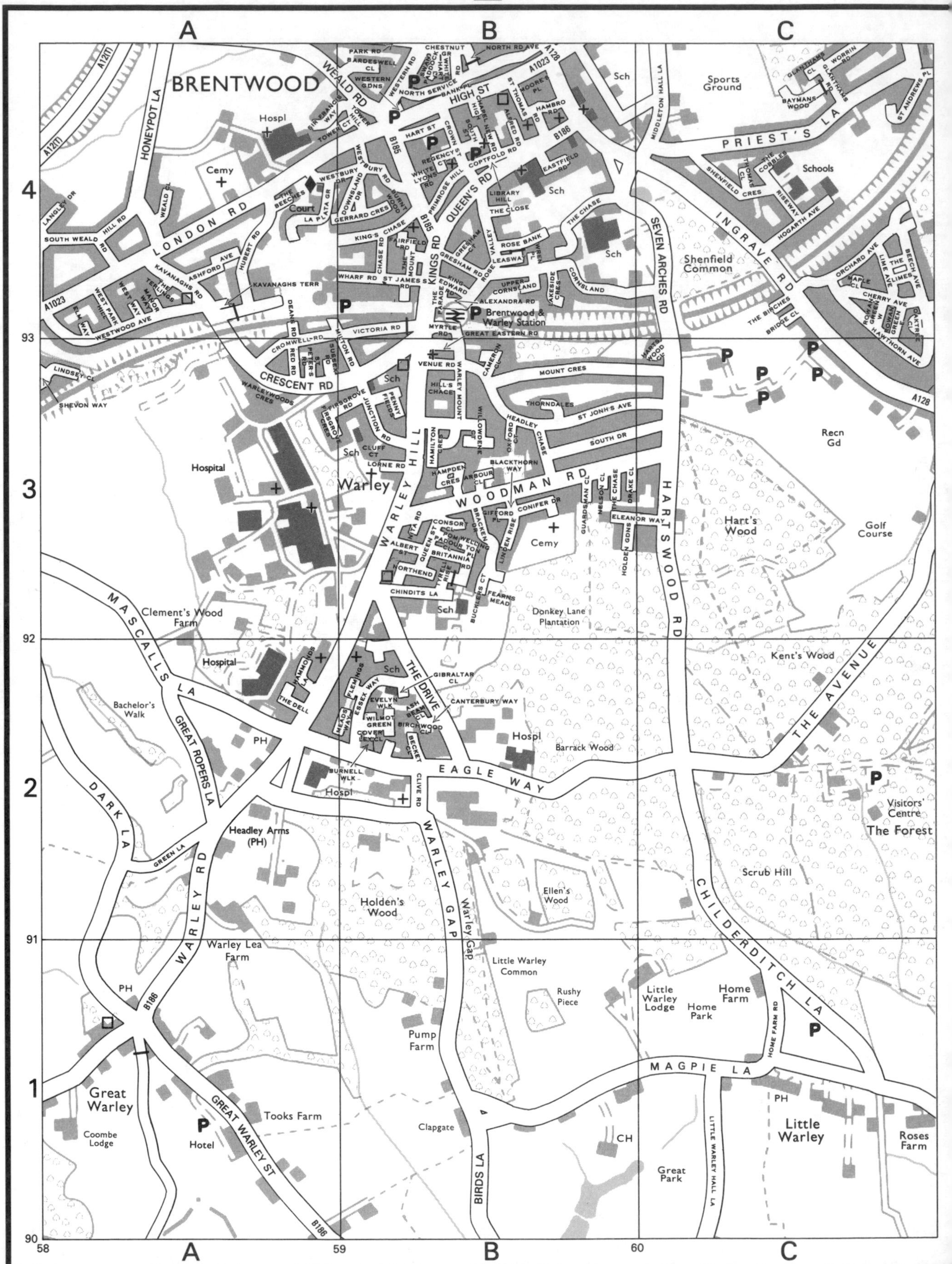
A
B
C
BRENTWOOD
Hospl
Cemy
Court
Sch
Sports Ground
Schools
PRIEST'S LA
Shenfield Common
INGRAVE RD
SEVEN ARCHES RD
Brentwood & Warley Station
LONDON RD
HIGH ST
WEALD RD
KINGS RD
QUEEN'S RD
HONEYPOT LA
CRESCENT RD
WESTWOOD AVE
A1023
A128
A12(T)
B185
B186
Recn Gd
Hospital
Warley
WARLEY HILL
WOODMAN RD
HARTSWOOD RD
Hart's Wood
Golf Course
Donkey Lane Plantation
Clement's Wood Farm
MASCALLS LA
Kent's Wood
THE AVENUE
THE DRIVE
Bachelor's Walk
GREAT ROPERS LA
PH
Barrack Wood
EAGLE WAY
Visitors' Centre
The Forest
DARK LA
Headley Arms (PH)
WARLEY RD
WARLEY GAP
Warley Gap
GREEN LA
Scrub Hill
Ellen's Wood
Holden's Wood
CHILDERDITCH LA
Warley Lea Farm
Little Warley Common
Rushy Piece
Little Warley Lodge
Home Park
Home Farm
HOME FARM RD
Pump Farm
MAGPIE LA
Great Warley
Tooks Farm
Clapgate
Coombe Lodge
Hotel
GREAT WARLEY ST
BIRDS LA
CH
Great Park
LITTLE WARLEY HALL LA
Little Warley
Roses Farm
93
92
91
90
58
59
60
1
2
3
4

157

167

147

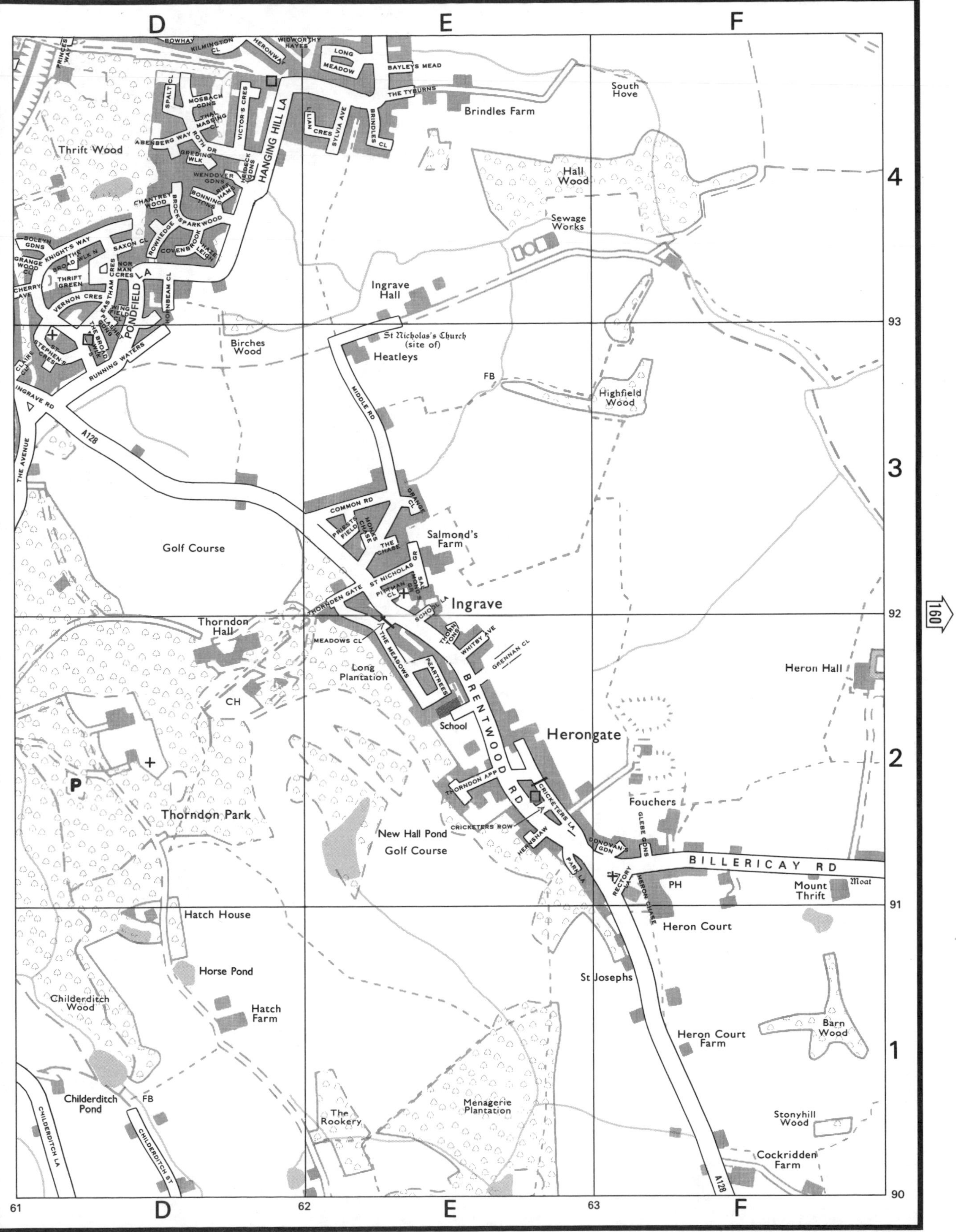
D
E
F
Thrift Wood
Hanging Hill La
Pondfield La
Brindles Farm
South Hove
Hall Wood
Sewage Works
Ingrave Hall
St Nicholas's Church (site of)
Heatleys
Birches Wood
Running Waters
Ingrave Rd
A128
The Avenue
FB
Highfield Wood
Middle Rd
Common Rd
Salmond's Farm
Golf Course
Ingrave
Thorndon Hall
Thorndon Gate
Long Plantation
CH
School
Herongate
Brentwood Rd
Heron Hall
P
Thorndon Park
New Hall Pond
Golf Course
Fouchers
Billericay Rd
PH
Mount Thrift
Moat
Heron Court
Hatch House
Horse Pond
St Josephs
Childerditch Wood
Hatch Farm
Heron Court Farm
Barn Wood
Childerditch Pond
Childerditch La
Childerditch St
The Rookery
Menagerie Plantation
Stonyhill Wood
Cockridden Farm
1
2
3
4
90
91
92
93
61
62
63

160

168

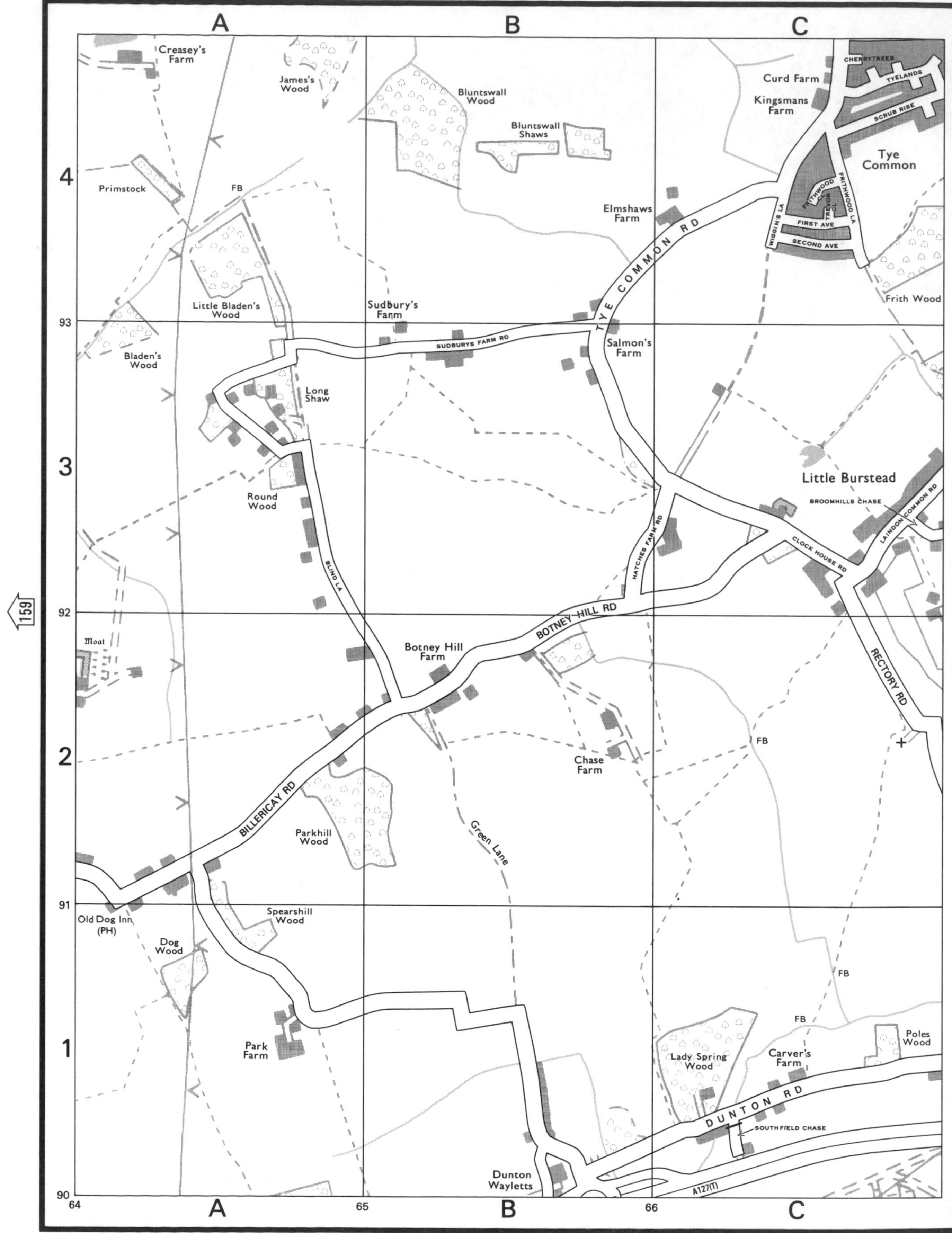
148
A
B
C
Creasey's Farm
James's Wood
Bluntswall Wood
Bluntswall Shaws
Curd Farm
Kingsmans Farm
CHERRYTREES
TYELANDS
SCRUB RISE
Tye Common
Primstock
FB
Elmshaws Farm
TYE COMMON RD
WIGGIN'S LA
FRITHWOOD CL
TREVOR CL
FRITHWOOD LA
FIRST AVE
SECOND AVE
Frith Wood
Little Bladen's Wood
Sudbury's Farm
SUDBURYS FARM RD
Salmon's Farm
Bladen's Wood
Long Shaw
Little Burstead
Round Wood
BROOMHILLS CHASE
LAINDON COMMON RD
HATCHES FARM RD
CLOCK HOUSE RD
BLIND LA
BOTNEY HILL RD
159
Moat
Botney Hill Farm
RECTORY RD
FB
Chase Farm
BILLERICAY RD
Parkhill Wood
Green Lane
Old Dog Inn (PH)
Spearshill Wood
Dog Wood
FB
FB
Poles Wood
Park Farm
Lady Spring Wood
Carver's Farm
DUNTON RD
SOUTHFIELD CHASE
Dunton Wayletts
A127(T)
4
93
3
92
2
91
1
90
64
65
66
169

149

D
E
F
Gatwick House
Bell Hill
Sch
White Farm
Browns Farm
South Green
Southend Farm
Brier Mount
Kennels
Schs
Sch
Laindon Common
Dukes Head (PH)
Blackmore Farm
Grange
Works
Gurnard's Farm
Great Burstead
Barleylands
River Crouch
Sewage Works
Council Depot
White's Farm
Noak Bridge
FB
Nursery
Benson's Farm
Prince of Wales (PH)
Laindon Barn
Barn Farm
Steeple View Farm
Compton Avenue
LAINDON RD
LAINDON COMMON RD
NOAK HILL RD
CHURCH ST
MILL RD
SOUTHEND RD
COXES FARM RD
OUTWOOD COMMON RD
GREENS FARM LA
GRANGE RD
KENNEL LA
BARLEYLANDS RD
RECTORY RD
NEW RD
DUNTON RD
WASH RD
SOUTHEND-ARTERIAL-RD
A127(T)
A129
A176
B1007
4
3
2
1
93
92
91
90
67
68
69

162

170

150
171
161
A
B
C
4
3
2
1
93
92
91
90
70
71
72
HOMESTEAD RD
GLEBE RD
CHURCH RD
Police Office
DURLEY AVE
HIGHCLIFF DR
CANFORD AVE
STUDLAND AVE
PARKSTONE AVE
BRANKSOME AVE
NEWHOUSE AVE
WOOLSHOTS RD
A129
Parsonage Farm
Crays Hall Farm
River Crouch
Woolshots Farm
LONDON RD
Crays Hall Cottages
CHURCH LA
Sch
Southlands
SOUTHLANDS RD
RAMSDEN VIEW RD
CORNER RD
Southacre Nursery
APPROACH RD
STACEY'S MOUNT
Shepherd & Dog (PH)
NORTH RD
UPPER RD
SOUTH RD
Crays Hill
HOPE RD
HIGH VIEW RISE
BROMFELDE RD
CRAYS HILL
BARNS RD
GRANITES CHASE
A129 SOUTHEND RD
River Crouch
Whites Bridge Farm
QUEENS RD
OAK AVE
CRAYS HILL RD
PITSEA VIEW RD
BORWICK LA
GARDINERS LA N
White's Bridge
Great Barns
HARDING'S ELMS RD
JUBILEE RD
OAK AVE
OAK RD
Nuttons Wood
BURY FARM LA
OAK LA
Great Wasketts
Summerhill Farm
WASH RD
Nursery
A127(T)
Portsea Ho Fm
PIPPS HILL RD N
SOUTHEND ARTERIAL RD
CHRISTOPHER MARTIN RD
Laindon Ponds
Pippshill
Nurseries
GARDINERS WAY
ILFORD TRADING ESTATE
Works
HERONSGATE TRADING ESTATE
OLYMPIC BUSINESS CENTRE
PAYCOCKE RD
THE ENTERPRISE CENTRE
PAYCOCKE CL
HONYWOOD RD
GOODVIEW RD
EASTFIELD RD
PH
BOWLERS CROFT
GARDINERS LA S
CRANES CL
ORION CT
Wks
A127(T)
MILES GRAY RD
Works
A1235
CHESTER HALL LA
BENTALLS
PIPPS HILL RD S
GARDINERS CL
ST PETER'S PAVEMENT
CRANES FARM RD
HOLDEN GDNS
HOLDEN RD
THEYDON CRES
PENDLE DR
Hotel
P
PIPPS HILL CL
A1235
MATCHING GREEN
Schs
WHITMORE CT
BATTLESWICK
WHITMORE WAY
DENYS DR

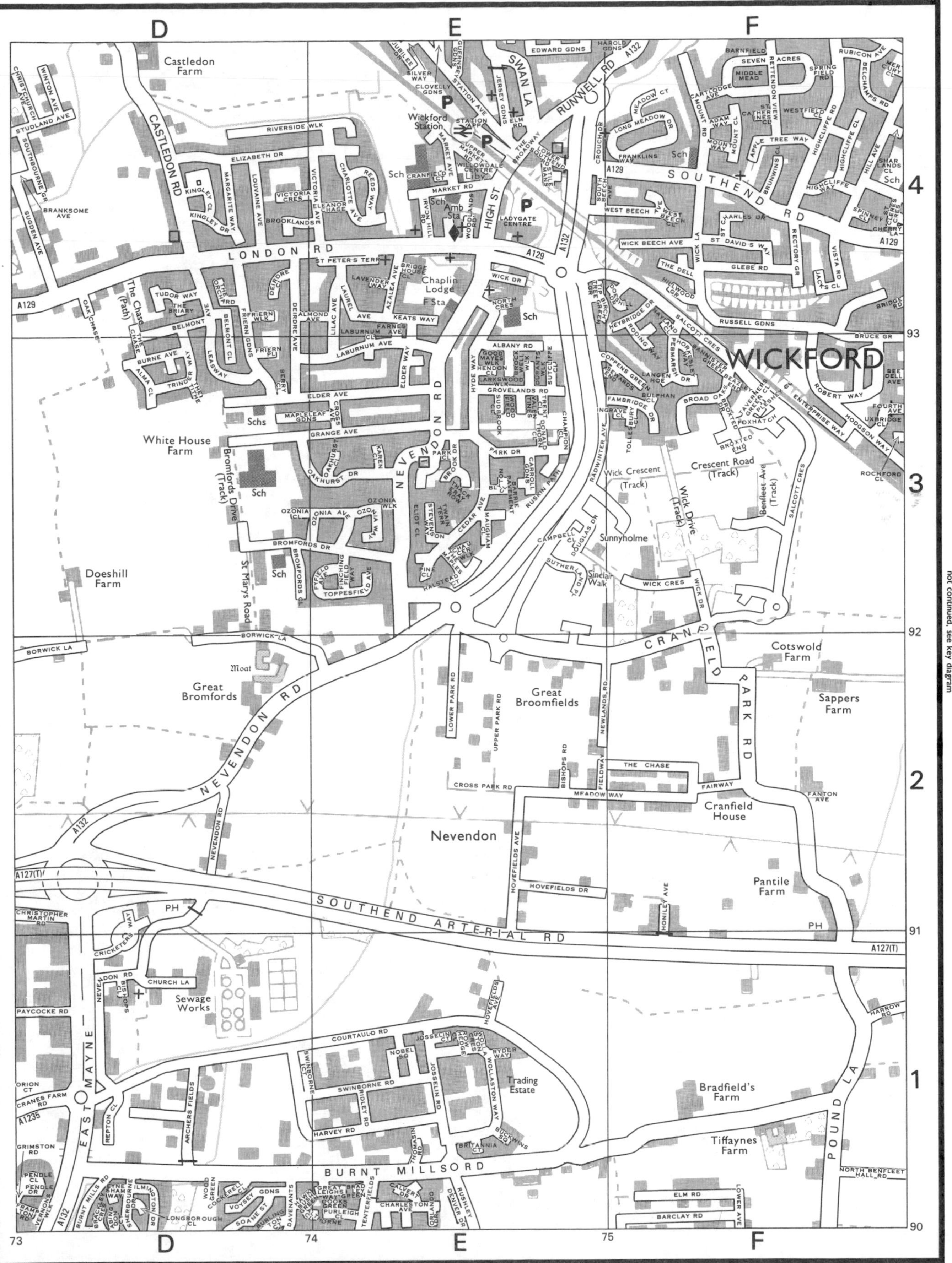

151
172
not continued, see key diagram

155

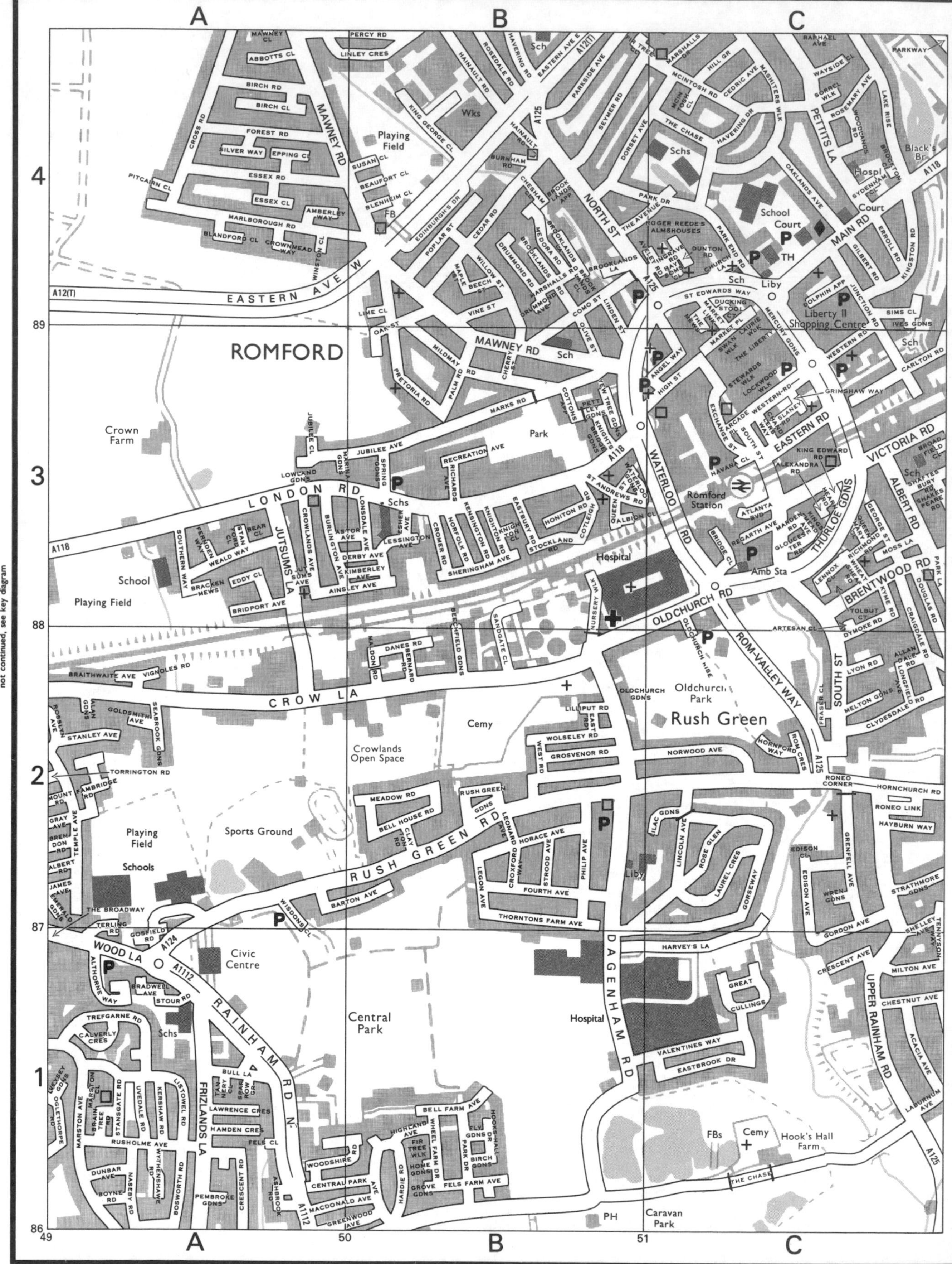

not continued, see key diagram

173

156

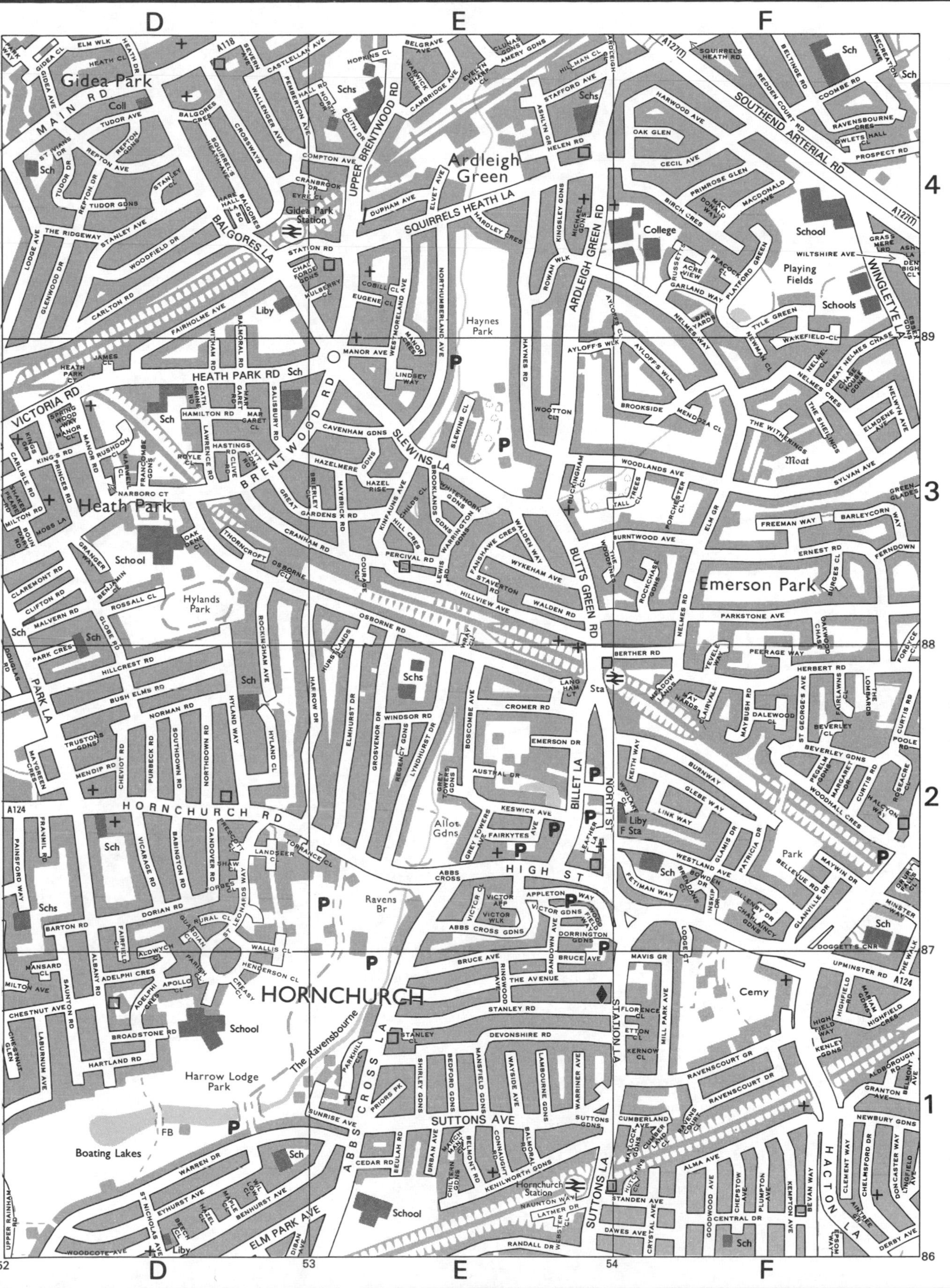
Gidea Park
Ardleigh Green
Heath Park
Emerson Park
HORNCHURCH
Haynes Park
Hylands Park
Harrow Lodge Park
Boating Lakes
Playing Fields
Cemy
Moat
Ravens Br
The Ravensbourne
Allot Gdns
Hornchurch Station
Gidea Park Station
MAIN RD
SQUIRRELS HEATH LA
UPPER BRENTWOOD RD
BRENTWOOD RD
HEATH PARK RD
SOUTHEND ARTERIAL RD
ARDLEIGH GREEN RD
BUTTS GREEN RD
HORNCHURCH RD
HIGH ST
NORTH ST
BILLET LA
STATION LA
SUTTONS LA
SUTTONS AVE
ABBS CROSS LA
ELM PARK AVE
HACTON LA
PARK LA
WINGLETYE LA
SLEWINS LA
BALGORES LA
UPMINSTER RD

166

174

157
175
165
A
B
C
4
3
2
1
89
88
87
86
55
56
57
Greathouse
Sutton's Farm
Prospect Farm
Cornlands Farm
Great Tomkyns
Little Tomkyns Farms
Emery Farm
Ingrebourne Farm
Mount Pleasant Farm
Upminster Lodge Farm
SOUTHEND ARTERIAL RD
A127(T)
The Rosary
Chapmans Farm
BIRD LA
TOMKYNS LA
FOLKES LA
HALL LA
Nursery
Lillyputts
School
Offices
Playing Fields
Ingrebourne River
Golf Course
CH
Cranham
FRONT LA
WINGLETYE LA
Upminster Station
Upminster Bridge Station
ST MARY'S LA
STATION RD
CORBETS TEY RD
UPMINSTER
Cranham Hall
PIKE LA
Liby
Sch
PH
B187
A124
B1421

158

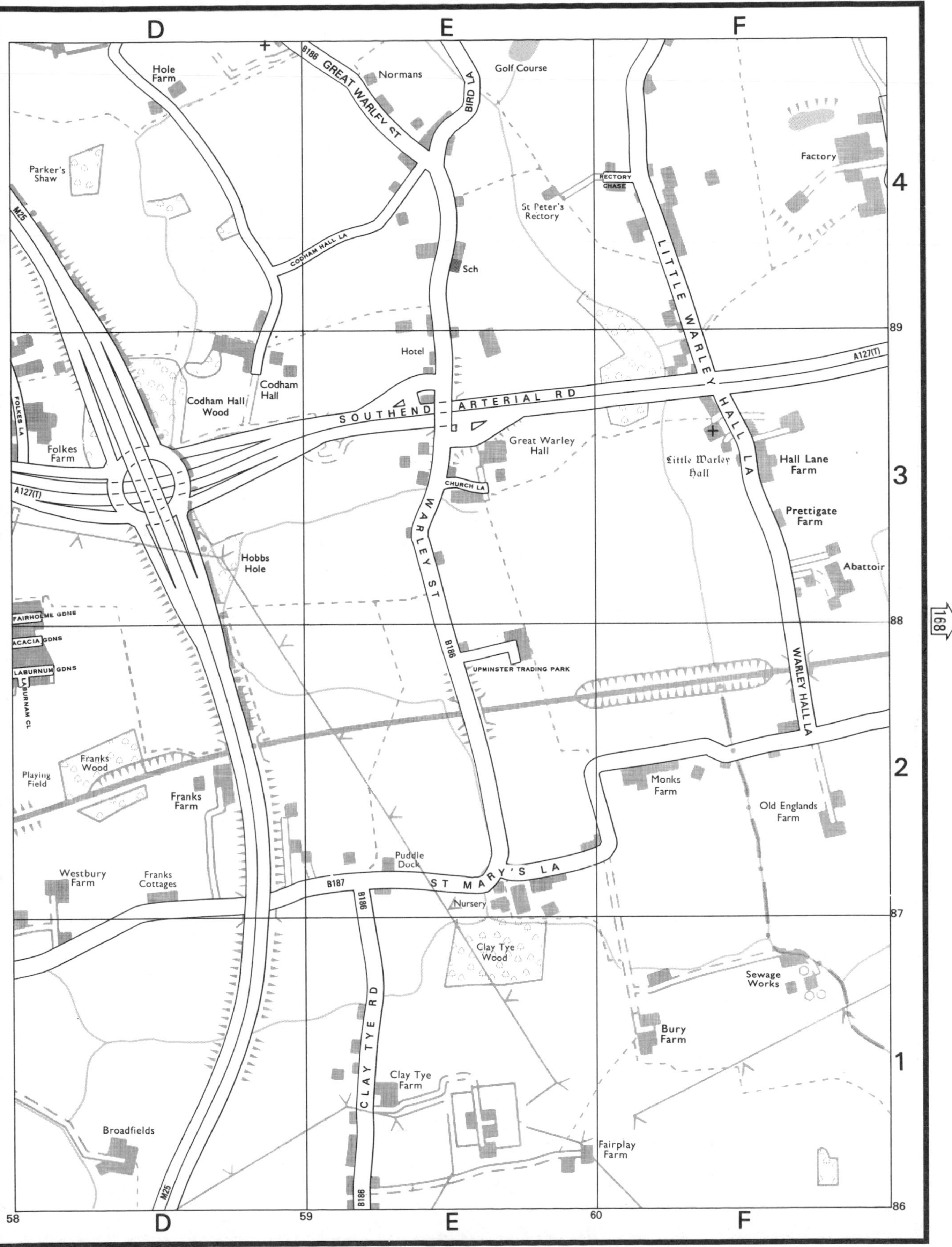
D
E
F
Hole Farm
B186 GREAT WARLEY ST
Normans
BIRD LA
Golf Course
Parker's Shaw
Factory
4
RECTORY CHASE
St Peter's Rectory
M25
CODHAM HALL LA
Sch
LITTLE WARLEY HALL LA
89
Hotel
A127(T)
Codham Hall
Codham Hall Wood
SOUTHEND ARTERIAL RD
FOLKES LA
Great Warley Hall
Little Warley Hall
Hall Lane Farm
Folkes Farm
3
A127(T)
CHURCH LA
WARLEY ST
Prettigate Farm
Hobbs Hole
Abattoir
FAIRHOLME GDNS
88
ACACIA GDNS
B186
LABURNUM GDNS
UPMINSTER TRADING PARK
LABURNUM CL
WARLEY HALL LA
Franks Wood
2
Playing Field
Monks Farm
Franks Farm
Old Englands Farm
Puddle Dock
Westbury Farm
Franks Cottages
B187
ST MARY'S LA
B186
Nursery
87
Clay Tye Wood
Sewage Works
CLAY TYE RD
Bury Farm
1
Clay Tye Farm
Broadfields
Fairplay Farm
M25
B186
86
58
D
59
E
60
F

168

176

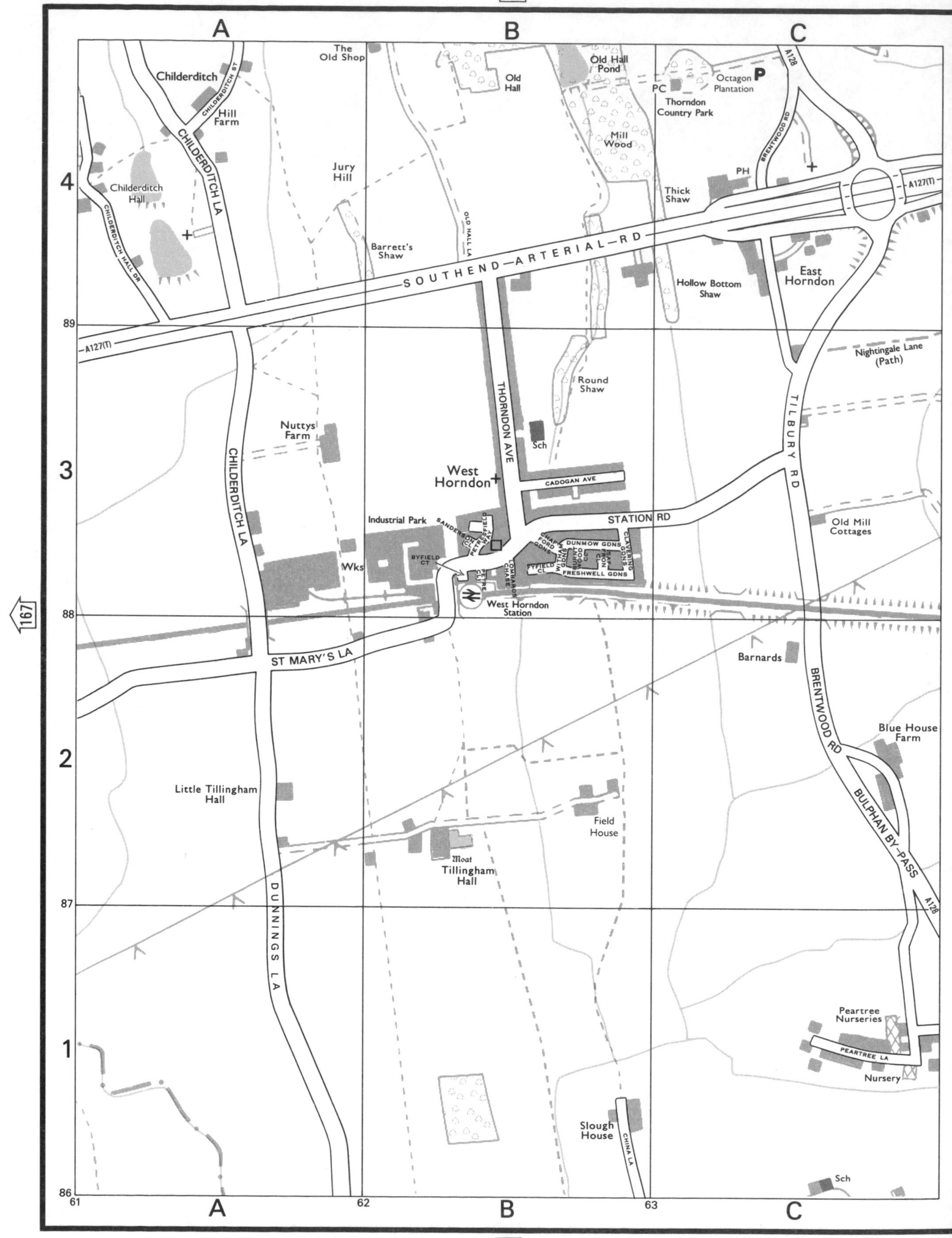
159
A
B
C
The Old Shop
Old Hall Pond
Old Hall
Childerditch
CHILDERDITCH ST
Hill Farm
PC
Octagon Plantation
P
Thorndon Country Park
A128
Mill Wood
BRENTWOOD RD
CHILDERDITCH LA
Jury Hill
PH
A127(T)
4
Childerditch Hall
Thick Shaw
CHILDERDITCH HALL DR
OLD HALL LA
Barrett's Shaw
SOUTHEND—ARTERIAL—RD
East Horndon
Hollow Bottom Shaw
89
A127(T)
Nightingale Lane (Path)
THORNDON AVE
Round Shaw
TILBURY RD
Nuttys Farm
Sch
3
CHILDERDITCH LA
West Horndon
CADOGAN AVE
STATION RD
Industrial Park
SANDERSON CL
PETRESFIELD WAY
Old Mill Cottages
DUNMOW GDNS
CLAVERING GDNS
FYFIELD CL
FRESHWELL GDNS
LOMBARDS CHASE
BYFIELD CT
Wks
West Horndon Station
167
88
ST MARY'S LA
Barnards
BRENTWOOD RD
2
Blue House Farm
Little Tillingham Hall
BULPHAN BY-PASS
Field House
Moat
Tillingham Hall
87
A128
DUNNINGS LA
Peartree Nurseries
1
PEARTREE LA
Nursery
Slough House
CHINA LA
Sch
86
61
62
63
A
B
C
177

160

Friern Manor Wood
Eastlands Spring
SOUTHEND-ARTERIAL-RD
A127(T)
NIGHTINGALE
B148
Automobile Research Centre
Green Meadows Nurseries
Brookman's Farm
Friern Manor
MERRYLANDS CHASE
SEAX WAY
SABLE WAY
CHRISTY WAY
FENTON WAY
BRAMSTON LINK
HORNSBY WAY
Southfields
Works
WEST MAYNE
BRAMSTON WAY
SAFFRON CT
BUXTON LINK
Sch
Moat
The Old Rectory
Dunton Hills Farm
WOODSTOCK CRES
WOODSTOCK GDNS
BROADWATER GREEN
KENNEDY AVE
MENZIES AVE
PALATINE PARK
DURHAM RD
MANDEVILLE WAY
HELMORES
ROWEN HALL
FRASER CL
PAXFORDS
BLACKMORES
Rectory
Dunton Park Caravan Site
CHURCH RD
Sewage Works
Dunton Hall
B1036
OSTERLEY DR
KENTON WAY
CHORLEY CL
AMERSHAM AVE
MAPLETREE LA
HOLLY GR
NIGHTINGALES
MAHONIA DR
LOWER DUNTON RD
WARWICK PL
STAFFORD GREEN
FOREST GLADE
FIRST AVE
CENTRAL AVE
SECOND AVE
THIRD AVE
FOURTH AVE
HILLCREST AVE
COBURG LA
HIGH BANK
SUNNYSIDE
LAKE VIEW
WEST HOOK
Poultry Farm
Dunton Poultry Farm
Lower Dunton Hall
Balgownie Farm
BULPHAN BY-PASS
BRENTWOOD RD
Garlesters
Motel
Noke Hall
Doesgate Farm
DOESGATE LA
OLD CHURCH HILL
Bentley Farm
Little Malgraves
Manor House
A128
CHURCH RD
D
E
F
4
3
2
1
89
88
87
86
64
66

170

178

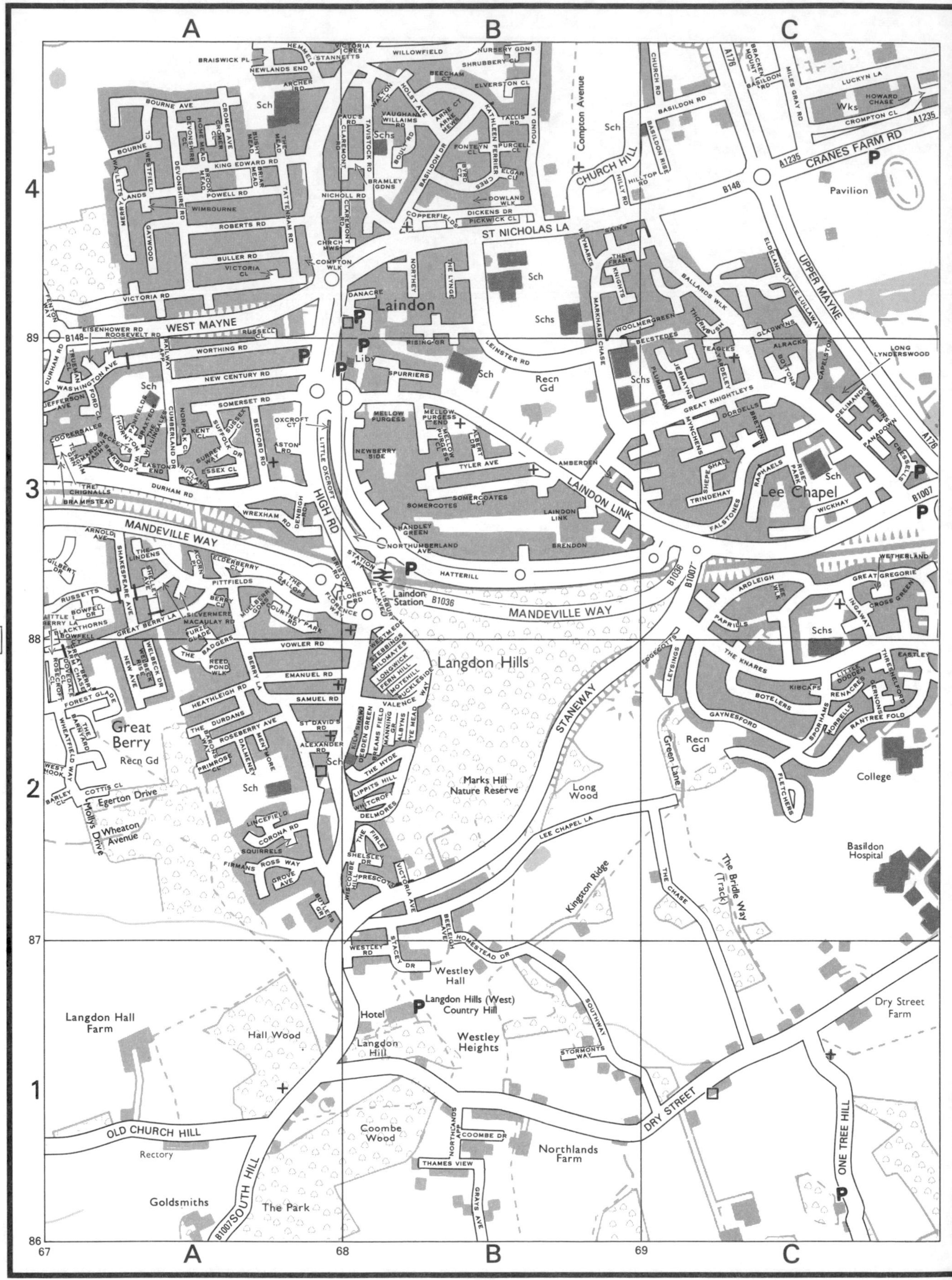
161
A
B
C
Laindon
Langdon Hills
Lee Chapel
Great Berry
Recn Gd
Marks Hill Nature Reserve
Long Wood
Westley Hall
Langdon Hills (West) Country Hill
Westley Heights
Hotel
Langdon Hill
Langdon Hall Farm
Hall Wood
Coombe Wood
Northlands Farm
Rectory
Goldsmiths
The Park
Dry Street Farm
Basildon Hospital
College
Pavilion
Laindon Station
WEST MAYNE
MANDEVILLE WAY
HIGH RD
LAINDON LINK
STANEWAY
ST NICHOLAS LA
UPPER MAYNE
CRANES FARM RD
OLD CHURCH HILL
SOUTH HILL
DRY STREET
ONE TREE HILL
LEE CHAPEL LA
Green Lane
The Bridle Way (Track)
Kingston Ridge
Compton Avenue
CHURCH HILL
4
3
2
1
89
88
87
86
67
68
69
169
179

162

D
E
F
BASILDON
Gloucester Park
Ghyllgrove
Fryerns
Barstable
Kingswood
Vange
Golf Course
Club House
Hospital
Tompkins Farm
Aviary and Wildlife Centre
Hawkesbury Manor
Marsh Farm
Marsh House
Vange Marshes
Vange Wharf
Vange Creek
Martinhole Wood
Hovels Farm
Water Works
Basildon Station
Training Centre
CRANES FARM RD
BROADMAYNE
WHITMORE WAY
THE FREMNELLS
SOUTHERNHAY
CLAY HILL RD
CHURCH RD
TIMBERLOG LA
SPARROWS HERNE
NETHER MAYNE
LONDON RD
HIGH RD
BELLS HILL RD
SOUTHEND RD
DRY ST
EAST MAYNE
A1235
A1321
A132
A176
A13
B1419
B1464
1
2
3
4
86
87
88
89
70
71
72

172

180

163

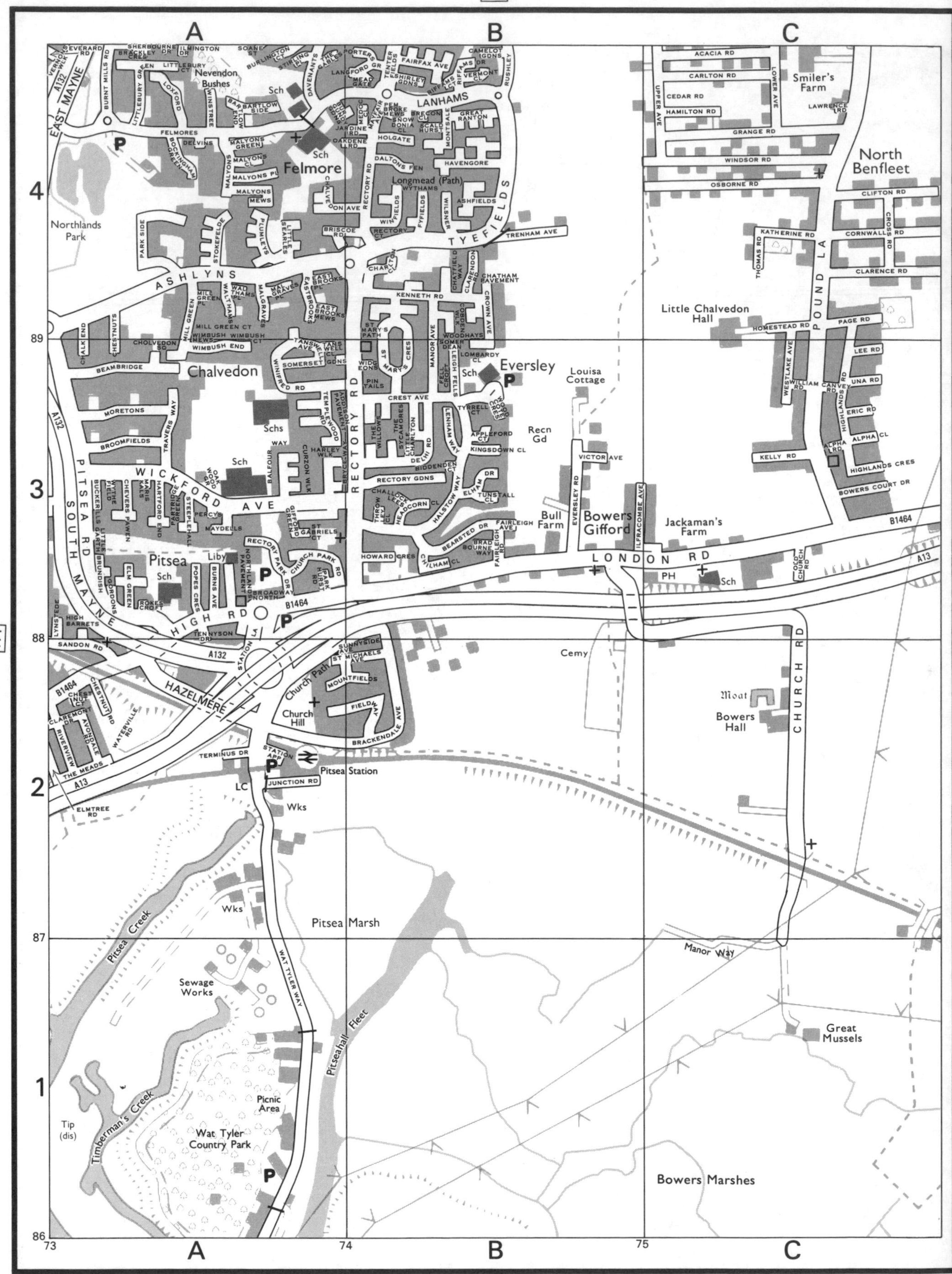
A
B
C
4
3
2
1
89
88
87
86
73
74
75
Nevendon Bushes
Felmore
LANHAMS
Longmead (Path)
Northlands Park
ASHLYNS
TYEFIELDS
TRENHAM AVE
Chalvedon
Schs
Sch
WICKFORD AVE
Eversley
Louisa Cottage
Recn Gd
VICTOR AVE
Bull Farm
Bowers Gifford
Jackaman's Farm
LONDON RD
B1464
A13
A132
PITSEA SOUTH MAYNE
EAST MAYNE
Pitsea
Liby
HIGH RD
HAZELMERE
Church Hill
Cemy
Moat
Bowers Hall
CHURCH RD
Pitsea Station
TERMINUS DR
JUNCTION RD
LC
Wks
Pitsea Marsh
Pitsea Creek
Sewage Works
WAT TYLER WAY
Pitseahall Fleet
Manor Way
Great Mussels
Tip (dis)
Timberman's Creek
Picnic Area
Wat Tyler Country Park
Bowers Marshes
Smiler's Farm
North Benfleet
ACACIA RD
CARLTON RD
CEDAR RD
HAMILTON RD
GRANGE RD
WINDSOR RD
OSBORNE RD
CLIFTON RD
KATHERINE RD
CORNWALLIS RD
CLARENCE RD
POUND LA
Little Chalvedon Hall
HOMESTEAD RD
PAGE RD
LEE RD
UNA RD
ERIC RD
ALPHA CL
KELLY RD
HIGHLANDS CRES
BOWERS COURT DR
RECTORY RD
CREST AVE
RECTORY GDNS
KINGSDOWN CL
MORETONS
BROOMFIELDS
BEAMBRIDGE
FELMORES
PH

171

181

164

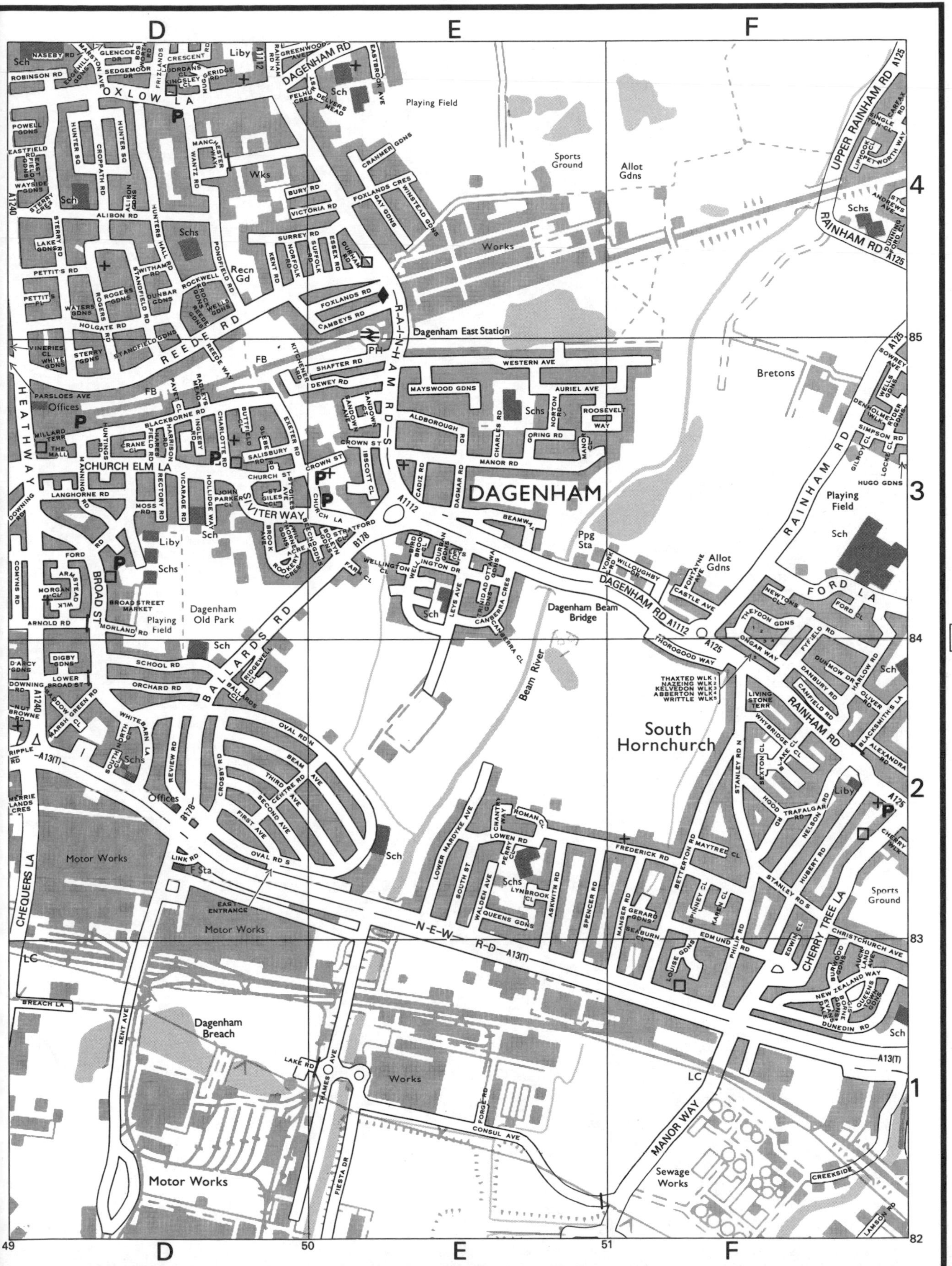

174

not continued, see key diagram

165

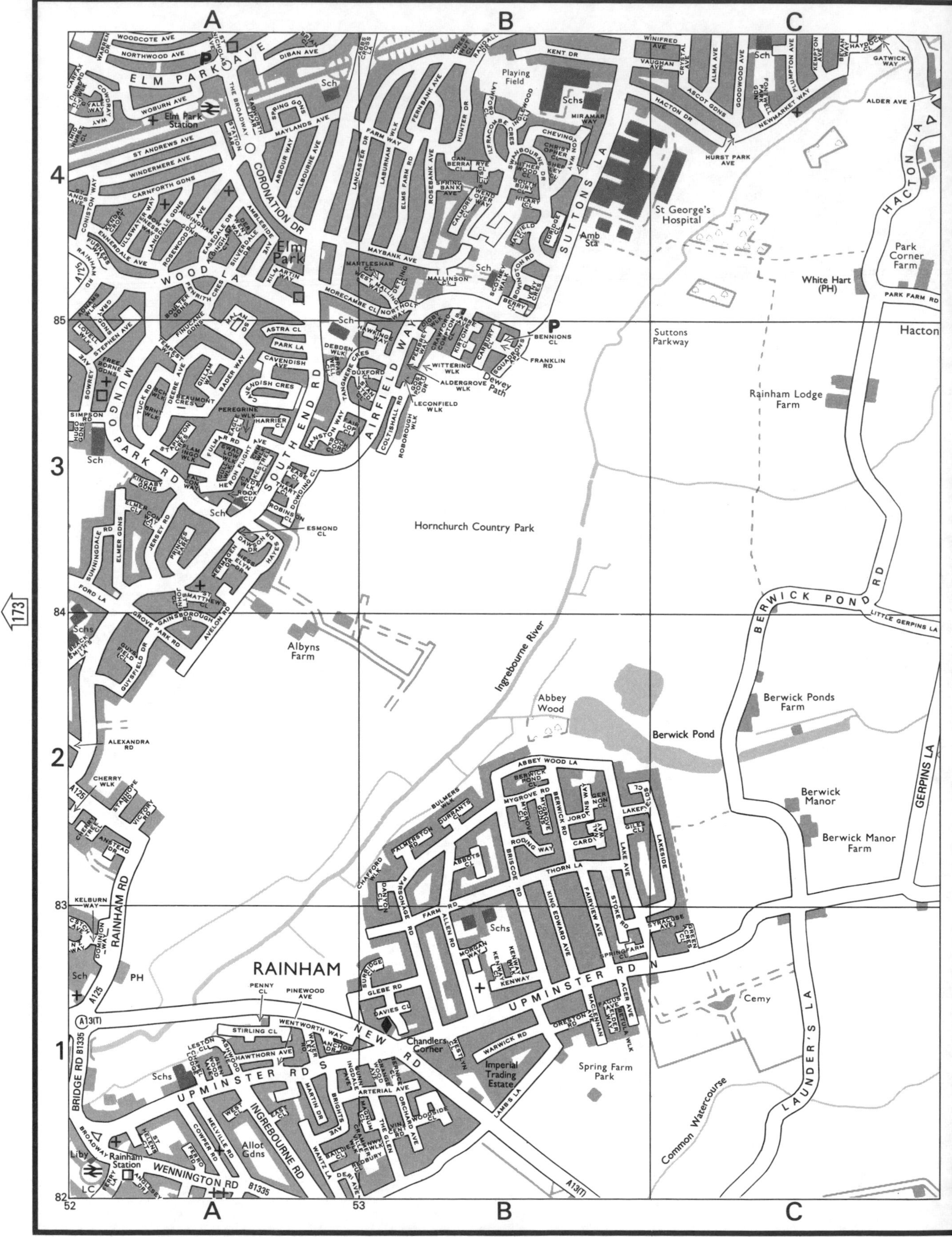

A
B
C
ELM PARK AVE
Elm Park Station
Elm Park
CORONATION DR
WOOD LA
SUTTONS LA
St George's Hospital
Playing Field
Schs
Sch
Amb Sta
Park Corner Farm
White Hart (PH)
PARK FARM RD
Hacton
HACTON LA
Suttons Parkway
Rainham Lodge Farm
SOUTH END RD
AIRFIELD WAY
MUNGO PARK RD
Dewey Path
Hornchurch Country Park
BERWICK POND RD
LITTLE GERPINS LA
Albyns Farm
Ingrebourne River
Abbey Wood
Berwick Pond
Berwick Ponds Farm
Berwick Manor
Berwick Manor Farm
GERPINS LA
RAINHAM RD
RAINHAM
UPMINSTER RD N
UPMINSTER RD S
NEW RD
Chandlers Corner
Imperial Trading Estate
Spring Farm Park
Cemy
LAUNDER'S LA
Common Watercourse
INGREBOURNE RD
Allot Gdns
Rainham Station
WENNINGTON RD
BRIDGE RD B1335
A13(T)
A125
B1335
4
3
2
1
85
84
83
82
52
53

173

182

166

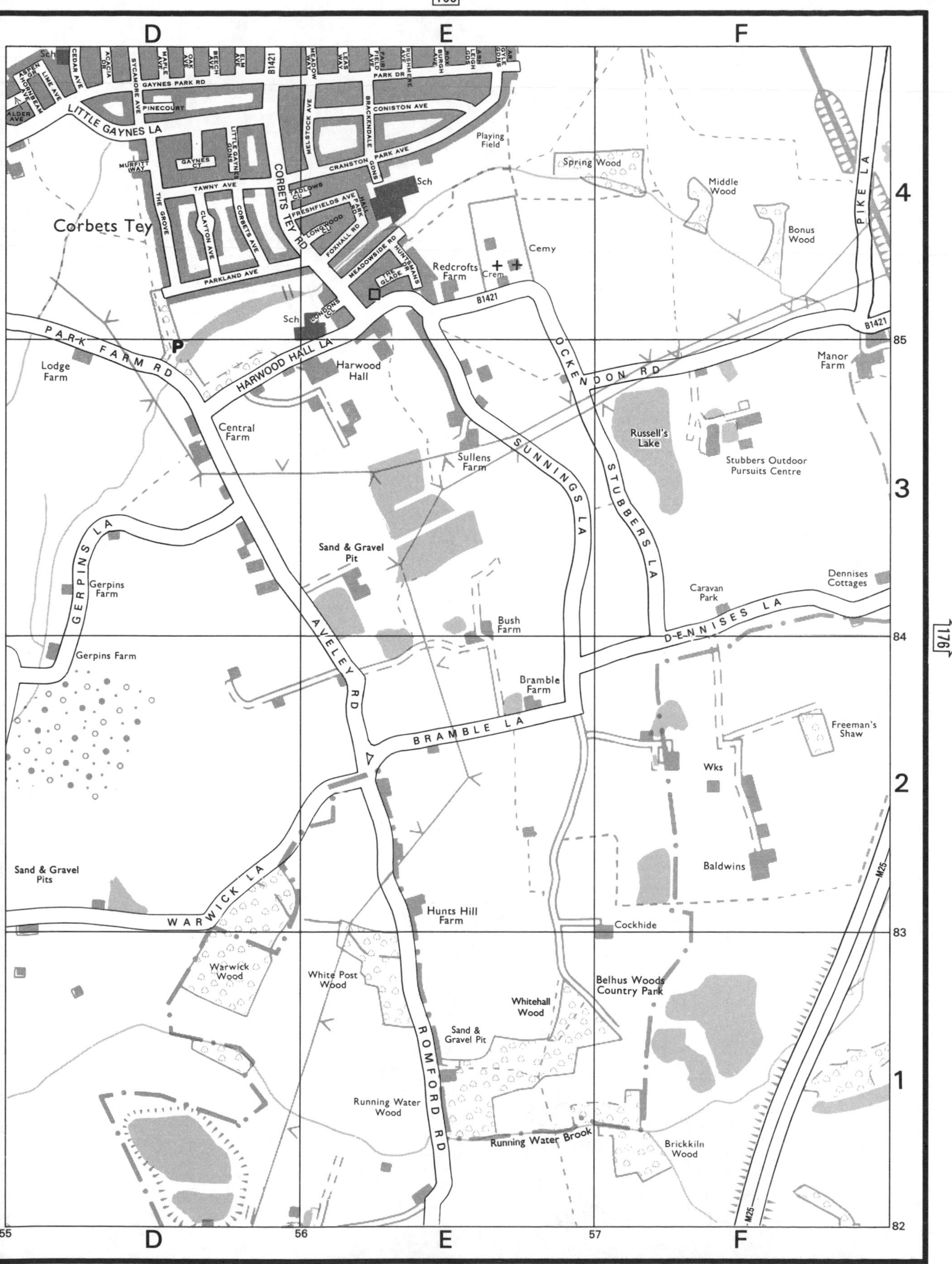
D
E
F
Corbets Tey
LITTLE GAYNES LA
GAYNES PARK RD
PINECOURT
CEDAR AVE
SYCAMORE AVE
CONISTON AVE
PARK DR
BRACKENDALE
MELSTOCK AVE
CORBETS TEY RD
CRANSTON PARK AVE
TAWNY AVE
THE GROVE
CLAYTON AVE
PARKLAND AVE
FRESHFIELDS AVE
FOXHALL RD
MEADOWSIDE RD
THE GLADE
HUNTSMANS DR
Sch
Playing Field
Spring Wood
Middle Wood
Bonus Wood
PIKE LA
Cemy
Crem
Redcrofts Farm
B1421
PARK FARM RD
HARWOOD HALL LA
Harwood Hall
Lodge Farm
OCKENDON RD
Manor Farm
Central Farm
Sullens Farm
SUNNINGS LA
STUBBERS LA
Russell's Lake
Stubbers Outdoor Pursuits Centre
GERPINS LA
Gerpins Farm
Sand & Gravel Pit
AVELEY RD
Bush Farm
Caravan Park
Dennises Cottages
DENNISES LA
Bramble Farm
BRAMBLE LA
Freeman's Shaw
Wks
Baldwins
Sand & Gravel Pits
WARWICK LA
Hunts Hill Farm
Cockhide
M25
Warwick Wood
White Post Wood
Whitehall Wood
Belhus Woods Country Park
Sand & Gravel Pit
ROMFORD RD
Running Water Wood
Running Water Brook
Brickkiln Wood
4
3
2
1
85
84
83
82
55
56
57

176

183

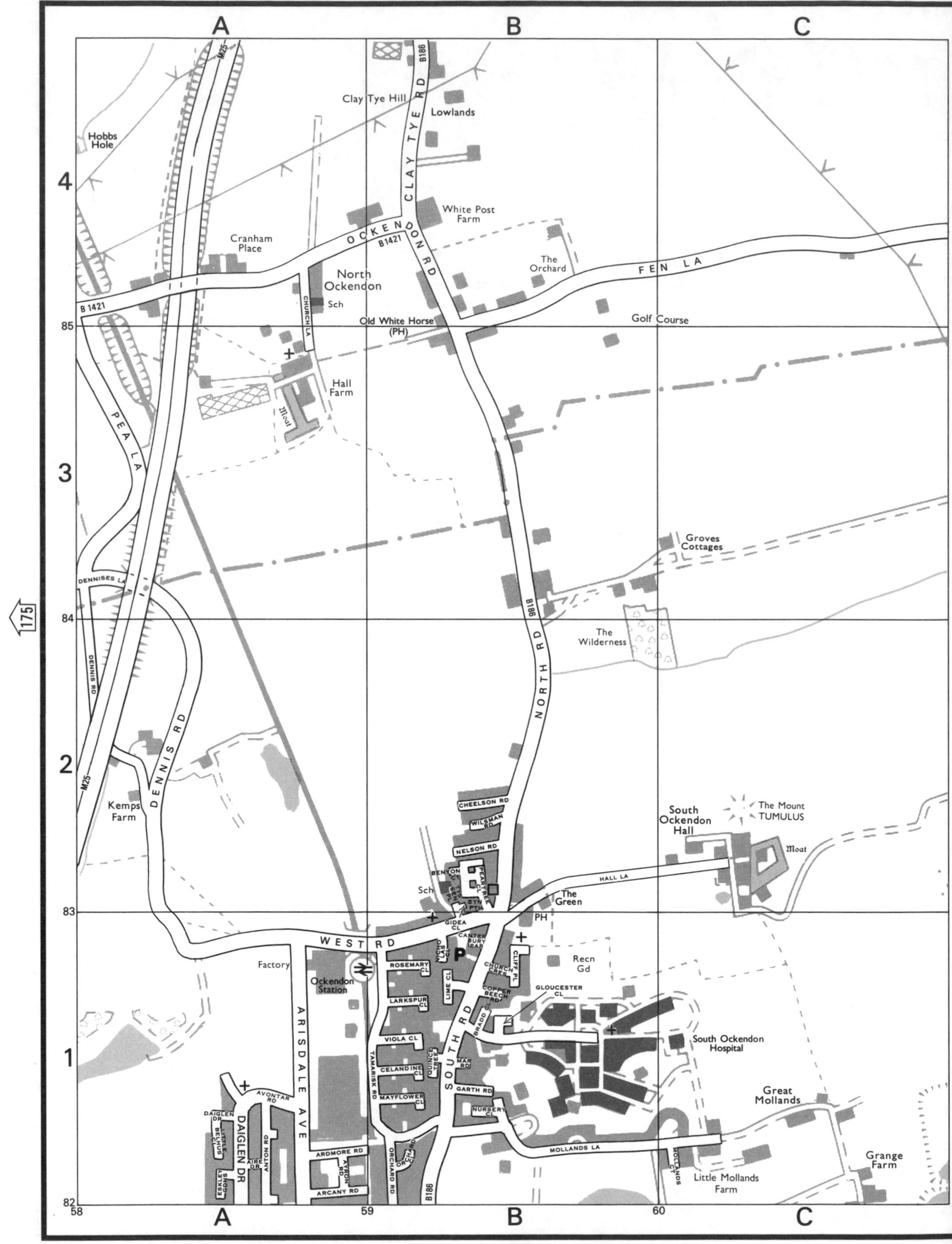
167
175
184
A
B
C
4
3
2
1
85
84
83
82
58
59
60
Hobbs Hole
Clay Tye Hill
Lowlands
CLAY TYE RD
B186
M25
White Post Farm
Cranham Place
OCKENDON RD
B1421
North Ockendon
Sch
CHURCH LA
The Orchard
FEN LA
B 1421
Old White Horse (PH)
Golf Course
Hall Farm
Moat
PEA LA
Groves Cottages
DENNISES LA
The Wilderness
NORTH RD
DENNIS RD
Kemps Farm
CHEELSON RD
WILSMAN RD
NELSON RD
South Ockendon Hall
The Mount TUMULUS
Moat
HALL LA
The Green
PH
Sch
GIDEA CL
WEST RD
Factory
Ockendon Station
ROSEMARY CL
LARKSPUR CL
LIME CL
CHURCH CRES
CLIFF PL
Recn Gd
GLOUCESTER CL
COPPER BEECH RD
SOUTH RD
ARISDALE AVE
VIOLA CL
CELANDINE CL
MAYFLOWER CL
TAMARISK RD
GARTH RD
NURSERY CL
South Ockendon Hospital
Great Mollands
AVONTAR RD
DAIGLEN DR
ANTON RD
AIRE DR
ARDMORE RD
ARCANY RD
ORCHARD RD
MOLLANDS LA
Grange Farm
Little Mollands Farm
HOLLANDS CT

168

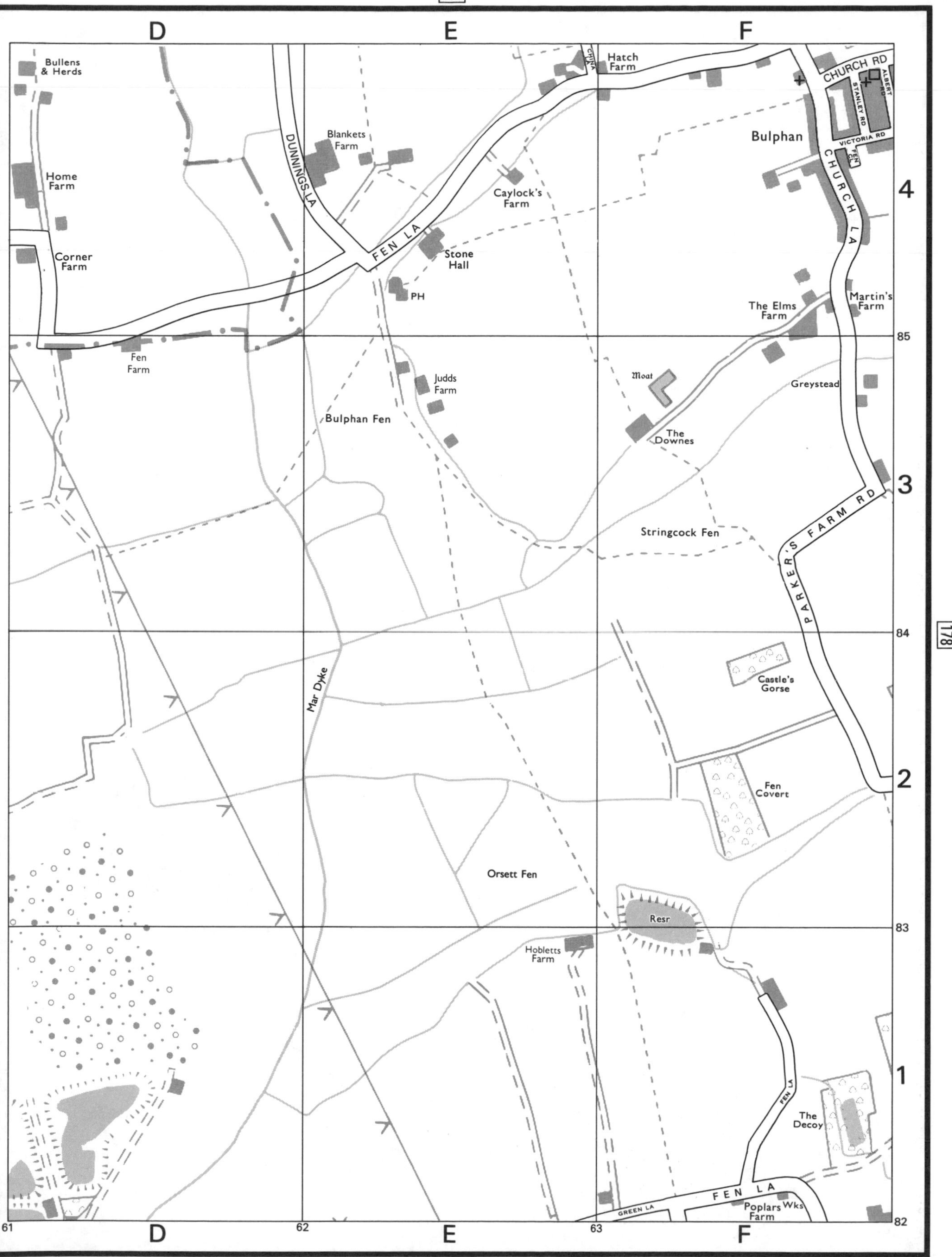
D
E
F
Bullens & Herds
Home Farm
Corner Farm
Fen Farm
Blankets Farm
DUNNINGS LA
FEN LA
Stone Hall
PH
Caylock's Farm
Hatch Farm
CHINA
CHURCH RD
ALBERT RD
STANLEY RD
VICTORIA RD
FEN LA
Bulphan
CHURCH LA
The Elms Farm
Martin's Farm
Judds Farm
Moat
The Downes
Greystead
Bulphan Fen
Stringcock Fen
PARKER'S FARM RD
Castle's Gorse
Mar Dyke
Fen Covert
Orsett Fen
Resr
Hobletts Farm
FEN LA
The Decoy
GREEN LA
FEN LA
Poplars Farm
Wks
4
3
2
1
85
84
83
82
61
62
63

178

185

169

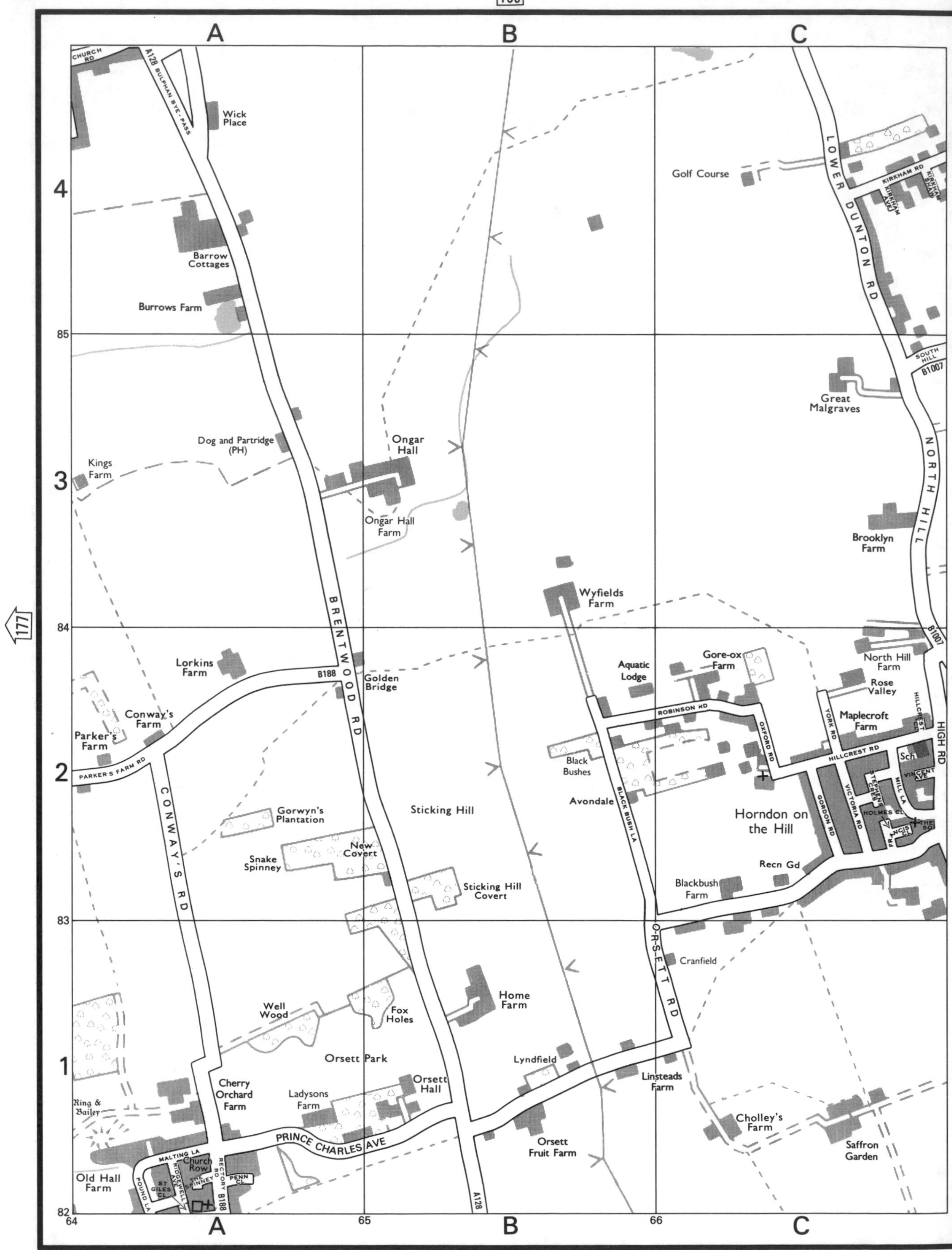

A
B
C
4
3
2
1
85
84
83
82
64
65
66
Wick Place
Golf Course
Barrow Cottages
Burrows Farm
LOWER DUNTON RD
KIRKHAM RD
SOUTH HILL
B1007
Great Malgraves
Dog and Partridge (PH)
Ongar Hall
Kings Farm
Ongar Hall Farm
NORTH HILL
Brooklyn Farm
Wyfields Farm
BRENTWOOD RD
Lorkins Farm
B188
Golden Bridge
Aquatic Lodge
Gore-ox Farm
North Hill Farm
Rose Valley
Conway's Farm
Parker's Farm
PARKER'S FARM RD
ROBINSON RD
OXFORD RD
YORK RD
Maplecroft Farm
HILLCREST RD
HIGH RD
Black Bushes
Avondale
BLACK BUSH LA
CONWAY'S RD
Gorwyn's Plantation
Sticking Hill
Horndon on the Hill
GORDON RD
VICTORIA RD
MILL LA
HOLMES CL
Snake Spinney
New Covert
Sticking Hill Covert
Recn Gd
Blackbush Farm
Cranfield
ORSETT RD
Home Farm
Well Wood
Fox Holes
Orsett Park
Lyndfield
Linsteads Farm
Cherry Orchard Farm
Ladysons Farm
Orsett Hall
Ring & Bailey
Cholley's Farm
Saffron Garden
PRINCE CHARLES AVE
Orsett Fruit Farm
MALTING LA
Church Row
Old Hall Farm
POUND LA
ST GILES CL
RIDGWELL AVE
THE SPINNEY
RECTORY RD
PENN CL
B188
A128
A128 BULPHAN BYE-PASS
CHURCH RD

177

186

170

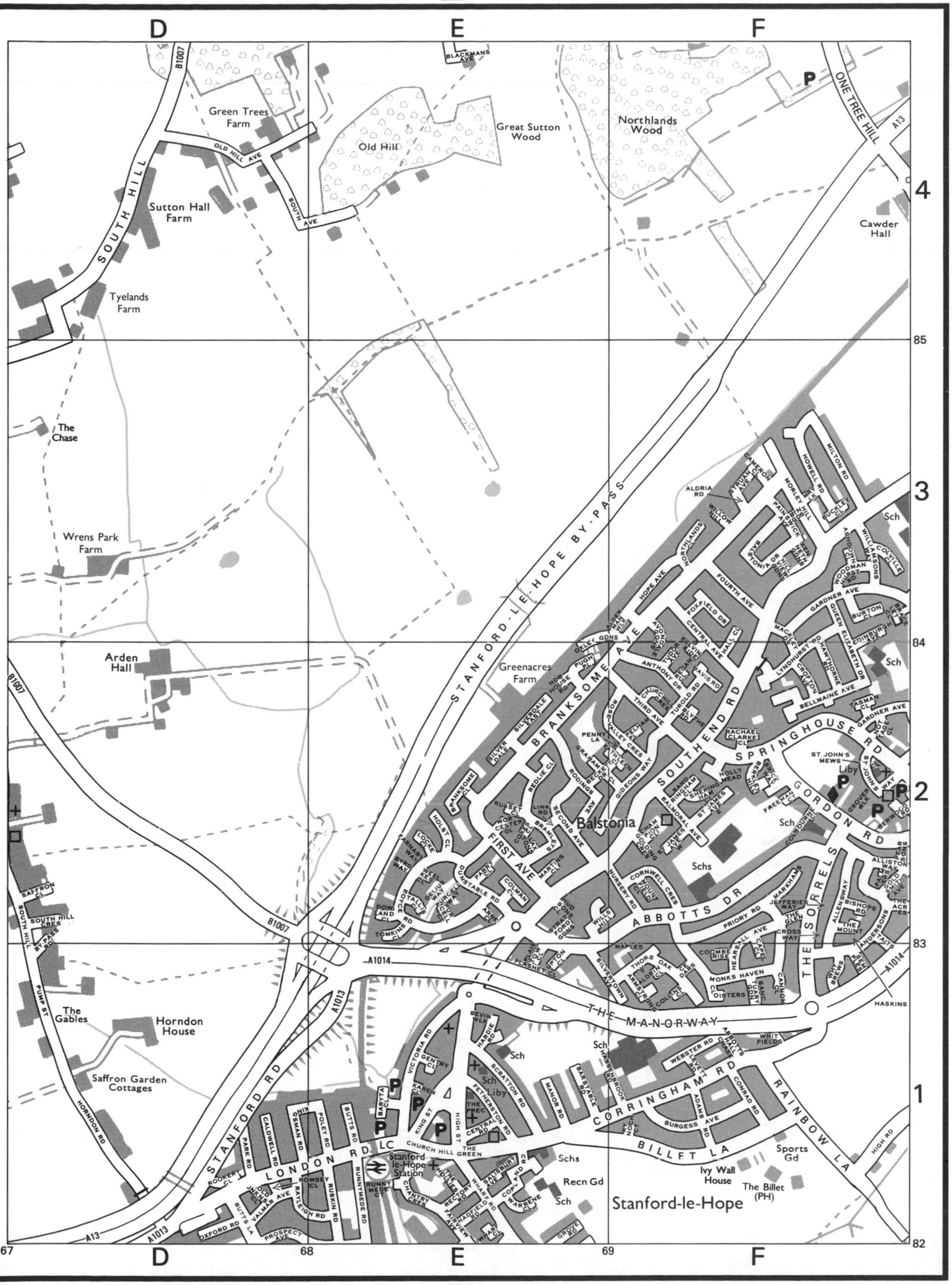

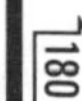

D
E
F
4
3
2
1
85
84
83
82
67
68
69
Green Trees Farm
Old Hill
Great Sutton Wood
Northlands Wood
Sutton Hall Farm
Tyelands Farm
Cawder Hall
SOUTH HILL
OLD HILL AVE
SOUTH AVE
BLACKMANS AVE
ONE TREE HILL
A13
B1007
The Chase
Wrens Park Farm
Arden Hall
Greenacres Farm
STANFORD-LE-HOPE BY-PASS
BRANKSOME AVE
SOUTHEND RD
SPRINGHOUSE RD
GORDON RD
FIRST AVE
SECOND AVE
THIRD AVE
FOURTH AVE
CENTRAL AVE
HOPE AVE
ABBOTTS DR
THE SORRELS
PRIORY RD
CORNWELL CRES
NURSERY RD
BALMORAL AVE
GIDEONS WAY
RODINGS
LINK RD
DUNSTABLE RD
COLMAN CL
HOLST CL
BRANKSOME CL
SILVER DALE
SILVERDALE EAST
FOXFIELD DR
GARDNER AVE
QUEEN ELIZABETH DR
BELLMAINE AVE
EDINBURGH AVE
WOODMAN AVE
HOWELL RD
MILTON RD
MORLEY HILL
BUCKLEY CL
ALDRIA RD
CAMERON CL
RACHAEL CLARKE CL
ST JOHN'S MEWS
Liby
Sch
Schs
Balstonia
ALLENSWAY
BISHOPS RD
THE MOUNT
ANDERSONS
JEFFERIES WAY
CROSS WAY
MONKS HAVEN
OISTERS
HEARSALL AVE
COOMBE RISE
MAPLES
SILVERTOWN AVE
THORS OAK
HASKINS
A1014
THE MANORWAY
A1013
Saffron Garden Cottages
The Gables
Horndon House
SAFFRON CL
SOUTH HILL CRES
PUMP ST
HORNDON RD
STANFORD RD
LONDON RD
CORRINGHAM RD
RAINBOW LA
BILLET LA
CONRAD RD
ADAMS RD
BURGESS AVE
WEBSTER RD
WHITFIELDS
MANOR RD
SCRATTON RD
VICTORIA RD
GENTRY CL
KING ST
HIGH ST
CHURCH HILL
THE GREEN
CENTRAL RD
BUTTS RD
POLEY RD
CALDWELL RD
PARK RD
ROOKERY CL
RUSKIN RD
RUNNYMEDE RD
RAYLEIGH RD
VALMAR AVE
OXFORD RD
BUTTS LA
PROSPECT AVE
Stanford-le-Hope Station
Schs
Recn Gd
Sports Gd
Ivy Wall House
The Billet (PH)
Stanford-le-Hope
HIGH RD
P

180

187

171

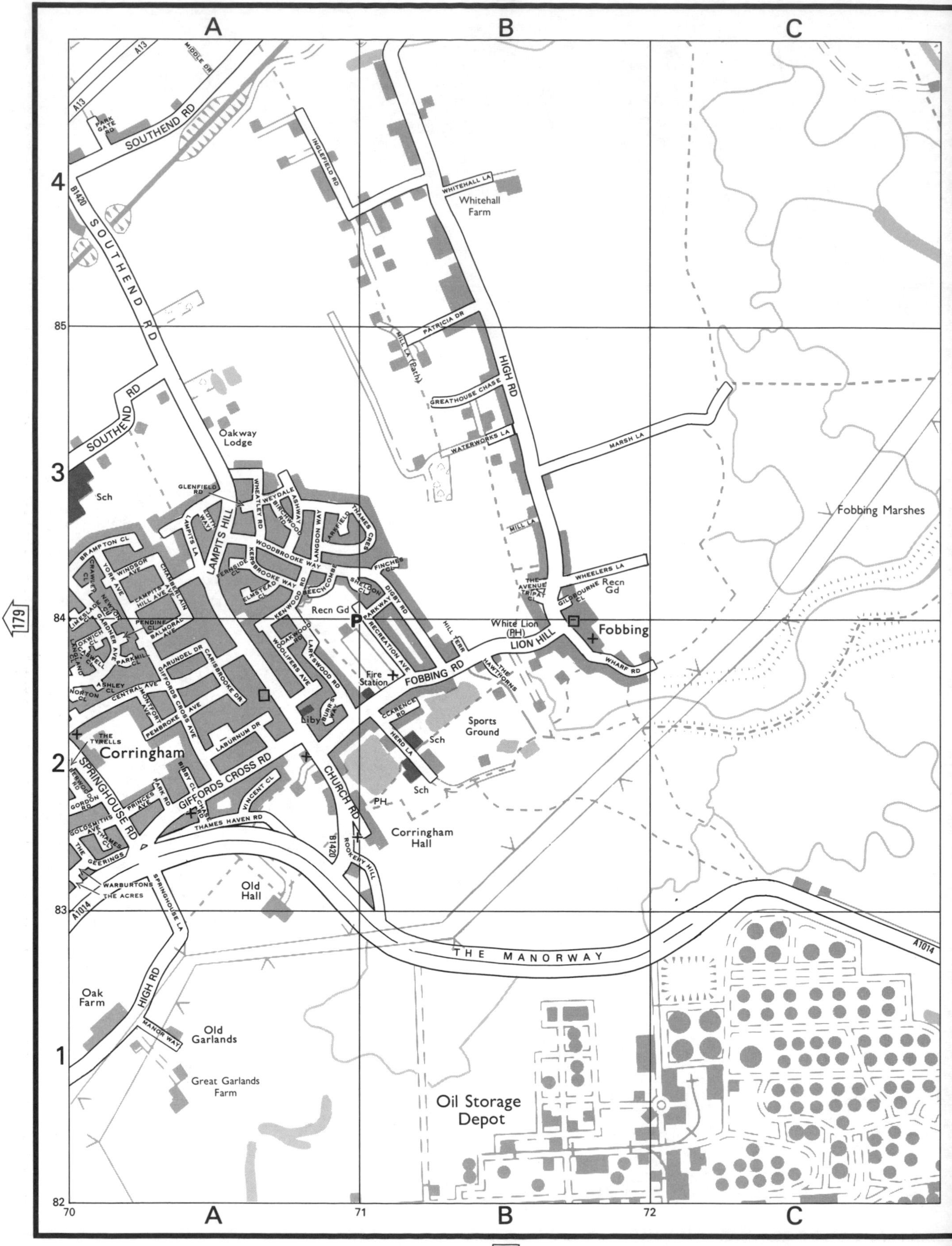

A
B
C
4
3
2
1
85
84
83
82
70
71
72
SOUTHEND RD
PARK GATE RD
MIDDLE DR
A13
B1420
INGLEFIELD RD
WHITEHALL LA
Whitehall Farm
PATRICIA DR
MILL LA (Path)
HIGH RD
GREATHOUSE CHASE
WATERWORKS LA
MARSH LA
Oakway Lodge
Sch
GLENFIELD RD
WHEATLEY RD
WEYDALE
BIRCHWOOD
ASHWAY
LANGDON WAY
LARKFIELD
THAMES CRES
LAMPITS HILL
LAMPITS LA
BRAMPTON CL
WINDSOR AVE
YORK AVE
CRAWLEY
LAMPITS HILL AVE
CHAMBERLAIN AVE
WOODBROOKE WAY
KERSBROOKE WAY
FERNSIDE CL
ELMSTEAD CL
KENWOOD RD
BEECHCOMBE
SHELDON
FINCHES CL
PARKWAY
DIGBY RD
MILL LA
WHEELERS LA
THE AVENUE
TRIPAT CL
GILDBOURNE CL
Recn Gd
Fobbing Marshes
Recn Gd
White Lion (PH)
LION HILL
Fobbing
WHARF RD
HILL TERR
RECREATION AVE
LIMESLADE CL
NEWTON CL
GARDINER AVE
PENDINE CL
BALMORAL AVE
PARKMILL CL
ARUNDEL DR
CARISBROOKE DR
WOODLIFERS AVE
OAKWOOD
LARKSWOOD RD
Fire Station
FOBBING RD
THE HAWTHORNS
ASHLEY CL
NORTON CL
CENTRAL AVE
MONTFORT AVE
GIFFORDS CROSS AVE
PEMBROKE AVE
LABURNUM DR
Liby
BURR'S WAY
CLARENCE RD
Sports Ground
HERD LA
Sch
THE TYRELLS
Corringham
SPRINGHOUSE RD
BIBBY CL
PARK RD
GIFFORDS CROSS RD
VINCENT CL
CHURCH RD
PH
Sch
GORDON RD
PRINCES AVE
GOLDSMITHS AVE
THAMES HAVEN RD
B1420
ROOKERY HILL
Corringham Hall
THE GEERINGS
WARBURTONS
THE ACRES
Old Hall
A1014
SPRINGHOUSE LA
THE MANORWAY
A1014
HIGH RD
Oak Farm
MANOR WAY
Old Garlands
Great Garlands Farm
Oil Storage Depot

179

188

172

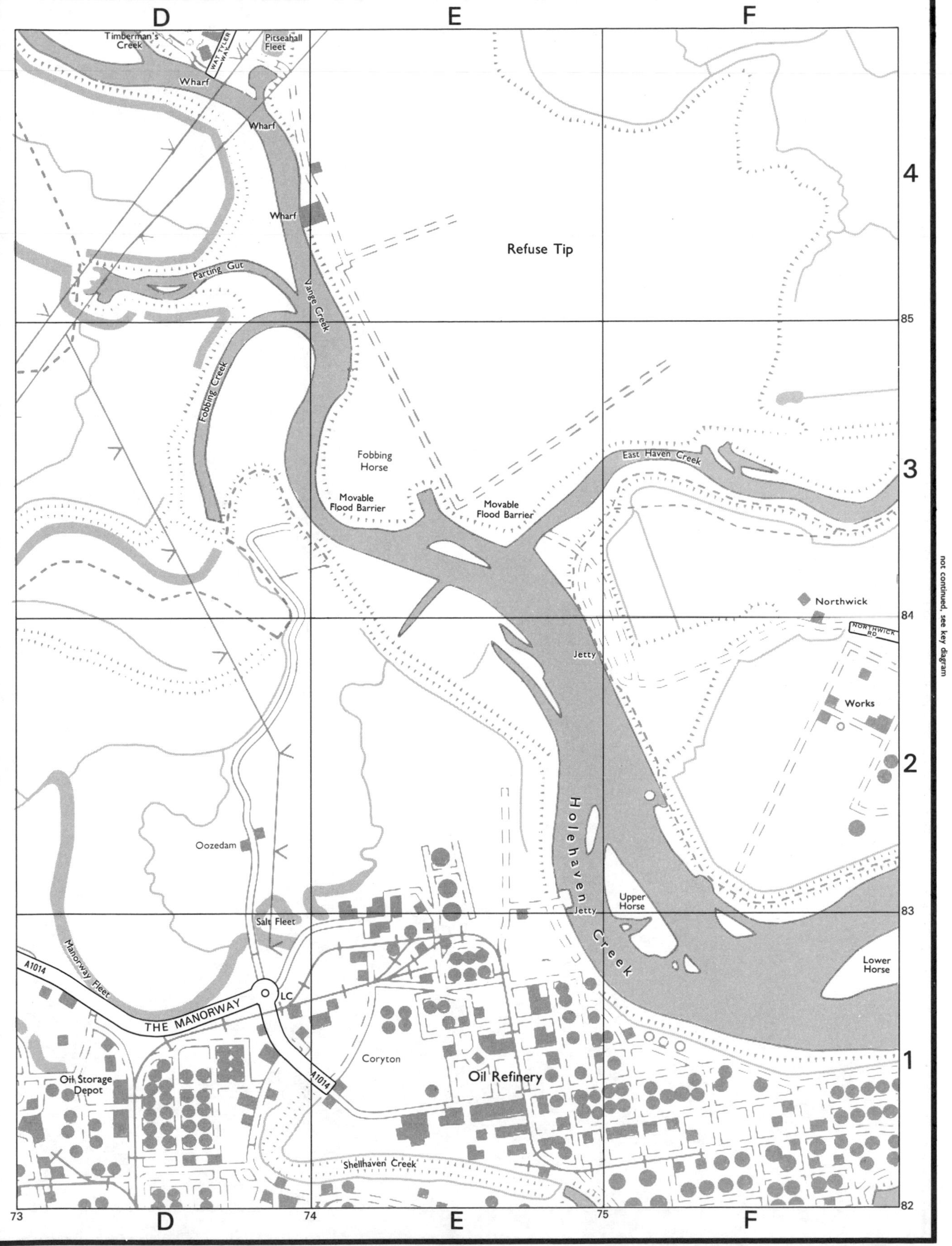

D
E
F
Timberman's Creek
Pitseahall Fleet
WAT TYLER WAY
Wharf
Wharf
Wharf
Refuse Tip
Parting Gut
Vange Creek
Fobbing Creek
Fobbing Horse
Movable Flood Barrier
Movable Flood Barrier
East Haven Creek
Northwick
NORTHWICK RD
Jetty
Works
Holehaven Creek
Oozedam
Upper Horse
Jetty
Salt Fleet
Lower Horse
Manorway Fleet
A1014
LC
THE MANORWAY
A1014
Coryton
Oil Refinery
Oil Storage Depot
Shellhaven Creek
4
3
2
1
85
84
83
82
73
74
75
not continued, see key diagram

189

174

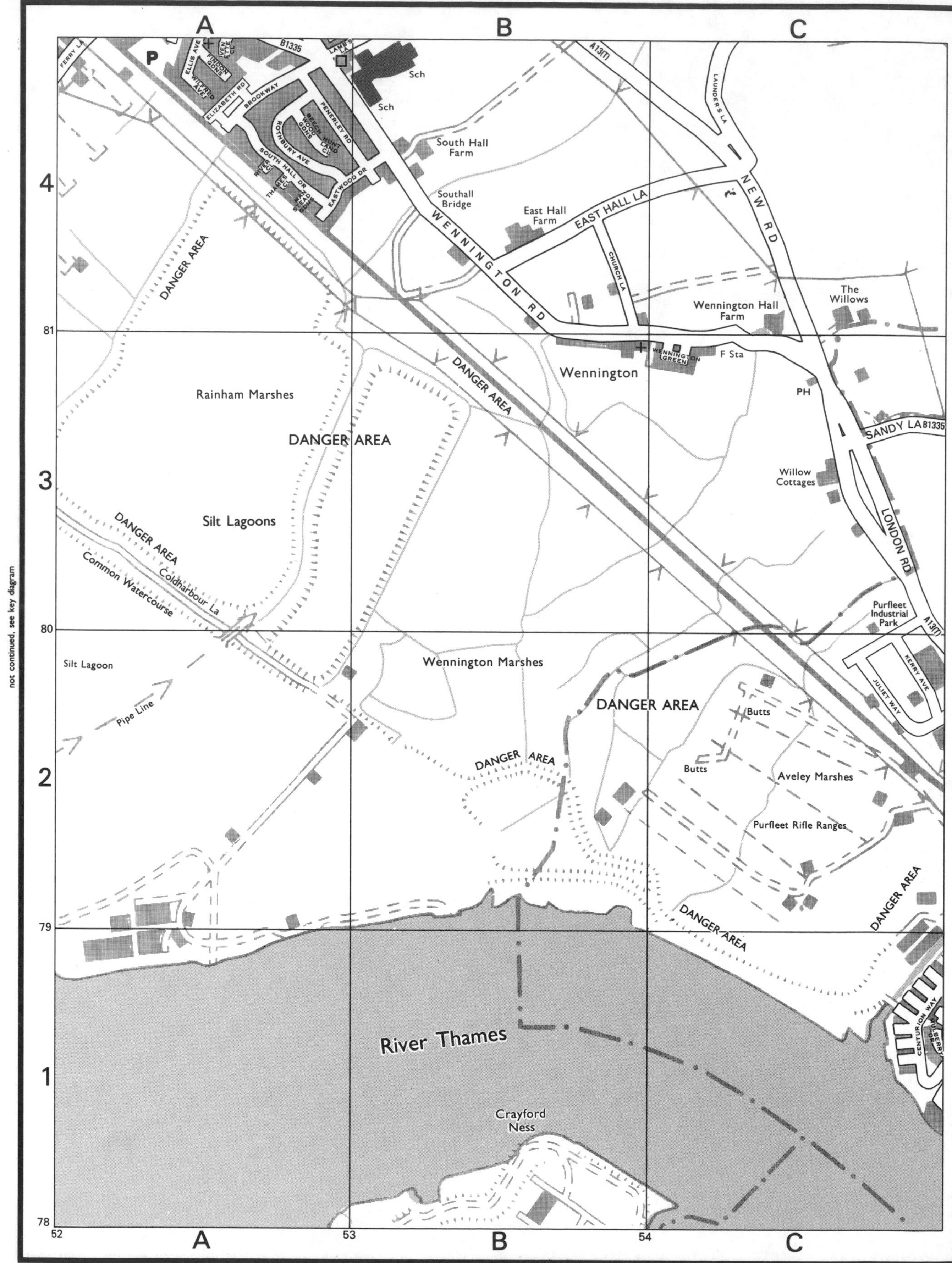

not continued, see key diagram

not continued, see key diagram

175

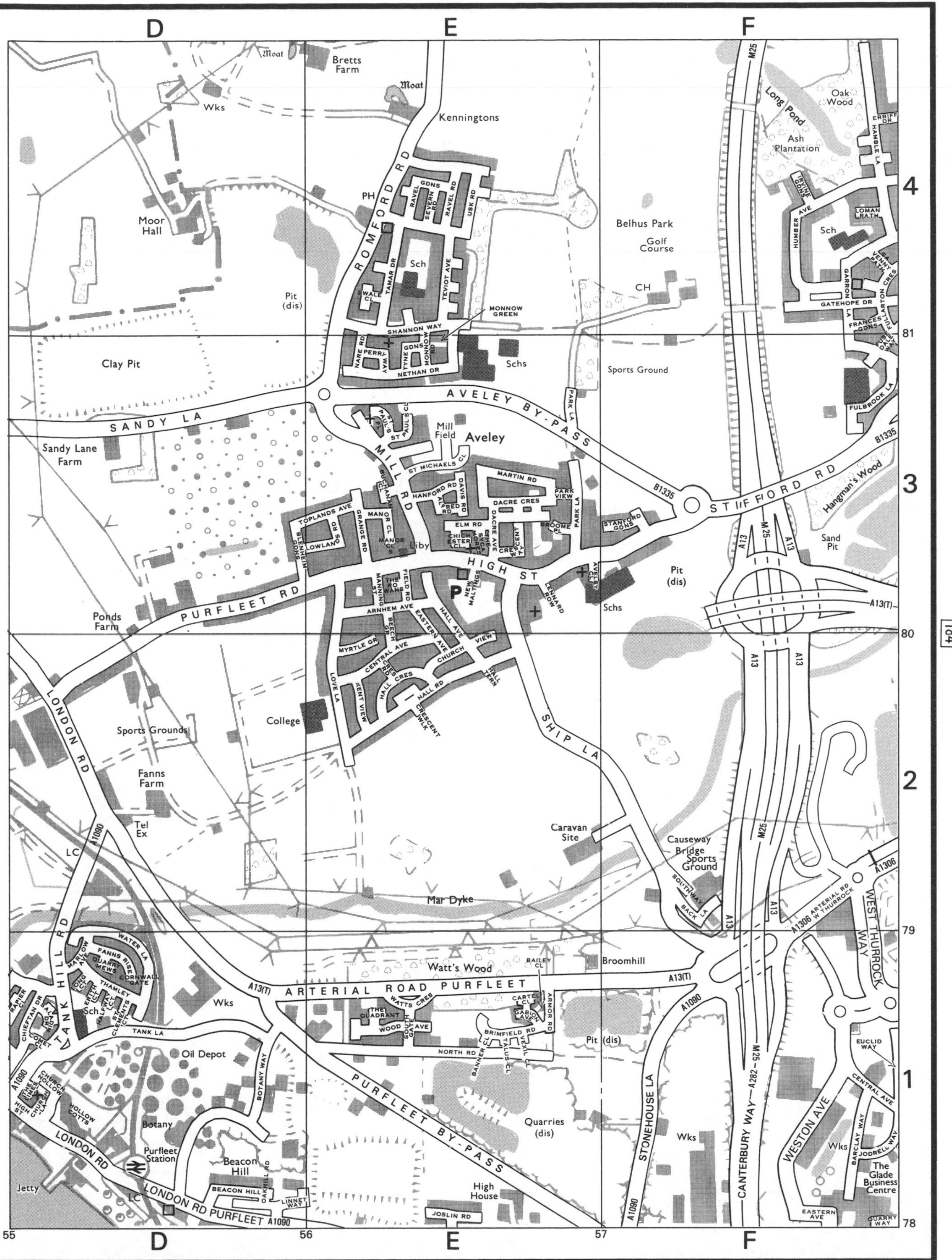

D
E
F
Moat
Bretts Farm
Moat
Wks
Kenningtons
Oak Wood
Long Pond
Ash Plantation
ERRIFF DR
HAMBLE LA
4
Moor Hall
PH
ROMFORD RD
RAVEL GDNS
SEVERN RD
RAVEL RD
USK RD
Belhus Park
Golf Course
IRVINE GDNS
HUMBER AVE
LOMAN PATH
Sch
Sch
TAMAR DR
TEVIOT AVE
SWALE CL
Pit (dis)
CH
GARRON LA
GATEHOPE DR
FRANCES GDNS
FULLARTON CRES
MONNOW GREEN
SHANNON WAY
81
Clay Pit
NARE RD
PERRY WAY
TYNE GDNS
MONNOW RD
NETHAN DR
Schs
Sports Ground
PARK LA
FULBROOK LA
AVELEY BY-PASS
SANDY LA
ST PAULS CL
ST PAUL'S RD
Mill Field
Aveley
Sandy Lane Farm
MILL RD
ST MICHAELS CL
B1335
MARTIN RD
STIFFORD RD
Hangman's Wood
3
BUCHANAN CL
HANFORD RD
DAVIS RD
ALFRED RD
PARK VIEW
DACRE CRES
TOPLANDS AVE
GRANGE RD
MANOR CL
ELM RD
DACRE AVE
CRESCENT WAY
BROOME PL
PARK LA
STANFORD GDNS
A13
M25
A13
Sand Pit
BLENHEIM GDNS
LOWLANDS RD
MANOR CL
Liby
HIGH ST
AVELEY CL
Pit (dis)
PURFLEET RD
MANNING ST
THE ROWANS
FIELD RD
NEW MALTINGS
LENNARD ROW
Schs
A13(T)
Ponds Farm
ARNHEM AVE
BEECH DR
EASTERN AVE
HALL AVE
VIEW
80
MYRTLE GR
CENTRAL AVE
CHURCH
HALL CRES
HALL RD
HALL TERR
A13
A13
LONDON RD
LOVE LA
KENT VIEW
CRESCENT WLK
College
SHIP LA
Sports Grounds
Fanns Farm
2
Tel Ex
Caravan Site
M25
A1090
LC
Causeway Bridge Sports Ground
A1306
SOUTHWAY
BACK LA
Mar Dyke
A13
A13
ARTERIAL RD W THURROCK
A1306
WEST THURROCK WAY
79
TANK HILL RD
WATER LA
FANNS RISE
QUARRY MEWS
CORNWALL GATE
MARLOW AVE
THAMLEY
LONG CT
Watt's Wood
BAILEY CL
Broomhill
A13(T)
ARTERIAL ROAD PURFLEET
Wks
WATTS CRES
CARTEL CL
GABION AVE
ARMOR RD
RAPIER CL
CHIEFTAN DR
COMET CL
Sch
HALFWAY CT
ST CLEMENTS CT
THE QUADRANT
WOOD AVE
SOUTH GATE
BRIMFIELD RD
A1090
TANK LA
Oil Depot
NORTH RD
BANNER CL
TALUS CL
VEXIL CL
Pit (dis)
EUCLID WAY
1
A1090
CHURCH HOLLOW
BOTANY WAY
PURFLEET BY-PASS
Quarries (dis)
STONEHOUSE LA
CANTERBURY WAY — A282 — M25
CENTRAL AVE
HIGH ST
HOLLOW COTTS
Botany
WESTON AVE
Wks
BARCLAY WAY
JODRELL WAY
LONDON RD
Purfleet Station
Beacon Hill
OAKHILL RD
Wks
Jetty
LC
BEACON HILL
LINNET WAY
High House
The Glade Business Centre
LONDON RD PURFLEET A1090
JOSLIN RD
A1090
EASTERN AVE
QUARRY WAY
78
55
56
57

184

190

176

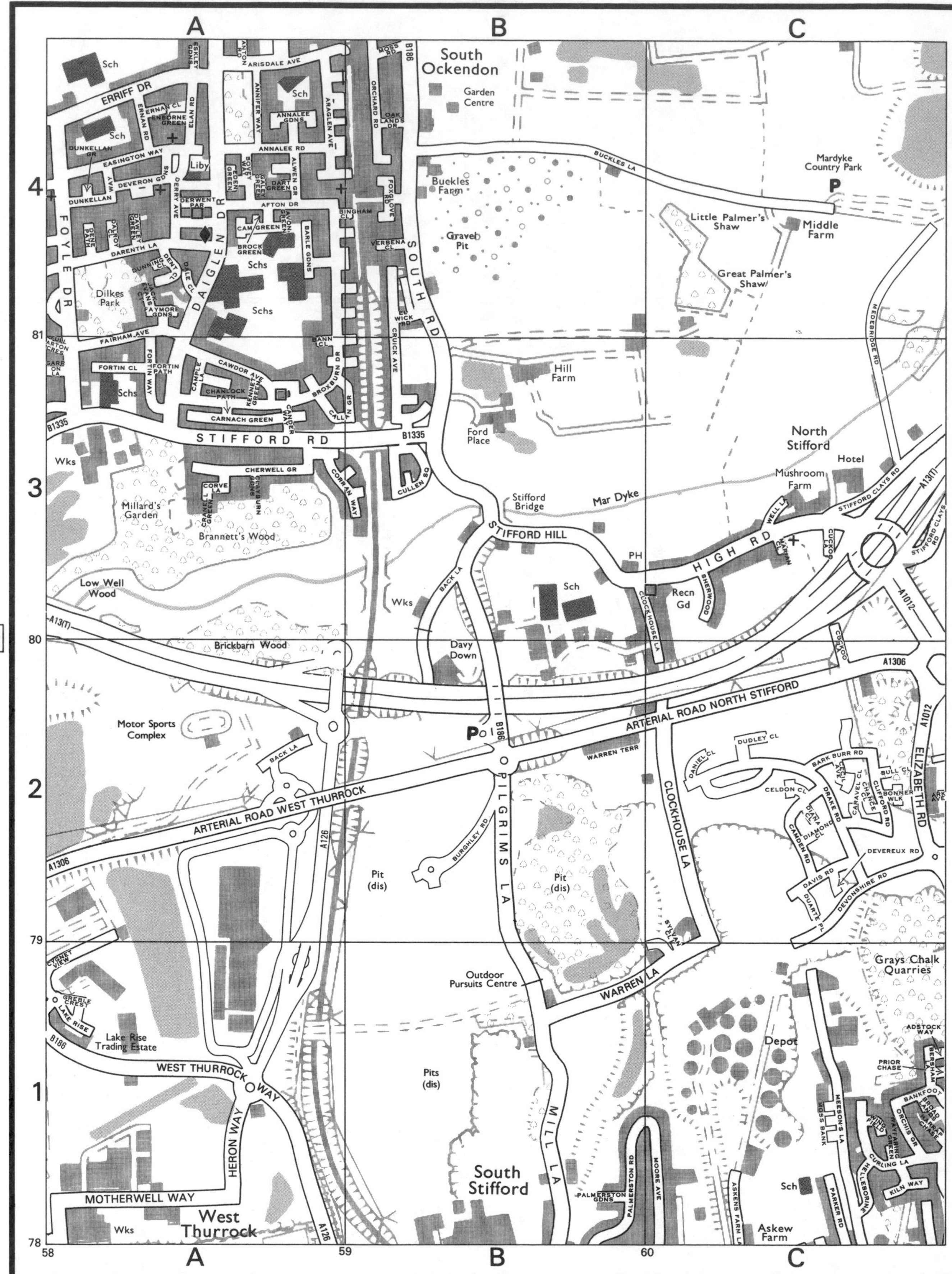

South Ockendon
Garden Centre
Buckles Farm
Gravel Pit
BUCKLES LA
Mardyke Country Park
Little Palmer's Shaw
Middle Farm
Great Palmer's Shaw
Hill Farm
Ford Place
North Stifford
Hotel
Mushroom Farm
Stifford Bridge
Mar Dyke
STIFFORD HILL
HIGH RD
PH
Sch
Recn Gd
STIFFORD RD
Wks
Millard's Garden
Brannett's Wood
Low Well Wood
Brickbarn Wood
Davy Down
Motor Sports Complex
ARTERIAL ROAD NORTH STIFFORD
ARTERIAL ROAD WEST THURROCK
PILGRIMS LA
CLOCKHOUSE LA
Pit (dis)
Outdoor Pursuits Centre
WARREN LA
Lake Rise Trading Estate
WEST THURROCK WAY
HERON WAY
MOTHERWELL WAY
West Thurrock
Pits (dis)
South Stifford
MILL LA
Depot
Grays Chalk Quarries
Askew Farm
ELIZABETH RD
Dilkes Park
FOYLE DR
ERRIFF DR
DAIGLEN DR
SOUTH RD
Schs
Liby
A
B
C
1
2
3
4
78
79
80
81
58
59
60

183

191

177

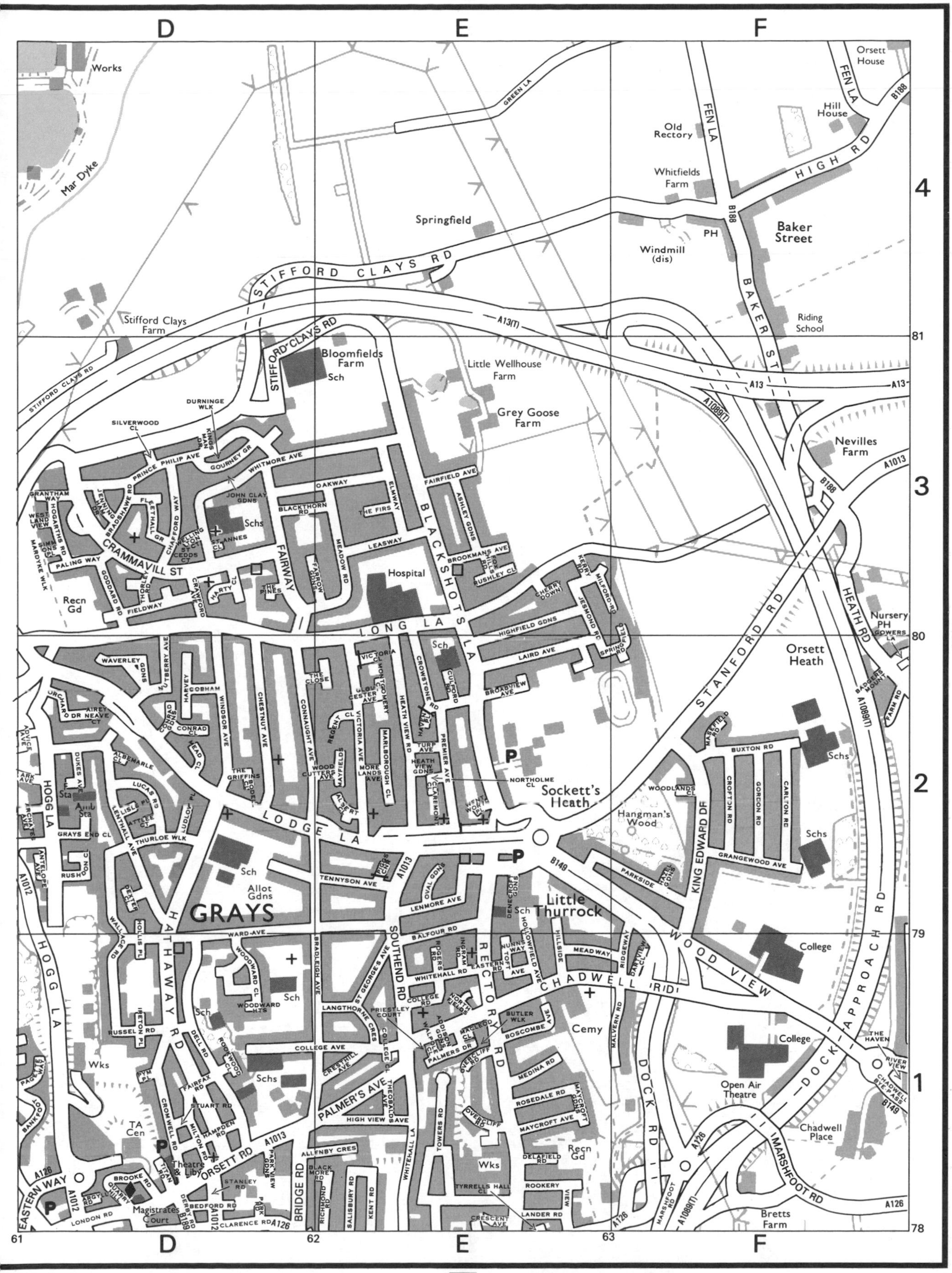

D E F

Works
Mar Dyke
Orsett House
Fen La
Hill House
High Rd
Old Rectory
Whitfields Farm
Springfield
Baker Street
PH
Windmill (dis)
Stifford Clays Rd
Stifford Clays Farm
Riding School
Bloomfields Farm
Sch
Little Wellhouse Farm
Grey Goose Farm
Nevilles Farm
Schs
Hospital
Recn Gd
Long La
Blackshots La
Stanford Rd
Heath Rd
Nursery PH
Orsett Heath
Sch
Sockett's Heath
Hangman's Wood
Lodge La
Schs
Sch
Allot Gdns
GRAYS
Little Thurrock
College
Wood View
Chadwell Rd
Cemy
Wks
College
Open Air Theatre
Chadwell Place
TA Cen
Theatre & Liby
Magistrates Court
Wks
Recn Gd
Dock Rd
Marshfoot Rd
Bretts Farm
Hogg La
Hathaway Rd
Southend Rd
Rectory Rd
Orsett Rd
Bridge Rd
Dock Approach Rd

4
3
2
1

81
80
79
78

61 62 63

D E F

186

192

178

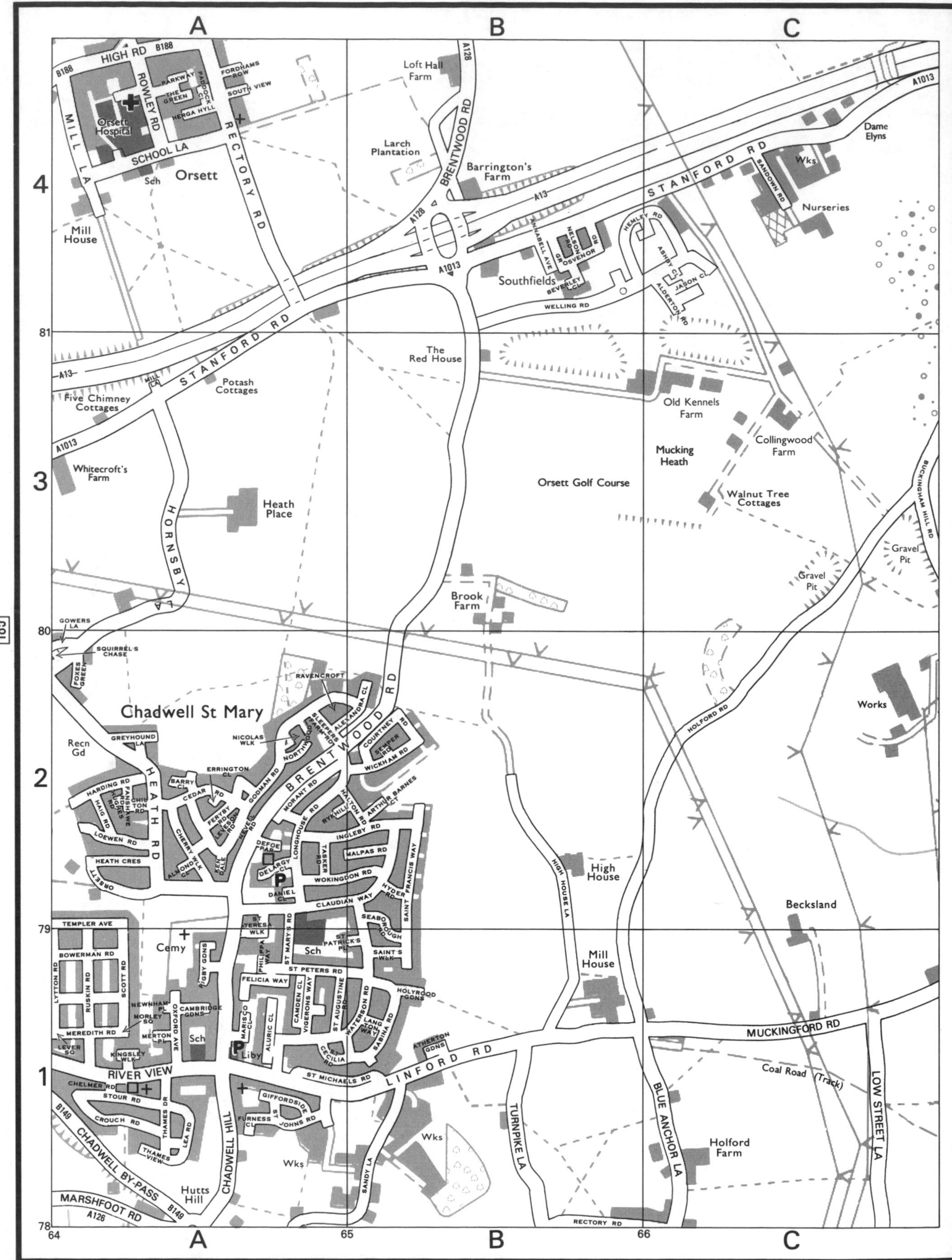

A
B
C
HIGH RD
B188
ROWLEY RD
PARKWAY
THE GREEN
PADDOCK CL
FORDHAMS ROW
SOUTH VIEW
HERGA HYLL
Orsett Hospital
MILL LA
SCHOOL LA
RECTORY RD
Sch
Orsett
Mill House
Loft Hall Farm
A128
BRENTWOOD RD
Larch Plantation
Barrington's Farm
A13
A1013
STANFORD RD
SANDOWN RD
Wks
Dame Elyns
Nurseries
ANNABELL AVE
NELSON RD
GROSVENOR RD
HEMLEY RD
ASHBY CL
JASON CL
ALDERTON RD
BEVERLEY CL
Southfields
WELLING RD
The Red House
Potash Cottages
Five Chimney Cottages
MILL LA
Old Kennels Farm
Mucking Heath
Collingwood Farm
Orsett Golf Course
Walnut Tree Cottages
Whitecroft's Farm
Heath Place
HORNSBY LA
BUCKINGHAM HILL RD
Gravel Pit
Gravel Pit
Brook Farm
GOWERS LA
SQUIRREL'S CHASE
FOXES GREEN
RAVENCROFT
ALEXANDRA CL
Chadwell St Mary
SLEEPERS FARM RD
NICOLAS WLK
NORTHWOOD
COURTNEY RD
SEMPER RD
WICKHAM RD
HOLFORD RD
Works
Recn Gd
GREYHOUND LA
ERRINGTON CL
BRENTWOOD RD
HARDING RD
HAIG RD
FANSHAWE
CHILTON RD
BARRY CL
CEDAR RD
FERBY RD
LEVESON RD
NEVELL RD
GODMAN RD
MORANT RD
RYKHILL
HALTON RD
ARTHUR BARNES CT
HEATH RD
LOEWEN RD
CHERRY WLK
INGLEBY RD
DEFOE PAR
LONGHOUSE RD
TASKER RD
MALPAS RD
SAINT FRANCIS WAY
HEATH CRES
ALMOND CL
KENDALE
DELARGY CL
WOKINGDON RD
HYDER RD
ORSETT RD
DANIEL CL
CLAUDIAN WAY
SEABOROUGH
High House
HIGH HOUSE LA
Becksland
TEMPLER AVE
ST TERESA WLK
ST MARY'S RD
ST PATRICK'S PL
SAINT'S WLK
Cemy
BOWERMAN RD
LYTTON RD
RUSKIN RD
SCOTT RD
RIGBY GDNS
PHILIPPA WAY
Sch
ST PETERS RD
FELICIA WAY
Mill House
NEWNHAM PL
MORLEY SQ
CAMBRIDGE GDNS
OXFORD AVE
CAMDEN CL
VIGERONS WAY
ST AUGUSTINE RD
WATERSON RD
LANGTON WAY
SABINA RD
HOLYROOD GDNS
MEREDITH RD
MERTON PL
MARISCO CL
ALURIC CL
LEVER SQ
KINGSLEY WLK
Sch
Liby
CECILIA RD
ATHERTON GDNS
LINFORD RD
MUCKINGFORD RD
RIVER VIEW
CHELMER RD
STOUR RD
ST MICHAELS RD
GIFFORDSIDE
Coal Road (Track)
CROUCH RD
THAMES DR
LEA RD
FURNESS CL
ST JOHNS RD
B149
CHADWELL BY-PASS
THAMES VIEW
CHADWELL HILL
Wks
Wks
SANDY LA
TURNPIKE LA
BLUE ANCHOR LA
Holford Farm
LOW STREET LA
Hutts Hill
MARSHFOOT RD
A126
RECTORY RD
64
65
66
78
79
80
81
1
2
3
4

185

193

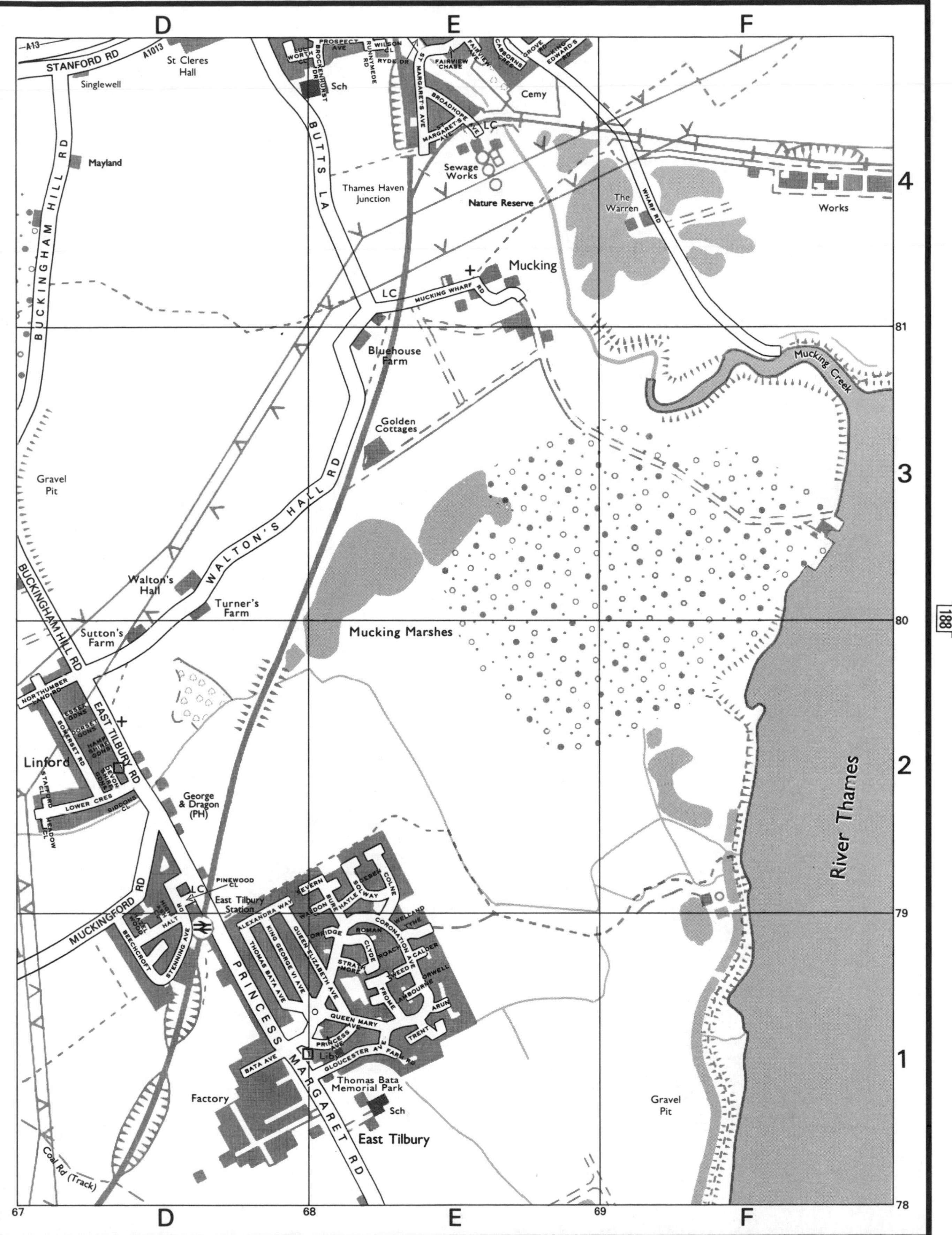

179
D
E
F
A13
STANFORD RD
A1013
St Cleres Hall
Singlewell
Sch
Cemy
LC
BUTTS LA
Mayland
BUCKINGHAM HILL RD
Sewage Works
Thames Haven Junction
Nature Reserve
The Warren
WHARF RD
Works
4
Mucking
LC
MUCKING WHARF RD
81
Bluehouse Farm
Mucking Creek
Golden Cottages
3
Gravel Pit
WALTON'S HALL RD
Walton's Hall
Turner's Farm
80
188
Sutton's Farm
Mucking Marshes
BUCKINGHAM HILL RD
EAST TILBURY RD
Linford
LOWER CRES
George & Dragon (PH)
2
River Thames
MUCKINGFORD RD
PINEWOOD CL
LC
East Tilbury Station
79
ALEXANDRA WAY
KING GEORGE VI AVE
THOMAS BATA AVE
QUEEN ELIZABETH AVE
CORONATION AVE
QUEEN MARY AVE
PRINCESS MARGARET RD
STENNING AVE
BEECHCROFT
1
BATA AVE
Liby
GLOUCESTER AVE
FARM RD
Thomas Bata Memorial Park
Sch
Factory
East Tilbury
Gravel Pit
Coal Rd (Track)
67
68
69
78
D
E
F
194

180

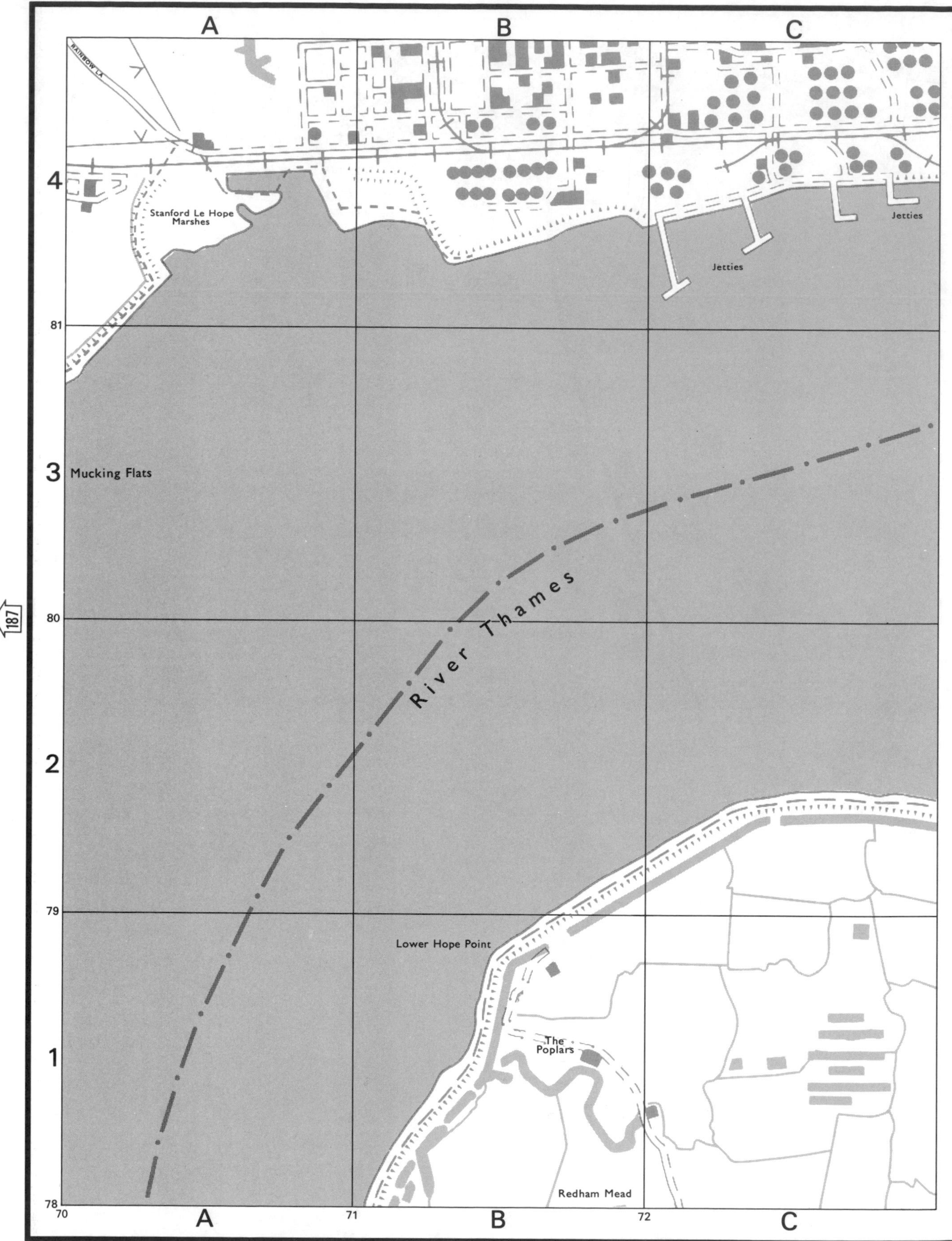

187

not continued, see key diagram

181

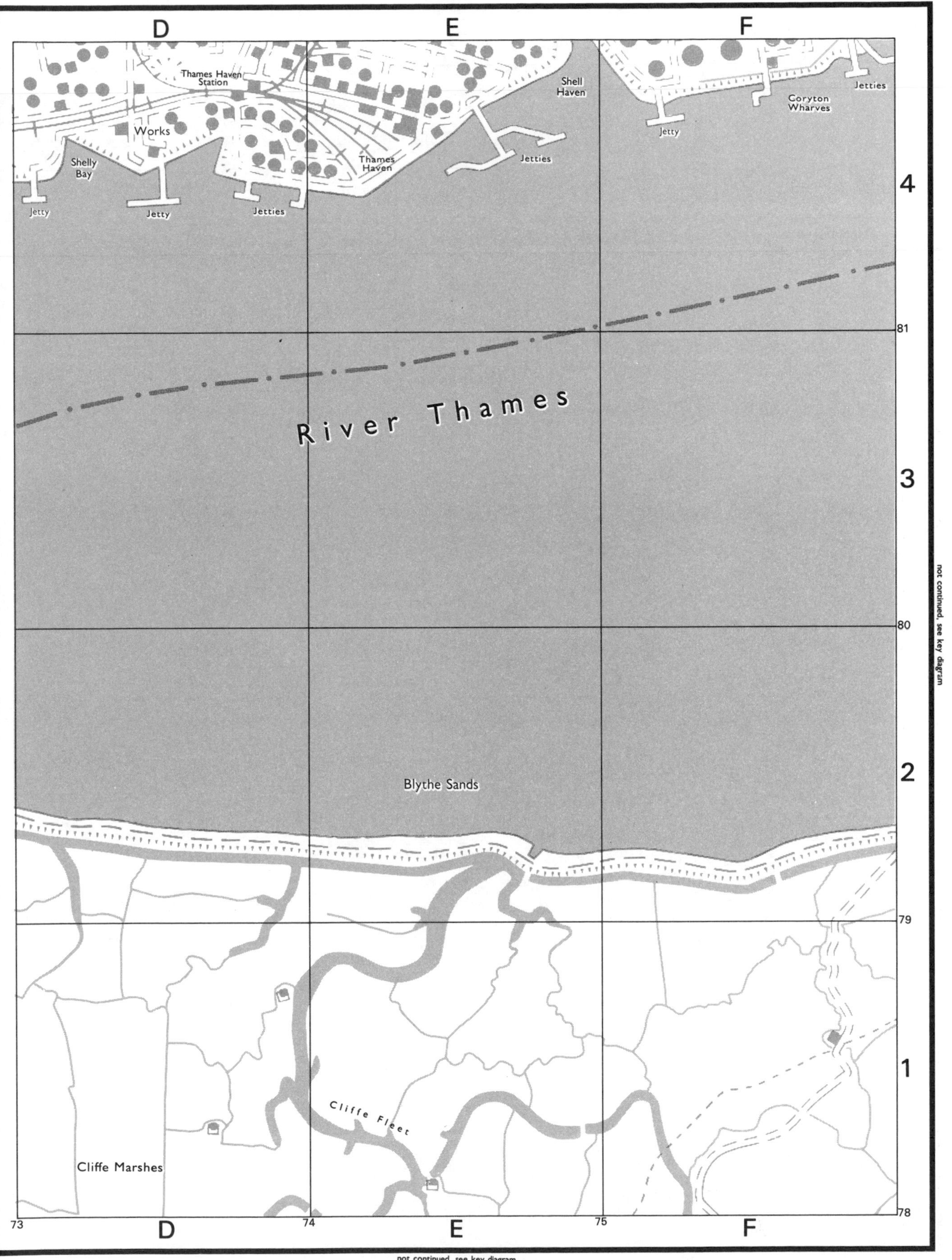

not continued, see key diagram

not continued, see key diagram

183

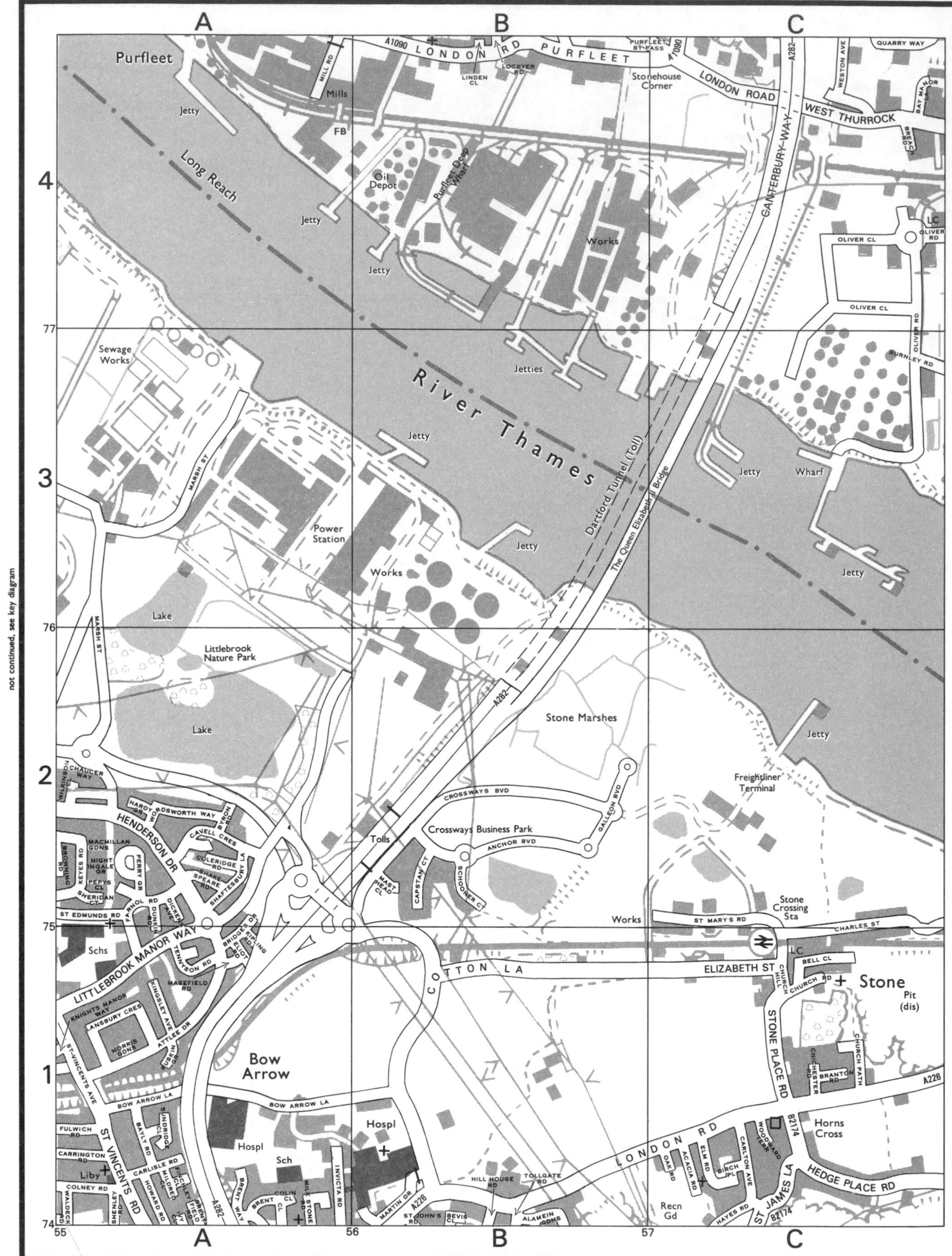
A
B
C
4
3
2
1
77
76
75
74
55
56
57
Purfleet
Jetty
Long Reach
Mills
FB
Oil Depot
Purfleet Deep Wharf
Works
Stonehouse Corner
LONDON ROAD
WEST THURROCK
CANTERBURY WAY
A1090 LONDON RD PURFLEET
PURFLEET BY-PASS
A1090
A282
LINDEN CL
LOCKYER RD
MILL RD
QUARRY WAY
WESTON AVE
OLIVER CL
OLIVER RD
BURNLEY RD
LC
Sewage Works
Jetties
River Thames
Dartford Tunnel (Toll)
The Queen Elizabeth II Bridge
Wharf
MARSH ST
Power Station
Works
Lake
Littlebrook Nature Park
Stone Marshes
Freightliner Terminal
CROSSWAYS BVD
Crossways Business Park
ANCHOR BVD
GALLEON BVD
Tolls
HENDERSON DR
CHAUCER WAY
WORDSWORTH WAY
BYRON RD
CAVELL CRES
MACMILLAN GDNS
NIGHTINGALE GR
PERRY GR
COLERIDGE RD
SHAKESPEARE RD
SHAFTESBURY LA
PEPYS CL
SHERIDAN CT
BROWNING RD
KEYES RD
ST EDMUNDS RD
FARNOL RD
DUNKIN RD
DICKENS AVE
LITTLEBROOK MANOR WAY
Schs
TENNYSON RD
BRIDGES DR
KIPLING RD
ELIOT RD
MASEFIELD RD
KINGSLEY AVE
KNIGHTS MANOR WAY
LANSBURY CRES
MORRIS GDNS
ATTLEE DR
RUSKIN GR
ST VINCENTS AVE
MAST HEAD CL
CAPSTAN CT
SCHOONER CT
Works
ST MARY'S RD
Stone Crossing Sta
CHARLES ST
COTTON LA
ELIZABETH ST
BELL CL
CHURCH HILL
CHURCH RD
Stone
Pit (dis)
STONE PLACE RD
CHICHESTER RD
BRANTON RD
CHURCH PATH
A226
Bow Arrow
BOW ARROW LA
Hospl
Sch
FULWICH RD
ST VINCENTS RD
CARRINGTON RD
Liby
COLNEY RD
CARLISLE RD
BAYLY RD
SUNDRIDGE CL
HOWARD RD
MILDRED CL
FINCHLEY CL
WALDECK RD
SHENLEY RD
A282
BRENT WAY
BRENT CL
COLIN CL
MILESTONE RD
INVICTA RD
MARTIN DR
A226
ST JOHN'S RD
BEVIS CL
HILL HOUSE RD
TOLLGATE RD
ALAMEIN GDNS
LONDON RD
OAK RD
ACACIA RD
ELM RD
BIRCH PL
CARLTON AVE
WOODWARD TERR
B2174
Horns Cross
HEDGE PLACE RD
Recn Gd
HAYES RD
ST JAMES LA
not continued, see key diagram

184

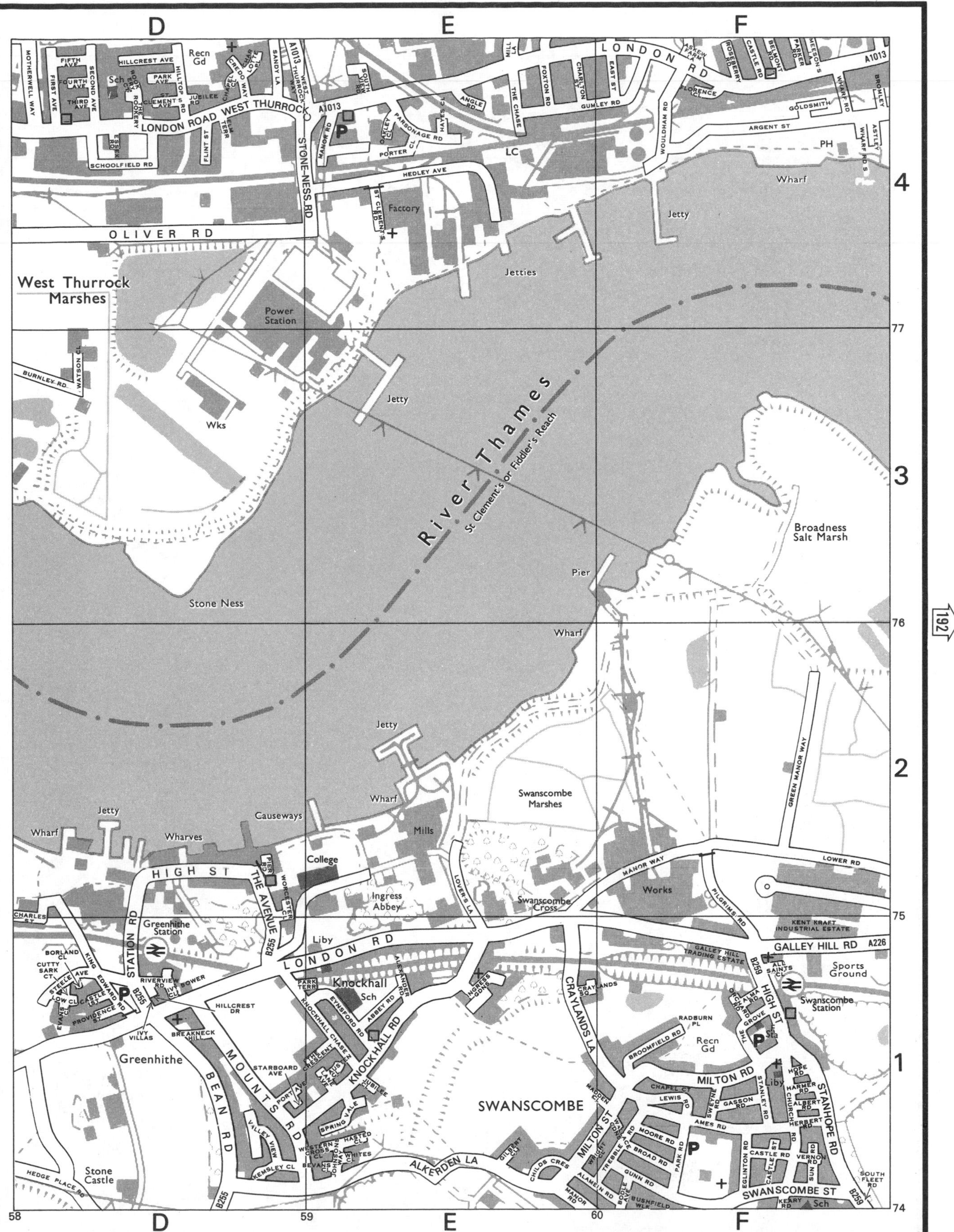

192

not continued, see key diagram

185

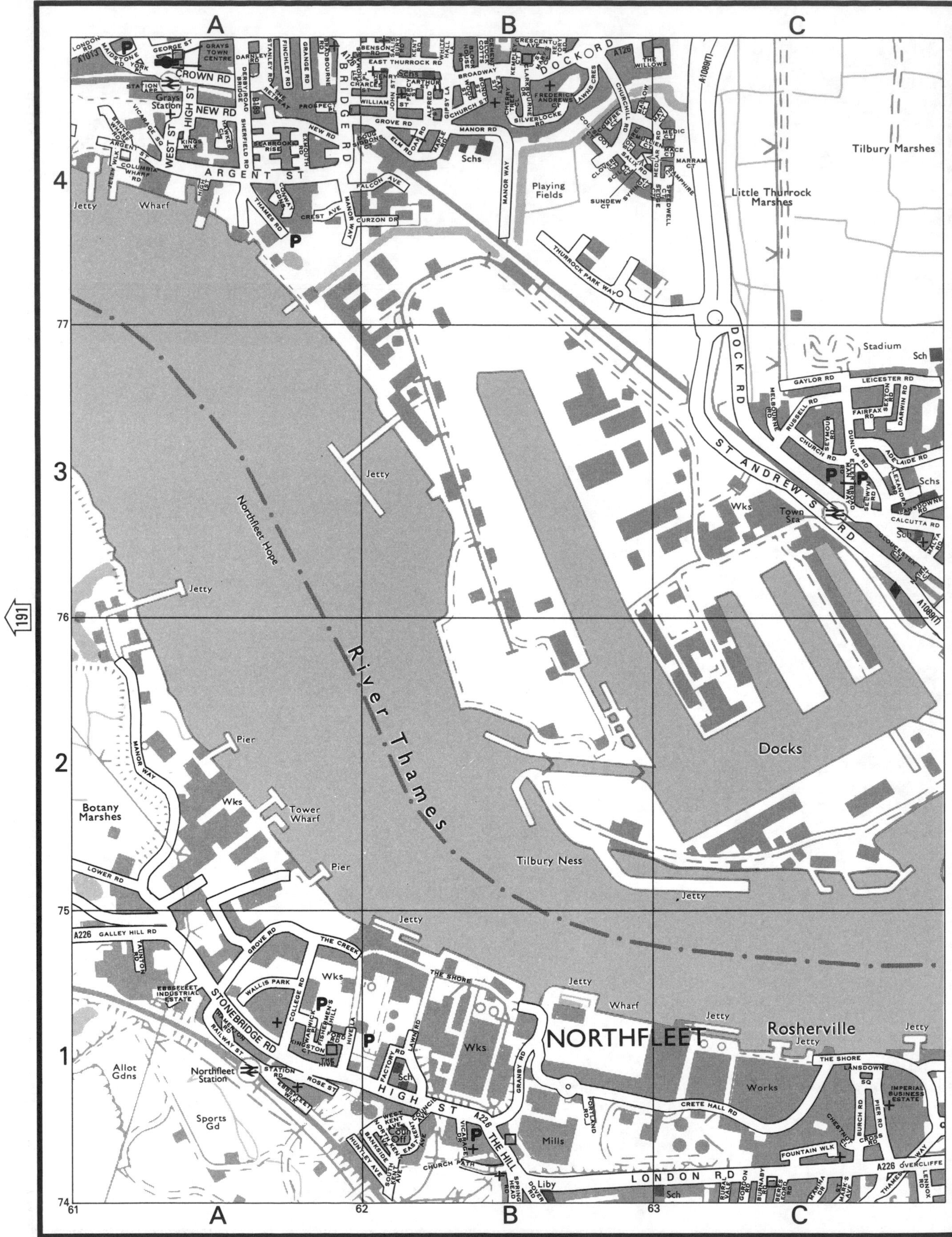

191

not continued, see key diagram

186

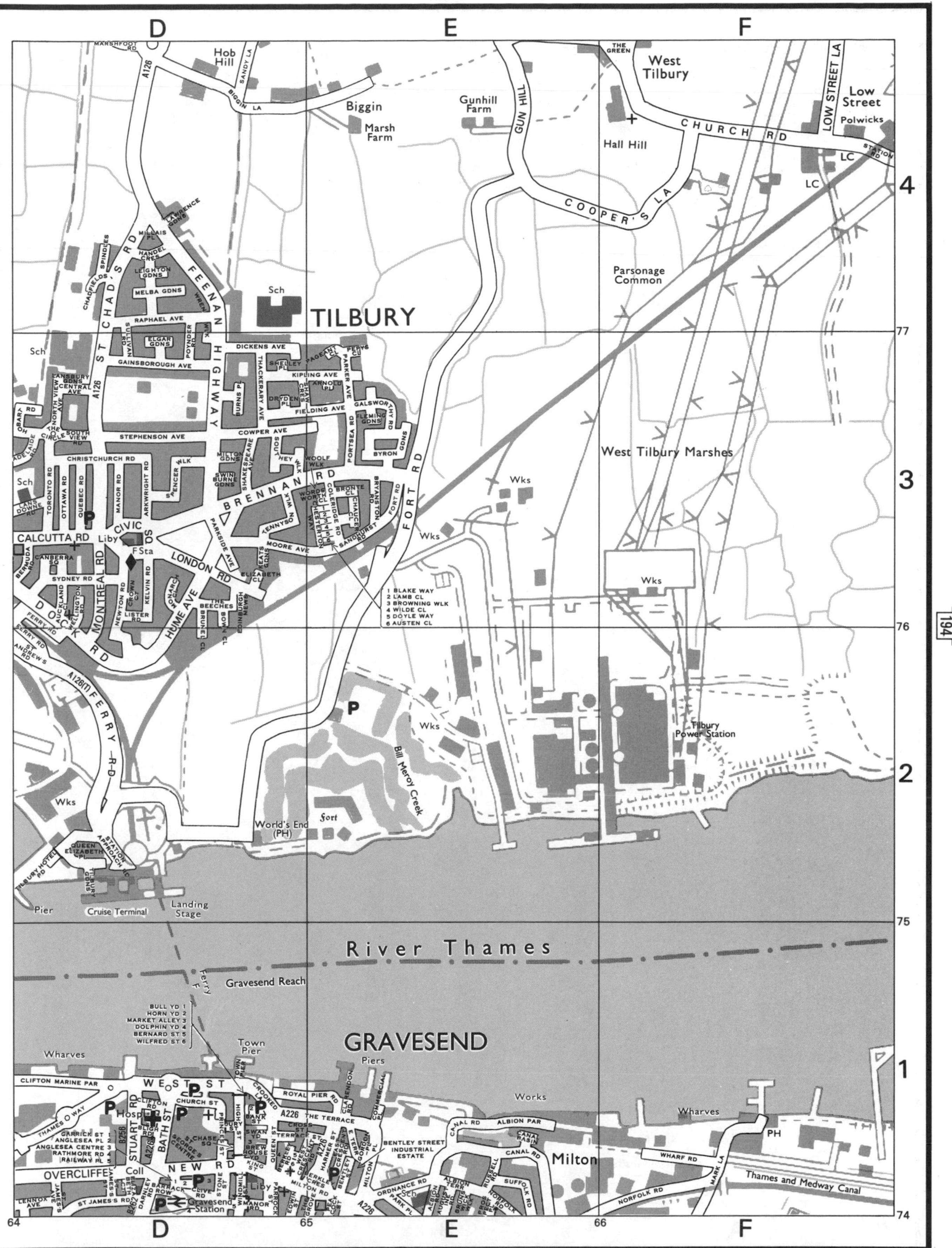

D
E
F
TILBURY
West Tilbury
Low Street
Hob Hill
Biggin
Marsh Farm
Gunhill Farm
Hall Hill
Polwicks
CHURCH RD
COOPER'S LA
GUN HILL
Parsonage Common
West Tilbury Marshes
FEENAN HIGHWAY
ST CHAD'S RD
BRENNAN RD
FORT RD
LONDON RD
CALCUTTA RD
DOCK RD
FERRY RD
Tilbury Power Station
Bill Meroy Creek
World's End (PH)
Fort
Cruise Terminal
Landing Stage
Pier
River Thames
Gravesend Reach
GRAVESEND
Town Pier
Wharves
Works
Milton
Thames and Medway Canal
1 BLAKE WAY
2 LAMB CL
3 BROWNING WLK
4 WILDE CL
5 DOYLE WAY
6 AUSTEN CL
BULL YD 1
HORN YD 2
MARKET ALLEY 3
DOLPHIN YD 4
BERNARD ST 5
WILFRED ST 6
GARRICK ST 1
ANGLESEA PL 2
ANGLESEA CENTRE 3
RATHMORE RD 4
RAILWAY PL 5
Gravesend Station
4
3
2
1
77
76
75
74
64
65
66

194

187

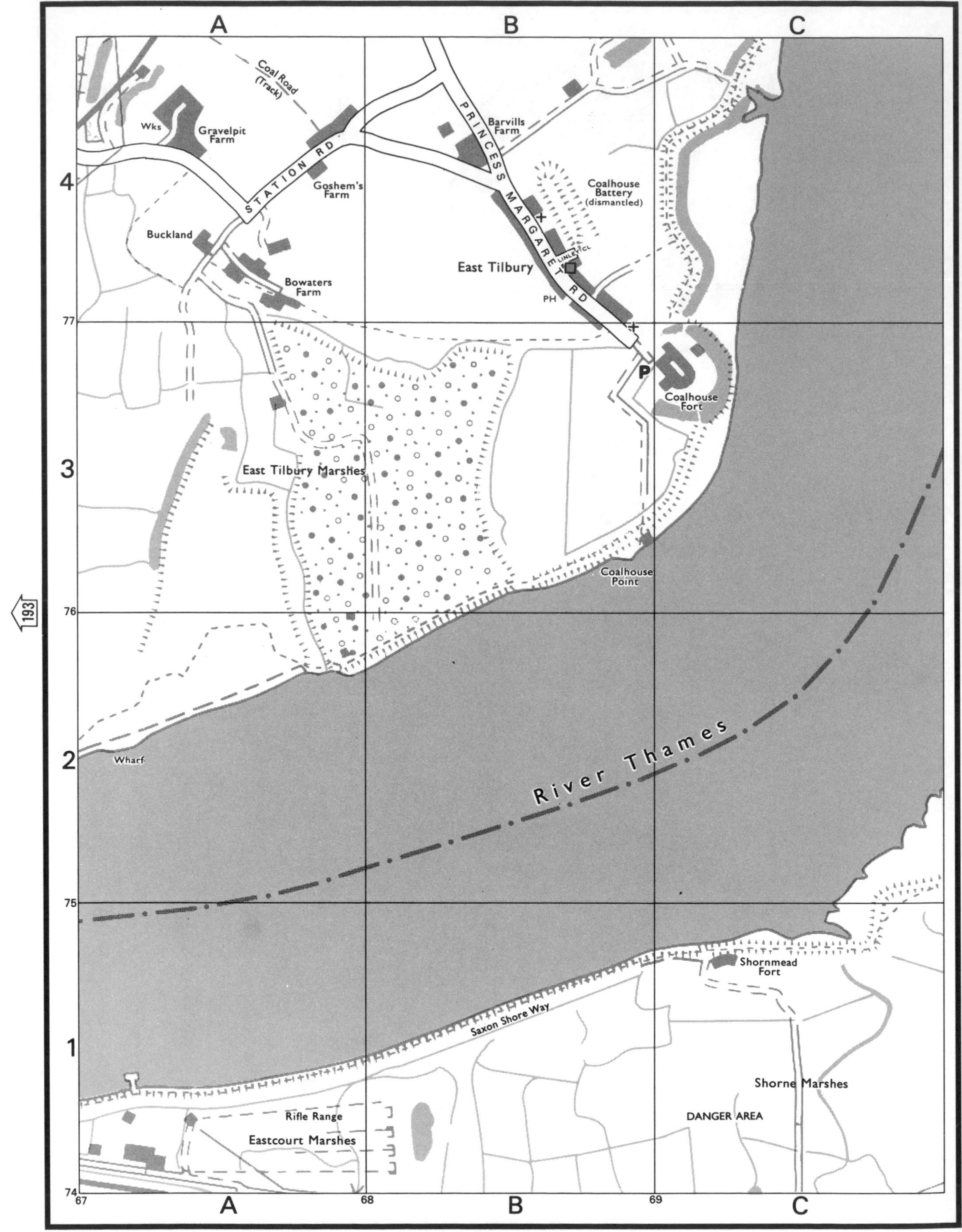

193

not continued, see key diagram

USER'S NOTES

EXPLANATION OF THE STREET INDEX REFERENCE SYSTEM

Street names are listed alphabetically and show the locality, the page number and a reference to the square in which the name falls on the map page.

Example:	Dellows La. Ugl. 48 A1
Dellows La.	This is the full street name, which may have been abbreviated on the map.
Ugl.	This is the abbreviation for the town, village or locality in which the street falls.
48	This is the page number of the map on which the street name appears.
A1	The letter and figure indicate the square on the map in which the centre of the street falls. The square can be found at the junction of the vertical column carrying the appropriate letter and the horizontal row carrying the appropriate figure.

ABBREVIATIONS USED IN THE INDEX
Road Names

Approach	App	Lane	La
Avenue	Ave	North	N
Boulevard	Bvd	Orchard	Orch
Broadway	Bwy	Parade	Par
By-Pass	By-Ps	Passage	Pas
Causeway	Cswy	Place	Pl
Common	Comm	Pleasant	Plea
Corner	Cnr	Precinct	Prec
Cottages	Cotts	Promenade	Prom
Court	Ct	Road	Rd
Crescent	Cres	South	S
Drive	Dr	Square	Sq
Drove	Dro	Street,Saint	St
East	E	Terrace	Terr
Gardens	Gdns	Walk	Wlk
Grove	Gr	West	W
Heights	Hts	Yard	Yd

Towns, Villages and Rural Localities

Abbess Roding .... Abb Rod 93 F2
Abridge .... Abr 142 A3
Anstey .... Ans 33 D3
Arkesden .... Arkes 23 F1
Ashdon .... Ash 4 A1
Ashen .... Ashe 9 E1
Aveley .... Ave 183 E3
Aythorpe Roding .... Ay Rod 81 D2
Bardfield Saling .... Ba Sal 53 E1
Barnston .... Barn 73 D2
Bartlow .... Bart 4 A4
Basildon .... Basil 171 E2
Berden .... Berd 46 A4
Billericay .... Bill 149 D1
Birchanger .... Birhr 57 F1
Birdbrook .... Bird 19 D4
Bishop's Stortford .... Bis St 68 A3
Black Notley .... Bl Not 76 C3
Blackmore .... Bla 133 F4
Bobbingworth .... Bobb 118 B4
Boreham .... Bore 112 C4
Braintree .... Brain 65 E2
Brent Pelham .... Br Pl 34 A1
Brentwood .... Brent 158 A4
Broomfield .... Broom 98 A1
Broxted .... Brox 49 F1
Canfield End .... Can E 71 D4
Chadwell St Mary ..... Cha S M 186 A2
Chelmsford .... Chelm 111 D2
Chigwell .... Chig 153 D4
Chingforth .... Ching 139 E2
Chipping Ongar .... Ch Ong 119 D1
Chrishall .... Chris 10 B2
Clare .... Cla 9 F4
Clavering .... Clav 35 E3
Corringham .... Corr 180 A2
Dagenham .... Dag 173 E3
Debden .... Deb 38 A4
Doddinghurst .... Dodd 133 E1
East Hanningfield .... E Han 138 C3
Eastwick .... East 89 D2
Elmdon .... Elm 11 D2
Elsenham .... Els 48 B1
Enfield .... Enf 126 A2
Epping .... Epp 116 A1
Epping Green .... Ep Gr 115 D4
Fairstead .... Fair 86 C3
Farnham .... Far 56 B3
Felstead .... Felst 74 A3
Finchingfield .... Finch 42 B3
Furneaux Pelham .... Fu Pel 45 D3
Fyfield .... Fyf 106 B1
Good Easter .... G Ea 95 E3
Gravesend .... Grave 193 E1
Grays .... Grays 185 D2
Great Baddow .... Gt Bad 124 C4
Great Bardfield .... Gt Ba 42 A1
Great Canfield .... Gt Can 81 E4
Great Chesterford .... Gt C 1 B1
Great Dunmow .... Gt Dun 72 B4
Great Easton .... Gt Ea 60 C4
Great Hallingbury .... Gt Ha 68 C2
Great Leighs .... Gt Le 85 F4
Great Saling .... Gt Sal 64 A4
Great Sampford......... Gt Sam 29 D2
Great Waltham .... Gt Wal 97 F4
Great Yeldham .... Gt Y 20 C1
Hadstock .... Had 3 E3
Harlow .... Harl 89 E1
Hatfield Broad Oak .... Hat B O 79 F3
Haverhill .... Hav 7 E4
Havering-atte-Bower ..... Hav B 155 F4
Helions Bumpstead .... Hel B 17 D4
Hempstead .... Hemp 16 C1
Henham .... Hen 48 C3
Heydon .... Hey 10 A2
High Easter .... H Ea 8 B1
High Laver .... H Lav 105 D3
High Ongar .... H Ong 119 E2
High Roding .... H Rod 81 F4
High Wych .... H Wy 77 D1
Hinxton .... Hinxt 1 A4
Hoddesdon .... Hod 100 A3
Hordon on the Hill .... Horn H 178 C2
Hornchurch .... Hornc 165 D1
Ingatestone .... Ing 135 E2
Kelvedon Hatch .... Kelv H 132 C1
Langley .... Langl 22 B1
Leadon Roding .... Lea Rod 94 B4
Lindsell .... Lind 52 A2
Little Baddow .... Lit Bad 112 C2
Little Bardfield .... Lit Ba 41 E1
Little Chesterford .... Lit C 12 C4
Little Chishill .... Lit Chis 21 F4
Little Dunmow .... Lit Dun 73 E4
Little Easton .... Lit Ea 60 C3
Little Hallingbury .... L Hal 78 B4
Little Laver .... Lit Lav 105 F4
Little Sampford .... Lit Sam 41 E4
Little Waltham .... Lit Wal 98 B3
Littlebury .... Litt 12 C2
Loughton .... Lou 140 C3
Lower Nazeing .... Lo Naz 113 E4
Magdalen Laver .... Mag Lav 104 D3
Manuden .... Man 46 C1
Margaret Roding .... Mar Rod 94 C2
Margaretting .... Marg 136 A4
Matching Green .... Match 92 B2
Meesden .... Mee 34 A3
Moreton .... More 105 E1
Mountnessing .... Mtssg 147 E4
Navestock Heath .... Nave H 144 B4
Newport .... New 36 C4
North Weald
Bassett .... N W Bas 117 E3
Nuthampstead .... Nut 21 D1
Panfield .... Pan 65 D4
Pleshey .... Ple 83 F1
Purfleet .... Pur 183 A4
Quendon .... Quen 36 C1
Radwinter .... Rad 27 F4
Rainham .... Rain 174 A1
Rayne .... Ray 64 C1
Rettendon .... Rett 151 F4
Ridgewell .... Ridge 20 A3
Romford .... Romf 164 B3
Roxwell .... Rox 109 D3
Royden .... Roy 101 D4
Runwell .... Runw 151 F1
Saffron Waldon .... Saff W 13 F1
Sandon .... Sand 125 E3
Sawbridgeworth .... Saw 77 E1
Shalford .... Shal 54 C4
Sheering .... Sheer 91 E4
South Hanningfield .... S Han 151 E4
South Ockendon .... S Ock 184 B4
Springfield .... Sprin 112 F3
Stambourne .... Stam 19 E1
Stanford le Hope .... Sta L H 179 F1
Stanford Rivers .... Sta R 131 E3
Stanstead Abbots .... Sta Ab 87 F2
Stanstead
Mountfitchet .... Stan M 57 E3
Stapleford Abbotts ..... Sta Abb 143 E2
Stapleford Tawney .... Sta T 130 B2
Stebbing .... Steb 62 C3
Steeple Bumpstead .... Ste B 18 A4
Stock .... Stock 136 C2
Stocking Pelham .... St Pel 45 F3
Stondon Massey .... Sto M 133 D3
Stone .... Stone 190 C1
Strethall .... Stret 11 F2
Sturmer .... Stur 7 F2
Swanscombe .... Swan 191 E1
Takeley .... Take 70 A4
Terling .... Terl 86 C1
Thaxted .... Thax 40 A2
Theydon Bois .... The B 128 B2
Thorley .... Thor 67 E1
Tilbury .... Tilb 193 E4
Toppesfield .... Topp 32 B4
Ugley .... Ugl 47 F3
Upminster .... Upm 166 B1
Waltham Abbey .... Wa Aby 126 C4
Wendens Ambo .... Wen A 24 C3
West Hanningfield .... W Han 138 A2
West Thurrock .... W Thu 184 A1
Wethersfield .... Weth 43 D2
White Roothing .... Wh Rot 93 E4
Wicken Bonhunt .... Wic Bon 36 A4
Wickford .... Wick 163 F3
Widdington .... Widd 37 E2
Willingale .... Will 107 E2
Wimbush .... Wim 27 E3
Woodford .... Woodf 152 B2
Writtle .... Writ 110 B1

Abberton Wlk. Rain 173 F2
Abbess Cl. Chelm 110 C1
Abbey Ct. Wa Aby 126 A3
Abbey La. Saff W 13 E1
Abbey Rd. Bill 148 C1
Abbey Rd. Swan 191 E1
Abbey St. Hinx 1 A2
Abbey View. Gt Ea 50 C1
Abbey Wood La. Rain 174 B2
Abbeyview. Wa Aby 126 B3
Abbots Cl. Brent 147 D1
Abbots Cl. Rain 174 B2
Abbots Ct. Bill 161 F1
Abbots Dr. Wa Aby 127 D3
Abbots Ride. Bill 149 E1
Abbotsford Gdns. Woodf 152 A2
Abbotsweld. Harl 102 B3
Abbotts Cl. Chelm 111 E2
Abbotts Cl. Romf 164 A4
Abbotts Cotts. Stur 8 A2
Abbotts Dr. Corr 179 F2
Abbotts Hall Chase. Sta L H 179 F1
Abbotts Rise. Sta Ab 87 E2
Abbotts Way. Bis St 67 F2
Abbotts Way. Sta Ab 87 E2
Abbs Cross. Hornc 165 E2
Abbs Cross Gdns. Hornc 165 E2
Abbs Cross La. Hornc 165 E1
Abenberg Way. Brent 159 D4
Abercrombie Way. Harl 102 B3
Abingdon Ct. Basil 163 D1
Abram's La. Chris 10 B2
Abridge Gdns. Romf 155 D2
Abridge Rd. Chig 141 F2
Abridge Rd. The B 142 A4
Acacia Ave. Hornc 164 C1
Acacia Dr. Upm 175 D4
Acacia Gdns. Upm 166 C2
Acacia Rd. Basil 172 C4
Acacia Rd. Stone 190 C1
Acer Ave. Rain 174 B1
Achilles Way. Brain 66 A3
Acorn Ave. Brain 65 E1
Acorn Mews. Harl 103 D3
Acorn Pl. Basil 170 A3
Acorn St. Hun 88 B4
Acorns The. Chig 153 F3
Acre Rd. Dag 173 D3
Acre View. Hornc 165 F4
Acres Ave. Ch Ong 118 C3
Acres End. Chelm 110 C2
Acres The. Corr 179 F2
Adam Way. Wick 163 F4
Adams Ct. Saff W 25 E4
Adams Rd. Sta L H 179 F1
Adderley Rd. Bis St 67 F4
Addison Gdns. Grays 185 E1
Addison Pavement. Basil 172 A3
Addison Rd. Woodf 153 E1
Adelaide Rd. Tilb 192 C3
Adelphi Cres. Hornc 165 D1
Admirals Wlk. Chelm 110 C2
Admirals Wlk. Hod 100 A2
Adnams Wlk. Hornc 174 A4
Adstock Way. Grays 184 C1
Advice Ave. Grays 185 D2
Aetheric Rd. Brain 65 F2
Afton Dr. S Ock 184 A4
Agister Rd. Chig 154 A3
Ainsley Ave. Romf 164 B3
Aintree Cres. Woodf 153 E1
Aintree Gr. Upm 165 F1
Aire Dr. S Ock 176 A1
Airey Neave Ct. Grays 185 D2
Airfield Way. Hornc 174 B3
Ajax Cl. Brain 66 A3
Alamein Gdns. Stone 190 B1
Alamein Rd. Chelm 110 C3
Alamein Rd. Swan 191 E1
Alan Gdns. Romf 164 A2
Albany Cl. Chelm 110 C3
Albany Ct. Epp 115 F1
Albany Rd. Brent 146 A2
Albany Rd. Hornc 165 D1
Albany Rd. Wick 163 E3
Albany View. Lou 140 A1
Albemarle Cl. Grays 185 D2
Albemarle Gdns. Brain 66 B3
Albert Cl. Grays 185 E2
Albert Dr. Basil 170 B3
Albert Rd. Brain 66 A2
Albert Rd. Dag 164 A2
Albert Rd. Horn H 177 F4
Albert Rd. Lou 152 B4
Albert Rd. Romf 164 C3
Albert Rd. Swan 191 F1
Albert Rd. Woodf 152 A1
Albert St. Brent 158 B3
Albert Terr. Lou 152 C4
Albion Cl. Romf 164 B3
Albion Hill. Lou 140 B2
Albion Par. Grave 193 E1
Albion Park. Lou 140 B2
Albion Rd. Grave 193 E1
Albion Terr. Grave 193 E1
Albyns. Basil 170 B2
Alconbury. Bis St 57 D1
Alcotes. Basil 171 F3
Aldborough Rd. Dag 173 E3
Aldborough Rd. Upm 165 F1
Alde Rd. Hav 7 D4
Aldeburgh Cl. Hav 6 C4
Aldeburgh Pl. Woodf 152 A3
Aldeburgh Way. Sprin 111 E3
Alder Ave. Upm 175 D4
Alder Cl. Bis St 67 E2
Alder Dr. Chelm 124 A3
Alderbury Rd. Stan M 57 F4
Aldergrove Wlk. Hornc 174 B3
Alderman Wlk. Corr 179 F3
Alderney Gdns. Runw 151 E1
Aldersgrove. Wa Aby 126 C3
Alderton Cl. Brent 146 A2
Alderton Cl. Lou 141 D3
Alderton Hall La. Lou 141 D3
Alderton Hill. Lou 140 C2
Alderton Rd. Grays 186 C4
Alderton Rise. Lou 141 D3
Alderton Way. Lou 140 C2
Alderwood Cl. Abr 142 A3
Alderwood Dr. Abr 142 A3
Aldingham Ct. Hornc 174 A4
Aldingham Gdns. Hornc 174 A4
Aldria Rd. Corr 179 F3
Aldridge Ave. Enf 126 A1
Aldridge Cl. Sprin 112 A2
Aldrin Cl. Corr 179 F1
Aldwych Cl. Hornc 165 D1
Alexander Ct. Sprin 111 F4
Alexander La. Brent 147 D2
Alexander Mews. Sand 125 E1
Alexander Rd. Basil 170 A2
Alexander Rd. Brain 65 F2
Alexander Rd. Swan 191 E1
Alexandra Cl. Grays 186 B2
Alexandra Rd. Brent 158 B4
Alexandra Rd. Rain 173 F2
Alexandra Rd. Romf 164 C3
Alexandra Rd. Tilb 192 C3
Alexandra Way. Grays 187 D2
Alf Lowne Ct. Grays 186 A2
Alfred Gdns. Runw 151 E1
Alfred Rd. Ave 183 E3
Alfred Rd. Brent 158 B4
Alfred Rd. Lou 152 B4
Alfred St. Grays 192 B4
Algers Cl. Lou 140 B2
Algers Rd. Lou 140 B2
Alghers Mead. Lou 140 B2
Alibon Gdns. Dag 173 D4
Alibon Rd. Dag 173 D4
Alienor Ave. Gt Ba 42 A1
Alison Cl. Wa Aby 127 D4
Alkerden La. Swan 191 E1
All Saints Cl. Bis St 68 A4
All Saints Cl. Chig 154 A4
All Saints Cl. Dodd 133 D2
All Saints Cl. Sprin 111 F2
All Saints Cl. Swan 191 F1
Allandale Rd. Hornc 164 C2
Allen Rd. Rain 174 B1
Allenby Cres. Grays 185 E1
Allenby Dr. Hornc 165 F2
Allende Ave. Harl 89 E1
Allens Cl. Bore 99 F1
Allens Rd. S Han 150 B3
Allensway. Corr 179 F2
Allington Wlk. Hav 6 C4
Allistonway. Corr 179 F2
Allmains Cl. Lo Naz 114 A3
Allnutts Rd. Epp 129 D3
Allysum Wlk. Bill 149 D2
Alma Ave. Hornc 165 F1
Alma Cl. Wick 163 D3
Alma Dr. Chelm 111 D1
Alma Rd. Swan 191 F1
Almond Ave. Wick 163 E4
Almond Cl. Grays 186 A2
Almonds Ave. Woodf 152 A4
Alpha Cl. Basil 172 C3
Alpha Cl. Brain 66 A1
Alpha Pl. Bis St 67 F4
Alpha Rd. Basil 172 C3
Alpha Rd. Brent 147 E2
Alracks. Basil 170 C3
Alsa Gdns. Els 48 B1
Alsa Leys. Els 48 B1
Alsa St. Stan M 47 F1
Altham Gr. Harl 89 F1
Althorne Cl. Basil 163 D1
Althorne Way. Dag 164 A1
Aluric Cl. Grays 186 A1
Alverstoke Rd. Romf 156 C2
Alwen Gr. S Ock 184 A4
Alwyne Ave. Brent 147 D2
Alyssum Cl. Bore 112 A3
Amanda Cl. Chig 153 E2
Amberden. Basil 170 B3
Amberley Rd. Lou 140 B1
Amberley Way. Romf 164 A4
Amberry Ct. Harl 89 E1
Ambleside. Epp 129 D4
Ambleside Ave. Hornc 174 A4
Amersham Ave. Basil 169 F3
Amersham Cl. Romf 156 C2
Amersham Dr. Romf 156 C2
Amersham Rd. Romf 156 C2
Amersham Wlk. Romf 156 C2
Amery Gdns. Romf 165 E4
Ames Rd. Swan 191 F1
Amesbury. Wa Aby 127 D4
Amesbury Cl. Epp 128 C4
Amesbury Dr. Ching 139 D2
Amesbury Rd. Epp 128 C4
Amoss Rd. Gt Bad 124 C4
Ampers End. Basil 171 E3
Amwell Ct. Hod 100 A4
Amwell Ct. Wa Aby 126 C3
Amwell La. Sta Ab 87 D3
Amwell St. Hod 100 A4
Anan Way. Romf 155 F1
Anchor Bvd. Stone 190 B2
Anchor Dr. Rain 174 A1
Anchor La. Abb Rod 93 E2
Anchor St. Bis St 68 A3
Anchor St. Chelm 111 D1
Anderson Ave. Chelm 110 C3
Anderson's La. Br Pel 33 D1
Andersons. Corr 179 F2
Andrew Cl. Brain 65 F3
Andrew Cl. Chig 153 E2
Andrews Cl. Lou 152 B4
Andrews Farm La. Gt Ea 61 E4
Andrews Pl. Chelm 110 C2
Andromeda Ct. Romf 156 B2
Angel Cl. Basil 171 E2
Angel La. Gt Dun 72 B4
Angel Way. Romf 164 C3
Angle Rd. Grays 191 E4
Angle Side. Brain 66 A1
Anglesea Centre. Grave 193 D1
Anglesea Pl. Grave 193 D1
Anglesey Cl. Bis St 67 E4
Anglesey Dr. Rain 174 A1
Anglia Way. Brain 66 A1
Ann Coles Cl. Ste B 18 B3
Annabell Ave. Grays 186 B4
Annalee Gdns. S Ock 184 A4
Annalee Rd. S Ock 184 A4
Anne Way. Woodf 153 E2
Annifer Way. S Ock 184 A4
Ansgar Rd. Saff W 25 F4
Anson Cl. Romf 155 D1
Anson Way. Brain 66 B2
Anstead Dr. Rain 174 A2
Antelope Ave. Grays 185 D2
Anthony Cl. Bill 161 E3
Anthony Dr. Corr 179 F2
Antlers Hill. Ching 139 D2
Anton Rd. S Ock 176 A1
Antonia Cl. Hav 7 F4
Anvil Way. Bill 149 D3
Anvil Way. Sprin 111 F4
Anworth Cl. Woodf 152 A2
Apollo Cl. Hornc 165 D1
Apple Tree Cl. Dodd 133 E1
Apple Tree Cres. Dodd 133 E1
Apple Tree La. Dodd 133 E1
Apple Tree Way. Wick 163 F4
Appleby Dr. Romf 156 B3
Appleby Green. Romf 156 B3
Appledore Cl. Romf 156 B1
Appleford Ct. Basil 172 B3
Appleton Fields. Bis St 67 F2
Appleton Rd. Lou 141 D3
Appleton Way. Hornc 165 E2
Appletree Wlk. Brain 66 A1
Approach Rd. Bill 162 B3
Approach The. Upm 166 A1
April Pl. Saw 77 F2
Apsley Cl. Bis St 67 F2
Apton Ct. Bis St 67 F4
Apton Fields. Bis St 67 F3
Apton Rd. Bis St 67 F4
Arabia Cl. Ching 139 E1
Araglen Ave. S Ock 184 A4
Aragon Cl. Romf 155 D2
Aragon Dr. Woodf 153 E2
Aragon Rd. Gt Le 85 F4
Arbour Cl. Brent 158 B3
Arbour La. Sprin 111 E2
Arbour Way. Hornc 174 A4
Arbutus Cl. Chelm 124 A3
Arcade Pl. Romf 164 C3
Arcade The. Romf 156 B3
Arcany Rd. S Ock 176 A1
Archate Ave. Grays 185 D2
Archer Rd. Basil 170 A4
Archers. Harl 102 A2
Archers Fields. Basil 163 D1
Archers Way. Chelm 124 B1
Archibald Rd. Romf 157 D1
Archway. Romf 156 A2
Ardleigh. Basil 170 C3
Ardleigh Cl. Hornc 165 E4
Ardleigh Ct. Brent 146 C1
Ardleigh Gdns. Brent 147 F2
Ardleigh Green Rd. Hornc 165 E4
Ardley Cres. Hat B O 79 D1
Ardmore La. Lou 140 A1
Ardmore Rd. S Ock 176 A1
Argent St. Grays 191 F4
Argent St. Grays 192 A4
Argus Cl. Romf 155 D1
Argyle Gdns. Upm 166 B1
Argyll Rd. Bore 112 A3
Argyll Rd. Grays 185 D1
Arisdale Ave. S Ock 176 A1
Ark Ave. Grays 185 D2
Arkwright Rd. Tilb 193 D3
Arkwrights. Harl 89 F1
Arlington Gdns. Romf 156 C1
Arlington Rd. Woodf 152 A2
Arlington Way. Bill 148 C3
Armor Rd. W Thu 183 E1
Armstead Wlk. Dag 173 D3
Armstrong Cl. Corr 179 F1
Arne Cl. Corr 179 E2
Arne Ct. Basil 170 B4
Arne Mews. Basil 170 B4
Arnhem Ave. Ave 183 E3
Arnhem Gr. Brain 65 F2
Arnhem Rd. Chelm 110 C3
Arnold Ave. Basil 170 A3
Arnold Ave East. Enf 126 A1
Arnold Pl. Tilb 193 E3
Arnold Rd. Dag 173 D3
Arnold Way. Chelm 124 B2
Arnolds Ave. Brent 147 E2
Arnolds Cl. Brent 147 E2
Arnolds Farm La. Mtssg 147 F3
Arrowsmith Cl. Chig 153 F3
Arrowsmith Path. Chig 153 F3
Arrowsmith Rd. Chig 153 F3
Arterial Ave. Rain 174 B1
Arterial Rd N Stifford. Grays 184 C2
Arterial Rd Purfleet. Pur 183 E1
Arterial Rd Purfleet. W Thu 183 E1
Arterial Rd W Thurrock. Grays 184 A2
Arterial Rd W Thurrock. W Thu 184 A2
Artesan Cl. Hornc 164 C2
Arthur Barnes Ct. Grays 186 B2
Arthur Ct. Chelm 110 C3
Arthur St. Grays 192 B4
Arun. Grays 187 E1
Arun Cl. Sprin 111 E3
Arundel Cl. Bill 149 E3
Arundel Dr. Corr 180 A2
Arundel Dr. Woodf 152 A2
Arundel Mews. Bill 149 E3
Arundel Rd. Romf 156 C1
Arundel Rd. Runw 151 E1
Arundel Way. Bill 149 E3
Ascension Rd. Romf 155 E2
Ascot Cl. Bis St 68 B4
Ascot Cl. Chig 153 F2
Ascot Gdns. Hornc 174 C4
Ash Bungalows. Brain 65 F2
Ash Cl. Brent 145 F2
Ash Gr. Chelm 124 B4
Ash Green. Bill 149 F1
Ash Groves. Saw 78 A1
Ash La. Hornc 165 F4
Ash Tree Cl. Chelm 110 C1
Ash Tree Cres. Chelm 110 C1
Ash Tree Field. Harl 89 D1
Ash Tree Wlk. Basil 171 F3
Ashbeam Cl. Brent 158 B2
Ashbourne Rd. Romf 156 B3
Ashbrook Rd. Dag 164 A1
Ashburnham Gdns. Upm 166 B2
Ashby Cl. Grays 186 C4
Ashby Cl. Hornc 166 A2
Ashby Rise. Bis St 57 D1
Ashdale. Bis St 67 E2
Ashdon Cl. Brent 147 E2
Ashdon Cl. Woodf 152 A2
Ashdon Rd. Saff W 14 B2
Ashdon Rd Comm Cntre. Saff W 14 A2
Ashdon Way. Basil 171 D3
Ashdown Cl. Corr 179 F3
Ashdown Wlk. Romf 155 D1
Ashen Cl. Ashe 9 E1
Ashen Hill. Ashe 9 E1
Ashen La. Cla 9 E2
Ashen Rd. Ashe 20 A4
Ashfield Cl. Gt Dun 61 E1
Ashfields. Basil 172 B4
Ashfields. Lou 140 C4
Ashford Ave. Brent 158 A4
Ashford Rd. Chelm 110 C1
Ashford Rd. Woodf 152 A1
Ashlea Cl. Hav 7 D3
Ashlea Rd. Hav 7 D3
Ashleigh Gdns. Upm 166 B1
Ashley Ave. Woodf 153 D1
Ashley Cl. Corr 180 A2
Ashley Gdns. Grays 185 E3
Ashlyn Gr. Hornc 165 E4
Ashlyns. Basil 172 A4
Ashlyns La. Bobb 104 C1
Ashlyns La. Mag Lav 104 C1
Ashlyns Rd. Epp 115 F1
Ashmour Gdns. Romf 155 E1
Ashton Pl. Sprin 112 A2
Ashton Rd. Romf 156 B1
Ashurst Dr. Sprin 111 E4
Ashvale Dr. Upm 166 C1
Ashvale Gdns. Romf 155 E3
Ashvale Gdns. Upm 166 C1
Ashway. Corr 180 A3
Ashwells Rd. Dodd 145 F3
Ashwood Ave. Rain 174 A1
Askew Farm La. Grays 184 C1
Askwith Rd. Rain 173 E2
Aspen Gr. Upm 175 D4
Aspin Mews. Saff W 13 F2
Aster Ct. Sprin 111 F3
Astley. Grays 191 F4
Aston Rd. Basil 170 A3
Astor Ave. Romf 164 B3
Astra Cl. Hornc 174 A3
Athelstan Cl. Romf 156 C1
Athelstan Gdns. Runw 151 E1
Athelstan Rd. Romf 156 C1
Atherton End. Saw 77 F2
Atherton Gdns. Grays 186 B1
Atherton Rd. Woodf 152 C1
Atholl Rd. Sprin 111 F3
Atlanta Blvd. Romf 164 C3
Atridge Chase. Bill 149 D2
Attlee Ct. Grays 185 D2
Attlee Dr. Stone 190 A1
Attwoods Cl. Chelm 124 B2
Aubrey Cl. Chelm 111 D4
Aubrietia Cl. Romf 156 B1
Auckland Ave. Rain 173 F1
Auckland Cl. Chelm 110 C3
Auckland Cl. Tilb 193 D3
Audleigh Pl. Chig 153 D2
Audley End. Saff W 25 D4
Audley End Rd. Saff W 25 E4
Audley Gdns. Lou 141 E4
Audley Gdns. Wa Aby 126 B3
Audley Rd. Gt Le 85 F4
Audley Rd. Saff W 13 F1
Audley Way. Basil 171 D3
Audrey Gdns. Bis St 67 F2
Augustine Rd. Grave 193 E1
Augustus Cl. Hav 7 E4
Aukingford Gdns. Ch Ong 118 C3
Aukingford Green. Ch Ong 118 C2
Auriel Ave. Dag 173 E3
Austen Cl. Lou 141 E3
Austen Cl. Swan 191 E1
Austen Cl. Tilb 193 E3
Austral Dr. Hornc 165 E2
Auton Croft. Saff W 25 E4
Aveley By-Ps. Ave 183 E3
Aveley Cl. Ave 183 E3
Aveley Rd. Ave 175 E2
Aveley Rd. Romf 164 C4
Aveley Rd. Upm 175 E2
Avelon Rd. Rain 174 A2
Avelon Rd. Romf 155 E2
Avenue Cl. Romf 156 C2
Avenue Ind Est. Romf 156 B1
Avenue Rd. Bis St 68 A3
Avenue Rd. Corr 171 D1
Avenue Rd. Gt Bad 124 B4
Avenue Rd. Ing 135 D2
Avenue Rd. Romf 156 C2
Avenue Rd. Roy 100 B3
Avenue Rd. The B 128 B2
Avenue Rd. Woodf 152 B2
Avenue The. Bill 149 D1
Avenue The. Brain 65 F2
Avenue The. Brent 158 C2
Avenue The. Corr 180 B3
Avenue The. Gt Dun 72 C4
Avenue The. Hornc 165 E1
Avenue The. Lo Naz 114 B3
Avenue The. Lou 140 C2
Avenue The. Lou 152 B4
Avenue The. Romf 164 B4
Avenue The. Swan 191 D2
Avey La. Wa Aby 126 C1
Avila Chase. Chelm 124 A1
Avon Green. S Ock 184 A4
Avon Rd. Chelm 110 B3
Avon Rd. Upm 166 B3
Avondale Cl. Lou 140 C1
Avondale Ct. Woodf 152 A1
Avondale Dr. Lou 140 C2
Avondale Gdns. Corr 179 F3
Avondale Rd. Basil 172 A2
Avontar Rd. S Ock 176 A1
Aylett Rd. Upm 166 B1
Ayletts. Basil 171 F3
Ayletts. Broom 98 A2
Ayloff's Wlk. Hornc 165 F3
Ayloffs Cl. Hornc 165 F4
Aylsham La. Romf 156 B3
Aylsham Rd. Hod 100 B4
Aynsley Gdns. Harl 103 E4
Aynsworth Ave. Bis St 57 D1
Ayr Green. Romf 155 F1
Ayr Way. Romf 155 F1
Ayron Rd. S Ock 176 A1
Azalea Ave. Wick 163 E4

Babington Rd. Hornc 165 D2
Back Hill. Had 3 D3
Back La. Gt Wal 84 A3
Back La. Hal 78 A4
Back La. Hinx 1 A2
Back La. Ing 135 D3
Back La. Lit Wal 98 B2
Back La. Lo Naz 101 E1
Back La. Ple 83 F1
Back La. Saw 78 A1
Back La. Stock 136 B1
Back La. W Thu 184 A2
Back Rd. Writ 110 A1

Bacon Link. Romf 155 D2
Badburgham Ct. Wa Aby 126 C3
Baddow Cl. Dag 173 D2
Baddow Hall Ave. Gt Bad 125 D4
Baddow Hall Cres. Gt Bad 125 D4
Baddow Place Ave. Gt Bad 125 D3
Baddow Rd. Chelm 111 E1
Baddow Rd. Chelm 124 C4
Baddow Rd. Gt Bad 124 C4
Baddows Cl. Woodf 152 B2
Bader Way. Rain 174 A3
Badgers. Bis St 67 F3
Badgers Cl. Chelm 124 A1
Badgers Mount. Grays 185 F2
Badgers The. Basil 170 A2
Bag La. Ing 134 C2
Bailey Bridge Rd. Brain 65 F3
Bailey Cl. Hav 7 E4
Bailey Cl. W Thu 183 E1
Baillie Cl. Rain 174 A1
Baker St. Chelm 111 D1
Baker St. Grays 185 F3
Baker's La. Bl Not 76 B3
Bakers Ct. Bis St 68 A4
Bakers La. Epp 115 F1
Bakers La. Felst 74 B2
Bakers La. Ing 135 D2
Bakers La. Stock 137 D4
Bakers Mead. Gt Wal 97 F4
Bakers Meadow. Dodd 133 E1
Bakers Mews. Ing 135 D2
Bakers Villas The. Epp 115 F1
Bakery Cl. Roy 101 E4
Bakery Ct. Stan M 57 E3
Baldocks Rd. The B 128 C2
Baldwin's Hill. Lou 140 C4
Balfour Rd. Grays 185 E1
Balfour Way. Basil 172 A3
Balgonie Rd. Ching 139 E1
Balgores Cres. Romf 165 D4
Balgores La. Romf 165 D4
Balgores Sq. Romf 165 D4
Ballards Cl. Dag 173 D2
Ballards Rd. Dag 173 D3
Ballards Wlk. Basil 170 C4
Balmoral Ave. Corr 179 F2
Balmoral Ave. Corr 180 A2
Balmoral Cl. Bill 149 F1
Balmoral Dr. Hav 6 C4
Balmoral Rd. Brent 146 A2
Balmoral Rd. Hornc 165 E1
Balmoral Rd. Romf 165 D3
Balstonia Dr. Corr 179 F3
Bamford Way. Romf 155 D3
Bampton Rd. Romf 156 C2
Bancroft Ave. Woodf 152 A4
Banes Down. Lo Naz 100 C1
Bangs Cl. Bart 5 D4
Bank Pl. Brent 158 B4
Bank St. Brain 65 F2
Bank St. Grave 193 D1
Bankart La. Sprin 111 F2
Bankfoot. Grays 185 D1
Banks La. Sta T 129 F4
Bankside. Grave 192 B1
Bann Cl. S Ock 184 A3
Banner Cl. W Thu 183 E1
Bannister Dr. Brent 147 E2
Bannister Green. Wick 163 F3
Bannister Green Villas. Felst 74 C3
Banson's La. Ch Ong 119 D2
Banson's Yd. Ch Ong 119 D2
Bansons Way. Ch Ong 119 D2
Banters La. Gt Le 76 A1
Banyards. Hornc 165 F4
Barbel Cl. Ches 126 A3
Barberry Cl. Romf 156 B2
Barclay Cl. Gt Bad 125 D3
Barclay Ct. Hod 100 A3
Barclay Oval. Woodf 152 A3
Barclay Rd. Basil 163 F1
Barclay Way. W Thu 183 F1
Bardeswell Cl. Brent 158 B4
Bardfield. Basil 171 F3
Bardfield Rd. Gt Sal 53 F1
Bardfield Rd. Thax 40 B1
Barfields. Lou 141 D3
Barfields Gdns. Lou 141 D3
Barfields Path. Lou 141 D3
Barham Cl. Romf 155 D1
Bark Burr Rd. Grays 184 C2
Barker Cl. Ste B 18 A3
Barkis Cl. Chelm 110 B4
Barle Gdns. S Ock 184 A4
Barley Cl. Basil 170 A2
Barley Cl. Hat B O 79 F1
Barley Croft. Harl 102 C2
Barley Field. Kelv H 132 C1
Barley Hills. Bis St 67 F2
Barleycorn Way. Hornc 165 F3
Barleylands Rd. Bill 161 F2
Barlow's Reach. Sprin 112 A2
Barn Green. Sprin 111 F4
Barn Hill. Harl 101 D2
Barn Mead. Bla 133 E2
Barn Mead. Harl 102 B3
Barn Mead. The B 128 C2
Barnaby Rudge. Chelm 110 C4
Barnaby Way. Chig 153 D4
Barnard Acres. Lo Naz 113 F4
Barnard Cl. Basil 171 F1
Barnard Cl. New 36 C4
Barnard Rd. Chelm 124 B1
Barnard Rd. Saw 77 F2
Barnards Field. Thax 40 A1
Barncroft Cl. Lou 141 D2
Barncroft Green. Lou 141 D2
Barncroft Rd. Lou 141 D2
Barnet Park Rd. Runw 151 F1
Barnfield. Epp 116 C3
Barnfield. Hat B O 80 A3
Barnfield. Wick 163 F4
Barnfield Cl. Hod 100 A4
Barnfield Cl. Lo Naz 100 C1
Barnfield Mews. Chelm 111 D3
Barns Rd. Bill 162 B3
Barnsley Rd. Romf 156 C2
Barnstaple Path. Romf 156 B3
Barnstaple Rd. Romf 156 B3
Barnston Green. Barn 73 D2
Barnston Way. Brent 147 E2
Barnyard The. Basil 170 A2
Barons Gate. Bis St 67 E4
Barons The. Bis St 67 E3
Barons Way. Basil 170 A2
Barrack La. Gt Wal 97 F4
Barrack Rd. G Ea 96 A3
Barrack Row. Grave 193 D1
Barrack Sq. Chelm 111 D1
Barrells Down Rd. Bis St 56 C1
Barrett La. Bis St 67 F4
Barrie Pavement. Wick 163 E3
Barrington Cl. Basil 171 F4
Barrington Cl. Gt Bad 125 D3
Barrington Cl. Lou 141 E3
Barrington Cl. Woodf 152 C1
Barrington Ct. Brent 147 E2
Barrington Gdns. Basil 171 F4
Barrington Green. Lou 141 E3
Barrington Pl. Ing 135 D2
Barrington Rd. Lou 141 E3
Barron's Cl. Ch Ong 118 C2
Barrows Rd. Harl 101 F4
Barry Cl. Grays 186 A2
Barryfields. Shal 54 C4
Barstable Rd. Corr 179 E1
Bartholomew Cl. Gt C 1 C1
Bartholomew Dr. Romf 156 B1
Bartholomew Rd. Bis St 67 F3
Bartlow End. Basil 172 A4
Bartlow Gdns. Romf 155 E1
Bartlow Rd. Bart 5 E2
Bartlow Rd. Had 3 E4
Bartlow Side. Basil 172 A4
Barton Ave. Romf 164 A2
Barton Cl. Chig 153 E4
Barton Rd. Hornc 165 D2
Bartram Ave. Brain 66 B2
Baryta Cl. Sta L H 179 E1
Basbow La. Bis St 67 F4
Basildon Ave. Woodf 153 D1
Basildon Dr. Basil 170 B4
Basildon Rd. Basil 170 C4
Basildon Rise. Basil 170 C4
Bassett Gdns. N W Bas 117 D3
Bassett's La. Will 121 D4
Bassingbourn Rd. Take 58 C1
Bata Ave. Grays 187 D1
Bates Rd. Romf 157 D2
Bath St. Grave 193 D1
Battle Ct. Ch Ong 119 D1
Battleswick. Basil 162 C1
Bawn Cl. Brain 66 A2
Bay Manor La. W Thu 190 C4
Bayleys Mead. Brent 159 E4
Bayly Rd. Stone 190 A1
Baymans Wood. Brent 158 C4
Baywood Sq. Chig 154 A3
Beach's Dr. Chelm 110 B2
Beacon Hill. Nave H 132 B1
Beacon Hill. Pur 183 D1
Beacon Hill Rd. Nave H 132 A1
Beaconfield Ave. Epp 116 A1
Beaconfield Rd. Epp 116 A1
Beaconfield Way. Epp 116 A1
Beacons The. Lou 128 A1
Beadle Way. Gt Le 86 A3
Beadles The. Lit Hal 78 A4
Beadon Dr. Brain 66 A1
Beam Ave. Dag 173 D2
Beambridge. Basil 172 A3
Beaminster Gdns. Woodf 153 D1
Beamish Cl. N W Bas 117 E3
Beams Cl. Bill 161 E4
Beams Way. Bill 161 E4
Beamway. Dag 173 E3
Bean Rd. Swan 191 D1
Beanfield Rd. H Wy 77 D2
Beansland Gr. Romf 154 C1
Bear Cl. Romf 164 A3
Beard's La. Elm 23 D3
Beardsley Dr. Sprin 111 F4
Bearing Cl. Chig 154 A3
Bearing Way. Chig 154 A3
Bearsted Dr. Basil 172 B3
Beatty Gdns. Brain 66 B2
Beatty La. Basil 171 F3
Beauchamps Cl. Spring 111 F4
Beaufort Cl. N W Bas 117 D2
Beaufort Cl. Romf 164 B4
Beaufort Gdns. Brain 66 A2
Beaufort Rd. Bill 148 C1
Beaufort Rd. Sprin 112 A2
Beauly Way. Romf 155 F1
Beaumaris. Woodf 152 B2
Beaumont Cl. Romf 156 B1
Beaumont Cres. Rain 174 A3
Beaumont Ct. Hav 7 D3
Beaumont Gdns. Brent 147 E2
Beaumont Hill. Gt Dun 61 E1
Beaumont Park Dr. Roy 101 D4
Beaumont Pl. Brain 66 A2
Beaumont Vale. Hav 7 D3
Beaumont Wlk. Chelm 110 B3
Beaver Rd. Chig 154 B3
Beazley End. Wick 163 F3
Bebington Cl. Bill 149 D2
Beckers Green Rd. Brain 66 B1
Becket Cl. Brent 158 B2
Beckett Dr. Corr 179 E2
Becketts. Basil 170 A3
Bedale Rd. Romf 157 D3
Bedford Cl. Brain 66 A2
Bedford Gdns. Hornc 165 E1
Bedford Rd. Basil 170 A3
Bedford Rd. Grays 185 D1
Bedford Rd. Woodf 152 A1
Bedwell Rd. Ugl 48 A2
Beech Ave. Brain 65 F3
Beech Ave. Brent 158 C4
Beech Ave. Lou 152 A4
Beech Ave. Upm 175 D4
Beech Cl. Hornc 165 D1
Beech Cl. Take 70 B4
Beech Ct. Basil 171 F3
Beech Dri. Saw 90 B4
Beech Gdns. Dag 173 E3
Beech Gr. Ave 183 E2
Beech Gr. Chig 153 F2
Beech Gr. Hav 6 C4
Beech Hill Gdns. Wa Aby 127 D1
Beech La. Woodf 152 A4
Beech Pl. Epp 128 C4
Beech Rd. Basil 171 F3
Beech Rd. Will 107 E2
Beech St. Romf 164 B4
Beech Tree Glade. Ching 139 F1
Beecham Ct. Basil 170 B4
Beechams La. Quen 47 F4
Beechcombe. Corr 180 A3
Beechcroft. Sta L H 187 D1
Beechcroft Rd. Woodf 152 A1
Beeches Cl. Chelm 110 C1
Beeches Cl. Saff W 25 E4
Beeches Ct. Chelm 110 C1
Beeches Rd. Chelm 110 C1
Beeches The. Brent 158 A4
Beeches The. Tilb 193 D3
Beeches The. Wen A 24 C3
Beechfield. Hod 87 D1
Beechfield. Saw 77 F1
Beechfield Gdns. Romf 164 B2
Beechfield Wlk. Wa Aby 126 B2
Beechlands. Bis St 67 F3
Beechwood Gdns. Rain 182 A4
Beedell Ave. Wick 163 F3
Beehive Chase. Bla 133 D2
Beehive Ct. Hat B O 79 D2
Beehive La. Basil 171 D3
Beehive La. Chelm 124 B3
Beehive La. Gt Bad 124 B3
Beeleigh Ave. Basil 170 B2
Beeleigh Cross. Basil 171 F4
Beeleigh East. Basil 171 F4
Beeleigh Link. Sprin 111 F2
Beeleigh West. Basil 171 E4
Beggarhill. Ing 134 C3
Begonia Cl. Sprin 111 F3
Bekeswell La. Chelm 123 F1
Belchamps Rd. Wick 163 F4
Belcher Rd. Hod 100 A4
Belchers La. Lo Naz 114 B4
Beldams La. Bis St 68 A3
Beldowes. Basil 171 E3
Belgrave Ave. Romf 156 B1
Belgrave Cl. Gt Bad 124 B4
Belgrave Rd. Bill 149 D2
Belgrave Terr. Woodf 152 A4
Bell Ave. Romf 156 A1
Bell Cl. Stone 190 C1
Bell Comm. Epp 128 C4
Bell Farm Ave. Dag 164 B1
Bell Hill Cl. Bill 161 D4
Bell House Rd. Romf 164 B2
Bell La. Hod 100 A3
Bell La. Pan 65 D4
Bell La. Thax 40 A2
Bell Lane. Gt Ba 42 A1
Bell Mead. Saw 77 F1
Bell St. Gt Bad 124 C3
Bell St. Saw 77 F1
Belle Vue. Chelm 111 D1
Belle Vue Rd. Romf 155 E2
Bellevue Rd. Bill 148 C1
Bellevue Rd. Hornc 165 F2
Bellfield. Basil 171 F2
Bellflower Path. Romf 156 B2
Bellhouse La. Dodd 145 F2
Bellmaine Ave. Corr 179 F2
Bellmead. Chelm 111 D1
Bells Chase. Gt Bad 124 C3
Bells Cl. Saff W 25 F4
Bells Hill. Bis St 67 F4
Bells Hill Rd. Basil 171 D1
Belmer Rd. Stan M 58 B2
Belmonde Dr. Sprin 111 F4
Belmont Ave. Upm 165 F1
Belmont Ave. Wick 163 D4
Belmont Cl. Sprin 111 F4
Belmont Cl. Wick 163 D4
Belmont Cl. Woodf 152 A3
Belmont Hill. New 25 D1
Belmont Rd. Grays 191 F4
Belmont Rd. Hornc 165 E1
Belsteads Farm La. Broom 98 C1
Belstedes. Basil 170 C3
Belsyns Rd. Gt Ba 42 A2
Beltinge Rd. Romf 165 F4
Belvawney Cl. Chelm 110 C3
Belvedere Ave. Woodf 153 D1
Belvedere Rd. Brent 157 F4
Belvoir The. Ing 135 D2
Bendlowes Rd. Gt Ba 42 B1
Benedict Dr. Chelm 110 C1
Benets Rd. Hornc 166 A2
Benfalls. Basil 162 A1
Benfield Way. Brain 66 A1
Benhooks Ave. Bis St 67 F3
Benhurst Ave. Hornc 165 D1
Benjamin Cl. Hornc 165 D3
Bennett's Ave. E Han 138 C2
Bennett's La. Gt Wal 73 F1
Bennions Cl. Hornc 174 B3
Bennison Dr. Romf 156 C1
Benrek Cl. Woodf 153 E1
Benskins Cl. Berd 46 A4
Benskins La. Hav B 144 B1
Benson Rd. Grays 192 B4
Bentfield End Cswy. Stan M 57 E4
Bentfield Gdns. Stan M 57 E4
Bentfield Rd. Stan M 57 E4
Bentley Cl. Bis St 67 F3
Bentley St. Grave 193 E1
Bentley Street Ind Est. Grave 193 E1
Bentley Way. Woodf 152 A4
Benton Gdns. Corr 179 F3
Benyon Ct. S Ock 176 B2
Benyon Path. S Ock 176 B2
Beran Way. Hornc 165 F1
Berbice La. Gt Dun 61 E1
Berdens. Basil 171 E3
Berecroft. Harl 102 B2
Beredens La. Romf 157 F1
Berens Cl. Runw 151 F1
Beresford Ct. Bill 148 C3
Beresford Dr. Woodf 152 B3
Beresford Rd. Ching 139 F1
Beresford Rd. Grave 192 C1
Berkeley Ave. Romf 155 E2
Berkeley Dr. Bill 149 D3
Berkley Ave. Woodf 153 D1
Berkley Cl. Hornc 166 A1
Berkley Cres. Grave 193 E1
Berkley Dr. Hornc 166 A1
Berkley Hill. Corr 179 F2
Berkley Rd. Grave 193 D1
Berkshire Way. Hornc 166 A4
Bermuda Rd. Tilb 193 D3
Bernard Cl. Chig 153 E2
Bernard Rd. Romf 164 B2
Bernard St. Grave 193 D1
Berners End. Barn 73 D2
Berners Wlk. Basil 171 E4
Bernice Cl. Rain 174 B1
Bernside. Brain 65 F1
Berry Cl. Basil 170 A3
Berry Cl. Hornc 174 B4
Berry Cl. Wick 163 D3
Berry La. Basil 170 A2
Bersham La. Grays 184 C1
Berther Rd. Hornc 165 F2
Berwick Ave. Chelm 111 D4
Berwick Cl. Ches 126 A3
Berwick La. Sta R 130 C3
Berwick Pond Cl. Rain 174 B2
Berwick Pond Rd. Upm 174 C3
Berwick Rd. Rain 174 B2
Berwood Rd. Corr 179 F2
Betony Cres. Bill 148 C3
Betony Rd. Romf 156 B2
Betoyne Cl. Bill 149 E1
Betterton Rd. Rain 173 F2
Betts La. Lo Naz 101 E1
Betula Wlk. Rain 174 B1
Beulah Rd. Epp 116 A1
Beulah Rd. Hornc 165 E1
Bevans Cl. Swan 191 E1
Beverley Cl. Grays 186 B4
Beverley Cl. Hornc 165 F2
Beverley Cres. Woodf 152 A2
Beverley Gdns. Hornc 165 F2
Beverley Rise. Bill 149 E1
Bevil Ct. Hod 87 D1
Bevin Wlk. Sta L H 179 E1
Bevis Cl. Stone 190 B1
Beyers Gdns. Hod 87 D1
Beyers Prospect. Hod 87 D1
Beyers Ride. Hod 87 D1
Bibby Cl. Corr 180 A2
Biddenden Ct. Basil 172 B3
Bideford Cl. Romf 156 B1
Biggin La. Grays 193 D4
Bigods La. Gt Dun 61 E2
Bilberry End. Had 3 E3
Billericay Rd. Brent 160 A2
Billet La. Hornc 165 E2
Billet La. Sta L H 179 F1
Billet Rd. Romf 154 C1
Bilton Rd. Chelm 110 C1
Bingham Cl. S Ock 184 A4
Bingley Rd. Hod 100 B3
Binley Rd. Sprin 111 F1
Birbeck Gdns. Woodf 152 A4
Birbeck Rd. Brent 147 E2
Birch Cl. Brain 65 E1
Birch Cl. Lou 152 B4
Birch Cl. Romf 164 A4
Birch Cres. Hornc 165 F4
Birch Gdns. Dag 164 B1
Birch Green. Wick 163 E4
Birch La. Stock 136 C2
Birch Pl. Stone 190 C1
Birch Rd. Romf 164 A4
Birchalls. Stan M 57 F4
Birchanger La. Birhr 57 F1
Birches The. Brent 158 C4
Birches The. N W Bas 117 D3
Birches Wlk. Chelm 124 A1
Birchwood. Birhr 57 E1
Birchwood. Wa Aby 126 C3
Birchwood Cl. Brent 158 B2
Birchwood Rd. Corr 180 A3
Bird La. Brent 167 E4
Bird La. Upm 166 B3
Birdbrook Cl. Brent 147 D2
Birdbrook Cl. Dag 173 E3
Birdbrook Rd. Stam 19 D2
Birdbush Ave. Saff W 25 E4
Birds Cl. Hinx 1 A2
Birds Farm Ave. Romf 155 D2
Birds Green. Will 107 D3
Birkdale Ave. Romf 157 D2
Biros Cl. S Han 150 B3
Birs Cl. Runw 151 E1
Biscay Cl. Hav 7 E4
Bishop Hall La. Chelm 111 D2
Bishop Rd. Chelm 111 D2
Bishop's Ave. Bis St 67 F2
Bishop's Hall Rd. Brent 146 A2
Bishop's Park Way. Bis St 67 D4
Bishops Ave. Brain 66 A2
Bishops Cl. Basil 163 D1
Bishops Rd. Corr 179 F2
Bishops Rd. Wick 163 E2
Bishopscourt Gdns. Sprin 111 F2
Bishopsfield. Harl 102 B3
Black Bush La. Horn H 178 B2
Black Ditch Rd. Wa Aby 126 B2
Black La. Lit Ba 41 F1
Blackacre Rd. The B 128 C1
Blackborne Rd. Dag 173 D3
Blackbush Spring. Harl 90 A1
Blackbushe. Bis St 57 E1
Blackhorse La. N W Bas 117 E3
Blacklands Cl. Saff W 25 E4
Blackley La. Gt Le 76 A2
Blacklock. Sprin 112 A2
Blackmans Ave. Corr 179 E4
Blackmore Ct. Wa Aby 127 D3
Blackmore Mead. Bla 133 F4
Blackmore Rd. Bla 134 B3
Blackmore Rd. Dodd 133 D2
Blackmore Rd. Grays 185 E1
Blackmore Rd. Ing 121 E2
Blackmore Rd. Ing 134 B3
Blackmore Rd. Kelv H 133 D2
Blackmore Rd. Lou 140 C1
Blackmores. Basil 169 F3
Blackshots La. Grays 185 E2
Blacksmith Cl. Bill 149 D3
Blacksmith Cl. Sprin 111 F4
Blacksmith Cl. Sta Ab 87 D4
Blacksmith's La. Rain 173 F2
Blacksmiths Alley. Bla 133 F4
Blacksmiths Hill. Cla 9 D2
Blacksmiths La. Bart 5 E3
Blacksmiths Way. H Wy 77 D1
Blackthorn Cl. Writ 110 A1
Blackthorn Rd. Grays 185 D3
Blackthorn Way. Brent 158 B3
Blackthorns. Basil 170 A2
Blackwater Cl. Sprin 111 E3
Blackwater Way. Brain 66 A2
Blade End. The B 128 C2
Bladon Cl. Brain 65 F4
Blake Cl. Rain 173 F2
Blake Dr. Brain 66 B2
Blake Hall Rd. Bobb 118 A3
Blake Way. Tilb 193 E3
Blakeborough Dr. Romf 156 C1
Blandford Cl. Romf 164 A4
Blandford Cres. Ching 139 E1
Blenheim Cl. Romf 164 B4
Blenheim Cl. Saw 90 B4
Blenheim Cl. Upm 166 C2

Blenheim Ct. Woodf 152 A2
Blenheim Gdns. Ave 183 D3
Blenheim Rd. Brent 146 A2
Blenheim Way. N W Bas 117 D2
Blenneim Cl. Brain 65 F4
Bligh Rd. Grave 193 D1
Blind La. Bill 160 A3
Blind La. Sand 125 F2
Blind La. W Han 137 F3
Blockhouse Rd. Grays 192 B4
Blois Rd. Ste B 18 B4
Blue Anchor La. Grays 186 C1
Bluebell Green. Sprin 111 F4
Bluebell Wood. Bill 148 C2
Bluehouse. Basil 171 D3
Bluemans. N W Bas 117 E4
Bluemans End. N W Bas 117 E4
Blunts Wall Rd. Bill 148 C1
Blyth Wlk. Upm 166 C3
Blyth's Meadow. Brain 65 F2
Blyth's Way. Ray 64 C1
Blythe Rd. Corr 179 F2
Blythe Rd. Roy 100 B3
Blythwood Gdns. Stan M 57 E3
Blyton Cl. Wick 163 E3
Boar Cl. Chig 154 A3
Boardman Ave. Ching 139 D2
Bobbingworth Mill. Bobb 118 A4
Bocking End. Brain 65 F2
Bockingham Green. Basil 172 A4
Bodell Cl. Grays 185 D2
Bodle Ave. Swan 191 F1
Bodmin Rd. Sprin 111 F3
Bogmoor Rd. Nut 21 D4
Bohun Cl. Gt Le 85 F4
Boleyn Cl. Bill 149 D3
Boleyn Ct. Lou 140 A1
Boleyn Gdns. Brent 159 D4
Boleyn Gdns. Dag 173 E3
Boleyn Way. Bore 99 F1
Boleyn Way. Woodf 153 E2
Boleyns Ave. Brain 65 F3
Bolford St. Thax 39 F1
Bolingbroke Cl. Gt Le 85 F4
Boltons The. Woodf 152 A3
Bond St. Chelm 111 E1
Bond St. Grays 192 B4
Bonington Chase. Sprin 111 F3
Bonington Rd. Hornc 174 B4
Bonks Hill. Saw 77 E1
Bonner Wlk. Grays 184 C2
Bonneting La. Clav 35 D1
Bonningtons. Brent 159 D4
Bonnygate. Basil 171 E4
Bootham Cl. Bill 148 C1
Bootham Rd. Bill 148 C1
Borda Cl. Chelm 111 D3
Border's La. Lou 141 D3
Boreham Rd. Gt Le 86 A2
Borland Cl. Stone 191 D1
Borough La. Saff W 25 E4
Borough The. Ch Ong 118 C1
Borradale Ct. Ste B 18 A3
Borwick La. Bill 162 C2
Bosanquet Rd. Hod 100 B4
Boscawen Gdns. Brain 66 B2
Boscombe Ave. Grays 185 E1
Boscombe Ave. Hornc 165 E2
Boscombe Ave. Wick 162 C4
Bosgrove. Ching 139 E1
Boswells Dr. Chelm 111 E1
Bosworth Cres. Romf 156 B2
Bosworth Rd. Dag 164 A1
Botany Way. Pur 183 D1
Botelers. Basil 170 C2
Botney Hill Rd. Bill 160 B2
Bouchers Mead. Sprin 111 F4
Bouchier Wlk. Rain 174 A3
Boult Rd. Basil 170 B4
Boulter Gdns. Hornc 174 A4
Boundary Dr. Brent 147 F1
Boundary Rd. Bis St 68 A3
Boundary Rd. Hav 7 E3
Boundary Rd. Romf 165 D3
Boundary Rd. Upm 166 A1
Bounderby Gr. Chelm 110 C3
Bourne Ave. Basil 170 A4
Bourne Cl. Basil 170 A4
Bourne Ct. Woodf 152 B1
Bourne End. Hornc 166 A2
Bourne Rd. Hav 7 D4
Bournebridge Cl. Brent 147 F1
Bournebridge La. Abr 143 D1
Bournebridge La. Sta Abb 143 D1
Bouverie Rd. Chelm 124 A4
Bovey Way. S Ock 184 A4
Bovingdon Rd. Brain 55 E1
Bow Arrow La. Stone 190 A1
Bowden Dr. Hornc 165 F2
Bower Cl. Romf 155 E2
Bower Farm Rd. Hav B 155 E4
Bower Hall Dr. Ste B 18 A3
Bower Hill. Epp 129 D4
Bower La. Basil 171 F4
Bower Vale. Epp 129 D4
Bowerman Rd. Grays 186 A1
Bowers Court Dr. Basil 172 C3
Bowes Dr. Ch Ong 119 D2
Bowfell Ct. Basil 170 A2
Bowfell Dr. Basil 170 A3
Bowhay. Brent 159 D4
Bowland Rd. Woodf 152 B2
Bowlers Croft. Basil 162 C1
Bowmont Cl. Brent 147 D2
Bown Cl. Tilb 193 D3
Bowness Way. Hornc 174 A4
Bowsers La. Ash 3 E2
Bowsers La. Saff W 3 E2
Boxmoor Rd. Romf 155 E3
Boxted Cl. Lou 140 C1
Boyce Rd. Corr 179 E2
Boyd Cl. Bis St 68 A4
Boyne Dr. Sprin 111 E3
Boyne Rd. Dag 164 A1
Boyton's La. Hemp 17 D1
Boytons. Basil 170 C3
Brabner Gdns. S Han 150 B2
Bracelet Cl. Corr 179 F3
Bracken Dr. Brent 158 B3
Bracken Dr. Chig 153 D2
Bracken Mews. Romf 164 A3
Bracken Mount. Basil 170 C4
Brackendale. Bill 149 E2
Brackendale Ave. Basil 172 B2
Brackendale Gdns. Upm 175 E4
Brackenden Dr. Sprin 111 E4
Brackley Cres. Basil 163 D1
Brackley Sq. Woodf 152 B2
Bradbourne Rd. Grays 192 A4
Bradbourne Way. Basil 172 B3
Bradbury Dr. Brain 65 E2
Bradd Cl. S Ock 176 B1
Bradford St. Brain 66 A3
Bradford St. Chelm 111 D1
Bradleigh Ave. Grays 185 E1
Bradley Common. Birhr 57 E2
Bradley Green. Basil 163 E1
Bradley Mews. Saff W 13 F1
Bradshawe Rd. Grays 185 D3
Bradwell Ave. Dag 164 A1
Bradwell Cl. Hornc 174 A3
Bradwell Green. Brent 147 E2
Bradwell Rd. Lou 140 C1
Brady Ave. Lou 141 E4
Braemar Ave. Chelm 124 A4
Braemar Gdns. Hornc 166 A3
Braintree Rd. Dag 164 A1
Braintree Rd. Felst 74 B3
Braintree Rd. Gt Ba 42 A1
Braintree Rd. Gt Dun 61 F1
Braintree Rd. Shal 54 C3
Braintree Rd. Weth 43 E1
Braiswick Pl. Basil 170 A4
Braithwaite Ave. Romf 164 A2
Bramble La. Lit Dun 62 C1
Bramble La. Upm 175 E2
Brambles The. Chig 153 E2
Bramley Cl. Brain 66 A1
Bramley Gdns. Basil 170 B4
Bramley Shaw. Wa Aby 126 C3
Bramleys. Corr 179 E2
Brampstead. Basil 170 A3
Brampton Cl. Corr 180 A3
Bramshill Cl. Chig 153 F3
Bramston Link. Basil 169 F4
Bramston Way. Basil 169 F3
Bramstone Cl. Chig 153 F2
Bramstone Cl. Gt Bad 124 C4
Bramwoods Rd. Gt Bad 124 C4
Bran End Fields. Steb 62 B4
Brancepeth Gdns. Woodf 152 A4
Branch Rd. Chig 154 A3
Brandon Cl. Bill 149 D3
Brandon Rd. Brain 65 E1
Branfill Rd. Upm 166 A1
Branksome Ave. Corr 179 F2
Branksome Ave. Wick 162 C4
Branksome Cl. Corr 179 E2
Branton Rd. Stone 190 C1
Bratherstone Ct. Bill 148 C2
Braxteds. Basil 170 A3
Braybrooke. Basil 171 D3
Brays Mead. Harl 102 C3
Brays Springs. Wa Aby 126 C3
Brazier Quay. Bis St 68 A3
Braziers Cl. Chelm 124 B2
Breach La. Dag 173 D1
Breach La. Gt Ea 51 E1
Breach Rd. W Thu 190 C4
Break Egg Hill. Bill 149 E2
Breakneck Hill. Swan 191 D1
Breams Field. Basil 170 B2
Brecon Cl. Basil 172 B4
Brempsons. Basil 171 D4
Brendans Cl. Hornc 165 F2
Brendon. Basil 170 B3
Brendon Pl. Chelm 110 C1
Brendon Rd. Dag 164 A2
Brennan Rd. Tilb 193 D3
Brent Cl. Stone 190 A1
Brent Way. Stone 190 A1
Brentfield Rd. Stone 190 A1
Brentwood Pl. Brent 146 B1
Brentwood Rd. Brent 159 E2
Brentwood Rd. Ch Ong 132 A4
Brentwood Rd. Grays 178 A2
Brentwood Rd. Horn H 178 A2
Brentwood Rd. Romf 165 D3
Bressey Gr. Woodf 152 A1
Bretons. Basil 170 C3
Brewery La. Stan M 57 F4
Brewery Rd. Hod 100 A3
Brewhouse Yd. Grave 193 D1
Brian Cl. Chelm 124 A3
Brian Cl. Hornc 174 A4
Briar Cl. Bill 161 E4
Briar Cl. Lou 152 B4
Briar Mead. Basil 170 A4
Briar Rd. Romf 156 B2
Briar View. Bill 161 E4
Briarleas Gdns. Upm 166 C2
Briars Wlk. Romf 156 C1
Briarswood. Sprin 111 E4
Briarwood. Kelv H 132 C1
Briary The. Wick 163 D4
Briceway. Corr 179 F2
Brick House La. Bore 99 F1
Brick Kiln La. Quen 36 B1
Brick Kiln La. Steb 62 B4
Brick Kiln Rd. Sand 125 E4
Brick Row. Chris 10 B2
Brickenden Ct. Wa Aby 126 C3
Brickfield Rd. Basil 171 E1
Brickfield Rd. Epp 116 B1
Bridge Ave. Upm 166 A1
Bridge Cl. Brent 158 C4
Bridge Cl. Romf 164 C3
Bridge Croft. Gt Wal 84 C1
Bridge Hill. Epp 128 C3
Bridge House Cl. Wick 163 E4
Bridge Rd. Grays 192 A4
Bridge Rd. More 105 E1
Bridge Rd. Rain 174 A1
Bridge St. Bill 161 F1
Bridge St. Bis St 67 F4
Bridge St. Finch 42 B3
Bridge St. Gt Ba 42 A1
Bridge St. Saff W 13 E1
Bridge St. Writ 110 B1
Bridgecote La. Bill 161 F1
Bridges Dr. Stone 190 A1
Bridgeways. Hod 100 A3
Bridgwater Cl. Romf 156 B3
Bridgwater Rd. Romf 156 B3
Bridgwater Wlk. Romf 156 B3
Bridle Cl. Hod 87 D1
Bridle Way. Hod 87 D1
Bridle Way. Sta Ab 87 D3
Bridle Way (N). Hod 87 D1
Bridle Way (S). Hod 87 D1
Bridleway. Bill 149 E3
Bridport Ave. Romf 164 A3
Bridport Rd. Sprin 111 E3
Bridport Way. Brain 66 B2
Brierley Cl. Hornc 165 E3
Brights Ave. Rain 174 A1
Brightside. Bill 148 C2
Brightside Cl. Bill 148 C2
Brimfield Rd. W Thu 183 E1
Brindles Cl. Brent 159 E4
Bringey The. Gt Bad 125 D3
Brinsmead Rd. Romf 157 D1
Briscoe Rd. Basil 172 A4
Briscoe Rd. Rain 174 B2
Brise Cl. Brain 66 A1
Bristow Rd. Basil 170 B3
Bristowe Ave. Gt Bad 125 D3
Britannia Ct. Basil 163 E1
Britannia Rd. Brent 158 B3
Britten Cres. Gt Bad 124 C4
Brittons La. S Han 149 F4
Brixton La. Man 47 E3
Brixton La. Quen 47 E3
Brixton La. Ugl 47 E3
Broad Green. Basil 171 E4
Broad Meadow. Kelv H 132 C1
Broad Oak. Woodf 152 A3
Broad Oakes Cl. Wim 26 C1
Broad Oaks. Wick 163 F3
Broad Rd. Brain 66 A4
Broad Rd. Swan 191 F1
Broad St. Dag 173 D3
Broad St. Hat B O 79 F3
Broad St. Hav 6 C4
Broad Street Market. Dag 173 D3
Broad Wlk. Harl 89 E1
Broad Wlk (N) The. Brent 159 D4
Broad Wlk (S) The. Brent 159 D3
Broadcroft Cres. Hav 6 C4
Broadfield. Bis St 56 C1
Broadfield. H Rod 81 F4
Broadfield. Harl 89 F1
Broadfield Cl. Romf 164 C3
Broadfield Rd. Take 70 C4
Broadfield Way. Lou 152 B4
Broadfields. H Wy 77 D1
Broadgate. Wa Aby 126 C3
Broadhope Ave. Sta L H 187 E4
Broadhurst Gdns. Chig 153 E3
Broadhurst Wlk. Rain 174 A3
Broadlands. Grays 184 C1
Broadleaf Ave. Bis St 67 E2
Broadley Rd. Harl 102 A2
Broadmayne. Basil 171 E3
Broadmead Rd. Woodf 152 A2
Broadoaks. Epp 128 C4
Broadstone Rd. Hornc 165 D1
Broadstrood. Lou 128 A1
Broadview Ave. Grays 185 E2
Broadwater Green. Basil 169 F3
Broadway. Grays 192 B4
Broadway. Gt Dun 62 A3
Broadway. Rain 174 A1
Broadway. Romf 156 A1
Broadway. Tilb 192 C3
Broadway Ave. Harl 90 A2
Broadway Cl. Woodf 152 A2
Broadway North. Basil 172 A3
Broadway The. Dag 164 A1
Broadway The. Gt Dun 61 F2
Broadway The. Hornc 174 A4
Broadway The. Lou 141 E3
Broadway The. Runw 163 E4
Broadway The. Woodf 152 A2
Brock Green. S Ock 184 A4
Brock Hill. Runw 151 E2
Brock Hill Dr. Runw 151 E2
Brockenhurst Dr. Sta L H 187 E4
Brocket Cl. Chig 153 F3
Brocket Rd. Hod 100 A3
Brocket Way. Chig 153 F3
Brockles Mead. Harl 102 B2
Brockley Cres. Romf 155 E2
Brockley Gr. Brent 147 D1
Brockley Rd. Chelm 111 E1
Brocks Mead. Gt Ea 60 C4
Brocksparkwood. Brent 159 D4
Brockton Cl. Romf 164 C4
Brockwell Wlk. Wick 163 E3
Brodie Rd. Ching 139 E1
Brograve Cl. Chelm 124 B2
Bromefield Ct. Wa Aby 127 D3
Bromfield. Saff W 25 F4
Bromfords Cl. Wick 163 D3
Bromfords Dr. Wick 163 E3
Bromley. Grays 191 F4
Brompton Cl. Bill 149 D3
Bronfelde Rd. Bill 162 B3
Bronte Cl. Tilb 193 E3
Brook Ave. Dag 173 D3
Brook Cl. Brain 65 E1
Brook Cl. Romf 155 F1
Brook Dr. Basil 171 E1
Brook Dr. Wick 163 E3
Brook End. Saw 77 E1
Brook End Rd. Sprin 112 A2
Brook Hill. Gt Wal 73 F1
Brook Hill. Lit Wal 98 B3
Brook La. Chelm 124 C2
Brook La. Dodd 133 E1
Brook La. Saw 77 E1
Brook La. Sprin 112 A1
Brook La. W Han 124 C2
Brook Mead. Basil 170 A4
Brook Mead. Gt Wal 97 F4
Brook Rd. Brent 157 F4
Brook Rd. Lou 140 A1
Brook Rd. Lou 140 C2
Brook Rd. Romf 155 F1
Brook Rd. Saw 77 F1
Brook Rd. Sta T 129 D3
Brook Rd. Stan M 57 F3
Brook Rise. Chig 153 D4
Brook Service Rd. Hav 7 D4
Brook St. Brent 157 F3
Brook St. Gt Ba 42 A1
Brook St. Lit Dun 73 E4
Brook View. Sand 125 E3
Brook View. Thax 40 A2
Brook Way. Chig 153 D4
Brookdale Ave. Upm 166 A1
Brookdale Cl. Upm 166 A1
Brooke Ave. Saff W 13 F1
Brooke Rd. Grays 185 D1
Brooker Rd. Wa Aby 126 B3
Brookfield Cl. Brent 147 E2
Brookfields. Ch Ong 118 C3
Brookfields. Saw 77 E1
Brookfields. Steb 62 B4
Brookhampton St. Hinx 1 A3
Brookhurst Cl. Sprin 111 E2
Brooklands. Wick 163 D4
Brooklands App. Romf 164 B4
Brooklands Cl. Romf 164 B4
Brooklands Gdns. Hornc 165 E3
Brooklands La. Romf 164 B4
Brooklands Park. Basil 169 F3
Brooklands Rd. Romf 164 B4
Brooklands Wlk. Chelm 124 A4
Brooklane Field. Harl 103 D3
Brooklyn Ave. Lou 140 C3
Brookmans Ave. Grays 185 E3
Brookmans Cl. Upm 166 C2
Brookmans Rd. Stock 136 B1
Brookside. Bill 149 E3
Brookside. Chig 153 E2
Brookside. Harl 101 F3
Brookside. Hod 100 A3
Brookside. Hornc 165 F3
Brookside. Wa Aby 126 C4
Brookside Cl. Bill 149 E3
Brooksies. Elm 22 C3
Brookway. Rain 182 A4
Broom Farm Rd. Els 48 B1
Broome Cl. Bill 149 E3
Broome Pl. Ave 183 E3
Broome Rd. Bill 149 E3
Broomfield. Harl 90 A2
Broomfield Ave. Lou 140 C2
Broomfield Cl. Romf 155 E2
Broomfield Rd. Chelm 111 D3
Broomfield Rd. Swan 191 F1
Broomfields. Basil 172 A3
Broomhall Cl. Broom 98 A1
Broomhall Rd. Broom 98 A1
Broomhill Rd. Woodf 152 A2
Broomhill Wlk. Woodf 152 A2
Broomhills Chase. Bill 161 D3
Broomstick Hall Rd. Wa Aby 126 C3
Broomwood Gdns. Brent 146 A2
Broomwood La. S Han 150 A4
Broseley Gdns. Romf 156 C3
Broseley Rd. Romf 156 C3
Brown's End Rd. Brox 59 F4
Browne Cl. Romf 155 D3
Browning Rd. Stone 190 A2
Browning Wlk. Tilb 193 E3
Brownings Ave. Chelm 111 D3
Brownlow Bend. Basil 171 E3
Brownlow Cross. Basil 171 E3
Brownlow Green. Basil 171 E3
Browns Ave. Runw 151 F1
Broxburn Dr. S Ock 184 A3
Broxhill Rd. Hav B 156 A4
Broxted Dr. Wick 163 F3
Broxted End. Wick 163 F3
Broxted Mews. Brent 147 E2
Bruce Ave. Hornc 165 E1
Bruce Gr. Chelm 124 A4
Bruce Rd. Writ 110 A1
Bruces Wharf Rd. Grays 192 A4
Brundish. Basil 172 A3
Brunel Cl. Tilb 193 D3
Brunel Rd. Brain 66 A1
Brunel Rd. Chig 152 C3
Brunswick Ave. Upm 166 C2
Brunswick Gdns. Woodf 153 E2
Brunswick Wlk. Grave 193 E1
Brunwin Rd. Ray 64 C1
Brunwins Cl. Wick 163 F4
Bryan Rd. Bis St 67 F4
Bryanston Rd. Tilb 193 E3
Bryant Ave. Romf 156 B1
Bryce Way. Basil 172 B3
Buchanan Cl. Ave 183 E3
Buck Hill. Bl Not 76 C3
Buckbean Path. Romf 156 B2
Buckenhoe Rd. Saff W 13 F2
Buckerills. Basil 172 A3
Buckhurst Way. Lou 152 B4
Buckingham Cl. Hornc 165 E3
Buckingham Hill Rd. Sta L H 187 D3
Buckingham Rd. Hav 6 C3
Bucklers Ct. Brent 158 B3
Buckles La. S Ock 184 B4
Buckley Cl. Corr 179 F3
Buckleys. Gt Bad 124 C4
Bucknells Mead. Ing 122 A2
Buckwins Sq. Basil 163 E1
Buckwoods Rd. Brain 66 A1
Buckwyns Chase. Bill 148 C3
Buckwyns Chase. Mtssg 148 C3
Buglers Rise. Writ 123 D4
Building End Rd. Chris 22 A4
Bull Cl. Grays 184 C2
Bull La. Dag 164 A1
Bull La. Langl 22 B1
Bull Yd. Grave 193 D1
Bullen Wlk. Chelm 124 B2
Buller Rd. Basil 170 A4
Bullfields. New 37 D4
Bullfields. Saw 77 F2
Bulmers Wlk. Rain 174 B2
Bulphan By-Ps. Horn H 169 D1
Bulphan Cl. Wick 163 F3
Bumpstead Rd. Hav 7 D2
Bumpstead Rd. Hel B 7 D2
Bundick's Hill. Chelm 110 C2
Bungalows The. Chig 153 F1
Bunting Cl. Chelm 124 A3
Bunting La. Bill 149 E1
Bunyan Rd. Brain 65 F2
Burch Rd. Grave 192 C1
Burches. Basil 161 F1
Burchwall Cl. Romf 155 E2
Bure. Grays 187 E2
Burford St. Hod 100 A3
Burfordstreet. Hod 100 A4
Burges Cl. Hornc 165 F3
Burgess Ave. Sta L H 179 F1
Burgess Field. Sprin 111 F2
Burghley Ave. Bis St 67 E4
Burghley Rd. Grays 184 B2
Burghstead Cl. Bill 149 D1
Burgoyne Hatch. Harl 90 A1
Burgundy Gdns. Basil 172 A4
Burland Rd. Brent 146 B1
Burland Rd. Romf 155 E2
Burleigh Cl. Bill 149 D3
Burley Rd. Bis St 68 A2
Burlington Ave. Romf 164 A3
Burlington Ct. Basil 163 D1
Burlington Pl. Woodf 152 A4
Burnaby Rd. Grave 192 C1
Burne Ave. Wick 163 D3

Burnell Wlk. Brent 158 B2
Burnells Way. Stan M 57 F4
Burnett Park. Harl 102 A2
Burney Dr. Lou 141 E3
Burnham Rd. Romf 164 B4
Burnham Rd. Sprin 111 E3
Burnley Rd. W Thu 191 D3
Burns Ave. Basil 172 A3
Burns Cres. Chelm 124 B4
Burns Pl. Tilb 193 D3
Burns Way. Brent 147 E2
Burnsall Cl. Saff W 25 F4
Burnside. Saw 77 E1
Burnside Cres. Chelm 111 D4
Burnside Terr. Harl 90 C2
Burnstie Rd. Felst 74 C3
Burnt Mill Cl. Harl 89 E2
Burnt Mills Rd. Basil 163 E1
Burnt Wood. Brent 158 B4
Burnthouse La. Mtssg 148 A4
Burntmill Cl. Harl 89 E2
Burntmill La. H Wy 89 E2
Burntwood Ave. Hornc 165 F3
Burntwood Cl. Bill 148 C1
Burntwood Cl. Horn H 168 B3
Burnway. Hornc 165 F2
Burr's Way. Corr 180 A2
Burrow Cl. Chig 153 F3
Burrow Green. Chig 153 F3
Burrow Rd. Chig 154 A3
Burses Way. Brent 147 D1
Burses Way. Brent 147 E2
Burslem Ave. Chig 154 A2
Burstead Dr. Bill 161 E4
Burton Cl. Corr 179 F3
Burton Cl. Hav 6 C4
Burton End. Hav 6 C4
Burton Pl. Sprin 111 F2
Burton Rd. Lou 141 E3
Burtons Mill. Saw 77 F2
Burwood Gdns. Rain 173 F1
Bury Farm La. Bill 162 B2
Bury Fields. Felst 74 A3
Bury La. Chris 10 B1
Bury La. Epp 115 E1
Bury La. Gt Wal 97 E4
Bury Lodge La. Stan M 58 A2
Bury Lodge La. Stan M 69 E4
Bury Rd. Ching 139 F2
Bury Rd. Dag 173 D4
Bury Rd. Epp 128 C4
Bury Rd. Harl 90 B2
Bury Rd. Wa Aby 139 F2
Bury Villas. Take 59 F2
Bury Water La. New 24 C1
Bush Elms Rd. Hornc 165 D2
Bush Fair. Harl 102 C3
Bush Hall Rd. Bill 149 E3
Bush Rd. Lit Sam 28 B1
Bush Rd. Woodf 152 B3
Bushey Croft. Harl 102 C3
Bushfield Wlk. Swan 191 F1
Bushfields. Lou 141 D2
Bushy Lea. Ch Ong 119 D1
Bushy Mead. Basil 170 A4
Butcher Row. Saff W 13 E1
Butcher's Hill. Hinx 1 A2
Butchers Pasture. Lit Ea 60 C3
Butler Cl. Saff W 13 F1
Butler Wlk. Grays 185 E1
Butlers Cl. Broom 98 A1
Butlers Dri. Wa Aby 126 B1
Butlers Gr. Basil 170 A2
Butlers La. Saff W 14 B3
Butneys. Basil 171 D4
Butt La. Man 46 C1
Butt's Green Rd. Sand 125 F2
Buttercross La. Epp 116 A1
Buttercup Cl. Bill 149 D2
Buttercup Cl. Romf 156 B1
Butterfield Rd. Bore 112 C4
Buttermere. Bl Not 76 B4
Buttersweet Rise. Saw 77 F1
Butterworth Gdns. Woodf 152 A3
Buttfield Cl. Dag 173 D3
Buttondene Cres. Lo Naz 100 A1
Butts Green Rd. Hornc 165 E3
Butts La. Sta L H 187 E4
Butts Rd. Sta L H 179 E1
Butts Way. Chelm 123 F2
Buttsbury. Stock 135 F1
Buxton Cl. Woodf 152 B2
Buxton Link. Basil 169 F3
Buxton Rd. Ching 139 E1
Buxton Rd. Grays 185 F2
Buxton Rd. The B 128 C2
Buxton Rd. Wa Aby 127 D3
By-Pass Rd. Horn H 179 F2
Byfield Ct. Horn H 168 B3
Byfleets. Basil 171 F2
Bylands Cl. Bis St 67 E3
Byng Gdns. Brain 66 B2
Bynghams. Harl 101 F3
Bynghams. Harl 102 A3
Byrd Ct. Basil 170 B4
Byrd Way. Corr 179 E2
Byrd's Farm La. Saff W 13 F2
Byron Gdns. Tilb 193 E3
Byron Rd. Brent 147 E1
Byron Rd. Chelm 111 E1
Byron Rd. Stone 190 A2
Byron Way. Romf 156 B1
Bysouth Cl. Woodf 153 D1

Cabborns Cres. Sta L H 187 E4
Cadiz Rd. Dag 173 E3
Cadogan Ave. Horn H 168 B3
Caernarvon Cl. Hornc 166 A2
Caernarvon Dr. Woodf 153 D1
Cage End. Hat B O 79 F3
Cage End Cl. Hat B O 79 F3
Cairns Ave. Woodf 152 C2
Calbourne Ave. Hornc 174 A4
Calcott Cl. Brent 146 A1
Calcutta Rd. Tilb 193 D3
Caldbeck. Wa Aby 126 B3
Caldbeck Way. Bl Not 76 B3
Calder. Grays 187 E1
Caldwell Rd. Sta L H 179 D1
Callan Gr. S Ock 184 B3
Calmore Cl. Hornc 174 B4
Calne Ave. Woodf 153 D1
Calverley Cl. Bis St 67 F2
Calverly Cres. Dag 164 A1
Calvert Dr. Basil 163 E1
Cam Green. S Ock 184 A4
Camberton Rd. Brain 65 F3
Cambeys Rd. Dag 173 E4
Camborne Ave. Romf 156 C2
Camborne Cl. Sprin 111 F3
Camborne Way. Romf 156 C2
Cambridge Ave. Romf 165 E4
Cambridge Gdns. Grays 186 A1
Cambridge Rd. Ching 139 E1
Cambridge Rd. Harl 90 B3
Cambridge Rd. Litt 12 C2
Cambridge Rd. New 25 D1
Cambridge Rd. Saw 77 F2
Cambridge Rd. Stan M 57 F4
Camden Cl. Grays 186 A1
Camden Rd. Grays 184 C2
Camellia Cl. Romf 156 C1
Camellia Cl. Sprin 111 F3
Camelot Gdns. Basil 172 B4
Cameron Cl. Brent 158 B3
Cameron Cl. Corr 179 F3
Cameron Cl. Ing 135 D2
Camoise Cl. Topp 32 A4
Campbell Cl. Chelm 124 A4
Campbell Cl. Romf 155 F2
Campbell Cl. Wick 163 E3
Campions. Lou 128 A1
Campions The. Stan M 57 F4
Cample La. S Ock 184 A3
Camps Rd. Bart 4 A4
Camps Rd. Hav 6 C4
Camps Rd. Hel B 6 A1
Canal Basin. Grave 193 E1
Canal Rd. Grave 193 E1
Canberra Cl. Chelm 110 C3
Canberra Cl. Dag 173 E3
Canberra Cl. Hornc 174 B4
Canberra Cres. Dag 173 E3
Canberra Sq. Tilb 193 D3
Cander Way. S Ock 184 A3
Candover Rd. Hornc 165 D2
Candytuft Rd. Sprin 111 F3
Caneland Ct. Wa Aby 126 C3
Canes La. N W Bas 103 F1
Canewdon Cl. Runw 151 F1
Canewdon Gdns. Runw 151 E1
Canfield. Bis St 67 F4
Canfield Rd. H Rod 81 F4
Canfield Rd. Rain 173 F2
Canfield Rd. Woodf 152 C2
Canford Ave. Wick 162 C4
Canford Cl. Gt Bad 124 C4
Cannon Circ. Finch 43 E3
Cannon Cl. Corr 179 F1
Cannon Leys. Chelm 124 B2
Cannons Cl. Bis St 57 D1
Cannons La. Fyf 106 C1
Cannons La. Hat B O 79 F3
Cannons Mead. Stan M 57 E4
Cannons Mead. Sto M 133 D3
Cannons Mill La. Bis St 57 D1
Canons Brook. Harl 102 A4
Canons Gate. Harl 89 D1
Canterbury Ave. Upm 166 C1
Canterbury Cl. Basil 171 F4
Canterbury Cl. Chig 153 F4
Canterbury Par. S Ock 176 B1
Canterbury Way. Brent 158 B2
Canterbury Way. Chelm 110 C2
Canterbury Way. W Thu 183 F1
Canuden Rd. Chelm 110 C1
Canvey Rd. Basil 172 C3
Canvey Wlk. Sprin 111 F3
Capel Cl. Chelm 111 D4
Capel Cl. Ray 64 C1
Capel Rd. Ray 64 C1
Capelston. Basil 170 C3
Capital Pl. Harl 102 A4
Capon Cl. Brent 146 A1
Cappell La. Sta Ab 87 E3
Capstan Ct. Stone 190 B2
Caravel Cl. Grays 184 C2
Carbis Cl. Ching 139 E1
Carbury Cl. Hornc 174 B3
Card's Rd. Sand 125 E3
Cardinal Dr. Woodf 153 E2
Cardinal Way. Rain 174 B2
Carfax Rd. Hornc 173 F4
Carisbrooke Cl. Hornc 166 A2
Carisbrooke Dr. Corr 180 A2
Carisbrooke Rd. Brent 146 A2
Carlisle Rd. Romf 165 D3
Carlisle Rd. Stone 190 A1
Carlton Ave. Stone 190 C1
Carlton Cl. Upm 166 A1
Carlton Rd. Basil 172 C4
Carlton Rd. Grays 185 F2
Carlton Rd. Romf 165 D4
Carlton Rd. Runw 151 E1
Carlyle Gdns. Bill 148 C3
Carmen St. Gt C 1 B2
Carnach Green. S Ock 184 A3
Carnation Cl. Sprin 111 F3
Carnation Dr. Saff W 13 F1
Carnel St. Gt C 1 B1
Carnforth Gdns. Hornc 174 A4
Carpenter Cl. Bill 148 C2
Carpenters Arms La. N W Bas 116 B3
Carriage Dr. Sprin 111 F4
Carrick Dr. Woodf 153 E1
Carrigans. Bis St 67 F4
Carrington Rd. Stone 190 A1
Carrington Way. Brain 65 F4
Carroll Gdns. Wick 163 E3
Carroll Hill. Lou 140 C3
Carruthers Cl. Runw 151 E1
Carruthers Dr. Runw 151 E1
Carsey Cl. S Han 150 B2
Carsey Hill. Bart 5 D3
Carson Rd. Bill 149 E3
Carswell Cl. Brent 147 E2
Cart La. Ching 139 F1
Cartel Cl 183 E1
Carter Cl. Romf 155 D2
Carter Dr. Romf 155 D2
Carters Croft. Ash 4 A1
Carters Hill. Man 47 D1
Carters La. Ep Gr 115 D4
Carters La. Hen 48 C3
Carters Leys. Bis St 67 E4
Carters Mead. Harl 103 E3
Cartersfield Rd. Wa Aby 126 B3
Carthagena Estate. Lo Naz 100 B2
Cartlodge Ave. Wick 163 F4
Cartwright Wlk. Sprin 111 F1
Cascade Cl. Lou 152 B4
Cascade Rd. Lou 152 B4
Cashmere Way. Basil 171 E1
Cassino Rd. Chelm 110 C3
Castell Rd. Lou 141 E4
Castle Ave. Hav 6 C4
Castle Ave. Rain 173 F3
Castle Cl. Gt Le 85 F3
Castle Cl. Hod 87 E1
Castle Cl. Romf 156 B4
Castle Cross. Saff W 13 F1
Castle Hill. Saff W 13 E1
Castle La. Hav 6 C4
Castle Rd. Grays 191 F4
Castle Rd. Hod 87 E1
Castle Rd. Swan 191 F1
Castle St. Bis St 67 F3
Castle St. Ch Ong 119 D1
Castle St. Saff W 13 E1
Castle St. Stone 191 D1
Castle St. Swan 191 F1
Castle Wlk. Hav 6 C4
Castledon Rd. S Han 151 D1
Castlellan Ave. Romf 165 D4
Caswell Cl. Corr 180 A2
Caswell Mews. Sprin 111 F1
Cater Wood. Bill 149 D2
Caterham Ave. Woodf 153 D1
Caterham Ct. Wa Aby 126 C3
Cates Cnr. Saff W 13 E1
Cathedral Wlk. Chelm 111 D2
Catherine Cl. Brent 146 A2
Catherine Rd. Romf 165 D3
Catherines Cl. Gt Le 86 A3
Catons La. Saff W 13 E1
Cattawade End. Basil 171 E4
Cattawade Link. Basil 171 E4
Causeway End Rd. Felst 74 B2
Causeway The. Bis St 67 F4
Causeway The. Br Pel 34 A1
Causeway The. Brain 65 F2
Causeway The. Deb 38 A4
Causeway The. Fu Pel 45 D2
Causeway The. Gt Bad 124 C4
Causeway The. Gt Dun 61 E1
Causeway The. Hav 6 C4
Causeway The. Langl 22 B2
Causeway The. Ridge 20 A4
Causeway The. Topp 32 A4
Causeway The. Writ 122 B4
Cautherly La. Sta Ab 87 D3
Cavell Cres. Stone 190 A2
Cavell Rd. Bill 149 E1
Cavendish Ave. Hornc 174 A3
Cavendish Ave. Woodf 152 A2
Cavendish Cres. Hornc 174 A3
Cavendish Ct. Saff W 13 F1
Cavendish Gdns. Brain 66 B3
Cavendish Way. Bill 161 E1
Cavenham Gdns. Hornc 165 E3
Cawdor Ave. S Ock 184 A3
Cawkell Cl. Stan M 57 E4
Cawkwell Cl. Sprin 112 A2
Caxton Rd. Hod 87 D1
Cecil Ave. Grays 184 C2
Cecil Ave. Hornc 165 F4
Cecil Cl. Bis St 68 B4
Cecil Rd. Hod 100 B4
Cedar Ave. Chelm 111 D2
Cedar Ave. Upm 175 D4
Cedar Ave. Wick 163 E3
Cedar Ave W. Chelm 111 D2
Cedar Cl. Brent 147 E1
Cedar Cl. Lou 152 B4
Cedar Cl. Saw 77 F1
Cedar Ct. Epp 129 D4
Cedar Gdns. Upm 166 B1
Cedar Green. Hod 100 A3
Cedar Park. Bis St 67 E2
Cedar Rd. Basil 172 C4
Cedar Rd. Brent 147 E2
Cedar Rd. Grays 186 A2
Cedar Rd. Hornc 165 E1
Cedar Rd. Romf 164 B4
Cedar Wlk. Wa Aby 126 B3
Cedars. Corr 179 F1
Cedars The. Lou 140 A1
Cedric Ave. Romf 159 E2
Celandine Cl. Bill 148 C2
Celandine Cl. S Ock 176 B1
Celedon Cl. Grays 184 C2
Cement Block Cotts. Grays 192 B4
Cemetery Rd. Bis St 67 F3
Central Ave. Ave 183 E2
Central Ave. Basil 169 F2
Central Ave. Bill 149 E3
Central Ave. Corr 180 A2
Central Ave. Harl 89 E1
Central Ave. Tilb 193 D3
Central Ave. W Thu 183 F1
Central Dr. Hornc 165 F1
Central Park Ave. Dag 164 A1
Central Rd. Harl 90 A2
Central Rd. Sta L H 179 E1
Central Sq. Chelm 111 D1
Centre Ave. Epp 128 C4
Centre Dr. Epp 128 C4
Centre Green. Epp 128 C4
Centre Rd. Dag 173 D2
Centre Way. Wa Aby 126 B2
Centurion Way. Pur 182 C1
Century Rd. Hod 100 A4
Chadfields. Tilb 193 D4
Chadwell By-Ps. Grays 186 A1
Chadwell Hill. Grays 186 A1
Chadwell Rd. Grays 185 F1
Chadwick Dr. Romf 156 B1
Chaffix. Felst 74 B3
Chafford Gdns. Horn H 168 B3
Chafford Way. Grays 185 D3
Chafford Wlk. Rain 174 B2
Chalford Wlk. Woodf 152 B2
Chalforde Gdns. Romf 165 D4
Chalgrove Cres. Woodf 152 C1
Chalk End. Basil 172 A3
Chalk La. Match 91 D1
Chalk St. Rett 151 F4
Chalklands. Saff W 13 F2
Chalklands. Sand 125 E2
Chalks Ave. Saw 77 E2
Chalkstone Way. Hav 7 E4
Chalky La. Chris 10 B1
Challacombe Cl. Brent 147 E1
Challis La. Brain 65 F1
Challock Lees. Basil 172 B3
Chalvedon Ave. Basil 172 A4
Chamberlain Ave. Corr 180 A3
Champion Cl. Corr 179 F2
Champion Cl. Wick 163 E3
Champion Rd. Upm 166 A1
Champions Green. Hod 87 D1
Champions Way. Hod 87 D1
Chance Cl. Grays 184 C2
Chancery Pl. Writ 110 A1
Chandler Rd. Lou 141 D4
Chandlers Way. Romf 164 C3
Chandlers Wlk. Kelv H 132 C1
Chandos Cl. Lou 152 A4
Chanlock Path. S Ock 184 A3
Chantreywood. Brent 159 D4
Chantry Cl. Bis St 67 F4
Chantry Cres. Sta L H 179 E1
Chantry Dr. Ing 135 D2
Chantry Rd. Bis St 67 F4
Chantry The. Harl 90 A1
Chantry Way. Bill 149 D1
Chantry Way. Rain 173 E2
Chanute Ave. Finch 43 E4
Chapel Cl. W Thu 191 D4
Chapel Croft. Ing 135 D2
Chapel Ct. Bill 149 D1
Chapel Ct. Swan 191 F1
Chapel Dr. Lit Wal 98 A3
Chapel End. Hod 100 A3
Chapel End Way. Stam 19 E1
Chapel Fields. Harl 103 E3
Chapel High. Brent 158 B4
Chapel Hill. Brain 66 A1
Chapel Hill. Stan M 57 E3
Chapel La. Chig 153 F4
Chapel La. Harl 103 E3
Chapel La. New 37 D4
Chapel La. Rox 108 C1
Chapel Lodge. Rain 174 A1
Chapel Rd. Epp 115 F1
Chapel Rd. Ridge 20 A4
Chapel Row. Bis St 67 F3
Chapel St. Bill 149 D1
Chapel St. Cla 9 D2
Chapel St. Ste B 18 B4
Chapelfields. Sta Ab 87 E2
Chaplaincy Gdns. Hornc 165 F2
Chaplemount Rd. Woodf 152 C2
Chaplin Cl. Bill 161 F1
Chaplin Cl. Chelm 124 A1
Charlbury Cl. Romf 156 B2
Charlbury Cres. Romf 156 B2
Charles Rd. Dag 173 E3
Charles St. Epp 129 D4
Charles St. Grays 192 B4
Charles St. Stone 191 D1
Charleston Ave. Basil 163 E1
Charlotte Ave. Wick 163 E4
Charlotte Gdns. Romf 155 D2
Charlotte Pl. W Thu 191 D4
Charlotte Rd. Dag 173 D3
Charlton Cl. Basil 172 B4
Charlton Mead La. Hod 100 B3
Charlton St. Grays 191 E4
Charlton Way. Hod 100 A3
Charnwood Ave. Chelm 110 C1
Charterhouse. Basil 171 E3
Charteris Rd. Woodf 152 A2
Charters. Gt Dun 61 E1
Charters Cross. Harl 102 B3
Chartwell Cl. Brain 65 F4
Chartwell Cl. Wa Aby 126 C3
Chase Cross Rd. Romf 155 E2
Chase House Gdns. Hornc 165 F3
Chase La. Chig 154 A4
Chase Rd. Brent 158 B4
Chase Rd. Corr 180 A2
Chase Sq. Grave 193 D1
Chase The. Barn 73 D2
Chase The. Basil 170 C2
Chase The. Bill 149 E1
Chase The. Bill 161 D1
Chase The. Bis St 67 F3
Chase The. Bl Not 76 B3
Chase The. Bore 112 C4
Chase The. Brain 65 F4
Chase The. Brent 158 B4
Chase The. Brent 159 E3
Chase The. Chig 153 E3
Chase The. Finch 42 B3
Chase The. Grays 191 E4
Chase The. Gt Bad 124 C3
Chase The. Hen 48 C3
Chase The. Hornc 164 C1
Chase The. Romf 164 C1
Chase The. Romf 164 C4
Chase The. Ste B 18 A4
Chase The. Upm 166 C1
Chase The. Wick 163 D3
Chase The. Wick 163 F2
Chaseside Cl. Romf 155 F2
Chaseway. Basil 171 F2
Chaseway The. S Han 150 A4
Chaseways. Saw 90 B4
Chaters Hill. Saff W 13 F1
Chatfield Way. Basil 172 B4
Chatham Pavement. Basil 172 B4
Chathamhall La. Lit Wal 98 A4
Chatley Rd. Gt Le 85 F4
Chatteris Ave. Romf 156 B2
Chaucer Cl. Tilb 193 E3
Chaucer Rd. Chelm 111 E1
Chaucer Rd. Romf 156 A2
Chaucer Way. Hod 87 D1
Chaucer Way. Stone 190 A2
Chaucer Wlk. Wick 163 E3
Chauntry Rd. Hav 6 C4
Cheelson Rd. S Ock 176 B2
Chelmer Ave. Lit Wal 98 A3
Chelmer Dr. Brent 147 F2
Chelmer Dr. Gt Dun 72 C4
Chelmer Lea. Gt Bad 124 C4
Chelmer Pl. Chelm 111 E2
Chelmer Rd. Brain 66 B1
Chelmer Rd. Grays 186 A1
Chelmer Rd. Hav 7 D4
Chelmer Rd. Sprin 111 F2
Chelmer Rd. Upm 166 B3
Chelmer Valley Rd. Chelm 111 E3
Chelmer Village Way. Sprin 112 A2
Chelmerton Ave. Gt Bad 124 C4
Chelmsford Ave. Romf 155 E2
Chelmsford Dr. Upm 165 F1
Chelmsford Rd. Barn 73 D2
Chelmsford Rd. Bla 121 D1
Chelmsford Rd. BO 79 E2
Chelmsford Rd. Brent 147 D3
Chelmsford Rd. Ch Ong 119 E2
Chelmsford Rd. Chelm 110 B1
Chelmsford Rd. Felst 74 A2

Chelmsford Rd. Gt Wal 98 A3
Chelmsford Rd. H Ong 119 E2
Chelmsford Rd. Mar Rod 94 B2
Chelmsford Rd. Woodf 152 A1
Chelsworth Cl. Romf 156 C2
Chelsworth Dr. Romf 156 C1
Cheltenham Gdns. Lou 140 C2
Chelwater. Gt Bad 124 B4
Chelwood Cl. Ching 139 D2
Chenies Dr. Bill 161 D1
Chenies Green. Bis St 67 E3
Chepstow Ave. Hornc 165 F1
Chepstow Cl. Bill 149 E3
Chequers. Bis St 67 E4
Chequers. Lou 140 A1
Chequers La. Dag 173 D2
Chequers La. Gt Dun 72 B4
Chequers Rd. Brent 144 C1
Chequers Rd. Lou 141 D2
Chequers Rd. Writ 109 F1
Chequers Wlk. Wa Aby 126 C3
Cheriton Ave. Woodf 153 D1
Cheriton Rd. Brain 66 B1
Cherry Ave. Brent 158 C4
Cherry Garden La. New 37 D4
Cherry Garden Rd. Gt Wal 97 F4
Cherry Gdns. Bill 148 C2
Cherry Gdns. Bis St 68 A4
Cherry Gdns. Saw 77 F2
Cherry St. Romf 164 B3
Cherry Tree Cl. Grays 192 B4
Cherry Tree Cl. Rain 174 A2
Cherry Tree La. Rain 173 F2
Cherry Tree Rd. Hod 100 A4
Cherry Tree Rise. Woodf 152 B3
Cherry Wlk. Grays 186 A2
Cherry Wlk. Rain 174 A2
Cherrydown. Grays 185 E3
Cherrydown East. Basil 171 D3
Cherrydown West. Basil 171 D3
Cherrydown Wlk. Romf 155 D1
Cherrygarden La. Chelm 124 A4
Cherrytrees. Bill 160 C4
Cherston Gdns. Lou 141 D3
Cherston Rd. Lou 141 D3
Cherwell Dr. Chelm 110 B3
Cherwell Gr. S Ock 184 A3
Chesfield Cl. Bis St 67 F3
Chesham Cl. Romf 164 B4
Chesham Dr. Bill 161 D1
Cheshire Cl. Hornc 166 A3
Chester Ave. Upm 166 C1
Chester Cl. Lou 141 E4
Chester Green. Lou 141 E4
Chester Hall La. Basil 162 A1
Chester Path. Lou 141 E4
Chester Pl. Chelm 111 D3
Chester Rd. Chig 153 D4
Chester Rd. Lou 141 D4
Chester Way. Basil 171 F4
Chesterford Gdns. Basil 171 F4
Chesterford Green. Basil 171 F4
Chesterton Way. Tilb 193 E3
Chestnut Ave. Bill 149 D1
Chestnut Ave. Grays 185 D2
Chestnut Ave. Hornc 165 D1
Chestnut Ave. Litt 12 B1
Chestnut Ave. Lou 152 B4
Chestnut Cl. Bis St 67 F3
Chestnut Cl. Grave 192 C1
Chestnut Cl. Hav 6 C4
Chestnut Cl. Hornc 174 B4
Chestnut Cl. Lou 152 B4
Chestnut Ct. Basil 172 A2
Chestnut Ct. New 37 D4
Chestnut Glen. Hornc 165 D1
Chestnut Gr. Brain 65 F1
Chestnut Gr. Brent 158 A4
Chestnut Gr. Chig 153 F2
Chestnut Rd. Basil 172 A2
Chestnut Way. Take 70 B4
Chestnut Wlk. Chelm 111 D3
Chestnut Wlk. Felst 74 B3
Chestnut Wlk. Woodf 152 A3
Chestnuts. Basil 172 A4
Chestnuts. Brent 147 D1
Chestwood Cl. Bill 149 D3
Cheveley Cl. Romf 156 C1
Chevely Cl. Epp 116 B1
Chevers Pawen. Basil 172 A3
Chevington Way. Hornc 174 B4
Cheviot Dr. Chelm 110 B3
Cheviot Rd. Hornc 165 D2
Chichester Cl. Ave 183 E3
Chichester Cl. Basil 171 F4
Chichester Dr. Sprin 111 E2
Chichester Rd. Saff W 25 F4
Chichester Rd. Stone 190 C1
Chickney Rd. Brox 49 E3
Chickney Rd. Hen 49 E3
Chieftan Dr. Pur 183 D1
Chignall Rd. Chelm 110 B3
Chignalls The. Basil 170 A3
Chigwell La. Chig 141 E2
Chigwell Park Dr. Chig 153 D3
Chigwell Rd. Woodf 152 B2
Chigwell Rise. Chig 153 D4
Chigwell View. Romf 155 D3
Childerditch Hall Dr. Brent 168 A4
Childerditch La. Brent 158 C1
Childerditch St. Brent 168 A4
Childers The. Woodf 152 C3
Childs Cl. Hornc 165 E3
Childs Cres. Swan 191 E1
Chilham Cl. Basil 172 B3
Chiltern Gdns. Hornc 165 E1
Chiltern Way. Woodf 152 A4
Chilton Cl. Gt Bad 124 B4
Chilton Rd. Grays 186 A2
Chimswell Way. Hav 6 B4
China La. Horn H 168 B1
Chindits La. Brent 158 B3
Chinnery Hill. Bis St 67 F3
Chippenham Cl. Romf 156 B3
Chippenham Gdns. Romf 156 B3
Chippenham Rd. Romf 156 B3
Chippenham Wlk. Romf 156 B2
Chipperfield Cl. Upm 166 C2
Chippingfield. Harl 90 B2
Chishill Rd. Hey 10 A2
Chittock Gate. Basil 171 F3
Chittock Mead. Basil 171 F3
Chivers Rd. Sto M 132 C2
Cholvedon Sq. Basil 172 A3
Chorley Cl. Basil 169 F3
Christchurch Ave. Rain 173 F1
Christchurch Ave. Wick 163 D4
Christchurch Rd. Tilb 193 D3
Christopher Cl. Hornc 174 B4
Christopher Martin Rd. Basil 162 C2
Christy Ave. Chelm 110 C2
Christy Way. Basil 169 F4
Chudleigh Rd. Romf 156 C3
Church Ave. Broom 98 A1
Church Cl. Kelv H 132 B1
Church Cl. Lou 140 C4
Church Cl. Mtssg 147 F4
Church Cres. Mtssg 147 F4
Church Cres. S Ock 176 B1
Church Cres. Saw 77 F1
Church Dr. Berd 46 A4
Church Elm La. Dag 173 D3
Church End. Gt Dun 61 F1
Church End. Harl 102 A3
Church End. Pan 65 D4
Church End Ave. Runw 151 F1
Church End La. Runw 151 F1
Church Field. Epp 116 A1
Church Field. Saff W 25 F4
Church Fields. Gt Y 20 C1
Church Gdns. Gt Dun 61 E1
Church Green. Broom 98 A1
Church Green. Hinx 1 A4
Church Green. Rox 109 D3
Church Hill. Ash 15 D4
Church Hill. Basil 170 B4
Church Hill. Epp 116 A1
Church Hill. Finch 42 B3
Church Hill. Hel B 17 E4
Church Hill. Lit Wal 98 B3
Church Hill. Lou 140 C3
Church Hill. Sta L H 179 E1
Church Hill. Stone 190 C1
Church Hollow. Pur 183 D1
Church La. Abr 142 C3
Church La. Bart 5 F2
Church La. Basil 163 D1
Church La. Bill 162 A3
Church La. Brain 65 F3
Church La. Brent 147 F1
Church La. Brent 167 E3
Church La. Can E 71 D4
Church La. Ch Ong 119 D4
Church La. Chelm 111 D1
Church La. Dag 173 E3
Church La. Deb 38 A4
Church La. Dodd 133 D1
Church La. Els 58 C4
Church La. Gt Le 85 E4
Church La. Gt Wal 84 A3
Church La. Horn H 177 F4
Church La. Kelv H 133 D1
Church La. Lou 140 C3
Church La. Marg 135 F3
Church La. N W Bas 117 D3
Church La. Pur 183 D1
Church La. Rain 182 B4
Church La. Ridge 20 A3
Church La. Romf 164 C4
Church La. S Han 151 E4
Church La. Sheer 91 E4
Church La. Sprin 111 E2
Church La. Sta Abb 143 E3
Church La. Take 70 A4
Church La. Thor 67 E2
Church La. Topp 32 A4
Church La. Upm 176 A4
Church La. W Han 138 A2
Church La. Writ 110 A1
Church Langley Way. Harl 103 E4
Church Leys. Harl 102 C4
Church Manor. Bis St 68 A4
Church Mead. Roy 88 A1
Church Mews. Basil 170 A4
Church Park. Cla 9 E2
Church Park Rd. Basil 172 A3
Church Path. Grave 192 B1
Church Path. Gt Am 87 D3
Church Path. Had 3 D3
Church Path. Saff W 13 E1
Church Path. Stone 190 C1
Church Rd. Bart 5 E3
Church Rd. Basil 169 E3
Church Rd. Basil 171 E3
Church Rd. Bill 161 F1
Church Rd. Chris 10 B2
Church Rd. Corr 180 A2
Church Rd. Grays 193 F4
Church Rd. Gt Ha 68 C2
Church Rd. Gt Ha 69 D3
Church Rd. Gt Y 20 C1
Church Rd. Harl 103 E3
Church Rd. Hav B 144 B1
Church Rd. Hemp 28 C4
Church Rd. Horn H 178 A4
Church Rd. Kelv H 132 B1
Church Rd. L Hal 68 A1
Church Rd. Lou 140 A1
Church Rd. More 105 E1
Church Rd. Mtssg 147 F4
Church Rd. Nave H 144 B1
Church Rd. Nave H 144 C4
Church Rd. Romf 157 D2
Church Rd. S Han 150 B2
Church Rd. Sta R 131 E3
Church Rd. Stam 19 E1
Church Rd. Stan M 57 E3
Church Rd. Stone 190 C1
Church Rd. Swan 191 F1
Church Rd. Tilb 192 C3
Church Rd. W Han 138 A2
Church Rd. Wa Aby 140 A4
Church Rd. Wick 150 B1
Church St. Bill 161 E3
Church St. Bis St 67 F4
Church St. Bla 133 F4
Church St. Chelm 111 D1
Church St. Dag 173 D3
Church St. Grave 193 D1
Church St. Grays 192 B4
Church St. Gt Bad 125 D3
Church St. Gt C 1 B1
Church St. Gt Dun 61 E1
Church St. Hen 48 C3
Church St. Hinx 1 A2
Church St. New 25 D1
Church St. Pan 65 F4
Church St. Saff W 13 E1
Church St. Saw 77 F1
Church St. Ste B 18 A4
Church St. Wa Aby 126 B3
Church St. Wen A 24 C3
Church St. Widd 37 E2
Church View. Ave 183 E2
Church View. Cla 8 B1
Church View. Upm 166 A1
Church Wlk. Litt 12 C2
Church Wlk. Saw 77 F1
Church Wlk. Stur 7 F2
Churchfield. Harl 90 A1
Churchfields. Hod 100 A2
Churchfields. Lou 140 C3
Churchfields. Woodf 152 A1
Churchfields Dr. Ste B 18 A3
Churchgate St. Harl 90 C2
Churchill Cl. Ch Ong 119 D2
Churchill Cres. Corr 179 F2
Churchill Rd. Brain 65 F4
Churchill Rd. Grays 192 B4
Churchill Rise. Sprin 111 F4
Chuzzlewit Dr. Chelm 110 C4
Cillocks Cl. Hod 100 A4
Circle The. Tilb 193 D3
Civic Sq. Tilb 193 D3
Clachar Cl. Sprin 112 A2
Claire Cl. Brent 159 D3
Clairmont Cl. Brain 65 F1
Clairvale. Hornc 165 F2
Clapton Hall La. Gt Dun 72 B3
Clare Ave. Runw 151 E1
Clare Mews. Ch Ong 119 D3
Clare Rd. Brain 65 F1
Claremont. Basil 170 B4
Claremont Cl. Grays 185 E2
Claremont Dr. Basil 172 A2
Claremont Gdns. Upm 166 B2
Claremont Gr. Woodf 152 B2
Claremont Rd. Hornc 165 D3
Clarence Ave. Upm 166 A1
Clarence Cl. Sprin 112 A2
Clarence Rd. Basil 172 C4
Clarence Rd. Brent 146 A2
Clarence Rd. Corr 180 B2
Clarence Rd. Grays 185 D1
Clarence Rd. Stan M 57 F4
Clarendon Rd. Basil 172 B4
Clarendon Rd. Grave 193 E1
Clarendon Rd. Hav 6 C3
Clarendon Rd. Take 70 C4
Clark Way. Broom 98 A1
Clarkbourne Dr. Grays 192 B4
Clarkhill. Harl 102 C3
Clarks La. Epp 128 C4
Clatterbury La. Clav 35 F3
Claudian Cl. Hav 7 E4
Claudian Way. Grays 186 A2
Claughton Way. Brent 147 E2
Claverhambury Rd. Wa Aby 114 A2
Clavering. Basil 171 F2
Clavering Gdns. Horn H 168 B3
Clavering Rd. Brain 65 F3
Clavering Way. Brent 147 E2
Clay Hill Rd. Basil 171 E3
Clay La. Steb 62 B4
Clay Pit Piece. Saff W 25 F3
Clay Tye Rd. Upm 167 E1
Clay's La. Lou 141 D4
Clayburn Circ. Basil 171 E3
Clayburn End. Basil 171 E3
Clayburn Gdns. S Ock 184 A3
Clayburn Side. Basil 171 E3
Claybury Rd. Woodf 152 C2
Claydon Cl. Bart 5 F2
Claydon Cres. Basil 171 E4
Claygate Cl. Hornc 174 A4
Clayhall Ave. Woodf 152 C1
Claypit Hill. Els 58 C3
Claypit Hill. Wa Aby 127 E2
Claypits Rd. Bore 99 F1
Claypits Villas. Thax 40 A1
Clayponds. Bis St 68 A4
Clays Meadow. Litt 12 C2
Clayside. Chig 153 E3
Clayton Ave. Upm 175 D4
Clayton Rd. Romf 164 B2
Claywall Bridge. Ste B 18 B4
Cleall Ave. Wa Aby 126 B3
Cleland Path. Lou 141 D4
Clematis Cl. Romf 156 B2
Clematis Tye. Sprin 111 F4
Clement Way. Upm 165 F1
Clement's La. Hav 6 C4
Clements Cl. Hav 6 C4
Clements Dr. Hav 6 C4
Clerks Piece. Lou 140 C3
Cleveland Rd. Basil 171 E3
Cleveland Rd. Woodf 152 A1
Cleves Ct. Bore 99 F1
Cleves Wlk. Woodf 153 E2
Clickett End. Basil 171 E3
Clickett Hill. Basil 171 E3
Clickett Side. Basil 171 E3
Cliff Pl. S Ock 176 B1
Clifield. Shal 54 C4
Clifford Ave. Woodf 153 D1
Clifford Rd. Grays 184 C2
Clifton Marine Par. Grave 193 D1
Clifton Rd. Basil 172 C4
Clifton Rd. Grave 193 D1
Clifton Rd. Hornc 165 D3
Clifton Rd. Lou 140 C3
Clifton Way. Brent 147 E1
Clinton Cres. Chig 153 F2
Clipped Hedge. Hat B O 79 D2
Clitheroe Rd. Romf 155 E3
Clive Rd. Brent 158 B2
Clive Rd. Grave 193 D1
Clive Rd. Romf 165 D3
Cliveden Cl. Brent 146 C1
Cliveden Cl. Chelm 110 C2
Clobbs Yd. Chelm 111 D4
Clock House Rd. Bill 160 C3
Clockhouse La. Grays 184 C2
Clockhouse La. Hav B 155 E2
Clockhouse La. Romf 155 E2
Clockhouse Way. Brain 66 B1
Cloisters. Corr 179 F1
Cloisters The. Brain 66 A3
Clopton Green. Basil 171 D4
Close The. Brent 158 B4
Close The. Deb 38 A4
Close The. Grays 185 E2
Close The. Gt Dun 72 C4
Close The. Hat B O 79 D2
Cloudberry Rd. Romf 156 B2
Clovelly Gdns. Romf 155 D1
Clovelly Gdns. Runw 163 E4
Clover Cl. Basil 171 F2
Clover Ct. Grays 192 B4
Clover Field. Harl 103 D3
Clover Leas. Epp 115 F1
Clover Way. Basil 171 F2
Cloverley Rd. Ch Ong 119 D1
Cloverleys. Lou 140 B3
Cluff Ct. Brent 158 B3
Clunas Gdns. Romf 165 E4
Clyde. Grays 187 E1
Clyde Cres. Chelm 110 B2
Clyde Cres. Upm 166 C3
Clyde Rd. Roy 100 B2
Clyde Way. Romf 155 F1
Clydesdale Rd. Brain 65 F1
Clydesdale Rd. Hornc 164 C2
Coach Mews. Bill 149 E3
Coach Rd. Hemp 16 C1
Cobbins The. Wa Aby 126 C3
Cobbinsbank. Wa Aby 126 B3
Cobbinsend Rd. Wa Aby 114 B1
Cobbles The. Brent 158 C4
Cobbles The. Upm 166 C2
Cobbs La. Take 59 F2
Cobbs Pl. Sprin 111 E2
Cobden Wlk. Basil 172 B4
Cobham. Grays 185 D2
Cobill Cl. Hornc 165 E4
Coburg Gdns. Woodf 152 C1
Coburg La. Basil 169 F2
Cock Green. Harl 102 A3
Cock La. Clav 34 C2
Cock La. Ing 121 F1
Cockerell Cl. Basil 163 D1
Codenham Green. Basil 171 D2
Codenham Straight. Basil 171 D2
Codham Hall La. Brent 167 D4
Codham Little Park Dr. Weth 55 E3
Coggeshall Rd. Brain 66 B2
Coggeshall Rd. Stis 66 B2
Cogmore. Elm 23 D4
Colbourne Cl. Corr 179 F2
Colchester Rd. Bore 112 A3
Colchester Rd. Romf 156 C1
Coldharbour Rd. Harl 102 A4
Coldnailhurst Ave. Brain 65 F3
Cole End La. Saff W 26 B3
Cole End La. Wim 26 B3
Cole Hill. Gt Le 86 A3
Colebrook Gdns. Lou 141 D4
Colebrook La. Lou 141 D4
Colebrook Path. Lou 141 D4
Colehills Cl. Clav 35 E2
Coleman's La. Lo Naz 113 F3
Coleridge Rd. Romf 156 A2
Coleridge Rd. Stone 190 A2
Coleridge Rd. Tilb 193 E3
Coleridge Wlk. Brent 147 E1
Coles Cl. Ch Ong 119 D3
Coles Green. Lou 141 D4
Colet Rd. Brent 147 E2
Colin Cl. Stone 190 A1
Collard Ave. Lou 141 E4
Collard Green. Lou 141 E4
College Ave. Grays 185 E1
College Cl. Grays 185 F1
College Gdns. Ching 139 E1
College Rd. Brain 65 F1
College Rd. Grave 192 A1
College Rd. Grays 185 E1
College Sq. Harl 102 B4
Colley Rd. Gt Bad 125 D3
Collier Row La. Romf 155 E1
Collier Row Rd. Romf 155 D2
Collingwood Cl. Brain 66 B3
Collingwood Rd. Basil 171 E2
Collingwood Terr. Basil 171 E3
Collingwood Wlk. Basil 171 E3
Collins Cl. Brain 65 F1
Collins Cl. Corr 179 F1
Collins Cross. Bis St 57 D1
Collins Meadow. Harl 102 A4
Collins Way. Brent 147 F2
Collops Villas. Steb 63 D2
Colman Cl. Corr 179 E2
Colne. Grays 187 E2
Colne Dr. Romf 156 C2
Colne Pl. Basil 171 E2
Colne Springs. Ridge 20 A3
Colne Valley. Upm 166 C3
Colne Valley Rd. Hav 7 D4
Colney Rd. Stone 190 A1
Colson Gdns. Lou 141 D3
Colson Green. Lou 141 D2
Colson Path. Lou 141 D3
Colson Rd. Lou 141 D3
Coltishall Rd. Hornc 174 B3
Colts The. Bis St 67 F2
Coltsfield. Stan M 57 F4
Coltsfoot Ct. Grays 192 B4
Coltsfoot Path. Romf 156 B2
Columbia Wharf Rd. Grays 192 A4
Columbine Way. Romf 156 C1
Colville Cl. Corr 179 F3
Colville Mews. Bill 148 C3
Colvin Chase. Chelm 124 A1
Colvin Gdns. Woodf 153 E2
Colyers Reach. Sprin 112 A1
Colyn Pl. Saff W 13 F2
Comet Cl. Pur 183 D1
Comfrey Ct. Grays 192 B4
Commercial Pl. Grave 193 E1
Common Hill. Saff W 13 E1
Common La. Chris 22 A4
Common La. Stock 136 C1
Common Rd. Brent 159 E3
Common Rd. Lo Naz 101 F1
Common Rd. Stock 136 C1
Commonfields. Harl 89 F1
Commonside Rd. Harl 102 C2
Como St. Romf 164 B4
Compton Ave. Brent 147 E1
Compton Ave. Romf 165 E4
Compton Wlk. Basil 170 A4
Comyns Pl. Writ 110 A1
Comyns Rd. Dag 173 D3
Condor Wlk. Rain 174 A3
Conduit La. Br Pel 33 D1
Conduit La. Hod 100 A3
Conduit La E. Hod 100 A3
Conduit St. Chelm 111 D1
Coney Green. Saw 77 E2
Congreve Rd. Wa Aby 126 C4
Conifer Ave. Romf 155 D3
Conifer Dr. Brent 158 B3
Coniston Ave. Upm 175 E4
Coniston Cl. Bl Not 76 B3
Coniston Way. Hornc 174 A4

Connaught Ave. Ching 139 E1
Connaught Ave. Grays 185 D2
Connaught Ave. Lou 140 B3
Connaught Gdns. Brain 66 A2
Connaught Hill. Lou 140 B3
Connaught Rd. Ching 139 F1
Connaught Rd. Hav 6 C4
Connaught Rd. Hornc 165 E1
Connaught Way. Bill 149 D3
Conrad Cl. Grays 185 D2
Conrad Gdns. Grays 185 D2
Conrad Rd. Sta L H 179 F1
Consort Cl. Brent 158 B3
Constable View. Sprin 111 F3
Constance Cl. Broom 98 A1
Consul Ave. Rain 173 E1
Convent Hill. Brain 66 A3
Convent La. Brain 66 A3
Conway Cl. Rain 174 A3
Conway Gdns. Grays 192 A4
Conway's Rd. Grays 178 A1
Conway's Rd. Horn H 178 A1
Conybury Cl. Wa Aby 127 D4
Conyers. Harl 89 E1
Conyers Way. Lou 141 D3
Cook Pl. Sprin 111 F2
Cook's Cl. Romf 155 E1
Cook's La. Gt Ba 41 F2
Cooks Green. Basil 163 E1
Cooks Spinney. Harl 90 A1
Coolgardie Ave. Chig 153 D4
Coombe Dr. Basil 170 B1
Coombe Rd. Romf 165 F4
Coombe Rise. Brent 146 C1
Coombe Rise. Chelm 111 D4
Coombe Rise. Corr 179 F1
Coombes Cl. Bill 148 C2
Cooper's La. Grays 193 F4
Cooper's Row. Chelm 111 D3
Coopers Cl. Chig 154 A4
Coopers Dr. Bill 161 E4
Coopers End Rd. Take 59 D2
Coopers Hill. Ch ong 119 D1
Coopers La. Gt Le 85 F4
Coopersale Common. Epp 116 B1
Coopersale La. The B 129 D2
Coopersale St. Epp 129 E4
Coopersales. Basil 170 A3
Copdoek. Basil 171 E4
Copeman Rd. Brent 147 E1
Copford Cl. Bill 149 E1
Copford Cl. Woodf 152 C2
Copford Rd. Bill 149 E1
Copland Cl. Broom 98 A1
Copland Cl. Gt Bad 124 C4
Copland Rd. Sta L H 179 E1
Coploe Rd. Hinx 1 A1
Coppens Green. Wick 163 F3
Copper Beech Cl. Woodf 153 D1
Copper Beech Ct. Lou 141 D4
Copper Beech Rd. S Ock 176 B1
Copper Ct. Saw 77 F1
Copperfield. Bill 161 E3
Copperfield. Chig 153 E2
Copperfield Gdns. Brent 146 B1
Copperfield Rd. Chelm 110 C4
Copperfields. Basil 170 B4
Copperfields Way. Romf 156 B1
Coppice Cl. Gt Dun 61 E1
Coppice Hatch. Harl 102 B3
Coppice La. Bill 161 F1
Coppice Path. Chig 154 A3
Coppice Row. The B 128 B2
Coppice The. Kelv H 132 C1
Coppings The. Hod 87 D1
Coppins Cl. Sprin 111 F2
Copse Hill. Harl 102 A3
Copse The. Bill 149 D2
Copse The. Bis St 68 B4
Copse The. Ching 139 F1
Copse The. Felst 74 C3
Coptfold Rd. Brent 158 B4
Copthall La. Thax 40 A2
Copthorne Ave. Woodf 153 D2
Copthorne Gdns. Hornc 166 A3
Copy Hill. Hel B 6 C1
Coram Green. Brent 147 E2
Corbets Ave. Upm 175 D4
Corbets Tey Rd. Upm 175 D4
Corcorans. Brent 146 B2
Cormorant Wlk. Chelm 124 B3
Cormorant Wlk. Rain 174 A3
Cornell Way. Romf 155 D3
Cornells La. Widd 37 F2
Corner Park. Saff W 13 F2
Corner Rd. Bill 162 B3
Cornflower Dr. Sprin 111 F3
Cornflower Gdns. Bill 148 C2
Cornflower Way. Romf 156 C1
Cornhill. Chelm 111 D1
Cornish Hall End Rd. Stam 19 D1
Cornmill. Wa Aby 126 A3
Cornsland. Brent 158 B4
Cornwall Cl. Hornc 166 A4
Cornwall Cres. Chelm 111 D4
Cornwall Gate. Pur 183 D1
Cornwall Gdns. Brain 66 A2
Cornwall Rd. Basil 172 C4
Cornwall Rd. Brent 146 A2
Cornwallis Pl. Saff W 13 F1
Cornwallis Rd. Hav 6 C3
Cornwell Cres. Corr 179 F2
Corona Rd. Basil 170 A2
Coronation Ave. Brain 65 F1
Coronation Ave. Grays 187 E1
Coronation Dr. Hornc 174 A4
Coronation Hill. Epp 115 F1
Coronation Rd. Bis St 67 F3
Corporation Rd. Chelm 111 D2
Corran Way. S Ock 184 B3
Corringham Rd. Sta L H 179 F1
Corve La. S Ock 184 A3
Cory Dr. Brent 147 D1
Costead Manor Rd. Brent 146 A1
Coteford Cl. Lou 141 D4
Cotelands. Basil 171 F2
Cotleigh Rd. Romf 164 B3
Cotswold Cres. Chelm 110 B3
Cotswold Gdns. Brent 147 F1
Cotswold Rd. Romf 156 C1
Cottage Pl. Chelm 111 D2
Cottesmore Ave. Woodf 153 D1
Cottis Cl. Basil 170 A2
Cotton La. Stone 190 B1
Cottons App. Romf 164 B3
Couchmore Ave. Woodf 152 C1
Council Ave. Grave 192 B1
Council Rd. Bis St 68 A4
Counting House La. Gt Dun 61 E1
Coupals Cl. Hav 7 E3
Coupals Rd. Hav 7 F3
Courage Cl. Hornc 165 E3
Courage Wlk. Brent 147 E2
Court Ave. Romf 157 D2
Court Rd. Broom 98 A2
Court Rd. Broom 98 A2
Court View. Ing 134 C1
Court Way. Romf 156 C1
Courtauld Rd. Basil 163 E1
Courtauld Rd. Brain 66 A2
Courtfield Cl. Hod 100 A2
Courtland Dr. Chig 153 E4
Courtlands. Bill 148 C1
Courtlands. Chelm 111 D3
Courtney Park Rd. Basil 170 A3
Courtney Rd. Grays 186 B2
Courtway. Woodf 152 B3
Courtway Cotts. Corr 180 B3
Coval Ave. Chelm 111 D2
Coval La. Chelm 111 D2
Covenbrook. Brent 159 D4
Coverley Cl. Brent 158 B2
Covert Rd. Chig 153 F2
Coverts The. Brent 147 D1
Coverts The. Writ 110 A1
Cow La. Gt C 2 A3
Cow Watering La. Writ 109 F2
Cowdray Way. Hornc 174 A4
Cowell Ave. Chelm 110 C3
Cowels Farm La. Thax 51 F3
Cowley Rd. Romf 156 A2
Cowper Ave. Tilb 193 D3
Cowper Rd. Rain 174 A1
Cowslip Mead. Basil 171 D3
Cowslip Rd. Woodf 152 A1
Cox Ley. Hat B O 79 D2
Coxes Cl. Corr 179 E2
Coxes Farm Rd. Bill 161 E4
Coxtie Green Rd. Brent 145 E2
Crabb's La. St Pel 45 F3
Crabtree Hill. Widd 37 D2
Craigdale Rd. Hornc 164 C2
Craiston Way. Gt Bad 124 C3
Crammavill St. Grays 185 D3
Crammerville Wlk. Rain 174 A1
Cramphorn Wlk. Chelm 110 C2
Cranborne Gdns. Upm 166 A1
Cranborne Rd. Hod 100 B4
Cranbourne Dri. Hod 87 E1
Cranbrook Dr. Romf 165 E4
Crane Cl. Dag 173 D3
Cranell Green. S Ock 184 A3
Cranes Cl. Basil 162 C1
Cranes Ct. Basil 171 E4
Cranes Farm Rd. Basil 171 D4
Cranes La. Basil 171 E4
Cranfield Ct. Runw 163 E4
Cranfield Park Rd. Wick 163 F2
Cranham Gdns. Upm 166 C2
Cranham Rd. Brox 49 F2
Cranham Rd. Hornc 165 D3
Cranleigh Gdns. Lou 140 C2
Cranmer Cl. Bill 149 D3
Cranmer Gdns. Dag 173 E4
Cranmore Cl. Els 48 B1
Cranston Park Ave. Upm 175 E4
Cranwell Gdns. Bis St 57 E1
Cranworth Cres. Ching 139 E1
Craven Gdns. Romf 155 D3
Craven Gdns. Romf 157 E2
Craven Gdns. Woodf 153 E1
Crawford Ave. Grays 185 D3
Crawford Cl. Bill 149 E3
Crawford Compton Cl. Hornc 174 B3
Crawley Cl. Corr 180 A3
Crayfields. Gt Dun 61 F1
Craylands. Basil 171 F4
Craylands La. Swan 191 E1
Craylands Sq. Swan 191 E1
Crays Hill. Bill 162 B3
Crays Hill Rd. Bill 162 B2
Crays View. Bill 161 D4
Creasey Cl. Hornc 165 D1
Credo Way. W Thu 191 D4
Cree Way. Romf 155 F2
Creek The. Grave 192 A1
Creek View. Basil 171 F2
Creekside. Rain 173 F1
Crescent Ave. Grays 192 B4
Crescent Ave. Hornc 164 C1
Crescent Cl. Bill 148 C2
Crescent Dr. Brent 146 C1
Crescent Gdns. Bill 148 C2
Crescent Rd. Ave 183 E2
Crescent Rd. Bill 148 C2
Crescent Rd. Bis St 68 A3
Crescent Rd. Brent 158 A3
Crescent Rd. Ching 139 F1
Crescent Rd. Dag 164 A1
Crescent Rd. Gt Bad 125 D4
Crescent Rd. Woodf 152 B1
Crescent The. Epp 128 C4
Crescent The. Gt Le 85 F3
Crescent The. Harl 90 B3
Crescent The. Lou 140 B2
Crescent The. Ste B 18 A4
Crescent The. Swan 191 E1
Crescent The. Upm 166 C2
Crescent View. Lou 140 B2
Crescent Way. Ave 183 E3
Crescent Wlk. Ave 183 E2
Cress Croft. Brain 66 B1
Cressages Cl. Felst 74 C3
Cressells. Basil 170 C3
Cresset Cl. Sta Ab 87 E2
Cressing Rd. Brain 66 B1
Crest Ave. Basil 172 B3
Crest Ave. Grays 192 A4
Crest The. Saw 77 E1
Cresthill Ave. Grays 185 E1
Crete Hall Rd. Grave 192 C1
Cricketers Cl. Broom 98 B1
Cricketers La. Brent 159 E2
Cricketers Row. Brent 159 E2
Cricketers Way. Wick 163 D1
Cricketfield La. Bis St 67 F4
Cricklade Ave. Romf 156 B2
Crina Wlk. Basil 171 F3
Cripsey Ave. Ch Ong 118 C3
Crittall Dr. Brain 65 E2
Crix Green Villas. Felst 75 E3
Croasdaile Rd. Stan M 57 F4
Croasdale Cl. Stan M 57 F4
Crocus Way. Sprin 111 F4
Croft Cl. Brain 66 A2
Croft Ct. Sprin 111 F4
Croft La. Hav 7 D3
Croft Lodge Cl. Woodf 152 A2
Croft The. Els 48 B1
Croft The. Lou 141 D4
Crofters. Saw 77 F2
Crofters End. Saw 77 F2
Crofton Ave. Corr 179 F2
Crofton Rd. Grays 185 F2
Cromer Ave. Basil 170 A4
Cromer Cl. Basil 170 A4
Cromer Rd. Hornc 165 E2
Cromer Rd. Romf 164 B3
Cromer Rd. Woodf 152 A3
Crompton Cl. Basil 170 C4
Crompton St. Chelm 110 C1
Cromwell Ave. Bill 149 D2
Cromwell Cl. Bis St 67 E4
Cromwell Rd. Brent 158 A3
Cromwell Rd. Grays 185 D1
Cromwell Rd. Saff W 25 F4
Crondon Park La. Stock 136 C2
Crooked La. Grave 193 D1
Crooked Mile. Wa Aby 126 B4
Crooked Way. Lo Naz 100 C1
Croppath Rd. Dag 173 D4
Crosby Rd. Dag 173 D2
Cross Ave. Wick 163 E3
Cross Green. Basil 170 C3
Cross Park Rd. Wick 163 E2
Cross Rd. Basil 172 C4
Cross Rd. Ching 139 F1
Cross Rd. Grave 192 C1
Cross Rd. Romf 164 A4
Cross Rd. Woodf 152 C2
Cross Roads. Wa Aby 140 A4
Cross St. Grave 193 D1
Cross St. Harl 102 B4
Cross St. Saff W 13 E1
Crossbow Rd. Chig 153 F3
Crossby Cl. Mtssg 147 F4
Crossfield Rd. Hod 100 A4
Crossfields. Lou 141 D2
Crossing Rd. Epp 129 D3
Crossway. Corr 179 F2
Crossway. Woodf 152 B3
Crossway The. Bill 149 E2
Crossways. Brent 147 D2
Crossways. Chelm 124 B4
Crossways. Romf 165 D4
Crossways Bvd. Stone 190 B2
Crouch Dr. Wick 163 E4
Crouch Rd. Grays 186 A1
Crouch St. Bill 161 F1
Crouch Valley. Upm 166 C2
Crow Green La. Brent 146 A2
Crow Green Rd. Brent 146 A3
Crow Green Rd. Dodd 145 F3
Crow La. Romf 164 A2
Crow St. Hen 48 C3
Crowland Rd. Hav 6 C4
Crowlands Ave. Romf 164 A3
Crown Ave. Basil 172 B4
Crown Cl. Saw 78 B1
Crown Cl. Sheer 91 E4
Crown Ct. Tilb 193 D3
Crown Gate. Harl 102 B4
Crown Hill. Wa Aby 127 F3
Crown Rd. Bill 149 D1
Crown Rd. Grays 192 A4
Crown Rd. Kelv H 145 E4
Crown St. Brent 158 B4
Crown St. Dag 173 E3
Crown St. Gt Ba 42 A1
Crown Terr. Bis St 68 A4
Crownfield. Hod 100 A1
Crownhill Rd. Woodf 152 C2
Crownmead Way. Romf 164 A4
Crows Field Cotts. W Han 137 F2
Crows Rd. Epp 115 F1
Crowsheath La. S Han 150 C3
Crowstone Rd. Grays 185 E2
Croxford Way. Romf 164 B2
Cruick Ave. S Ock 184 B3
Crummock Cl. Bl Not 76 B3
Crunch Croft. Stur 7 F3
Crushes Cl. Brent 147 F2
Crystal Ave. Hornc 165 F1
Cuckoo La. T Thu 184 C3
Cuckoos La. Gt Can 71 D2
Culford Rd. Grays 185 E2
Cullen Sq. S Ock 184 B3
Cullings Ct. Wa Aby 126 C3
Culpeper Cl. Woodf 153 D2
Culverdown. Basil 171 D3
Cumberland Ave. Hornc 165 F1
Cumberland Cl. Brain 66 A2
Cumberland Cl. Hornc 165 F1
Cumberland Cres. Chelm 111 D4
Cumberland Dr. Basil 170 A3
Cumley Rd. Ch Ong 117 F1
Cumming Rd. S Han 151 D1
Cummings Hall La. Romf 156 B4
Cunningham Rise. N W Bas 117 E3
Cunnington Rd. Brain 66 B2
Cupthall Cl. Gt Ha 68 C2
Curlew Cres. Basil 171 D2
Curling La. Grays 184 C1
Curling Tye. Basil 171 E4
Curling Wlk. Basil 171 E4
Currants Farm Rd. Brain 65 F3
Curtis Mill La. Sta Abb 143 F3
Curtis Rd. Hornc 165 F2
Curzon Dr. Grays 192 A4
Curzon Way. Sprin 112 A1
Curzon Wlk. Basil 172 A3
Cusak Rd. Sprin 111 F1
Cutforth Rd. Saw 77 F2
Cutmore Pl. Chelm 123 F4
Cuton Hall La. Bore 112 A3
Cutty Sark Cl. Stone 191 D1
Cygnet View. W Thu 184 A1
Cypress Cl. Wa Aby 126 B3
Cypress Dr. Chelm 124 B3
Cypress Gr. Chig 153 F2
Cypress Rd. Romf 156 B2

D'Arcy Gdns. Dag 173 D2
Dacre Ave. Ave 183 E3
Dacre Ave. Woodf 153 D1
Dacre Cl. Chig 153 E3
Dacre Cres. Ave 183 E3
Dacre Gdns. Chig 153 E3
Daffodil Ave. Brent 146 A2
Daffodil Way. Sprin 111 F4
Dagenham Rd. Rain 173 F3
Dagenham Rd. Romf 164 B1
Dagmar Rd. Dag 173 E3
Dagnam Park Cl. Romf 157 D3
Dagnam Park Dr. Romf 156 C3
Dagnam Park Gdns. Romf 157 D2
Dagnam Park Sq. Romf 157 D2
Dagnets La. Gt Le 76 B1
Dagwood La. Dodd 133 D1
Dahlia Cl. Sprin 111 F3
Daiglen Dr. S Ock 184 A4
Daines Rd. Bill 149 E1
Dairy Rd. Sprin 111 F2
Daisley Rd. Lind 52 A2
Daisleys La. Gt Le 86 A1
Daisy Ct. Bore 112 A3
Daisy Rd. Woodf 152 A1
Dakyn Dr. Stock 136 B2
Dale Cl. S Ock 184 A4
Dale Ct. Saw 77 E1
Dale Gdns. Woodf 152 A3
Dale The. Wa Aby 126 C3
Daleside Gdns. Chig 153 E4
Dalewood Cl. Hornc 165 F2
Dallwood Way. Brain 66 A2
Dalmeney. Basildon 170 A2
Dalroy Cl. S Ock 184 A4
Dalrymple Cl. Sprin 111 E2
Dalton Gdns. Bis St 67 F2
Daltons Fen. Basil 172 B4
Danacre. Basil 170 B4
Danbury Cl. Brent 145 F2
Danbury Down. Basil 171 F4
Danbury Rd. Lou 140 C2
Danbury Rd. Rain 173 F2
Danbury Way. Woodf 152 B2
Dane Acres. Bis St 67 E4
Dane O'Coys Rd. Bis St 56 C1
Dane Park. Bis St 67 E4
Dane Rd. Chelm 110 C1
Dane St. Bis St 68 A4
Danemead. Hod 87 D1
Danes Rd. Romf 164 A2
Danes Way. Brent 146 A2
Daniel Cl. Grays 184 C2
Daniel Cl. Grays 186 A2
Danyon Cl. Rain 174 B2
Darby Dri. Wa Aby 126 B3
Darcy Cl. Brent 147 D1
Darell Way. Bill 149 E1
Darenth La. S Ock 184 A4
Dark La. Brent 158 A2
Dark La. Romf 157 F2
Darlington Ct. Brent 146 A2
Darlington Gdns. Romf 156 B3
Darlington Path. Romf 156 B3
Darnay Rise. Chelm 110 B3
Darnley Rd. Grave 193 D1
Darnley Rd. Grays 192 A4
Darnley Rd. Woodf 152 A1
Darrell Cl. Chelm 111 D3
Dart Cl. Upm 166 B3
Dart Green. S Ock 184 A4
Dartfields. Romf 156 B2
Dartmouth Rd. Sprin 111 F3
Dartview Cl. Grays 185 F1
Darwin Cl. Brain 65 F1
Darwin Rd. Tilb 192 C3
Dashes The. Harl 89 F1
Davenants. Basil 163 D1
Daventry Gdns. Romf 156 B3
Daventry Green. Romf 156 B3
Daventry Rd. Romf 156 B3
David Ave. Runw 151 E1
David Dr. Romf 157 D2
David's Wlk. Bill 149 E1
Davids Way. Chig 153 F2
Davies Cl. Rain 174 B1
Davinia Cl. Woodf 152 C2
Davis Rd. Ave 183 E3
Davis Rd. Grays 184 C2
Daw St. Bird 19 D4
Daw St. Finch 42 C2
Dawes Ave. Hornc 165 F1
Dawley Green. S Ock 184 A4
Daws Cl. Writ 109 F1
Daws Hill. Wa Aby 139 E3
Dawson Cl. Saff W 13 F1
Dawson Dr. Rain 174 A3
Daylop Dr. Chig 154 A4
Days Cl. Chelm 111 D4
Days La. Dodd 146 A4
De Bohun Ct. Saff W 13 F1
De Mandeville Rd. Els 48 B1
De Vigier Ave. Saff W 14 A1
Deacon Way. Woodf 152 C2
Deadman's La. Gt Bad 124 B2
Deal Cl. Brain 65 F3
Dealtree Cl. Dodd 133 D2
Dean Rd. Bart 4 A4
Dean Rogers Pl. Brain 65 F4
Dean Way. Chelm 110 C1
Deanery Gdns. Brain 65 F4
Deanery Hill. Brain 65 F4
Deans Rd. Brent 158 A3
Debden Cl. Woodf 152 B2
Debden Dr. Wim 26 C1
Debden Green. Basil 170 B2
Debden La. Lou 128 B1
Debden Rd. Lou 128 A1
Debden Rd. New 37 E4
Debden Rd. Saff W 25 E4
Debden Rd. Saff W 25 F3
Debden Wlk. Hornc 174 A3
Deben. Grays 187 E2
Deben Rd. Hav 7 D4
Dedham Cl. Bill 149 E1
Dedham Rd. Bill 149 E1
Dee Cl. Upm 166 C3
Dee Way. Romf 155 F1
Deepdene. Basil 171 D3
Deepdene. Ing 135 D2
Deepdene Path. Lou 141 D3
Deepdene Rd. Lou 141 D3
Deer Park. Harl 102 A3
Deerbank Rd. Bill 149 E2
Deere Ave. Rain 174 A3
Deerleap Gr. Ching 139 D2
Deerleap Way. Brain 66 B2
Defoe Par. Grays 186 A2
Defoe Way. Romf 155 D2
Deirdre Ave. Wick 163 D4
Deirdre Cl. Wick 163 D4
Delafield Rd. Grays 185 E1
Delamere Rd. Chelm 110 C1

Delargy Cl. Grays 186 A2
Delhi Rd. Basil 172 B3
Delimands. Basil 170 C3
Delius Way. Corr 179 E2
Dell Cl. Woodf 152 A4
Dell La. Bis St 68 A4
Dell La. L Hal 78 A4
Dell Rd. Grays 185 D1
Dell The. Basil 171 D2
Dell The. Brent 158 A2
Dell The. Gt Bad 124 C3
Dell The. Gt Dun 61 F1
Dell The. Wick 163 F4
Dell The. Woodf 152 A4
Dellfield Ct. Harl 90 B2
Dellows La. Ugl 48 A1
Dells Cl. Ching 139 D2
Dells The. Bis St 67 F4
Delmar Gdns. Runw 151 E1
Delmores. Basil 170 B2
Delta Rd. Brent 147 E2
Delvers Mead. Dag 173 E4
Delvins. Basil 172 A4
Denbigh Cl. Hornc 166 A4
Denbigh Rd. Basil 170 A3
Dencourt Cres. Basil 171 F3
Dene Ct. Chelm 110 B3
Dene Path. S Ock 184 A4
Dene Rd. Lou 140 C1
Denecroft Gdns. Grays 185 E2
Denehurst Gdns. Woodf 152 A3
Deneway. Basil 171 E1
Dengayne. Basil 171 E3
Denholme Wlk. Rain 173 F3
Dennis Rd. Ave 176 A2
Dennis Rd. S Ock 176 A2
Dennises La. Upm 175 F3
Denny Ave. Wa Aby 126 B3
Denny Ct. Bis St 57 D1
Dent Cl. S Ock 184 A4
Denver Dr. Basil 163 E1
Denys Dr. Basil 162 C1
Derby Ave. Romf 164 B3
Derby Ave. Upm 166 A1
Derby Cl. Bill 149 E3
Derby Rd. Grays 185 D1
Derby Rd. Roy 100 B2
Derby Road Bridge. Grays 192 A4
Derham Gdns. Upm 166 B1
Deri Ave. Rain 174 A1
Derry Ave. S Ock 184 A4
Derwent Par. S Ock 184 A4
Derwent Way. Bl Not 76 B4
Derwent Way. Chelm 110 B2
Derwent Way. Hornc 174 A4
Detling Cl. Hornc 174 B4
Devereux Rd. Grays 184 C2
Devereux Way. Bill 149 D3
Deveron Gdns. S Ock 184 A4
Deveron Way. Romf 155 F1
Devoils La. Bis St 67 F4
Devon Cl. Lou 152 A4
Devonshire Cl. Basil 170 A4
Devonshire Gdns. Brain 66 A2
Devonshire Gdns. Sta L H 187 D2
Devonshire Rd. Basil 170 A4
Devonshire Rd. Grays 184 C2
Devonshire Rd. Hornc 165 E1
Dewes Green Rd. Berd 46 A4
Dewey Rd. Dag 173 E3
Dewlands. Basil 171 D4
Dewsbury Cl. Romf 156 C2
Dewsbury Gdns. Romf 156 B2
Dewsbury Rd. Romf 156 C2
Dewsgreen. Basil 171 F2
Dexter Cl. Grays 185 D2
Deyncourt Gdns. Upm 166 B1
Deynes Rd. Deb 38 A4
Diamond Cl. Grays 184 C2
Diana Cl. Grays 184 C2
Diana Cl. Woodf 152 A1
Diban Ave. Hornc 174 A4
Dickens Ave. Stone 190 A2
Dickens Ave. Tilb 193 D3
Dickens Dr. Basil 170 B4
Dickens Pl. Chelm 110 B4
Dickens Rise. Chig 153 D4
Dicky Moors. Gt Wal 97 F4
Digby Gdns. Dag 173 D2
Digby Rd. Corr 180 B3
Digby Wlk. Hornc 174 B3
Dimsdale Cres. Bis St 68 A3
Dinant Link Rd. Hod 100 A4
Disney Cl. Ing 135 D2
Ditchfield Rd. Hod 87 D1
Dixon Ave. Chelm 110 C2
Dobb's Weir Rd. Roy 100 B2
Dock Approach Rd. Grays 185 F1
Dock Rd. Grays 185 F1
Dock Rd. Tilb 192 C3
Docklands Ave. Ing 135 E2
Doctor's La. Ashe 9 E1
Doddenhill Cl. Saff W 13 F2
Doddinghurst Rd. Brent 146 B2
Doddinghurst Rd. Dodd 133 E1
Doesgate La. Horn H 169 E1
Doeshill Dr. Wick 163 F4
Dog Chase. Weth 43 E2
Dog Kennel La. Ing 135 E4
Dogden La. Man 46 C1
Doggett's Cnr. Hornc 165 F1
Dolby Rise. Sprin 111 F1
Dolphin App. Romf 164 C4
Dolphin Gdns. Bill 148 C3
Dolphin Way. Bis St 68 A4
Dolphin Yd The. Grave 193 D1
Dombey Cl. Chelm 110 C4
Dominion Dr. Romf 155 D2
Dominion Way. Rain 174 A1
Domsey La. Lit Wal 98 C2
Don Way. Romf 155 F2
Donald Thorn Cl. Wick 163 E3
Donald Way. Chelm 124 B4
Doncaster Way. Upm 165 F1
Doncel Ct. Ching 139 E1
Donovan's Gdn. Brent 159 E2
Dorchester Ave. Hod 100 A4
Dorchester Rd. Bill 149 D3
Dordells. Basil 170 C3
Dorewards Ave. Brain 65 F4
Dorian Rd. Hornc 165 D2
Dorking Rd. Romf 156 B3
Dorking Rise. Romf 156 B3
Dorking Wlk. Romf 156 B3
Dorkins Way. Upm 166 C2
Dorrington Gdns. Hornc 165 E2
Dorset Ave. Gt Bad 124 C3
Dorset Ave. Romf 164 B4
Dorset Cl. Gt Bad 124 C3
Dorset Gdns. Sta L H 187 D2
Dorset Way. Bill 149 D3
Dorvis La. Ash 4 A1
Doubleday Rd. Lou 141 E3
Doublet Mews. Bill 149 E3
Doug Siddons Ct.Greys 192 B4
Douglas Ave.Romf 156 C1
Douglas Cl. Chelm 124 B2
Douglas Dr. Wick 163 E3
Douglas Rd. Ching 139 F1
Douglas Rd. Hornc 164 C3
Douglas Wlk. Chelm 124 A4
Dove Cl. Bis St 67 F2
Dove Cl. Stan M 57 F4
Dove Crofts. H Rod 81 F4
Dove La. Chelm 124 A3
Dovedale Ave. Woodf 153 D1
Dovedale Cl. Basil 170 A2
Dovehouse Croft. Harl 90 A1
Dovehouse Rd. Hav 7 D4
Dover Cl. Brain 65 F3
Dover Cl. Romf 155 E1
Dover Rd. Grave 192 B1
Doves La. Gt Dun 72 A1
Dowding Cl. Hornc 174 A3
Dowland Cl. Corr 179 E2
Dowland Wlk. Basil 170 B4
Downey Cl. Basil 171 E4
Downhall Rd. Hat B O 92 B3
Downham Rd. Runw 151 E2
Downham Rd. S Han 150 B3
Downham Rd. S Han 150 B4
Downing Rd. Dag 173 D2
Downing Rd. Dag 173 D3
Downlands. Wa Aby 126 C3
Downs Cres. Gt Dun 61 E1
Downs Cres. Hav 6 C4
Downs Gr. Basil 171 F2
Downs Pl. Hav 6 C4
Downs The. Gt Dun 61 E1
Downs The. Harl 102 C4
Downsland Dr. Brent 158 B4
Downsway. Sprin 111 E3
Downton Dr. Hav 6 C4
Dowsett La. S Han 150 B3
Doyle Way. Tilb 193 E3
Drake Cl. Brent 158 B3
Drake Gdns. Brain 66 B2
Drake Rd. Grays 184 C2
Drakes La. Lit Wal 99 D4
Draper's Chase. Felst 75 E4
Draper's Crnr. Ch Ong 118 B1
Drapers La. Hel B 6 A1
Drayson Cl. Wa Aby 126 C4
Drayton Ave. Lou 140 C2
Dreys The. Saff W 26 B4
Driberg Way. Brain 66 A1
Driftway. Basil 171 F2
Drive The. Brent 158 B2
Drive The. Chelm 111 D3
Drive The. Ching 139 E1
Drive The. Harl 89 F1
Drive The. Hod 100 A4
Drive The. Lou 140 B1
Drive The. Lou 140 C3
Drive The. Romf 155 E2
Drive The. Romf 156 C1
Drive The. Saw 77 F1
Drive The. Thax 39 F2
Drive The. Woodf 152 A1
Drood Cl. Chelm 110 C4
Droveway. Lou 141 D4
Druce The. Clav 35 E2
Drummond Ave. Romf 164 B4
Drummond Rd. Romf 164 B4
Drummonds The. Epp 116 A1
Drummonds The. Lou 152 A4
Drury La. Ay Rod 81 E1
Drury La. Brain 65 F2
Drury La. Ridge 20 A3
Dry St. Basil 170 C1
Dryden Cl. Chig 153 F2
Dryden Pl. Tilb 193 D3
Drysdale Ave. Ching 139 D2
Duarte Pl. Grays 184 C2
Duchess Cl. Bis St 67 E4
Duck La. N W Bas 116 B3
Duck St. Lit Ea 60 C3
Duck St. Wen A 24 C3
Duckend Farm La. Thax 51 F3
Ducketts Mead. Roy 88 A1
Ducking Stool Ct. Romf 164 C4
Duckling La. Saw 77 F1
Dudbrook Rd. Nave H 132 A1
Duddery Hill. Hav 7 D4
Duddery Rd. Hav 7 D4
Dudley Cl. Grays 184 C2
Dudley Gdns. Romf 156 B2
Dudley Rd. Romf 156 B2
Duffield Rd. Gt Bad 124 B3
Duffries Cl. Gt Wal 97 F4
Duggers La. Brain 66 A1
Duke St. Chelm 111 D2
Duke St. Hod 100 A4
Duke's Pl. Brent 146 B1
Dukes Ave. Grays 185 D2
Dukes Ave. The B 128 C2
Dukes Cl. N W Bas 117 D2
Dukes Farm Cl. Bill 149 E3
Dukes Farm Rd. Bill 149 D3
Dukes La. Sprin 111 F2
Dukes La. Will 107 E3
Dukes Orchard. Hat B O 79 F3
Dukes Park Ind Est. Sprin 111 F2
Dukes Rd. Bill 149 E2
Dukes Rd. Brain 65 F3
Dukes Ride. Bis St 67 E4
Dulverton Rd. Romf 156 B2
Dumney La. Gt Le 85 F4
Dunbar Ave. Dag 164 A1
Dunbar Gdns. Dag 173 D4
Duncan Rise. Gt Y 20 C1
Dunedin Rd. Rain 173 F1
Dunfane. Bill 149 E3
Dunkellan Gr. S Ock 184 A4
Dunkellan Way. S Ock 184 A4
Dunkin Rd. Stone 190 A2
Dunlop Rd. Tilb 192 C3
Dunmore Rd. Sprin 112 A2
Dunmow Cl. Lou 140 C2
Dunmow Dr. Rain 173 F2
Dunmow Gdns. Horn H 168 B3
Dunmow Rd. Abb Rod 93 F1
Dunmow Rd. Ay Rod 81 E2
Dunmow Rd. Birhr 68 C4
Dunmow Rd. Bis St 68 A4
Dunmow Rd. Fyf 106 C3
Dunmow Rd. Gt Ba 52 C4
Dunmow Rd. H Rod 81 E2
Dunmow Rd. Hat B O 79 F3
Dunmow Rd. Lit Ba 52 C4
Dunmow Rd. Ray 64 B1
Dunmow Rd. Take 70 C4
Dunning Cl. S Ock 184 A4
Dunningford Cl. Romf 173 F4
Dunnings La. Horn H 168 A1
Dunoon Cl. Brain 66 B2
Dunspring La. Woodf 153 D1
Dunstable Cl. Romf 156 B2
Dunstable Rd. Corr 179 E2
Dunstable Rd. Romf 156 B2
Dunstalls. Harl 102 A2
Dunster Cl. Romf 155 E1
Dunster Cres. Hornc 166 A1
Dunster Dr. Hav 6 C4
Dunton Rd. Basil 160 C1
Dunton Rd. Romf 164 C4
Durants Wlk. Wick 163 E3
Durban Gdns. Dag 173 E3
Durban La. Bill 161 F1
Durdans The. Basil 170 A2
Durham Ave. Romf 165 E4
Durham Ave. Woodf 152 B3
Durham Cl. Gt Ba 42 A1
Durham Cl. Saw 77 E1
Durham Cl. Sta Ab 87 D3
Durham Rd. Basil 169 F3
Durham Rd. Dag 173 E4
Durley Ave. Wick 162 C4
Durnell Way. Lou 141 D3
Durninge Wlk. Grays 185 D3
Durrants Cl. Rain 174 B2
Durrington Cl. Basil 171 E3
Dury Falls Cl. Hornc 166 A2
Duxford Cl. Hornc 174 B3
Duxford Rd. Hinx 1 A4
Dyer's Way. Romf 156 A2
Dyers Rd. Stam 19 F1
Dymchurch Cl. Woodf 153 D1
Dymoke. Hornc 164 C2
Dymokes Way. Hod 87 D1
Dytchleys La. Nave H 145 D3
Dytchleys Rd. Nave H 144 C3
Eagle Cl. Rain 174 A3
Eagle Cl. Wa Aby 127 D3
Eagle La. Brain 65 F3
Eagle La. Kelv H 132 C1
Eagle Terr. Woodf 152 A2
Eagle Way. Brent 158 B2
Earl Mountbatten Way. Bill 148 C2
Earls Cl. Bis St 67 E3
Earls Path. Lou 140 B3
Earlsfield Dr. Sprin 111 F2
Easedale Dr. Hornc 174 A4
Easington Way. S Ock 184 A4
East Cl. Rain 174 A1
East Crescent Rd. Grave 193 E1
East Dene Dr. Romf 156 B3
East Dri. Saw 77 F1
East Entrance. Dag 173 D2
East Gate. Harl 89 E1
East Hall La. Rain 182 B4
East Kent Ave. Grave 192 B1
East Mayne. Basil 163 D1
East Park. Harl 90 B2
East Park. Saw 77 F1
East Rd. Bis St 68 A4
East Rd. Harl 90 A2
East Rd. Romf 164 B2
East Sq. Basil 171 D3
East St. Brain 66 A2
East St. Grays 191 F4
East St. Grays 192 B4
East St. Saff W 13 F1
East Terr. Grave 193 E1
East Thorpe. Basil 171 E3
East Thurrock Rd. Grays 192 B4
East Tilbury Rd. Sta L H 187 D2
East View. Writ 109 F1
East View Cl. Rad 27 F4
East Way. Wa Aby 126 B2
East Wlk. Basil 171 D3
East Wlk. Harl 89 E1
Eastbrook Ave. Dag 173 E4
Eastbrook Dr. Romf 164 C1
Eastbrook Rd. Wa Aby 126 C3
Eastbrooks. Basil 172 A4
Eastbrooks Mews. Basil 172 A4
Eastbrooks Pl. Basil 172 A4
Eastbury Rd. Romf 164 B3
Eastby Cl. Saff W 25 F4
Eastend La. Els 59 E4
Eastern App. Sprin 111 F3
Eastern Ave. Ave 183 E2
Eastern Ave. Hav 6 C4
Eastern Ave E. Romf 155 F1
Eastern Ave W. Romf 164 A4
Eastern Cres. Chelm 110 C3
Eastern Rd. Grays 185 E1
Eastern Rd. Romf 164 C3
Eastern Way. Grays 185 D1
Eastfield Gdns. Dag 173 D4
Eastfield Rd. Bill 161 F1
Eastfield Rd. Brent 158 B4
Eastfield Rd. Dag 173 D4
Eastgate. Basil 171 D3
Eastgate. Gt C 1 B1
Eastham Cres. Brent 159 D4
Easton End. Basil 170 A3
Eastwick Hall La. E Wick 89 D3
Eastwick Rd. East 89 D2
Eastwick Rd. H Wy 89 F3
Eastwood Cl. Woodf 152 A1
Eastwood Dr. Rain 182 A4
Eastwood Rd. Woodf 152 A1
Eaton Cl. Bill 149 D3
Eaton Dr. Romf 155 D2
Eaton Rd. Upm 166 C1
Ebbsfleet Ind Est. Grave 192 A1
Ebbsfleet Wlk. Grave 192 A1
Eccleston Gdns. Bill 149 D3
Echo Hts. Ching 139 D1
Eckersley Rd. Chelm 111 E2
Eddy Cl. Romf 164 A3
Eden Green. S Ock 184 A4
Eden Rd. Hav 7 D4
Eden Way. Chelm 110 B3
Edenhall Cl. Romf 156 B3
Edenhall Glen. Romf 156 B3
Edenhall Rd. Romf 156 B3
Edens Cl. Bis St 68 A4
Edens Mount. Saw 77 F2
Edgecotts. Basil 170 C2
Edgehill Gdns. Dag 173 D4
Edinburgh Ave. Corr 179 F3
Edinburgh Gdns. Brain 66 B2
Edinburgh Mews. Tilb 193 D3
Edinburgh Pl. Harl 90 A2
Edinburgh Way. Harl 89 F2
Edinburgh's Dr. Romf 164 B4
Edison Ave. Hornc 164 C2
Edison Cl. Brain 65 F1
Edison Cl. Hornc 164 C2
Edith Cavell Way. Ste B 18 A3
Edith Way. Corr 180 A3
Edmund Cl. Hav 6 C4
Edmund Rd. Rain 173 F1
Edridge Cl. Hornc 174 B4
Edward Cl. Bill 148 C3
Edward Ct. Wa Aby 126 C3
Edward Dr. Chelm 124 B4
Edward Gdns. Runw 163 E4
Edwards Cl. Brent 147 F2
Edwards Way. Brent 147 F2
Edwin Cl. Rain 173 F1
Edwin St. Grave 193 D1
Egbert Gdns. Runw 151 E1
Egg Hall. Epp 116 A1
Eggshell La. Ste B 18 C1
Eglington Rd. Ching 139 E1
Eglinton Rd. Swan 191 F1
Ehringshausen Way. Hav 7 D4
Eisenhower Rd. Basil 170 A3
Elan Rd. S Ock 184 A4
Eldeland. Basil 170 C4
Elder Ave. Wick 163 E3
Elder Way. Rain 174 B1
Elder Way. Wick 163 E3
Elderberry Cl. Basil 170 A3
Elderfield. Harl 90 B2
Eldon Rd. Roy 100 B2
Eldred Gdns. Upm 166 C2
Eleanor Chase. Wick 163 E4
Eleanor Way. Brent 158 C3
Eleanor Way. Wa Aby 126 A3
Eleven Acre Rise. Lou 140 C3
Elgar Cl. Basil 170 B4
Elgar Cl. Lou 152 B4
Elgar Gdns. Tilb 193 D3
Elgin Ave. Chelm 111 D1
Elgin Ave. Romf 157 D2
Elham Dr. Basil 172 B3
Eliot Cl. Wick 163 E3
Eliot Rd. Stone 190 A1
Elizabeth Cl. Lo Naz 113 E4
Elizabeth Cl. Romf 155 D1
Elizabeth Cl. Saff W 13 F1
Elizabeth Cl. Tilb 193 D3
Elizabeth Ct. Grave 193 D1
Elizabeth Dr. The B 128 C2
Elizabeth Dr. Wick 163 D4
Elizabeth Rd. Bis St 67 F3
Elizabeth Rd. Brent 146 A2
Elizabeth Rd. Grays 184 C2
Elizabeth Rd. Rain 182 A4
Elizabeth St. Stone 190 C1
Elizabeth Way. Harl 89 D1
Elizabeth Way. Saff W 13 F1
Elkins The. Romf 155 F1
Ellen Way. Bl Not 76 B4
Ellenborough Cl. Bis St 67 E3
Ellerman Rd. Tilb 192 C3
Elliott Gdns. Romf 156 A2
Ellis Ave. Rain 182 A4
Ellmore Cl. Romf 156 A1
Elm Ave. Upm 175 D4
Elm Bungalows. Brain 65 E2
Elm Cl. Broom 111 D4
Elm Cl. Els 48 B1
Elm Cl. Ep Gr 115 D4
Elm Cl. Gt Bad 124 C3
Elm Cl. Hav 6 C4
Elm Cl. Lou 152 B4
Elm Cl. Romf 155 D1
Elm Cl. Take 70 B4
Elm Cl. Wa Aby 126 B3
Elm Ct. Elm 11 D2
Elm Gdns. N W Bas 117 D3
Elm Gr. Hornc 165 F3
Elm Gr. Saff W 13 E1
Elm Gr. Woodf 152 A3
Elm Green. Basil 172 A3
Elm Green. Bill 149 F1
Elm Grove. Bis St 68 A4
Elm Park Ave. Hornc 165 D1
Elm Rd. Ave 183 E3
Elm Rd. Basil 163 F1
Elm Rd. Bis St 67 F4
Elm Rd. Chelm 124 A4
Elm Rd. Grays 192 B4
Elm Rd. Hod 100 A3
Elm Rd. Romf 155 D1
Elm Rd. Runw 163 E4
Elm Rd. Stone 190 C1
Elm Terr. W Thu 191 D4
Elm Way. Bore 99 F1
Elm Way. Brent 158 A3
Elm Wlk. Ray 64 C1
Elm Wlk. Romf 165 D4
Elmbridge. Harl 90 C2
Elmbridge Rd. Chig 154 A2
Elmbrook Cl. Bis St 67 F2
Elmdene Ave. Hornc 165 F3
Elmer Ave. Hav B 155 F4
Elmer Cl. Rain 174 A3
Elmer Gdns. Rain 174 A3
Elmhurst Cl. Bis St 67 F4
Elmhurst Cl. Hav 7 D4
Elmhurst Dr. Hornc 165 E2
Elmhurst Dr. Woodf 152 A1
Elmhurst Way. Lou 140 C1
Elmores. Lou 141 D3
Elms Dr. Chelm 111 D2
Elms Farm Rd. Hornc 174 B4
Elms The. Ch Ong 119 D1
Elms The. Gt C 1 C2
Elmslie Cl. Woodf 152 C2
Elmstead Cl. Corr 180 A3
Elmtree Ave. Kelv H 132 C1
Elmtree Rd. Basil 172 A2
Elmway. Grays 185 E3
Elmwood. Saw 77 F1
Elsenham Cres. Basil 171 F3
Elverston Cl. Basil 170 B4
Elvet Ave. Romf 165 E4

Elwick Rd. S Ock 184 B4
Ely Gdns. Dag 164 B1
Ely Pl. Chig 153 D3
Emanuel Rd. Basil 170 A2
Emberson Ct. Sprin 111 F2
Emberson Way. N W Bas 117 E3
Emerald Gdns. Dag 164 A2
Emerson Dr. Hornc 165 E2
Emma's Cres. Sta Ab 87 D2
Emmaus Way. Chig 153 D3
Emson Cl. Saff W 13 E1
Emsworth Rd. Woodf 153 D1
Enborne Green. S Ock 184 A4
Endway The. Gt Ea 60 C4
Endway The. Ste B 18 B4
Engayne Gdns. Upm 166 A2
England's La. Lou 141 D4
Engleric. Chris 10 B2
Ennerdale Ave. Bl Not 76 B3
Ennerdale Ave. Hornc 174 A4
Enterprise Centre The. Basil 162 C1
Enterprise Ct. Brain 66 A1
Enterprise Way. Wick 163 F3
Epping Cl. Chelm 110 C1
Epping Cl. Romf 164 A4
Epping Glade. Ching 139 E2
Epping La. Sta T 143 E4
Epping La. The B 142 A4
Epping New Rd. Lou 140 A2
Epping New Rd. Wa Aby 140 A2
Epping Rd. Bobb 118 B3
Epping Rd. Ch Ong 117 E1
Epping Rd. Ch Ong 118 B3
Epping Rd. Epp 116 B2
Epping Rd. Harl 101 E3
Epping Rd. Lo Naz 101 E3
Epping Rd. N W Bas 117 D2
Epping Rd. Roy 101 D4
Epping Rd. Sta T 116 B2
Epping Rd. Wa Aby 128 A2
Epping Way. Ching 139 D2
Epsom Cl. Bill 149 E3
Epsom Way. Hornc 165 F1
Eric Rd. Basil 172 C3
Erick Ave. Chelm 111 D4
Eridge Cl. Sprin 111 E4
Eriswell Rd. Hav 7 D4
Erith Cres. Romf 155 E1
Erith Ct. Pur 183 D1
Ernan Cl. S Ock 184 A4
Ernan Rd. S Ock 184 A4
Ernest Rd. Hornc 165 F3
Erriff Dr. S Ock 184 A4
Errington Cl. Grays 186 A2
Erroll Rd. Romf 164 C4
Esdaile Gdns. Upm 166 B2
Esdaile La. Hod 100 A3
Esher Ave. Romf 164 B3
Esk Way. Romf 155 F2
Eskley Gdns. S Ock 184 A4
Esmond Cl. Rain 174 A3
Essex Ave. Chelm 111 D4
Essex Cl. Basil 170 A3
Essex Cl. Romf 164 A4
Essex Gdns. Hornc 166 A3
Essex Gdns. Sta L H 187 D2
Essex Hill. Elm 11 D1
Essex Rd. Brain 66 A2
Essex Rd. Ching 139 F1
Essex Rd. Dag 173 E4
Essex Rd. Hod 100 B3
Essex Rd. Romf 164 A4
Essex Rd. W Thu 191 D4
Essex Rd. Woodf 152 A1
Essex Regiment Way. Broom 111 E4
Essex Regiment Way. Lit Wal 85 D1
Essex Regiment Way. Lit Wal 98 B3
Essex Way. Brent 158 B2
Estella Mead. Chelm 110 C4
Ethelburga Rd. Romf 157 D1
Ethelred Gdns. Runw 151 E1
Etheridge Green. Lou 141 E3
Etheridge Rd. Lou 141 E3
Etton Cl. Hornc 165 F1
Euclid Way. Ave 183 F1
Eugene Cl. Hornc 165 E4
Evans Cl. Stone 191 D1
Evansdale. Rain 173 F1
Evelyn Rd. Felst 75 E2
Evelyn Sharp Cl. Romf 165 E4
Evelyn Wlk. Brent 158 B2
Everard Rd. Basil 172 A4
Everest Rise. Bill 148 C1
Everitt Rd. Saff W 13 F1
Eversleigh Gdns. Upm 166 B2
Eversley Rd. Basil 172 B3
Eves Cres. Chelm 111 D3
Ewan Rd. Romf 156 C1
Ewanrigg Terr. Woodf 152 B2
Ewellhurst Rd. Woodf 152 C1
Exchange St. Romf 164 C3
Exchange Way. Chelm 111 D1
Exeter Cl. Basil 171 F4
Exeter Cl. Brain 66 A3
Exeter Rd. Dag 173 D3
Exeter Rd. Sprin 111 F3
Exley Cl. Ing 135 D2
Exmoor Cl. Chelm 110 B1
Exmoor Cl. Woodf 153 E1
Exmouth Rd. Grays 192 A4
Eyhurst Ave. Hornc 165 D1
Eynesham Way. Basil 163 D1
Eynsford Rd. Swan 191 E1
Eyre Cl. Romf 165 D4
Factory Rd. Grave 192 B1
Faggoters La. H Lav 105 D4
Faggots Yd. Brain 65 F3
Fagus Ave. Rain 174 B1
Fair Leas. Saff W 13 F2
Fair Mead. Basil 171 E4
Fairbank Cl. Ch Ong 118 C1
Faircross Ave. Romf 155 E2
Fairfax Ave. Basil 172 B4
Fairfax Mead. Sprin 111 F1
Fairfax Rd. Grays 185 D1
Fairfax Rd. Tilb 192 C3
Fairfield. Ing 135 E2
Fairfield Ave. Grays 185 E3
Fairfield Ave. Upm 166 B1
Fairfield Cl. Hornc 165 D2
Fairfield Rd. Brain 65 F1
Fairfield Rd. Brent 158 B4
Fairfield Rd. Ch Ong 118 C1
Fairfield Rd. Chelm 111 D2
Fairfield Rd. Epp 116 A1
Fairfield Rd. Hod 100 A4
Fairfield Rd. Woodf 152 A2
Fairfield Rise. Bill 148 C1
Fairford Cl. Romf 157 D2
Fairford Way. Romf 157 D2
Fairham Ave. S Ock 184 A3
Fairholme Ave. Romf 165 D4
Fairholme Gdns. Upm 166 C2
Fairhouse Ct. Basil 171 E3
Fairkytes Ave. Hornc 165 E2
Fairlands Ave. Lou 152 A4
Fairlawn Dr. Woodf 152 A2
Fairlawns Cl. Hornc 165 F2
Fairleigh Ave. Basil 172 B3
Fairleigh Rd. Basil 172 B3
Fairlight Ave. Woodf 152 A2
Fairlop Cl. Hornc 174 A3
Fairlop Gdns. Basil 171 E3
Fairlop Gdns. Woodf 153 E2
Fairlop Rd. Woodf 153 E1
Fairmead Rd. Wa Aby 140 A3
Fairmeadside. Lou 140 B2
Fairoak Gdns. Romf 155 F1
Fairstead. Basil 171 D3
Fairview. Bill 149 D1
Fairview Ave. Brent 147 F2
Fairview Ave. Rain 174 B1
Fairview Ave. Sta L H 179 E1
Fairview Chase. Sta L H 187 E4
Fairview Cl. Chig 153 F3
Fairview Dr. Chig 153 F3
Fairview Gdns. Woodf 152 A1
Fairview Rd. Basil 171 F3
Fairview Rd. Chig 153 F3
Fairway. Bis St 68 B3
Fairway. Grays 185 D3
Fairway. Gt Bad 124 B4
Fairway. Saw 77 F1
Fairway. Wick 163 E2
Fairway. Woodf 152 B3
Fairway The. Harl 103 D3
Fairway The. Upm 166 B2
Fairways. Wa Aby 126 C3
Fairy Hall La. Ray 65 D1
Fairycroft Rd. Saff W 13 F1
Falcon Ave. Grays 192 B4
Falcon Cl. Hav 7 E4
Falcon Cl. Saw 77 E1
Falcon Cl. Wa Aby 127 D3
Falcon Way. Basil 171 E2
Falcon Way. Chelm 124 A3
Falcon Way. Rain 174 A3
Falconer Rd. Chig 154 A3
Falconer Rd. Hav 7 E3
Falconers Park. Saw 77 E1
Falkenham End. Basil 171 E4
Falkenham Path. Basil 171 E4
Falkenham Rise. Basil 171 E4
Falkenham Row. Basil 171 E4
Falkirk Cl. Hornc 166 A2
Falkland Cl. Bore 112 C4
Falkner Cl. Stock 136 C2
Fallow Cl. Chig 153 F3
Fallowden La. Ash 14 C4
Falmouth Rd. Sprin 111 F3
Falstones. Basil 170 C3
Fambridge Dr. Wick 163 F3
Fambridge Rd. Dag 164 A2
Fanns Rise. Pur 183 D1
Fanshawe Cres. Hornc 165 E3
Fanshawe Rd. Grays 186 A2
Fanton Ave. Wick 163 F2
Faraday Cl. Brain 65 F1
Farm Cl. Brent 147 E1
Farm Cl. Dag 173 E3
Farm Cl. Lou 152 B4
Farm End. Wa Aby 139 F2
Farm Hill Rd. Wa Aby 126 B3
Farm Rd. Grays 185 F2
Farm Rd. Grays 187 E1
Farm Rd. Rain 174 B1
Farm Way. Hornc 174 B4
Farm Way. Lou 152 B3
Farmadine. Saff W 13 F1
Farmadine Gr. Saff W 13 F1
Farmbridge End Rd. G Ea 95 E2
Farmer Ct. Wa Aby 127 D3
Farnaby Way. Corr 179 E2
Farnes Ave. Wick 163 E4
Farnes Dr. Romf 156 B1
Farnham Cl. Saw 77 E1
Farnham Rd. Romf 156 B3
Farnley Rd. Ching 139 F1
Farnol Rd. Stone 190 A2
Farriers. Sta Ab 87 D3
Farriers Dr. Bill 149 D3
Farringdon Ave. Romf 156 B2
Farrow Gdns. Grays 185 E3
Farrow Rd. Chelm 123 F4
Farthing Centre The. Chelm 111 D1
Farthingale La. Wa Aby 127 D3
Fastnet Cl. Hav 7 E4
Fauners. Basil 171 D3
Faversham Ave. Ching 139 F1
Faversham Cl. Chig 154 A4
Fawkner Cl. Sprin 111 F1
Fawkon Wlk. Hod 100 A3
Fawn Rd. Chig 153 F3
Fawters Cl. Brent 147 E2
Faymore Gdns. S Ock 184 A4
Fearns Mead. Brent 158 B3
Feathers Hill. Hat B O 79 F3
Feenan Highway. Tilb 193 D3
Feering Dr. Basil 171 F3
Feering Green. Basil 171 F3
Feering Rd. Bill 149 E1
Feering Row. Basil 171 F3
Felhurst Cres. Dag 173 E4
Felicia Way. Grays 186 A1
Fell Rd. Bird 19 D4
Fellcroft. Basil 172 B3
Felmongers. Harl 90 A1
Felmores. Basil 172 A4
Fels Cl. Dag 164 A1
Fels Farm Ave. Dag 164 B1
Felstead Ave. Woodf 153 D1
Felstead Cl. Brent 147 E2
Felstead Rd. Lou 140 C1
Felstead Rd. Romf 155 E2
Felsted Rd. Bill 149 E1
Fen Cl. Brent 147 E3
Fen Cl. Horn H 177 F4
Fen La. Grays 177 F1
Fen La. Horn H 177 E4
Fen La. Upm 176 C4
Fencepiece Rd. Chig 153 E2
Fencepiece Rd. Woodf 153 E2
Fennels. Harl 102 B2
Fennes Rd. Brain 55 F1
Fentiman Way. Hornc 165 F2
Fenton Rd. Hav 7 D4
Fenton Way. Basil 169 F4
Ferguson Ave. Romf 156 B1
Ferguson Ct. Romf 156 B1
Fern Cl. Bill 149 D2
Fern Gr. Hav 6 C4
Fern Hill. Basil 170 B2
Fern Hill La. Harl 102 C2
Fernbank. Bill 148 C1
Fernbank. Lou 140 A1
Fernbank Ave. Hornc 174 B4
Ferndale Rd. Romf 155 E1
Fernden Way. Romf 164 A3
Ferndown. Hornc 165 F3
Fernhall La. Wa Aby 127 E4
Fernie Cl. Chig 154 A3
Fernie Rd. Brain 65 E1
Fernside. Lou 140 A1
Fernside Cl. Corr 180 A3
Ferro Rd. Rain 174 A1
Ferry La. Rain 182 A4
Ferry Rd. Tilb 193 D2
Feryby Rd. Grays 186 A2
Feryngs Cl. Harl 90 B2
Fesants Croft. Harl 90 A2
Fetherston Rd. Sta L H 179 E1
Field Cl. Abr 142 A3
Field Cl. Lou 152 B4
Field Gate La. Ugl 48 A2
Field Rd. Ave 183 E3
Field Way. Hod 87 E1
Fieldfare. Bill 161 E4
Fielding Ave. Tilb 193 E3
Fielding Way. Brent 147 E2
Fieldway. Basil 172 B2
Fieldway. Grays 185 D3
Fieldway. Sta Ab 87 D2
Fieldway. Wick 163 E2
Fiesta Dr. Rain 173 E1
Fifth Ave. Chelm 111 D3
Fifth Ave. Harl 89 E1
Fifth Ave. W Thu 191 D4
Finches Cl. Corr 180 B3
Finchingfield Ave. Woodf 152 B2
Finchingfield Rd. Stam 31 E4
Finchingfield Rd. Ste B 18 B3
Finchingfield Way. Wick 163 E3
Finchingfields. Kelv H 132 C1
Finchley Ave. Chelm 124 A4
Finchley Cl. Stone 190 A1
Finchley Rd. Grays 192 A4
Finchmoor. Harl 102 B3
Findon Gdns. Rain 182 A4
Fingrith Hall La. Bla 120 C1
Fingrith Hall La. H Ong 120 C3
Finucane Gdns. Rain 174 A3
Fir Park. Harl 102 A3
Fir Tree Cl. Romf 164 B4
Fir Tree Rise. Chelm 124 A3
Fir Tree Wlk. Dag 164 B1
Firbank Rd. Romf 155 D3
Firecrest Rd. Chelm 124 B3
Firecrest Rd. Gt Bad 124 B3
Firham Park Ave. Romf 157 D2
Firlands. Bis St 67 F3
Firle The. Basil 170 B2
Firmans. Basil 170 A2
Firs Dr. Lou 141 D4
Firs Dr. Writ 110 A1
Firs The. Brent 146 A2
Firs The. Grays 185 E3
Firs Wlk. Woodf 152 A3
Firsgrove Cres. Brent 158 A3
Firsgrove Rd. Brent 158 B3
First Ave. Basil 169 F2
First Ave. Bill 160 C4
First Ave. Chelm 111 D3
First Ave. Corr 179 E2
First Ave. Dag 173 D2
First Ave. Dodd 133 E3
First Ave. Harl 89 F1
First Ave. W Thu 191 D4
Fisher Cl. Hav 7 E4
Fisher Way. Brain 66 B2
Fishermen's Hill. Grave 192 A1
Fishers Cl. Ches 126 A3
Fishmarket St. Thax 40 A1
Fitzilian Ave. Romf 156 C1
Fitzpiers. Saff W 13 F1
Fitzroy Cl. Bill 149 D2
Fitzwalter Pl. Chelm 110 C2
Fitzwalter Rd. Bore 112 C4
Fitzwilliams Ct. Harl 90 C2
Five Acres. Harl 102 C3
Five Acres. Stan M 57 F4
Five Oaks La. Hav B 154 C3
Five Oaks La. Romf 154 C3
Flagstaff Rd. Wa Aby 126 A3
Flamingo Wlk. Rain 174 A3
Flanders Cl. Brain 65 F3
Flavian Cl. Hav 7 E4
Fleet Ave. Upm 166 B3
Fleet Cl. Upm 166 B3
Fleethall Gr. Grays 185 D3
Fleetway. Basil 171 F2
Fleming Cl. Brain 65 F1
Fleming Gdns. Romf 156 B1
Fleming Gdns. Tilb 193 E3
Flemings. Brent 158 B2
Fletcher Rd. Chig 153 F3
Fletchers. Basil 170 C2
Flint St. W Thu 191 D4
Flintwich Manor. Chelm 110 C4
Flitch Ind Est The. Gt Dun 72 B4
Flitch La. Gt Dun 72 C4
Florence Cl. Grays 191 F4
Florence Cl. Harl 103 E3
Florence Cl. Hornc 165 F1
Florence Rd. Basil 170 B3
Florence Way. Basil 170 A3
Flux's La. Epp 129 D3
Fobbing Farm Cl. Basil 171 D2
Fobbing Rd. Corr 180 B2
Fodderwick. Basil 171 D3
Fold Croft. Harl 89 D1
Fold The. Basil 171 D3
Folkes La. Upm 166 C4
Folly Mill La. Thax 51 D3
Folly View. Sta Ab 87 D2
Fontayne Ave. Chig 153 E3
Fontayne Ave. Rain 173 F3
Fontayne Ave. Romf 155 F1
Fonteyn Cl. Basil 170 B4
Fonteyne Gdns. Woodf 152 B1
Fontwell Park Gdn. Hornc 174 C4
Forbes Cl. Hornc 165 D2
Ford Cl. Basil 170 A3
Ford Cl. Rain 173 F3
Ford End. Woodf 152 A2
Ford La. Rain 173 F3
Ford Rd. Dag 173 D3
Ford Rd. Grave 192 A1
Fordham Cl. Hornc 166 A2
Fordhams Row. Grays 186 A4
Fordson Rd. Bore 112 A3
Fordwater Cl. Stur 8 A2
Fordyce Cl. Hornc 165 F2
Fore St. Bill 161 F1
Fore St. Harl 90 B2
Forebury Ave. Saw 77 F1
Forebury Cres. Saw 77 F1
Forebury The. Saw 77 F1
Forefield Green. Sprin 111 F4
Forelands Pl. Saw 77 F1
Foremark Cl. Chig 153 F2
Forest App. Ching 139 F1
Forest App. Woodf 152 A2
Forest Ave. Chig 153 D3
Forest Ave. Ching 139 F1
Forest Cl. Wa Aby 127 D1
Forest Cl. Woodf 152 A3
Forest Ct. Ching 139 F1
Forest Dr. Chelm 110 C1
Forest Dr. The B 128 C2
Forest Edge. Lou 152 B4
Forest Glade. Basil 169 F2
Forest Glade. Basil 170 A2
Forest Glade. N W Bas 116 C2
Forest Heights. Lou 152 A4
Forest House Fields. Chig 153 F3
Forest Ind Park. Chig 153 F1
Forest La. Chig 153 D3
Forest Rd. Chig 154 A2
Forest Rd. Lou 140 C3
Forest Rd. Romf 164 A4
Forest Rd. Woodf 152 A4
Forest Rd. Woodf 154 A2
Forest Side. Ching 139 F1
Forest Side. Lou 140 B1
Forest Side. The B 128 B3
Forest View. Ching 139 E1
Forest View Rd. Lou 140 B3
Forest Way. Lou 140 C3
Forest Way. Woodf 152 A3
Forester Ct. Bill 148 C2
Foresthall Rd. Birhr 57 F2
Forge Rd. Rain 173 E1
Forres Cl. Hod 100 A4
Forsythia Cl. Sprin 111 F4
Fort Rd. Tilb 193 E3
Fort William Rd. Basil 171 D1
Forth Rd. Upm 166 B3
Forties Cl. Hav 7 E4
Fortin Cl. S Ock 184 A3
Fortin Path. S Ock 184 A3
Fortin Way. S Ock 184 A3
Fortune Cl. Gt Le 86 A4
Fortunes The. Harl 102 C3
Foster St. Match 103 F3
Fosters Cl. Woodf 152 A1
Fosters Cl. Writ 109 F1
Fountain Farm. Harl 102 C3
Fountain Pl. Wa Aby 126 B3
Fountain Rd. G Ea 95 E2
Fountain Wlk. Grave 192 C1
Four Acres. Gt C 1 C2
Four Acres. Saff W 13 F1
Four Acres The. Saw 78 A1
Four Ash Hill. Bird 8 C1
Four Wants The. Ch Ong 119 D2
Fourth Ave. Basil 169 F2
Fourth Ave. Chelm 111 D3
Fourth Ave. Corr 179 F3
Fourth Ave. Harl 102 A4
Fourth Ave. Romf 164 B2
Fourth Ave. W Thu 191 D4
Fourways. Els 48 B1
Fowlmere Rd. Hey 10 A3
Fox Burrow Rd. Hav B 154 B3
Fox Burrows La. Writ 110 A1
Fox Cl. Romf 155 D3
Fox Cres. Chelm 110 C2
Fox Hatch. Kelv H 132 C1
Fox's Rd. Ashe 9 F1
Foxborough Chase. Stock 137 D3
Foxdells La. Bis St 56 C1
Foxes Gr. Brent 148 B1
Foxes Green. Grays 186 A2
Foxfield Dr. Corr 179 F3
Foxglove Rd. S Ock 184 B4
Foxglove Way. Sprin 111 F3
Foxgloves The. Bill 148 C2
Foxhall Rd. Upm 175 E4
Foxhatch. Wick 163 F3
Foxhills Rd. Grays 185 E3
Foxholes Rd. Gt Bad 124 C3
Foxhunter Wlk. Bill 149 D3
Foxlands Cres. Dag 173 E4
Foxlands Rd. Dag 173 E4
Foxleigh. Bill 161 D4
Foxleigh Cl. Bill 161 D4
Foxley Cl. Lou 141 D4
Foxley Dri. Bis St 68 A4
Foxton Rd. Grays 191 E4
Foxton Rd. Hod 100 A3
Foyle Dr. S Ock 184 A4
Foys Wlk. Bill 161 E4
Frambury La. New 36 C4
Frame The. Basil 170 B4
Frampton Rd. Basil 163 D1
Frampton Rd. Epp 116 C3
Frances Gdns. S Ock 183 F4
Francis Cl. Hav 6 C4
Francis Cl. Horn H 178 C2
Francis Rd. Brain 65 E1
Francombe Gdns. Romf 165 D3
Frankland Cl. Woodf 152 B3
Franklin Rd. Hornc 174 B3
Franklins Way. Wick 163 F4
Franklyn Gdns. Chig 153 E2
Franmil Rd. Hornc 165 D2
Fraser Cl. Basil 169 F3
Fraser Cl. Chelm 124 B4
Fraser Cl. Romf 164 C2
Frating Cres. Woodf 152 A2
Frederica Rd. Ching 139 E1
Frederick Rd. Rain 173 F2
Fredrick Andrews Ct. Grays 192 B4
Freeborne Gdns. Rain 174 A3

Freeman Ct. Corr 179 F2
Freeman Way. Hornc 165 F3
Freemantle Rd. Woodf 153 E1
Freewood La. Elm 11 D2
Fremnells The. Basil 171 E4
French's Cl. Sta Ab 87 D2
Freshfields Ave. Upm 175 E4
Freshwater Dr. Basil 171 F2
Freshwaters. Harl 89 F1
Freshwell Gdns. Horn H 168 B3
Freshwell Gdns. Saff W 13 E1
Freshwell St. Saff W 13 E1
Frettons. Basil 171 F3
Friar's Ave. Brent 147 D1
Friar's Cl. Brent 147 D1
Friars Gate Cl. Woodf 152 A3
Friars La. Brain 66 A2
Friars La. Hat B O 79 E1
Friars The. Chig 153 F3
Friars Wlk. Chelm 111 D1
Friars Wood. Bis St 68 B4
Friarscroft. Hod 100 A2
Friary La. Woodf 152 A3
Friedburg Ave. Bis St 67 E2
Friends Wlk. Saff W 25 E4
Friern Gdns. Wick 163 D4
Friern Pl. Wick 163 D3
Friern Wlk. Wick 163 D4
Frimley Ave. Hornc 166 A2
Frinton Rd. Romf 155 D2
Friston Path. Chig 153 F3
Frithwood Cl. Bill 160 C4
Frithwood La. Bill 160 C4
Frizlands La. Dag 164 A1
Frobisher Way. Brain 66 B2
Froden Brook. Bill 161 E3
Froden Cl. Bill 161 E4
Froden Ct. Bill 161 E3
Frog St. Kelv H 145 F4
Frogge St. Hinx 1 A2
Frome. Grays 187 E1
Front La. Upm 166 C2
Fry Cl. Romf 155 D2
Fryerning La. Ing 135 D2
Fryth The. Basil 171 F4
Fulbrook La. S Ock 183 F3
Fulfen Way. Saff W 25 E4
Fullarton Cres. S Ock 183 F4
Fuller Ct. Bis St 68 A4
Fuller's La. Romf 155 E2
Fullers Cl. Romf 155 E2
Fullers Cl. Wa Aby 127 D3
Fullers Mead. Harl 103 E4
Fullwell Ave. Woodf 153 D1
Fulmar Rd. Rain 174 A3
Fulton Cres. Bis St 68 B4
Fulwich Rd. Stone 190 A1
Furlong Way. Sta Ab 87 D3
Furlongs. Basil 171 E2
Furlongs The. Ing 135 D2
Furness Cl. Grays 186 A1
Furness Way. Hornc 174 A4
Furrowfelde. Basil 171 D2
Further Meadow. Writ 123 D4
Furze Farm Cl. Romf 154 C1
Furze Glade. Basil 170 A3
Furze La. S Han 150 A4
Furze La. Stock 137 D1
Fusedale Way. S Ock 183 F3
Fyfield Ave. Wick 163 E3
Fyfield Cl. Horn H 168 B3
Fyfield Rd. Ch Ong 119 D3
Fyfield Rd. More 105 F2
Fyfield Rd. Rain 173 F2
Fyfield Rd. Will 107 E2
Fyfield Rd. Woodf 152 B2
Fyfields. Basil 172 B4

Gabion Ave. W Thu 183 E1
Gablefields. Sand 125 E3
Gables The. Basil 172 A4
Gabriel Cl. Romf 155 E2
Gaces Acre. New 25 D1
Gadsden Cl. Upm 166 C3
Gaiger Cl. Sprin 111 E4
Gainsborough Ave. Tilb 193 D3
Gainsborough Cl. Bill 149 D1
Gainsborough Cres. Sprin 111 F2
Gainsborough Rd. Rain 174 A2
Gainsborough Rd. Woodf 152 C2
Gainsford End Rd. Topp 32 A3
Gainsthorpe Rd. Bobb 118 B4
Gales Way. Woodf 152 C2
Galey Green. S Ock 184 A4
Gall End La. Stan M 57 F4
Galleon Bvd. Stone 190 B2
Galleons Hill. Rox 109 E3
Galley Green. Hod 87 D1
Galley Hill Rd. Swan 191 F1
Galley Hill Trad Est. Swan 191 F1
Galleydene Ave. Chelm 124 B2
Galleyhill Rd. Wa Aby 126 C4
Galleywood Cres. Romf 155 E2
Galleywood Rd. Chelm 124 A3
Galleywood Rd. Gt Bad 124 C3
Gallops The. Basil 170 A3
Galloway Cl. Bis St 67 F4
Galloway Rd. Bis St 56 C1
Gallows Green Rd. Lind 51 F1
Gallows Hill. Saff W 25 E4
Galsworthy Rd. Tilb 193 E3
Gambleside. Basil 171 F2
Ganels Cl. Bill 161 E4
Ganels Rd. Bill 161 E4
Gangies Hill. H Wy 77 D2
Ganley Cl. Bill 149 D1
Gannet Cl. Hav 7 E4
Gant Ct. Wa Aby 126 C3
Gap The. Arkes 23 F1
Garbutt Rd. Upm 166 B1
Garden Fields. Sta R 131 F3
Garden Fields. Steb 62 B3
Garden Terrace Rd. Harl 90 B2
Garden Way. Lou 128 A1
Gardeners. Gt Bad 124 B3
Gardens The. Dodd 133 D2
Gardiners Cl. Basil 162 B1
Gardiners La N. Bill 162 C2
Gardiners La S. Basil 162 C1
Gardiners Way. Basil 162 B1
Gardner Ave. Corr 180 A2
Garfield Rd. Ching 139 E1
Garland Way. Hornc 165 F4
Garnetts. Take 70 A4
Garnetts Bungalows. Felst 74 B3
Garnetts La. Felst 74 B3
Garnon Mead. Epp 116 B2
Garrettlands. Sand 125 F3
Garrick St. Grave 193 D1
Garron La. S Ock 183 F4
Garry Cl. Romf 155 F2
Garry Way. Romf 155 F2
Garth Rd. S Ock 176 B1
Gascoigne Way. Bill 149 E1
Gascoyne Cl. Romf 156 B2
Gasson Rd. Swan 191 F1
Gate Lodge Sq. Bill 161 F1
Gate Lodge Way. Bill 161 F1
Gatehope Dr. S Ock 183 F4
Gatehouse Villas. Gt Dun 72 C4
Gateway. Basil 171 D3
Gatwick Cl. Bis St 57 D1
Gatwick View. Bill 161 D4
Gatwick Way. Hornc 174 C4
Gauden Rd. Brain 65 F4
Gavenny Path. S Ock 183 F4
Gawlers. Berd 46 A4
Gay Bowers. Basil 171 E4
Gay Gdns. Dag 173 E4
Gay Links. Basil 171 D4
Gaylor Rd. Tilb 192 C3
Gaynes Ct. Upm 175 D4
Gaynes Hill Rd. Woodf 152 C2
Gaynes Park Rd. Upm 175 D4
Gaynes Rd. Upm 166 A1
Gaynesford. Basil 170 C2
Gaywood. Basil 170 A4
Geary Ct. Brent 146 B1
Geddings Rd. Hod 100 A3
Geerings The. Corr 180 A2
Geisthorp Ct. Wa Aby 127 D3
Gelsthorpe Rd. Romf 155 D2
Generals La. Bore 99 D1
Gentry Cl. Sta L H 179 E1
Geoffrey Ave. Romf 157 D2
George Avey Croft. N W Bas 117 D3
George Gent Cl. Ste B 18 A3
George La. Woodf 152 A1
George Rd. Brain 65 E1
George St. Chelm 111 D1
George St. Grays 192 A4
George St. Romf 164 C3
George St. Saff W 13 E1
George Yd. Brain 65 F2
Georges Dr. Brent 145 F2
Gepps Cl. H Ea 82 B1
Gerard Ave. Bis St 67 F2
Gerard Gdns. Rain 173 F2
Gernon Cl. Broom 98 A2
Gernon Cl. Rain 174 B2
Gernons. Basil 170 C2
Gerpins La. Upm 175 D3
Gerrard Cres. Brent 158 B4
Ghyllgrove. Basil 171 D4
Gibbons Ct. Gt Dun 61 E1
Gibbs Croft. Harl 102 C2
Gibbs Field. Bis St 67 E3
Gibcracks. Basil 171 F3
Gibraltar Cl. Brent 158 B2
Gibson Cl. N W Bas 117 E3
Gibson Cl. Saff W 13 E1
Gibson Gdns. Saff W 13 E1
Gibson Way. Saff W 13 E1
Gidea Ave. Romf 165 D4
Gidea Cl. Romf 165 D4
Gidea Cl. S Ock 176 B2
Gideons Way. Corr 179 F2
Giffins Cl. Brain 65 F1
Gifford Green. Basil 172 A3
Gifford Pl. Brent 158 B3
Giffords Cross Ave. Corr 180 A2
Giffords Cross Rd. Corr 180 A2
Giffordside. Grays 186 A1
Gilbert Cl. Swan 191 E1
Gilbert Dr. Basil 170 A3
Gilbert Rd. Romf 164 C4
Gilbert Way. Brain 66 B3
Gilbey Ave. Bis St 68 A3
Gilbey Cres. Stan M 57 F4
Gilbey Green. New 24 C1
Gilchrist Way. Brain 65 F2
Gilda Terr. Brain 65 D1
Gildbourne Cl. Corr 180 B3
Gilden Cl. Harl 90 C2
Gilden Way. Harl 90 C2
Gilders. Saw 77 E1
Giles Cl. Rain 174 B2
Gillam Way. Rain 174 A3
Gillian Cres. Romf 156 B1
Gilmore Way. Gt Bad 125 D3
Gilmour Rise. Bill 148 C1
Gilpin Way. Bl Not 76 B4
Gilpin's Gallop. Sta Ab 87 D2
Gilroy Cl. Rain 173 F3
Gilsland. Wa Aby 126 C2
Gilson Cl. Sprin 111 F1
Gilwell Cl. Ching 139 D3
Ginns Rd. St Pel 45 E3
Gippeswyck. Basil 171 E4
Gipping Cl. Hav 6 C3
Gipsy La. Grays 192 B4
Gipsy La. Stan M 57 E2
Girton Rd. Hav 7 D4
Gisborne Gdns. Rain 173 F1
Glade The. Basil 171 E2
Glade The. Brent 147 D1
Glade The. Upm 175 E4
Glade The. Woodf 152 A4
Glade The. Woodf 152 C1
Gladeway The. Wa Aby 126 B3
Gladstone Ct. Chelm 111 D1
Gladstone Rd. Hod 100 A4
Gladstone Rd. Lou 140 B1
Gladwyns. Basil 170 C4
Glamis Dr. Hornc 165 F2
Glanmead. Brent 146 C1
Glanmire. Bill 149 E3
Glanthams Cl. Brent 158 C4
Glanthams Rd. Brent 158 C4
Glanville Dr. Hornc 165 F2
Glastonbury Ave. Woodf 152 B2
Glebe Ave. Brain 65 F3
Glebe Ave. Woodf 152 A2
Glebe Cres. Broom 98 A1
Glebe Ct. Bis St 68 A4
Glebe End. Els 48 B1
Glebe Field. Basil 171 E4
Glebe Gdns. Brent 159 E2
Glebe La. Lit Ea 60 C3
Glebe Rd. Ch Ong 118 C1
Glebe Rd. Chelm 111 D2
Glebe Rd. Dag 173 D3
Glebe Rd. Rain 174 B1
Glebe Rd. Wick 150 C1
Glebe Rd. Wick 163 F4
Glebe The. Mag Lav 104 B3
Glebe The. Saff W 25 F4
Glebe Way. Hornc 165 F2
Glebelands. Chig 154 A4
Glebelands. Harl 89 F2
Glebelands Ave. Woodf 152 A1
Glebeway. Woodf 152 B3
Glen Cres. Woodf 152 A2
Glen Faba Rd. Roy 100 C3
Glen Hazel. Bla 133 E2
Glen Rd. Basil 171 F2
Glen Rise. Woodf 152 A2
Glen The. Corr 179 F2
Glen The. Rain 174 B1
Glencoe Dr. Dag 173 D4
Glencree. Bill 149 E3
Glendale Cl. Brent 146 C1
Glendower Rd. Ching 139 E1
Gleneagles Cl. Romf 156 C2
Glenester Cl. Hod 87 D1
Glenfield Rd. Corr 180 A3
Glengall Rd. Woodf 152 A2
Glenmere. Basil 171 E1
Glenmire Terr. Sta Ab 87 E2
Glenside. Bill 149 E1
Glenside. Chig 153 D2
Glenton Cl. Romf 155 F2
Glenton Way. Romf 155 F2
Glenwood Ave. Rain 174 A1
Glenwood Dr. Romf 165 D4
Globe Cres. Far 56 B3
Globe Rd. Hornc 165 D3
Globe Rd. Woodf 152 B2
Gloucester Ave. Chelm 124 B3
Gloucester Ave. Grays 185 E2
Gloucester Ave. Grays 187 E1
Gloucester Ave. Hornc 166 A4
Gloucester Cl. S Ock 176 B1
Gloucester Cres. Chelm 111 D3
Gloucester Ct. Tilb 192 C3
Gloucester Gdns. Brain 66 A2
Gloucester Pl. Bill 149 D3
Gloucester Rd. Brent 146 A2
Gloucester Rd. Hav 6 C3
Gloucester Rd. Romf 164 C3
Glovers Field. Kelv H 132 C1
Glovers La. N W Bas 103 F2
Goat Hall La. Chelm 124 A2
Goatsmoor La. S Han 149 F3
Gobions. Basil 171 D2
Gobions Ave. Romf 155 E2
Goddard Rd. Grays 185 D3
Goddard Way. Saff W 13 F2
Goddard Way. Sprin 111 F1
Godfrey Way. Gt Dun 61 E1
Godfrey's Mews. Chelm 111 D1
Godlings Way. Brain 65 F1
Godman Rd. Grays 186 A2
Godsafe. Harl 90 C2
Godwin Cl. Wa Aby 139 E4
Gold Cl. Els 48 A1
Gold St. Saff W 13 E1
Goldcrest Dr. Bill 149 E1
Golden La. Rad 16 A1
Goldenacres. Sprin 111 F4
Goldhanger Cross. Basil 171 F4
Goldhaze Cl. Woodf 152 B2
Golding Cres. Corr 179 F2
Golding Thoroughfare. Sprin 111 F2
Golding's Hill. Lou 127 F1
Goldingham Ave. Lou 141 E4
Goldings. Bis St 68 A4
Goldings Cres. Basil 171 F2
Goldings Rd. Lou 141 D4
Goldings Rise. Lou 141 D4
Goldington Cres. Bill 148 C3
Goldlay Ave. Chelm 111 E1
Goldlay Gdns. Chelm 111 E1
Goldlay Rd. Chelm 111 E1
Goldsmith. Grays 191 F4
Goldsmith Ave. Romf 164 A2
Goldsmiths Ave. Corr 180 A2
Goodliffe Park. Birhr 57 D1
Goodmans La. Gt Le 85 F2
Goodmayes Wlk. Wick 163 E3
Goodview Rd. Bill 162 A1
Goodwin Stile. Bis St 67 E3
Goodwins Cl. Litt 12 C2
Goodwood Ave. Brent 147 F2
Goodwood Ave. Hornc 174 C4
Goodwood Cl. Hod 100 A4
Goose La. Gt Ha 78 C4
Goose La. Lit Hal 79 D4
Gooshays Dr. Romf 156 C2
Gooshays Gdns. Romf 156 C2
Gordon Ave. Hornc 164 C1
Gordon Cl. Bill 148 C2
Gordon Pl. Grave 193 E1
Gordon Rd. Basil 171 E3
Gordon Rd. Brent 147 D1
Gordon Rd. Chelm 124 A3
Gordon Rd. Ching 139 F1
Gordon Rd. Corr 179 F2
Gordon Rd. Grave 192 C1
Gordon Rd. Grays 185 F2
Gordon Rd. Horn H 178 C2
Gordon Rd. Wa Aby 126 A3
Gordon Rd. Woodf 152 A1
Gordons. Basil 172 A3
Gore La. Brain 65 D1
Gore The. Basil 171 D4
Gorfield Rd. Take 59 D2
Goring Cl. Romf 155 E1
Goring Rd. Dag 173 E3
Gorseway. Romf 164 C2
Gosfield Rd. Dag 164 A1
Goshawk Dr. Chelm 124 A3
Gosport Dr. Hornc 174 B3
Gossetts The. Mar Rod 94 C2
Gould Cl. More 105 E1
Goulton Rd. Broom 98 A1
Gourney Gr. Grays 185 D3
Government Row. Enf 126 A1
Gowers Ave. Gt Bad 124 C3
Gowers La. Grays 185 F2
Gowers The. Harl 90 A1
Grace Cl. Chig 153 F2
Grace Gdns. Bis St 67 F2
Grafton Pl. Sprin 112 A2
Graham Cl. Bill 149 E3
Graham Cl. Brent 147 E2
Graham Cl. Corr 179 F2
Grailands. Bis St 67 E4
Grampian Gr. Chelm 110 B3
Granary Meadow. Dodd 133 F2
Granary The. Roy 88 A1
Granby Rd. Grave 192 B1
Grandville Cl. Bill 148 C3
Grange Ave. Wick 163 E3
Grange Ave. Woodf 152 A2
Grange Cl. Brent 159 E3
Grange Cl. Woodf 152 A2
Grange Cres. Chig 153 E3
Grange Ct. Lou 140 B2
Grange Ct. Wa Aby 126 B3
Grange La. Lit Dun 73 E4
Grange La. Roy 101 E4
Grange Park. Bis St 56 C1
Grange Rd. Ave 183 E3
Grange Rd. Basil 172 C4
Grange Rd. Bill 161 E4
Grange Rd. Bis St 68 A4
Grange Rd. Grays 192 A4
Grange Rd. Hinx 11 D4
Grange Rd. Ple 83 F1
Grange Rd. Romf 156 A2
Grange Rd. Runw 151 E1
Granger Way. Hornc 165 D3
Grangeside. Bis St 57 D1
Grangeway. Woodf 152 B3
Grangewood Ave. Grays 185 F2
Grangewood Ave. Rain 174 B1
Grangewood Cl. Brent 159 D4
Granites Chase. Bill 161 F3
Granta Cl. GT C 1 B1
Grantham Way. Grays 185 D3
Granton Ave. Upm 165 F1
Granville Gdns. Hod 87 D1
Granville Rd. Epp 116 A1
Granville Rd. Woodf 152 A1
Grapnells. Basil 171 F2
Grasmere Cl. Bl Not 76 B3
Grasmere Cl. Lou 140 C4
Grassmere Rd. Hornc 165 F4
Gratmore Green. Basil 171 F2
Gravel Cl. Chig 154 A4
Gravel Hill. Wa Aby 127 D1
Gravel La. Chig 142 A1
Gravelly La. Rox 109 E2
Gray Ave. Dag 164 A2
Gray Gdns. Rain 174 A3
Gray's La. Weth 43 F2
Graylands. The B 128 C1
Grays Ave. Basil 170 B1
Grays Ct. Bis St 67 F4
Grays End Cl. Grays 185 D2
Grays Town Centre. Grays 192 A4
Grays Wlk. Brent 147 E1
Great Berry Farm Chase. Basil 170 A2
Great Berry La. Basil 170 A3
Great Brays. Harl 103 D4
Great Canfield Rd. Gt Can 70 B3
Great Cob. Sprin 111 F3
Great Cullings. Romf 164 C1
Great Eastern Rd. Brent 158 B3
Great Fox Meadow. Kelv H 132 C1
Great Gardens Rd. Hornc 165 E3
Great Godfreys. Rox 109 F1
Great Gregorie. Basil 170 C3
Great Gregories La. The B 128 C3
Great Hadham Rd. Bis St 67 E3
Great Knightleys. Basil 170 C3
Great Lawn. Ch Ong 119 D2
Great Leighs Way. Basil 163 E1
Great Leylands. Harl 103 D4
Great Meadow. Lo Naz 100 A1
Great Mistley. Basil 171 E3
Great Nelmes Chase. Hornc 165 F3
Great Oaks. Basil 171 D3
Great Oaks. Brent 147 D2
Great Oaks. Chig 153 E3
Great Owl Rd. Chig 153 D4
Great Oxcroft. Basil 170 A3
Great Plumtree. Harl 89 F1
Great Ranton. Basil 172 B4
Great Ropers La. Brent 158 A2
Great Spenders. Basil 171 E4
Great Sq. Brain 65 F2
Great Warley St. Brent 158 A1
Great Yeldham Rd. Topp 32 B4
Greathouse Chase. Corr 180 B3
Grebe Cres. W Thu 184 A1
Greding Wlk. Brent 159 D4
Green Cl. Ep Gr 115 D4
Green Cl. Sprin 111 E2
Green Cl. Writ 110 A1
Green Glade. The B 128 C1
Green Glades. Hornc 166 A3
Green La. Bill 161 D1
Green La. Brent 158 A2
Green La. Grays 185 E4
Green La. Kelv H 145 E4
Green La. Lo Naz 113 D4
Green La. Match 104 A4
Green La. Rox 109 E3
Green La. Wa Aby 139 E3
Green Lane. Chig 153 E4
Green Manor Way. Grave 191 F2
Green Shaw. Brent 146 A1
Green St. Gt Can 70 C1
Green St. Ing 134 B2
Green The. Bis St 67 F2
Green The. Bla 133 F4
Green The. Chelm 110 C2
Green The. Ching 139 E1
Green The. Cla 9 E2
Green The. Grays 186 A4
Green The. Grays 193 F4
Green The. S Ock 176 B2
Green The. Saff W 13 E2
Green The. Sta L H 179 E1
Green The. The B 128 B2
Green The. Wa Aby 126 B3
Green The. Woodf 152 A3
Green The. Writ 110 A1
Green Trees. Epp 129 D4
Green Wlk. Ch Ong 119 D1
Green Wlk. Woodf 152 C2
Green Wlk The. Ching 139 E1
Greenacre La. Stock 149 F4
Greenacres. Ep Gr 115 F2
Greenacres Cl. Rain 174 C1
Greenbank Cl. Romf 156 B4
Greenbanks. Upm 166 C1
Greenfield St. Wa Aby 126 B3
Greenfields. Bill 161 D4
Greenfields. Chelm 124 B1
Greenfields. Lou 141 D3
Greenfields. Stan M 57 F4
Greenfields Cl. Bill 161 D4

Greenfields Cl. Lou 141 D3
Greenfields Way. Brent 158 B2
Greenfields Way. Hav 6 C3
Greenhill. Lou 140 B1
Greenhill Park. Bis St 67 E3
Greenhills. Harl 102 C4
Greenleas. Wa Aby 126 C3
Greenock Way. Romf 155 F2
Greens Cl The. Lou 141 D4
Greens Farm La. Bill 161 E4
Greenstead. Saw 77 F1
Greenstead Ave. Woodf 152 B2
Greenstead Cl. Brent 147 F1
Greenstead Cl. Woodf 152 B2
Greenstead Gdns. Woodf 152 B2
Greensted Rd. Ch Ong 118 B1
Greensted Rd. Lou 140 C1
Greensted The. Basil 171 F3
Greenway. Bill 149 E1
Greenway. Bis St 68 B3
Greenway. Brent 147 D1
Greenway. Romf 157 D2
Greenway. Woodf 152 B3
Greenway Gdns. Bl Not 76 B4
Greenway The. Runw 151 E2
Greenways. Chelm 111 D3
Greenways. Saff W 25 F4
Greenwood Ave. Dag 173 D4
Greenwood Cl. Hav 6 C4
Greenwood Gdns. Woodf 153 E2
Greenwood Rd. Chig 154 A3
Greenyard. Wa Aby 126 B3
Grenfell Ave. Hornc 164 C2
Grennan Cl. Brent 159 E2
Grenville Gdns. Woodf 152 B2
Grenville Rd. Brain 65 F1
Gresham Ct. Brent 158 B4
Gresham Rd. Brent 158 B4
Grey Hollow. Quen 47 E4
Grey Ladys. Chelm 124 A1
Grey Towers Ave. Hornc 165 E2
Grey Towers Gdns. Hornc 165 E2
Greyfriars. Brent 147 D1
Greygoose Park. Harl 102 A3
Greyhound La. Grays 186 A2
Greystone Gdns. Woodf 153 E1
Gridiron Pl. Upm 166 A1
Griffin Ave. Upm 166 C3
Griffin's Wood Cotts. Ep Gr 128 B4
Griffins The. Grays 185 D2
Grimshaw Way. Romf 164 C3
Grimston Rd. Basil 162 C1
Grimstone Cl. Romf 155 D2
Grinstead La. L Hal 78 B3
Grosvenor Cl. Gt Bad 124 B4
Grosvenor Cl. Lou 141 D4
Grosvenor Dr. Hornc 165 E2
Grosvenor Dr. Lou 141 E4
Grosvenor Gdns. Bill 149 D2
Grosvenor Gdns. Upm 166 B2
Grosvenor Gdns. Woodf 152 A2
Grosvenor Path. Lou 141 E4
Grosvenor Rd. Grays 186 B4
Grosvenor Rd. Romf 164 B2
Grove Ave. Basil 170 A2
Grove Ct. Wa Aby 126 A3
Grove Gdns. Dag 164 B1
Grove Hill. Stan M 57 F4
Grove Hill. Woodf 152 A1
Grove La. Chig 153 F4
Grove La. Epp 116 A1
Grove Park Rd. Rain 174 A2
Grove Pl. Bis St 67 F4
Grove Rd. Bill 148 C1
Grove Rd. Chelm 111 D1
Grove Rd. Grave 192 A1
Grove Rd. Grays 192 B4
Grove Rd. Sta L H 187 E4
Grove Rd. Woodf 152 A1
Grove The. Bill 149 E2
Grove The. Brent 157 F3
Grove The. Grave 193 E1
Grove The. Gt Ha 68 C2
Grove The. Swan 191 F1
Grove The. Upm 175 D4
Grove Villas. Gt Sal 64 A4
Grovelands Rd. Wick 163 E3
Grovelands Way. Grays 184 C1
Grover Wlk. Corr 179 F2
Grovesnor Cl. Bis St 67 E2
Grubb's Hill. Wa Aby 113 E1
Guardian Cl. Hornc 165 D2
Guardsman Cl. Brent 158 B3
Gubbins La. Romf 156 C1
Guelph's La. Thax 40 A2
Guernsey Gdns. Runw 151 E1
Guernsey Way. Brain 65 E1
Guildford Gdns. Romf 156 C2
Guildford Rd. Romf 156 C2
Guildhall Way. Ash 14 C4
Guilfords. Harl 90 B3
Gull Wlk. Rain 174 A3
Gumley Rd. Grays 191 F4
Gun Hill. Tilb 193 E4
Gun Hill Pl. Basil 171 E3
Gunn Rd. Swan 191 F1
Gutters La. Chelm 111 D4
Guysfield Cl. Rain 174 A2
Guysfield Dr. Rain 174 A2
Gwyn Cl. Bore 99 F1
Gwynne Park Ave. Woodf 152 C2

Habgood Rd. Lou 140 C3
Hacton Dr. Hornc 174 C4
Hacton La. Hornc 165 F1
Hadfield Rd. Sta L H 179 E1
Hadham Rd. Bis St 67 E4
Hadleigh Ct. Saff W 13 F1
Hadrian Cl. Hav 7 E4
Haggers Cl. Gt C 1 B1
Haig Ct. Chelm 111 D1
Haig Rd. Grays 186 A2
Hailes Wood. Els 48 B1
Hailey Ave. Hod 87 D1
Hailsham Cl. Romf 156 B3
Hailsham Gdns. Romf 156 B3
Hailsham Rd. Romf 156 B3
Hainault Gr. Chelm 110 C1
Hainault Gr. Chig 153 E3
Hainault Rd. Chig 153 E3
Hainault Rd. Romf 154 A1
Hainault Rd. Romf 164 B4
Halchfields. Gt Wal 97 F4
Halcyon Way. Hornc 165 F2
Haldon Cl. Chig 153 F3
Hale End. Romf 156 A2
Halesworth Cl. Romf 156 C2
Halesworth Rd. Romf 156 C2
Half Acres. Bis St 67 F4
Half Moon La. Epp 128 C4
Halfhides. Wa Aby 126 B3
Halfway Ct. Pur 183 D1
Halidon Rise. Romf 157 D2
Hall Ave. Ave 183 E3
Hall Chase. H Ea 83 F4
Hall Cl. Corr 179 F2
Hall Cl. Gt Bad 125 D3
Hall Cl. Hen 48 C3
Hall Cres. Ave 183 E2
Hall Green La. Brent 147 E1
Hall La. Br Pel 33 D3
Hall La. Brent 146 C2
Hall La. Ing 135 E1
Hall La. Mtssg 148 A4
Hall La. Ridge 20 A3
Hall La. S Ock 176 B2
Hall La. Sand 125 E3
Hall La. Stock 137 E3
Hall La. Upm 166 B3
Hall Park Rd. Upm 175 E4
Hall Rd. Ave 183 E2
Hall Rd. Els 58 C4
Hall Rd. Pan 65 D3
Hall Rd. Romf 165 D4
Hall St. Chelm 111 D1
Hall Terr. Ave 183 E2
Hallam Cl. Dodd 133 D2
Hallam Ct. Bill 148 C2
Halling Hill. Harl 89 F1
Hallingbury Cl. L Hal 68 A1
Hallingbury Rd. Bis St 68 A2
Hallingbury Rd. Saw 78 A2
Hallmores. Hod 100 A2
Hallwood Cres. Brent 146 C1
Halstead Ct. Wick 163 E3
Halstead Way. Brent 147 E2
Halstow Way. Basil 172 B3
Halt Dr. Sta L H 187 D2
Halton Rd. Grays 186 B2
Hamble La. S Ock 183 F4
Hambro Rd. Brent 158 B4
Hamden Cres. Dag 164 A1
Hamel Way. Widd 37 E2
Hamerton Rd. Grave 192 A1
Hamilton Ave. Hod 100 A4
Hamilton Ave. Romf 155 E1
Hamilton Cres. Brent 158 B3
Hamilton Dr. Romf 156 C1
Hamilton Mews. Saff W 13 F1
Hamilton Rd. Basil 172 C4
Hamilton Rd. Romf 165 D3
Hamilton Rd. Take 70 C4
Hamlet Cl. Romf 155 D2
Hamlet Hill. Roy 101 D2
Hamlet Rd. Chelm 111 D1
Hamlet Rd. Hav 7 D4
Hamlet Rd. Romf 155 D2
Hammarskjold Rd. Harl 89 E1
Hammonds La. Bill 161 E4
Hammonds La. Brent 158 A2
Hammonds Rd. Hat B O 80 A3
Hammonds Rd. Lit Bad 112 C2
Hammonds Rd. Sand 112 C2
Hampden Cl. N W Bas 117 D2
Hampden Cres. Brent 158 B3
Hampden Rd. Grays 185 D1
Hampden Rd. Romf 155 D2
Hampit Rd. Arkes 23 E1
Hampshire Gdns. Sta L H 187 D2
Hampshire Rd. Hornc 166 A4
Hampton Mead. Lou 141 D3
Hampton Rd. Gt Bad 124 C3
Hamstel Rd. Harl 89 E1
Hanbury Rd. Chelm 123 F4
Hance La. Ray 64 C1
Hand La. Saw 77 E1
Handel Cres. Tilb 193 D4
Handley Green. Basil 170 B3
Hanford Rd. Ave 183 E3
Hanging Hill. Brent 147 E1
Hanging Hill La. Brent 147 E1
Hannards Way. Chig 154 A3
Hanover Cl. Basil 171 F3
Hanover Ct. Hod 100 A4
Hanover Dr. Basil 171 F3
Hanover Gdns. Woodf 153 E2
Hanover Pl. Saff W 13 E1
Hansells Mead. Roy 101 D4
Hanson Cl. Lou 141 E4
Hanson Dr. Lou 141 E4
Hanson Gr. Lou 141 E4
Harberts Rd. Harl 102 A4
Harbourer Cl. Chig 154 A3
Harbourer Rd. Chig 154 A3
Hardie Rd. Dag 164 B1
Hardie Rd. Sta L H 179 E1
Harding Rd. Grays 186 A2
Harding's Elms Rd. Bill 162 A2
Harding's La. Ing 135 D4
Hardley Cres. Hornc 165 E4
Hardwick Rd. Hav 7 D4
Hardy Gr. Stone 190 A2
Hare Hall La. Romf 165 D4
Hare St. Harl 102 A4
Harebel Way. Romf 156 B2
Harebell Cl. Bill 148 C2
Harefield. Harl 90 A1
Hares Chase. Bill 148 C2
Haresfield Rd. Dag 173 D3
Harewood Dr. Woodf 152 C1
Harewood Hill. The B 128 C2
Harewood Rd. Brent 146 A2
Harewood Rd. Chelm 110 C1
Harford Cl. Ching 139 D1
Harford Rd. Ching 139 D1
Hargrave Cl. Stan M 57 F4
Harkilees Way. Brain 65 F3
Harkness Cl. Romf 156 C3
Harlesden Cl. Romf 156 C2
Harlesden Rd. Romf 156 C2
Harlesden Wlk. Romf 156 C2
Harley Wlk. Basil 172 A3
Harlings Gr. Chelm 111 E2
Harlow Common. Match 103 F3
Harlow Gdns. Romf 155 E2
Harlow Rd. Match 91 E2
Harlow Rd. More 105 E1
Harlow Rd. Rain 173 F2
Harlow Rd. Roy 88 B1
Harlow Rd. Saw 90 B4
Harlow Rd. Sheer 91 D4
Harlton Ct. Wa Aby 126 C3
Harmer Rd. Swan 191 F1
Harmer St. Grave 193 E1
Harness Cl. Sprin 111 F4
Harold Court Rd. Romf 157 D2
Harold Cres. Wa Aby 126 B4
Harold Gdns. Runw 151 F1
Harold Rd. Brain 65 F1
Harold Rd. Woodf 152 A1
Harold View. Romf 156 C1
Harpers La. Dodd 133 E1
Harrap Chase. Grays 184 C1
Harrier Cl. Rain 174 A3
Harriescourt. Wa Aby 127 D4
Harrison Cl. Brent 147 E2
Harrison Dr. Brain 66 A1
Harrison Dr. N W Bas 117 D3
Harrison Rd. Dag 173 D3
Harrisons. Birhr 57 E1
Harrods Ct. Bill 149 F1
Harrow Cres. Romf 156 A2
Harrow Dr. Hornc 165 E2
Harrow Hill. Topp 31 F3
Harrow Way. Gt Bad 125 D3
Hart Cres. Chig 153 F3
Hart Rd. Harl 90 B3
Hart St. Brent 158 B4
Hart St. Chelm 111 D1
Hart Wood Rd. Brent 158 C3
Hartford End. Basil 172 A3
Hartland Rd. Epp 116 A1
Hartland Rd. Hornc 165 D1
Hartley Cl. Sprin 112 A2
Harts Gr. Woodf 152 A3
Hartswood Cl. Brent 158 C3
Harty Cl. Grays 185 D3
Harvard Wlk. Hornc 174 A4
Harvey. Grays 185 D2
Harvey Gdns. Lou 141 D3
Harvey Rd. Basil 163 E1
Harvey Way. Hemp 16 C1
Harvey Way. Saff W 13 F1
Harvey's La. Romf 164 C1
Harveyfields. Wa Aby 126 B3
Harwater Dr. Lou 140 C4
Harwood Ave. Hornc 165 F4
Harwood Hall La. Upm 175 E3
Haselfoot Rd. Bore 112 C4
Haskins. Corr 179 F1
Haslemere Rd. Runw 151 E1
Haslewood Ave. Hod 100 A3
Hassenbrook Rd. Sta L H 179 F1
Hasted Cl. Swan 191 E1
Hastings Rd. Romf 165 D3
Hastings The. Runw 151 E1
Hastingwood Rd. Mag Lav 104 A3
Hastingwood Rd. N W Bas 103 F2
Hatch Green. L Hal 78 A4
Hatch Rd. Brent 146 A2
Hatch Side. Chig 153 D3
Hatches Farm Rd. Bill 160 B3
Hatfield Cl. Brent 147 E1
Hatfield Cl. Hornc 174 B4
Hatfield Cl. Woodf 153 D1
Hatfield Dr. Bill 149 E1
Hatfield Gr. Chelm 110 B1
Hatfields. Lou 141 D3
Hathaway Rd. Grays 185 D1
Hatherleigh Way. Romf 156 B1
Hatherley The. Basil 171 E4
Hatterill. Basil 170 B3
Havana Cl. Romf 164 C3
Haven Cl. Basil 171 F2
Haven Pl. Grays 185 E2
Haven Rise. Bill 161 E3
Haven The. Grays 185 F1
Havengore. Basil 172 B4
Havengore. Sprin 111 F3
Haverhill Rd. Bart 5 F3
Haverhill Rd. Ching 139 E1
Haverhill Rd. Hel B 6 B1
Haverhill Rd. Ste B 7 D1
Havering Dr. Romf 164 C4
Havering Rd. Romf 155 E2
Havers La. Bis St 67 F3
Havis Rd. Corr 179 F2
Havisham Way. Chelm 110 C4
Haward Rd. Hod 100 B4
Hawes La. Wa Aby 126 B1
Hawfinch Wlk. Chelm 124 A3
Hawk Cl. Wa Aby 127 D3
Hawkbush Green. Basil 163 D1
Hawkdene. Ching 139 E2
Hawkenbury. Harl 102 A3
Hawkes Cl. Grays 192 A4
Hawkesbury Bush La. Basil 171 D1
Hawkhurst Cl. Chelm 110 C1
Hawkhurst Gdns. Romf 155 E2
Hawkinge Way. Hornc 174 B3
Hawkins Way. Brain 66 B2
Hawksmoor Green. Brent 147 E2
Hawksmouth. Ching 139 E1
Hawksway. Basil 171 D2
Hawkswood Rd. S Han 151 D3
Hawkwood Cres. Ching 139 D2
Hawsted. Lou 140 A1
Hawthorn Ave. Brent 158 C3
Hawthorn Ave. Rain 174 A1
Hawthorn Cl. Chelm 124 B3
Hawthorn Cl. Take 70 B4
Hawthorn Rd. Hod 100 A4
Hawthorn Rd. Woodf 152 B3
Hawthorn Rise. Thor 67 F2
Hawthorne Rd. Corr 179 F2
Hawthorns. Harl 102 C2
Hawthorns. Harl 103 D2
Hawthorns. Woodf 152 A4
Hawthorns The. Corr 180 B2
Hawthorns The. Lou 141 D3
Hay Green La. Dodd 133 F2
Hay La. Brain 66 B2
Hayburn Way. Hornc 164 C2
Haycroft. Bis St 68 B4
Hayden Way. Romf 155 E1
Haydens Rd. Harl 102 A4
Haydock Cl. Hornc 174 C4
Hayes Cl. Chelm 111 D1
Hayes Cl. Grays 191 E4
Hayes Dr. Rain 174 A3
Hayes Rd. Stone 190 C1
Hayle. Grays 187 E2
Hayley Bell Gdns. Bis St 67 F2
Haymeads La. Bis St 68 B3
Haynes Rd. Hornc 165 E3
Haysoms Cl. Romf 164 C4
Haytor Cl. Brain 66 B1
Haywards Cl. Brent 147 F2
Haywood Ct. Wa Aby 126 C3
Hazel Cl. Hav 6 C4
Hazel Cl. Hornc 165 D1
Hazel Gdns. Grays 185 F2
Hazel Gr. Brain 65 F1
Hazel Rise. Hornc 165 E3
Hazelbrouck Gdns. Chig 153 E2
Hazeldon Cl. Lit Wal 98 B3
Hazeleigh. Brent 159 D4
Hazeleigh Gdns. Woodf 152 C3
Hazelend Rd. Stan M 57 D2
Hazell Cres. Romf 155 D1
Hazelmere. Basil 172 A2
Hazelmere Gdns. Hornc 165 E3
Hazelwood. Lou 140 B2
Hazelwood. Sta L H 187 D1
Hazelwood Gdns. Brent 146 A2
Hazelwood Park Cl. Chig 153 F3
Headcorn Cl. Basil 172 B3
Headingley Cl. Chig 153 F2
Headland Ave. Hav 6 C4
Headley Chase. Brent 158 B3
Headley Rd. Bill 149 E2
Heard's La. Brent 146 C3
Heard's La. Finch 30 B3
Hearn Rd. Romf 164 C3
Hearsall Ave. Chelm 111 D4
Heath Cl. Romf 165 D4
Heath Dr. Chelm 124 A3
Heath Dr. Romf 156 A1
Heath Dr. The B 128 C2
Heath Park Ct. Romf 165 D3
Heath Park Rd. Romf 165 D3
Heath Rd. Grays 186 A2
Heath Rd. S Han 150 A2
Heath Row. Bis St 57 D1
Heath View Gdns. Grays 185 E2
Heath View Rd. Grays 185 E2
Heathcote Ave. Woodf 152 C1
Heather Ave. Romf 155 E1
Heather Bank. Bill 149 E1
Heather Cl. Brent 146 A2
Heather Cl. Romf 155 E1
Heather Ct. Sprin 111 F3
Heather Dr. Romf 155 F1
Heather Gdns. Romf 155 F1
Heather Glen. Romf 155 E1
Heather Way. Romf 155 E1
Heathfield Rd. Chelm 111 D4
Heathleigh Rd. Basil 170 A2
Heathway. Dag 173 D3
Heathway. Woodf 152 B3
Heaton Ave. Romf 156 A2
Heaton Cl. Romf 156 B2
Heaton Grange Rd. Romf 155 F1
Heaton Way. Romf 156 B2
Hedge Place Rd. Stone 190 C1
Hedgerow The. Basil 171 F2
Hedgerows. Bore 112 A3
Hedgerows. Saw 77 F1
Hedingham Rd. Hornc 166 A2
Hedley Ave. W Thu 191 E4
Heideck Gdns. Brent 159 D4
Heighams. Harl 101 F3
Heights The. Lou 140 C4
Helen Rd. Hornc 165 E4
Helford Way. Upm 166 B3
Helions Bumpstead Rd. Hav 7 D3
Helions Park Ave. Hav 7 D4
Helions Park Gdns. Hav 7 D4
Helions Park Gr. Hav 7 D4
Helions Rd. Harl 102 A4
Helions Rd. Ste B 18 A3
Helions Service Rd. Hav 7 D4
Helions Wlk. Hav 7 D4
Helleborine. Grays 184 C1
Helmons La. W Han 138 A2
Helmores. Basil 169 F3
Helmsdale Cl. Romf 155 F2
Helmsdale Rd. Romf 155 F2
Helpeston. Basil 171 E3
Helston Rd. Sprin 111 F3
Hemley Rd. Grays 186 C4
Hemmels. Basil 170 A4
Hemnall St. Epp 116 A1
Hemnall St. Epp 128 C4
Hempstead Cl. Woodf 152 A4
Henbone Path. Romf 156 B2
Henderson Cl. Hornc 165 D1
Henderson Dr. Stone 190 A2
Hendon Cl. Wick 163 E3
Hendon Gdns. Romf 155 E2
Hengist Gdns. Runw 151 E1
Henham Cl. Bill 149 E1
Henham Rd. Deb 38 C2
Henham Rd. Els 48 C1
Henham Rd. Hen 48 C1
Henniker Gate. Sprin 112 A2
Henry Rd. Chelm 111 D2
Henry St. Grays 192 B4
Henry's Wlk. Chig 153 E2
Henwood Side. Lou 152 C2
Herald Cl. Bis St 67 E3
Herbert Rd. Hornc 165 F2
Herbert Rd. Swan 191 F1
Herd La. Corr 180 B2
Hereford Wlk. Basil 171 F4
Hereward Cl. Wa Aby 126 B4
Hereward Gdns. Runw 151 E1
Hereward Green. Lou 141 E4
Hereward Way. Weth 43 E2
Herga Hyll. Grays 186 A4
Herington Gr. Brent 147 D1
Hernshaw. Brent 159 E2
Heron Cl. Lou 140 A1
Heron Cl. Saw 77 E1
Heron Ct. Bis St 68 A4
Heron Dale. Basil 171 E3
Heron Flight Ave. Rain 174 A3
Heron Way. Upm 166 C2
Heron Way. W Thu 184 A1
Herons La. Fyf 106 B1
Herons Wood. Harl 89 D1
Heronsgate Trdng Est. Basil 162 C1
Heronswood. Wa Aby 126 C3
Heronway. Brent 147 D1
Heronway. Woodf 152 B3
Hertford Dr. Basil 171 E1
Hertford La. Elm 10 C3
Hesselyn Dr. Rain 174 A3
Heybridge Dr. Wick 163 F4
Heybridge Dr. Woodf 153 E1
Heybridge Rd. Ing 135 D1
Heycroft Way. Gt Bad 124 C3
Heydon La. Elm 10 C2
Heythrop The. Ing 135 D2
Heythrop The. Sprin 111 E2

Hicks Way. Stur ... 7 F3
Hickstars La. Bill ... 161 E4
Hides The. Harl ... 89 E1
High Ash Cl. Sta L H ... 187 D1
High Bank. Basil ... 169 F2
High Barrets. Basil ... 172 A3
High Beech Rd. Lou ... 140 C3
High Bridge Rd. Sprin ... 111 E1
High Chelmer. Chelm ... 111 D1
High Cl. Hey ... 10 A3
High Cloister. Bill ... 149 D1
High Easter Rd. Barn ... 72 C1
High Easter Rd. Lea Rod ... 94 B4
High Elms. Chig ... 153 F3
High Elms. Upm ... 166 C2
High Elms. Woodf ... 152 A3
High Fields. Gt Dun ... 72 B4
High Gables. Lou ... 140 B2
High House Estate. Harl ... 90 C2
High House La. Grays ... 186 B2
High La. Match ... 91 F3
High La. Stan M ... 57 F4
High Mead. Chig ... 153 E4
High Meadow. Bill ... 149 E1
High Meadow. Gt Dun ... 72 B4
High Meadows. Chig ... 153 E3
High Pastures. Sheer ... 91 E4
High Rd. Basil ... 170 A3
High Rd. Basil ... 172 A3
High Rd. Bill ... 161 E1
High Rd. Chig ... 153 D4
High Rd. Corr ... 180 A1
High Rd. Corr ... 180 B3
High Rd. Ep Gr ... 128 B3
High Rd. Grays ... 185 F4
High Rd. Horn H ... 178 C2
High Rd. Lou ... 140 B2
High Rd. N W Bas ... 116 B3
High Rd. N W Bas ... 117 E3
High Rd. T Thu ... 184 C3
High Rd. Woodf ... 152 A1
High Rd Buckhurst Hill. Woodf 152 A4
High Rd Knighton. Lou ... 152 A4
High Rd Knighton. Woodf ... 152 A4
High Rd Woodford Green. Woodf ... 152 A3
High Silver. Lou ... 140 B3
High St. Ave ... 183 E3
High St. Bart ... 5 F2
High St. Bill ... 149 D1
High St. Bis St ... 67 F4
High St. Brain ... 65 F1
High St. Brent ... 158 B4
High St. Ch Ong ... 119 D2
High St. Chelm ... 111 D1
High St. Chris ... 10 B2
High St. Clav ... 35 E2
High St. Deb ... 38 A4
High St. Els ... 48 B1
High St. Epp ... 128 C4
High St. Grave ... 192 B1
High St. Grave ... 193 D1
High St. Grays ... 192 A4
High St. Gt Ba ... 42 A1
High St. Gt Bad ... 124 C4
High St. Gt C ... 1 C1
High St. Gt Dun ... 72 B4
High St. Harl ... 90 B2
High St. Hat B O ... 79 F3
High St. Hav ... 7 D4
High St. Hemp ... 16 C1
High St. Hen ... 48 C3
High St. Hinx ... 1 A4
High St. Hod ... 100 A3
High St. Hornc ... 165 E2
High St. Hun ... 88 A1
High St. Ing ... 135 D2
High St. Litt ... 12 C4
High St. New ... 37 D4
High St. Pur ... 183 D1
High St. Romf ... 164 C3
High St. Saff W ... 13 E1
High St. Sta Ab ... 87 E2
High St. Sta L H ... 179 E1
High St. Steb ... 62 C3
High St. Stock ... 136 C2
High St. Swan ... 191 D2
High St. Swan ... 191 F1
High St. Weth ... 43 E2
High St. Wick ... 163 E4
High St. Widd ... 37 E2
High St. Woodf ... 153 E1
High Stile. Gt Dun ... 72 B4
High View. Birhr ... 57 E2
High View Ave. Grays ... 185 E1
High View Cl. Lou ... 140 B2
High View Rise. Bill ... 162 B3
High View School La. Chig ... 153 F3
High Wych La. Saw ... 77 D1
High Wych Rd. H Wy ... 89 F4
High Wych Rd. Saw ... 77 E1
Higham Rd. Woodf ... 152 A2
Higham View. N W Bas ... 117 D3
Highbury Ave. Hod ... 100 A4
Highcliff Dr. Wick ... 162 C4
Highcliffe Cl. Wick ... 163 F4
Highcliffe Rd. Wick ... 163 F4
Highcliffe Way. Wick ... 163 F4
Highcross La. Can E ... 71 E3
Highfield. Harl ... 103 D4
Highfield App. Bill ... 161 E4
Highfield Ave. Bis St ... 68 B3
Highfield Cl. Brain ... 66 A3
Highfield Cl. Romf ... 155 E2
Highfield Cres. Hornc ... 165 F1
Highfield Ct. Bill ... 161 E4
Highfield Gdns. Grays ... 185 E3
Highfield Green. Epp ... 128 C4
Highfield Link. Romf ... 155 E2
Highfield Pl. Epp ... 128 C4
Highfield Rd. Bill ... 161 E4
Highfield Rd. Chelm ... 110 C2
Highfield Rd. Hornc ... 165 F1
Highfield Rd. Romf ... 155 E2
Highfield Rd. Woodf ... 152 C2
Highfield Stile Rd. Brain ... 66 A3
Highfield Way. Hornc ... 165 F1
Highfields. Deb ... 38 A4
Highfields. Hen ... 48 C3
Highfields. Langl ... 22 B1
Highfields. Saff W ... 13 F1
Highgate Gr. Saw ... 77 E1
Highland Ave. Brent ... 146 B1
Highland Ave. Dag ... 164 B1
Highland Ave. Lou ... 140 C2
Highland Gr. Bill ... 149 D1
Highland Rd. Corr ... 171 D1
Highland Rd. Lo Naz ... 100 C1
Highland Rd. Thor ... 67 F2
Highlands Ave. Basil ... 171 E2
Highlands Cres. Basil ... 172 C3
Highlands Rd. Basil ... 172 C3
Highmead. Stan M ... 57 F4
Hightrees. Stock ... 136 B1
Highview Cres. Brent ... 147 E2
Highview Gdns. Upm ... 166 A1
Highwood Cl. Brent ... 146 A1
Highwood La. Lou ... 141 D2
Highwood Rd. Ing ... 122 A3
Hilary Cl. Hornc ... 174 B4
Hill Ave. Wick ... 163 F4
Hill Cres. Chelm ... 111 E1
Hill Cres. Hornc ... 165 E3
Hill Crest Rd. Ch Ong ... 117 F1
Hill Ct. Basil ... 171 E3
Hill Gr. Romf ... 164 C4
Hill House Rd. Stone ... 190 B1
Hill La. Stur ... 7 F2
Hill Rd. Brent ... 158 A4
Hill Rd. Chelm ... 111 E1
Hill Rd. Hemp ... 28 B4
Hill Rd. The B ... 128 C1
Hill Rise. Upm ... 166 A1
Hill St. Saff W ... 13 E1
Hill Terr. Corr ... 180 B2
Hill The. Grave ... 192 B1
Hill The. Harl ... 90 B2
Hill Top. Lou ... 141 D3
Hill Top Cl. Lou ... 141 D3
Hill Top La. Saff W ... 25 F4
Hill Top View. Lou ... 152 C2
Hill View Rd. Sprin ... 111 E2
Hill Way The. Mtssg ... 147 F4
Hill's Chace. Brent ... 158 B3
Hillary Cl. Sprin ... 111 E2
Hillary Mount. Bill ... 149 D1
Hillcrest Ave. Basil ... 169 F2
Hillcrest Ave. W Thu ... 191 D4
Hillcrest Cl. Horn H ... 178 C2
Hillcrest Dr. Swan ... 191 D1
Hillcrest Rd. Horn H ... 178 C2
Hillcrest Rd. Hornc ... 165 D2
Hillcrest Rd. Lou ... 140 B2
Hillcrest Rd. Woodf ... 152 A1
Hillcrest View. Basil ... 171 E2
Hillcrest Way. Epp ... 129 D4
Hillcroft. Lou ... 141 D4
Hilldene Ave. Romf ... 156 B3
Hilldene Cl. Romf ... 156 B3
Hillfoot Ave. Romf ... 155 E1
Hillfoot Rd. Romf ... 155 E1
Hillhouse. Wa Aby ... 126 C3
Hillhouse Cl. Bill ... 149 D2
Hillhouse Dr. Bill ... 149 D2
Hillington Gdns. Woodf ... 152 B1
Hillman Cl. Hornc ... 165 E4
Hillrise Rd. Romf ... 155 E2
Hills Cl. Brain ... 65 F2
Hills Rd. Lou ... 140 A1
Hillside. Grays ... 185 E1
Hillside. Harl ... 103 E3
Hillside Ave. Bis St ... 68 A4
Hillside Ave. Woodf ... 152 B3
Hillside Cl. Bill ... 149 D1
Hillside Cl. Woodf ... 152 B3
Hillside Cres. Sta Ab ... 87 D2
Hillside Gdns. Brain ... 65 F1
Hillside Gr. Chelm ... 124 A4
Hillside La. Sta Ab ... 87 D2
Hillside Mews. Chelm ... 124 A4
Hillside Rd. Bill ... 149 D1
Hillside Rd. Lit Dun ... 73 F3
Hillside Wlk. Brent ... 157 F4
Hilltop Rd. Basil ... 170 C4
Hilltop Rd. W Thu ... 191 D4
Hillview Ave. Hornc ... 165 E3
Hillview Gdns. Corr ... 179 F3
Hillway. Bill ... 149 E1
Hillwood Cl. Brent ... 147 D1
Hillwood Gr. Brent ... 147 D1
Hillwood Gr. Wick ... 163 F4
Hilly Field. Harl ... 102 C2
Hilly Rd. Basil ... 170 B4
Hillyfields. Lou ... 141 D4
Hind Cl. Chig ... 153 F3
Hipkins. Bis St ... 67 F2
Hishbridge St. Wa Aby ... 126 C4
Hitch Common Rd. New ... 36 C4
Hitchin Cl. Romf ... 156 B3
Hitherwood Cl. Hornc ... 174 B4
Hive La. Grave ... 192 A1
Hive The. Grave ... 192 A1
Hobart Cl. Chelm ... 110 C3
Hobart Rd. Tilb ... 193 D3
Hobart Rd. Woodf ... 153 E1
Hobbs Cross Rd. Harl ... 90 C2
Hobbs Cross Rd. The B ... 129 E2
Hobhouse Rd. Corr ... 179 E2
Hoblongs Ind Est. Gt Dun ... 72 C3
Hobtoe Rd. Harl ... 89 D1
Hockerill St. Bis St ... 68 A4
Hockley Cl. Basil ... 171 E3
Hockley Dr. Romf ... 156 A1
Hockley Green. Basil ... 171 F3
Hockley Rd. Basil ... 171 E3
Hoddesdon Rd. Sta Ab ... 87 E2
Hodings Rd. Harl ... 89 E1
Hoe La. Abr ... 142 B2
Hoe La. Gt Wal ... 97 F3
Hoe La. Lo Naz ... 101 D1
Hoe St. Rox ... 109 E2
Hoe The. Bill ... 161 D2
Hoecroft. Lo Naz ... 100 C1
Hoestock Rd. Saw ... 77 E1
Hog Hill Rd. Romf ... 155 D2
Hog's La. Chris ... 10 B2
Hogarth Ave. Brent ... 158 C4
Hogarth Reach. Lou ... 140 C2
Hogarths Rd. Grays ... 185 D3
Hogg La. Grays ... 185 D1
Holbech Rd. Basil ... 171 F4
Holbrook Cl. Bill ... 149 E1
Holbrook Rd. Hav ... 6 C3
Holdbrook Way. Romf ... 156 C1
Holden Gdns. Basil ... 162 C1
Holden Gdns. Brent ... 158 B3
Holden Rd. Basil ... 162 C1
Holden Way. Upm ... 166 B2
Holecroft. Wa Aby ... 126 C3
Holford Rd. Grays ... 186 C2
Holgate. Basil ... 172 B4
Holgate Rd. Dag ... 173 D4
Holiday Hill. W Han ... 137 F2
Hollands Rd. Hav ... 7 D3
Hollands Wlk. Basil ... 171 E1
Holley Gdns. Bill ... 149 D2
Hollidge Way. Dag ... 173 D3
Hollies The. Sta L H ... 179 E1
Hollis Lock. Sprin ... 112 A2
Hollis Pl. Grays ... 185 D1
Hollow Cotts. Pur ... 183 D1
Hollow La. Broom ... 110 C4
Hollow Rd. Ashe ... 9 F2
Hollow Rd. Chris ... 10 B1
Hollow Rd. Elm ... 11 E2
Hollow Rd. Felst ... 75 D2
Hollow Rd. Widd ... 37 D2
Holloway Cres. Lea Rod ... 94 B4
Hollowfield Ave. Grays ... 185 E1
Holly Cl. Lou ... 152 B4
Holly Ct. Bill ... 149 D1
Holly Dr. Ching ... 139 D1
Holly Field. Harl ... 102 B3
Holly Gr. Basil ... 169 F3
Holly Way. Chelm ... 124 B4
Hollybank. Basil ... 169 F2
Hollycross Rd. Ware ... 87 D4
Hollyford. Bill ... 149 E3
Hollyhock Rd. Saff W ... 13 F1
Hollymead. Corr ... 179 F2
Hollywood Cl. Gt Bad ... 124 C3
Holme Rd. Hornc ... 166 A2
Holmes Cl. Horn H ... 178 C2
Holmes Meadow. Harl ... 102 A1
Holmwood Ave. Brent ... 147 D2
Holst Ave. Basil ... 170 B4
Holst Cl. Corr ... 179 E2
Holt Cl. Chig ... 153 F3
Holt The. Chig ... 153 E2
Holt Way. Chig ... 153 F3
Holyfield Rd. Wa Aby ... 113 E2
Holyrood Gdns. Grays ... 186 B1
Home Cl. Harl ... 102 C4
Home Cl. Ste B ... 18 B4
Home Farm Rd. Brent ... 155 E1
Home Gdns. Dag ... 164 B1
Home Mead. Basil ... 170 A4
Home Mead. Chelm ... 124 B1
Home Mead. Writ ... 110 A1
Home Meadows. Bill ... 149 D1
Homebridge. Gt Sam ... 29 D2
Homecroft Gdns. Lou ... 141 D3
Homefield. Wa Aby ... 127 D4
Homefield Cl. Bill ... 161 E3
Homefield Cl. Chelm ... 110 B3
Homefield Cl. Epp ... 116 A1
Homefield Rd. Hav ... 6 C3
Homelands Gr. S Han ... 150 B2
Homelye Chase. Gt Dun ... 62 A1
Homestead. Sprin ... 111 D4
Homestead Dr. Basil ... 170 B1
Homestead Rd. Basil ... 172 C4
Homestead Rd. Wick ... 162 B4
Homeway. Romf ... 157 D2
Honey Bourne. Bis St ... 67 F3
Honey Brook. Wa Aby ... 126 C3
Honey Cl. Bla ... 133 E2
Honey Cl. Gt Bad ... 124 B3
Honey La. Clav ... 34 C2
Honey La. Wa Aby ... 126 C3
Honeycroft. Lou ... 141 D3
Honeyhill. Harl ... 102 C2
Honeymeade. Saw ... 90 B4
Honeypot La. Basil ... 171 D4
Honeypot La. Brent ... 158 A4
Honeypot La. Stock ... 136 B1
Honeysuckle Cl. Brent ... 146 A2
Honeysuckle Cl. Romf ... 156 B2
Honiley Ave. Wick ... 163 E2
Honiton Rd. Romf ... 164 B3
Honywood Rd. Basil ... 162 C1
Hoo The. Harl ... 90 B3
Hood Gdns. Brain ... 66 B2
Hood Rd. Rain ... 173 F2
Hood Wlk. Romf ... 155 D1
Hook End La. Dodd ... 133 E3
Hook End Rd. Dodd ... 133 E2
Hook Field. Harl ... 102 C3
Hook La. Sta Abb ... 143 D2
Hooks Hall Dr. Dag ... 164 B1
Hookstone Way. Woodf ... 152 B2
Hoover Dr. Basil ... 169 F3
Hope Ave. Corr ... 179 F3
Hope Cl. Mtssg ... 147 F4
Hope Cl. Woodf ... 152 B2
Hope Rd. Bill ... 162 B3
Hope Rd. Swan ... 191 F1
Hopgrounds The. Finch ... 42 B3
Hopkins Cl. Romf ... 165 E4
Hopkins Mead. Sprin ... 112 A1
Hoppit Mead. Brain ... 65 F1
Hoppit Rd. Wa Aby ... 126 A3
Hoppits The. H Lav ... 105 E2
Horace Ave. Romf ... 164 B2
Horace Rd. Bill ... 149 E2
Horkesley Way. Wick ... 163 F3
Horksley Gdns. Brent ... 147 E2
Horn La. Woodf ... 152 A2
Horn Yd. Grave ... 193 D1
Hornbeam Ave. Upm ... 175 D4
Hornbeam Cl. Brent ... 159 D4
Hornbeam Cl. Chelm ... 124 A3
Hornbeam Cl. Lou ... 152 B4
Hornbeam Cl. The B ... 128 C1
Hornbeam La. Wa Aby ... 139 F2
Hornbeam Rd. Lou ... 152 B4
Hornbeam Rd. The B ... 128 B1
Hornbeam Way. Bill ... 161 E1
Hornbeams The. Harl ... 89 E1
Hornchurch Rd. Hornc ... 165 D2
Horndon Cl. Romf ... 155 E1
Horndon Green. Romf ... 155 E1
Horndon Rd. Horn H ... 179 F2
Horndon Rd. Romf ... 155 E1
Hornford Way. Romf ... 164 C2
Hornminster Glen. Hornc ... 166 A1
Hornsby La. Grays ... 186 A3
Hornsby Sq. Basil ... 169 F4
Hornsby Way. Basil ... 169 F4
Hornsea Villas. Steb ... 62 B4
Horse and Groom La. Chelm 124 A2
Horsecroft Pl. Harl ... 101 F4
Horsecroft Rd. Harl ... 101 F4
Horseman Ct. Kelv H ... 132 C1
Horseman Side. Nave H ... 144 B2
Horses La. Kelv H ... 145 E3
Horseshoe Cl. Bill ... 149 D3
Horseshoe Cl. Wa Aby ... 127 D3
Horseshoe Hill. Wa Aby ... 127 E4
Horseshoe La. Hav ... 6 C4
Horsley Cross. Basil ... 171 D4
Hospital App. Broom ... 98 A2
Houblon Dr. Chelm ... 124 B1
Houblons Hill. Epp ... 116 B1
Houchin Dr. Fyf ... 106 B1
Hovefields Ave. Wick ... 163 E2
Hovefields Dr. Wick ... 163 E2
Howard Chase. Basil ... 171 D4
Howard Cl. Brain ... 66 B2
Howard Cl. Wa Aby ... 126 B3
Howard Cres. Basil ... 172 B3
Howard Dr. Sprin ... 112 A1
Howard Lodge Rd. Nave H ... 132 B1
Howard Rd. Saff W ... 13 F1
Howard Rd. Stone ... 190 A1
Howard Rd. Upm ... 166 B1
Howard Way. Harl ... 89 F1
Howards Cl. Bore ... 112 C4
Howe Cl. Romf ... 155 D1
Howe La. Gt Sam ... 29 D3
Howell Rd. Corr ... 179 F3
Howfield Green. Hod ... 87 D1
Hows Mead. N W Bas ... 117 E4
Hoylake Gdns. Romf ... 157 D2
Hubbard Chase. Hornc ... 166 A3
Hubbards Cl. Hornc ... 166 A3
Hubert Rd. Brent ... 158 A4
Hubert Rd. Rain ... 173 F2
Hucknall Cl. Romf ... 156 C2
Hudson Cl. Hav ... 7 E3
Hudson's Hill. Weth ... 43 E2
Hudsons Cl. Corr ... 179 E2
Hughes Rd. Grays ... 186 A2
Hugo Gdns. Rain ... 174 A3
Hull Gr. Harl ... 102 A2
Hull Green. Match ... 92 B1
Hull's La. Sand ... 125 F4
Hullett's La. Dodd ... 145 F2
Hulse Ave. Romf ... 155 D1
Hulton Cl. Bore ... 112 C4
Humber Ave. S Ock ... 183 F4
Humber Dr. Upm ... 166 B3
Humber Rd. Sprin ... 111 E3
Hume Ave. Tilb ... 193 D3
Humphrey Cl. Woodf ... 152 C1
Humphrey's Farm La. Gt Wal ... 97 E4
Hungerdown. Ching ... 139 E1
Hunnable Rd. Brain ... 65 F1
Hunsdon Rd. Sta Ab ... 88 A3
Hunt's Cl. Writ ... 123 D4
Hunt's Dr. Writ ... 123 D4
Hunter Ave. Brent ... 147 D2
Hunter Dr. Hornc ... 174 B4
Hunter Rd. Brain ... 66 B1
Hunter Sq. Dag ... 173 D4
Hunter's Gr. Romf ... 155 D3
Hunters Ave. Bill ... 161 D4
Hunters Chase. Brent ... 148 B1
Hunters Hall Rd. Dag ... 173 D4
Hunters Way. Saff W ... 25 E4
Hunters Way. Sprin ... 111 F4
Huntings Rd. Dag ... 173 D3
Huntland Cl. Rain ... 182 A4
Huntley Ave. Grave ... 192 B1
Hunts La. Hinx ... 1 A4
Hunts Mead. Bill ... 149 D1
Huntsman Rd. Chig ... 154 A3
Huntsmans Dr. Upm ... 175 E4
Hurlock Rd. Bill ... 149 D1
Hurrell Down. Bore ... 99 F1
Hurrells La. Lit Bad ... 112 C2
Hurricane Way. N W Bas ... 117 D2
Hursley Rd. Chig ... 153 F3
Hurst Park Ave. Hornc ... 174 C4
Hurst Rd. Lou ... 140 C1
Hurst Way. Sprin ... 111 F1
Hurstlands Cl. Hornc ... 165 E3
Hurstleigh Gdns. Woodf ... 153 D1
Hurstwood Ave. Brent ... 146 A1
Hutchins Cl. Hornc ... 165 F1
Hutton Cl. Woodf ... 152 A2
Hutton Dr. Brent ... 147 E1
Hutton Gate. Brent ... 147 D1
Hutton Rd. Brent ... 147 E2
Hutton Village. Brent ... 147 F1
Hyacinth Ct. Sprin ... 111 F4
Hycliffe Gdns. Chig ... 153 E3
Hyde Mead. Lo Naz ... 113 F4
Hyde The. Basil ... 170 B2
Hyde Way. Wick ... 163 E3
Hyder Rd. Grays ... 186 B2
Hyland Cl. Hornc ... 165 D2
Hyland Way. Hornc ... 165 D2
Hylands Cl. Barn ... 73 D2
Hyll Cl. Gt C ... 1 B2
Hythe Cl. Brain ... 65 F3

Ian Rd. Bill ... 148 C2
Ibbetson Path. Lou ... 141 D3
Ibscott Cl. Dag ... 173 E3
Ickleton Rd. Elm ... 11 D2
Ickleton Rd. Gt C ... 1 B1
Ickleton Rd. Hinx ... 1 A3
Icknield Cl. Hinx ... 1 A2
Ilford Trad Est. Basil ... 162 C1
Ilfracombe Ave. Basil ... 172 B3
Ilfracombe Cres. Hornc ... 174 B4
Ilgars Rd. Runw ... 151 F1
Ilmington Dr. Basil ... 163 D1
Imperial Bsns Est. Grave ... 192 C1
Ingatestone By-Ps. Ing ... 135 D3
Ingatestone Rd. Bla ... 133 F4
Ingatestone Rd. Ing ... 121 F1
Ingatestone Rd. Stock ... 136 A1
Ingatestone Rd. Woodf ... 152 A2
Ingaway. Basil ... 170 C3
Ingels Mead. Epp ... 115 F1
Ingham Rd. Hav ... 7 D4
Ingleby Gdns. Chig ... 154 A4
Ingleby Rd. Dag ... 173 D3
Ingleby Rd. Grays ... 186 B2
Inglefield Rd. Corr ... 180 A4
Ingleglen. Hornc ... 166 A2
Ingleside Ct. Saff W ... 13 E1
Inglewood Cl. Chig ... 153 F2
Inglewood Cl. Hornc ... 174 B4
Ingram Rd. Grays ... 185 E1
Ingrave Cl. Wick ... 163 F3
Ingrave Rd. Brent ... 158 C4
Ingrave Rd. Romf ... 164 C4
Ingrebourne Gdns. Upm ... 166 B2
Ingrebourne Rd. Rain ... 174 A1
Ingress Gdns. Swan ... 191 E1
Ingreway. Romf ... 157 D2
Inkerpole Pl. Sprin ... 111 F2

Inmans Row. Woodf 152 A3
Inskip Dr. Hornc 165 F2
Institute Rd. Epp 116 B1
Inverness Dr. Chig 153 F2
Invicta Rd. Stone 190 A1
Ireton Pl. Grays 185 D1
Iris Cl. Brent 146 A2
Iris Cl. Sprin 111 F3
Iris Path. Romf 156 B2
Irons Way. Romf 155 E2
Irvine Gdns. S Ock 183 F4
Irvine Way. Bill 149 D1
Irving Cl. Bis St 67 E2
Irvon Hill Rd. Wick 163 E4
Isbell Gdns. Romf 155 F2
Isis Dr. Upm 166 C3
Iver Rd. Brent 146 A2
Ives Gdns. Romf 164 C4
Ivy Barn La. Marg 122 B1
Ivy Bower Cl. Swan 191 D1
Ivy Chimneys Rd. Epp 128 C4
Ivy Cl. Stone 190 A1
Ivy Lodge La. Romf 157 D1
Ivy Terr. Hod 100 B4
Ivy Todd Hill. Deb 38 A4
Ivybridge. Hod 100 A2
Ixworth Rd. Hav 6 C3

Jacaranda Cl. Sprin 111 F3
Jack Evans Ct. S Ock 184 A4
Jack Stevens Cl. Harl 103 E3
Jack's La. Take 70 B4
Jackdaw Cl. Bill 161 E4
Jacklin Green. Woodf 152 A3
Jacks Cl. Wick 163 F4
Jackson Pl. Gt Bad 124 B3
Jackson Sq. Bis St 67 F4
Jackson's La. Gt C 1 B2
Jackson's Sq. Gt C 1 B2
Jacksons Cl. Ch Ong 119 D1
Jacksons La. Bill 149 E1
Jacksons Mews. Bill 149 E1
Jacobs Ave. Romf 156 C1
Jacqueline Gdns. Bill 149 D3
James Ave. Dag 164 A2
James Cl. Romf 165 D3
James Sq. Bill 149 F1
James St. Epp 116 C3
Janmead. Brent 147 D1
Janus Cl. Hav 7 E3
Jardine Rd. Basil 172 B4
Jarvis Way. Romf 156 C1
Jasmine Cl. Sprin 111 F4
Jason Cl. Brent 157 F4
Jason Cl. Grays 186 C4
Jay Cl. Hav 7 E4
Jaywick Rd. Hav 7 D4
Jeffcut Rd. Sprin 111 F1
Jefferies Way. Corr 179 F2
Jefferson Ave. Basil 170 A3
Jeffery Rd. Gt Bad 125 F4
Jekylls La. Finch 30 B2
Jellicoe Way. Brain 66 B2
Jenkins Dr. Els 48 B2
Jenkins La. Bis St 68 B3
Jenner Cl. Brain 65 F1
Jenner Mead. Sprin 112 A2
Jenningham Dr. Grays 185 D3
Jenny Path. Romf 156 B2
Jericho Pl. Bla 133 F4
Jermayns. Basil 170 C3
Jernigham Ave. Woodf 153 D1
Jerounds. Harl 102 A3
Jersey Cl. Hod 100 A4
Jersey Gdns. Runw 163 E4
Jersey Rd. Rain 174 A3
Jersey Way. Brain 65 E1
Jervis Rd. Bis St 67 F3
Jesmond Rd. Grays 185 E3
Jessel Dr. Lou 141 E4
Jetty Wlk. Grays 192 A4
Jocelyns. Harl 90 B2
Jodrell Way. W Thu 183 F1
John Clay Gdns. Grays 185 D3
John Ct. Hod 87 D1
John English Ave. Brain 65 F2
John Henry Keene Meml Hms. Chelm 111 D2
John Parker Cl. Dag 173 D3
John Ray St. Brain 66 A2
John St. Grays 192 B4
John Tibauld Ct. Ste B 18 A3
Johns Rd. Bis St 57 D1
Johns The. Ch Ong 119 D2
Johnson Rd. Gt Bad 125 D3
Johnsons Way. Swan 191 E1
Johnston Rd. Woodf 152 A3
Jollyboys La S. Felst 74 B2
Jordans Cl. Dag 173 D4
Jordans Way. Rain 174 B2
Joslin Rd. W Thu 183 E1
Josselin Ct. Basil 163 E1
Josselin Rd. Basil 163 E1
Joyce Ct. Wa Aby 126 B3
Joyners Field. Harl 102 B2
Jubilee Ave. Broom 98 A1
Jubilee Ave. Romf 164 B3
Jubilee Cl. Romf 164 A3
Jubilee Cl. Swan 191 E1
Jubilee Ct. Gt Dun 61 E1
Jubilee Ct. Wa Aby 126 C3
Jubilee Dr. Runw 163 E4
Jubilee Rd. Bill 162 B2
Jubilee Rd. W Thu 191 D4
Judith Ave. Romf 155 D2
Julian Cl. Broom 98 A1
Julian Cl. Hav 7 E4
Julien Court Rd. Brain 66 A2
Juliet Way. Pur 182 C2
Junction Rd. Basil 172 A2
Junction Rd. Brent 158 B3
Junction Rd. Romf 164 C4
Juniper Cl. Bill 149 E2
Juniper Dr. Chelm 124 A3
Juniper Rd. Bore 112 C4
Juniper Way. Romf 156 C1
Jupiter Cl. Hav 7 E3
Jury St. Grave 193 D1
Justinian Cl. Hav 7 E3
Jutsums Ave. Romf 164 A3
Jutsums La. Romf 164 A3

Kandlewood. Brent 147 D1
Kangels The. Langl 22 B1
Karen Cl. Brent 146 B1
Karen Cl. Rain 173 F2
Karen Cl. Sta L H 179 E1
Karen Cl. Wick 163 E3
Kate's La. Ash 15 E4
Katherine Gdns. Woodf 153 E2
Katherine Rd. Basil 172 C4
Katherine's Way. Harl 102 A3
Kathleen Cl. Corr 179 F2
Kathleen Ferrier Cres. Basil 170 B4
Kavanaghs Rd. Brent 158 A4
Kavanaghs Terr. Brent 158 A4
Kay Cl. Gt Le 86 A4
Keary Rd. Swan 191 F1
Keats Ave. Brain 76 C4
Keats Ave. Romf 156 A2
Keats Cl. Chig 153 E2
Keats Gdns. Tilb 193 D3
Keats Way. Wick 163 E4
Keats Wlk. Brent 147 E1
Kecksy's. Saw 77 F2
Keefield. Harl 102 A2
Keene Way. Chelm 124 A2
Keighley Rd. Romf 156 C2
Keith Ave. Runw 151 E1
Keith Way. Hornc 165 F2
Kelburn Way. Rain 174 A1
Kelly Rd. Basil 172 C3
Kelsie Way. Chig 153 F2
Kelston Rd. Woodf 153 D1
Kelvedon Cl. Bill 149 E1
Kelvedon Cl. Brent 147 F2
Kelvedon Cl. Chelm 111 D3
Kelvedon Green. Kelv H 132 C1
Kelvedon Hall La. Kelv H 132 A2
Kelvedon Rd. Bill 149 E1
Kelvedon Way. Woodf 152 C2
Kelvedon Wlk. Rain 173 F2
Kelvin Rd. Tilb 193 D3
Kelvinside. Corr 179 F2
Kempe Rd. Finch 42 B3
Kempley Ct. Grays 192 B4
Kempton Ave. Hornc 165 F1
Kemsley Cl. Swan 191 D1
Kendal Ave. Epp 129 D4
Kendal Croft. Hornc 174 A4
Kendale. Grays 186 A2
Kenilworth Ave. Romf 157 D2
Kenilworth Cl. Bill 148 C1
Kenilworth Gdns. Hornc 165 E1
Kenilworth Gdns. Lou 140 C2
Kenilworth Pl. Bill 161 F1
Kenley Gdns. Hornc 165 F1
Kennedy Ave. Basil 169 F3
Kennel La. Bill 161 E4
Kennet Cl. Upm 166 C3
Kennet Green. S Ock 184 A3
Kennet Way. Chelm 110 B3
Kenneth Gdns. Corr 179 F3
Kenneth Rd. Basil 172 B4
Kenning Rd. Hod 100 A4
Kensington Dr. Woodf 152 B1
Kensington Gdns. Bill 149 D2
Kensington Rd. Brent 146 A2
Kensington Rd. Romf 164 B3
Kent Ave. Dag 173 D1
Kent Cl. Basil 170 A3
Kent Cres. Bis St 67 F2
Kent Dr. Hornc 174 B4
Kent Gdns. Brain 66 A2
Kent Kraft Ind Est. Grave 191 F1
Kent Rd. Dag 173 D4
Kent Rd. Grays 185 E1
Kent View. Ave 183 E2
Kent View Rd. Basil 171 F2
Kentings The. Brain 65 F1
Kenton Way. Basil 169 F3
Kents La. Mag Lav 104 B1
Kents Yd. Litt 12 C2
Kenway. Rain 174 B1
Kenway. Romf 155 E1
Kenway Cl. Rain 174 B1
Kenway Wlk. Rain 174 B1
Kenwood Rd. Corr 180 A3
Kenworthy Rd. Brain 65 F1
Kerby Rise. Sprin 111 F1
Kernow Cl. Hornc 165 F1
Kerril Croft. Harl 89 D1
Kerry Ave. Pur 182 C2
Kerry Cl. Upm 166 C2
Kerry Dr. Upm 166 C2
Kerry Rd. Grays 185 E3
Kersbrooke Way. Corr 180 A3
Kersey Gdns. Romf 156 C2
Kershaw Rd. Dag 164 A1
Kesteven Cl. Chig 153 F2
Kestrel Cl. Chig 154 B3
Kestrel Cl. Rain 174 A3
Kestrel Rd. Wa Aby 127 D3
Kestrel Wlk. Chelm 124 A2
Keswick Ave. Hornc 165 E2
Ketleys. Chelm 124 B2
Ketleys View. Pan 65 D4
Kettering Rd. Romf 156 C2
Kettlebury Way. Ch Ong 118 C1
Kevin Cl. Bill 161 E4
Keyes Rd. Stone 190 A2
Keyes Way. Brain 66 B2
Keys The. Brent 158 B2
Keysers Rd. Lo Naz 100 A1
Kibcaps. Basil 170 C2
Kidder Rd. Ray 64 C1
Kielder Cl. Chig 153 F2
Kilbarry Wlk. Bill 149 E3
Kilmartin Way. Hornc 174 A4
Kilmington Cl. Brent 159 D4
Kiln Field. Bla 133 E2
Kiln La. Harl 103 E4
Kiln Rd. N W Bas 117 D2
Kiln Shaw. Basil 170 B2
Kiln Way. Grays 184 C1
Kilnfield. Ch Ong 118 C1
Kilworth Ave. Brent 147 D2
Kimberley Ave. Romf 164 B3
Kimberley Cl. Bis St 68 A3
Kimberley Rd. Ching 139 F1
Kimberley Way. Ching 139 F1
Kimberly Dr. Bill 161 F1
Kimpton Ave. Brent 146 B1
Kimpton's Cl. Ch Ong 118 C3
Kinfauns Ave. Hornc 165 E3
King Alfred Rd. Romf 156 C1
King Edward Ave. Rain 174 B1
King Edward Dr. Grays 185 F2
King Edward Rd. Basil 170 A4
King Edward Rd. Brent 158 B4
King Edward Rd. Romf 164 C3
King Edward Rd. Stone 191 D1
King Edward's Rd. Sta L H 187 E4
King George Cl. Romf 164 B4
King George Rd. Wa Aby 126 B3
King George VI Ave. Grays 187 D1
King George's Rd. Brent 146 A2
King Henry's Mews. Enf 126 A1
King St. Bis St 67 F4
King St. Grave 193 D1
King St. H Ong 120 A2
King St. Saff W 13 E1
King St. Sta L H 179 E1
King Street Mews. Bis St 67 F4
King's Ave. Lou 152 B4
King's Ave. Woodf 152 B3
King's Chase. Brent 158 B4
King's Green. Lou 140 C3
King's Hill. Lou 140 C4
King's La. Elm 11 D2
King's Rd. Brain 65 F3
King's Rd. Ching 139 E1
King's Rd. Romf 165 D3
Kingaby Gdns. Rain 174 A3
Kingfisher Cl. Brent 147 D1
Kingfisher Cl. Hav 7 E4
Kingfisher Cl. Sta Ab 87 E2
Kingfisher Rd. Upm 166 C2
Kingfisher Way. Bis St 68 A4
Kingfishers. Basil 171 E2
Kingfishers. Ing 135 E2
Kingley Cl. Wick 163 D4
Kingley Dr. Wick 163 D4
Kings Cres. Bill 161 D1
Kings Ct. Bis St 68 A4
Kings Ct. Lou 152 B4
Kings Gdns. Upm 166 C2
Kings Gr. Romf 165 D3
Kings Head Hill. Ching 139 D1
Kings La. Stis 66 C2
Kings Lynn Dr. Romf 156 B2
Kings Mews. Chig 153 E4
Kings Pl. Lou 152 B4
Kings Rd. Bill 161 D1
Kings Rd. Brent 158 B4
Kings Rd. Chelm 110 C2
Kings Way. Bill 161 E3
Kings Wlk. Grays 192 A4
Kingsbridge Cir. Romf 156 C2
Kingsbridge Cl. Brain 65 F4
Kingsbridge Cl. Romf 156 C2
Kingsbridge Rd. Bis St 68 A4
Kingsbridge Rd. Romf 156 C2
Kingsdon La. Harl 103 E4
Kingsdown Cl. Basil 172 B3
Kingsfield. Hod 100 A4
Kingshill Ave. Romf 155 E3
Kingsland. Harl 102 B3
Kingsley Ave. Stone 190 A1
Kingsley Cl. Dag 173 D4
Kingsley Gdns. Hornc 165 E4
Kingsley Rd. Brent 147 E1
Kingsley Rd. Lou 141 E3
Kingsley Rd. Woodf 153 E1
Kingsley Wlk. Grays 186 A1
Kingsman Dr. Grays 185 D3
Kingsman Rd. Sta L H 179 D1
Kingsmead. Saw 77 F1
Kingsmead Ave. Romf 164 C3
Kingsmead Cl. Roy 101 D4
Kingsmead Hill. Roy 101 D4
Kingsmead Rd. Bis St 68 A4
Kingsmoor Rd. Harl 102 A3
Kingston Ave. Sprin 111 F2
Kingston Cres. Sprin 111 F2
Kingston Ct. Grave 192 A1
Kingston Hill Ave. Romf 154 C1
Kingston Rd. Romf 164 C4
Kingsway. Woodf 152 B3
Kingswood Cl. Bill 149 E1
Kingswood Ct. Basil 171 F3
Kingswood Rd. Basil 171 E3
Kinnaird Way. Woodf 152 C2
Kipling Ave. Tilb 193 E3
Kipling Cl. Chelm 111 D3
Kipling Rd. Stone 190 A1
Kirby Cl. Chig 153 F2
Kirby Cl. Lou 140 C1
Kirby Cl. Romf 157 D3
Kirby Rd. Basil 171 F3
Kirk Pl. Sprin 111 F2
Kirkham Ave. Horn H 178 C4
Kirkham Rd. Horn H 178 C4
Kirkham Shaw. Horn H 178 C4
Kirkland Ave. Woodf 153 D1
Kirklees. Chelm 111 D2
Kirkmans Rd. Chelm 124 B2
Kirton Cl. Hornc 174 B3
Kitchener Rd. Dag 173 D3
Kitson Way. Harl 89 E1
Knapton Cl. Sprin 111 E4
Knares The. Basil 170 C2
Knebworth Ct. Bis St 67 E3
Knight St. Saw 77 F1
Knight's Way. Brent 159 D4
Knightbridge Wlk. Bill 149 D2
Knighton Cl. Romf 164 B3
Knighton Cl. Woodf 152 A3
Knighton Dr. Woodf 152 A3
Knighton La. Lou 152 A4
Knighton Rd. Romf 164 B3
Knights. Basil 170 B4
Knights Manor Way. Stone 190 A1
Knights Rd. Brain 66 B1
Knights Way. Gt Dun 61 E1
Knights Way. Woodf 153 E2
Knights Wlk. Abr 142 A3
Knightsbridge Gdns. Romf 164 B3
Knockhall Chase. Swan 191 E1
Knockhall Rd. Swan 191 E1
Knole La. Elm 23 D4
Knoll The. Bill 149 D2
Knowle The. Basil 171 E2
Knowle The. Hod 100 A3
Kyme Rd. Hornc 164 C3
Kynance Cl. Romf 156 B4
Kynaston Rd. Pan 65 D4

La Plata Gr. Brent 158 A4
Laburnam Cl. Upm 167 D2
Laburnam Wlk. Hornc 174 B4
Laburnham Gdns. Upm 166 C2
Laburnum Ave. Hornc 165 D1
Laburnum Ave. Wick 163 E3
Laburnum Cl. Wick 163 E4
Laburnum Dr. Chelm 124 B3
Laburnum Dr. Corr 180 A2
Laburnum Rd. Epp 116 B1
Laburnum Rd. Hod 100 A4
Lady La. Chelm 124 B4
Ladyfields. Lou 141 E3
Ladyfields Cl. Lou 141 E3
Ladygate Centre. Wick 163 E4
Ladys Hill. Nave H 131 F1
Ladyshot. Harl 90 A1
Ladywell Prospect. Saw 78 A1
Lagonda Ave. Chig 153 F2
Laindon Common Rd. Bill 161 D3
Laindon Link. Basil 170 B3
Laing Cl. Chig 153 E2
Laird Ave. Grays 185 E2
Lake Ave. Bill 149 D2
Lake Ave. Rain 174 B2
Lake Gdns. Dag 173 D4
Lake Rd. Dag 173 D1
Lake Rd. Lo Naz 100 C1
Lake Rise. Romf 164 C4
Lake Rise. W Thu 184 A1
Lake View. Basil 169 F2
Lakefields Cl. Rain 174 B2
Lakeland Cl. Chig 154 A3
Lakeside. Bill 149 D2
Lakeside. Rain 174 C3
Lakeside Cres. Brent 158 B4
Lakin Cl. Sprin 112 A2
Lamb Cl. Tilb 193 E3
Lamb's La. Rain 174 B1
Lambert Cross. Saff W 13 F2
Lambourne. Grays 187 E1
Lambourne Cres. Basil 171 F3
Lambourne Cres. Chig 154 A4
Lambourne Dr. Brent 147 F2
Lambourne Gdns. Hornc 165 E1
Lambourne Rd. Chig 154 A4
Lambs Meadow. Woodf 152 B1
Lamerton Rd. Woodf 153 D1
Lamlighters Cl. Wa Aby 127 D3
Lampits. Hod 100 A3
Lampits Hill. Corr 180 A3
Lampits Hill Ave. Corr 180 A3
Lampits La. Corr 180 A3
Lamson Rd. Rain 173 F1
Lancaster Cl. Brent 146 A2
Lancaster Dr. Hornc 174 B4
Lancaster Rd. N W Bas 117 D3
Lancaster Way. Bis St 67 E4
Lancaster Way. Brain 65 F2
Lancelot Rd. Chig 153 F2
Lancer Way. Bill 148 C2
Lancing Rd. Romf 156 C2
Lander Rd. Grays 185 E1
Landermere. Basil 171 D4
Landscape Rd. Woodf 152 A2
Landscape View. Saff W 25 E3
Landseer Cl. Hornc 165 D2
Landview Gdns. Ch Ong 118 C1
Lane Ave. Swan 191 E1
Langdale. Bl Not 76 B4
Langdale Gdns. Chelm 124 B4
Langdale Gdns. Hornc 174 A4
Langdon Way. Corr 180 A3
Langemore Way. Bill 149 D1
Langenhoe. Wick 163 F3
Langfield Cl. Lo Naz 100 C1
Langford Gr. Basil 172 B4
Langford Green. Brent 147 E2
Langford Rd. Woodf 152 B2
Langfords. Lou 152 B4
Langham Cres. Bill 161 D4
Langham Ct. Hornc 165 E2
Langhorne Rd. Dag 173 D3
Langland Cl. Corr 180 A2
Langley Ave. Finch 43 E4
Langley Cl. Romf 156 B2
Langley Dr. Brent 158 A4
Langley Meadow. Lou 141 E4
Langleys. Basil 171 D2
Langston Rd. Lou 141 E2
Langthorne Cres. Grays 185 E1
Langton Ave. Chelm 110 C3
Langton Way. Grays 186 B1
Lanhams. Basil 172 B4
Lansbury Cres. Stone 190 A1
Lansbury Gdns. Tilb 193 D3
Lansdowne Rd. Tilb 192 C3
Lansdowne Rd. Woodf 152 A1
Lansdowne Sq. Grave 192 C1
Lapwing Rd. Runw 151 E1
Larch Cl. Bill 161 E1
Larch Gr. Chelm 124 B3
Larches The. Bore 112 C4
Larchwood. Bis St 67 E3
Larchwood Ave. Romf 155 D2
Larchwood Cl. Romf 155 E2
Larchwood Gdns. Brent 146 A2
Lark's La. Gt Wal 97 F3
Larkfield. Corr 180 A3
Larkin Cl. Brent 147 E1
Larkshall Rd. Ching 139 E1
Larkspur Cl. S Ock 176 B1
Larkswood. Harl 103 E3
Larkswood Rd. Corr 180 A2
Larkswood Wlk. Wick 163 E3
Larsen Dri. Wa Aby 126 B3
Lascelles Cl. Brent 146 A2
Latchett Rd. Woodf 152 A1
Latchetts Shaw. Basil 171 D2
Latchford Pl. Chig 154 A3
Latching Cl. Romf 156 B3
Latchingdon Gdns. Woodf 152 C2
Latchmore Bank. L Hal 68 A1
Lathcoates Cres. Gt Bad 124 C4
Latimer Dr. Bill 161 D1
Latimer Dr. Hornc 165 E1
Latton Green. Harl 102 C2
Launceston Cl. Romf 156 B1
Launder's La. Rain 174 C1
Laundry La. Lo Naz 113 F3
Laundry La. Mtssg 147 E4
Laurel Ave. Wick 163 E4
Laurel Cl. Brent 147 D2
Laurel Cl. Chig 153 E2
Laurel Cres. Romf 164 C2
Laurel Gdns. Ching 139 D1
Laurel Gr. Chelm 124 A4
Laurence Croft. Writ 110 A1
Laurie Wlk. Romf 164 C3
Lavender Ave. Brent 146 A2
Lavender Cl. Romf 156 B2
Lavender Ct. Sprin 111 F3
Lavender Way. Wick 163 E4
Lawford Cl. Hornc 174 B4
Lawford La. Writ 110 B1
Lawn La. Sprin 111 E3
Lawn Rd. Grave 192 B1

Lawn The. Harl 90 A2
Lawns Cres. Grays 192 B4
Lawns The. Sprin 111 E3
Lawns Way. Romf 155 E2
Lawrence Ave. Saw 77 F2
Lawrence Ave. Sta Ab 87 E2
Lawrence Cres. Dag 164 A1
Lawrence Gdns. Bla 133 F4
Lawrence Gdns. Tilb 193 D4
Lawrence Hill. Ching 139 D1
Lawrence Moorings. Saw 77 F1
Lawrence Rd. Basil 172 C4
Lawrence Rd. Romf 165 D3
Laws Cl. Saff W 25 E4
Lawton Rd. Lou 141 D3
Laxtons. Corr 179 E2
Layer Rd. Hav 6 C4
Lea Cl. Bis St 57 D1
Lea Cl. Brain 66 B1
Lea Gr. Bis St 57 D1
Lea Rd. Grays 186 A1
Lea Rd. Hod 100 B4
Lea Rd. Wa Aby 126 A3
Lea Valley Rd. Ching 139 D2
Leach Cl. Gt Bad 125 D4
Leaden Cl. Lea Rod 94 B4
Leafy Way. Brent 147 E1
Leamington Cl. Romf 157 D2
Leamington Rd. Romf 157 D3
Leapingwell Cl. Sprin 112 A2
Leas The. Ing 135 D1
Leas The. Upm 166 B2
Leasway. Brent 158 B4
Leasway. Grays 185 E3
Leasway. Upm 175 E4
Leasway. Wick 163 D3
Leat Cl. Saw 77 F2
Leathart Cl. Hornc 174 A3
Leather La. Brain 65 F2
Leather La. Hav 6 C4
Leather La. Hornc 165 E2
Leatherbottle Hill. Stock 137 D1
Leaview. Wa Aby 126 A3
Leaway. Bill 161 D4
Lechmere App. Woodf 152 B1
Lechmere Ave. Chig 153 E3
Lechmere Ave. Woodf 152 B1
Leconfield Wlk. Hornc 174 B3
Lee Chapel La. Basil 170 B2
Lee Cl. Sta Ab 87 E2
Lee Gardens Ave. Hornc 166 A2
Lee Gr. Chig 153 D4
Lee Rd. Basil 172 C3
Lee Wlk. Basil 170 C3
Lee Woottens La. Basil 171 D2
Leez La. Felst 74 C1
Legg St. Chelm 111 D2
Legions Way. Bis St 68 A4
Legon Ave. Romf 164 B2
Leicester Rd. Tilb 192 C3
Leigh Dr. Els 48 B1
Leigh Dr. Romf 156 B3
Leigh Fells. Basil 172 B3
Leighs Rd. Lit Wal 98 C4
Leighs Rifleman. Bill 148 C2
Leighton Gdns. Tilb 193 D4
Leinster Rd. Basil 170 B3
Leiston Rd. Hav 6 C4
Lenham Way. Basil 172 B3
Lenmore Ave. Grays 185 E2
Lennard Row. Ave 183 E3
Lennox Ave. Grave 193 D1
Lennox Cl. Romf 164 C3
Lennox Rd. Grave 192 C1
Lenthall Ave. Grays 185 D2
Lenthall Rd. Lou 141 E3
Leon Dr. Basil 171 E2
Leonard Ave. Romf 164 B2
Leonard Rd. Basil 171 D1
Leonard Way. Brent 157 F3
Lessington Ave. Romf 164 B3
Leston Cl. Rain 174 A1
Leveller Row. Bill 148 C2
Levens Way. Bl Not 76 B3
Lever Sq. Grays 186 A1
Leverton Way. Wa Aby 126 B3
Leveson Rd. Grays 186 A2
Levett Rd. Sta L H 179 F1
Lewes Rd. Romf 156 B3
Lewis Cl. Brent 146 C1
Lewis Dr. Chelm 124 A3
Lewis Rd. Hornc 165 E3
Lewis Rd. Swan 191 F1
Lexington Way. Upm 166 C3
Ley Field. Take 70 B4
Ley The. Brain 66 B1
Leybourne Dr. Sprin 111 F4
Leyburn Cres. Romf 156 C2
Leyburn Rd. Romf 156 C2
Leycroft Cl. Lou 141 D2
Leyfields. Ray 64 C1
Leyland Gdns. Woodf 152 B3
Leys Ave. Dag 173 E3
Leys Cl. Dag 173 E3
Leys The. Basil 171 E2
Leys The. Sprin 111 F3
Leyside. Ray 64 C1
Leysings. Basil 170 C2
Leywood Cl. Brain 66 B1
Liberty The. Romf 164 C3
Library Hill. Brent 158 B4
Lichfield Cl. Chelm 110 C2
Lichfield Terr. Upm 166 C1
Lichfields The. Basil 171 F4
Lilac Ave. Wick 163 E4
Lilac Cl. Brent 146 A2
Lilac Cl. Chelm 124 B3
Lilac Gdns. Romf 164 C2
Lilac Rd. Hod 100 A4
Lilford Rd. Bill 149 E2
Lilian Cres. Brent 159 E4
Lilian Gdns. Woodf 152 A1
Lilley Cl. Brent 157 F3
Lilliard Cl. Hod 87 D1
Lilliput Rd. Romf 164 B2
Lily Cl. Sprin 111 F3
Lilystone Cl. Stock 136 B1
Lime Ave. Brent 158 C4
Lime Ave. Upm 175 D4
Lime Cl. Lou 152 B4
Lime Cl. Romf 164 B4
Lime Cl. S Ock 176 B1
Lime Gr. Chig 153 F2
Lime Gr. Dodd 133 E1
Lime Meadow. Saff W 14 B1
Lime Pl. Bill 161 E1
Lime Wlk. Chelm 124 B3
Limefields.Saff W 13 F2
Limekiln La. Stan M 57 E3
Limerick Gdns. Upm 166 C2
Limes Ave. Chig 153 E2
Limes Cres. Bis St 68 A4
Limes The. Brent 158 C4
Limes The. Chelm 124 A1
Limes The. Ing 135 E2
Limes The. Pur 183 D1
Limeslade Cl. Corr 180 A2
Lincefield. Basil 170 A2
Lincoln Ave. Romf 164 C2
Lincoln Cl. Bis St 67 E3
Lincoln Cl. Hornc 166 A3
Lincoln Hill. Anst 33 D3
Lincoln Rd. Basil 171 F4
Lincoln Rd. Woodf 152 A1
Lincolns Fields. Epp 115 F1
Lincolns La. Brent 145 E2
Linda Gdns. Bill 148 C2
Linden Cl. Chelm 124 B4
Linden Cl. Pur 190 B4
Linden Cres. Woodf 152 A2
Linden Rise. Brent 158 B3
Linden St. Romf 164 B4
Lindens The. Basil 170 A3
Lindens The. Bis St 67 F3
Lindens The. Brain 66 A1
Lindens The. Lou 140 C2
Lindens The. Stock 136 C1
Lindfield Rd. Romf 156 C3
Lindford Dr. Basil 171 F3
Lindhurst Dr. S Han 150 B2
Lindon Rd. Runw 151 E2
Lindsell Green. Basil 171 F3
Lindsell La. Basil 171 F3
Lindsell La. Lind 52 A2
Lindsey Cl. Bis St 56 C1
Lindsey Cl. Brent 158 A3
Lindsey Rd. Bis St 56 C1
Lindsey St. Ep Gr 115 F2
Lindsey Way. Hornc 165 E3
Linford Cl. Harl 102 B3
Linford End. Harl 102 B3
Linford Rd. Grays 186 B1
Lingcroft. Basil 171 D2
Lingfield Ave. Upm 166 A1
Lingmere Cl. Chig 153 E4
Lingrove Gdns. Woodf 152 A4
Link Rd. Corr 179 E2
Link Rd. Dag 173 D2
Link Way. Bis St 67 F3
Link Way. Hornc 165 F2
Linkdale. Bill 161 D4
Links Ave. Romf 156 A1
Links Dr. Chelm 123 F4
Links Rd. Woodf 152 A3
Links The. Bill 148 C2
Linkside. Chig 153 E3
Linkside Rd. Bis St 68 B3
Linkway. Basil 171 D3
Linkway Rd. Brent 157 F4
Linley Cl. Grays 194 B4
Linley Cres. Romf 164 B4
Linnet Dr. Chelm 124 A3
Linnet Way. Pur 183 D1
Linnets. Basil 171 D2
Linnetts La. Stur 8 A2
Linton Cl. Saff W 25 F4
Linton Ct. Romf 155 F1
Linton Rd. Had 3 D4
Linwood. Saw 77 F1
Lion Hill. Corr 180 B2
Lion La. Bill 149 D1
Lion Meadow. Ste B 18 A4
Lionfield Terr. Sprin 111 E2
Liphook Cl. Hornc 173 F4
Lippits Hill. Basil 170 B2
Lippitts Hill. Wa Aby 139 F4
Lisa Cl. Bill 149 D3
Lisle Pl. Grays 185 D2
Lister Rd. Brain 76 C4
Lister Rd. Tilb 193 D3
Listowel Rd. Dag 164 A1
Littell Tweed. Sprin 112 A2
Little and Great Sir Hughes La. W Han 125 D1
Little Aston Rd. Romf 157 D2
Little Belhus Cl. S Ock 176 A1
Little Bentley. Basil 171 D4
Little Berry La. Basil 170 A2
Little Brays. Harl 103 D4
Little Cattins. Harl 101 F2
Little Charlton. Basil 172 B3
Little Chishill Rd. Lit Chis 21 E4
Little Chittock. Basil 171 F3
Little Dodden. Basil 170 C2
Little Dorrit. Chelm 110 C4
Little Dragons. Lou 140 B3
Little Garth. Basil 172 A3
Little Gaynes Gdns. Upm 175 D4
Little Gaynes La. Upm 175 D4
Little Gerpins La. Upm 174 C2
Little Gregories La. The B 128 B3
Little Grove Field. Harl 102 B4
Little Heath. L Hal 78 C2
Little Hyde La. Ing 135 D3
Little Larchmount. Saff W 25 E4
Little Laver Rd. Lit Lav 105 F3
Little Laver Rd. More 105 F3
Little London Hill. Finch 42 B4
Little Lullaway. Basil 170 C4
Little Meadow. Writ 110 A1
Little Nell. Chelm 110 C4
Little Norsey Rd. Bill 149 E2
Little Oaks. Basil 171 D3
Little Oxcroft. Basil 170 A3
Little Pluckett's Way. Lou 140 B1
Little Pynchons. Harl 102 C3
Little Russets. Brent 147 F1
Little Searles. Basil 172 A4
Little Spenders. Basil 171 E2
Little Sq. Brain 65 F2
Little Stile. Writ 123 D4
Little Walden Rd. Saff W 13 F3
Little Waltham Rd. Broom 98 B1
Little Warley Hall La. Brent 167 F3
Little Warley Hall La. Horn H 167 F3
Little Wlk. Harl 102 B4
Littlebrook Manor Way. Stone 190 A1
Littlebury Ct. Basil 172 A4
Littlebury Ct. Kelv H 132 C1
Littlebury Green. Basil 172 A4
Littlebury Green Rd. Litt 12 B2
Littlehurst La. Bill 161 F1
Littlethorpe. Basil 171 F2
Littleton Ave. Ching 139 F1
Livingstone Cl. Ch Ong 119 D1
Livingstone Terr. Rain 173 F2
Llewellyn Cl. Sprin 111 E2
Loates Pasture. Stan M 57 E4
Lobelia Cl. Bore 112 A3
Locarno Ave. Runw 151 F1
Locke Cl. Corr 179 E2
Locke Cl. Rain 173 F3
Lockwood Wlk. Romf 164 C3
Lockyer Rd. Pur 190 B4
Lodge Ave. Gt Bad 124 C4
Lodge Ave. Romf 165 D4
Lodge Cl. Chig 154 A4
Lodge Cres. Bore 112 C4
Lodge Ct. Hornc 165 F2
Lodge Hall. Harl 102 C2
Lodge La. Grays 185 D2
Lodge La. Hav B 155 D2
Lodge La. Romf 155 D2
Lodge La. Wa Aby 126 B2
Lodge Rd. Brain 65 F1
Lodge Rd. Wa Aby 128 A3
Lodge Rd. Writ 123 D4
Loewen Rd. Grays 186 A2
Loftin Way. Gt Bad 124 B4
Loman Path. S Ock 183 F4
Lombards Chase.. Horn H 168 B3
Lombards The. Hornc 165 F2
Lombardy Cl. Basil 172 B3
Lombardy Pl. Chelm 111 D2
London Hill. Chelm 123 F1
London Rd. Abr 142 A3
London Rd. Basil 171 E2
London Rd. Bill 148 C1
London Rd. Bill 163 D4
London Rd. Bis St 68 A3
London Rd. Bl Not 76 B3
London Rd. Brain 65 F1
London Rd. Brent 158 A4
London Rd. Chelm 123 F4
London Rd. Grave 192 C1
London Rd. Grays 191 F4
London Rd. Gt C 1 B1
London Rd. Gt Le 76 B3
London Rd. Harl 90 B1
London Rd. Litt 12 C1
London Rd. N W Bas 103 E1
London Rd. New 24 C2
London Rd. New 37 D3
London Rd. Pur 183 D1
London Rd. Romf 164 A3
London Rd. Saff W 25 E4
London Rd. Saw 77 F1
London Rd. Sta L H 179 D1
London Rd. Sta R 131 D1
London Rd. Sta T 130 C1
London Rd. Stone 190 C1
London Rd. Swan 191 E1
London Rd. Tilb 193 D3
London Rd. Wen A 24 C4
London Rd. Wick 163 D4
London Rd. Widd 37 D3
London Rd Purfleet. Pur 190 B4
London Rd W Thurrock. W Thu 191 D4
Londons Cl. Upm 175 E4
Long Acre. Harl 90 A2
Long Banks. Harl 102 B2
Long Border Rd. Take 58 C1
Long Brandocks. Writ 110 A1
Long Croft. Stan M 57 E4
Long Croft Dri. Ches 126 A3
Long Ct. Pur 183 D1
Long Deacon Rd. Ching 139 F1
Long Fields. Ch Ong 119 D1
Long Gages. Basil 171 D4
Long Green. Chig 153 F3
Long Green La. Ba Sal 53 E1
Long Horse Croft. Saff W 25 F4
Long La. Arkes 23 F3
Long La. Grays 185 E3
Long La. Ray 75 F4
Long Ley. Harl 102 C4
Long Ley. Langl 22 B1
Long Lynderswood. Basil 170 C3
Long Meadow. Bis St 67 E3
Long Meadow. Brent 159 E4
Long Meadow Dr. Wick 163 F4
Long Riding. Basil 171 E3
Long Ridings Ave. Brent 147 D2
Long St. Wa Aby 127 F4
Long Wlk. Wa Aby 126 A4
Long Wood. Harl 102 B2
Longacre. Basil 171 E4
Longacre. Chelm 123 E4
Longacres. Brain 66 A1
Longaford Way. Brent 147 E1
Longborough Cl. Basil 163 D1
Longcroft. Take 70 B4
Longcroft Rise. Lou 141 D2
Longcrofts. Wa Aby 126 C3
Longfellow Dr. Brent 147 E1
Longfield. Harl 103 D3
Longfield. Lou 140 B2
Longfield Ave. Hornc 164 C2
Longfield Rd. Gt Bad 124 C4
Longhedges. Saff W 13 F1
Longhouse Rd. Grays 186 A2
Longland Bridge. Sheer 91 E4
Longleaf Dr. Brain 76 C4
Longleat Cl. Chelm 110 C4
Longmead Ave. Gt Bad 124 C4
Longmead Cl. Brent 146 C1
Longmeads Cl. Writ 110 A1
Longmore Ave. Gt Bad 124 C4
Longport Cl. Chig 154 A2
Longrise. Bill 161 D4
Longshots Cl. Broom 98 A1
Longstomps Ave. Chelm 124 A4
Longtail. Bill 149 E3
Longtown Cl. Romf 156 B3
Longtown Rd. Romf 156 B3
Longview Way. Romf 155 E1
Longwick. Basil 170 B2
Longwood Cl. Upm 175 E4
Lonsdale Ave. Brent 147 E2
Lonsdale Ave. Romf 164 B3
Looe Gdns. Woodf 153 D1
Loompits Way. Saff W 25 E4
Loop Rd. Wa Aby 126 A4
Lord's Ave. Bis St 67 D4
Lord's Croft La. Hav 7 D4
Lordship Cl. Brent 147 E1
Lordship Rd. Writ 110 A1
Lordswood View. Lea Rod 94 B4
Lorne Rd. Brent 158 B3
Lorraine Cl. Bill 161 E3
Lorrimore Cl. Bill 148 C3
Loughton La. The B 128 B1
Loughton Way. Lou 140 C1
Louise Gdns. Rain 173 F1
Louvaine Ave. Wick 163 D4
Love La. Ave 183 E2
Love La. Ch Ong 119 D2
Love La. Lou 152 C2
Lovell Wlk. Rain 174 A3
Lover's La. Swan 191 E2
Loves Wlk. Gt Bad 124 C4
Loves Wlk. Writ 123 D4
Lovet Rd. Harl 102 A4
Lovibond Pl. Sprin 111 F2
Low Cl. Stone 191 D1
Low Hall Cl. Ching 139 D1
Low Hill Rd. Roy 101 D3
Low Street La. Grays 186 C1
Lowe Cl. Chig 154 A3
Lowe The. Chig 154 A3
Lowen Rd. Rain 173 E2
Lower Alderton Hall La. Lou 141 D2
Lower Anchor St. Chelm 111 D1
Lower Ave. Basil 172 C4
Lower Bedfords Rd. Romf 156 A2
Lower Broad St. Dag 173 D2
Lower Bury La. Epp 128 C4
Lower Cloister. Bill 149 D1
Lower Cres. Sta L H 187 D2
Lower Downs Slade. Hav 7 D4
Lower Dunton Rd. Basil 169 F3
Lower Dunton Rd. Horn H 169 E2
Lower Green. Chelm 124 B1
Lower Island Way. Wa Aby 126 A2
Lower Mardyke Ave. Rain 173 E2
Lower Meadow. Harl 102 C2
Lower Mill Field. Gt Dun 72 C4
Lower Park Cres. Bi St 67 F3
Lower Park Rd. Lou 141 D4
Lower Park Rd. Wick 163 E2
Lower Queen's Rd. Lou 152 B4
Lower Rd. Grave 191 F2
Lower Rd. L Hal 78 B4
Lower Rd. Lou 141 D4
Lower Rd. Mtssg 147 E3
Lower Rd. Sta Ab 87 D3
Lower Southend Rd. Wick 163 E4
Lower St. Bill 161 F1
Lower St. Stan M 57 F4
Lower Stock Rd. Stock 137 E2
Lower Stock Rd. W Han 137 E2
Lower Swaines. Epp 115 F1
Lowfield. Saw 77 F1
Lowfield La. Hod 100 A3
Lowland Gdns. Romf 164 A3
Lowlands Rd. Ave 183 E3
Lowshoe La. Romf 155 D1
Loxford. Basil 172 A4
Lucas Ave. Chelm 124 B3
Lucas Ct. Wa Aby 126 C3
Lucas Rd. Grays 185 D2
Lucerne Way. Romf 156 B2
Luck's La. Gt Wal 84 C1
Lucksfield Way. Gt Bad 124 C3
Luckyn La. Basil 170 C4
Luctons Ave. Lou 140 B1
Ludham Hall La. Bl Not 76 B4
Ludlow Pl. Grays 185 D2
Lukin's Dr. Gt Dun 72 B4
Lulworth Cl. Sta L H 187 D4
Lulworth Dr. Hav 6 C4
Lulworth Dr. Romf 155 D3
Luncies Rd. Basil 171 F3
Lundy Cl. Hav 7 E4
Lupin Dr. Sprin 111 F3
Lupin Mews. Sprin 111 F3
Luppits Cl. Brent 147 D1
Lushes Rd. Lou 141 D3
Luther King Rd. Harl 102 B4
Luthers Cl. Kelv H 132 C1
Luxborough La. Woodf 152 C3
Lynbrook Cl. Rain 173 E2
Lynceley Grange. Epp 116 A1
Lynch The. Hod 100 A3
Lyndale. Kelv H 132 C1
Lyndhurst Dr. Hornc 165 E2
Lyndhurst Rd. Corr 179 F2
Lyndhurst Rise. Chig 153 D3
Lyndhurst Way. Brent 147 E1
Lynfords Dr. Runw 151 F1
Lynge The. Basil 170 B4
Lynmouth Ave. Chelm 124 B4
Lynmouth Gdns. Chelm 111 E1
Lynross Cl. Romf 156 C1
Lynstede. Basil 172 A3
Lynton Ave. Romf 155 D1
Lynton Dr. Sprin 111 F3
Lynwood Cl. Romf 155 D2
Lynwood Cl. Woodf 152 B1
Lynwood Dr. Romf 155 D2
Lyon Cl. Chelm 124 A2
Lyon Rd. Hornc 164 C2
Lyons Hall Rd. Brain 66 B4
Lyster Ave. Gt Bad 125 D4
Lytton Cl. Lou 141 E3
Lytton Rd. Grays 186 A1
Lytton Rd. Romf 165 D3
Lyttons Way. Hod 87 D1

Maberly Ct. Saff W 13 E1
Mabey's Wlk. H Wy 77 D1
Macaulay Rd. Basil 170 A3
Macdonald Ave. Dag 164 A1
Macdonald Ave. Hornc 165 F4
Macdonald Way. Horne 165 F4
Mace Ct. Grays 192 C4
Mackley Dr. Corr 179 F3
Maclennan Ave. Rain 174 B1
Macleod Cl. Grays 185 E1
Macmillan Gdns. Stone 190 A2
Macon Way. Upm 166 C3
Madden Cl. Swan 191 F1
Maddox Rd. Harl 102 C4
Madeira Gr. Woodf 152 B2
Madeline Pl. Chelm 110 C3
Madells. Epp 128 C4
Madles La. Stock 136 C1
Magdalen Gdns. Brent 147 F1
Magdalen Gdns. Thax 40 A1
Magnaville Rd. Bis St 67 F2
Magnolia Cl. Chelm 124 A3
Magnolia Way. Brent 146 A2
Magnolias. Bill 161 E3
Magnum Cl. Rain 174 B1
Magpie La. Brent 158 C1

Magpies. Ep Gr 115 D4
Magwitch Cl. Chelm 110 C4
Mahonia Dr. Basil 169 F3
Maida Ave. Ching 139 D1
Maida Way. Ching 139 D1
Maidstone Ave. Romf 155 E1
Maidstone Rd. Grays 192 A4
Mailers La. Man 46 C1
Main Rd. Bore 112 B4
Main Rd. Broom 98 A1
Main Rd. Felst 75 F2
Main Rd. Gt Le 85 F4
Main Rd. Romf 165 D4
Main St. Bart 5 D3
Maitland Rd. Stan M 57 F3
Maizey Ct. Brent 146 A2
Makemores. Ray 64 C1
Malan Sq. Rain 174 A3
Maldon Rd. Gt Bad 125 E4
Maldon Rd. Marg 123 E1
Maldon Rd. Romf 164 B2
Maldon Rd. Sand 125 E4
Maldon Wlk. Woodf 152 B2
Malford Gr. Woodf 152 A1
Malgraves. Basil 172 A4
Malgraves Pl. Basil 172 A4
Malin Cl. Hav 7 E4
Mall The. Dag 173 D3
Mallard Cl. Upm 166 C2
Mallard Rd. Chelm 124 A3
Mallard Way. Brent 147 D1
Mallards Rd. Woodf 152 A2
Mallards Rise. Harl 103 E4
Mallinson Cl. Hornc 174 B4
Mallion Ct. Wa Aby 126 C3
Mallories. Harl 89 F1
Mallory Way. Bill 149 D1
Mallow Ct. Grays 192 B4
Mallow Gdns. Bill 148 C3
Mallows Green. Harl 102 A2
Mallows Green Rd. Man 46 C1
Malpas Rd. Grays 186 B2
Malta Rd. Tilb 192 C3
Maltese Rd. Chelm 111 D2
Malting La. Epp 116 A1
Malting La. Grays 178 A1
Maltings Dr. Epp 116 A1
Maltings Hill. More 105 F2
Maltings Rd. Gt Bad 125 D3
Maltings The. Gt Dun 61 E1
Maltings The. Ray 65 D1
Maltings The. Thax 40 A1
Malvern Cl. Chelm 110 B3
Malvern Dr. Woodf 152 B3
Malvern Gdns. Lou 140 C2
Malvern Rd. Grays 185 F1
Malvern Rd. Hornc 165 D3
Malyons. Basil 172 A4
Malyons Cl. Basil 172 A4
Malyons Green. Basil 172 A4
Malyons Mews. Basil 172 A4
Malyons Pl. Basil 172 A4
Manchester Way. Dag 173 D4
Mandela Ave. Harl 89 F1
Mandeville Cl. Harl 103 E3
Mandeville Rd. Saff W 25 E4
Mandeville Way. Basil 169 F3
Mandeville Way. Basil 170 A3
Mandeville Way. Broom 98 A2
Manford Cross. Chig 154 A3
Manford Way. Chig 153 F3
Manning Gr. Basil 170 B2
Manning Rd. Dag 173 D3
Manning St. Ave 183 E3
Mannings Cl. Saff W 25 F4
Mannock Dr. Lou 141 E4
Manor Ave. Basil 172 B3
Manor Ave. Hornc 165 E3
Manor Cl. Ave 183 E3
Manor Cl. Dag 173 E3
Manor Cl. Romf 165 D3
Manor Cl. S Han 150 B2
Manor Cl S. Ave 183 E3
Manor Cres. Hornc 165 E3
Manor Cres. Lit Wal 98 A3
Manor Ct. Wa Aby 126 B3
Manor Dr. Gt Bad 124 C4
Manor Hatch Cl. Harl 103 D4
Manor La. Gt C 1 B1
Manor Links Dr. Bis St 68 B4
Manor Rd. Abr 142 C1
Manor Rd. Bis St 68 A4
Manor Rd. Chelm 111 E1
Manor Rd. Chig 153 E3
Manor Rd. Dag 173 E3
Manor Rd. Grave 193 D1
Manor Rd. Grays 192 B4
Manor Rd. Harl 90 B3
Manor Rd. Hav 7 D4
Manor Rd. Hod 100 A4
Manor Rd. Lit Ea 60 C3
Manor Rd. Lou 140 B2
Manor Rd. Romf 165 D3
Manor Rd. Sta L H 179 E1
Manor Rd. Stan M 57 F3
Manor Rd. Swan 191 E1
Manor Rd. Tilb 193 D3
Manor Rd. W Thu 191 E4
Manor Rd. Wa Aby 126 B3
Manor Rd. Wa Aby 127 D1
Manor St. Brain 66 A2
Manor Way. Brent 158 A4
Manor Way. Grave 192 A2
Manor Way. Grays 192 A4
Manor Way. Rain 173 F1
Manor Way. Sta L H 180 A1
Manor Way. Swan 191 F2
Manorway. Woodf 152 B3
Manorway The. Sta L H 180 B1
Mansard Cl. Hornc 165 D1
Manser Rd. Rain 173 F2
Mansfield. H Wy 77 D1
Mansfield Gdns. Hornc 165 E1
Mansfield Hill. Ching 139 D1
Mansfields. Writ 109 F1
Manstead Gdns. Rain 182 A4
Manston Dri. Bis St 57 D1
Manston Rd. Harl 102 C4
Manston Way. Hornc 174 A3
Maple Ave. Bis St 67 E4
Maple Ave. Brain 65 E1
Maple Ave. Upm 175 D4
Maple Cl. Bis St 67 E4
Maple Cl. Brent 158 C4
Maple Cl. Chig 153 F3
Maple Cl. Hornc 165 D1
Maple Cl. Lou 152 B4
Maple Ct. Sta Ab 87 E2
Maple Dr. Chelm 124 A3
Maple Gate. Lou 141 D4
Maple Gr. Bis St 67 E4
Maple La. Wim 27 E3
Maple Mead. Bill 161 E4
Maple Rd. Grays 192 B4
Maple Spring. Bis St 67 E4
Maple Springs. Wa Aby 127 D4
Maple St. Romf 164 B4
Maple Tree La. Basil 169 F3
Maplecroft La. Lo Naz 100 C1
Mapleford Sweep. Basil 171 E2
Mapleleaf Gdns. Wick 163 D3
Maples. Corr 179 F1
Maples The. Harl 102 A2
Maples The. Wick 163 E3
Maplestead. Basil 171 E4
Mapletree La. Ing 134 C4
Maplin Gdns. Basil 171 F3
Mar Rd.S Ock 176 B1
Marchmant Cl. Hornc 165 E1
Marconi Rd. Chelm 111 D2
Marcus Cl. Hav 7 E4
Marden Ash. Basil 170 A3
Marden Rd. Romf 164 C3
Mardyke Rd. Harl 90 A1
Mardyke Wlk. Grays 185 D3
Margaret Ave. Brent 147 D2
Margaret Ave. Ching 139 D2
Margaret Cl. Romf 165 D3
Margaret Cl. Wa Aby 126 B3
Margaret Dr. Hornc 165 F2
Margaret Rd. Epp 116 A1
Margaret Rd. Romf 165 D3
Margaret St. Thax 40 A2
Margaret Way. Saff W 13 E1
Margaretting Rd. Chelm 123 F1
Margaretting Rd. Writ 123 D3
Margarite Way. Wick 163 D4
Margeth Rd. Bill 161 E2
Mariam Gdns. Hornc 165 F1
Marian Cl. T Thu 184 C3
Marigold Cl. Sprin 111 F3
Marigold Pl. Harl 90 A2
Marina Dr. Grave 192 C1
Marina Gdns. Romf 164 B3
Marion Cl. Chig 153 E2
Marisco Cl. Grays 186 A1
Mariskals. Basil 172 A3
Marjorams Ave. Lou 141 D4
Mark Ave. Ching 139 D2
Mark Hall Moors. Harl 90 A2
Mark La. Grave 193 F1
Mark's Ave. Ch Ong 119 D2
Market Alley. Grave 193 D1
Market Ave. Runw 163 E4
Market Hill. Hav 7 D4
Market Hill. Saff W 13 E1
Market Link. Romf 164 C4
Market Pavement. Basil 171 D3
Market Pl. Abr 142 A3
Market Pl. Brain 65 F2
Market Pl. Gt Dun 61 E1
Market Pl. Ing 135 D2
Market Pl. Romf 164 C3
Market Rd. Chelm 111 D1
Market Rd. Wick 163 E4
Market Row. Saff W 13 E1
Market Sq. Basil 171 D3
Market Sq. Bis St 67 F4
Market Sq. Wa Aby 126 B3
Market St. Bis St 67 F4
Market St. Brain 65 F2
Market St. Harl 90 B2
Market St. Saff W 13 E1
Markfield Gdns. Ching 139 D1
Markhams. Corr 179 F2
Markhams Chase. Basil 170 B4
Marking's Field. Saff W 13 F1
Markland Cl. Chelm 124 B2
Marks Cl. Bill 148 C2
Marks Cl. Ing 134 C1
Marks Gdns. Brain 66 B1
Marks Hall La. Mar Rod 94 C2
Marks La. Rett 151 F4
Marks Rd. Romf 164 B3
Markwell Wood. Harl 102 A1
Markwells. Els 48 B1
Marlands. Saw 77 F2
Marlands Rd. Woodf 152 C1
Marlborough Cl. Bis St 67 F3
Marlborough Cl. Grays 185 E2
Marlborough Cl. Upm 166 C2
Marlborough Gdns. Upm 166 C2
Marlborough Rd. Brain 66 A2
Marlborough Rd. Brent 146 A2
Marlborough Rd. Chelm 111 D1
Marlborough Rd. Romf 164 A4
Marlborough Rd. Woodf 152 A1
Marlborough Way. Bill 149 D3
Marlescroft Way. Lou 141 D2
Marlow Ave. Pur 183 D1
Marlowe Cl. Bill 149 D3
Marlowe Cl. Woodf 153 E1
Marney Cl. Gt Bad 124 C4
Marney Dr. Basil 171 F3
Marple Gdns. Wa Aby 126 B4
Marram Ct. Grays 192 C4
Marsh Green Rd. Dag 173 D2
Marsh Hill. Wa Aby 113 F2
Marsh La. Corr 180 B3
Marsh La. Harl 90 C3
Marsh La. Sta Ab 87 E2
Marsh St. Stone 190 A3
Marshalls Dr. Romf 164 C4
Marshalls Rd. Brain 65 F1
Marshalls Rd. Romf 164 B4
Marshbarnes. Bis St 67 E4
Marshfoot Rd. Grays 185 F1
Marston Ave. Dag 164 A1
Marston Beck. Sprin 112 A1
Marston Cl. Dag 164 A1
Marston Dr. Bis St 57 D1
Marston Rd. Hod 100 A4
Marston Rd. Woodf 152 C1
Martin Cl. Bill 149 D1
Martin Dr. Rain 174 A1
Martin Dr. Stone 190 B1
Martin Rd. Ave 183 E3
Martindale Ave. Bill 161 E1
Martingale Cl. Bill 149 E3
Martingale Dr. Sprin 111 F4
Martingale Rd. Bill 149 E3
Martins Cl. Corr 179 E2
Martlesham Cl. Hornc 174 B4
Marvens. Chelm 124 B2
Marwell Cl. Romf 165 D3
Mary McArthur Pl. Stan M 57 F4
Mary Park Gdns. Bis St 67 F2
Marylon Rd. Chig 154 A3
Mascalls Gdns. Brent 157 F3
Mascalls La. Brent 158 A2
Mascalls The. Gt Bad 124 C4
Mascalls Way. Gt Bad 124 C4
Masefield Cl. Romf 156 B1
Masefield Cres. Romf 156 B1
Masefield Dr. Upm 166 B2
Masefield Rd. Grays 185 F2
Masefield Rd. Stone 190 A1
Mashbury Rd. G Ea 96 B3
Mashbury Rd. Gt Wal 97 D4
Mashiters Hill. Romf 155 E1
Mashiters Wlk. Romf 164 C4
Mason Way. Wa Aby 126 C3
Masthead Cl. Stone 190 B2
Matching Field. Kelv H 132 C1
Matching Green. Basil 171 E4
Matching La. Bis St 67 E4
Matching Rd. Hat B O 79 D1
Matching Rd. Match 91 D2
Matfield Cl. Sprin 111 E4
Mathams Dr. Bis St 67 E3
Matlock Gdns. Hornc 165 F1
Matthews Cl. Romf 156 C1
Maugham Cl. Wick 163 E3
Mavis Gr. Hornc 165 F1
Mawney Cl. Romf 155 D1
Mawney Rd. Romf 164 A4
May Ct. Grays 192 C4
May Wlk. Chelm 124 B4
Maybank Ave. Hornc 174 B4
Maybank Ave. Woodf 152 A1
Maybank Rd. Woodf 152 B1
Maybrick Rd. Hornc 165 E3
Maybush Rd. Hornc 165 F2
Maycroft Ave. Grays 185 E1
Maycroft Gdns. Grays 185 E1
Maydells. Basil 172 A3
Mayes Cl. Bis St 68 B4
Mayes La. Sand 125 F3
Mayes Pl. Thax 51 D3
Mayfair Ave. Basil 172 B4
Mayfair Gdns. Woodf 152 A2
Mayfield. Wa Aby 126 B3
Mayfield Ave. Woodf 152 A2
Mayfield Cl. Harl 90 C2
Mayfield Gdns. Brent 146 B1
Mayfield Park. Bis St 67 E2
Mayfield Rd. Writ 110 A1
Mayfields. Grays 185 E2
Mayflower Cl. Lo Naz 100 C1
Mayflower Cl. S Ock 176 B1
Mayflower Rd. Bill 149 D1
Mayflower Way. Ch Ong 119 D2
Maygreen Cres. Hornc 165 D2
Maylands Ave. Hornc 174 A4
Maylands Dr. Bl Not 76 B4
Maylands Way. Romf 157 E2
Mayling Rd. Brain 65 E1
Maylins Dri. Saw 77 E1
Maynard Cl. Gt Dun 61 E1
Maynard Ct. Wa Aby 126 C3
Maynards. Hornc 165 F2
Mayne Crest. Sprin 111 F3
Maypole Cl. Saff W 25 E4
Maypole Cres. Chig 153 E2
Maypole Dr. Chig 154 A4
Maypole The. Thax 39 F2
Maysent Ave. Brain 65 F3
Mayswood Gdns. Dag 173 E3
Maytree Cl. Rain 173 F2
Maytree Gdns. Ugl 48 A2
Maywin Dr. Hornc 165 F2
Maze Green Rd. Bis St 67 E4
Mazoe Cl. Bis St 67 F3
Mazoe Rd. Bis St 67 F3
Mc Adam Cl. Hod 100 A4
McIntosh Cl. Romf 164 C4
McIntosh Rd. Romf 164 C4
Mckenzie Rd. Hod 100 A2
Mead Cl. Grays 185 D2
Mead Cl. Romf 156 A1
Mead Ct. Stan M 57 E4
Mead Ct. Wa Aby 126 A3
Mead Path. Chelm 123 F4
Mead The. Abr 142 A3
Mead The. Basil 170 A4
Mead The. Thax 40 A2
Mead View. St Pel 45 F3
Mead Wlk. Ch Ong 118 C1
Meade Cl. Bill 149 E3
Meade Rd. Bill 149 E3
Meadgate. Basil 172 B4
Meadgate. Lo Naz 100 B2
Meadgate Ave. Gt Bad 124 C4
Meadgate Ave. Woodf 152 C3
Meadow Cl. Ching 139 D1
Meadow Cl. Pan 65 D4
Meadow Cl. Sta L H 187 D2
Meadow Ct. Wick 163 F4
Meadow La. Runw 151 F2
Meadow Rd. Epp 115 F1
Meadow Rd. Grays 185 E3
Meadow Rd. Gt C 1 B2
Meadow Rd. Lou 140 C2
Meadow Rd. Romf 164 B2
Meadow Rise. Bill 149 E1
Meadow Rise. Bla 133 F4
Meadow Side. Chelm 111 D2
Meadow Way. Chig 153 E4
Meadow Way. Saw 78 A1
Meadow Way. Upm 166 B1
Meadow Way. Wick 163 E2
Meadow Way The. Bill 149 E1
Meadowcroft. Stan M 57 F4
Meadowcross. Wa Aby 126 C3
Meadowford. New 24 C1
Meadowgate. Stock 136 C1
Meadowlands. Bis St 57 D1
Meadowlands. Hornc 165 F2
Meadows La. Brent 159 E2
Meadows The. Brent 159 E2
Meadows The. Saw 78 A1
Meadowside. Brain 65 F3
Meadowside Rd. Upm 175 E4
Meadowside.. Chelm 111 E2
Meads Cl. Ing 135 D2
Meads The. Basil 172 A2
Meads The. Ing 135 D2
Meads The. Upm 166 C1
Meads The. Wic Bon 36 A4
Meadside. Weth 43 D2
Meadsway. Brent 158 B2
Meadway. Grays 185 E1
Meadway. Hod 100 A2
Meadway. Romf 156 A1
Meadway. Woodf 152 B3
Meadway The. Lou 140 B1
Meadway The. Lou 140 C2
Mearns Pl. Sprin 111 F2
Medebridge Rd. Grays 184 C3
Medic Ct. Grays 192 C4
Medina Rd. Grays 185 E1
Medlar Rd. Grays 192 C4
Medlar's Mead. Hat B O 79 F3
Medley Rd. Ray 64 C1
Medoc Cl. Basil 172 B4
Medora Rd. Romf 164 B4
Medway Cl. Chelm 110 B2
Meeson's La. Grays 184 C1
Meeting La. Ridge 20 A4
Melba Ct. Writ 110 B1
Melba Gdns. Tilb 193 D4
Melbourne Ave. Chelm 110 C3
Melbourne Rd. Tilb 192 C3
Melksham Cl. Romf 156 C2
Melksham Dr. Romf 156 C2
Melksham Gdns. Romf 156 C2
Mellish Gdns. Woodf 152 A3
Mellor Cl. Ing 135 D2
Mellow Purgess. Basil 170 B3
Mellow Purgess Cl. Basil 170 B3
Mellow Purgess End. Basil 170 B3
Melstock Ave. Upm 175 E4
Melton Gdns. Hornc 164 C2
Melville Rd. Rain 174 A1
Melville Rd. Romf 155 D2
Mendip Rd. Chelm 110 B3
Mendip Rd. Hornc 165 D2
Mendoza Cl. Hornc 165 F3
Menish Way. Sprin 112 A2
Mentmore. Basil 170 A2
Menzies Ave. Basil 169 F3
Meon Cl. Sprin 111 E3
Mercer Rd. Bill 149 E3
Mercia Cl. Gt Bad 125 D3
Mercury Cl. Wick 163 F4
Mercury Gdns. Romf 164 C3
Meredene. Basil 171 F3
Meredith Rd. Grays 186 A1
Merefield. Saw 77 F1
Meriden Cl. Woodf 153 E1
Meridian Way. Sta Ab 87 D3
Merlin Cl. Chig 154 A3
Merlin Cl. Romf 155 E2
Merlin Cl. Wa Aby 127 D3
Merlin Gdns. Romf 155 E2
Merlin Gr. Woodf 153 E2
Merlin Pl. Chelm 110 C3
Merlin Rd. Romf 155 E2
Merlin Way. N W Bas 117 D3
Merlin Way. Runw 151 E1
Mermagen Dr. Rain 174 A3
Merricks La. Basil 171 F1
Merrielands Cres. Dag 173 D2
Merring Way. Harl 101 F4
Merryhill Cl. Ching 139 D1
Merrylands. Basil 170 A4
Merrylands Chase. Basil 169 E4
Mersey Ave. Upm 166 B3
Mersey Fleet Way. Brain 66 B1
Mersey Way. Chelm 110 B3
Merton Pl. Grays 186 A1
Merton Pl. Litt 12 C2
Messant Cl. Romf 156 C1
Methersgate. Basil 171 E4
Mews Ct. Chelm 111 D1
Mews Pl. Woodf 152 A3
Mews The. Romf 164 C4
Mews The. Stan M 57 F4
Meynell Rd. Romf 156 A2
Micawber Way. Chelm 110 B4
Michael Gdns. Hornc 165 E4
Michaels Rd. Bis St 57 D1
Mid Colne. Basil 171 E2
Middle Boy. Abr 142 B3
Middle Cloister. Bill 149 D1
Middle Crockerford. Basil 171 F2
Middle Dr. Corr 180 A4
Middle Green. Dodd 133 E1
Middle King. Brain 66 B1
Middle Mead. Wick 163 F4
Middle Mead Cl. W Han 137 F2
Middle Rd. Brent 159 E3
Middle Rd. Wa Aby 126 A4
Middle Row. Bis St 67 F3
Middle St. Clav 35 E2
Middle St. Lo Naz 114 A4
Middlefield Ave. Hod 100 A4
Middlefield Rd. Hod 100 A4
Middlemead. S Han 138 B2
Middlemead. W Han 138 B2
Middleton Hall La. Brent 158 C4
Middleton Rd. Brent 146 C1
Midhurst Cl. Hornc 174 A4
Milburn Cres. Chelm 110 B1
Milch La. Felst 75 F3
Mildmay Rd. Chelm 111 D1
Mildmay Rd. Romf 164 B3
Mildmayes. Basil 170 B2
Mildred Cl. Stone 190 A1
Mile Cl. Wa Aby 126 B3
Mile Stone Rd. Stone 190 A1
Miles Cl. Harl 102 A4
Miles Gray Rd. Basil 161 F1
Milford Rd. Grays 185 E3
Milkwell Gdns. Woodf 152 A2
Mill Causeway. Chris 10 B3
Mill Chase. Ste B 18 B3
Mill Cl. Els 48 B1
Mill Cl. Gt Ba 42 A1
Mill Cl. Rox 109 D3
Mill Ct. Can E 71 D4
Mill End. Thax 40 A1
Mill Field. Barn 73 D2
Mill Field. Harl 90 B2
Mill Green. Basil 172 A4
Mill Green Ct. Basil 172 A4
Mill Green Pl. Basil 172 A4
Mill Green Rd. Ing 134 C4
Mill Hill. Brain 66 A1
Mill Hill. Brent 146 C1
Mill Hill. Chelm 123 F1
Mill Hill. Far 56 C3
Mill Hill. Hav 7 D4
Mill La. Bla 133 E2
Mill La. Broom 98 B1

Mill La. Corr 180 B3
Mill La. Felst 84 B4
Mill La. Finch 30 C2
Mill La. Grays 184 B1
Mill La. Grays 186 A4
Mill La. Gt Dun 61 E1
Mill La. Gt Le 86 A4
Mill La. H Lav 105 E3
Mill La. H Ong 119 E1
Mill La. Harl 90 C2
Mill La. Hinx 1 A2
Mill La. Hinx 1 A4
Mill La. Horn H 178 C2
Mill La. Ing 135 D3
Mill La. Kelv H 132 C1
Mill La. L Hal 78 C2
Mill La. Litt 12 C2
Mill La. Mee 34 A3
Mill La. Nave H 144 A4
Mill La. Ray 75 F4
Mill La. S Han 150 A3
Mill La. Saff W 13 F1
Mill La. Saw 77 F2
Mill La. Steb 62 C3
Mill La. Stock 136 C1
Mill La. Wen A 25 D3
Mill La. Woodf 152 A3
Mill Park Ave. Hornc 165 F1
Mill Race. Sta Ab 87 E2
Mill Rd. Ave 183 E3
Mill Rd. Bill 161 E3
Mill Rd. Cla 8 C1
Mill Rd. Deb 38 A4
Mill Rd. Felst 74 A2
Mill Rd. Finch 42 B3
Mill Rd. G Ea 82 B3
Mill Rd. Gt Ba 42 A1
Mill Rd. Hav 7 D4
Mill Rd. Hel B 17 E4
Mill Rd. Hen 48 C2
Mill Rd. Pur 190 A4
Mill Rd. Ridge 20 A3
Mill Rd. Stam 19 E2
Mill Rd. Stock 136 C1
Mill Rd. Wim 27 D2
Mill Side. Stan M 57 F3
Mill St. Bis St 68 A3
Mill St. N W Bas 103 F3
Mill Vue Rd. Sprin 111 F1
Millais Pl. Tilb 193 D4
Millard Terr. Dag 173 D3
Millbank Ave. Ch Ong 118 C1
Millbrook Gdns. Romf 155 F1
Millcroft. Bis St 57 D1
Miller's Cl. Barn 73 D2
Miller's La. Chig 142 A1
Millers Cl. Brain 66 A4
Millers Cl. Chig 154 A4
Millers Croft. Gt Bad 124 C3
Millers Croft. Gt Dun 61 F1
Millers Green Rd. Will 107 D2
Millers La. Sta Ab 87 E2
Millers Row. Finch 30 B3
Millersdale. Harl 102 A2
Millfield. H Ong 119 E2
Millfields. Saw 77 F2
Millfields. Stan M 57 F3
Millfields. Writ 110 A1
Millfields Way. Hav 7 D4
Millhoo Ct. Wa Aby 126 C3
Milligans Chase. Chelm 124 A1
Mills Way. Brent 147 E1
Millsmead Way. Lou 140 C4
Millson Bank. Sprin 112 A2
Millwell Cres. Chig 153 E3
Milner Pl. Bill 148 C3
Milton Ave. Hornc 164 C1
Milton Ct. Wa Aby 126 B3
Milton Gdns. Tilb 193 D3
Milton Pl. Chelm 111 D3
Milton Pl. Grave 193 E1
Milton Rd. Brent 158 B3
Milton Rd. Corr 179 F3
Milton Rd. Grave 193 E1
Milton Rd. Grays 185 D1
Milton Rd. Romf 165 D3
Milton Rd. Swan 191 F1
Milton St. Swan 191 E1
Milton St. Wa Aby 126 B3
Milwards. Harl 102 A2
Mimosa Cl. Brent 146 A2
Mimosa Cl. Romf 156 B2
Mimosa Cl. Sprin 111 F3
Minchen Rd. Harl 90 A1
Minerva Cl. Hav 7 E3
Minster Way. Hornc 166 A1
Miramar Way. Hornc 174 B4
Mistley End. Basil 171 E3
Mistley Path. Basil 171 E3
Mistley Rd. Harl 90 A1
Mistley Side. Basil 171 E3
Mitchell Circ. Finch 43 E3
Mitton Vale. Sprin 111 F1
Moat Cl. Dodd 133 E2
Moat Cl. S Han 150 B2
Moat Edge Gdns. Bill 149 D2
Moat Farm. Bird 19 D4
Moat Field. Basil 171 E4
Moat Rd. Bird 19 E4
Moatside. Anst 33 D4
Mole Hall La. Widd 37 F2
Molesworth. Hod 87 D1
Molineaux Ct. Bill 149 D2
Mollands. Basil 171 F2
Mollands Ct. S Ock 176 C1
Mollands La. S Ock 176 B1
Mollison Ave. Enf 126 A2
Molrams La. Gt Bad 125 D3
Momples Rd. Harl 90 A1
Monarch Cl. Tilb 193 D3
Monkchester Cl. Lou 141 D4
Monkham's Ave. Woodf 152 A3
Monkham's Dr. Woodf 152 A3
Monkham's La. Woodf 152 B3
Monks Chase. Brent 159 E3
Monks Cl. Hod 100 A2
Monks Haven. Corr 179 F1
Monks Hill. Saff W 25 F4
Monksbury. Harl 103 D3
Monksgrove. Lou 141 D2
Monkside. Basil 171 E4
Monkswick Rd. Harl 89 F1
Monkswood Ave. Wa Aby 126 B3
Monnow Green. Ave 183 E3
Monnow Rd. Ave 183 E3
Monoux Cl. Bill 149 E1
Mons Ave. Bill 149 E1
Montague Way. Bill 149 D2
Montfort Ave. Corr 180 A2
Montfort Gdns. Woodf 153 E2
Montgomery Cl. Grays 185 E2
Montgomery Cl. Sprin 111 F4
Montgomery Cres. Romf 156 B3
Montpelier Cl. Bill 149 D3
Montreal Rd. Tilb 193 D3
Montrose Ave. Romf 156 B1
Montrose Cl. Woodf 152 A3
Montrose Rd. Sprin 111 F2
Montsale. Basil 172 B4
Moon Hall La. Hav 7 D3
Moor Hall Rd. Harl 90 C2
Moor Hall Rd. Match 91 D2
Moor La. Upm 166 C2
Moor's La. Ray 64 B2
Moore Ave. Grays 184 C1
Moore Ave. Tilb 193 D3
Moore Cl. Bill 149 E3
Moore Rd. Swan 191 F1
Moore's Pl. Brent 158 B4
Moores Ave. Basil 171 E1
Moorescroft. Kelv H 132 C1
Moorfields. Harl 102 B2
Moorland Cl. Romf 155 D2
Moors La. Lit Dun 73 E4
Moran Ave. Chelm 111 D4
Morant Gdns. Romf 155 D3
Morant Rd. Grays 186 A2
Moray Cl. Romf 155 F2
Moray Way. Romf 155 F2
Morecambe Cl. Hornc 174 A4
Moreland Rd. Runw 151 E1
Morelands Ave. Grays 185 E2
Moremead. Wa Aby 126 B3
Mores La. Kelv H 145 E3
Moreton Bridge. Bobb 105 E1
Moreton Bridge. More 105 E1
Moreton Gdns. Woodf 152 C3
Moreton Rd. Bobb 118 A4
Moreton Rd. Ch Ong 118 C3
Moreton Rd. Fyf 106 A2
Moreton Rd. More 106 A2
Moreton Rd. More 118 C3
Moretons. Basil 172 A3
Moretons. Chelm 124 A1
Morgan Cl. Dag 173 D3
Morgan Cres. The B 128 C2
Morgan Way. Rain 174 B1
Morgan Way. Woodf 152 C2
Morland Rd. Dag 173 D3
Morley Gr. Harl 89 E1
Morley Hill. Corr 179 F3
Morley Link. Corr 179 F3
Morley Sq. Grays 186 A1
Mornington Rd. Ching 139 E1
Mornington Rd. Lou 141 E3
Mornington Rd. Woodf 152 A3
Morningtons. Harl 102 B2
Morrells. Basil 170 C2
Morris Ave. Bill 149 E1
Morris Ct. Wa Aby 126 C3
Morris Gdns. Stone 190 A1
Morris Harp. Saff W 13 F2
Morris Rd. Chelm 111 E1
Morris Rd. Romf 156 A2
Mosbach Gdns. Brent 159 D4
Moss Bank. Grays 184 C1
Moss Cl. Basil 171 F2
Moss Dr. Basil 171 F2
Moss La. Romf 164 C3
Moss La. Romf 165 D3
Moss Path. Chelm 124 B2
Moss Rd. Dag 173 D3
Moss Rd. S Ock 184 B4
Moss Wlk. Chelm 124 A3
Mossford La. Woodf 153 E1
Motehill. Basil 170 B2
Motherwell Way. W Thu 184 A1
Mott St. Wa Aby 139 F4
Motts Yd. Steb 62 C3
Moules La. Had 3 E3
Moulsham Chase. Chelm 124 B4
Moulsham Dr. Chelm 124 A4
Moulsham Hall La. Gt Le 75 F1
Moulsham St. Chelm 111 D1
Moulsham Thrift. Chelm 124 A3
Moultrie Way. Upm 166 C3
Mount Ave. Brent 147 D1
Mount Ave. Romf 157 E2
Mount Cl. Wick 163 F4
Mount Cres. Brent 158 B3
Mount Dr. Stan M 57 F3
Mount Echo Ave. Ching 139 D1
Mount Echo Dr. Ching 139 D1
Mount Pleasant Ave. Brent 147 F2
Mount Pleasant Cotts. Saff W 25 E4
Mount Pleasant Rd. Chig 153 E3
Mount Pleasant Rd. Romf 155 E2
Mount Pleasant Rd. Saff W 25 F4
Mount Rd. Brain 66 A2
Mount Rd. Dag 164 A2
Mount Rd. Hav 7 D4
Mount Rd. Sta T 129 F4
Mount Rd. Wick 163 F4
Mount The. Bill 149 F2
Mount The. Brent 158 B4
Mount The. Corr 179 F2
Mount The. Romf 156 B4
Mount View. Bill 149 F1
Mount View Rd. Ching 139 E1
Mount Way. Wick 163 F4
Mountain's Farm Rd. Gt Dun 72 B2
Mountbatten Ct. Lou 152 B4
Mountbatten Rd. Brain 66 B3
Mountbatten Way. Sprin 111 F4
Mountfield Cl. Corr 179 F2
Mountfields. Basil 172 B2
Mountfitchet Rd. Stan M 57 F3
Mounthill Ave. Sprin 111 E2
Mountnessing La. Dodd 133 F1
Mountnessing La. Mtssg 148 B3
Mountnessing Rd. Bill 148 C2
Mountnessing Rd. Dodd 134 A2
Mountney Cl. Ing 134 C1
Mounts Rd. Swan 191 D1
Mowbray Rd. Harl 90 A2
Mowbrays Cl. Romf 155 E1
Mowbrays Rd. Romf 155 E1
Mowbrey Gdns. Lou 141 E4
Mucking Wharf Rd. Sta L H 187 E4
Muckingford Rd. Grays 186 C1
Muckingford Rd. Sta L H 187 D1
Muggeridge Rd. Dag 173 D4
Mulberry Cl. Romf 165 E4
Mulberry Ct. Bis St 68 A3
Mulberry Dr. Pur 182 C1
Mulberry Green. Harl 90 B2
Mulberry Hill. Brent 146 C1
Mulberry Terr. Harl 90 A2
Mulberry Way. Sprin 111 E3
Mulberry Way. Woodf 152 A1
Mullberry Gdns. Basil 170 A3
Mullien Ct. Grays 192 B4
Mullins Rd. Brain 65 F3
Mullions The. Bill 148 C2
Mundon Rd. Brain 66 B1
Mungo Park Rd. Rain 174 A3
Murchison Cl. Chelm 110 C3
Murchison Rd. Hod 87 D1
Murfitt Way. Upm 175 D4
Murray Cl. Brain 65 F3
Murrell Lock. Sprin 112 A2
Murthering La. Nave 144 A3
Murtwell Dr. Chig 153 E2
Museum St. Saff W 13 E1
Muskham Rd. Harl 90 A2
Mutlow Cl. Wen A 24 C3
Mutlow Hill. Wen A 24 C3
Mutton Row. Sta R 131 E4
Myddylton Pl. Saff W 13 E1
Mygrove Cl. Rain 174 B2
Mygrove Gdns. Rain 174 B2
Mygrove Rd. Rain 174 B2
Myln Meadow. Stock 136 C1
Mynchens. Basil 170 C3
Myrtle Gr. Ave 183 E2
Myrtle Rd. Brent 158 B3
Myrtle Rd. Romf 156 B2
Nabbott Rd. Chelm 110 C1
Nags Head La. Brent 157 E2
Nails La. Bis St 67 F4
Nairn Ct. Tilb 192 C3
Nalla Gdns. Chelm 111 D4
Napier Ct. Chelm 110 C3
Narboro Ct. Romf 165 D3
Nare Rd. Ave 183 E3
Naseby Rd. Dag 164 A1
Naseby Rd. Woodf 152 C1
Nash Dr. Broom 98 A2
Nathan Cl. Upm 166 C2
Nathan's La. Writ 122 C3
Nation Way. Ching 139 E1
Nats La. Wen A 24 C3
Naunton Way. Hornc 165 E1
Navarre Gdns. Romf 155 D3
Navestock Cres. Woodf 152 B1
Navestock Side. Kelv H 145 E4
Navigation Rd. Chelm 111 E1
Nayland Cl. Wick 163 F4
Nayland Rd. Hav 6 C3
Nayling Rd. Brain 65 E1
Nazeing Common. Lo Naz 114 B4
Nazeing New Rd. Hod 100 A1
Nazeing Rd. Lo Naz 100 B1
Nazeing The. Basil 171 F3
Nazeing Wlk. Rain 173 F3
Neal Ct. Wa Aby 126 C3
Neave Cres. Romf 156 B1
Nelmes Cl. Hornc 165 F3
Nelmes Cres. Hornc 165 F3
Nelmes Rd. Hornc 165 F3
Nelmes Way. Hornc 165 F4
Nelson Cl. Brent 158 B3
Nelson Cl. Romf 155 D1
Nelson Gdns. Brain 66 B2
Nelson Rd. Basil 171 F3
Nelson Rd. Bis St 68 A3
Nelson Rd. Grays 186 B4
Nelson Rd. Rain 173 F2
Nelson Rd. S Ock 176 B2
Nelwyn Ave. Hornc 165 F3
Nethan Dr. Ave 183 E3
Nether Mayne. Basil 171 D2
Nether Priors. Basil 171 E3
Netherfield La. Sta Ab 87 E2
Netherhall Rd. Roy 100 C3
Netherpark Dr. Romf 155 F1
Netteswell Cross. Harl 89 F1
Netteswell Rd. Harl 89 F2
Nevell Rd. Grays 186 A2
Nevendon Rd. Basil 163 D1
Nevendon Rd. Wick 163 E3
Nevill Way. Lou 140 C2
Neville Rd. Saff W 13 F1
Neville Rd. Woodf 153 E1
Neville Shaw. Basil 171 D3
Nevin Dr. Ching 139 E1
Nevis Cl. Romf 155 F2
New Ave. Basil 170 A2
New Barn La. Gt Ha 68 B1
New Barn La. L Hal 68 A1
New Barns Way. Chig 153 D4
New Bowers Way. Sprin 111 F3
New Century Rd. Basil 170 A3
New Dukes Way. Sprin 111 F3
New Farm Dr. Abr 142 B3
New Forest La. Chig 153 D2
New Hall Dr. Romf 156 C1
New House La. Ash 15 E2
New London Rd. Chelm 111 D1
New Maltings. Ave 183 E3
New Meadgate Terr. Gt Bad 124 B4
New Nabbots Way. Sprin 111 F4
New North Rd. Chig 153 F2
New Path. Bis St 67 F3
New Place Gdns. Upm 166 B1
New Pond La. Saff W 13 E1
New Rd. Abr 142 B2
New Rd. Bart 5 E4
New Rd. Bill 161 D2
New Rd. Brent 158 B4
New Rd. Broom 98 A1
New Rd. Dag 173 E2
New Rd. Els 48 B1
New Rd. Grave 193 D1
New Rd. Grays 192 A4
New Rd. Gt Bad 125 D3
New Rd. Harl 90 B2
New Rd. Hinx 1 A4
New Rd. Hod 100 A2
New Rd. Ing 135 E2
New Rd. Ing 135 E3
New Rd. Rain 174 B1
New Rd. Ray 64 C1
New Rd. Saff W 13 F1
New River Ave. Sta Ab 87 D2
New River Cl. Hod 100 A4
New St. Brain 65 F1
New St. Chelm 111 D2
New St. Gt Dun 72 B4
New St. Saw 77 F2
New Street Fields. Gt Dun 72 B4
New Street Pas. Gt Dun 72 B4
New Waverley Rd. Bill 161 F1
New Writtle St. Chelm 111 D1
New Zealand Way. Rain 173 F1
Newberry Side. Basil 170 B3
Newbiggen St. Thax 39 F2
Newbury Cl. Bis St 67 F4
Newbury Cl. Romf 156 B3
Newbury Gdns. Romf 156 B3
Newbury Gdns. Upm 165 F1
Newbury Rd. Romf 156 B3
Newbury Wlk. Romf 156 B3
Newcastle Ave. Chig 154 A2
Newcourt Rd. Sprin 111 E2
Newcroft. Saff W 13 F1
Newhall Ct. Wa Aby 126 C3
Newhouse Ave. Wick 162 C4
Newhouse La. Bobb 105 E1
Newland Ave. Gt Ba 42 A1
Newlands Cl. Bill 149 D2
Newlands Cl. Brent 147 E1
Newlands End. Basil 170 A4
Newlands Rd. Bill 149 D2
Newlands Rd. Wick 163 E2
Newlands Rd. Woodf 152 A4
Newman Cl. Hornc 165 F3
Newmans Cl. Lou 141 D3
Newmans Dr. Brent 147 E1
Newmans La. Lou 141 D3
Newmarket Rd. Gt C 1 B2
Newmarket Way. Hornc 174 C4
Newnham Cl. Brain 65 F1
Newnham Cl. Lou 140 B2
Newnham Pl. Grays 186 A1
Newpasture La. Steb 63 E3
Newpiece. Lou 141 D3
Newport Cl. Gt Bad 125 D3
Newport Dr. Quen 36 C2
Newport Rd. Saff W 25 E3
Newports. Saw 77 E1
Newteswell Dr. Wa Aby 126 B4
Newton Cl. Brain 65 F1
Newton Cl. Corr 180 A3
Newton Cl. Hod 87 D1
Newton Dr. Saw 77 E1
Newton Green. Gt Dun 61 E1
Newton Rd. Chig 154 A3
Newton Rd. Tilb 193 D3
Newtons Cl. Rain 173 F3
Newtown Rd. Bis St 67 F3
Nicholas Cl. S Ock 176 B1
Nicholas Cl. Writ 110 A1
Nicholas Ct. Chelm 110 C3
Nicholl Rd. Basil 170 B4
Nicholl Rd. Epp 128 C4
Nicholls Field. Harl 103 D4
Nickleby Rd. Chelm 110 B3
Nicola Mews. Woodf 153 D2
Nicolas Wlk. Grays 186 A2
Nightingale Ave. Upm 166 C2
Nightingale Gr. Stone 190 A2
Nightingale La. Brent 169 E4
Nightingale Mews. Saff W 13 F1
Nightingales. Basil 169 F3
Nightingales. Wa Aby 126 C3
Nine Ashes Rd. Bla 120 B1
Nine Ashes Rd. H Ong 120 B1
Nine Ashes Rd. Sto M 133 D3
Nineacres. Brain 66 A1
Ninefields. Wa Aby 126 C3
Nita Rd. Brent 158 B3
Noak Hill. Bill 161 E2
Noak Hill Cl. Bill 161 E2
Noak Hill Rd. Bill 161 D2
Noak Hill Rd. Romf 156 B4
Noakes Ave. Gt Bad 124 C3
Nobel Sq. Basil 163 E1
Nobles The. Bis St 67 E3
Nonsuch Cl. Woodf 153 D2
Norfolk Cl. Basil 170 A3
Norfolk Dr. Chelm 111 D4
Norfolk Gdns. Brain 66 A2
Norfolk Rd. Dag 173 D4
Norfolk Rd. Grave 193 F1
Norfolk Rd. Romf 164 B3
Norfolk Rd. Upm 166 A1
Norfolk Way. Bis St 67 F3
Norman Ave. Bis St 67 E3
Norman Cl. Romf 155 D1
Norman Cl. Wa Aby 126 B3
Norman Cres. Brent 159 D4
Norman Ct. Stan M 57 F4
Norman Ct. Woodf 152 A3
Norman Rd. Hornc 165 D2
Norman's Way. Stan M 57 F4
Normanhurst. Brent 147 E2
Normansfield. Gt Dun 72 C4
Norris Cl. Bis St 68 B4
Norris Cl. Brain 66 B3
Norris Rd. Hod 100 A3
Norsey Cl. Bill 149 D2
Norsey Dr. Bill 149 E2
Norsey Rd. Bill 149 E2
Norsey View Dr. Bill 149 D3
North Ave. Chelm 110 C3
North Ave. Hav 6 C4
North Barn. Lo Naz 100 A1
North Benfleet Hall Rd. Wick 163 F1
North Circular Rd. Woodf 152 B1
North Cl. Chig 154 A3
North Cl. Dag 173 D2
North Colne. Basil 171 E2
North Cres. Ste B 18 A4
North Cres. Wick 163 E4
North Crockerford. Basil 171 F2
North Dell. Sprin 111 F4
North Dr. Brent 148 B1
North Dr. Gt Bad 124 C4
North Dr. Romf 165 E4
North End. Lou 140 B1
North End Rd. Hinx 1 A4
North Gate. Harl 89 E1
North Gr. Harl 103 D4
North Gunnels. Basil 171 D3
North Hall Rd. Hen 37 D1
North Hill. Horn H 178 C3
North Hill Dr. Romf 156 B3
North Hill Green. Romf 156 B3
North Kent Ave. Grave 192 B1
North Pl. Harl 90 A3
North Pl. Wa Aby 126 A3
North Rd. Bill 162 B3
North Rd. Brent 146 B1

North Rd. Hav B 155 F4
North Rd. Hod 100 A4
North Rd. S Ock 176 B2
North Rd. Take 70 B4
North Rd. W Thu 183 E1
North Road Ave. Brent 158 A4
North Service Rd. Brent 158 B4
North St. Bis St 67 F4
North St. Gt Dun 61 E1
North St. Hornc 165 E2
North St. Lo Naz 100 C1
North St. Romf 164 B4
North St. Ste B 18 A4
North Terr. Bis St 67 F4
North View Ave. Tilb 193 D3
Northallerton Way. Romf 156 B3
Northampton Meadow. Gt Ba 42 A1
Northbrooks. Harl 102 B4
Northdene. Chig 153 E3
Northdown Rd. Hornc 165 D2
Northend. Brent 158 B3
Northey. Basil 170 B4
Northfield. Finch 42 B3
Northfield. Lou 140 B3
Northfield Cl. Bill 149 E1
Northfield Rd. Saff W 25 F4
Northfield Rd. Saw 77 F2
Northfields. Grays 185 E1
Northgate End. Bis St 67 F4
Northolt Ave. Bis St 57 D1
Northlands App. Basil 170 B1
Northlands Cl. Corr 179 F3
Northlands Pavement. Basil 172 A3
Northolme Cl. Grays 185 E2
Northolt Way. Hornc 174 B4
Northumberland Ave. Basil 170 B3
Northumberland Ave. Hornc 165 E4
Northumberland Cl. Brain 66 A2
Northumberland Ct. Sprin 111 F2
Northumberland Rd. Sta L H 187 D2
Northview Dr. Woodf 152 B1
Northwood. Grays 186 A2
Northwood Ave. Hornc 174 A4
Norton Cl. Corr 180 A2
Norton Heath Rd. Will 120 C4
Norton La. H Ong 120 B3
Norton Rd. Chelm 111 D2
Norton Rd. Dag 173 E3
Norton Rd. Hav 6 C3
Norton Rd. Ing 135 D2
Norway Wlk. Rain 174 B1
Norwich Wlk. Basil 171 F4
Norwood Ave. Romf 164 C2
Norwood End. Basil 171 E4
Norwood End. Fyf 106 B3
Notley Rd. Brain 65 F1
Nottage Cl. Corr 179 F2
Nunns Way. Grays 185 F1
Nursery Cl. Bis St 67 F3
Nursery Cl. S Ock 176 B1
Nursery Cl. Woodf 152 A3
Nursery Dr. Brain 66 A3
Nursery Fields. Saw 77 E1
Nursery Gdns. Basil 170 B4
Nursery Rd. Bis St 67 F3
Nursery Rd. Chelm 124 A4
Nursery Rd. Corr 179 F2
Nursery Rd. Dodd 133 E3
Nursery Rd. Hod 87 D1
Nursery Rd. Lo Naz 100 B1
Nursery Rd. Lou 140 B3
Nursery Rise. Gt Dun 72 B4
Nursery Wlk. Romf 164 B3
Nutberry Ave. Grays 185 D2
Nutbrowne Rd. Dag 173 D2
Nuthatch Cl. Bill 161 E4
Nyssa Cl. Woodf 152 C2
Nyth Cl. Upm 166 B3

Oak Ave. Bill 162 B2
Oak Ave. Uph 175 D4
Oak Bungalows. Brain 65 F2
Oak Chase. Wick 163 D4
Oak Cl. Wa Aby 126 B3
Oak Dene Cl. Hornc 165 D3
Oak Dri. Saw 90 B4
Oak End. Harl 102 C3
Oak Glade. Epp 116 B1
Oak Glen. Hornc 165 F4
Oak Hill. Weth 55 D4
Oak Hill Rd. Sta Abb 143 F1
Oak Ind Park. Gt Dun 72 C3
Oak La. Bill 162 B2
Oak Lodge Ave. Chig 153 E3
Oak Lodge Tye. Bore 112 A3
Oak Piece. N W Bas 117 E3
Oak Rd. Bill 162 B2
Oak Rd. Epp 115 F1
Oak Rd. Grays 192 B4
Oak Rd. Romf 156 C1
Oak Rd. S Han 150 B3
Oak Rd. Stone 190 C1
Oak Rise. Lou 152 B4
Oak St. Bis St 67 F3
Oak St. Romf 164 B3
Oak Wood Gr. Basil 172 A3
Oakbank. Brent 147 F2
Oakdale Rd. Woodf 152 A1
Oakdene Rd. Basil 172 B4
Oakfield. Steb 63 D2
Oakhill Rd. Pur 183 D1
Oakhurst Cl. Wick 163 E3
Oakhurst Cl. Woodf 153 E1
Oakhurst Dr. Wick 163 E3
Oakhurst Gdns. Ching 139 F1
Oakland Gdns. Brent 147 E2
Oaklands Ave. Romf 164 C4
Oaklands Cl. Bis St 57 D1
Oaklands Cl. Bl Not 76 B4
Oaklands Cres. Chelm 124 A4
Oaklands Dr. Bis St 57 D1
Oaklands Dr. Harl 103 E4
Oaklands Dr. S Ock 184 B4
Oaklands Park. Bis St 57 D1
Oaklea Ave. Sprin 111 F2
Oakleigh Ct. Bis St 67 E4
Oakleigh Rise. Epp 129 D4
Oakley Cl. W Thu 191 E4
Oakley Dr. Bill 148 C3
Oakley Dr. Romf 157 D3
Oakley Rd. Brain 65 F4
Oakmoor Way. Chig 153 F3
Oakroyd Ave. Gt Dun 72 C4
Oaks Ave. Romf 155 E1
Oaks The. Bill 161 E3
Oaktree Cl. Brent 158 C4
Oakway. Grays 185 E3
Oakwood. Wa Aby 126 C3
Oakwood Ave. Brent 147 F2
Oakwood Chase. Hornc 165 F3
Oakwood Cl. Woodf 152 C2
Oakwood Hill. Lou 141 D2
Oakwood Hill Ind Est. Lou 141 D2
Oakwood Rd. Corr 180 A2
Oasthouse Ct. Saff W 13 E1
Oates Rd. Romf 155 D3
Ockelford Ave. Chelm 110 C3
Ockendon Rd. S Ock 176 B3
Ockendon Rd. Upm 175 F3
Ogard Rd. Hod 100 B4
Oglethorpe Rd. Dag 164 A1
Okehampton Rd. Romf 156 B2
Okehampton Sq. Romf 156 B2
Old Barns La. Ing 121 E2
Old Church Hill. Corr 170 A1
Old Church La. Mtssg 147 F3
Old Church Rd. Basil 172 C3
Old Church Rd. Mtssg 147 F4
Old Clements La. Hav 6 C4
Old Court Rd. Chelm 111 E2
Old Croft Cl. G Ea 95 E3
Old Crown La. Kelv H 145 E4
Old Farm Ct. Bill 149 D2
Old Forge Rd. Bore 112 C4
Old Hall La. Brent 168 B4
Old Highway. Hod 100 B4
Old Hill Ave. Corr 179 D4
Old House La. Harl 101 F3
Old House La. Lo Naz 113 F4
Old Jenkins Cl. Sta L H 179 D1
Old Mead La. Hen 48 B2
Old Mead Rd. Els 48 B2
Old Mead Rd. Hen 48 B2
Old Mill La. L Hal 78 A3
Old Mill Rd. Saff W 25 F4
Old Nazeing Rd. Lo Naz 100 A1
Old Oaks. Wa Aby 126 C4
Old Orchard. Harl 102 B3
Old Rd. Harl 90 B3
Old Rd. Nave H 144 C3
Old Rectory Rd. Sta R 131 D3
Old Rope Wlk. Hav 6 C4
Old Shire La. Wa Aby 127 D2
Old Southend Rd. Sand 138 B4
Old Station Rd. Lou 140 C2
Old Street Hill. Hat B O 79 E3
Old Vicarage The. Finch 42 B3
Oldbury Ave. Gt Bad 124 C4
Oldchurch Gdns. Romf 164 B2
Oldchurch Rd. Romf 164 C3
Oldchurch Rise. Romf 164 C2
Oldhouse Croft. Harl 89 F1
Oldwyk. Basil 171 F2
Olive St. Romf 164 B3
Oliver Cl. W Thu 190 C4
Oliver Rd. Brent 147 D2
Oliver Rd. Rain 173 F2
Oliver Rd. W Thu 191 D4
Oliver Way. Chelm 110 C4
Ollard's Gr. Lou 140 B3
Olympic Bsns Centre. Basil 162 C1
One Tree Hill. Corr 170 C1
Ongar Rd. Abr 142 B4
Ongar Rd. Brent 146 A1
Ongar Rd. Ch Ong 119 D4
Ongar Rd. Dodd 132 B2
Ongar Rd. Fyf 106 B1
Ongar Rd. Gt Dun 72 B3
Ongar Rd. Kelv H 132 B2
Ongar Rd. Mar Rod 94 B2
Ongar Rd. Sto M 132 C4
Ongar Rd. Writ 122 A4
Ongar Way. Rain 173 F2
Onslow Gdns. Ch Ong 119 D2
Orange St. Thax 40 A1
Orange Tree Cl. Chelm 124 B3
Orange Tree Hill. Hav B 155 F3
Orchard Ave. Bill 149 E3
Orchard Ave. Brent 158 C4
Orchard Ave. Rain 174 B1
Orchard Ave. Wick 150 C1
Orchard Cl. Gt Bad 124 B3
Orchard Cl. Hav 6 C4
Orchard Cl. New 36 C4
Orchard Cl. Ridge 20 A3
Orchard Cl. S Ock 176 B1
Orchard Cl. Saff W 25 E4
Orchard Cl. Sheer 91 E4
Orchard Cl. Sta Ab 87 E2
Orchard Cl. Writ 110 A1
Orchard Croft. Harl 90 A1
Orchard Dr. Brain 66 A1
Orchard Dr. Grays 185 D2
Orchard Dr. The B 128 C2
Orchard Gdns. Wa Aby 126 B3
Orchard La. Brent 145 F2
Orchard La. Lou 152 B3
Orchard Lea. Saw 77 E1
Orchard Piece. Bla 133 F4
Orchard Pightle. Had 3 E3
Orchard Rd. Bis St 57 D1
Orchard Rd. Dag 173 D2
Orchard Rd. Romf 155 D1
Orchard Rd. S Ock 184 B4
Orchard Rd. Swan 191 F1
Orchard St. Chelm 111 D1
Orchard The. Wick 163 D4
Orchard Way. Chig 154 A4
Orchards N The. Epp 129 D4
Orchards S The. Epp 129 D4
Orchards The. Saw 77 F2
Orchis Gr. Grays 184 C1
Orchis Way. Romf 156 C2
Ordnance Rd. Enf 126 A1
Ordnance Rd. Grave 193 E1
Oreston Rd. Rain 174 B1
Orford Cres. Sprin 111 E3
Orford Rd. Hav 6 C3
Organ La. Ching 139 E1
Orion Ct. Basil 163 D1
Orion Way. Brain 66 A2
Orkney Cl. Hav 7 E4
Orlando Dr. Basil 163 E1
Ormonde Rise. Lou 140 B1
Orsett End. Basil 171 E4
Orsett Heath Cres. Grays 186 A2
Orsett Rd. Grays 185 D1
Orsett Rd. Horn H 178 C1
Orsett Terr. Woodf 152 B2
Orton Cl. Marg 136 A4
Orwell. Grays 187 E1
Osborne Cl. Hornc 165 D3
Osborne Rd. Basil 171 E3
Osborne Rd. Basil 172 C4
Osborne Rd. Brent 146 A2
Osborne Rd. Hod 100 A2
Osborne Rd. Hornc 165 E3
Osborne Rd. Lou 140 A1
Osea Way. Sprin 111 F3
Osprey Way. Chelm 124 A3
Osterley Dr. Basil 169 F3
Ottawa Gdns. Dag 173 E3
Ottawa Rd. Tilb 193 D3
Outing's La. Dodd 133 D2
Outwood Common Rd. Bill 149 F1
Outwood Farm Cl. Bill 149 F1
Outwood Farm Rd. Bill 149 F1
Oval Gdns. Grays 185 E2
Oval Rd N. Dag 173 D2
Oval Rd S. Dag 173 D2
Over Hall La. Ash 4 B1
Overcliff Rd. Grays 185 E1
Overcliffe. Grave 193 D1
Ovington Gdns. Bill 149 D3
Owen Gdns. Woodf 152 C2
Owlets Hall Cl. Horne 165 F4
Oxcroft. Bis St 67 F2
Oxcroft Ct. Basil 170 A3
Oxendon Dri. Hod 100 A3
Oxford Ave. Grays 186 A1
Oxford Ave. Hornc 166 A4
Oxford Ct. Brent 158 B3
Oxford Ct. Sprin 111 F3
Oxford Rd. Horn H 178 C2
Oxford Rd. Romf 156 C2
Oxford Rd. Sta L H 179 D1
Oxford Rd. Woodf 152 B3
Oxley Cl. Romf 156 B1
Oxley Gdns. Corr 179 F3
Oxleys Rd. Wa Aby 127 D4
Oxleys The. Harl 90 C2
Oxlow La. Dag 173 D4
Oxney Mead. Writ 122 C4
Oxney Villas. Felst 74 B3
Oxwich Cl. Corr 180 A2
Oyster Pl. Sprin 111 F2
Ozier Ct. Saff W 25 F4
Oziers. Els 48 B1
Ozonia Ave. Wick 163 E3
Ozonia Cl. Wick 163 D3
Ozonia Way. Wick 163 E3
Ozonia Wlk. Wick 163 E3

Paceheath Cl. Romf 155 E2
Paddock Cl. Bill 161 E4
Paddock Cl. Grays 186 A4
Paddock Dr. Sprin 111 F4
Paddock Mead. Harl 102 B2
Paddock The. Bis St 67 E2
Paddock The. Hod 100 A2
Paddock The. Stock 136 C2
Paddocks The. H Rod 81 F4
Paddocks The. Ing 135 D2
Padgets The. Wa Aby 126 C3
Padham's Green Rd. Mtssg 148 B4
Page Rd. Basil 172 C4
Pageant Cl. Tilb 193 E3
Pagel Mead. Basil 171 D3
Pages Cl. Bis St 67 E3
Pages La. Romf 157 D1
Paget Ct. Els 48 B1
Paget Dr. Bill 149 D3
Pagette Way. Grays 185 D1
Paglesfield. Brent 147 E2
Paignton Ave. Sprin 111 E3
Paines Brook Rd. Romf 156 C2
Paines Brook Way. Romf 156 C2
Painsford Way. Hornc 165 D2
Painswick Ave. Corr 179 F3
Pakes Way. The B 128 C1
Palace Gdns. Lou 140 B1
Palatine Park. Basil 169 F3
Paley Gdns. Lou 141 E3
Paling Way. Grays 185 D3
Palm Cl. Chelm 124 B3
Palm Rd. Corr 171 D1
Palm Rd. Romf 164 B3
Palmer's Ave. Grays 185 E1
Palmers. Corr 179 F2
Palmers Croft. Sprin 112 A1
Palmers Dr. Grays 185 E1
Palmers Gr. Lo Naz 100 C1
Palmers Hill. Epp 116 A1
Palmers La. Bis St 67 F4
Palmers La. Chris 10 B2
Palmerston Gdns. Grays 184 B1
Palmerston Rd. Grays 184 B1
Palmerston Rd. Lou 140 B1
Palmerston Rd. Rain 174 B2
Pamela Gdns. Bis St 67 F2
Pamplins. Basil 170 C3
Pan La. E Han 138 C3
Pan Wlk. Chelm 110 B3
Panadown. Basil 170 C3
Pancroft. Abr 142 A3
Panfield La. Brain 65 F3
Panfields. Basil 170 A3
Paprills. Basil 170 C3
Parade The. Brent 158 B4
Paradise Rd. Wa Aby 126 B3
Paradise Rd. Writ 123 D4
Paringdon Rd. Harl 102 B2
Parish Cl. Hornc 165 D1
Park Ave. Bis St 67 F2
Park Ave. Brent 147 E1
Park Ave. Chelm 110 C2
Park Ave. Harl 103 E3
Park Ave. Upm 166 C2
Park Ave. W Thu 191 D4
Park Ave. Woodf 152 A3
Park Bvd. Romf 155 F1
Park Cl. N W Bas 117 D2
Park Cl. Wick 163 E3
Park Cres. Hornc 165 D2
Park Ct. Harl 89 E1
Park Dr. Dag 164 B1
Park Dr. Hat B O 79 D1
Park Dr. Ing 135 E2
Park Dr. Romf 164 C4
Park Dr. Upm 175 E4
Park Dr. Wick 163 E3
Park End Rd. Romf 164 C4
Park Farm La. Nut 21 E1
Park Farm Rd. Upm 175 D3
Park Fields. Roy 101 D4
Park Gate Rd. Corr 180 A4
Park Hill. Harl 90 A2
Park Hill. Lou 140 B2
Park La. Ave 183 E3
Park La. Bart 5 F2
Park La. Bis St 67 F2
Park La. Brent 159 E2
Park La. Harl 89 E1
Park La. Hornc 165 D2
Park La. Hornc 174 A3
Park La. Langl 22 A2
Park La. Ple 83 F2
Park La. S Han 150 B2
Park La. Saff W 13 E1
Park La. Topp 32 A4
Park Mead. Harl 89 D1
Park Meadow. Dodd 133 F1
Park Pl. Grave 193 E1
Park Rd. Brent 158 A4
Park Rd. Chelm 111 D1
Park Rd. Corr 180 A2
Park Rd. Els 48 B1
Park Rd. Grays 185 D1
Park Rd. Gt C 1 C3
Park Rd. Hav 6 B4
Park Rd. Hod 100 A3
Park Rd. Lit Ea 60 C2
Park Rd. Ple 83 F2
Park Rd. Sta L H 179 D1
Park Rd. Stan M 57 F3
Park Rd. Swan 191 F1
Park Side. Basil 172 A4
Park Side. Bill 149 E1
Park Side. Lou 152 A4
Park Side. Steb 62 B3
Park St. Thax 40 A1
Park Terr. Swan 191 E1
Park View. Ave 183 E3
Park View. Hod 100 A3
Park View Cres. Gt Bad 124 C3
Park View Gdns. Grays 185 D1
Park Way. Brent 146 C1
Parker Ave. Tilb 193 E3
Parker Rd. Chelm 111 E1
Parker Rd. Grays 184 C1
Parker's Farm Rd. Horn H 177 F3
Parkes Rd. Chig 153 F3
Parkhall Rd. Gos 55 F4
Parkhill Cl. Hornc 165 E1
Parkhill Rd. Ching 139 E1
Parkhurst Rd. Basil 172 A3
Parkland Ave. Romf 155 F1
Parkland Ave. Upm 175 D4
Parkland Cl. Hod 87 D1
Parkland Rd. Woodf 152 A2
Parkland Way. Ch Ong 118 C1
Parklands. Bill 149 D2
Parklands. Chig 153 E4
Parklands. Epp 116 B1
Parklands. Wa Aby 126 B4
Parklands Cl. Chig 153 E4
Parklands Dr. Sprin 111 E2
Parklards Way. Chelm 124 B1
Parkmead. Lou 141 D2
Parkmill Cl. Corr 180 A2
Parkmore Cl. Woodf 152 A3
Parkside. Grays 185 F2
Parkside Ave. Romf 155 F1
Parkside Ave. Tilb 193 D3
Parkstone Ave. Hornc 165 F3
Parkstone Ave. Wick 162 C4
Parkway. Bart 5 E3
Parkway. Chelm 111 D1
Parkway. Corr 180 B3
Parkway. Grays 186 A4
Parkway. Romf 155 F1
Parkway. Saw 77 F1
Parkway. Woodf 152 B3
Parnall Rd. Harl 102 B2
Parndon Mill La. Harl 89 D2
Parndon Wood Rd. Harl 102 B2
Parrock St. Grave 193 D1
Parrotts Field. Hod 100 A4
Parry Cl. Corr 179 E2
Parsloe Rd. Harl 102 A2
Parsloes Ave. Dag 173 D3
Parsonage Cl. Broom 98 A1
Parsonage Farm La. Gt Sam 29 D2
Parsonage Field. Dodd 133 E1
Parsonage La. Barn 73 E2
Parsonage La. Birhr 57 F2
Parsonage La. Bis St 68 B4
Parsonage La. Clav 35 D2
Parsonage La. Gt Wal 84 C1
Parsonage La. Marg 136 A4
Parsonage Leys. Harl 102 C4
Parsonage Rd. Rain 174 B1
Parsonage Rd. Take 70 B4
Parsonage Rd. W Thu 191 E4
Partridge Ave. Chelm 110 C3
Partridge Green. Basil 172 A3
Partridge Rd. Harl 102 C3
Parvills. Wa Aby 126 B4
Paschal Way. Gt Bad 124 C4
Pasfield. Wa Aby 126 B3
Paske Ave. Hav 6 C4
Paslowes. Basil 171 F2
Passingham Ave. Bill 161 E3
Passingham Cl. Bill 161 E3
Patching Hall La. Chelm 111 D4
Paternoster Cl. Wa Aby 126 C3
Paternoster Hill. Wa Aby 126 C4
Paternoster Row. Hav B 144 B1
Pathways. Basil 171 F3
Patmore Cl. Bis St 67 E4
Patmore Fields. Ugl 47 F3
Patmore Rd. Wa Aby 126 C3
Patmore Way. Romf 155 D3
Patricia Dr. Corr 180 B4
Patricia Dr. Hornc 165 F2
Patricia Gdns. Bill 161 E4
Patricia Gdns. Bis St 67 F3
Pattiswick Cnr. Basil 171 F4
Pattiswick Sq. Basil 171 F4
Pattocks. Basil 171 F3
Paul's Rd. Basil 170 B4
Pauline Gdns. Bill 148 C2
Pauls La. Hod 100 A3
Pavet Cl. Dag 173 D3
Pavilion Ct. Hav 7 D4
Pawle Cl. Gt Bad 125 D4
Paxfords. Basil 169 F3
Paycock Rd. Harl 102 A3
Paycocke Cl. Basil 162 C1
Paycocke Rd. Basil 162 C1
Paynes La. Lo Naz 113 E4
Paynters Hill. Basil 171 F2
Paynters Mead. Basil 171 F2
Pea La. Upm 176 A3
Peacock Cl. Hornc 165 F4

Peacock St. Grave 193 E1
Peacocks. Harl 101 F3
Peal Rd. Saff W 25 F4
Pear Tree Mead. Harl 103 D3
Pearce Manor. Chelm 123 F4
Pearmain Cl. Runw 151 E1
Pearsons. Corr 179 F2
Peartree Cl. Dodd 133 E1
Peartree Cl. S Ock 176 B2
Peartree Cl.. Brain 66 A1
Peartree Gdns. Romf 155 D1
Peartree La. Dodd 133 E1
Peartree La. Horn H 168 C1
Peartrees. Brent 159 E2
Pease Cl. Hornc 174 A3
Peaslands Rd. Saff W 25 F4
Pebmarsh Dr. Wick 163 F3
Peck's Hill. Lo Naz 100 C1
Pedlars End. More 105 E1
Peel Cres. Brain 65 F2
Peel Dr. Woodf 152 C1
Peel Pl. Woodf 152 C1
Peel Rd. Sprin 111 F2
Peel Way. Romf 156 C1
Peerage Way. Hornc 165 F2
Pegasus Way. Brain 65 F3
Pegelm Gdns. Hornc 165 F2
Peggotty Cl. Chelm 110 C3
Peggy's Wlk. Litt 12 C2
Peldon Pavement. Basil 171 E4
Pelham Pl. Corr 179 F2
Pelham Rd. Clav 35 E2
Pemberton Ave. Ing 135 D2
Pemberton Ave. Romf 165 D4
Pembrey Way. Hornc 174 B3
Pembroke Ave. Corr 180 A2
Pembroke Cl. Bill 149 D3
Pembroke Cl. Hornc 166 A4
Pembroke Gdns. Dag 164 A1
Pembroke Mews. Basil 172 B4
Pembroke Pl. Chelm 111 D4
Pendine Cl. Corr 180 A2
Pendle Cl. Basil 163 D1
Pendle Dr. Basil 162 C1
Penerley Rd. Rain 182 A4
Penhurst Rd. Woodf 153 D2
Penistone Wlk. Romf 156 B2
Penlow Rd. Harl 102 B3
Penn Cl. Grays 178 A1
Penn Gdns. Romf 155 D2
Pennine Rd. Chelm 110 B3
Pennington Cl. Romf 155 D3
Pennington La. Stan M 47 E1
Penningtons. Bis St 67 E3
Penny Cl. Rain 174 A1
Penny La. Corr 179 F2
Penny's La. Marg 135 F4
Pennyfields. Brent 158 B3
Pennymead. Harl 90 A1
Pennystone Rd. Saff W 25 F4
Penrith Cres. Hornc 174 A4
Penrith Rd. Chig 153 F2
Penrith Rd. Romf 157 D2
Penshurst. Harl 90 B2
Penticton Rd. Brain 65 E1
Pentire Cl. Upm 166 C3
Pentland Ave. Chelm 111 D3
Pentlow Hawke Cl. Hav 7 D4
Pentlow Way. Lou 140 C1
Pentney Rd. Ching 139 E1
Penwood Cl. Bill 149 E3
Penzance Cl. Sprin 111 F3
Penzance Gdns. Romf 157 D2
Penzance Rd. Romf 157 D2
Peony Cl. Brent 146 A2
Pepper Hill. Gt Am 87 D2
Pepples La. Wim 27 D1
Pepys Cl. Stone 190 A2
Pepys Cl. Tilb 193 E3
Percival Rd. Hornc 165 E3
Percy Rd. Romf 164 B4
Percy St. Grays 192 B4
Percys. Basil 172 A3
Peregrin Rd. Wa Aby 127 D3
Peregrine Cl. Basil 171 D2
Peregrine Cl. Bis St 67 E3
Peregrine Dr. Chelm 124 A2
Peregrine Rd. Chig 154 A3
Peregrine Wlk. Rain 174 A3
Perriclose. Sprin 111 E4
Perrin Pl. Chelm 111 D1
Perry Cl. Rain 173 E2
Perry Gr. Stone 190 A2
Perry Green. Basil 171 D4
Perry Hill. Lo Naz 113 F4
Perry Hill. Sprin 111 E2
Perry Rd. Harl 102 B2
Perry Spring. Basil 171 E3
Perry Spring. Harl 103 E3
Perry St. Bill 149 E3
Perry Way. Ave 183 E3
Perryfield. Match 92 B1
Pertwee Dr. Gt Bad 124 C3
Peter St. Stock 136 C1
Peterborough Ave. Upm 166 C2
Peterborough Way. Basil 171 F4
Petersfield. Chelm 111 D4
Petersfield Ave. Romf 156 C3
Petersfield Cl. Romf 157 D2
Peterswood. Harl 102 B2
Petlands. Saff W 13 F4
Petre Cl. Horn H 168 B3
Petre Cl. Ing 135 D1
Petrebrook. Sprin 112 A2
Petrel Way. Chelm 124 B3
Petresfield Way. Horn H 168 B3
Pettit's Pl. Dag 173 D4
Pettit's Rd. Dag 173 D4
Pettits Bvd. Romf 155 F1
Pettits Cl. Romf 155 F1
Pettits La. Romf 164 C4
Pettits La N. Romf 155 F1
Pettley Gdns. Romf 164 B3
Petts La. Saff W 13 F4
Petunia Cres. Sprin 111 F3
Petworth Way. Hornc 173 F4
Peverells. Wim 26 B1
Phelips Rd. Harl 102 A2
Philan Way. Romf 155 E2
Philip Ave. Romf 164 B2
Philip Cl. Brent 146 A2
Philip Rd. Rain 173 F1
Philippa Way. Grays 186 A1
Philips Cl. Ray 64 C1
Philips Rd. Ray 64 C1
Phillida Rd. Romf 157 D1
Phillips Chase. Brain 66 A3
Philpot End La. Gt Dun 72 A2
Phoenix Gr. Chelm 124 A4
Pick Hill. Wa Aby 127 D4
Pickwick Ave. Chelm 110 B3
Pickwick Close. Basil 170 B4
Pier Rd. Grave 192 C1
Pier Rd. Swan 191 D2
Piercing Hill. The B 128 B2
Pierrefitte Way. Brain 65 F2
Pig La. Bis St 68 A2
Piggotts Way. Bis St 67 F3
Piggs Cnr. Grays 185 E2
Pightle The. Finch 42 B3
Pightle The. Hav 7 D4
Pigstye Green Rd. Will 121 D4
Pike La. Upm 175 F4
Pike Way. N W Bas 117 D2
Pilgrim Cl. Brain 65 F3
Pilgrim's La. Dodd 145 E3
Pilgrims Cl. Bill 149 D1
Pilgrims Cl. Brent 145 F2
Pilgrims Cl. Gt C 1 B1
Pilgrims La. Grays 184 B2
Pilgrims Wlk. Bill 149 D1
Pilgrims' Rd. Swan 191 F2
Pimpernel Way. Romf 156 B2
Pincey Rd. Take 58 C1
Pinchpools Rd. Man 47 D2
Pindar Rd. Hod 100 B4
Pine Cl. Ing 135 E2
Pine Cl. Wick 163 E3
Pine Cres. Brent 147 E2
Pine Dr. Ing 135 E2
Pine Gr. Bis St 68 A3
Pinecourt. Upm 175 D4
Pinecroft. Brent 147 D1
Pinelands. Bis St 56 C1
Pines Hill. Stan M 57 E3
Pines Rd. Chelm 110 B3
Pines The. Bill 161 E1
Pines The. Grays 185 D3
Pines The. Woodf 152 A4
Pinewood Ave. Rain 174 A1
Pinewood Cl. Harl 103 E4
Pinewood Cl. Sta L H 187 D2
Pinewood Rd. Hav B 155 E3
Pinewood Way. Brent 147 E2
Pinkeneys. Hey 10 B3
Pinkney Cl. Wim 26 C1
Pinmill. Basil 171 E3
Pinnacles. Wa Aby 126 C3
Pintail Rd. Woodf 152 A2
Pintails. Basil 172 B3
Pipchin Rd. Chelm 110 C3
Piper's Tye. Chelm 124 B2
Piperell Way. Hav 7 D3
Pipers Cl. Hav 7 E4
Pipps Hill Cl. Basil 162 A1
Pipps Hill Rd. Basil 162 A1
Pipps Hill Rd N. Bill 162 A1
Pishiobury Dri. Saw 90 B4
Pitcairn Cl. Romf 164 A4
Pitsea Rd. Basil 172 A3
Pitsea View Rd. Bill 162 B2
Pitseaville Gr. Basil 171 F3
Pitt Chase. Gt Bad 124 C3
Pittfields. Basil 170 A3
Pittman Cl. Brent 159 E3
Pittman's Field. Harl 89 F1
Place Farm La. Kelv H 133 D1
Plain The. Epp 116 A1
Plains Field. Brain 66 B1
Plaistow Cl. Corr 179 E1
Plane Tree Cl. Chelm 124 A3
Plantation Cl. Saff W 25 F3
Plantation Rd. Bore 99 F1
Plashet Cl. Corr 179 E1
Plashet Gdns. Brent 159 D3
Plashets. Saw 78 B1
Plashetts. Basil 171 E4
Platford Green. Hornc 165 F4
Plaw Hatch Cl. Bis St 68 A4
Playfield Ave. Romf 155 E1
Playhouse Sq. Harl 102 B4
Pleasant Rd. Bis St 67 F4
Pleasant Valley. Saff W 25 E4
Pleshey Cl. Wick 163 F3
Pleshey Rd. Gt Wal 84 A3
Plough Rise. Upm 166 C2
Plover Gdns. Upm 166 C2
Plover Wlk. Chelm 124 A2
Plovers Barron. Bla 133 E2
Plovers Mead. Bla 133 E2
Ployters Rd. Harl 102 B2
Plumberow. Basil 170 C3
Plumleys. Basil 172 A4
Plumpton Ave. Hornc 165 F1
Plumpton Rd. Hod 100 B4
Plums La. Ba Sal 53 F2
Plumtree Ave. Gt Bad 124 C3
Plumtree Mead. Lou 141 D3
Plymouth Rd. Sprin 111 F3
Pocklington Cl. Sprin 112 A2
Pods La. Ray 64 B1
Pole Hill Rd. Ching 139 E1
Poley Rd. Sta L H 179 E1
Pollard Cl. Chig 154 A3
Pollard Hatch. Harl 102 A3
Pollards Cl. Lou 140 B2
Pollards Green. Sprin 111 F1
Pollards Villas. Ba Sal 53 E1
Polsteads. Basil 171 F2
Pomfret Mead. Basil 171 D3
Pompadour Cl. Brent 158 B3
Pond Cross Farm. New 37 D4
Pond Cross Way. New 37 D4
Pond Wlk. Upm 166 C1
Pondfield La. Brent 159 D4
Pondfield Rd. Dag 173 D4
Ponds Rd. Chelm 124 A1
Pontypool Wlk. Romf 156 B2
Pool's La. Ing 121 F2
Poole Rd. Hornc 165 F2
Poore St. Arkes 36 A4
Poore St. Wic Bon 36 A4
Popes Cres. Basil 172 A3
Poplar Cl. Bla 133 F4
Poplar Cl. Chelm 124 B3
Poplar Cl. Ing 135 D1
Poplar Dr. Brent 147 E2
Poplar Row. The B 128 C1
Poplar Shaw. Wa Aby 126 C3
Poplar St. Romf 164 B4
Poplars The. Abr 142 A3
Poppy Cl. Brent 146 A2
Poppy Green. Bore 112 A3
Porchester Cl. Hornc 165 F3
Porchester Rd. Bill 149 D3
Pork Hall La. Gt Le 86 A3
Port Ave. Swan 191 D1
Port La. L Hal 68 A1
Porter Cl. Grays 191 E4
Porters. Basil 172 B4
Porters Cl. Brent 146 A1
Portland Cl. Brain 66 A2
Portland Pl. Bis St 67 F4
Portland Rd. Bis St 67 F4
Portland Rd. Grave 192 B1
Portman Dr. Bill 149 D3
Portman Dr. Woodf 152 B1
Portmore Gdns. Romf 155 D3
Portnoi Cl. Romf 155 E1
Portreath Pl. Chelm 111 D4
Portsea Rd. Tilb 193 E3
Post Meadow. Bill 161 E3
Post Office Rd. Chelm 111 D4
Post Office Rd. Harl 89 E1
Post Office Rd. Ing 135 D2
Potash Rd. Bill 149 E3
Potash Rd. Match 92 B2
Potter St. Bis St 67 F4
Potter St. Harl 103 E3
Potters Cl. Lou 140 C4
Potters Field. Harl 103 E3
Pottery La. Chelm 111 D3
Poulteney Rd. Stan M 57 F4
Pound Cl. Lo Naz 113 F4
Pound Fields. Writ 123 D4
Pound Gate. Steb 62 B3
Pound La. Basil 170 B4
Pound La. Basil 172 C4
Pound La. Grays 178 A1
Pound La Cent. Bill 161 E1
Pound La N. Bill 161 E1
Pound Wlk. Saff W 13 F1
Poundfield Rd. Lou 141 D2
Powdermill La. Wa Aby 126 A3
Powdermill Way. Wa Aby 126 A3
Powell Gdns. Dag 173 D4
Powell Rd. Basil 170 A4
Powell Rd. Lou 140 B1
Poynder Rd. Tilb 193 D3
Poynings Way. Romf 156 C1
Pratts Farm La. Lit Wal 98 B2
Precinct The. Sta L H 179 E1
Premier Ave. Grays 185 E2
Prentice Pl. Harl 103 E3
Prescott. Basil 170 B2
Prescott Cl. Hornc 165 D2
Prescott Green. Lou 141 E3
Preston Rd. Romf 156 B3
Prestwick Dr. Bis St 57 D1
Prestwood Dr. Romf 155 E3
Pretoria Cres. Ching 139 E1
Pretoria Rd. Ching 139 E1
Pretoria Rd. Romf 164 B3
Priest's La. Brent 158 C4
Priestley Ct. Grays 185 E1
Priests Ave. Romf 155 E1
Priests Field. Brent 159 E3
Primary La. Saw 78 B1
Primrose Cl. Basil 170 A2
Primrose Field. Harl 102 C3
Primrose Glen. Hornc 165 F4
Primrose Hill. Brent 158 B4
Primrose Hill. Chelm 110 C2
Primrose Hill. Hav 6 C4
Primrose Rd. Woodf 152 A1
Primula Way. Bore 112 A3
Prince Charles Ave. Grays 178 A1
Prince Edward Rd. Bill 149 E1
Prince Philip Ave. Grays 185 D3
Prince's Rd. Nave H 145 D4
Princes Ave. Corr 180 A2
Princes Ave. Woodf 152 B3
Princes Cl. Bill 149 E3
Princes Cl. N W Bas 117 E3
Princes Ct. Bill 149 E3
Princes Gate. Bis St 67 E4
Princes Mews. Bill 149 E3
Princes Park. Rain 174 A3
Princes Rd. Chelm 124 A4
Princes Rd. Lou 152 B4
Princes Rd. Romf 165 D3
Princes St. Grave 193 D1
Princes Way. Brent 147 D1
Princes Way. Lou 152 B4
Princesfield Rd. Wa Aby 127 D3
Princess Ave. Grays 187 E1
Princess Margaret Rd. Grays 187 D1
Princess Way. Hav 6 C4
Printers Way. Harl 90 A3
Prior Chase. Grays 184 C1
Priors Cl. Basil 171 E3
Priors East. Basil 171 E3
Priors Pk. Hornc 165 E1
Priors Wood Rd. Take 70 B4
Priory Ave. Harl 90 B3
Priory Ave. Hav 6 C4
Priory Cl. Brent 146 A2
Priory Cl. Chelm 110 C1
Priory Cl. Hinx 1 A2
Priory Cl. Hod 100 A3
Priory Cl. Woodf 152 A1
Priory Ct. Harl 103 D3
Priory Dr. Stan M 57 F3
Priory Gr. Romf 156 C4
Priory Mead. Dodd 133 E2
Priory Path. Romf 156 C4
Priory Rd. Corr 179 F2
Priory Rd. Lou 140 C3
Priory Rd. Romf 156 C4
Priory The. Bill 149 E3
Priory The. Writ 110 A1
Proctors Way. Bis St 68 A2
Progress Ct. Brain 65 F2
Prospect Ave. Sta L H 187 E4
Prospect Bsns Park. Lou 141 E3
Prospect Pl. Grave 193 E1
Prospect Pl. Grays 192 A4
Prospect Pl. Romf 155 E1
Prospect Pl. Saff W 13 F1
Prospect Rd. Horne 165 F4
Prospect Rd. Woodf 152 B3
Prospect Way. Brent 147 F3
Providence St. Stone 191 D1
Provident Sq. Chelm 111 E1
Prower Cl. Bill 149 D1
Prykes Dr. Chelm 111 D1
Pryors Cl. Bis St 68 A3
Pryors Rd. Chelm 124 B1
Puckleside. Basil 170 B2
Pudding La. Chig 141 F1
Pugh Pl. Corr 179 E2
Pump Hill. Gt Bad 124 C4
Pump Hill. Lou 140 C4
Pump La. Ep Gr 115 D4
Pump La. Ple 83 F1
Pump La. Sprin 111 F3
Pump St. Corr 179 D1
Purbeck Ct. Gt Bad 124 C3
Purbeck Rd. Hornc 165 D2
Purcell Cl. Basil 170 B4
Purcell Cl. Corr 179 E2
Purcell Cole. Writ 110 A1
Purcell Way. Corr 179 E2
Purfleet By-Ps. W Thu 183 E1
Purfleet Rd. Ave 183 D3
Purford Green. Harl 103 D4
Purleigh Ave. Woodf 152 C2
Purleigh Cl. Basil 163 E1
Purley Cl. Woodf 153 D1
Purlieu Way. The B 128 C2
Pyenest Rd. Harl 102 A3
Pygot Pl. Brain 65 F2
Pym Pl. Grays 185 D1
Pyms Rd. Chelm 124 A2
Pynchbek. Bis St 67 F2
Pynchon Paddocks. L Hal 78 B4
Pyne Gate. Chelm 124 A1
Pynest Green La. Wa Aby 127 D1
Pyrles La. Lou 141 D4
Pytt Field. Harl 103 D4

Quadrant The. W Thu 183 E1
Quaker La. Wa Aby 126 B3
Quaker's La. Hav 7 D4
Quarles Cl. Romf 155 D2
Quarry Hill. Grays 185 D1
Quarry Mews. Pur 183 D1
Quarry Spring. Harl 103 D4
Quarry Way. W Thu 190 C4
Quebec Rd. Tilb 193 D3
Queen Edith Dr. Ste B 18 A3
Queen Elizabeth Ave. Grays 187 E1
Queen Elizabeth Dr. Corr 179 F2
Queen Elizabeth Pl. Tilb 193 D2
Queen Mary Ave. Grays 187 E1
Queen Mary Cl. Romf 164 C3
Queen St. Brent 158 B3
Queen St. Chelm 111 D1
Queen St. Fyf 106 C1
Queen St. Grave 193 D1
Queen St. Romf 164 B3
Queen's Alley. Epp 128 C4
Queen's Ave. Woodf 152 A3
Queen's Cl. Saw 77 F2
Queen's Cl. Stan M 57 F4
Queen's Dri. Ches 126 A3
Queen's Gdns. Pan 65 D4
Queen's Grove Rd. Ching 139 E1
Queen's Rd. Brent 158 B4
Queen's Rd. Chelm 111 E1
Queen's Rd. Lou 152 B4
Queenborough La. Brain 76 B4
Queens Cres. Bis St 67 F3
Queens Gate Mews. Bill 148 C3
Queens Gdns. Rain 173 E2
Queens Gdns. Upm 166 C3
Queens Park Ave. Bill 149 D3
Queens Park Rd. Romf 157 D1
Queens Rd. Bill 161 E1
Queens Rd. Bill 162 A2
Queens Rd. Brain 65 F3
Queens Rd. Lou 140 C3
Queens Rd. N W Bas 117 D3
Queens St. Hav 7 D4
Queens Wlk. Ching 139 E1
Queensland Cres. Chelm 110 C3
Queenstown Gdns. Rain 173 F1
Queensway. Ch Ong 118 C3
Queensway. Hav 6 C4
Queenswood Ave. Brent 147 E2
Quendon Dri. Wa Aby 126 B3
Quendon Rd. Basil 171 F4
Quennell Way. Brent 147 E1
Quickset Rd. Elm 11 E3
Quicksie Hill. Arkes 23 F1
Quilp Dr. Chelm 110 C4
Quilters Cl. Basil 171 E4
Quilters Straight. Basil 171 E4
Quince Tree. S Ock 176 B1
Quinion Cl. Chelm 110 B4
Quinton Way. Wa Aby 126 B2
Quorn The. Ing 135 D2

Rachael Clarke Cl. Corr 179 F2
Radburn Cl. Harl 103 D2
Radburn Pl. Swan 191 F1
Radford Cres. Bill 149 D2
Radford Ct. Bill 149 D2
Radford Way. Bill 149 D2
Radley Green Rd. Rox 121 E4
Radley Green Rd. Will 121 E4
Radley's La. Woodf 152 A1
Radleys Mead. Dag 173 D3
Radwinter Ave. Wick 163 E3
Radwinter Rd. Ash 15 D4
Radwinter Rd. Saff W 14 A1
Radwinter Rd. Saff W 14 C1
Rahn Rd. Epp 129 D4
Raider Cl. Romf 155 D1
Railey Rd. Saff W 25 F4
Railway App. Basil 170 A3
Railway Cotts. Wen A 24 C3
Railway Pl. Grave 193 D1
Railway Sq. Chelm 111 D2
Railway St. Brain 66 A2
Railway St. Chelm 111 D2
Railway St. Grave 192 A1
Rainbow La. Sta L H 179 F1
Rainbow Rd. Match 91 F2
Rainham Rd. Dag 173 F3
Rainham Rd N. Dag 164 A1
Rainham Rd S. Dag 173 E4
Rainsford Ave. Chelm 110 C2
Rainsford La. Chelm 110 C1
Rainsford Rd. Chelm 110 C2
Rainsford Rd. Stan M 57 F4
Ram Gorse. Harl 89 D1
Ramsay Dr. Basil 171 F2
Ramsden Dr. Romf 155 D2
Ramsden Park Rd. Wick 150 B1
Ramsden View Rd. Wick 162 C3
Ramsey Gdns. Romf 156 B1
Ramshaw Dr. Sprin 111 F2
Rana Ct. Brain 65 F2
Rana Dr. Brain 65 F2

Randall Cl. Gt Dun 61 E1
Randall Dr. Hornc 165 E1
Randalls Dr. Brent 147 F2
Randolph Ave. Finch 43 E3
Rands Rd. H Rod 81 F4
Randulph Terr. Sprin 111 E2
Ranger's Rd. Ching 140 A1
Ranger's Rd. Lou 140 A1
Rantree Fold. Basil 170 C2
Ranworth Ave. Hod 87 D1
Raphael Ave. Tilb 193 D4
Raphael Dr. Sprin 111 F4
Raphael.Ave. Romf 164 C4
Raphaels. Basil 170 C3
Rapier Cl. Pur 183 D1
Rathmore Rd. Grave 193 D1
Ratty's La. Hod 100 B3
Ravel Gdns. Ave 183 E4
Ravel Rd. Ave 183 E4
Raven Cl. Bill 148 C2
Raven Cres. Bill 148 C2
Raven La. Bill 148 C2
Raven Rd. Woodf 152 B1
Ravencroft. Grays 186 A2
Ravens Cres. Felst 74 C3
Ravensbourne Cres. Romf 165 F4
Ravensbourne Dr. Chelm 110 C1
Ravensbourne Gdns. Woodf 153 D1
Ravenscourt Cl. Hornc 165 F1
Ravenscourt Dr. Basil 171 F3
Ravenscourt Dr. Hornc 165 F1
Ravenscourt Gr. Hornc 165 F1
Ravensdale. Basil 171 D2
Ravensfield. Basil 171 F3
Ravensmere. Epp 116 A1
Ravenswood Cl. Romf 155 D3
Rawdon Dri. Hod 100 A3
Ray Lodge Rd. Woodf 152 B2
Ray Mead. Gt Wal 97 F4
Ray Rd. Romf 155 D3
Ray The. Sprin 111 F3
Rayburn Rd. Hornc 166 A2
Rayfield. Epp 116 A1
Rayfield Cl. Barn 73 D2
Rayleigh Cl. Brain 66 B2
Rayleigh Cl. Brent 147 E2
Rayleigh Rd. Brent 147 E2
Rayleigh Rd. Sta L H 179 D1
Rayleigh Rd. Woodf 152 B2
Rayley La. N W Bas 117 D4
Raymond Gdns. Chig 154 A4
Rayne Rd. Brain 65 E2
Raynham Rd. Bis St 68 B4
Rayside. Basil 171 E3
Read Ct. Wa Aby 127 D3
Readers Ct. Gt Bad 124 C3
Readings The. Harl 102 C3
Rebecca Meade. Gt Ea 60 C4
Recreation Ave. Corr 180 B2
Recreation Ave. Romf 156 C1
Recreation Ave. Romf 164 B3
Recreation Ave. Romf 165 F4
Recreation Ground. Stan M 57 F3
Recreation Rd. Hav 6 C4
Recreation Wlk.. S Han 150 B3
Rectory Chase. Brent 167 F4
Rectory Chase. Dodd 133 E1
Rectory Cl. Hun 88 B4
Rectory Cl. Ing 135 D2
Rectory Cl. Lit Wal 98 B3
Rectory Cl. Litt 12 C2
Rectory Cl. Stock 136 B1
Rectory Cl. Thor 67 E2
Rectory Ct. Basil 172 B4
Rectory Field. Harl 102 A3
Rectory Gdns. Basil 172 B3
Rectory Gdns. Upm 166 C1
Rectory Gr. Wick 163 F4
Rectory La. Ash 4 A1
Rectory La. Chelm 111 D2
Rectory La. Far 56 B3
Rectory La. Gt Le 85 E4
Rectory La. Harl 102 A3
Rectory La. Lou 141 D3
Rectory Park Dr. Basil 172 A3
Rectory Rd. Basil 172 B3
Rectory Rd. Bill 160 C2
Rectory Rd. Dag 173 D3
Rectory Rd. Grays 185 E1
Rectory Rd. Grays 186 A4
Rectory Rd. Grays 186 B1
Rectory Rd. Sta L H 179 E1
Rectory Rd. Writ 123 D4
Rectory Wood. Harl 89 E1
Red Lion Cres. Harl 103 E3
Red Lion Ct. Bis St 68 A4
Red Lion La. Harl 103 E3
Red Oaks Mead. The B 128 B1
Red Rd. Brent 150 A3
Red White and Blue Rd. Bis St 57 D1
Red Willow. Harl 101 F3
Redbury Cl. Rain 174 A1
Redcar Rd. Romf 156 C3
Redcliff Rd. Chelm 111 D1
Redden Court Rd. Romf 165 F4
Reddings Cl. Saff W 25 F4
Redfern Gdns. Romf 156 B1
Redgates La. Saff W 14 C2
Redgates Pl. Sprin 111 F2
Redgrave Rd. Basil 171 F2
Redinge The. Bill 161 E4
Redings The. Upm 166 B3
Redlie Cl. Corr 179 E2
Redmayne Dr. Chelm 124 A4
Redrick La. H Wy 89 F3
Redricks La. Saw 90 C4
Redriff Rd. Romf 155 D1
Redrose La. Bla 120 C1
Redruth Cl. Sprin 111 F3
Redruth Gdns. Romf 156 C3
Redruth Rd. Romf 156 C3
Redruth Wlk. Romf 156 C3
Redvers Cl. Bis St 57 D1
Redwing Dr. Bill 161 E4
Redwood Cl. Woodf 152 A4
Redwood Dr. Writ 109 F1
Redwood Gdns. Chig 154 A3
Reed Pond Wlk. Basil 170 A2
Reed Pond Wlk. Romf 156 A1
Reede Gdns. Dag 173 D4
Reede Rd. Dag 173 D3
Reede Way. Dag 173 D3
Reedings Way. Saw 77 F2
Reeds La. Hav 7 D4
Reeds Way. Wick 163 E4
Reeves Cl. Sto M 133 D3
Reeves La. Roy 101 E3
Regan Cl. Corr 179 F2
Regarder Rd. Chig 154 A3
Regarth Ave. Romf 164 C3
Regency Cl. Bis St 67 F4
Regency Cl. Chig 153 E3
Regency Cl. Runw 151 E1
Regency Cl. Sprin 111 E2
Regency Ct. Brent 158 B4
Regency Ct. Harl 103 D3
Regency Gdns. Hornc 165 E2
Regent Cl. Grays 185 E2
Regent Rd. Epp 115 F1
Regina Rd. Chelm 111 E2
Reginald Rd. Romf 157 D1
Rembrandt Gr. Sprin 111 F3
Renacres. Basil 170 C2
Rennie Rd. Chelm 111 E1
Renoir Pl. Sprin 111 F4
Renown Cl. Romf 155 D1
Repton Ave. Romf 165 D4
Repton Cl. Basil 163 D1
Repton Dr. Romf 165 D4
Repton Gdns. Romf 165 D4
Repton Gr. Woodf 152 C1
Repulse Cl. Romf 155 D1
Retford Cl. Romf 157 D2
Retford Path. Romf 157 D2
Retford Rd. Romf 157 D2
Retreat The. Brent 146 A1
Retreat The. Brent 147 D2
Retreat The. Grays 192 A4
Retreat Way. Chig 154 A4
Rettendon Gdns. Runw 151 F1
Rettendon View. Wick 163 F4
Reubens Rd. Brent 147 D2
Review Rd. Dag 173 D2
Reynard Ct. Gt Bad 124 C3
Rhodes Ave. Bis St 67 F3
Ribble Cl. Woodf 152 B2
Rich Cl. Gt Le 85 F4
Richards Ave. Romf 164 B3
Richmond Cl. Bis St 67 E4
Richmond Rd. Ching 139 E1
Richmond Rd. Grays 185 E1
Richmond Rd. Romf 164 C3
Richmond Rd. Runw 151 E1
Richmond Rd. Sprin 112 A2
Ricketts Dr. Bill 148 C2
Rickling. Basil 171 F2
Rickling Green Rd. Quen 36 C1
Rickling Rd. Wic Bon 36 A3
Riddings La. Harl 103 D2
Ridgeway. Bill 161 D4
Ridgeway. Brent 147 D1
Ridgeway. Grays 185 F1
Ridgeway. Ing 135 D1
Ridgeway. Woodf 152 B3
Ridgeway The. Brain 66 A1
Ridgeway The. Ching 139 E1
Ridgeway The. Romf 156 C1
Ridgeway The. Romf 165 D4
Ridgewell Ave. Grays 178 A1
Ridgewell Cl. Dag 173 D2
Ridgewell Rd. Bird 8 C1
Ridgewell Rd. Gt Y 20 C2
Ridings The. Bis St 67 E2
Ridings The. Gt Bad 124 B4
Ridley Cl. Romf 156 A1
Ridley Gdns. Els 48 B1
Ridley Rd. Basil 163 E1
Ridley Rd. Chelm 111 D4
Riffams Ct. Basil 172 B4
Riffams Dr. Basil 172 B4
Riffhams. Brent 159 D4
Riffhams Dr. Gt Bad 125 D4
Rifle Hill. Brain 65 F1
Rigby Gdns. Grays 186 A1
Rignals La. Chelm 124 B2
Ringwood Ave. Horne 165 E1
Ripley View. Lou 128 A1
Ripple Rd. Dag 173 D2
Rippleside. Basil 171 F3
Risdens. Harl 102 B3
Rise Park. Basil 170 C3
Rise Park Bvd. Romf 155 F1
Rise Park Par. Romf 155 F1
Rise The. Lou 140 B1
Risebridge Chase. Romf 155 F2
Risebridge Rd. Romf 156 A1
Riseway. Brent 158 C4
Rising Gr. Basil 170 B3
Rising The. Bill 149 E1
River Ave. Hod 100 A4
River Cl. Ches 126 A3
River Cl. Rain 182 A4
River Cotts. Bore 112 C4
River Dr. Upm 166 B3
River Meads. Stan 87 E2
River Rd. Brent 157 F3
River Rd. Lou 140 C1
River View. Brain 65 F1
River View. Grays 186 A1
River Way. Harl 90 A3
River Way. Lou 141 D2
Riverfield La. Saw 77 F2
Rivermead. Chelm 111 D2
Rivermill. Harl 89 E1
Riversdale Rd. Romf 155 D2
Riverside. Bis St 67 F4
Riverside. Gt Dun 61 F1
Riverside Ave. Lo Naz 100 A1
Riverside Cotts. Sta Ab 87 E2
Riverside Ct. Ching 139 D2
Riverside Wlk. Bis St 67 F4
Riverside Wlk. Wick 163 D4
Riversmead. Hod 100 A3
Rivertons. Basil 171 F2
Riverview. Basil 172 A2
Riverview Ct. Basil 171 F2
Riverview Rd. Swan 191 D1
Rivington Ave. Woodf 152 B1
Roach. Grays 187 E1
Robert Cl. Bill 148 C1
Robert Cl. Chig 153 F3
Robert Suckling Ct. Ste B 18 A3
Robert Wallace Cl. Bis St 56 C1
Robert Way. Wick 163 F3
Roberts Cl. Romf 156 A1
Roberts Rd. Basil 170 A4
Robin Cl. Bill 149 E3
Robin Cl. Bill 161 E1
Robin Cl. Romf 155 E2
Robin Hood Rd. Brent 146 B1
Robin Hood Rd. Els 48 B1
Robin Way. Chelm 124 A3
Robinia Cl. Chig 153 F2
Robins The. Bla 133 E2
Robinson Cl. Bis St 67 F3
Robinson Cl. Hornc 174 A3
Robinson Rd. Dag 173 D4
Robinson Rd. Horn H 178 C2
Robinsway. Wa Aby 126 C3
Robjohns Rd. Chelm 123 F4
Roborough Wlk. Hornc 174 B3
Rochelle Cl. Thax 40 A2
Rochester Way. Basil 171 F4
Rochford Ave. Brent 147 D2
Rochford Ave. Lou 141 E3
Rochford Ave. Wa Aby 126 B3
Rochford Cl. Hornc 174 A3
Rochford Cl. Wick 163 F3
Rochford Green. Lou 141 E3
Rochford Rd. Bis St 57 D1
Rochford Rd. Chelm 111 E1
Rock Gdns. Dag 173 D4
Rockall Cl. Hav 7 E4
Rockchase Gdns. Hornc 165 F3
Rockingham Ave. Hornc 165 D3
Rockwell Rd. Dag 173 D4
Roden Cl. Harl 90 C2
Roding Ave. Woodf 152 C2
Roding Cl. Fyf 106 B1
Roding Dr. Kelv H 132 C1
Roding La. Chig 153 D4
Roding La. Lov 153 D4
Roding La N. Woodf 152 C1
Roding Rd. Lou 140 C2
Roding View. Ch Ong 119 D2
Roding View. Lou 140 B1
Roding Way. Rain 174 B2
Roding Way. Wick 163 F3
Rodings Ave. Corr 179 E2
Rodings The. Woodf 152 B2
Rodney Cres. Hod 100 A4
Rodney Gdns. Brain 66 B2
Rodney Rd. Ch Ong 118 C1
Rodney Way. Chelm 123 F4
Rodney Way. Romf 155 D1
Roebuck La. Lou 140 B1
Roebuck Rd. Chig 154 A2
Roger Reede's Almshouses. Romf 164 C4
Rogers Gdns. Dag 173 D4
Rogers Rd. Dag 173 D4
Rogers Rd. Grays 185 E1
Rokeby Gdns. Woodf 152 A1
Rokells. Basil 171 D4
Rokescroft. Basil 172 A3
Rolands Cl. Chelm 111 D4
Rollestons. Writ 122 C4
Rom Cres. Romf 164 C2
Rom Valley Way. Romf 164 C2
Roman. Grays 187 E1
Roman Cl. Rain 173 E2
Roman Rd. Chelm 111 D1
Roman Rd. Lit Wal 98 A3
Roman St. Hod 100 A4
Roman Vale. Harl 90 B3
Roman Way. Bill 161 D4
Roman Way. Hav 7 E4
Roman Way. Litt 12 C2
Romans Pl. Writ 110 A1
Romans Way. Writ 110 A1
Romeland. Wa Aby 126 B3
Romford Rd. Ave 183 E4
Romford Rd. Chig 154 B3
Romford Rd. Romf 154 B3
Romford Rd. Sta R 131 F4
Romney Chase. Hornc 166 A3
Romney Cl. Brain 65 F3
Romney Rd. Bill 148 C1
Romsey Cl. Sta L H 179 D1
Ronald Rd. Romf 157 D1
Roneo Cnr. Hornc 164 C2
Roneo Link. Hornc 164 C2
Roodegate. Basil 171 D3
Rook Cl. Rain 174 A3
Rook End La. Deb 38 A3
Rookery Cl. Gt C 1 B2
Rookery Cres. Dag 173 D3
Rookery Ct. W Thu 191 D4
Rookery Hill. Corr 180 B2
Rookery La. Wen A 24 C2
Rookery Rd. H Ong 120 B2
Rookery The. Stan M 57 F4
Rookery The. W Thu 191 D4
Rookery View. Grays 185 E1
Rookes. Saff W 13 E2
Rookwood Ave. Lou 141 E3
Rookwood Cl. Grays 185 D1
Rookwood Gdns. Lou 141 E3
Rookwood Way. Hav 7 D3
Rookyards. Basil 171 F3
Roos Hill. Saff W 25 F3
Roosevelt Rd. Basil 170 A3
Roosevelt Way. Dag 173 E3
Roper's Chase. Writ 123 D4
Rose Acre. Basil 171 F3
Rose Ave. Woodf 152 A1
Rose Bank. Brent 158 B4
Rose Glen. Chelm 124 B4
Rose Glen. Romf 164 C2
Rose Hill. Brain 66 A1
Rose La. Bill 149 D1
Rose La. Gt C 1 C1
Rose St. Grave 192 A1
Rose Vale. Hod 100 A3
Rose Valley. Brent 158 B4
Rose Valley Cres. Corr 179 F2
Roseacre Cl. Hornc 165 F2
Roseacres. Saw 77 E2
Roseacres. Take 70 B4
Rosebank. Wa Aby 126 C3
Rosebank Ave. Hornc 174 B4
Rosebay Ave. Bill 148 C3
Roseberry Ave. Basil 170 A2
Roseberry Cl. Upm 166 C3
Roseberry Gdns. Upm 166 C3
Rosebery Rd. Grays 191 F4
Rosebery. Bis St 68 B3
Rosebery Rd. Chelm 124 A4
Rosecroft Cl. Basil 170 A2
Rosedale Rd. Grays 185 E1
Rosedale Rd. Romf 164 B4
Rosefinch Cl. Hav 7 E4
Roselaine. Basil 171 D4
Rosemary Ave. Brain 65 F2
Rosemary Ave. Romf 164 C4
Rosemary Cl. Gt Dun 61 E1
Rosemary Cl. Harl 90 B2
Rosemary Cl. S Ock 176 B1
Rosemary Cres. Gt Dun 61 E1
Rosemary La. Gt Dun 61 E1
Rosemary La. Steb 62 B4
Rosemead Gdns. Brent 147 E3
Rosemount. Harl 102 A3
Rosemount Cl. Woodf 152 C2
Rosewood Ave. Hornc 174 A4
Roslings Cl. Chelm 110 B3
Roslyn Gdns. Romf 155 F1
Ross Cl. Hav 7 E4
Ross Cl. Saff W 25 F3
Ross Way. Basil 170 A2
Rossall Cl. Hornc 165 D3
Rossdene Gdns. Lea Rod 94 B4
Rossendale. Chelm 110 C1
Rosslyn Ave. Dag 164 A2
Rosslyn Ave. Romf 156 C1
Rosslyn Rd. Bill 148 C1
Roth Dr. Brent 159 D4
Rothbury Ave. Rain 182 A4
Rothbury Rd. Chelm 110 B1
Rothesay Ave. Chelm 124 A4
Rothmans Ave. Gt Bad 124 C3
Roughtallys. N W Bas 116 C2
Roughtons. Chelm 124 B2
Round Coppice Rd. Stan M 69 D4
Round Coppice Rd. Take 58 A1
Roundacre. Basil 171 D3
Roundaway Rd. Woodf 152 C1
Roundhills. Wa Aby 126 C3
Roundmead Ave. Lou 141 D4
Roundmead Cl. Lou 141 D4
Roundwood Ave. Brent 147 D1
Roundwood Gr. Brent 147 D1
Rounton Rd. Wa Aby 126 C3
Rous Chase. Chelm 124 A1
Rous Rd. Lou 140 C1
Rover Ave. Chig 153 F2
Row The. Hen 48 C3
Rowan Green E. Brent 158 C4
Rowan Green W. Brent 158 C4
Rowan Wlk. Hornc 165 E4
Rowans The. Ave 183 E3
Rowans The. Bill 161 E4
Rowans Way. Lou 140 C3
Rowenhall. Basil 169 F3
Rowhedge. Brent 159 D4
Rowhedge Cl. Basil 163 E1
Rowland Cres. Chig 153 F3
Rowley Hill. Stur 7 F3
Rowley Mead. N W Bas 116 B3
Rowley Rd. Grays 186 A4
Rowney Ave. Wim 26 C1
Rowney Gdns. Saw 90 B4
Rowney Wood. Saw 77 E1
Rowntree Way. Saff W 25 E4
Roxburgh Ave. Upm 166 B1
Roxwell Ave. Chelm 110 B2
Roxwell Gdns. Brent 147 E2
Roxwell Rd. Chelm 110 B2
Roxwell Rd. Writ 110 B2
Roxwell Way. Woodf 152 B2
Royal Pier Rd. Grave 193 E1
Roycroft Cl. Woodf 152 A1
Roydon Bridge. Basil 171 E4
Roydon Cl. Lou 140 C1
Roydon Lodge Chalet Est. Roy 88 B1
Roydon Rd. Harl 88 C1
Roydon Rd. Sta Ab 87 F2
Royle Cl. Romf 165 D3
Royston Ave. Basil 161 E1
Royston La. Hinx 11 D4
Royston Rd. Romf 157 D2
Royston Rd. Wen A 24 B3
Rubens Gate. Sprin 111 F4
Rubicon Ave. Wick 163 F4
Rue De St Lawrence. Wa Aby 126 B3
Rumbold Rd. Hod 100 B4
Rumbullion Dr. Bill 148 C2
Rundells. Harl 103 D2
Rundells Wlk. Basil 171 F4
Running Mare La. Chelm 124 A2
Running Waters. Brent 159 D3
Runnymede Ct. Sta L H 179 E1
Runnymede Rd. Sta L H 179 E1
Runwell Gdns. Runw 151 E1
Runwell Rd. Runw 151 F1
Rural Cl. Hornc 165 D2
Rural Vale. Grave 192 C1
Rush Cl. Sta Ab 87 E2
Rush Green Gdns. Romf 164 B2
Rush Green Rd. Romf 164 B2
Rushden Gdns. Woodf 153 D1
Rushdene Rd. Bill 148 C1
Rushdene Rd. Brent 146 B1
Rushdon Cl. Grays 185 D2
Rushdon Cl. Romf 165 D3
Rushes Ct. Bis St 68 A3
Rushes Mead. Harl 102 C3
Rushfield. Saw 77 F1
Rushleigh Green. Bis St 67 E2
Rushley. Basil 163 E1
Rushley Cl. Grays 185 E3
Rushleydale. Sprin 111 F3
Rushmere Ave. Upm 166 B1
Rusholme Ave. Dag 164 A1
Ruskin Ave. Upm 166 B2
Ruskin Ave. Wa Aby 126 C3
Ruskin Gdns. Romf 156 A2
Ruskin Gr. Stone 190 A1
Ruskin Path. Wick 163 E3
Ruskin Rd. Chelm 111 F1
Ruskin Rd. Grays 186 A1
Ruskin Rd. Sta L H 179 E1
Ruskins The. Ray 64 C1
Russel Rd. Grays 185 D1
Russell Cl. Basil 170 A4
Russell Cl. Brent 146 A1
Russell Gdns. Chelm 124 A2
Russell Gdns. Wick 163 F4
Russell Rd. Grave 193 E1
Russell Rd. Lou 140 B1
Russell Rd. Tilb 192 C3
Russell Way. Chelm 123 F4
Russet Cl. Brain 66 A1
Russet Cl. Corr 179 E2
Russets. Chelm 124 B2
Russetts. Basil 170 A3
Russetts. Hornc 165 F4
Rustic Cl. Upm 166 C2
Rutherford Cl. Bill 149 D3
Rutherford St. Broom 98 A1
Rutland App. Hornc 166 A3
Rutland Cl. Basil 170 A3
Rutland Dr. Hornc 166 A3
Rutland Gdns. Brain 66 A2
Rutland Rd. Chelm 111 D4

Rydal Way. Bl Not 76 B3
Ryde Dr. Sta L H 187 E4
Ryder Gdns. Rain 173 F3
Ryder Way. Basil 163 E1
Rye Cl. Hornc 174 B4
Rye Hill Rd. Ep Gr 102 C1
Rye Hill Rd. Harl 102 C1
Rye Hill Rd. N W Bas 102 C1
Rye Mead. Basil 170 B2
Rye Rd. Hod 100 B4
Rye Rd. Sta Ab 87 E1
Rye St. Bis St 56 C1
Rye Wlk. Ing 135 D1
Ryecroft. Harl 102 A4
Ryecroft Ave. Woodf 153 D1
Ryedene. Basil 171 F2
Ryedene Cl. Basil 171 F2
Ryedene Pl. Basil 171 F2
Ryefeld Cl. Hod 87 D1
Ryes La. Hat B O 79 D4
Rykhill. Grays 186 A2
Ryle The. Writ 123 D4
Rylstone Way. Saff W 25 F4

Sabina Rd. Grays 186 B1
Sabines Rd. Nave H 144 C3
Sable Way. Basil 169 F4
Sackville Cl. Chelm 110 C2
Sackville Cres. Romf 156 C1
Saddle Rise. Sprin 111 F4
Saddleworth Rd. Romf 156 B2
Saddleworth Sq. Romf 156 B2
Sadlers Cl. Bill 149 E3
Sadlers Mead. Harl 103 D4
Saffro Ct. Basil 169 F3
Saffron Cl. Grays 179 D2
Saffron Cl. Horn H 168 B3
Saffron Cl. Weth 43 E2
Saffron Gdns. Weth 43 E2
Saffron Rd. Romf 155 E1
Saffron Wlk. Bill 149 D1
Sages. Hen 48 C3
Sages End Rd. Hel B 17 D4
Sailing Green. Bill 161 F1
Sains. Basil 170 B4
St Agnes Rd. Bill 161 E2
St Alban's Cres. Woodf 152 A1
St Alban's Rd. Epp 116 B1
St Alban's Rd. Woodf 152 A2
St Albans Ave. Upm 166 C1
St Andrew's Rd. Tilb 192 C3
St Andrews Ave. Hornc 174 A4
St Andrews Cl. N W Bas 117 E4
St Andrews Pl. Brent 158 C4
St Andrews Rd. Bore 99 F1
St Andrews Rd. Romf 164 B3
St Anne's Rd. Mtssg 147 E4
St Annes Cl. Grays 185 D3
St Anthony's Ave. Woodf 152 B2
St Anthony's Dr. Chelm 124 B4
St Augustine Rd. Grays 186 A1
St Barnabas Rd. Woodf 152 B2
St Botolph's Way. Hav 6 C4
St Catherine's Ct. Hod 100 A2
St Catherine's Rd. Chelm 110 C1
St Catherines Cl. Wick 163 F4
St Cecilia Rd. Grays 186 A1
St Cedds Ct. Grays 185 D3
St Chad's Rd. Tilb 193 D4
St Charles Dr. Wick 163 F4
St Charles Rd. Brent 146 A1
St Clair Cl. Woodf 152 C1
St Clement's Ave. W Thu 191 D4
St Clement's Rd. W Thu 191 E4
St Clements. Thax 40 A1
St Clements Ct. Pur 183 D1
St Cleres Cres. Wick 163 F4
St Cross Ct. Hod 100 A2
St Cuthbert's Rd. Hod 87 E1
St David's Rd. Basil 170 A2
St David's Way. Wick 163 F4
St Dunstan's Rd. Hun 88 B4
St Ediths Ct. Bill 149 D1
St Ediths La. Bill 149 D1
St Edmund's Way. Harl 90 B2
St Edmunds Fields. Gt Dun 61 F1
St Edmunds La. Gt Dun 61 F1
St Edmunds Rd. Stone 190 A2
St Edwards Way. Romf 164 C4
St Egberts Way. Ching 139 E1
St Fabian's Dr. Chelm 110 C2
St Gabriels Ct. Basil 172 A3
St George's Ave. Grays 185 E1
St George's Ave. Hornc 165 F2
St George's Centre. Grave 193 D1
St Georges Cl. Dodd 133 D2
St Gile's Ave. Dag 173 D3
St Giles Cl. Dag 173 D3
St Giles Cl. Grays 178 A1
St Helens Ct. Rain 174 A1
St Helens Wlk. Bill 148 C2
St Ivians Dr. Romf 165 D4
St James Ave. Ch Ong 119 D1
St James Ave E. Corr 179 F2
St James Ave W. Corr 179 F2
St James La. Stone 190 C1
St James Park. Chelm 110 B2
St James Rd. Basil 171 E3
St James Rd. Brain 65 F3
St James' Ct. Hav 6 C4
St James's Ave. Grave 193 D1
St James's Rd. Brent 158 B4
St James's Rd. Grave 193 D1
St James's St. Grave 193 D1
St John Ave. Brain 65 F1
St John's Ave. Brent 158 B3
St John's Ave. Chelm 124 A4
St John's Ave. Harl 90 B2
St John's Cres. Stan M 57 F4
St John's Ct. Lou 140 A1
St John's Green. Writ 110 A1
St John's La. Stan M 57 F4
St John's Mews. Corr 179 F2
St John's Rd. Bill 149 D2
St John's Rd. Chelm 124 A4
St John's Rd. Epp 115 F1
St John's Rd. Lou 140 C4
St John's Rd. Stan M 57 F4
St John's Rd. Stone 190 B1
St John's Rd. Writ 110 A1
St John's Way. Corr 179 F2
St Johns Cl. Gt C 1 B1
St Johns Cl. Rain 174 A3
St Johns Cl. Saff W 25 F4
St Johns Rd. Grays 186 A1
St Johns Rd. Romf 155 E3
St Johns Wlk. Harl 90 B2
St Kilda's Rd. Brent 146 B1
St Lawrence Rd. Upm 166 B1
St Leonards Cl. Saff W 25 D1
St Leonards Rd. Lo Naz 113 F4
St Leonards Way. Hornc 165 D2
St Margaret's Ave. Sta L H 187 E4
St Margaret's Rd. Hod 87 D1
St Margaret's Rd. Sprin 111 F2
St Margaret's Rd. Sta L H 187 E4
St Mark's Ave. Grave 192 C1
St Martin's Mews. Ch Ong 119 D1
St Martins Cl. Wh Rot 93 E4
St Mary's Ave. Bill 149 D1
St Mary's Ave. Brent 147 D2
St Mary's Cl. Gt Bad 124 C3
St Mary's Cl. Pan 65 D4
St Mary's Cres. Basil 172 B3
St Mary's Ct. Grays 192 B4
St Mary's Dr. Stan M 57 F3
St Mary's La. Horn H 167 E2
St Mary's La. Upm 167 E2
St Mary's Mead. Broom 98 A2
St Mary's Path. Basil 172 B4
St Mary's Pl. Lit Dun 73 E4
St Mary's Rd. Brain 66 A2
St Mary's Rd. Grays 186 A1
St Mary's Wlk. Ste B 18 A3
St Marys Rd. Stone 190 C2
St Marys Way. Chig 153 D3
St Matthew's Cl. Rain 174 A3
St Michael's Cl. Harl 89 F1
St Michael's Dr. Rox 109 D3
St Michael's La. Brain 65 F1
St Michael's Rd. Brain 65 F1
St Michael's Rd. Chelm 124 A4
St Michael's Rd. Hod 100 A2
St Michaels Ave. Basil 172 B2
St Michaels Cl. Ave 183 E3
St Michaels Rd. Grays 186 A1
St Michaels Wlk. Chelm 124 B1
St Mildreds Rd. Chelm 124 A4
St Nazaire Rd. Chelm 110 C3
St Neots Rd. Romf 156 C2
St Nicholas Ave. Hornc 165 D1
St Nicholas Field. Berd 46 A4
St Nicholas Gr. Brent 159 E3
St Nicholas La. Basil 170 B4
St Patrick's Pl. Grays 186 B1
St Paul's Cl. Ave 183 E3
St Paul's Pl. Ave 183 E3
St Pauls Gdns. Bill 149 D2
St Pauls Way. Wa Aby 126 B3
St Peter's Ave. Ch Ong 118 C3
St Peter's Cl. Brain 65 F2
St Peter's Pavement. Basil 162 C1
St Peter's Rd. Brain 65 F2
St Peter's Rd. Brent 158 A3
St Peter's Rd. Chelm 110 C1
St Peter's Terr. Wick 163 E4
St Peter's Wlk. Brain 65 F2
St Peters Rd. Grays 186 A1
St Peters Wlk. Bill 148 C2
St Peters's-in-the-Fields. Brain 65 F2
St Ronans Cres. Woodf 152 A2
St Stephen's Cres. Brent 159 D3
St Teresa Wlk. Grays 186 A1
St Thomas' Rd. Brent 158 B4
St Thomas's Cl. Wa Aby 127 D3
St Thomas's Pl. Grays 192 B4
St Valerie. Take 70 B4
St Vincent Chase. Brain 66 A3
St Vincents Ave. Stone 190 A1
St Vincents Rd. Chelm 124 A4
St Vincents Rd. Stone 190 A1
St Winifred's Cl. Chig 153 E3
Saint Francis Way. Grays 186 B2
Saint's Wlk. Grays 186 B1
Sakins Croft. Harl 102 C3
Salcombe Pk. Lou 183 D1
Salcombe Rd. Brain 66 B1
Salcott Cres. Wick 163 F3
Salerno Way. Chelm 110 C3
Salesbury Dr. Bill 149 E1
Salisbury Ave. Basil 170 B3
Salisbury Ave. Sta L H 179 E1
Salisbury Cl. Bis St 67 F3
Salisbury Gdns. Lou 152 B4
Salisbury Rd. Dag 173 D3
Salisbury Rd. Grays 185 E1
Salisbury Rd. Hod 100 B4
Salisbury Rd. Romf 165 D3
Salix Rd. Grays 192 B4
Salmond's Gr. Brent 159 E3
Saltash Rd. Chig 153 E2
Salter Pl. Sprin 111 F1
Salway Cl. Woodf 152 A2
Samantha Mews. Hav B 155 F4
Samphire Ct. Grays 192 C4
Samuel Manor. Sprin 111 F2
Samuel Rd. Basil 170 A2
Sanctuary Gdn. Corr 179 F1
Sanderson Cl. Horn H 168 B3
Sandford Ave. Lou 141 E3
Sandford Mill Rd. Sprin 112 A1
Sandford Rd. Chelm 111 F2
Sandgate Cl. Romf 164 B2
Sandhurst Rd. Tilb 193 E3
Sandle Rd. Bis St 68 A4
Sandon Hall Bridleway. Sand 125 E2
Sandon Hill. Gt Wal 84 A3
Sandon Pl. Ch Ong 119 D1
Sandon Rd. Basil 171 F3
Sandown Ave. Dag 173 E3
Sandown Ave. Hornc 165 E1
Sandown Ct. Dag 173 E3
Sandown Rd. Grays 186 C4
Sandpiper Cl. Hav 7 D4
Sandpiper Wlk. Chelm 124 B3
Sandpit La. Brent 145 F1
Sandpit Rd. Brain 65 F2
Sandringham Cl. Corr 179 F2
Sandringham Rd. Brent 146 A2
Sandwich Cl. Brain 65 F3
Sandy La. Ave 183 D3
Sandy La. Grays 186 B1
Sandy La. Rain 183 D3
Sandy La. W Thu 191 D4
Sappers Cl. Saw 77 F1
Sarre Ave. Hornc 174 B3
Saunders Ave. Brain 65 F2
Saunton Rd. Hornc 165 D1
Savill Row. Woodf 152 A3
Saville Cl. Clav 35 D2
Savoy Wood. Harl 102 A2
Sawbridgeworth Rd. Saw 78 C2
Sawkins Ave. Gt Bad 124 B3
Sawkins Cl. Gt Bad 124 B3
Sawkins Gdns. Gt Bad 124 B3
Sawney Brook. Writ 110 A1
Sawpit La. Berd 46 B4
Sawyer's Chase. Abr 142 A3
Sawyer's Hall La. Brent 146 B1
Saxon Cl. Brent 159 D4
Saxon Cl. Romf 156 C1
Saxon Cl. Runw 151 F1
Saxon Way. Chelm 111 D4
Saxon Way. Saff W 13 E1
Saxon Way. Wa Aby 126 B3
Sayes Gdns. Saw 77 F1
Sayesbury Ave. Saw 77 F2
Sayesbury Rd. Saw 77 F1
Saywell Brook. Sprin 112 A1
Scaldhurst. Basil 172 B4
Scarletts. Basil 171 E4
Scholars Rd. Ching 139 E1
School Green La. N W Bas 117 E3
School La. Abb Rod 93 F1
School La. Abb Rod 107 D4
School La. Brent 159 E2
School La. Broom 98 A1
School La. Brox 59 E3
School La. Elm 23 D4
School La. Grays 186 A4
School La. Gt Le 85 F4
School La. H Ea 82 A2
School La. Harl 89 F1
School La. Hav 6 C4
School La. Hen 48 C3
School La. Mag Lav 104 B3
School La. New 24 C1
School La. Stock 136 B1
School Rd. Bill 149 D1
School Rd. Dag 173 D2
School Rd. G Ea 95 E3
School Rd. Kelv H 132 C1
School Rd. Ray 75 F4
School Rd. S Han 150 C3
School Rd. Sta R 131 D4
School St. Gt C 1 B1
School View Rd. Chelm 110 C2
School Villas. Brox 49 F1
School Wlk. Brain 65 F2
Schoolfield Rd. W Thu 191 D4
Schooner Ct. Stone 190 B2
Scilla Ct. Grays 192 B4
Scoter Cl. Woodf 152 A2
Scotland Rd. Lou 140 B1
Scotney Walk. Hornc 174 B4
Scott Ave. Finch 43 E3
Scott Ave. Sta Ab 87 D2
Scott Rd. Bis St 67 F3
Scott Rd. Grays 186 A1
Scotts Cl. Hornc 174 B4
Scotts Wlk. Chelm 110 B3
Scratton Rd. Sta L H 179 E1
Scrub Rise. Bill 160 C4
Scurvy Hall La. Lit Wal 85 D1
Seaborough Rd. Grays 186 B1
Seabrook Gdns. Bore 99 F1
Seabrook Gdns. Romf 164 A2
Seabrook Rd. Gt Bad 125 D3
Seabrooke Rise. Grays 192 A4
Seaburn Cl. Rain 173 F1
Seaforth Cl. Romf 155 F2
Seaforth Gdns. Woodf 152 B3
Seamans La. Stock 137 E1
Seaview Ave. Basil 171 E2
Seax Ct. Basil 169 F4
Seax Way. Basil 169 F4
Sebastian Ave. Brent 147 D2
Sebert Cl. Bill 161 E4
Second Ave. Basil 169 F2
Second Ave. Bill 160 C4
Second Ave. Chelm 111 D3
Second Ave. Corr 179 E2
Second Ave. Dag 173 D2
Second Ave. Dodd 133 E3
Second Ave. Harl 102 C4
Second Ave. W Thu 191 D4
Sedge Ct. Grays 192 C4
Sedge Green. Lo Naz 100 C2
Sedge Green. Roy 100 C2
Sedgefield Cl. Romf 156 C3
Sedgefield Cres. Romf 156 C3
Sedgemoor Dr. Dag 173 D4
Sedley Rise. Lou 140 C4
Sedop Cl. Saff W 25 E4
Seeleys. Harl 90 B2
Selsdon Cl. Romf 155 E1
Selwood Rd. Brent 157 F4
Selworthy Cl. Bill 161 E4
Selwyn Rd. Tilb 192 C3
Semper Rd. Grays 186 B2
Semples. Corr 179 F1
Settle Rd. Brent 157 D3
Seven Acres. Wick 163 F4
Seven Arches Rd. Brent 158 C4
Seven Ash Green. Sprin 111 E3
Sevenoaks Cl. Romf 156 B3
Seventh Ave. Chelm 111 D3
Severn. Grays 187 D2
Severn Ave. Romf 165 D4
Severn Dr. Upm 166 C3
Severn Rd. Ave 183 E4
Severns Field. Epp 116 A1
Sewards End. Wick 163 F3
Sewardstone Gdns. Ching 139 D2
Sewardstone Rd. Ching 139 D3
Sewardstone Rd. Wa Aby 139 D3
Sewardstone Way. Wa Aby 126 B2
Sewell Harris Cl. Harl 90 A1
Sexton Cl. Rain 173 F2
Sexton Rd. Tilb 192 C3
Seymer Rd. Romf 164 B4
Seymour Rd. Ching 139 D1
Seymour Rd. Tilb 192 C3
Seymour St. Chelm 111 D1
Seymours. Harl 101 F3
Seymours. Harl 102 A3
Seymours. Lou 141 D4
Shaftenhoe End Rd. Nut 21 D4
Shafter Rd. Dag 173 E3
Shaftesbury La. Stone 190 A2
Shaftesbury Rd. Ching 139 E1
Shaftesbury Rd. Epp 116 A1
Shaftesbury Rd. Romf 164 C3
Shaftsbury. Lou 140 B3
Shakespeare Ave. Basil 170 A3
Shakespeare Ave. Bill 149 E1
Shakespeare Ave. Tilb 193 D3
Shakespeare Rd. Romf 164 C3
Shakespeare Rd. Stone 190 A2
Shakespeare Sq. Woodf 153 E2
Shakeston Cl. Writ 123 D4
Shakletons. Ch Ong 119 D2
Shalford Rd. Bill 149 E1
Shalford Rd. Ray 64 C2
Shangani Rd. Bis St 67 F3
Shanklin Ave. Bill 149 D1
Shannon Cl. Hav 7 E4
Shannon Way. Ave 183 E4
Sharlands Cl. Wick 163 F4
Sharpecroft. Harl 102 B4
Sharpington Cl. Chelm 124 B2
Shaw Cl. Hornc 165 D2
Shaw Cres. Brent 147 E3
Shaw Cres. Tilb 193 D3
Shaw Dr. Finch 43 E4
Shawbridge. Harl 102 B3
Shearers Way. Bore 99 F1
Sheds La. Saff W 13 F1
Sheepcote La. Man 46 C2
Sheepcotes La. Lit Wal 98 B3
Sheering Dri. Harl 90 C2
Sheering Lower Rd. Harl 90 C4
Sheering Lower Rd. Saw 78 A1
Sheering Mill La. Saw 77 F1
Sheering Rd. Harl 90 C3
Sheering Rd. Sheer 91 D3
Sheffield Dr. Romf 157 D3
Sheffield Gdns. Romf 157 D3
Sheila Cl. Romf 155 D2
Sheila Rd. Romf 155 D2
Sheilings The. Hornc 165 F3
Sheldon Ave. Woodf 153 D1
Sheldon Cl. Corr 180 A3
Shelley Ave. Basil 170 A3
Shelley Ave. Hornc 164 C1
Shelley Cl. Ch Ong 118 C3
Shelley Gr. Lou 140 C3
Shelley Pl. Tilb 193 D3
Shelley Rd. Brent 147 E1
Shelley Rd. Chelm 111 E1
Shellow Rd. Will 107 E2
Shelsley Dr. Basil 170 B2
Shenfield Cres. Brent 158 C4
Shenfield Gdns. Brent 147 D2
Shenfield Green. Brent 147 D1
Shenfield Pl. Brent 146 C1
Shenfield Rd. Brent 146 C1
Shenfield Rd. Woodf 152 A2
Shenley Rd. Stone 190 A1
Shenstone Gdns. Romf 156 B1
Shepeshall. Basil 170 C3
Shepherds Hill. Romf 157 D1
Shepherds Way. Saff W 13 F1
Shepley Cl. Hornc 174 B4
Shepley Mews. Enf 126 A1
Sheppard Dr. Sprin 112 A2
Sheppards. Harl 101 F3
Sherborne Gdns. Romf 155 D3
Sherborne Rd. Sprin 111 E3
Sherbourne Dr. Basil 163 D1
Sherfield Rd. Grays 192 A4
Sheridan Cl. Romf 156 B2
Sheridan Ct. Stone 190 A2
Sheringham Ave. Romf 164 B3
Sheringham Cl. Corr 179 F2
Shernbroke Rd. Wa Aby 126 C3
Sherwood. T Thu 184 C3
Sherwood Dr. Chelm 110 B1
Shetland Rd. Hav 7 E4
Shevon Way. Brent 157 F3
Shillibeer Wlk. Chig 153 F4
Shingle Ct. Wa Aby 127 D3
Ship La. Ave 183 E2
Ship Rd. Stock 137 E3
Ship Rd. W Han 137 E3
Shire Cl. Bill 149 E3
Shire Cl. Sprin 111 F4
Shire Hill. Saff W 13 F1
Shire Hill La. Saff W 25 F4
Shirley Gdns. Basil 172 B4
Shirley Gdns. Hornc 165 E1
Shonks Mill Rd. Nave H 131 E1
Shooters Dr. Lo Naz 100 C1
Shore The. Grave 192 B1
Short Croft. Kelv H 132 C1
Short La. S Han 150 B2
Shortacre. Basil 171 E3
Shortcroft. Bis St 68 B4
Shorter Ave. Brent 146 C1
Shortlands. Basil 171 D3
Shortlands Ave. Ch Ong 118 C3
Shrubberies The. Chig 153 E3
Shrubberies The. Woodf 152 A1
Shrubberies The. Writ 122 C4
Shrubbery Cl. Basil 170 B4
Shrubbery The. Upm 166 B1
Shrublands. Saff W 13 F2
Shrublands Cl. Chelm 111 E1
Shrublands Cl. Chig 153 E2
Sibneys Green. Harl 102 C2
Siddons Cl. Sta L H 187 D2
Sidmouth Rd. Sprin 111 F3
Sidney Rd. The B 128 B2
Sidney Terr. Bis St 67 F3
Silver Birch Ave. N W Bas 116 C2
Silver Birches. Brent 147 D1
Silver La. Will 108 A1
Silver St. Abr 142 A3
Silver St. Anst 33 D3
Silver St. Stan M 57 E3
Silver St. Wa Aby 126 B3
Silver St. Weth 43 D2
Silver Way. Romf 164 A4
Silver Way. Runw 163 E4
Silverdale. Corr 179 E2
Silverdale Dr. Hornc 174 A4
Silverdale East. Corr 179 E2
Silverlocke Rd. Grays 192 B4
Silvermead. Woodf 152 A1
Silvermere. Basil 170 A3
Silvermere Ave.. Romf 155 D3
Silvertown Ave. Corr 179 E1
Silverwood Cl. Grays 185 D3
Simmons Pl. Grays 185 D3
Simpson Rd. Rain 173 F3
Sims Cl. Romf 164 C4
Singleton Cl. Hornc 173 F4
Sir Francis Way. Brent 158 A4
Siviter Way. Dag 173 D3
Six Bells Ct. Brain 65 F3
Sixth Ave. Chelm 111 D3
Skarnings Ct. Wa Aby 127 D3
Skeins Way. Clav 35 E2
Skerry Rise. Chelm 111 D4
Skiddaw Cl. Bl Not 76 B4

Skinner's La. Chelm 124 A2
Skitts Hill. Brain 66 A1
Skreens Ct. Chelm 110 B2
Skreens Park Rd. Rox 108 C3
Skylark Cl. Bill 149 E1
Skylark Wlk. Chelm 124 A3
Slade's La. Chelm 124 A2
Slades The. Basil 171 F2
Slaney Rd. Romf 164 C3
Sleepers Farm Rd. Grays 186 A2
Slewins Cl. Hornc 165 E3
Slewins La. Hornc 165 E3
Sloane Mews. Bill 148 C3
Slough Rd. H Ea 82 A1
Smallgains La. Stock 149 F4
Smart Cl. Romf 156 A1
Smart's La. Lou 140 C3
Smeaton Cl. Wa Aby 126 C4
Smeaton Rd. Chig 152 C3
Smith's End La. Nut 21 D4
Smithers Dr. Gt Bad 125 D3
Smiths Field. Ray 64 C1
Smiths Green. Deb 38 B4
Smythe Cl. Bill 149 E3
Smythe Rd. Bill 149 E3
Snake's La E. Woodf 152 B2
Snake's La W. Woodf 152 A2
Snakes Hill. Kelv H 145 E3
Snakes La. Stan M 48 A1
Snelling Gr. Gt Bad 124 C3
Snowdonia Cl. Basil 172 B4
Snowdrop Cl. Sprin 111 F4
Snowdrop Path. Romf 156 B2
Soames Mead. Sto M 133 D3
Soane St. Basil 163 D1
Solid La. Dodd 145 F4
Solway. Grays 187 E2
Somerby Cl. Hod 100 A1
Somercoates. Basil 170 B3
Somercoates Ct. Basil 170 B3
Somerdean. Basil 172 B3
Somerset Cl. Woodf 152 A1
Somerset Gdns. Basil 172 A3
Somerset Gdns. Hornc 166 A2
Somerset Pl. Chelm 111 D4
Somerset Rd. Basil 170 A3
Somerset Rd. Enf 126 A1
Somerset Rd. Sta L H 187 D2
Sorrel Ct. Grays 192 B4
Sorrel Wlk. Romf 164 C4
Sorrell Cl. Lit Wal 98 A3
Sorrells The. Corr 179 F2
South Ave. Ching 139 E1
South Ave. Corr 179 D4
South Beech Ave. Wick 163 E4
South Cl. Dag 173 D2
South Colne. Basil 171 E2
South Crockerford. Basil 171 F2
South Dr. Brent 158 B3
South Dr. Romf 165 E4
South End Rd. Hornc 174 A3
South End Rd. Rain 174 A3
South Gate. Harl 102 B4
South Gate. W Thu 183 E1
South Gunnels. Basil 171 D3
South Hall Dr. Rain 182 A4
South Hanningfield Rd. Rett 151 E4
South Hanningfield Rd. S Han 151 E4
South Hanningfield Way. Hunw 151 E2
South Hill. Horn H 179 D4
South Hill Cres. Grays 179 D2
South Kent Ave. Grave 192 B1
South Mayne. Basil 172 A3
South Par. Wa Aby 126 B3
South Pl. Harl 90 A2
South Primrose Hill. Chelm 110 C2
South Rd. Bill 162 B3
South Rd. Bis St 68 A3
South Rd. Harl 90 A2
South Rd. S Ock 184 B4
South Rd. Saff W 25 F4
South Rd. Take 70 B4
South Ridge. Bill 149 E1
South Riding. Basil 171 F3
South St. Bis St 67 F3
South St. Brain 65 F1
South St. Brent 158 B4
South St. Gt C 1 B1
South St. Gt Wal 97 F4
South St. Rain 173 E2
South St. Romf 164 C2
South St. Sta Ab 87 E2
South View. Grays 186 A4
South View. Gt Dun 72 B4
South View Dr. Upm 166 A1
South View Rd. Lou 140 C2
South View Rd. Tilb 193 D3
South View Rd. W Thu 191 E4
South Wash Rd. Bill 161 F1
South Way. Wa Aby 126 B2
South Weald Dri. Wa Aby 126 B3
South Weald Rd. Brent 158 A4
South Wlk. Basil 171 D3
Southall Way. Brent 157 F3
Southborough Rd. Chelm 124 A4
Southbourne Gr. Wick 163 D4
Southbrook. Saw 77 F1
Southbury Cl. Hornc 174 B4
Southcote Cres. Basil 171 F4
Southcote Row. Basil 171 F4
Southcote Sq. Basil 171 F4
Southdale. Chig 153 E2
Southdown Rd. Hornc 165 D2
Southend Arterial Rd. Basil 162 B1
Southend Arterial Rd. Brent 167 E3
Southend Arterial Rd. Hornc 165 F4
Southend Arterial Rd. Romf 156 B1
Southend Arterial Rd. Upm 166 B3
Southend La. Wa Aby 127 D3
Southend Rd. Bill 161 E3
Southend Rd. Corr 179 F2
Southend Rd. Grays 185 E1
Southend Rd. Gt Bad 125 E2
Southend Rd. Sand 125 E2
Southend Rd. W Han 125 E2
Southend Rd. Woodf 152 A1
Southend-Arterial-Rd. Basil 161 E1
Souther Cross Rd. G Ea 95 E3
Southern Dr. Lou 140 C2
Southern Lodge. Harl 102 B3
Southern Way. Harl 102 B3
Southern Way. Romf 164 A3
Southernhay. Basil 171 D3
Southernhay. Lou 140 B2
Southey Wlk. Tilb 193 D3
Southfield. Hinx 1 A2
Southfield Chase. Basil 160 C1
Southfield Rd. Hod 100 A4
Southfleet Rd. Swan 191 F1
Southlands Chase. Sand 125 F1
Southlands Rd. Bill 162 C3
Southmill Rd. Bis St 68 A3
Southview Rd. Basil 171 F3
Southwark Path. Basil 171 F4
Southway. Basil 170 B1
Southway. W Thu 183 F2
Sovereign Ct. Harl 102 A3
Sowerberry Cl. Chelm 110 C4
Sowrey Ave. Rain 174 A3
Spains Hall Pl. Basil 171 E3
Spains Hall Rd. Will 107 F1
Spalding Ave. Chelm 110 C3
Spalding Way. Gt Bad 124 C4
Spalt Cl. Brent 159 D4
Spareleaze Hill. Lou 140 C3
Sparepenny La N. Gt Sam 29 D2
Sparepenny La S. Gt Sam 29 D2
Sparkbridge. Basil 170 A3
Sparks La. Ridge 20 A3
Sparrow Gr. Dag 164 A1
Sparrow's La. Hat B O 79 F1
Sparrows Herne. Basil 171 D2
Sparrowsend Hill. Saff W 25 D3
Speedwell Ct. Grays 192 C4
Spellbrook La E. Spel 77 F4
Spellbrook La W. Spel 77 F4
Spencer Cl. Els 48 B2
Spencer Cl. Stan M 57 F3
Spencer Cl. Woodf 152 B3
Spencer Rd. Gt C 1 B2
Spencer Rd. Rain 173 E2
Spencer Sq. Brain 65 F4
Spencer Wlk. Tilb 193 D3
Spencers Croft. Harl 103 D3
Spenders Cl. Basil 171 E4
Spenlow Dr. Chelm 110 B4
Spenser Cres. Upm 166 B2
Spey Way. Romf 155 F2
Spicers La. Harl 90 B2
Spillbutters. Dodd 133 D2
Spilsby Rd. Romf 156 C2
Spindle Rd. Hav 6 B4
Spindles. Tilb 193 D4
Spinney Cl. Rain 173 F2
Spinney Cl. Wick 163 F4
Spinney The. Bill 149 D2
Spinney The. Brain 66 B1
Spinney The. Brent 147 E2
Spinney The. Ch Ong 119 D1
Spinney The. Grays 178 A1
Spinning Wheel Mead. Harl 103 D3
Spires The. Gt Bad 124 C3
Spital La. Brent 157 F4
Sporhams. Basil 170 C2
Spots Wlk. Chelm 124 B2
Spriggs La. Bla 121 D1
Spring Gdns. Hornc 174 A4
Spring Gdns. Romf 164 B3
Spring Gdns. Woodf 152 B2
Spring Gr. Lou 140 B2
Spring Hill. Saff W 13 D1
Spring Hills. Harl 89 D1
Spring Pond Cl. Gt Bad 124 C4
Spring Pond Meadow. Dodd 133 E3
Spring Rise. Chelm 124 B1
Spring Vale. Swan 191 E1
Springbank Ave. Hornc 174 B4
Springfield. Epp 128 C4
Springfield Ave. Brent 147 F1
Springfield Cl. Ch Ong 118 C3
Springfield Cl. Rain 174 B1
Springfield Gdns. Upm 166 B1
Springfield Gdns. Woodf 152 B2
Springfield Green. Sprin 111 F2
Springfield Park Ave. Chelm 111 E1
Springfield Park Hill. Chelm 111 E1
Springfield Park La. Chelm 111 F1
Springfield Park Par. Chelm 111 E1
Springfield Park Rd. Chelm 111 E1
Springfield Pl. Sprin 111 E3
Springfield Rd. Bill 149 D3
Springfield Rd. Chelm 111 E2
Springfield Rd. Ching 139 F1
Springfield Rd. Grays 185 F2
Springfield Rd. Sprin 111 E2
Springfield Rd. Wick 163 F4
Springfields. Basil 171 F2
Springfields. Gt Dun 72 B4
Springfields. Wa Aby 126 C3
Springhall La. Saw 77 F1
Springhall Rd. Saw 77 F1
Springhead Rd. Grave 192 B1
Springhill Rd. Saff W 25 E4
Springhouse La. Sta L H 180 A2
Springhouse Rd. Corr 179 F2
Springmead. Bl Not 76 B4
Springwell Rd. Lit C 13 D3
Springwood Ct. Brain 65 E2
Springwood Dr. Brain 65 E2
Springwood Way. Romf 165 D3
Spruce Cl. Bill 161 E1
Spruce Hill. Harl 102 C2
Spur Cl. Abr 142 A3
Spurriers. Basil 170 B3
Squadrons App. Hornc 174 B3
Square The. Horn H 178 C2
Square The. Saw 77 F1
Square The. Stock 136 C1
Square The. Woodf 152 A3
Squirrel's Chase. Grays 186 A2
Squirrel's Heath Ave. Romf 165 D4
Squirrells Ct. Chelm 110 C3
Squirrels. Basil 170 A2
Squirrels Cl. Bis St 67 F4
Squirrels Heath La. Hornc 165 E4
Squirrels Heath Rd. Romf 156 C1
Stablecroft. Sprin 111 F4
Stables The. Lou 140 B1
Stacey Dr. Basil 170 B1
Stacey's Mount. Bill 162 B3
Stackfield. Harl 90 A2
Staddles. L Hal 78 A4
Stafford Ave. Hornc 165 E4
Stafford Cl. Sta L H 187 D2
Stafford Dr. Hod 100 A2
Stafford Green. Basil 169 F2
Staffords. Harl 90 C2
Stag La. Lou 152 A4
Stagden Cross. Basil 171 F3
Staggart Green. Chig 154 A2
Stambourne Rd. Gt Y 20 B2
Stambourne Rd. Ridge 19 F3
Stambourne Rd. Topp 32 A4
Standen Ave. Hornc 165 F1
Standfield Gdns. Dag 173 D3
Standfield Rd. Dag 173 D4
Standingford. Harl 102 A2
Standrums. Gt Dun 72 B4
Stane Cl. Bis St 56 C1
Stanes Rd. Brain 65 F3
Staneway. Basil 170 B2
Stanford Cl. Romf 164 A3
Stanford Cl. Woodf 152 C3
Stanford Ct. Wa Aby 127 D3
Stanford Gdns. Ave 183 F3
Stanford Rd. Grays 186 C4
Stanford Rd. Sta L H 179 D1
Stanford Rivers Rd. Ch Ong 132 A4
Stanford-Le-Hope By-Ps. Corr 179 E3
Stanhope Rd. Rain 174 A2
Stanhope Rd. Swan 191 F1
Stanley Ave. Dag 164 A2
Stanley Ave. Romf 165 D4
Stanley Cl. Hornc 165 E1
Stanley Cl. Romf 165 D4
Stanley Pl. Ch Ong 119 D1
Stanley Pl. Stan M 57 F3
Stanley Rd. Ching 139 E1
Stanley Rd. Grays 192 A4
Stanley Rd. Gt C 1 C2
Stanley Rd. Horn H 177 F4
Stanley Rd. Hornc 165 E1
Stanley Rd. Rain 173 F2
Stanley Rd. Swan 191 F1
Stanley Rd N. Rain 173 F2
Stanley Rise. Sprin 111 F2
Stanleys Farm Rd. Saff W 25 F4
Stanmore Way. Lou 141 D4
Stannetts. Basil 170 A4
Stansgate Rd. Dag 164 A1
Stanstead Abbots By-Ps. Sta Ab 87 E1
Stanstead Dr. Hod 100 A4
Stanstead Rd. Hod 87 D1
Stansted Cl. Bill 149 E1
Stansted Cl. Chelm 110 C1
Stansted Cl. Hornc 174 B3
Stansted Rd. Birhr 57 D2
Stansted Rd. Bis St 57 D2
Stansted Rd. Els 48 B1
Stanway Cl. Chig 153 F3
Stanway Rd. Wa Aby 127 D3
Stanwyck Dr. Chig 153 E3
Stanwyck Gdns. Romf 156 A3
Staple Tye. Harl 102 B3
Staple's Rd. Lou 140 C3
Stapleford Gdns. Romf 155 D2
Stapleford Rd. Sta Abb 143 D3
Stapleford Tawney. Sta T 130 B2
Stapleford Tawney. Sta T 143 E4
Stapleton Cres. Rain 174 A3
Star La. Epp 116 A1
Star La. Gt Dun 61 E1
Star La. Ing 135 E2
Star Mead. Thax 40 A1
Starboard Ave. Swan 191 D1
Starch House La. Woodf 153 E1
Starling Cl. Lou 140 A1
Starr Rd. Hen 48 C3
Station App. Basil 170 B3
Station App. Basil 172 A2
Station App. Brain 66 A1
Station App. Grays 192 A4
Station App. Runw 163 E4
Station App. Woodf 152 B3
Station Approach Rd. Tilb 193 D2
Station Ave. Runw 163 E4
Station La. Basil 172 A2
Station La. Hornc 165 F1
Station La. Ing 135 D2
Station Par. Hornc 174 A4
Station Pass. Woodf 152 A1
Station Rd. Bill 148 C1
Station Rd. Bis St 68 A4
Station Rd. Brain 65 F1
Station Rd. Chig 153 D4
Station Rd. Ching 139 E1
Station Rd. Cla 8 B1
Station Rd. Els 48 B1
Station Rd. Epp 129 D4
Station Rd. Felst 73 F3
Station Rd. Grave 192 A1
Station Rd. Grays 194 A4
Station Rd. Gt Dun 72 C4
Station Rd. Harl 90 B2
Station Rd. Hav 7 D4
Station Rd. Hod 100 A2
Station Rd. Horn H 168 B3
Station Rd. Lit Dun 73 F3
Station Rd. Lou 140 C2
Station Rd. N W Bas 117 D2
Station Rd. New 37 D4
Station Rd. Ray 64 C1
Station Rd. Romf 165 E4
Station Rd. Runw 151 E1
Station Rd. Saff W 25 E4
Station Rd. Saw 77 F2
Station Rd. Sta Ab 87 E2
Station Rd. Stan M 57 F3
Station Rd. Swan 191 D1
Station Rd. Take 70 B4
Station Rd. Upm 166 B1
Station Rd. Wen A 24 C3
Station Rd Ind Est. Gt Dun 72 C4
Station St. Saff W 13 E1
Station Way. Basil 171 D3
Station Way. Woodf 152 B3
Staverton Rd. Hornc 165 E3
Stebbing Rd. Felst 74 A4
Stebbings. Basil 170 B2
Steeds Way. Lou 140 C3
Steele Ave. Stone 191 D1
Steen Cl. Ing 135 D2
Steeple Bumpstead Rd. Hel B 17 E4
Steeple View. Bis St 67 F4
Steeple Way. Dodd 133 D1
Steeplehall. Basil 172 A3
Steerforth Cl. Chelm 110 B4
Stenning Ave. Sta L H 187 D1
Stephen Ave. Rain 174 A3
Stephen Cl. Hav 6 C4
Stephen Marshall Ave. Finch 42 B3
Stephens Cl. Romf 156 B3
Stephens Cres. Horn H 178 C2
Stephenson Ave. Tilb 193 D3
Stephenson Rd. Brain 66 A1
Sterry Cres. Dag 173 D4
Sterry Gdns. Dag 173 D3
Sterry Rd. Dag 173 D4
Stevens La. Felst 74 C3
Stevens Way. Chig 153 F3
Stevenson Way. Wick 163 E3
Stewards Cl. Epp 129 D3
Stewards Green Rd. Epp 129 D3
Stewards Wlk. Romf 164 C3
Stewardstone St. Wa Aby 126 B3
Stewart Ave. Upm 166 A1
Stewart Rd. Chelm 124 A4
Stewarts The. Bis St 67 F3
Stewarts Way. Man 46 C1
Stifford Clays Rd. Grays 185 D4
Stifford Hill. S Ock 184 B3
Stifford Hill. W Thu 184 B3
Stifford Rd. S Ock 184 A3
Stile Croft. Harl 103 D3
Stilemans. Wick 163 E4
Stirling Cl. Rain 174 A1
Stirling Dr. Hav 6 C4
Stirling Pl. Basil 172 A4
Stirrup Cl. Sprin 111 F4
Stock Hill. Stock 149 E4
Stock La. Ing 135 E2
Stock Rd. Bill 149 E3
Stock Rd. Bill 149 E3
Stock Rd. Chelm 137 D4
Stock Rd. Stock 137 D4
Stockfield Ave. Hod 100 A4
Stockland Rd. Romf 164 B3
Stocks La. Kelv H 132 C1
Stocksfield. Kelv H 132 C1
Stockwell Cl. Bill 161 E4
Stoke Ave. Chig 154 A2
Stoke Rd. Rain 174 B1
Stokefelde. Basil 172 A4
Stonards Hill. Epp 129 E4
Stonards Hill. Lou 140 C2
Stondon Rd. Ch Ong 119 D1
Stone Cross. Harl 89 E1
Stone Ness Rd. W Thu 191 D4
Stone Place Rd. Stone 190 C1
Stone St. Grave 193 D1
Stonebridge Rd. Grave 192 A1
Stonebridge Wlk. Chelm 111 D1
Stonechat Rd. Bill 161 E4
Stonehill Rd. Rox 108 C2
Stonehouse La. W Thu 183 F1
Stoneleigh. Saw 77 E2
Stoney Common. Stan M 57 F3
Stoney Common Rd. Stan M 57 E3
Stoneycroft Rd. Woodf 152 C2
Stoneyfield Dr. Stan M 57 F3
Stonleigh Dri. Hod 87 D1
Stony Hills. S Han 150 A3
Stony La. Bobb 118 B4
Stony La. Thax 40 A1
Stony Path. Lou 140 C4
Stony Wood. Harl 102 C4
Stonyshotts. Wa Aby 126 C3
Stormonts Way. Basil 170 B1
Storr Gdns. Brent 147 E2
Stort Lodge. Bis St 67 E4
Stort Mill. Harl 90 A3
Stort Rd. Bis St 67 F3
Stortford Hall Park. Bis St 68 A4
Stortford Rd. Can E 71 E4
Stortford Rd. Clav 35 E2
Stortford Rd. Gt Dun 72 A4
Stortford Rd. Hod 100 B4
Stortford Rd. L Hal 78 C2
Stortford Rd. Lea Rod 94 A3
Stour Rd. Dag 164 A1
Stour Rd. Grays 186 A1
Stour Vale. Cla 8 B2
Stour Vale. Cla 8 B2
Stour Valley Rd. Hav 7 D4
Stour Way. Upm 166 C3
Stow The. Harl 89 F1
Stradbroke Dr. Chig 153 D2
Stradbroke Gr. Lou 140 B1
Stradbroke Park. Chig 153 D2
Strafford Ave. Woodf 153 D1
Straight Rd. Romf 156 D2
Straits The. Wa Aby 126 A4
Stratford Cl. Dag 173 E3
Stratford Gdns. Corr 179 E2
Strathmore. Grays 187 E1
Strathmore Gdns. Hornc 164 C2
Stratton Rd. Romf 157 D3
Stratton Wlk. Romf 157 D3
Strawberry Cl. Brain 66 A1
Strawbrook Hill. Gt Le 85 F2
Street The. Ashe 9 E1
Street The. Berd 46 A4
Street The. Bird 19 D4
Street The. Chelm 124 A1
Street The. Cla 9 E2
Street The. Fu Pel 45 D2
Street The. Gt Ha 69 D2
Street The. Gt Hal 69 D2
Street The. H Ea 82 B1
Street The. H Ong 119 E2
Street The. Lit Dun 73 E4
Street The. Lit Wal 98 A3
Street The. Man 46 C1
Street The. Ple 83 F1
Street The. Ray 64 C1
Street The. Rox 109 D3
Street The. Saw 78 C1
Street The. Sheer 91 E4
Street The. Topp 32 A4
Strethall Rd. Litt 12 B2
Strood Ave. Romf 164 B2
Struan Ave. Corr 179 F3
Strudwick Cl. Brain 65 F1
Stuart Cl. Brent 146 A2
Stuart Cl. Gt Bad 125 D4
Stuart Rd. Grave 193 D1
Stuart Rd. Grays 185 D1
Stuart Way. Bill 149 F1
Stuarts Way. Brain 66 A1
Stubbers La. Upm 175 F3
Stubbs La. Brain 66 B1
Stublands. Basil 171 F3
Studland Ave. Wick 162 C4
Stump La. Sprin 111 E2
Sturmer End Ind Est. Hav 7 E3
Sturmer Rd. Hav 7 E3
Sturrocks. Basil 171 F2
Styles. Lit Ba 41 E1
Sudbrook Cl. Wick 163 E3
Sudbury Rd. S Han 151 D3
Sudburys Farm Rd. Bill 160 B3
Sudicamps Ct. Wa Aby 127 D3
Suffolk Dr. Basil 170 A3
Suffolk Dr. Sprin 112 A2
Suffolk Rd. Dag 173 E4

Suffolk Rd. Grave 193 E1
Suffolk Way. Hornc 166 A4
Sugar La. Si Hed 44 C4
Sugden Ave. Wick 163 D4
Sullivan Rd. Tilb 193 D3
Summerdale. Bill 149 D1
Summerfield Rd. Lou 140 B2
Summerfields. Ing 135 E2
Summerhill Rd. Saff W 25 E4
Summit Dr. Woodf 152 B1
Summit The. Lou 140 C4
Sun Ray Ave. Brent 147 F2
Sun Rd. Swan 191 F1
Sun St. Bill 149 D1
Sun St. Saw 78 A1
Sun St. Wa Aby 126 B3
Sunbank. Gt Dun 72 C4
Sundew Ct. Grays 192 B4
Sundridge Cl. Stone 190 A1
Sunflower Cl. Sprin 111 F3
Sunflower Way. Romf 156 B1
Sunnedon. Basil 171 E3
Sunningdale. Bis St 67 F3
Sunningdale Ave. Rain 174 A1
Sunningdale Rd. Chelm 110 C2
Sunningdale Rd. Rain 174 A3
Sunnings La. Upm 175 E3
Sunnycroft Gdns. Upm 166 C2
Sunnydene Cl. Romf 156 C2
Sunnymede. Chig 154 A4
Sunnyside. Basil 169 F2
Sunnyside. Brain 65 F2
Sunnyside. Stan M 57 F3
Sunnyside Ave. Basil 172 B2
Sunnyside Dr. Ching 139 E1
Sunnyside Gdns. Upm 166 B1
Sunnyside Rd. Epp 129 D4
Sunrise Ave. Chelm 111 D3
Sunrise Ave. Hornc 165 E1
Sunset Ave. Ching 139 D1
Sunset Ave. Woodf 152 A3
Surman Cres. Brent 147 E1
Surrey Dr. Hornc 166 A4
Surrey Rd. Dag 173 D4
Surrey Way. Basil 170 A3
Surridge Cl. Rain 174 B1
Susan Cl. Romf 164 B4
Sussex Ave. Romf 156 C2
Sussex Cl. Basil 170 A3
Sussex Cl. Bore 112 C4
Sussex Cl. Hod 100 A4
Sussex Rd. Brent 158 A3
Sutcliffe Cl. Wick 163 E3
Sutherland Pl. Wick 163 E3
Sutton Acres. L Hal 78 B4
Sutton Cl. Lou 140 C1
Sutton Mead. Sprin 112 A2
Suttons Ave. Hornc 165 E1
Suttons Gdns. Hornc 165 E1
Suttons La. Hornc 174 B4
Swale Cl. Ave 183 E4
Swallow Dale. Basil 171 E2
Swallow Path. Chelm 124 A2
Swallow Rd. Runw 151 E1
Swallow Wlk. Rain 174 A3
Swallows. Harl 90 B2
Swallows The. Bill 161 E4
Swan Ave. Upm 166 C2
Swan La. Hav 7 D4
Swan La. Kelv H 132 C1
Swan La. Runw 151 E1
Swan La. Stock 136 B3
Swan Mead. Basil 171 E2
Swan Paddock. Brent 158 B4
Swan Pike Rd. Enf 126 A1
Swan Side. Brain 65 F2
Swan Wlk. Romf 164 C3
Swan Yd. Grave 193 D1
Swanbourne Dr. Hornc 174 B4
Swanscombe St. Swan 191 F1
Swanshope. Lou 141 D4
Swanstead. Basil 171 F2
Sweet Mead. Saff W 13 F2
Sweyne Rd. Swan 191 F1
Sweyns. Harl 103 E3
Swift Cl. Upm 166 C2
Swinborne Ct. Basil 163 D1
Swinborne Rd. Basil 163 E1
Swinbourne Dr. Brain 65 E2
Swinburne Gdns. Tilb 193 D3
Swindon Cl. Romf 156 C3
Swindon Gdns. Romf 156 C3
Swindon La. Romf 156 C3
Swiss Ave. Chelm 111 D2
Sycamore Ave. Upm 175 D4
Sycamore Dr. Brent 146 B1
Sycamore Field. Harl 102 A3
Sycamore Gr. Brain 65 E1
Sycamore Way. Chelm 124 B3
Sycamores The. Ave 183 E3
Sycamores The. Basil 172 B3
Sycamores The. Bis St 68 A3
Sydenham Cl. Romf 164 C4
Sydner Cl. Gt Bad 125 D3
Sydney Rd. Tilb 193 D3
Sydney Rd. Woodf 152 A3
Sydney Rd. Woodf 153 E1
Syers Field. Weth 44 A1
Sylvan Ave. Hornc 165 F3
Sylvan Cl. Chelm 124 A3
Sylvan Cl. Grays 184 C1
Sylvan Tryst. Bill 149 D2
Sylvan Way. Basil 169 F4
Sylvan Way. Chig 154 A4
Sylvester Gdns. Chig 154 A3
Sylvesters. Harl 101 F3
Sylvia Ave. Brent 159 E4
Symmons Cl. Ray 64 C1
Syracuse Ave. Rain 174 C1
Syringa Ct. Grays 192 B4
Tabor Ave. Brain 65 F2
Tabor's Hill. Gt Bad 124 C4
Tabors Ave. Gt Bad 124 C4
Tabrums Way. Upm 166 C2
Tadlows Cl. Upm 175 D4
Tadworth Par. Hornc 174 A4
Taits. Corr 179 F1
Takeley Cl. Romf 155 E1
Takeley Cl. Wa Aby 126 B3
Takely End. Basil 171 D3
Takely Ride. Basil 171 D3
Talbrook. Brent 157 F4
Talisman Wlk. Bill 149 E3
Tall Trees Cl. Hornc 165 F3
Tallis Cl. Corr 179 E2
Tallis Rd. Basil 170 B4
Tallon Rd. Brent 147 F2
Tally-Ho Dr. Brent 148 B1
Talus Cl. W Thu 183 E1
Tamar Cl. Upm 166 C3
Tamar Dr. Ave 183 E4
Tamar Rise. Sprin 111 E3
Tamar Sq. Woodf 152 A2
Tamarisk Rd. S Ock 176 B1
Tan House La. Nave H 145 D3
Tanfield Dr. Bill 149 D1
Tangent Rd. Romf 156 B1
Tangmere Cres. Hornc 174 A3
Tank Hill Rd. W Thu 183 D1
Tank La. Pur 183 D1
Tanners Way. Hun 88 B4
Tanners Way. Saff W 13 F1
Tannery Cl. Dag 164 A1
Tanswell Ave. Basil 172 A3
Tanswell Cl. Basil 172 A3
Tansy Cl. Romf 156 C2
Tany's Dell. Harl 90 A2
Tanyard The. Thax 40 A1
Tapley Rd. Chelm 110 C4
Tarnworth Rd. Romf 157 D2
Tasker Rd. Grays 186 A2
Tasman Cl. Corr 179 F2
Tasman Ct. Chelm 110 C3
Tasman Rd. Hav 7 E4
Tatsfield Ave. Lo Naz 113 E4
Tattenham Rd. Basil 170 A4
Tattersall Way. Chelm 123 F4
Taunton Cl. Chig 153 F2
Taunton Rd. Romf 156 B3
Taunton Rd. Sprin 111 F3
Taunton Rd. Swan 192 A1
Taverners Green Cl. Wick 163 F3
Taverners Way. Ching 139 F1
Taverners Way. Hod 100 A3
Tavistock Cl. Romf 156 B1
Tavistock Dr. Bill 148 C3
Tavistock Rd. Basil 170 B4
Tavistock Rd. Sprin 111 F3
Tawney Comm. Sta T 130 B4
Tawneys Rd. Harl 102 C3
Tawny Ave. Upm 175 D4
Tay Way. Romf 155 F1
Taylifers. Harl 102 A2
Taylor Ave. Chelm 110 C3
Taylor Cl. Romf 155 D2
Taylors Ave. Hod 100 A3
Taylors End Rd. Take 58 C1
Teagles. Basil 170 C3
Tees Cl. Upm 166 B3
Tees Dr. Romf 156 B4
Tees Rd. Sprin 111 E3
Telford Rd. Brain 66 A1
Tempest Way. Rain 174 A3
Templar's Ct. Hav 6 C4
Temple Ave. Dag 164 A2
Temple Bank. Harl 90 A3
Temple Cl. Bill 148 C3
Temple Mead. Roy 88 A1
Templer Ave. Grays 186 A2
Templewood Rd. Basil 172 A3
Tendring Rd. Harl 102 C3
Tennyson Ave. Grays 185 E2
Tennyson Ave. Wa Aby 126 C3
Tennyson Cl. Brain 76 C4
Tennyson Dr. Basil 172 A3
Tennyson Rd. Brent 147 E1
Tennyson Rd. Chelm 110 C3
Tennyson Rd. Romf 156 B2
Tennyson Rd. Stone 190 A1
Tennyson Way. Hornc 164 C1
Tennyson Wlk. Tilb 193 D3
Tensing Gdns. Bill 149 D1
Tenterfields. Basil 172 B4
Tenterfields. Gt Dun 72 C4
Tenterfields. New 24 C1
Tercel Path. Chig 154 A3
Terling. Basil 171 D3
Terling Rd. Dag 164 A1
Terlings The. Brent 158 A4
Terminal Rd N. Take 59 D2
Terminal Rd S. Take 59 E2
Terminus Dr. Basil 172 A2
Terminus St. Harl 102 B4
Tern Cl. Hav 7 E4
Tern Gdns. Upm 166 C2
Tern Way. Brent 157 F3
Terrace St. Grave 193 D1
Terrace The. Grave 193 E1
Teviot Ave. Ave 183 E4
Thackerary Ave. Tilb 193 D3
Thackeray Row. Wick 163 E3
Thalmassing Cl. Brent 159 D4
Thames Ave. Chelm 110 B2
Thames Cl. Brain 66 B1
Thames Cl. Corr 180 A2
Thames Cl. Rain 182 A4
Thames Cres. Corr 180 B3
Thames Dr. Grays 186 A1
Thames Haven Rd. Corr 180 A2
Thames Rd. Grays 192 A4
Thames View. Basil 170 B1
Thames View. Grays 186 A1
Thames Way. Grave 192 C1
Thameshill Ave. Romf 155 E1
Thamley. Pur 183 D1
Thane Ave. Dag 173 E1
Thatchers Cl. Lou 141 E4
Thaxted Rd. Deb 38 B3
Thaxted Rd. Lou 140 C1
Thaxted Rd. Saff W 25 F4
Thaxted Rd. Wim 26 B2
Thaxted Way. Wa Aby 126 B3
Thaxted Wlk. Rain 173 F3
Thele Ave. Sta Ab 87 E2
Thele Estate. Sta Ab 87 F2
Theobalds Ave. Grays 185 E1
Thetford Pl. Bill 161 E1
Theydon Cres. Basil 162 C1
Theydon Ct. Wa Aby 127 D3
Theydon Gdns. Rain 173 F3
Theydon Gr. Epp 116 A1
Theydon Gr. Woodf 152 B2
Theydon Park Rd. The B 128 C1
Theydon Pl. Epp 128 C4
Theydon Rd. Epp 128 B3
Theydon Rd. The B 128 B3
Third Ave. Basil 169 F2
Third Ave. Chelm 111 D3
Third Ave. Corr 179 F2
Third Ave. Dag 173 D2
Third Ave. Harl 102 B4
Third Ave. W Thu 191 D4
Thirlmere Cl. Bl Not 76 B4
Thirtieth St. Take 58 C2
Thistle Mead. Lou 141 D3
Thistledene Ave. Hav B 155 D3
Thistledown. Basil 171 E3
Thistledown. Pan 65 D4
Thistledown Ct. Basil 171 E3
Thistley Cres. Quen 36 C1
Thistley Green Rd. Brain 66 A4
Thoby La. Mtssg 134 B1
Thomas Bata Ave. Grays 187 D1
Thomas Cl. Brent 158 C4
Thomas Rd. Basil 172 C4
Thomasin Rd. Basil 163 E1
Thorley High. Thor 67 F1
Thorley Hill. Bis St 67 F3
Thorley La. Bis St 67 F2
Thorley La. Thor 67 E2
Thorley Park Rd. Bis St 67 F2
Thorley Rd. Grays 185 D3
Thorn Gr. Bis St 68 A3
Thorn La. Rain 174 B2
Thornbera Cl. Bis St 67 F2
Thornbera Gdns. Bis St 67 F2
Thornbera Rd. Bis St 67 F2
Thornbury Cl. Hod 87 D1
Thornbush. Basil 170 C4
Thorncroft. Hornc 165 D3
Thorncroft. Saff W 13 F1
Thorndales. Brent 158 B3
Thornden Gate. Brent 159 E3
Thorndon App. Brent 159 E2
Thorndon Ave. Horn H 168 B3
Thornfield Rd. Bis St 67 F4
Thornhill. N W Bas 117 E3
Thornridge. Brent 146 A1
Thornton Pl. Stock 136 C1
Thornton Rd. Take 70 C4
Thornton Way. Basil 170 A3
Thorntons. Brent 159 E2
Thorntons Farm Ave. Romf 164 B1
Thornwood Cl. Woodf 152 A1
Thornwood Rd. N W Bas 116 B3
Thorogood Way. Rain 173 F2
Thorolds. Basil 171 F2
Thorrington Cross. Basil 171 E3
Thors Oak. Corr 179 F1
Three Horseshoes Rd. Harl 102 A3
Three Mile Hill. Chelm 123 E1
Thremhall Ave. Birhr 68 C4
Thremhall Ave. Stan M 69 E4
Thremhall Ave. Take 58 C1
Threshelford. Basil 170 C2
Thrift Green. Brent 159 D4
Thrifts Mead. The B 128 C1
Throwley Cl. Basil 172 B3
Thurgood Rd. Hod 100 A4
Thurlby Cl. Woodf 152 C3
Thurloe Gdns. Romf 164 C3
Thurloe Wlk. Grays 185 D2
Thurlow Gdns. Chig 153 E2
Thurrock Park Way. Grays 192 B4
Thurso Cl. Romf 157 D2
Thurstans. Harl 102 B2
Thynne Rd. Bill 149 E1
Tiberius Cl. Hav 7 E4
Tickenhall Dr. Harl 103 E4
Tidworth Ave. Runw 151 F1
Tidy's La. Epp 116 A1
Tilbury Gdns. Tilb 193 D2
Tilbury Hotel Rd. Tilb 193 D2
Tilbury Mead. Harl 103 D3
Tilbury Rd. Horn H 168 C3
Tilbury Rd. Ridge 20 B4
Tilegate Rd. Harl 102 C3
Tilegate Rd. Mag Lav 104 C3
Tillingham Ct. Wa Aby 127 D3
Tillingham Green. Basil 170 A3
Tillwicks Rd. Harl 102 C4
Tilney Dr. Lou 152 A4
Tilney Turn. Basil 171 F2
Timberdene Ave. Woodf 153 E1
Timberlog Cl. Basil 171 F3
Timberlog La. Basil 171 F3
Timbermans View. Basil 171 F2
Timpsons La. Sprin 111 F2
Tindal Sq. Chelm 111 D1
Tindal St. Chelm 111 D1
Tindall Cl. Romf 156 C1
Tindon End Rd. Lit Sam 28 B1
Tine Rd. Chig 153 F3
Tinker Ave. Finch 43 E3
Tinkler Side. Basil 171 D3
Tiplers Bridge. S Han 150 A3
Tipps Cross La. Dodd 133 D2
Tips Cross Mead. Dodd 133 D2
Tiptree Cl. Hornc 166 A2
Tiptree Cres. Woodf 153 D1
Tiptree Gr. Wick 163 E4
Titan Rd. Grays 185 D1
Tithe The. Wick 163 D3
Tithelands. Harl 101 F3
Tithelands. Harl 102 A3
Tiverton Ave. Woodf 153 D1
Tiverton Gr. Romf 157 D3
Tobruk Rd. Chelm 110 C3
Toddbrook. Harl 102 A4
Toft Ave. Grays 185 E1
Tolbut Ct. Romf 164 C3
Tollesbury Cl. Wick 163 F3
Tollgate Rd. Stone 190 B1
Tom's La. Finch 42 A3
Tomkins Cl. Corr 179 E2
Tomkyns La. Upm 166 B4
Tomlyns Cl. Brent 147 F2
Tomswood Hill. Woodf 153 D2
Tomswood Rd. Chig 153 D2
Tonbridge Rd. Romf 156 B2
Toot Hill Rd. Ch Ong 117 F1
Top House Rise. Ching 139 E1
Top Rd. Wim 27 F2
Toplands Ave. Ave 183 E3
Toppesfield Ave. Wick 163 E3
Toppesfield Rd. Gt Y 32 C4
Tor Bryan. Ing 135 D1
Toronto Rd. Tilb 193 D3
Torquay Rd. Sprin 111 E3
Torrance Cl. Hornc 165 E2
Torridge. Grays 187 E1
Torrington Cl. Sprin 111 F3
Torrington Dr. Lou 141 E3
Torrington Gdns. Lou 141 E3
Torrington Rd. Dag 164 A2
Torver Cl. Bl Not 76 B3
Tot La. Birhr 57 E2
Totnes Wlk. Sprin 111 F3
Toucan Way. Basil 171 D2
Tovey Ave. Hod 100 A4
Tovey Cl. Lo Naz 113 F4
Tower Ave. Chelm 110 C2
Tower Cl. N W Bas 117 E4
Tower Cl. Woodf 153 D2
Tower Ct. Brent 158 B4
Tower Ct. Ch Ong 119 D1
Tower Hill. Brent 158 B4
Tower Rd. Epp 115 F1
Tower Rd. Writ 109 F1
Towers Rd. Grays 185 E1
Town Croft. Chelm 111 D3
Town Mead Rd. Wa Aby 126 B3
Town Pier. Grave 193 D1
Town Sq. Basil 171 D3
Town St. Thax 40 A1
Townfield St. Chelm 111 D2
Towngate. Basil 171 D3
Tracyes Rd. Harl 103 D3
Traddles Ct. Chelm 110 C3
Trafalgar Rd. Rain 173 F2
Trafalgar Way. Bill 149 D3
Trafalgar Way. Brain 66 A2
Trafford Cl. Chig 153 F2
Trap's Hill. Lou 140 C3
Travers Way. Basil 172 A3
Trebble Rd. Swan 191 F1
Tredgetts. Ash 4 A1
Tree Tops. Brent 146 B1
Trefgarne Rd. Dag 164 A1
Tregelles Rd. Hod 100 A4
Trehearn Rd. Chig 153 E2
Trelawney Rd. Chig 153 E2
Trenchard Cres. Sprin 111 E4
Trenham Ave. Basil 172 B4
Trent. Grays 187 E1
Trent Ave. Upm 166 B3
Trent Cl. Wick 163 E3
Trent Rd. Chelm 110 B3
Trent Rd. Lou 140 A1
Trentbridge Cl. Chig 153 F2
Trescoe Gdns. Romf 155 E3
Trevor Cl. Bill 160 C4
Trevor Rd. Woodf 152 A2
Trimble Cl. Ing 135 D2
Trimley Cl. Basil 171 E4
Trindehay. Basil 170 C3
Trinder Way. Wick 163 D3
Tring Cl. Romf 156 C3
Tring Gdns. Romf 156 C3
Tring Green. Romf 156 C3
Tring Wlk. Romf 156 C3
Trinidad Gdns. Dag 173 E3
Trinity Cl. Bill 161 E3
Trinity Cl. Bis St 67 F3
Trinity Cl. Chelm 111 E2
Trinity Rd. Bill 161 E3
Trinity Rd. Chelm 111 E1
Trinity Rd. Woodf 153 E1
Trinity St. Bis St 67 F3
Trinity Way. Bis St 67 F3
Tripat Cl. Corr 180 B3
Tripton Rd. Harl 102 C4
Troopers Dr. Romf 156 B3
Trotter's Gap. Sta Ab 87 F2
Trotters Field. Brain 66 A2
Trotters Rd. Harl 103 D3
Trotwood. Chig 153 E2
Trotwood Cl. Chelm 110 C4
Trowbridge Rd. Romf 156 C3
Trueloves La. Ing 134 C2
Trueman Cl. Basil 170 A3
Trumpeter Ct. Bill 148 C2
Truro Wlk. Romf 156 B2
Trustons Gdns. Hornc 165 D2
Tuck Rd. Rain 174 A3
Tucker's Row. Bis St 67 F3
Tudor Ave. Corr 179 F2
Tudor Ave. Romf 165 D4
Tudor Cl. Brent 146 C2
Tudor Cl. Chig 153 D3
Tudor Cl. Hun 88 B4
Tudor Cl. Ing 135 D1
Tudor Cl. Woodf 152 A3
Tudor Cres. Woodf 153 D2
Tudor Ct. Bill 161 F1
Tudor Dr. Romf 165 D4
Tudor Gdns. Romf 165 D4
Tudor Gdns. Upm 166 B1
Tudor Way. Wa Aby 126 B3
Tudor Way. Wick 163 D4
Tufter Rd. Chig 153 F3
Tugby Pl. Chelm 110 C3
Tukes Way. Saff W 25 F4
Tulip Cl. Brent 146 A2
Tulip Cl. Romf 156 B2
Tulip Cl. Sprin 111 F4
Tumbler Rd. Harl 103 D4
Tunnmeade. Harl 90 A1
Tunstall Ave. Chig 154 A2
Tunstall Cl. Basil 172 B3
Tupman Cl. Chelm 110 B3
Turkey Oaks. Chelm 111 E2
Turners Cl. Ch Ong 118 C1
Turnpike La. Grays 186 B1
Turold Rd. Corr 179 F2
Turp Ave. Grays 185 E2
Turpin Ave. Romf 155 D2
Turpin's La. Chig 152 C3
Turpins The. Basil 171 E4
Tusser Ct. Gt Bad 124 B4
Tuttlebee La. Lou 152 A4
Twain Terr. Wick 163 E3
Tweed. Grays 187 E1
Tweed Glen. Romf 155 E2
Tweed Green. Romf 155 E2
Tweed Way. Romf 155 E2
Twentieth St. Take 58 C2
Twentyfirst St. Take 58 C2
Twentyman Cl. Woodf 152 A3
Twitten La. Chelm 124 A1
Twyford Bury La. Bis St 68 A2
Twyford Cl. Bis St 68 A3
Twyford Gdns. Bis St 67 F2
Twyford Rd. Bis St 68 A3
Tyburns The. Brent 159 E4
Tycehurst Hill. Lou 140 C3
Tye Common Rd. Bill 160 B4
Tye Green Rd. Els 58 B3
Tye Green Village. Harl 102 C3
Tyefields. Basil 172 B4
Tyelands. Bill 160 C4
Tyle Green. Hornc 165 F4
Tyler Ave. Basil 170 B3
Tylers. Saff W 14 C1

Tylers Ave. Bill 149 E3
Tylers Cl. Chelm 124 A3
Tylers Cl. Lou 140 C1
Tylers Rd. Roy 101 E2
Tylney Croft. Harl 102 B3
Tyne. Grays 187 E1
Tyne Cl. Upm 166 B3
Tyne Gdns. Ave 183 E3
Tyne Way. Chelm 110 B3
Tynfield Rd. Hod 87 D1
Tyrell Rise. Brent 158 B3
Tyrells Cl. Sprin 111 F2
Tyrells Cl. Upm 166 A1
Tyrells The. Corr 180 A2
Tyrells Way. Gt Bad 124 C4
Tyrone Cl. Bill 161 E3
Tyrone Rd. Bill 161 E3
Tyrrell Ct. Basil 172 B3
Tyrrells Hall Cl. Grays 185 E1
Tyrrells Rd. Bill 161 E3
Tysea Cl. Harl 102 C3
Tysea Hill. Nave H 143 F1
Tysea Hill. Sta Abb 143 F1
Tysea Rd. Harl 102 C3
Tyssen Pl. S Ock 176 B2
Tythe Cl. Sprin 111 F4

Udall Gdns. Romf 155 D2
Ullswater Cl. Bl Not 76 B3
Ullswater Way. Hornc 174 A4
Una Rd. Basil 172 C3
Underwood Rd. Woodf 152 B2
Unwin Pl. Stock 136 C1
Upland Cl. Bill 148 C2
Upland Court Rd. Romf 156 C1
Upland Croft Rd. Romf 156 C1
Upland Dr. Bill 148 C2
Upland Rd. Bill 148 C2
Upland Rd. Ep Gr 115 F3
Uplands Dr. Sprin 111 E4
Uplands Rd. Woodf 152 C2
Uplands The. Lou 140 C3
Upminster Rd. Hornc 165 F1
Upminster Rd N. Rain 174 B1
Upminster Rd S. Rain 174 A1
Upminster Trad Pk. Brent 167 E2
Upper Ave. Basil 172 C4
Upper Brentwood Rd. Romf 165 E4
Upper Bridge Rd. Chelm 111 D1
Upper Chase. Chelm 124 A4
Upper Cornsland. Brent 158 B4
Upper Farm Rd. Ashe 20 B4
Upper Hook. Harl 102 C3
Upper Market Rd. Runw 163 E4
Upper Marsh La. Hod 100 A3
Upper Mayne. Basil 170 C4
Upper Mealines. Harl 103 D3
Upper Mill Field. Gt Dun 72 C4
Upper Moors. Gt Wal 97 F4
Upper Park. Harl 89 D1
Upper Park. Lou 140 B2
Upper Park Rd. Wick 163 E2
Upper Rainham Rd. Hornc 164 C1
Upper Rd. Bill 162 B3
Upper Roman Rd. Chelm 111 D1
Upper Ryle. Brent 146 A1
Upper Stonyfield. Harl 102 A4
Upper Swaines. Epp 115 F1
Upsheres. Saff W 25 F4
Upshire Rd. Wa Aby 127 D3
Upton Cl. Corr 179 E1
Upway The. Basil 171 E4
Urban Ave. Hornc 165 E1
Urban Rd. Bis St 68 A4
Usk Rd. Ave 183 E4
Usterdale Rd. Saff W 13 F2
Uvedale Rd. Dag 164 A1
Uxbridge Cl. Wick 163 F3

Valance Ave. Ching 139 F1
Valance Rd. Clav 35 D4
Vale Cl. Brent 145 F2
Vale End. Chelm 124 B2
Vale The. Basil 171 E2
Vale The. Bill 149 E4
Vale The. Brent 146 B1
Vale The. Woodf 152 A2
Valence Way. Basil 170 B2
Valentines. Stock 136 C1
Valentines. Wick 163 E3
Valentines Way. Romf 164 C1
Valiant Cl. Romf 155 D1
Valletta Cl. Chelm 111 D2
Valley Bridge. Chelm 111 D3
Valley Cl. Lou 140 C2
Valley Cl. Wa Aby 126 B4
Valley Hill. Lou 140 C2
Valley Rd. Bill 149 E1
Valley Rd. Brain 66 A2
Valley Side. Ching 139 D1
Valley View. Swan 191 D1
Valmar Ave. Sta L H 179 D1
Van Dieman's La. Chelm 124 B4
Van Dieman's Rd. Chelm 124 B4
Vandenbury Circ. Finch 43 E3
Vange Corner Dr. Corr 171 D1
Vange Hill Dr. Basil 171 F2
Vange Park Rd. Basil 171 D1
Vanguard Cl. Romf 155 D1
Vanguard Way. Brain 66 A2
Vantorts Cl. Saw 77 F1
Vantorts Rd. Saw 77 F1
Varden Cl. Chelm 110 C3
Vaughan Ave. Hornc 174 B4
Vaughan Cl. Ray 64 C1
Vaughan Willaims Rd. Basil 170 B4
Vauxhall Dr. Brain 65 E1
Velizy Ave. Harl 102 B4
Vellacotts. Chelm 111 D4
Venette Cl. Rain 182 A4
Venmore Dr. Gt Dun 72 C4
Venue Rd. Brent 158 B3
Veny Cres. Hornc 174 B4
Vera Rd. S Han 151 D1
Verbena Cl. S Ock 184 B4
Verderers Rd. Chig 154 A3
Vere Rd. Lou 141 E3
Vermeer Ride. Sprin 111 F4
Vermont Cl. Basil 172 B4
Vernon Ave. Woodf 152 A2
Vernon Cnr. Stock 136 B1
Vernon Cres. Brent 159 D4
Vernon Rd. Romf 155 E3
Vernon Rd. Swan 191 F1
Vernon Way. Brain 66 B3
Vernon's Cl. Hen 48 C2
Vernons Wlk. Basil 163 D1
Veronica Cl. Romf 156 B2
Vexil Cl. W Thu 183 F1
Veysey Gdns. Dag 164 A1
Viaduct Rd. Chelm 111 D1
Viaduct The. Woodf 152 A1
Vicarage Cl. Brent 157 F3
Vicarage Cl. Gt Sal 64 A4
Vicarage Cl. Rox 109 D3
Vicarage Dr. Grave 192 B1
Vicarage La. Berd 46 A4
Vicarage La. Chig 153 E4
Vicarage La. Gt Bad 124 C3
Vicarage La. N W Bas 117 D4
Vicarage La. Thax 40 A2
Vicarage La. Ugl 47 F3
Vicarage Mews. Gt Bad 124 C3
Vicarage Rd. Chelm 124 A4
Vicarage Rd. Dag 173 D3
Vicarage Rd. Epp 116 B1
Vicarage Rd. Finch 42 B3
Vicarage Rd. Hornc 165 D2
Vicarage Rd. Ple 83 F1
Vicarage Rd. Rox 109 E3
Vicarage Rd. Woodf 152 C2
Vicarage Sq. Grays 192 A4
Vicarage Wood. Harl 90 A1
Victor App. Hornc 165 E2
Victor Ave. Basil 172 B3
Victor Cl. Hornc 165 E2
Victor Gdns. Hornc 165 E2
Victor Wlk. Hornc 165 E2
Victor's Cres. Brent 159 D4
Victoria Ave. Basil 170 B2
Victoria Ave. Grays 185 E2
Victoria Ave. Romf 155 D2
Victoria Ave. Saff W 13 F1
Victoria Ave. Wick 163 E4
Victoria Cl. Basil 170 A4
Victoria Cl. Grays 185 E2
Victoria Cres. Basil 170 B4
Victoria Cres. Chelm 111 D2
Victoria Cres. Wick 163 D4
Victoria Gdns. Saff W 25 F4
Victoria Rd. Basil 170 A4
Victoria Rd. Basil 171 E1
Victoria Rd. Brent 158 B4
Victoria Rd. Brent 158 B4
Victoria Rd. Chelm 111 E2
Victoria Rd. Ching 139 F1
Victoria Rd. Dag 173 E4
Victoria Rd. Horn H 177 F4
Victoria Rd. Horn H 178 C2
Victoria Rd. Lou 152 B4
Victoria Rd. Romf 164 C3
Victoria Rd. Sta L H 179 E1
Victoria Rd. Wa Aby 126 B3
Victoria Rd. Woodf 152 A1
Victoria Rd. Writ 109 F1
Victoria Rd S. Chelm 111 D1
Victoria St. Brain 66 A1
Victory Rd. Rain 174 A2
Victory Way. Romf 155 D1
Vienna Cl. Woodf 152 C1
View Cl. Chig 153 E3
Vigerons Way. Grays 186 A1
Vignoles Rd. Romf 164 A2
Viking Way. Brent 146 A2
Viking Way. Runw 151 E1
Village Gate. Sprin 112 A2
Village The. Will 107 E2
Villiers Pl. Bore 99 F1
Villiers-Sur-Marne Ave. Bis St 67 E3
Vincent Ave. Horn H 178 C2
Vincent Cl. Chig 153 E2
Vincent Cl. Corr 180 A2
Vincent Rd. Rain 174 B1
Vincent Way. Bill 149 D3
Vine Gr. H Wy 89 F3
Vine St. Gt Ba 42 A1
Vine St. Romf 164 B4
Vineries Cl. Dag 173 D3
Vineway. Brent 146 B1
Vineyards The. Gt Bad 124 C4
Viola Cl. S Ock 176 B1
Violet Cl. Sprin 111 F4
Violet Rd. Woodf 152 A1
Violets La. Fu Pel 45 D2
Virginia Gdns. Woodf 153 E1
Vista Rd. Wick 163 F4
Vowler Rd. Basil 170 A2
Voysey Gdns. Basil 163 D1

Wadham Cl. Ing 135 D2
Wagon Mead. Hat B O 79 D2
Wainfleet Ave. Romf 155 E1
Wainsfield Villas. Thax 40 A1
Wainwright Ave. Brent 147 E2
Wakefield Ave. Bill 149 D1
Wakefield Cl. Gt C 1 B2
Wakefield Cl. Hornc 165 F3
Wakelin Chase. Ing 135 D2
Waldeck Rd. Stone 190 A1
Waldegrave. Basil 171 D2
Waldegrave Gdns. Upm 166 A2
Walden Ave. Rain 173 E2
Walden Ave. Wim 26 C1
Walden Rd. Ash 14 C3
Walden Rd. Gt C 1 C1
Walden Rd. Had 3 D3
Walden Rd. Hornc 165 E3
Walden Rd. Lit C 12 C4
Walden Rd. Litt 12 C2
Walden Rd. Rad 27 E4
Walden Rd. Saff W 14 B1
Walden Rd. Thax 39 F3
Walden Rd. Wen A 24 C3
Walden Way. Chig 153 F2
Walden Way. Hornc 165 E3
Waldgrooms. Gt Dun 61 E1
Waldon. Grays 187 E2
Waldringfield. Basil 171 D4
Walford Pl. Sprin 111 F1
Walfords Cl. Harl 90 B2
Walk The. Gt Ba 42 A1
Walk The. Hornc 165 F1
Walker Ave. Fyf 106 B1
Walker's Hoppet. Lou 140 C4
Walkers Cl. Sprin 111 E4
Wall Chase. Gt Wal 83 F4
Wallace Cres. Chelm 124 B4
Wallace Gdns. Swan 191 F1
Wallace Rd. Grays 185 D1
Wallace's La. Bore 99 F2
Wallasea Gdns. Sprin 111 F3
Wallenger Ave. Romf 165 D4
Wallers Cl. Woodf 152 C2
Wallers Way. Hod 87 D1
Wallflower Ct. Sprin 111 F3
Wallis Cl. Hornc 165 D2
Wallis Park. Grave 192 A1
Walmer Cl. Romf 155 D1
Walnut Dri. Bis St 67 E2
Walnut Gr. Brain 65 F1
Walnut Tree Ave. Saw 77 F2
Walnut Tree Cl. Hod 100 A3
Walnut Tree Cres. Saw 77 F2
Walnut Way. Lou 152 B4
Walpole Cl. Grays 185 E1
Walsingham Way. Bill 149 D3
Walters Cl. Chelm 124 B2
Waltham Cl. Brent 147 E2
Waltham Glen. Chelm 124 B4
Waltham Rd. Bore 99 F3
Waltham Rd. Lo Naz 113 F3
Waltham Rd. Lo Naz 114 A3
Waltham Rd. Terl 86 C1
Waltham Rd. Woodf 152 C2
Waltham Way. Ching 139 D1
Walthams. Basil 172 A4
Walthams Pl. Basil 172 A4
Walton Ct. Basil 170 B4
Walton Gdns. Brent 147 E2
Walton Gdns. Wa Aby 126 A3
Walton Rd. Hod 100 B4
Walton Rd. Romf 154 C2
Walton's Hall Rd. Sta L H 187 D3
Wambrook Cl. Brent 147 E1
Wannock Gdns. Woodf 153 D2
Wansford Cl. Brent 157 F4
Wansford Rd. Woodf 152 B1
Wantz La. Rain 174 A1
Wantz Rd. Dag 173 D4
Wantz Rd. Marg 136 A4
Warburtons. Corr 180 A2
Ward Ave. Grays 185 D1
Ward Cres. Bis St 67 F3
Warden Ave. Romf 155 E3
Ware Rd. Gt Am 87 D1
Ware Rd. Hod 100 A4
Warehouse Rd. Steb 62 C2
Warehouse Villas. Steb 63 D2
Wares Rd. G Ea 95 F3
Warescot Cl. Brent 146 A1
Warescot Rd. Brent 146 A1
Warley Gap. Brent 158 B2
Warley Hall La. Horn H 167 F2
Warley Hill. Brent 158 B3
Warley Mount. Brent 158 B3
Warley Rd. Brent 157 F1
Warley Rd. Upm 157 F1
Warley Rd. Woodf 152 A2
Warley Rd. Woodf 153 D1
Warley St. Brent 167 E3
Warleywoods Cres. Brent 158 A3
Warner Cl. Bill 149 E1
Warner Dr. Brain 65 E2
Warners. Gt Dun 72 B4
Warners Cl. Woodf 152 A3
Warren Cl. Broom 98 A2
Warren Cl. Take 70 B4
Warren Ct. Chig 153 E3
Warren Dr. Hornc 165 D1
Warren Field. Epp 129 D4
Warren Hill. Lou 140 B2
Warren La. Grays 184 B1
Warren La. Kelv H 146 A4
Warren La. Writ 110 B2
Warren Pond Rd. Ching 139 F1
Warren Rd. Brain 66 B1
Warren Rd. Ching 139 E1
Warren Rd. S Han 151 E4
Warren Terr. Grays 184 B2
Warren The. Bill 148 C2
Warrene Cl. Sta L H 179 E1
Warriner Ave. Horne 165 E1
Warrington Gdns. Hornc 165 E3
Warrington Sq. Bill 148 C2
Warwick Cl. Brain 66 A2
Warwick Gdns. Romf 165 E4
Warwick La. Upm 175 D2
Warwick Pl. Basil 169 F2
Warwick Pl. Grave 192 A1
Warwick Pl. Kelv H 145 E3
Warwick Rd. Bis St 68 A3
Warwick Rd. Rain 174 B1
Warwick Rd. Take 70 C4
Warwick Sq. Chelm 110 C2
Wash Rd. Bill 161 F1
Wash Rd. Brent 147 E2
Wash The. St Pel 45 E3
Washington Ave. Basil 170 A3
Wat Tyler Way. Basil 172 A1
Watch House Rd. Steb 62 C3
Watchouse Rd. Chelm 124 B2
Water Hall La. Shal 54 C4
Water La. Bis St 67 F4
Water La. Brox 60 B4
Water La. Deb 26 A1
Water La. Hel B 17 E4
Water La. New 25 D1
Water La. Pur 183 D1
Water La. Rad 27 F4
Water La. Roy 101 F2
Water La. Shal 54 C2
Water La. Stan M 57 F3
Water La. Ste B 18 A3
Water La. Stur 7 F3
Waterhouse La. Chelm 110 C1
Waterhouse Moor. Harl 102 C4
Waterhouse St. Chelm 110 C1
Waterloo Gdns. Romf 164 B3
Waterloo La. Chelm 111 E1
Waterloo Rd. Brent 146 B1
Waterloo Rd. Romf 164 C3
Waterloo Rd. Woodf 153 E1
Watermans Way. N W Bas 117 D2
Waters Gdns. Dag 173 D4
Waterside. Stan M 57 F3
Watermeet. Harl 102 A2
Waterson Rd. Grays 186 B1
Waterville Rd. Basil 172 A2
Waterworks La. Corr 180 B3
Watery La. Gt Dun 72 A1
Watery La. Lit Lav 105 E4
Watery La. Man 46 B1
Wates Way. Brent 146 B1
Watling La. Thax 39 F2
Watling St. Thax 40 A2
Watlington Rd. Harl 90 B2
Watson Cl. Grays 191 D3
Watson Gdns. Romf 156 B1
Watts Cl. Barn 73 D2
Watts Cres. W Thu 183 E1
Wavell Cl. Sprin 111 E4
Waveney Dr. Sprin 111 E3
Waveney Terr. Hav 7 D4
Waverley Cl. Woodf 152 B1
Waverley Cres. Romf 156 B2
Waverley Cres. Runw 151 E2
Waverley Gdns. Grays 185 D2
Waverley Gdns. Woodf 153 E1
Waverley Rd. Bill 161 F1
Waverley Rd. Rain 174 A1
Waverley Rd. Woodf 152 B1
Way Bank La. Cla 8 C4
Wayback The. Saff W 13 F1
Waycross Rd. Upm 166 C3
Wayfaring Green. Grays 184 C1
Wayletts. Basil 170 A4
Wayre St. Harl 90 B2
Wayre The. Harl 90 B2
Wayside Ave. Hornc 165 E1
Wayside Cl. Romf 164 C4
Wayside Gdns. Dag 173 D4
Waytemore Rd. Bis St 67 F3
Weald Bridge Rd. Mag Lav 104 C1
Weald Bridge Rd. N W Bas 104 C1
Weald Cl. Brent 158 A4
Weald Hall La. N W Bas 116 C3
Weald Park Way. Brent 157 F4
Weald Rd. Brent 145 F1
Weald Way. Romf 164 A3
Wear Dr. Sprin 111 E3
Weaverhead Cl. Thax 40 A2
Weaverhead La. Thax 40 A2
Weavers. Basil 171 F2
Weavers Cl. Bill 149 D1
Webster Cl. Hornc 165 E1
Webster Cl. Wa Aby 127 D3
Webster Pl. Stock 136 C1
Webster Rd. Sta L H 179 F1
Weddell Rd. Hav 7 E3
Wedgewood Cl. Epp 116 A1
Wedhey. Harl 102 B4
Wedlake Cl. Hornc 165 F2
Wedmore Ave. Woodf 153 D1
Wednesbury Gdns. Romf 156 C2
Wednesbury Green. Romf 156 C2
Wednesbury Rd. Romf 156 C2
Wedow Rd. Thax 40 A2
Weelkes Cl. Corr 179 E2
Weight Rd. Chelm 111 E1
Weind The. The B 128 C2
Weir Wynd. Bill 149 D1
Welbeck Dr. Basil 170 A2
Welbeck Rise. Basil 170 A2
Well Field. Writ 110 A1
Well La. Chelm 124 A1
Well La. Dodd 145 F3
Well La. Harl 89 D1
Well La. Harl 102 A4
Well La. Stock 136 C1
Well La. T Thu 184 C3
Well Mead. Bill 161 E4
Well's St. Chelm 111 D2
Well-Green Cl. Saff W 25 F4
Welland. Grays 187 E1
Welland Ave. Chelm 110 B3
Weller Gr. Chelm 110 C4
Wellesley. Harl 102 A2
Wellesley Rd. Brent 146 B1
Wellfields. Lou 141 D3
Welling Rd. Grays 186 B4
Wellington Cl. Brain 66 B2
Wellington Cl. Chelm 110 B3
Wellington Cl. Dag 173 E3
Wellington Ct. Grays 185 D3
Wellington Dr. Dag 173 E3
Wellington Hill. Wa Aby 127 D1
Wellington Mews. Bill 149 D2
Wellington Pl. Brent 158 B3
Wellington Rd. N W Bas 117 D2
Wellington Rd. Tilb 193 D3
Wellingtonia Ave. Hav B 155 F4
Wellmeads. Chelm 124 A4
Wells Ct. Sprin 111 E3
Wells Gdns. Basil 171 F4
Wells Gdns. Dag 173 D4
Wells Gdns. Rain 173 F3
Wellstye Green. Basil 171 F4
Wenden Rd. Saff W 25 D4
Wendene. Basil 171 F2
Wendover Gdns. Brent 159 D4
Wendover Way. Hornc 174 B4
Wenham Gdns. Brent 147 E2
Wenlocks La. Bla 133 F3
Wennington Green. Rain 182 C3
Wennington Rd. Rain 182 B4
Wensley Ave. Woodf 152 A2
Wensley Cl. Romf 155 D3
Wensleydale Ave. Woodf 152 C1
Wentworth Cres. Brain 65 F3
Wentworth Dri. Bis St 67 E3
Wentworth Way. Rain 174 A1
Wesley End Rd. Stam 19 E2
Wesley Gdns. Bill 148 C3
West Ave. Chelm 110 C3
West Beech Ave. Wick 163 F4
West Beech Cl. Wick 163 F4
West Cl. Hod 100 A4
West Cl. Rain 174 A1
West Cloister. Bill 149 D1
West Crescent Rd. Grave 193 E1
West Croft. Bill 149 E1
West Dene Dr. Romf 156 B3
West Dr. Weth 43 E2
West Fields. Saff W 25 F4
West Gate. Harl 102 B4
West Gr. Woodf 152 B3
West Hanningfield Rd. Sand 124 C1
West Hanningfield Rd. W Han 124 C1
West Hill Rd. Hod 100 A4
West Hook. Basil 169 F2
West Kent Ave. Grave 192 B1
West Lawn. Chelm 124 B1
West Malling Way. Hornc 174 B4
West Mayne. Basil 169 F3
West Park Ave. Bill 149 D2
West Park Cres. Bill 149 D1
West Park Dr. Bill 149 D1
West Park Hill. Brent 158 A4
West Rd. Bis St 67 F3
West Rd. Harl 90 A2
West Rd. Romf 164 B2
West Rd. S Ock 176 A1
West Rd. Saff W 25 E4
West Rd. Saw 77 E2
West Rd. Stan M 57 F3

West Ridge. Bill 149 D1
West Sq. Chelm 111 D1
West Sq. Harl 89 E1
West St. Grave 193 D1
West St. Grays 192 A4
West Thorpe. Basil 171 E3
West Thurrock Way. W Thu 183 F1
West Thurrock Way. W Thu 184 A1
West View. Lou 140 C3
West Way. Brent 158 A4
West Way. Wa Aby 126 A1
West Wlk. Harl 102 B4
Westall Rd. Lou 141 E3
Westbourne Ct. Hav 7 D4
Westbourne Dr. Brent 157 F3
Westbourne Gdns. Bill 149 D3
Westbourne Gr. Gt Bad 124 B4
Westbury Dr. Brent 158 B4
Westbury La. Lou 152 B4
Westbury Rd. Brent 158 B4
Westbury Rd. Lou 140 B1
Westbury Terr. Upm 166 C1
Westcroft Ct. Hod 100 A2
Westerdale. Sprin 111 E4
Westergreen Meadow. Brain 65 F1
Westerings The. Gt Bad 124 C3
Western Ave. Brent 146 B1
Western Ave. Dag 173 E3
Western Ave. Epp 128 C4
Western Ave. Romf 156 B1
Western Ave. W Thu 183 F1
Western Cross Cl. Swan 191 E1
Western Gdns. Brent 158 B4
Western Mews. Bill 149 D1
Western Rd. Bill 149 D1
Western Rd. Lo Naz 100 C1
Western Rd. Romf 164 C3
Westfield. Basil 170 A4
Westfield. Harl 102 C4
Westfield. Lou 140 B2
Westfield Ave. Chelm 111 D2
Westfield Cl. Bis St 67 F4
Westfield Cl. Wick 163 F4
Westfield Rd. Bis St 67 F4
Westlake Ave. Basil 172 C3
Westland Ave. Hornc 165 F2
Westland View. Grays 185 D3
Westley La. Saff W 13 E3
Westley Rd. Basil 170 B1
Westlyn Cl. Rain 174 B1
Westmede. Basil 170 B3
Westmede. Chig 153 E2
Westminster Cl. Woodf 153 E1
Westminster Gdns. Brain 66 A2
Westminster Gdns. Ching 139 F1
Westminster Gdns. Woodf 153 E1
Westmoreland Ave. Hornc 165 E4
Weston Ave. W Thu 183 F1
Weston Cl. Brent 147 E1
Westview Dr. Woodf 152 B1
Westway. Chelm 123 F4
Westwood Ave. Brent 158 A3
Wetherfield. Stan M 57 E4
Wetherland. Basil 170 C3
Weydale. Corr 180 A3
Weymarks. Basil 170 B4
Weymouth Rd. Sprin 111 F3
Whadden Chase. Ing 135 D2
Whalebone La N. Romf 154 C1
Wharf Cl. Sta L H 179 E1
Wharf Rd. Bis St 67 F3
Wharf Rd. Brent 158 B4
Wharf Rd. Chelm 111 E1
Wharf Rd. Corr 180 B2
Wharf Rd. Grave 193 F1
Wharf Rd. Grays 191 F4
Wharf Rd. Sta L H 187 E4
Wharf Rd S. Grays 191 F4
Wharley Hook. Harl 102 C3
Wheat Croft. Bis St 67 F2
Wheatear Pl. Bill 149 E1
Wheatfield Way. Basil 170 A2
Wheatfield Way. Chelm 110 C2
Wheatley Ave. Brain 66 B2
Wheatley Cl. Saw 77 E1
Wheatley Rd. Corr 180 A3
Wheatsheaf Rd. Romf 164 C3
Wheel Farm Dr. Dag 164 B1
Wheeler's Hill. Lit Wal 98 C3
Wheelers. Epp 115 F1
Wheelers Cl. Lo Naz 100 C1
Wheelers Fm Gdns. N W Bas 117 D3
Wheelers La. Corr 180 B3
Wheelers La. Nave H 145 D3
Whinhams Way. Bill 148 C2
Whist Ave. Runw 151 F1
Whitakers Way. Lou 140 C4
Whitbreads Farm La. Lit Wal 85 F3
Whitby Ave. Brent 159 E2
Whitchurch Rd. Romf 156 C3
Whitcroft. Basil 170 B2
White Bear. Stan M 57 F4
White Cotts. Fair 86 B2
White Gdns. Dag 173 D3
White Hall. Abr 142 A3
White Hart La. Brent 158 A4
White Hart La. Romf 155 D1
White Hart La. Sprin 111 F4
White Horse La. New 25 D1
White Lyons Rd. Brent 158 B4
White Post Field. Saw 77 E1
White St. Gt Dun 72 B4
Whitebarn La. Dag 173 D2
Whitebarns. Fu Pel 45 D3
Whitebarns Cres. Fu Pel 45 D3
Whiteditch La. New 24 C1
Whitehall Cl. Chig 154 A4
Whitehall Cl. Lo Naz 100 C1
Whitehall Gdns. Ching 139 E1
Whitehall La. Bis St 56 C1
Whitehall La. Corr 180 B4
Whitehall La. Grays 185 E1
Whitehall La. Woodf 152 A4
Whitehall Rd. Bis St 56 C1
Whitehall Rd. Ching 139 F1
Whitehall Rd. Grays 185 E1
Whitehall Rd. Woodf 152 A4
Whitehills Rd. Lou 141 D3
Whitehouse Cres. Gt Bad 124 B4
Whitehouse Rd. Steb 62 C3
Whitelands. Bla 133 E2
Whitelands Cl. Runw 151 F1
Whitelands Way. Romf 156 B1
Whitemead. Broom 98 A1
Whites Cl. Swan 191 E1
Whites Hill. Stock 150 A4
Whites La. Gt Le 85 F3
Whiteshot Way. Saff W 13 F1
Whiteshott. Basil 171 D2
Whitethorn Gdns. Chelm 124 B4
Whitethorn Gdns. Hornc 165 E3
Whitewaites. Harl 89 F1
Whiteways. Bill 149 F2
Whiteways. Gt C 1 B1
Whitfields. Sta L H 179 F1
Whitley Rd. Hod 100 A4
Whitley's Chase. Finch 30 B3
Whitmore Ave. Grays 185 D3
Whitmore Ct. Basil 171 F4
Whitmore Way. Basil 171 E4
Whittingstall Rd. Hod 100 A4
Whittington Rd. Brent 147 E2
Whittington Way. Bis St 67 F2
Whybrews. Corr 179 F1
Whybridge Cl. Rain 173 F2
Whytewaters. Basil 171 F2
Whyverne Cl. Sprin 111 F3
Wick Beech Ave. Wick 163 F4
Wick Cres. Wick 163 F3
Wick Dr. Wick 163 E4
Wick Dr. Wick 163 F3
Wick Glen. Bill 148 C2
Wick La. Wick 163 F4
Wicken Rd. New 36 C4
Wickets Way. Chig 153 F2
Wickfield Ash. Chelm 110 B3
Wickford Ave. Basil 172 A3
Wickford Cl. Romf 156 C3
Wickford Dr. Romf 156 C3
Wickham Pl. Basil 171 E3
Wickham Rd. Grays 186 B2
Wickhay. Basil 170 C3
Wicklands Rd. Hun 88 B4
Wicklow Ave. Chelm 110 B3
Wicks Cl. Brain 65 E2
Wid Cl. Brent 147 E2
Widecombe Cl. Romf 156 B1
Widford Chase. Chelm 123 F4
Widford Cl. Chelm 123 F4
Widford Gr. Chelm 123 F4
Widford Park Pl. Chelm 123 F4
Widford Rd. Chelm 123 F4
Widgeons. Basil 172 B3
Widworthy Hayes. Brent 147 D1
Wiggin's La. Bill 160 C4
Wigley Bush La. Brent 157 F4
Wigton Rd. Romf 156 C3
Wigton Way. Romf 156 C3
Wilde Cl. Tilb 193 E3
Wilfred Ave. Rain 182 A4
Wilfred St. Grave 193 D1
Wilkes Rd. Brent 147 E2
Wilkinson Cl. Stone 190 A2
Wilkinsons Mead. Sprin 112 A2
Will's Ayley La. Saff W 14 C1
William Cl. Romf 155 E1
William Rd. Basil 172 C3
William St. Grays 192 B4
Williams Rd. Broom 98 A1
Williamsons Way. Corr 179 F3
Willingale Cl. Brent 147 F2
Willingale Cl. Lou 141 E4
Willingale Cl. Woodf 152 B2
Willingale Rd. Fyf 106 C1
Willingale Rd. H Ong 120 C3
Willingale Rd. Lou 141 E4
Willingales The. Basil 170 A3
Willinghall Cl. Wa Aby 126 B4
Willoughby Dr. Rain 173 F3
Willoughby Dr. Sprin 111 F1
Willoughby's La. Brain 66 B4
Willow Cl. Bis St 67 F4
Willow Cl. Brent 147 D2
Willow Cl. Broom 98 A1
Willow Cl. Dodd 133 E1
Willow Cl. Hornc 165 D1
Willow Cl. Lou 152 B4
Willow Green. Ing 135 D2
Willow Mead. Saw 77 F1
Willow Path. Wa Aby 126 C3
Willow St. Ching 139 E1
Willow St. Romf 164 B4
Willow Walk. Upm 166 C2
Willow Way. Romf 157 D2
Willowbank. Chelm 124 A2
Willowdale Centre. Runw 163 E4
Willowdene. Brent 145 F2
Willowdene Ct. Brent 158 B3
Willowfield. Basil 170 B4
Willowfield. Bill 161 E1
Willowfield. Harl 102 B3
Willowherb Wlk. Romf 156 B2
Willowhill. Corr 179 F3
Willowmead. Chig 154 A4
Willowmead. S Han 150 B2
Willows The. Basil 172 B3
Willows The. Bill 161 E4
Willows The. Bore 112 C4
Willows The. Grays 192 B4
Willows The. Gt C 1 B2
Wills Hill. Corr 179 E2
Wilmot Green. Brent 158 B2
Wilshire Ave. Sprin 111 F2
Wilsman Rd. S Ock 176 B2
Wilsner. Basil 172 B4
Wilson Cl. Sta L H 187 E4
Wilthorne Gdns. Dag 173 D3
Wilton Cl. Bis St 68 A4
Wilton Dr. Romf 155 E2
Wiltshire Ave. Hornc 165 F4
Wimbish Wlk. Wim 26 C1
Wimborne Cl. Lou 152 B4
Wimborne Cl. Saw 77 E1
Wimbourne. Basil 170 A4
Wimbush Ct. Basil 172 A4
Wimbush End. Basil 172 A3
Wimbush Mews. Basil 172 A4
Wincanton Gdns. Woodf 153 D1
Wincanton Rd. Romf 156 B4
Wincelow Hall Rd. Hemp 16 B1
Winchelsea Dr. Gt Bad 124 C4
Winchester Ave. Upm 166 C1
Winchester Cl. Bis St 67 E2
Winchester Gdns. Bill 161 E1
Wind Hill. Mag Lav 105 D2
Windermere Ave. Hornc 174 A4
Windermere Dr. Bl Not 76 B3
Windhill. Bis St 67 F4
Windhill Fields. Bis St 67 F4
Windhill Old Rd. Bis St 67 F4
Windmill Cl. Gt Dun 61 F1
Windmill Cl. Upm 166 A1
Windmill Cl. Wa Aby 126 C3
Windmill Fields. Harl 90 C2
Windmill Gdns. Brain 66 A4
Windmill Heights. Bill 161 D4
Windmill Hill. Saff W 13 D2
Windmill Meadows. Ay Rod 81 E1
Windmill St. Grave 193 D1
Windmill Way. Kelv H 132 C1
Windmills The. Broom 98 A2
Windrush Dr. Sprin 111 E3
Windsor Ave. Corr 180 A3
Windsor Ave. Grays 185 D2
Windsor Gdns. Bis St 67 D4
Windsor Gdns. Brain 66 A2
Windsor Gdns. Runw 151 E1
Windsor Rd. Basil 172 C4
Windsor Rd. Brent 146 A2
Windsor Rd. Hornc 165 E2
Windsor Rd. S Han 150 B2
Windsor Way. Chelm 110 C1
Windsors The. Lou 152 C4
Windy Hill. Brent 147 E1
Winfields. Basil 172 B4
Wingate Cl. Brain 65 F2
Wingfield. Grays 184 C1
Wingfield Cl. Brent 159 D4
Wingfield Gdns. Upm 166 C3
Wingletye La. Hornc 166 A2
Wingrave Cres. Brent 157 F3
Wingway. Brent 146 B1
Winifred Ave. Hornc 174 C4
Winifred Rd. Basil 172 A3
Winsey Chase. Finch 42 B3
Winstanley Rd. Saff W 25 F4
Winstead Gdns. Dag 173 E4
Winston Cl. Romf 164 A4
Winstree. Basil 172 A4
Winters Way. Wa Aby 127 D3
Winton Ave. Wick 163 D4
Wiscombe Hill. Basil 170 B2
Wisdons Cl. Dag 164 A2
Wisemans Gdns. Saw 77 E1
Wissants. Harl 102 A2
Witchards. Basil 171 D3
Witchtree La. Hemp 16 C2
Witham Cl. Lou 140 C2
Witham Gdns. Horn H 168 B3
Witham Rd. Dag 173 D4
Witham Rd. Romf 165 D3
Witherings The. Hornc 165 F3
Withersfield Rd. Hav 6 C4
Wittering Wlk. Hornc 174 B3
Woburn Ave . Bis St 67 E4
Woburn Ave. Hornc 174 A4
Woburn Ave. The B 128 C1
Woburn Pl. Bill 148 C3
Wokingdon Rd. Grays 186 A2
Wollaston Cres. Basil 163 E1
Wollaston Way. Basil 163 E1
Wolmers Hey. Gt Wal 97 F4
Wolseley Rd. Chelm 111 D1
Wolseley Rd. Romf 164 B2
Wolsey Gdns. Woodf 153 E2
Wood Ave. W Thu 183 E1
Wood Dale. Gt Bad 124 C3
Wood End. Widd 37 E2
Wood Green. Basil 163 D1
Wood La. Dag 164 A1
Wood La. Hornc 174 A4
Wood La. Mee 34 A3
Wood La. Will 107 F2
Wood Meads. Epp 116 A1
Wood St. Chelm 124 A4
Wood St. Grays 192 B4
Wood View. Grays 185 F1
Woodberry Down. Epp 116 C3
Woodberry Way. Ching 139 E1
Woodbine Cl. Harl 102 B3
Woodbridge Cl. Romf 156 B4
Woodbridge La. Romf 156 B4
Woodbrook Cres. Bill 148 C2
Woodbrook Gdns. Wa Aby 126 C3
Woodbrooke Way. Corr 180 A3
Woodbury Hill. Lou 140 C4
Woodcock Cl. Hav 7 E4
Woodcote Ave. Hornc 174 A4
Woodcote Cres. Basil 172 B3
Woodcroft. Harl 102 B3
Woodcroft Ave. Sta Ab 87 E2
Woodcutters Ave. Grays 185 E2
Woodedge Cl. Ching 139 F1
Woodfield. Wick 163 E3
Woodfield Cl. Stan M 57 F3
Woodfield Dr. Romf 165 D4
Woodfield Rd. Brain 66 A2
Woodfield Terr. Stan M 57 F3
Woodfield Way. Hornc 165 E2
Woodfields. Stan M 57 F3
Woodfines The. Hornc 165 E3
Woodford Ct. Wa Aby 127 D3
Woodford Rd. Woodf 152 A1
Woodford Trad Est. Woodf 152 B1
Woodgreen Rd. Wa Aby 127 E3
Woodhall Cres. Hornc 165 F2
Woodhall Gr. Bis St 67 E3
Woodhall Hill. Broom 97 E1
Woodhall Rd. Chelm 111 D4
Woodham Way. Sta Ab 87 E2
Woodhays. Basil 172 B4
Woodhill. Harl 102 C3
Woodhouse La. Broom 98 A2
Wooding Gr. Harl 102 A4
Woodland Ave. Brent 147 E2
Woodland Cl. Brent 147 E2
Woodland Cl. Woodf 152 A4
Woodland Rd. Chelm 111 D2
Woodland Rd. Ching 139 E1
Woodland Rd. Lou 140 C3
Woodland Way. Ch Ong 118 C1
Woodland Way. The B 128 C2
Woodland Way. Woodf 152 A4
Woodlands. Bis St 68 B4
Woodlands. Brain 66 B2
Woodlands. Epp 129 D4
Woodlands Ave. Hornc 165 F3
Woodlands Cl. Basil 171 F2
Woodlands Cl. Grays 185 F2
Woodlands Cl. Hod 100 A3
Woodlands Cl. Ing 135 E2
Woodlands Dr. Basil 171 E1
Woodlands Dr. Hod 100 A2
Woodlands Rd. Romf 157 D1
Woodlands Rd. Romf 164 C4
Woodlands Rd. Wick 163 E4
Woodman La. Wa Aby 139 F2
Woodman Path. Chig 153 F2
Woodman Rd. Brent 158 B3
Woodman Rd. Chig 153 F3
Woodmanhurst Rd. Corr 179 F3
Woodmill Mews. Hod 100 A4
Woodredon Cl. Roy 101 D4
Woodredon Farm La. Wa Aby 127 E2
Woodridden Hill. Wa Aby 127 E2
Woodroffe Cl. Sprin 112 A2
Woods Rd. Gt Wal 84 A3
Woodshire Rd. Dag 164 A1
Woodside. Birhr 68 B4
Woodside. Lou 152 B4
Woodside. N W Bas 116 B2
Woodside Cl. Brent 147 E2
Woodside Cl. Rain 174 B1
Woodside Rd. Woodf 152 A3
Woodstock Ave. Romf 157 D2
Woodstock Cres. Basil 169 F3
Woodstock Gdns. Basil 169 F3
Woodview Dr. Gt Le 86 A4
Woodview Rd. Gt Dun 72 B4
Woodville Rd. Woodf 152 A1
Woodward Cl. Grays 185 D1
Woodward Hts. Grays 185 D1
Woodward Terr. Stone 190 C1
Woodwards. Harl 102 B3
Woodway. Brent 147 D1
Woolf Wlk. Tilb 193 E3
Woolhampton Way. Chig 154 A4
Woolifers Ave. Corr 180 A2
Woollard St. Wa Aby 126 B3
Woollard Way. Bla 133 F4
Woolmergreen. Basil 170 C4
Woolmers Mead. Ple 83 F1
Woolmongers La. H Ong 133 D4
Woolnough Cl. Ste B 18 A3
Woolpack La. Brain 65 F3
Woolpits Rd. Ba Sal 53 F1
Woolshots Rd. Wick 162 C4
Wootton Cl. Hornc 165 E3
Worcester Ave. Upm 166 C1
Worcester Cl. Brain 66 A1
Worcester Cl. Corr 179 E2
Worcester Cl. Swan 191 D2
Worcester Cres. Woodf 152 B3
Worcester Ct. Gt Bad 125 D3
Wordsworth Cl. Romf 156 B1
Wordsworth Cl. Tilb 193 E3
Wordsworth Ct. Chelm 111 D3
Wordsworth Rd. Brain 65 F4
Wordsworth Way. Stone 190 A2
Wormley Ct. Wa Aby 127 D3
Wormyngford Ct. Wa Aby 127 D3
Worrin Cl. Brent 146 C1
Worrin Rd. Brent 146 C1
Wortham Pl. Hav 7 D4
Worthing Rd. Basil 170 A3
Wouldham Rd. Grays 191 F4
Wraglins The. Bis St 68 A3
Wrangley Ct. Wa Aby 127 D3
Wratting Rd. Hav 7 D4
Wray Cl. Hornc 165 E2
Wraysbury Dr. Bill 161 E1
Wren Cl. Bill 149 E1
Wren Gdns. Hornc 164 C2
Wren Pl. Brent 158 B4
Wren Wlk. Tilb 193 D4
Wrenbrook Rd. Bis St 67 F3
Wrens The. Harl 102 A4
Wrexham Rd. Basil 170 A3
Wrexham Rd. Romf 156 B4
Wright Cl. Swan 191 E1
Wright's Green La. L Hal 78 B4
Wright's Piece. Hen 49 D3
Wrights La. Bla 133 E2
Wrightsbridge Rd. Romf 156 C4
Writtle Rd. Chelm 123 F4
Writtle Rd. Marg 122 C1
Writtle Walk. Rain 173 F2
Writtle Wlk. Basil 171 F4
Wroths Path. Lou 140 C4
Wyatt's Green Rd. Dodd 133 F2
Wyatts Green La. Bla 133 E2
Wych Elm. Harl 89 E1
Wych Elm Cl. Hornc 166 A2
Wych Elm Rd. Hornc 166 A3
Wychford Dri. Saw 77 E1
Wyes's Rd. Ing 122 A3
Wyfields. Woodf 153 D1
Wykeham Ave. Hornc 165 E3
Wykeham Rd. Writ 110 A1
Wykes Green. Basil 171 E4
Wyldwood Cl. Harl 90 B3
Wynndale Rd. Woodf 152 A1
Wynters. Basil 171 D2
Wynyard Rd. Saff W 13 F1
Wythams. Basil 172 B4
Wythefield. Basil 172 A3
Wythenshawe Rd. Dag 164 A1

Yale Way. Hornc 174 A4
Yardeley. Basil 170 C3
Yardley Cl. Ching 139 D2
Yardley Hall La. Thax 39 E3
Yardley La. Ching 139 D2
Yarmouth Pl. Hav 7 D4
Yarwood Rd. Chelm 111 F1
Yeldham Lock. Sprin 112 A1
Yeldham Pl. Hav 7 D4
Yellowpine Way. Chig 154 A3
Yelverton Cl. Romf 156 B1
Yeomen Way. Woodf 153 E2
Yevele Way. Hornc 165 F2
Yew Cl. Lou 152 B4
Yew Tree Cl. Brent 147 D2
Yew Tree Gdns. Chelm 124 B3
Yew Tree Gdns. Romf 164 B3
Yew Wlk. Hod 100 A3
Yewlands. Hod 100 A3
Yewlands. Saw 77 F1
York Ave. Corr 180 A3
York Cl. Brent 146 C1
York Cres. Lou 140 C3
York Gdns. Brain 66 A2
York Hill. Lou 140 C3
York Pl. Grays 192 A4
York Rd. Bill 149 D3
York Rd. Brent 146 C1
York Rd. Chelm 124 A4
York Rd. Dag 173 E3
York Rd. Hav 6 C4
York Rd. Horn H 178 C2
York Rd. N W Bas 117 D2
Yorkes. Harl 102 C3

Zambesi Rd. Bis St 67 F3

ORDNANCE SURVEY

STREET ATLASES

The Ordnance Survey / Philip's County Street Atlases provide unique and definitive mapping of entire counties

Counties available

- **Berkshire**
- **Buckinghamshire**
- **East Essex**
- **West Essex**
- **North Hampshire**
- **South Hampshire**
- **Hertfordshire**
- **East Kent**
- **West Kent**
- **Nottinghamshire**
- **Oxfordshire**
- **Surrey**
- **East Sussex**
- **West Sussex**
- **Warwickshire**

The County Street Atlases are revised and updated on a regular basis and new titles are added to the series. Many counties are now available in full-size hardback and softback editions as well as handy pocket-size versions.

The series is available from all good bookshops or by mail order direct from the publisher. However, the order form opposite may not reflect the complete range of titles available so it is advisable to check by telephone before placing your order. Payment can be made by credit card or cheque/postal order in the following ways:

By phone *Phone your order through on our special Credit Card Hotline on 0933 410511. Speak to our customer service team during office hours (9am to 5pm) or leave a message on the answering machine, quoting CSA94, your full credit card number plus expiry date and your full name and address*

By post *Simply fill out the order form opposite (you may photocopy it) and send it to:*
Cash Sales Department, Reed Book Services, PO Box 5, Rushden, Northants, NN10 6YX

STREET ATLASES

CSA94

	Hardback	Softback	Pocket	
	QUANTITY TOTAL		QUANTITY TOTAL	
	£12.99	£8.99	£4.99	
East Essex	£__.__ ISBN 0-540-05848-3	£__.__ ISBN 0-540-05866-1	£__.__ ISBN 0-540-05850-5	£__.__
West Essex	£__.__ ISBN 0-540-05849-1	£__.__ ISBN 0-540-05867-X	£__.__ ISBN 0-540-05851-3	£__.__
North Hampshire	£__.__ ISBN 0-540-05852-1	£__.__ ISBN 0-540-05853-X	£__.__ ISBN 0-540-05854-8	£__.__
South Hampshire	£__.__ ISBN 0-540-05855-6	£__.__ ISBN 0-540-05856-4	£__.__ ISBN 0-540-05857-2	£__.__
Nottinghamshire	£__.__ ISBN 0-540-05858-0	£__.__ ISBN 0-540-05859-9	£__.__ ISBN 0-540-05860-2	£__.__
East Sussex	£__.__ ISBN 0-540-05875-0	£__.__ ISBN 0-540-05874-2	£__.__ ISBN 0-540-05873-4	£__.__
West Sussex	£__.__ ISBN 0-540-05876-9	£__.__ ISBN 0-540-05877-7	£__.__ ISBN 0-540-05878-5	£__.__
	£10.99		£4.99	
Berkshire	£__.__ ISBN 0-540-05738-X		£__.__ ISBN 0-540-05835-1	£__.__
Buckinghamshire	£__.__ ISBN 0-540-05660-X		£__.__ ISBN 0-540-05711-8	£__.__
Hertfordshire	£__.__ ISBN 0-540-05720-7		£__.__ ISBN 0-540-05840-8	£__.__
East Kent	£__.__ ISBN 0-540-05661-8			£__.__
West Kent	£__.__ ISBN 0-540-05662-6			£__.__
Oxfordshire	£__.__ ISBN 0-540-05665-0			£__.__
Warwickshire	£__.__ ISBN 0-540-05642-1			£__.__
	£10.99		£3.99	
Surrey	£__.__ ISBN 0-540-05694-4		£__.__ ISBN 0-540-05708-8	£__.__

I enclose a cheque/postal order for £__.__ *made payable to* ***Reed Book Services*** *or please debit my* ◂*Access* ◂*American Express* ◂*Visa account by* £__.__

Name

Address

Postcode

Account number

Expiry date

Signature

Please tick this box if you do not wish your name to be used by other carefully selected organisations that may wish to send you information about other products and services

◆ ***Free postage and packing*** ◆ *All available titles will normally be dispatched within 5 working days of receipt of order, but please allow up to 28 days for delivery.*